MY MAGPIE EYES ARE HUNGRY FOR THE PRIZE

For Penelope

THE CREATION RECORDS STORY

My Magpie Eyes are Hungry for the Prize

David Cavanagh

First published in Great Britain in 2000 by
Virgin Publishing Ltd
Thames Wharf Studios
Rainville Road
London
W6 9HA

A catalogue record for this book is available from the British Library.

ISBN 1 8522 7775 0

Typeset by Phoenix Photosetting, Chatham, Kent
Printed and bound in Great Britain by Mackays of Chatham PLC, Chatham, Kent

Contents

Prologue: The Indie Dream

When this book was commissioned in 1997, Creation Records still existed. Alan McGee – the founder and self-styled 'President' of the label – was looking forward to a third album from Oasis, which seemed certain to bring consolidation and high times to his company. Fourteen years after its first release, Creation had become one of the most famous record labels in the world. Dragged into celebrity, McGee was being hailed as a brilliant entrepreneur-Svengali and had recently been asked to sit on a Government cultural industries think-tank.

But as he and I embarked on the marathon sequence of interviews in which he would recount his side of the Creation story, he was reminded of a time – the first 29 years of his life, in fact – when success had eluded him like a buttered eel. These memories were vital, because the key to understanding Alan McGee is not the years when he roared with vindication. It is the decades of disappointment and frustration that went before.

In 1983 McGee, then 22, opened a music club in central London called the Living Room, booking young guitar bands and out-of-favour punk veterans. That same month, he put out his first record on Creation. These were small gestures, hardly noticed at the time, for the 1980s was a decade of musical bipartisanism like no other. The chart-pop produced by Britain's major labels (EMI, CBS, Phonogram, RCA, Polydor) was clean, air-conditioned and technically perfect, but sounded, to those who had come from a punk background like McGee, cynical, lacking in atmosphere and banal. Creation was an independent (or 'indie') label; its aim was to provide an alternative to the mainstream by recapturing some of the pop magic of the 60s and the punky anger of the late 70s.

To the consumers of today, 'indie' means Travis, Coldplay and Stereophonics, bands that play guitars and don't sound like Britney Spears. But the original meaning of indie was something quite different. It described a culture of independence that was almost a form of protest: a means of recording and releasing music that had nothing to do with the major labels. The groups on indie labels didn't play the same game as Phil Collins or Eurythmics, and nor did they sound anything like them. Partly because the indies didn't have much money to spend on recording, and partly because the groups were spirited rather than skilled instrumentalists, indie records often sounded as though they came from a place beneath musical society – an austere underside to the affluent city life bustling above them. When you heard them on John Peel's Radio 1 show at night, these records moved in shadows and you suspected they would be uncomfortable, or even invisible, in daylight. And so they were. For almost the entirety of the 80s, the majority of indie bands went unplayed by Radio 1 during the day. With very few exceptions, most of them didn't sell enough records to get into the charts.

To many indie acts of that period, signing to a major label would have been the ultimate sellout. But it was also the only chance some of them would ever have of coming off unemployment benefit, and a few signed with lighter hearts than others, risking derision from their peers or – in one or two cases – fantasising about the stardom they imagined awaited them.

Others had a different dream, however. They dreamed of going it alone, controlling their own destiny and building a new music structure that would be self-sufficient and ethical, the absolute antithesis to the commercially orientated major labels whose values they despised. And that is the context in which the story of Alan McGee and Creation must be seen.

Creation was not one of the leading UK indie labels initially, and nor was it one of the first. Throughout its life, it was a reactive rather than proactive label, reflecting McGee's changing tastes. The reason Creation succeeded where other labels failed is not because McGee is a success and his rivals are all failures, but because he persevered when they gave up; because he took risks while they played safe and because he found Oasis just when he needed them.

The indie revolution in the late 70s and early 80s cut the music industry in two, creating both an opening and a vocation for McGee, a man who otherwise might never have been heard of. Certain important developments in the mid-80s enabled indie labels like Creation to operate as underground irritants and counter-attractions to all that was going on overground, several times making dogged, doomed attempts to wage war on the Top 40. Finally, the events of the late 80s and early 90s made it possible for McGee to mount a series of increasingly powerful bids for mainstream acceptance. Then, and only then, did he find the prize he was looking for.

In this book, I have looked at some of the indie labels that predated Creation, inspired McGee and taught him his life-lessons. Four labels were particularly crucial: Postcard, Cherry Red, Whaam! and Rough Trade (which doubled as Creation's distribution company for many years). In the years in which they were most active and/or influential, Postcard, Cherry Red and Whaam! did not have a single hit record between them. Today, they are unknown save by the cognoscenti. Had they not existed, however, there would have been no *(What's The Story) Morning Glory?*, no *Screamadelica*, no *Loveless*.

Geoff Travis and Iain McNay, the founders of Rough Trade and Cherry Red respectively, were indie dreamers and pioneers. Travis is simply a colossus in independent music and his amazing career deserves a book of its own. McNay, who came up with the idea for the indie charts in 1980, is a fascinating individual and a business-man no less ambiguous than the spiritual gurus he followed in the 80s. Alan Horne at Postcard, Dan Treacy at Whaam! and Mike Alway at Cherry Red were all gifted mavericks who play telling roles in this story. Yet for all their talents, not one of these men made it quite as far as Alan McGee did. If *My Magpie Eyes are Hungry for the Prize* proves anything, it is that talent is never enough. To end up where McGee did – not just at number 1 in the charts but in the House of Commons discussing Government policy – you need luck, self-belief, arrogance and a streak of ruthlessness to compare with any politician. Oh, and a couple of brothers named Gallagher don't hurt.

Did McGee sell out the indie dream? He would argue that he never believed in it for a second. 'Alan never wanted to be small fry,' observes a former Creation publicist. 'He was a rough kid from Glasgow and he wanted to succeed in his own right.' Maybe so, but the nineteen-year-old McGee who arrived in London in 1980 must have been dreaming of something or else he would never have made the journey. What happened to him in London is the story of an out-sider becoming an insider; the story of how unpopular music became popular; the story of one man's independence and how he fought to keep it. My own personal feeling is that, in the 21st century music business at least, stories of independence are history. In every sense of the word.

Part One

Creating and Destroying

1 The Galvanised Latecomer

URING THE MONTH OF MAY 1976, the Glasgow *Evening Times* gave a great deal of coverage to a court case arising from the death of a local teenage glue-sniffer. It was Scotland's twelfth such fatality since 1970, and all of them had been young. But in the days following the trial Dr Joyce Watson, a medical officer for the Greater Glasgow Health Board, warned that this statistic was only the tip of the iceberg. An estimated 2,000 children in the city – some as young as five – regularly sniffed glue or other legally obtained solvents, and there were 2,000 more doing exactly the same in surrounding towns. From out of nowhere, Greater Glasgow had an epidemic on its hands.

It was debatable whether the city was ready for a solvent abuse scare. Having seen its hopes of staging the 1984 Olympic Games collapse in cantankerous bickering earlier in 1976, Glasgow was in low spirits generally, and the district council had a perennial struggle to keep the region's poor image in check. The routine depiction in the London media of Glasgow as a violent, poverty-stricken no-go area had been a matter of grave concern for some time, and the situation had recently deteriorated. A series of damning reports in the mid-70s had found unusually high incidences in Glasgow of alcoholism, vandalism, worker absenteeism and – shockingly – infant mortality. In 1975, Harold Wilson's Labour Government had been asked to spend £700 million to help eradicate some of the more urgent problems facing what the *Glasgow Herald* called 'Britain's most deprived city'. In the light of such anxieties, Dr Watson's report on glue-sniffing might very well have gone no further, had it not been for one decisive factor.

The *Evening Times* – Glasgow's six-days-a-week tabloid – was enjoying its centenary year, insofar as it ever enjoyed anything. Conservative and parochial, the *Times* had been moving through the 1970s as reluctantly as a proprietor of a corner shop trying out the new-fangled supermarket: nose crinkled in distaste, eyes narrowing at the prices. It was not a paper for the young. When it tried to be, it invariably revealed a well-meaning ineffectuality. On Saturdays, the city's various youth clubs would be listed beneath the moth-eaten slogan 'Read the *Times* and keep in touch with the young world'. The Wednesday pop column, fogeyishly, would feature a smiling band of thirty-year-old local hopefuls called Whisky Mac, or Sweet Breeze, or Topaz, each one audaciously tipped by the writer for the top. In an effort to underline its importance to Glasgow family life, the *Times* had lately been promoting its wares vigorously. What better than a campaign to stamp out the menace of teenage glue-sniffing?

The *Evening Times* campaign was launched on 10 June, 1976. In a leader headlined 'The Whiff Of Death', the paper itemised the health risks and called for the sale of solvents to be made illegal to under-16s. Within twenty-four hours, several politicians and churchmen had declared their support. By the end of that month, the *Times* was running macabre stories of glue-induced hallucinations and tragedies almost on a daily basis. True, some were not very credible – one article began: 'Last week a boy bit a dog six times' – but there was no doubting the veracity of others, and in August another teenager died. The shock seemed to send the *Times* flying off the rails. It concocted a thin story about four American musicians who had no connection with Glasgow whatsoever, and splashed it all over the front page.

In the summer of 1976, the only Glaswegians who had heard of punk rock were those who read the London-published weekly music papers *Sounds*, *New Musical Express* and *Melody Maker*. The high-cir-culation *NME* had, for almost a year, been reporting on the New York club CBGBs, which had come alive as a focal point for the new rock talent on America's east coast. Articles in the *NME* about New York groups such as Television, Talking Heads and the Ramones had become common. To Glaswegians, these bands were completely inaccessible. As interesting and as exotic as they were to read about, none had issued any records in Britain nor played concerts in Scotland.

The Sex Pistols, who emerged in London in the spring of 1976, were a different matter. For one thing, they were recognisably a product of inner-city Britain, and their folio of anti-authoritarian protests and grudges needed no translation for someone growing up in 1970s Glasgow. Just as importantly, their verbal attacks on the music industry resonated poignantly in a city that depended on – and was expected to be grateful for – passing visits from the major London groups.

But although the angry rhetoric of the Sex Pistols struck a chord north of the border, it appeared somehow to reverberate from a far-away land. Lacking the network of small venues that had launched the Pistols down south, Glasgow was by comparison rooted in the musical dark ages of 1972. 'The music scene in Glasgow at that point was very much hard rock and progressive rock,' says Billy Sloan, a local journalist and broadcaster. 'It was bands playing "Smoke On The Water" and "All Right Now". Punk took a good six months to get here. Four hundred and fifty miles [from London] doesn't seem a lot when you're sitting for an hour on the Shuttle, but in 1976 it could have been Australia.'

The first punk band to release an album was New York's Ramones, whose self-titled LP started drifting into Glasgow on import in May 1976. Copies were quickly snapped up by *NME* readers eager to put a sound to the photographs, and by July the album was widely available. The word of mouth on it was strong: the tunes were abrupt and amusing, yet deceptively conceptual, extrapolating truth and meaning from the plight of the inarticulate urban loser. *The Ramones* became something of a totem for bored Glaswegian youth.

Somewhere around the middle of August, a journalist on the *Evening Times* discovered that one song on the album had the title 'Now I Wanna Sniff Some Glue'. Having reported a glue-related death only days before, the paper furiously demanded the immediate withdrawal of *The Ramones* from Glasgow's shops, claiming in a front-page editorial: 'A record on [the subject of] glue-sniffing is bound to sow the seeds of the idea in the minds of impressionable youngsters.' The *Times* explained to its readers that the Ramones' style of music – punk rock – appealed to people of 'about sixteen'. The band, its music and its fans were condemned by councillors and local MPs, and by spokesmen for the Greater Glasgow Health Board and the Royal Society for the Prevention of Accidents.

It was ironic that Glasgow of all cities became the first in Britain to associate punk rock with juvenile delinquency. Arguably, it was the city that least tolerated its young people to begin with. Throughout 1976 and 1977, there would be little joy for any Glaswegian who declared himself a punk rocker; as a result, the region's part in the unfolding punk story would be a mere cameo. Four months before the release of the first Sex Pistols record – and long before a punk concert took place locally – punk rock in Glasgow was doomed.

Despite being a Labour-controlled body for much of the 70s, Glasgow District Council was famously and fiercely conservative. Much of the city fathers' methodology revealed a suspicion of modern thinking, as well as an innate dislike of what could be termed left-field culture. Some of their judgments – for example, their banning in 1971 of Ken Russell's film *The Devils* – appeared to cross the line between civic affairs and theology. As teenagers were finding, Glasgow's social climate of puritanism and prohibition made the city as dull as a town half the size.

'In Glasgow now, there's a new age of consumer enlightenment,' says Steven Daly, a musician and journalist who turned 16 in 1976. 'There are fabulous bars, places where you can buy any fashions you want, loads of great restaurants ... But back then, there was just so little – almost nothing – to do. It's almost impossible to stress how boring and nullifying it was there. You have to understand that punk rock in Glasgow took place against a backdrop of total repression. There was no record industry. There was nowhere adequate to rehearse. There was no welcome. Nothing was accommodated or accepted. It was like trying to plant a seed on concrete.'

While the likes of Status Quo, Led Zeppelin and Queen dominated the UK rock market that year, the Sex Pistols made tentative in-roads into the Midlands and the north, playing twice in Birmingham and Manchester, and once in Liverpool. In November, it was announced that the Pistols would undertake a full-scale British tour to promote their debut single, 'Anarchy In The UK', including a concert on 15 December at the Glasgow Apollo.

The world-renowned, 3,500-seat Apollo was a bizarre setting for the city's inaugural punk gig. Grandiose and extraordinarily atmospheric, it had a creaking balcony, yards upon yards of purple art deco carpet and the dimensions of Doctor Who's Tardis. It was patrolled by the most notorious of security men – these bouncers threw punches if someone so much as rose from his seat. Full of history and spilt blood, the Apollo intimidated audiences and musicians alike. 'It was the only place I was ever booed *on* to the stage,' recalled the Scots singer B.A. Robertson years later. 'I know a lot of people who never played again after they played the Apollo.'

On 2 December, 1976, the Fleet Street tabloids in England reported that the Sex Pistols, appearing live on a London television show the previous evening, had sworn repeatedly at their middle-aged host, Bill Grundy. As the media storm spread north – prompting the *Evening Times*, inevitably, to jog its readers' memories about the glue-crazed Ramones – the Lord Provost of Glasgow, Peter McCann, called the Sex Pistols 'filth'. The chairman of the council's licensing committee, Robert Gray, let it be known that he would close the Apollo on the night of the Pistols' performance, as he believed the audience would be in danger. (This was certainly true. At the mercy of the Apollo bouncers, the audience was almost constantly in danger.)

In a well-informed editorial on 7 December, the *Glasgow Herald* commented: 'So, for Glaswegians, there will be no Johnny Rotten, no nihilism and safety pins (delicately worn in earlobes), no spitting, and none of the other highly unappealing, absurd and adolescent artefacts of the "blank generation". And few Glaswegians will feel deprived.'

As for Robert Gray, his reaction was rather more down-to-earth. 'We feel we have enough problems in Glasgow without importing yobbos,' he said simply.

In January 1977, London began to show the first signs of punk ennui. An exasperated *NME* journalist wrote that month: 'There can scarcely be anyone left in London who is not a member of a punk rock band.' In Glasgow, it was a different story. There was hardly anyone who was. Nothing was happening anywhere. Fans of punk rock – there were perhaps a few dozen in the city – relied heavily on the London music papers for information, guidance and vicarious thrills. By March 1977, not a single punk band had played in Glasgow.

Gradually – even apologetically – a few such bands managed to slip under the council's net. In March, the Damned supported T. Rex at a poorly-attended gig at the Apollo. A couple of double bills in May brought over the American groups Television, Blondie, Talking Heads and (to the consternation of the *Evening Times*) the Ramones. For all that, there was no scene – no punk community – and Glasgow languished at least a year behind Liverpool and Manchester.

'The first punk that I saw [in Glasgow] was a guy walking down Royal Exchange Square,' recalls journalist Tommy Udo, at that time a teenager living in Beith, a short train journey from the city centre. 'He was wearing a shirt and tie, which was unusual in itself, a skinny black tie. The shirt had numbers from a [rubber] stamp all over it. He looked so different because there was a kind of homogenous late 70s look in Glasgow: university sweatshirts, aviator sunglasses, flared denim ... He had his eyebrows shaved off and this really strange bowl haircut.'

The punk's name was Jim Kerr, although he often referred to himself as Pripton Weird. He was one of two singers in a band called Johnny and the Self Abusers, based in Toryglen on Glasgow's south side. One of the first of the new wave of local groups to play in public, the Self Abusers caused a stir by wearing mascara and using their own light show. By the proletarian standards of 1977, they were decadent and theatrical. 'They were a good rock and roll band,' says punk fan John (Jake) Black. 'It was Lou Reed make-up and all that. And they had a wee Dansette record-player with a wee dayglo skull, and they'd turn the record-player on and the skull would go round and round. But Jim was already a pompous git, always trying to articulate these big, arty ideas.' At a concert in the Saints and Sinners pub in St Vincent Street, followers of Johnny and the Self Abusers had smashed glasses and destroyed furnishings, leading to a blanket ban on punks. One fewer place to go at night.

Jake Black was a 16-year-old from a working-class estate in Possilpark to the north of the city, and a walking example of how punk rock could overturn a young Glaswegian's life. As a boy, Black had run with a local gang, feeling strong emotional ties to his area. Even as a teenager, he'd seldom ventured further than a mile or two from his home. Now, awakened to the Sex Pistols and the seductive dangers of urban punk rock, he was making a beeline for the city centre, where he met former heavy metal kids, disco fans and non-aligned oddballs from every part of Glasgow – all of whom had thrown in their lot with punk.

For a territorially conscious city like Glasgow, it was a new-look youth trend, de-regionalised, deregulated and mobile. But because it was new, the punks had to keep their wits about them. 'People wanted to fight you – older people, too,' says the singer and song-writer Edwyn Collins. 'I'd be in my teens and people in their late twenties would be chasing me down Sauchiehall Street and Argyle Street. At this time there were probably only a hundred hardcore people into punk in Glasgow. The majority – the proletariat – hated it. They fucking hated it.'

Jake Black was well aware of the risks, and much more able to handle the blows than the gangling, effeminate Collins. But with a mind wired on Drynamil pills and fortified wine, Black couldn't help visualising the vast improvement to Glasgow's landscape if the punks were to prevail. 'I thought we were going to change the world,' he says. 'I thought we were going to change the face of Glasgow forever.'

For that to happen, a whole new entertainment scene needed to be created from scratch. Manchester and Liverpool were already giv-ing birth to their own punk bands, punk record labels and punk venues. Yet in Glasgow these were impossibly daunting proposi-tions. The city-wide resistance to punk was compounded by archaic licensing laws, which obliged audiences to remain politely seated while watching a band play – and in any case, there was virtually no active promotion of live music other than at the Apollo.

Admittedly, new bands were forming. Edwyn Collins was the singer in one of them, the Nu-Sonics, who rehearsed in affluent west-end Bearsden. But the Nu-Sonics never played gigs. Johnny and the Self Abusers were the city's hottest new attraction, but had no reputation outside Glasgow. Nor did the Exile, who had recorded a self-financed EP; nor the Jolt, an R&B-influenced trio; nor the Backstabbers, a raw outfit inspired by the Stooges. None of these bands came close to rivalling Edinburgh's Rezillos, let alone Manchester's Buzzcocks, in terms of profile.

Only when punk rock had become a commercial force in the UK singles and album charts was Glasgow finally ignited. On 22 June, 1977, the city saw its first proper punk gig when Top 20 recording artists the Stranglers played at the City Hall. For a variety of reasons, it was an absurd and far-reaching occasion.

The initial thought, when the concert was announced, was that a serious chink had appeared in the council's armour. To allow the dreaded Stranglers – banned up and down Britain by councils not nearly as sensitive as Glasgow's – to play in a municipal building seemed an unaccountable lapse of the councillors' judgment. The

Stranglers had shrouded their music in the imagery of violence, were confrontational performers skilled in crowd manipulation, and had had a single, 'Peaches', blackballed by Radio 1 for obscenity. Then there was the question of the City Hall security. 'The Apollo was a very controlled environment – the bouncers were thugs in suits,' says Tommy Udo. 'But the City Hall was a council-owned venue. It was policed entirely by old men in commissionaires' uniforms.' Glasgow's punks would really be able to stretch out and get to know each other.

A month before, Peter McCann had stood down as Lord Provost and been succeeded by Labour councillor David Hodge. Like his predecessor, Hodge wasn't much of a punk rock enthusiast. Although he had green-lighted the Stranglers concert, he could not afford to be too blasé. Glasgow had recently enjoyed its first public relations triumph in some years when the Queen began her Jubilee tour of Britain with a walkabout in the city. In a bid to keep the goodwill flowing, Hodge had publicly promised a crackdown on troublemakers. With the Stranglers due at the City Hall, he thought it a good idea to send along a chaperon.

Bill Aitken was a Tory councillor of the old school. The new chairman of the licensing committee, he was, at 31, not much older than the Stranglers' guitarist Hugh Cornwell. In facial resemblance, however, Aitken was closer to Harold Pinter. As the council's crack undercover punk agent, he was hard to miss – and he was spotted by fans even before entering the building. 'Do you think they would take me as a councillor?' one punk asked him. 'Listen, son, there are bigger morons than you in the city chambers,' Aitken was heard to reply.

Jake Black was no more a Stranglers fan than Aitken was, but had gone to the concert in the hope of meeting girls. Halfway through the show, when Cornwell gestured to fans in the front rows to climb up and join the band onstage, Black stayed where he was and watched the disorder that ensued. 'A couple of people got up and were simulating sex,' he says. 'There were scuffles, and a bit of pushing and shoving, and then millions of cozzers [police] turned up.' Seven arrests were made. 'But it was nothing out of hand,' Black adds. 'It wasn't a full-blown rammie.' In other words, it was no white riot.

The following day's *Evening Times* reported the events as though a desecration had occurred. 'Punk rock will never again be heard in any of Glasgow's theatres or halls,' it wrote. 'After a night of paint-spraying, spittle, songs with swear words and home-made "cocktails", the unanimous verdict from city officials was "never again".' Bill Aitken told the paper: 'It's a wonder there wasn't a fatality. Twice the stage was invaded as this crowd, suffering from induced hysteria, went on the rampage.' David Hodge added: 'If these people with their depraved minds want to hear this type of thing, fair enough. But let them do it in private.'

Among the readers of the *Evening Times* that day was a recent punk convert named Alan McGee. The 16-year-old son of a south-side panel-beater, he had been in the audience at the City Hall him-self. He read the write-up in the *Times* with a mixture of excitement and bewilderment.

The McGees lived in Mount Florida, a neighbourhood of high-rises and tenements overlooking the national football stadium, Hampden Park. Alan, the only son in a working-class family of five, was pas-sionate about music, football and little else. A year before, he had been listening mostly to heavy rock: having experienced the glam explosion – Bowie, Slade, T. Rex – as part of the wide-eyed *Top Of The Pops* generation of 1972–3, he had graduated, as many did, to the long-haired, albums-based groups on the Apollo circuit such as Deep Purple and Uriah Heep, with a smattering of Bob Dylan as an occa-sional respite from the machismo.

Although McGee had read about punk rock in the music papers, he had taken a while to commit himself to it. Tuning in to the local commercial station Radio Clyde in May 1977, he'd heard 'God Save The Queen' by the Sex Pistols. He liked its corrosive riff and bitter, risqué lyrics, and looked forward to hearing the song again. Within days, it had been banned by Radio Clyde, by every other commercial station in Britain, by Radio 1, by *Top Of The Pops* and by many chain-stores.

McGee was impressed: the simple emotion of enjoying a pop record had made him a dissident. The following week, he bought three punk singles – 'God Save The Queen', 'Go Buddy Go'/'Peaches' by the Stranglers and 'Sheena Is A Punk Rocker' by the Ramones. A few days of intensive listening later, he had turned into a fully-fledged zealot. 'I was religious about punk rock,' he says. 'It was the first thing I'd ever believed in.'

The appeal for McGee was not so much the anti-monarchist howl of 'God Save The Queen' as the broader realisation that punk rock was a movement made up of people just like himself. It was music for the white disenfranchised teenager, just as glam-rock had been music for their younger, optimistic selves. And by now, at 16, McGee was far from optimistic. He was about to leave school, and was under pressure from his parents to take an electrician's apprenticeship. A serial truant, he had few other prospects.

'My family thought I was a bit of a waster,' he says. 'I didn't talk about it but I felt quite alienated growing up. I was invisible with women. I had red hair with freckles, and glasses. Women were so far off my agenda they didn't even come into it. So when punk came along, I was like: "I can be part of this. This is my world. I can go along and be accepted." ' McGee had rolled up at City Hall – it was his first punk gig – with the darting eyes and dry mouth of the galvanised latecomer. Now that he'd seen the Stranglers, he was insatiable for more. But that *Evening Times* report worried him. Was it all off now?

In the past, McGee had daydreamed of a career in pop music, without really knowing what he was dreaming about, or having the vaguest idea of how it could be achieved. 'He never actually spelt it out – "I want to be a pop star",' says Colin Dobbins, a friend from Mount Florida. 'In the 70s, if you'd said that, you would have got slagged. It was more that he loved music and wanted to play it.' After leaving school with one O level, McGee bought a guitar and decided to form a punk band. Dobbins was unable to help – he worked for Scottish Television and had no spare time. The situation with McGee's other close friend, Bobby Gillespie, was rather more complicated.

The son of the prominent SOGAT union official Robert Gillespie, Bobby was a particularly single-minded and emphatic individual by teenagers' standards. The deeply embedded Glasgow rivalry between Protestants and Catholics was much less important to the Gillespies than it was to other households. 'I guess our family was unique because my dad was left-wing,' Bobby suggested in an interview a quarter of a century later. 'Other people I knew had pictures of the Queen or the Pope on the wall. My dad had a picture of the Black Panthers.'

A year younger than McGee, Gillespie had turned up on his doorstep one day in 1976 and asked to be taken to a Thin Lizzy concert at the Apollo. The two teenagers developed a friendship as they saw more and more gigs together. 'Me and Bobby were intense friends, almost like brothers,' says McGee. 'Out of the whole crowd of people I grew up with, he was definitely the most interesting. [He was] quite individual in his point of view. He used to do my head in because he was so intense. Often when we were coming back from gigs, I would get off the train two stops early and say I wanted to go for a walk, just so I could stop him talking.'

Since the football-mad Gillespie, typically, was taking his time before making his mind up about punk, McGee was forced to look further afield for people to join his band. Hooking up with a fellow guitar player, he started a group called the Lunatic Fringe. However, neither of the boys was very competent and rehearsals soon petered out. McGee was obliged to do what his parents had hoped and become an apprentice electrician.

The city fathers of Glasgow, their fingers burnt by the carnage at City Hall, had meanwhile rallied to head the punks off at the pass. *Music Week*, a trade magazine published in London, revealed that Glasgow District Council had started refusing licences for live entertainment 'at the last minute'. One punk promoter who said he'd take the risk was warned to expect a police raid. The city was bringing down the shutters.

For the next two months, at the instigation of Arthur Haggerty, the manager of Bruce's Record Shop, the nascent Glasgow punk scene moved to the unlikely location of a businessmen's hotel in Paisley, a town seven miles away. The Silver Thread Hotel had a function room, which it would hire out for weddings and funeral lunches. At night, the room was the setting for a discotheque. By August, as the 6,600 workforce of the nearby Chrysler Linwood plant began construction of the new Sunbeam hatchback, the Silver Thread disco was playing host to punk fans every Wednesday. 'To put it in perspective,' says Edwyn Collins, 'it was a two hundred capacity venue which was run by a guy called Disco Harry, who was dressed up as John Travolta and was probably in his mid-to-late forties. He had a medallion and a Hawaiian shirt under a white jacket. It was incredible.'

As Disco Harry and Arthur Haggerty knew very well, Paisley fell within the jurisdiction of the county of Renfrewshire, where punk concerts had not been outlawed. The two men started booking the cream of the new wave – the Buzzcocks, XTC, Elvis Costello and the Saints – and chartered buses full of punks from Glasgow city centre to the Silver Thread. By September, the hotel was a *de facto* punk headquarters, and the best gig within forty miles.

In Mount Florida, Alan McGee was spending long, tedious weeks making tea for the older electricians. On his first day at the firm, they had pinned him to the ground, removed his trousers and underpants, and daubed his genitals with paint. 'It was an initiation ceremony,' he remembers. 'They painted my bollocks with this orange metallic paint – it takes about six weeks to get off – and I took it, so to speak, on the chin. Then as a joke they went to paint me a second time and I chased them about with a metal bar. After that, I was left alone and put in the corner of, like, "loony".'

Unaware of the events at the Silver Thread, McGee was gleaning most of his information about punk from a programme called *Street Sounds* on Radio Clyde. The DJ, Brian Ford, had a notice-board service on which local bands could advertise for musicians. Listening one evening, McGee learned that the Drains required a bass guitarist. The Drains turned out to be a 15-year-old guitar player named Andrew Innes and his next-door neighbour, a drummer. Grammar schoolboys, they made McGee a little uncomfortable; it was not in his nature to fraternise with clever kids like these. However, he had to concede that Innes was easily the most accomplished musician he had met: the skilful guitarist was also able to teach McGee the rudiments of the bass. After engineering the sacking of the drummer for being, as he would later put it, 'a middle-class twat', McGee introduced Innes to Bobby Gillespie in the autumn of 1977.

Glasgow's two-month moratorium on punk had brought an unexpected wave of sympathy from some of the movement's former opponents. One or two councillors even admitted to the papers that punks were – when you looked behind the spiky hair and safety pins – no worse than football supporters. At a council meeting towards the end of August, permission was granted for the Clash to play at the Apollo in October. McGee and Colin Dobbins were in the audience that night, and with them was Bobby Gillespie. 'The Clash were the most exciting thing I had ever seen in my life,' says McGee. 'They stood like stormtroopers across the stage, man, it was unbelievable. Better still, Bobby had caught punk and was massively into it.'

Speaking to *NME* in 1989, Gillespie recalled the following incident from his Glasgow past: 'There were these hippies who used to live across the road from me. They were into Yes, Genesis, Joni Mitchell ... They used to scream abuse at me because I bought records by the Clash and Sex Pistols, so I set fire to their house in the name of rock 'n' roll because they were complacent, soulless, dope-smoking dead-heads, too stoned to live ...'

Whether or not this really happened – and the extraordinary phraseology suggests it ought to be taken with a pinch of salt – it is undeniable that Gillespie was consumed by punk. A late starter even for Glasgow, he was transformed into a true believer, astonishing his friends. 'He was born again. He was obsessed,' says McGee. The wiry Gillespie was soon persuaded that he had star quality as a singer, and was talked into joining a new band called Captain Scarlet and the Mysterons.

'We'd go round to Innes' house and get drunk,' Gillespie later recalled. 'McGee would have a bass and Innes would have a guitar – they'd be playing, like, Pistols songs and Clash songs, Jam songs, and I'd be rolling around on the floor screaming "No Fun" or "White Riot" or whatever ... I never thought I could do that until I'd seen Innes playing "Pretty Vacant". I thought: fucking hell, man, this is incredible, I want a piece of this. But even then I didn't think I wanted to be a singer.'

In November 1977, with the city's doors now opened to visiting punk bands, a record was released that recalled the restriction and fear of the previous spring. 'Saints And Sinners', a single by Johnny and the Self Abusers, commemorated the trashing of the St Vincent Street venue by overexcited first-wave punks. Shortly before the record came out, however, the Self Abusers split up. A few of the original members advertised for fresh faces to join their new band. Seeing an opportunity to break out of his Mount Florida doldrums, Alan McGee phoned the number and was invited to a house in Toryglen to try out for the role of rhythm guitarist. In less than an hour, he was on his way home. He had failed his audition for Simple Minds.

2 The Sound of Young Scotland

WHEN JOHN PEEL OPENED the package containing the first single by a group called the Television Personalities in 1977, he was amused to see that the covering letter was signed 'Nicholas Parsons'. Whoever the sender was, it was unlikely to be the prim host of ITV's Saturday evening quiz show *Sale Of The Century*. The note went on to list the members of the Television Personalities as Hughie Green, Bruce Forsyth and Bob Monkhouse: stolid pillars of light entertainment all. That night on his Radio 1 show, Peel played the single – a shambolic slice of tower-block angst entitled '14th Floor' – and read out the letter for good measure.

The Television Personalities lived in Chelsea, the birthplace of punk in England. Dan Treacy, the band's singer and main writer, had watched the story unfold from his parents' seventh-floor flat in the King's Road, situated at a diagonal to Malcolm McLaren and Vivienne Westwood's boutique, Sex. Further up the King's Road was the Roebuck, the pub where Johnny Rotten had first been introduced by McLaren to Steve Jones, Paul Cook and Glen Matlock. Opposite Sex was the laundrette where Treacy's mother worked during the day, and which was used by some of the Pistols' entourage.

In 1977, as the notoriety of Sex and the Sex Pistols spread, the King's Road became the centrepoint and commercial heartland of punk. To the irritation of those living locally, the area was invaded at weekends by swarms of punks with safety pins, dog collars and leather jackets, heading in a two-way parade towards Sex at the westernmost end and Sloane Square tube station to the east. 'The first six months was just total shock horror,' Dan Treacy recalled in 1986. 'People were scared to go out on a Saturday.'

Treacy and his fellow Television Personalities Joe Foster and Ed Ball were punk fans to a degree – they had seen gigs by the Pistols, the Clash, the Stranglers and the Damned at early stages in their careers – but the cartoon-like aspect of the King's Road at weekends had convinced them that the movement now merited an injection of satire. 'It didn't take long for the whole punk thing to become a tabloid farce,' says Ed Ball. 'I saw the Pistols on *So It Goes* and thought they were exciting. But the cynicism was there in us quite early on.'

Once they had learned the basics of how to make their own record (from a brief correspondence with a south London group called the Desperate Bicycles), the Television Personalities made '14th Floor' with money saved by Treacy from his job at Swan Song, a record company owned by Led Zeppelin. Unbeknown to Robert Plant and Jimmy Page, they effectively bankrolled the first musical steps taken by their tea boy.

The Television Personalities' name was both an afterthought and a signifier. Chosen by Treacy as he was composing his letter to John Peel, it had the effect of sounding at once groovy and perverse: punks weren't supposed to like middle-aged TV hosts, let alone use their names as aliases. However, Treacy's wheeze was wholly in keeping with the oblique worldview of these partly overdeveloped, partly naive teenagers. It was particularly germane to boys who had grown up in Chelsea, a chichi area since the 1960s. Even in the mid-70s, the King's Road had retained the fashion influence of the previous decade. There was a plethora of clothes shops, and stars from sport and TV were a frequent sight. '[Footballers] Peter Osgood and Alan Hudson drank in the Chelsea Drugstore pub,' says Ball. 'I remember seeing John Cleese walking down the King's Road in 1972 or 1973, going to a restaurant. He was dressed quite bizarrely in his Ministry of Silly Walks suit with a flower sticking out of his buttonhole.'

As children in the 60s, the three friends had been shaped by series such as *The Prisoner* and *The Avengers*. In their teens, they had discovered and become passionate about 60s movies depicting Swinging London – *Smashing Time*, *The Knack*, *Georgy Girl* – as well as mod and psychedelic music (the Who, the Pink Floyd) and pop art. In the three principal characters in Lindsay Anderson's film *If...*, they had found parallels to their own eccentric relationships and to their hated Catholic school, the London Oratory. 'I don't think we wanted to relive the 60s,' says Ball. 'We wanted to be of our time. But the idea of being an anachronism, and the faddy coolness of being isolated, were very appealing.' Or as Joe Foster puts it: 'We thought it would be pretty nice to be a boy and not have to be a man.'

For these reasons, the Television Personalities were appreciably stranger in their attitude to culture than many of the punk bands springing up around them. 'We were always interested in being a peculiar band,' says Foster. 'We were interested in being either a really weird psychedelic band, or something like Roxy Music that would have some weird instrument in there somewhere.' The simplicity of punk rock let the Television Personalities off the hook, removing the need to become proficient as musicians and enabling them to articulate their oddness in an elementary one-two-three-four idiom.

John Peel not only played '14th Floor' on his radio show, he also wrote about it in his weekly column for *Sounds*, twinning it with 'Read About Seymour', a single by a Midlands band called Swell Maps which had come out at the same time. The two records shared a sense of fun and games, Swell Maps' single ending in much banging and clattering as if the band had suddenly started fighting. '14th Floor' was sung by Treacy with the cockney impudence of TV's *Please Sir!*, a world of graffiti'd walls, flicked rulers and shouts of 'oy-oy!' disturbing the classroom hush. Neither Swell Maps nor the Television Personalities were yet known nationally, and gigs by either band were extremely rare.

For their second release, in 1978, the Television Personalities spent £22 and four hours recording an EP that wittily pinpointed the childish, points-scoring nature of being a metropolitan punk fan. Named after the LWT presenter who had conducted the infamous interview with the Sex Pistols, the *Where's Bill Grundy Now?* EP was released on the band's own King's Road label. But it was soon apparent that the demand for the record was exhausting the Television Personalities' resources. They were going to need help.

Taking advantage of Glasgow's new mood of tolerance, Arthur Haggerty of Bruce's Record Shop gave up his involvement in the Silver Thread Hotel and began to promote punk concerts within Glasgow itself. At Christmas 1977, he organised a gig by the Backstabbers – whom he also managed – but this disintegrated into violence when gatecrashers stormed the stage. In January, Haggerty tried his luck with reggae, booking Birmingham's Steel Pulse to play in Satellite City, a disco above the Apollo, with three local groups making up the bill. In the audience that night was a 19-year-old Glasgow University botany student named Alan Horne.

Horne came from Saltcoats, an unexciting holiday resort on the west coast of Scotland. As a child, he had aspired to be a jockey, but a difficult adolescence had sent him retreating into his shell with severe shyness and depression. Obsessed with movies and music, of which he had an encyclopaedic knowledge, the lisping, bespectacled youth indulged in elaborate fantasies of show business, success and power.

Shortly before accepting his university place in 1976, Horne took drastic steps to confront his shyness head-on. Packing a rucksack, he embarked alone on a rail journey through Europe, forcing himself to approach strangers with an unfamiliar assertiveness. When he returned to Saltcoats, he was almost unrecognisable. His timid personality had veered to the opposite extreme – he was a verbally aggressive, witheringly sarcastic, arrogant bully.

These changes brought him perfectly into line with the point-of-sale hostility of punk, and he began to be noticed on the Glasgow music scene the following year. He would hang around in Bruce's Record Shop with a notebook, sneering at the stupidity of the shop's clientele. 'He was really obnoxious,' recalls the Backstabbers' guitarist James King. 'He was offensive to your face. But it wasn't the kind of offensiveness that made you want to beat the shit out of him. You just thought: who is this dick?'

Horne attended punk gigs as and when they were drip-fed to Glasgow, enjoying the police presence, the element of danger, the paranoia. 'Everybody was scared and watching everybody,' he remembers. 'It was a really uptight experience.' As an uptight person himself, Horne had found his milieu. To his delight, a rumour circulated that he had walked into the Stranglers' dressing-room and berated them for being a bunch of phonies. Suddenly, he had a reputation.

But although it suited Horne's purposes to be respected as a card-carrying militant punk, he was actually nothing of the kind. Bored with almost all punk music, he was also contemptuous of the consensus politics that went with it. Where Mount Florida's Alan McGee saw in punk a broad church where everyone was welcome, Horne saw dim-witted dogma that lacked humour – and for Horne, there were few crimes more heinous than lacking humour. Believing that a new generation of outrageous bands was needed to recapture the original spirit of the Sex Pistols, he pinned his hopes on a young group called Oscar Wild, which, by the by, included Alan Horne on vocals. Throughout 1977, Horne dipped into his university grant to finance Oscar Wild, but it was not a sound investment. A luckless five-piece, they played only one concert in their short lifetime – in Troon in Ayrshire, to an audience of bikers.

But if Horne had virtually given up on punk, its sister genre – reggae – still held his interest. He had been running a weekly reggae disco, Channel One, and had been intrigued to learn that Arthur Haggerty was planning to bring Steel Pulse to Glasgow. Horne didn't like the band as such, but he admired the artful Haggerty and suspected the gig might be fun. He arrived at Satellite City just in time to catch the first of the support groups.

They were an unusual bunch. The singer-guitarist wore a dark blue Marks & Spencer velvet jacket, quite a stylish touch for a Glasgow punk. He also had his right arm in a sling, which Horne presumed to be some kind of art statement. They began their set with 'We're Gonna Have A Real Good Time Together' by the Velvet Underground, another point in their favour. It meant they had heard *1969: The Velvet Underground Live*, a very cool record to own in 1978. However, they were musically untogether and ungainly, and the crowd hated them.

For one song, they brought a friend onstage. As the band improvised, the friend shouted a refrain from a recent hit by Chic: 'Yowsa

yowsa yowsa! I wanna boogie witchoo! Yowsa yowsa yowsa! I wanna boogie witchoo!' The audience hooted and yelled, but Horne knew that he was watching something revolutionary for Glasgow. 'They had a magical hipness,' he recalls. 'The Velvets and chart disco – the best white and the best black rhythm guitar sound. I had to get to know them.'

The band was the Nu-Sonics, fronted by Edwyn Collins. With a handful of gigs to their name, they were the artiest, most fey group in the city. While their peers were writing songs about housing estates, or playing Clash covers, the Nu-Sonics provoked a reaction with the theme tune from the *Mary Tyler Moore Show*. 'They weren't like any of the other Glasgow bands,' says journalist Tommy Udo, who was at Satellite City that night. 'I'd never seen anyone as camp as Edwyn Collins in front of a Glasgow audience. There was total abuse: "You fucking poof!" '

The Nu-Sonics stayed in Horne's memory, and five months later he and Edwyn Collins met for the first time at a David Bowie concert in the Apollo. There was considerable friction. The Nu-Sonics needed all the fans they could get, but they had good reason not to consort with Horne: he was rumoured to be flirting with Nazism. After the Satellite City gig, he'd spoken to the Nu-Sonics' drummer Steven Daly (who informed him that Collins' sling was not an art statement at all – he had cut his hand accidentally with a Stanley knife), and Daly had reported back to a shocked Collins that Horne sported a swastika badge. Horne had also suggested to Daly that the Nu-Sonics play the 'yowsa yowsa yowsa' song at their next gig, only this time with Horne dressed in lederhosen and singing 'Springtime For Hitler' from *The Producers*. Collins wanted nothing to do with the idea.

In the Apollo foyer, Horne, podgy and pugnacious in Harris tweed and a black beret, glimpsed the tall, plaid-shirted Collins standing nearby. 'Look at that fucking lanky wimp – you're John Boy Walton,' he said loudly. 'Shut your mouth, fat boy,' retorted Collins. At this, Horne began to giggle.

'He was very, very awkward,' Horne recalls. 'He *was* John Boy Walton. But I knew he was also Jonathan Richman. And that was really weird because Jonathan Richman's a one-off. You just don't meet people like that. It wasn't like a copy thing. [Edwyn] just was that way. I was captivated by him.'

Like Horne, Collins was tiring of punk rock. Initially excited by literate New York acts like Television and Richard Hell, he'd grown disillusioned with the more populist and clichéd British bands, and now felt as excluded as he had in 1975 when everyone at school had been carrying Pink Floyd's *Wish You Were Here*. 'I was the posh, boho end of Glasgow punk,' he says. 'A lot of the hardcore types thought I was a snobby dilettante.' Most of them assumed – wrongly – that he was gay.

The Nu-Sonics had rejected punk's yob-like orthodoxy, as Collins believed the best English bands had: his favourites were the Buzzcocks, the eccentric Subway Sect and the all-female Slits. The Nu-Sonics' problem was that Glasgow, being a year behind the times, had only just familiarised itself with the orthodoxy, and a backlash generated in middle-class Bearsden would be unlikely to muster much support.

Though fearful of Horne's suspected Nazi sympathies, Collins went along to the large Victorian flat in Glasgow's student neigh-bourhood where Horne lived, to see if it had potential as a Nu-Sonics rehearsal space. As he and Horne got talking, Collins' worries abated and he began to laugh out loud. This was not a racist. This was a full-blown misanthrope. Horne showed him copies of *Swankers*, a fanzine he published and distributed to local shops. It was a virulent, nihilistic piece of work whose singular aim, Horne explained, was to ridicule and infuriate his flatmate, Oscar Wild's guitarist Brian Taylor – or, as the Warhol-influenced Horne had renamed him, Brian Superstar. *Swankers* was full of stories about Superstar, each one grossly libellous.

'It was a horrible, horrible fanzine,' says Collins. 'The thing that was probably most offensive was he had this picture [headlined] "Carnage At Auschwitz", with a caption he'd written at the bottom of the page saying: "Good carnage, but not great carnage". Horrible, nasty, student humour. But he put a lot of effort into it. I think he made about three issues – solely to annoy Brian Superstar. That's the kind of person he was.'

Behind his Milky Bar Kid veneer, Horne was deceptively danger-ous, a troubled soul too ruinous and loveless even for the most gra-tuitous excesses of punk. Steven Daly comments: 'Alan's whole drive in life – his animus – was … It's like when your school-teacher would say to you: "You just want to spoil it for everybody else." That's all Alan wanted to do. He didn't want any of that right-wing bullshit. He didn't want to join any organisation. He just wanted to spoil it for everybody else.'

By 1979, Collins was Horne's wry lieutenant and co-conspirator. Two effete misfits – one heterosexual, one secretly gay – in a grace-less time and place, they were united, in Horne's phrase, 'by a com-plete loathing of all the naffness around us'. Whatever the Nu-Sonics did next, it was certain that Horne would be involved.

'There was a sea change in '79,' says Collins. 'Nobody was inter-ested in what punk had become. It seemed to arty types like us to be a debasement. All of a sudden you got the identikit Sid Vicious look in Glasgow. Everyone was wearing leather jackets, bondage trousers and spiky hair. Suddenly it was all clones, and they'd look at you aggressively because you were carrying an umbrella.'

In May, the Nu-Sonics started to perform under a new name,

Orange Juice. The sweet-toothed appellation mocked the thuggish-ness of the Sham 69-type bands whose popularity in Glasgow had snowballed. All over the city, slow-off-the-mark punks were making up for lost time with a shower of phlegm every night. 'I did a gig at Partick Borough Hall,' recalls James King. 'This was after spitting at gigs had become unfashionable in London. I came offstage and my trousers were filthy from being gobbed on. As far as the audience were concerned, it was still 1977.'

When Orange Juice played at the Glasgow School of Art, they had pints of beer thrown at them and were threatened with a beating. The assailants were a duo called the Dyeletics, furious because Orange Juice wouldn't let them sing an impromptu song of their own. 'We were going to give them a doing when they got offstage. Then we felt sorry for them. They were all nice boys,' Jake Black of the Dyeletics says.

Jake Black's crowd of first-wave Glasgow punks had watched aghast as the movement went first commercial, then professional – to the point where Siouxsie and the Banshees' second album sounded to them like progressive rock. Black had recognised the members of Orange Juice from the Satellite City club eighteen months before, but took some convincing that their Velvet Underground-indebted noise was the way forward for Glasgow.

'The Nu-Sonics had been one of the worst bands ever,' he says. 'They thought they were doing all this twee pop music with nice melodies, but it was just this mad thrash. And early Orange Juice was like that as well. The very early gigs were frenetic. They were obsessed with that Velvets' guitar sound – pure tin. Ed [Collins] was gifted, but they were all self-taught boys, they weren't musos. And they cultivated that Andy Warhol's Factory look. Ed had his big fringe and that. It was Cuban heels, tight denims and turtlenecks. Ed was the first guy that I saw wearing Ray-Bans as a fashion accessory, which were not considered cool in 1979.'

But although Orange Juice were shrill and amateurish in concert, something important was happening behind the scenes. They were being given a crash course in Alan Horne's 'magical hipness', absorb-ing the best pop, rock and soul records from the 60s and 70s which Horne had been collecting since his early teens. 'He had accumu-lated a huge box, a huge chest of 45s,' says Collins. 'One column was all the Elektra singles: Love and the Doors. Then he would have all the Kinks EPs, the Small Faces' "Here Come The Nice" and all the rest. Then he'd have all the records on blue [label] Stax, a few Northern Soul singles ... He had a huge frame of reference. If you wanted to go and hear rare Dylan things, or something like "Different Drum" by the Stone Poneys, he would have it in his box. He read magazines religiously. He was fanatical about music.'

Another influence on Orange Juice was the preppiness, or weird 'straightness', of Talking Heads. Drummer Steven Daly actually looked like a Talking Head: smart, clean-cut, rather abnormally normal. As the sensible member of Orange Juice – he had a job as a civil servant – Daly was wary of Horne's growing influence on the band, and particularly on Collins. 'Steven had no confidence in Edwyn,' says Horne. 'He thought he was an idiot. The side of Edwyn that I thought was a star, Steven thought was an arsehole ... The group was always in a state of collapse.'

Like a Hydra-headed Professor Higgins, Horne indirectly and directly pushed Collins and Orange Juice in a variety of musical directions. Their rhythmic bedrock was the motorised wrist action of Lou Reed in the Velvet Underground of 1969. From Philadelphia soul, they took their dance-orientated beat and a lightness of touch. Already over-reaching, and with little thought of expediency, they threw in diverse elements of 60s pop, American west coast folk-rock and Nashville country music. In theory, they were mixing roots they did not have with techniques they could not emulate. In essence, they were juxtaposing forms that resisted juxtaposition. What gave it legitimacy, aside from the fact that Horne and Collins seemed to like the results, was the context of British alternative music in 1979.

Out of punk's sinister atmosphere had emerged a compelling new strand of rock that had outgrown the petulant ululations of 1977 and slowed itself down to the pulses of dub reggae, Roxy Music, American funk or – most unhurried of all – the sombre ice-shifts of David Bowie's Berlin albums *Low* and *Heroes*. In many groups, the synthesizer or the saxophone had replaced the guitar as the lead instrument. Magazine, Public Image Ltd, the Pop Group, Joy Division, the Human League and the Gang Of Four – some of the most acclaimed bands of the period – had shaken off punk's fetters to produce landmark records in 1978–9. Post-punk music, as it was speculatively tagged, had no ground rules but it did have certain distinctive characteristics. The records often came in cryptic, shadowy sleeves. The titles of the songs were inclined to be psyche-related and of one-word length. And the lyrics would contemplate alienation, paranoia and morbidity. Intensely ideas-based, post-punk music appealed to four judicious, overlapping audiences: intelligent teenagers, ex-punks, young males and students. Crucially, it had the backing of the weekly rock press and Radio 1's John Peel.

Orange Juice both belonged in this changing world and stood back from it. Horne, who had had enough alienation to last him a lifetime, loathed at least three of the aforementioned post-punk groups. Moreover, the lyrics of Collins' songs were not dark or gloomy in the slightest – on the contrary, they were amusing and romantic. But the nationwide shift towards a more abstract underground music had done Horne and Orange Juice two big favours. It had educated the palate of the listeners, giving them a taste for records that had an edge – be it a slightly out of tune vocal or a jarring clash of musical components – and thereby an all-important cachet of modernism. And secondly, it had placed several key people in the media who would go out on a limb for a band in the regions that was doing something a little different.

The dilemmas that faced Orange Juice on their home turf – where crowds reacted with disdain and promoters thought twice of booking them – would soon cease to matter.

In the 1960s, both Glasgow and Edinburgh had enjoyed thriving live music circuits. However, in neither city was there a pop industry as such, and few outlets existed for bands to make records. One or two independent labels had been started around the time of R&B and Merseybeat, notably Alp (short for Andy Lothian Productions, a leading Scottish promoter of the day), which secured a national distribution deal with Polydor and received some Radio Luxembourg support in 1966 for a single by the Perth-based Vikings. But in 1967, when Alp folded, the Vikings were forced to join the trail of Scottish bands heading south.

With these acts, the same story was repeated again and again. A major London record company, seeing a passion and a fire in Scottish groups that their English counterparts often lacked, would bring them down to record a single. The band would make the journey with high hopes; many of the Scottish hitmakers of the following decade – Gerry Rafferty, Frankie Miller, Alex Harvey, Gallagher and Lyle – had brief stints on London labels in the mid-60s. The trouble was that disc jockeys in England would not play records by unknown Scots.

By the end of the 60s, live music in Glasgow and Edinburgh was dying out in the face of gang violence, venue closures and the end of the dancehall boom. Glasgow's stringent licensing laws all but killed off its music scene. During the first half of the 70s, the only record labels in Scotland were those that served the folk community – the 'haggis and heather' scene. To achieve commercial success in those years – as Nazareth, the Bay City Rollers, the Sensational Alex Harvey Band and the Average White Band all did – it was necessary to leave Scotland and relocate to London or America. And although punk rock inspired plenty of Scots to form bands in 1977, very few amounted to anything outside Scotland.

Only the Skids from Fife – signed by Virgin in 1978 on the day that British Rail's Intercity 125 cut the journey to London by a critical three hours – and the Rezillos, from Edinburgh, made a dent nationally. 'There wasn't any confidence in Scottish music,' says Edwyn Collins. 'Even when the Rezillos had a national profile, people didn't really take them very seriously. It didn't seem like any of the groups could actually build a career.' And besides, as Jake Black points out, there was a deep suspicion among Scottish punks of any band that sought to make its name in London. 'Everybody was reactionary towards the idea of people becoming commercially successful,' he says. 'That was not *de rigueur*. You would be betraying your local following if you were to get sucked into the corporate quagmire in England.'

Realistically, a Scottish band could not afford to ignore London, assuming it possessed a modicum of ambition. But in 1977, ignoring London was precisely what Lenny Love, an Edinburgh-based promotions rep for Island Records, was obliged to do. He was the manager of the Rezillos, Edinburgh's own manic boy-girl outfit surfing the punk wave. Once the Rezillos had built up a following in the city, Love tried to interest the major London labels, only to meet with scorn and incomprehension. No one was ready for Scottish punk, it seemed. Back in Edinburgh, Love explained his predicament to his friend Bruce Findlay, owner of the Bruce's Record Shop chain. Findlay had himself taken a young band under his wing – the Valves – and was planning to bypass the London companies and start his own indie label north of the border. He advised Love to do the same.

In the summer of 1977, Love founded Sensible Records – the first punk/new wave label in Scotland – and pressed up a few thousand copies of 'Can't Stand My Baby', a single by the Rezillos. He found a distributor, Scotia, which served the Scottish market. Then, like every other indie label owner in Britain, Love sat back and waited for John Peel to play his record. The Rezillos were fortunate: Peel loved the song.

Soon Love had a national buzz. Scotia started shipping 'Can't Stand My Baby' to Rough Trade – London's foremost indie record shop – in batches of hundreds. Within a few weeks, 'Can't Stand My Baby' had hit 7,000 sales and rising, and Love was hanging on for dear life. 'It was great that Scotland had local bands that could justify having their own records out,' he says. 'I didn't really think about England, or anywhere else in the world for that matter. I didn't expect [the record] to sell outside Edinburgh, to tell you the truth.'

But England was where it counted, and when Bruce Findlay launched his own label Zoom in September, it was clear that England did not care for anything he had to offer. 'I saw the immediate punk explosion falter,' Findlay later recalled, 'and I knew Zoom had to get financial support to survive.' He took a band called the Zones to a London label, Arista, in 1978, and later that same year delivered a second act, Simple Minds. Findlay took on Simple Minds' management in 1980. The job had once been turned down by Arthur Haggerty.

Lenny Love returned home one night in 1977 to find a message on his answering machine from Seymour Stein, the head of Sire Records in America. Stein, who had signed Talking Heads and the

Ramones in 1976, was one of the New York punk scene's chief executives and he wanted the Rezillos for Sire. When he got them, it was
the end of Sensible.

The spotlight now fell on Bob Last, an Englishman studying in
Edinburgh who had been the Rezillos' road manager. Inspired by the
eye-catching use of collage on an early Buzzcocks sleeve, Last
started the Fast Product label in December 1977 with the intention
of combining music and design in hard-hitting audio-visual packages. Fast Product's house style, a farrago of humorously incongru-
ous slogans and photographs, attracted the sort of aficionado who
liked records to look arty and highbrow, but it also talked a language
that the market in general was becoming used to hearing. In
essence, this said: records should be brilliant for an instant, relevant
for a moment and forgotten in a flash. Quite the most knowing indie
label of its time, Fast Product was manna to the choosy new wave
collector. As Brian Hogg noted in his book *All That Ever Mattered:
The History Of Scottish Rock and Pop*: '[Fast Product's] notion of corporate identity encouraged fans to buy every release – complete the
set, so to speak – irrespective of artist, or, more perversely, merit.'

Putting the icing on the post-modernist cake, Fast Product was a
Scottish label whose roster consisted almost entirely of English
bands. In a display of enlightened largesse that most record companies would have thought suicidal, Last actively encouraged these
bands to leave Fast Product if they received a better offer – and the
Gang Of Four and the Human League did just that. After licensing a
single for UK release by San Francisco punks the Dead Kennedys,
Fast Product wound itself down at the beginning of 1980.

If Last had shown that he could run a chic Scottish indie label that
also meant something in England, this still didn't get around the fact
that nobody had ever done it in Glasgow. The man who would do it
– Alan Horne – was not the type to be influenced by an Edinburgh
intellectual such as Last. Horne's motivation would come in time,
but it had to be idiomatic of Horne. It had to be bloody-minded. It
had to be perverse. And above all, it had to be mean-spirited.

Orange Juice hardly played any more in Glasgow, and were to all
intents and purposes an art-school secret. Wearing his managerial
hat, Horne ordered them to get professional or risk missing their
chance. An offended Steven Daly left the band in 1979 and swore
never to talk to Horne again. To show Orange Juice what kind of
business acumen they were losing, Daly motivated himself to
finance, release and promote two singles – one by an Edinburgh
band called Josef K, and one by the Fun Four, a Glasgow group comprised of Daly and three ex-Backstabbers. From his desk at the
Maryhill DHSS, where he worked as a clerk, Daly priced studios,
contacted sleeve-printers and approached a pressing plant, ordering
1,000 copies of each single.

Horne's curiosity was roused. If Daly could do all of that unaided, he thought to himself, it surely couldn't be so difficult. Hmmm ... The scheming Horne volunteered to drive Daly to the pressing plant in London and helped him distribute copies to Rough Trade and John Peel, using the long car journey to sweet-talk Daly into rejoining Orange Juice. 'We'll make a record ourselves, Steven,' he promised. 'But we can't do it without you.' And it'll be miles better than either of yours, he added to himself.

With bad grace, Daly agreed to return to Orange Juice and play drums on the first single to be released on Postcard, a label launched by Horne. Horne's dreams for Postcard were as petty as they were grandiose. He wanted to obliterate Daly's two singles – but he also envisaged a seethingly productive school of excellence that would not only recreate the bohemian spirit of the Factory under Warhol, but also bear comparison, ultimately, with two of the most illustrious homes-of-the-hits in black American history.

'The label was based along the lines of Stax and Motown,' Edwyn Collins told Brian Hogg. 'Alan saw himself as a cross between Berry Gordy and Andy Warhol.' Nor was Horne joking. 'I was thinking: well, there's all that [music] there, and we're going to come in *here* and be the main thing, and all that will just go away,' he says. 'Echo and the Bunnymen? The Clash? Joy Division? They won't matter. They'll all fade away. All that shite: gone.'

In an eight-track studio below a tailor's shop in Paisley, Orange Juice recorded their debut single, 'Falling And Laughing', for just under £100. The tiny budget exposed all the flaws in the performance – wayward tunefulness, erratic drumming, structural fragility – but these were pardonable blemishes for the post-punk times. Towering above them, in any case, was the extraordinary presence of Collins, whose fruity vocal and arch, cleverly rhymed lyric were completely new for Scotland. Slurring his way down a slalom of unexpected chord changes, he made it hard to guess his true age. Twenty years old, he sounded younger and strikingly gauche. It was the voice of – as one journalist would put it – 'lovesick schoolboys'; the voice of John Gordon Sinclair in the hit Scottish film of the following year, *Gregory's Girl*.

Exhilarated by the recording, Orange Juice and Horne pressed up around 1,000 copies of 'Falling And Laughing', of which roughly 200 were circulated to shops, radio stations and fanzines in Glasgow and Edinburgh. The remaining 800 were put in the boot of Horne's father's Austin Maxi as Horne and Collins headed for London.

Their first visit was to Rough Trade, the leading indie emporium in the south of England. Opened as a reggae-and-imports record shop in 1976, it had moved into distribution in 1977 and – in 1978 – started its own label, Rough Trade Records. The company's founder and label boss, Geoff Travis, was a Cambridge graduate with a Jimi

Hendrix Experience-style Afro and an intense whisper of a voice. Horne and Collins knew that he was a man who could potentially be of great value to them. In his undemonstrative way, Travis was just as important a figure in indie music as John Peel.

Travis played 'Falling And Laughing' on the spot, liked it and agreed to take 300 copies. Horne and Collins were delighted. Getting back in the car, they called in at Small Wonder – another London indie shop – who told them the single was terrible but took 100 anyway. They returned to Glasgow in good cheer.

But now Horne came to the hurdle at which every Glasgow label before Postcard had fallen: making headway with the London media. Horne knew that a rave review in the *NME*, *Sounds* or *Melody Maker* could make the difference between an indie hit and a lonely wait on Rough Trade's shelves. He and Collins drove back to London the next week, walking into the offices of the music papers one by one.

At the *NME*, they left a copy of 'Falling And Laughing' for Danny Baker, a well-known fan of soul music. At *Melody Maker*, *Sounds*, *Smash Hits* and even *Cosmopolitan*, they introduced themselves as the two brightest sparks north of London – why, they were musicians, entrepreneurs, fanzine editors, label managers and talent-spotters. 'I remember walking into *Melody Maker* and looking at the place, and it was all hippies,' says Horne. 'I thought there'd be a punk somewhere, just somebody of our age. They were all old men in cowboy boots.' At each destination, he and Collins took care to stress their youth and their foreignness, presuming that no journalist would want to miss out on the breaking story of Glasgow's pop renaissance.

That evening, they cold-called John Peel at Broadcasting House. The avuncular Peel was used to unannounced visits from young bands and made a point of listening to every record he was given. He was liked and respected by the punk generation, which made what happened next all the more exceptional. 'I waited in the foyer while Alan went up to see him,' says Collins. 'This was about fifteen minutes before Peel was due on the air at ten o'clock. And I know what Alan said to him because Peel repeated the conversation on the air the next night. Alan said: "Listen, all that Liverpool stuff you play – the Bunnymen and the Teardrop Explodes – that's all just a *nice bore*." That was one of Alan's favourite phrases at the time – "a nice bore". He said: "You always catch on a year after every other cunt. I mean, really, we are the future and either you'll get wise to that or you'll look very stupid." '

Peel, 20 years Horne's senior, was taken aback. It was risky stuff. 'Peel, the next night, played "Falling And Laughing",' remembers Collins, 'but he said: "I'm only going to play this once, because I was confronted last night by a horrible, truculent youth." ' In a single journey, Horne and Collins had promoted Orange Juice brilliantly –

with no overheads apart from petrol – and made an unforgettable impression. Or so they imagined.

A week later, the results started coming in. Danny Baker at the *NME* had reviewed the B-side of 'Falling And Laughing' by mistake. The *Sounds* notice was kind, but the journalist wrote incorrectly that Orange Juice no longer existed under that name; he also had the temerity to list Postcard alongside other contemporary Scottish labels such as Bob Last's new venture Pop Aural and Daly's one-off label Absolute. *Smash Hits* overlooked 'Falling And Laughing' altogether. Only in *Melody Maker* was the praise unqualified: '[A] lovely, lilting Glaswegian record … the best flighty rhythm I've heard in a long time.'

In general, the single was reviewed less favourably than those released on more established indie labels by the Teardrop Explodes, Wah! Heat, Swell Maps and the Fall. For Horne and Collins, pushing to the front of the queue was going to be harder than they thought.

Postcard was only one of several hundred indie labels that started up in Britain in the late 70s and early 80s. Coming from every corner of the land, they found their terminus more often than not at the Ladbroke Grove address of Rough Trade. The most identifiable brand name in the independent sector, Rough Trade was a shop, a record label, a distribution company, a music publisher – and even the title of a song on Stiff Little Fingers' album *Inflammable Material*, which, needless to say, was released on Rough Trade Records.

Of all the various Rough Trade activities, the record label was Geoff Travis' main interest by the start of 1980. He saw the purpose of Rough Trade as helping musicians make the records they wanted to make, and this didn't just mean paying studio bills. The credits on *Inflammable Material* listed Travis as a co-producer.

Like Travis himself, Rough Trade was not anti-Top 40 so much as oblivious to it. With a constant turnover of independent product from all over the world, the shop had learned to play to its strengths and be generous in its orders. Nikki Sudden of Swell Maps paints a picture of a vast indie clearing-house run on principles of near-philanthropy. Prior to agreeing a deal with Rough Trade in 1978, Swell Maps had released their single 'Read About Seymour' on their own label, using one of Rough Trade's competitors as their distributor. Nine months after its release, 'Read About Seymour' had sold less than half of its 2,200 pressing run. Strolling into the Rough Trade shop at 202 Kensington Park Road, Sudden was asked: 'How many copies of that single have you got left?' 'About twelve hundred,' he admitted. 'We'll take the lot,' they told him.

By 1979, Travis' business partner Richard Scott, a former manager of the reggae band Third World, had turned Rough Trade's ailing mail order service into an efficient distribution utility, building up a network of friends in like-minded indie shops up and down the country. Each shop would order product from the Rough Trade mothership as it arrived from London, regional Britain, mainland Europe, America, Australia or Jamaica.

But Rough Trade Distribution was more than just a means of getting a record from A to B. It centralised the anarchic indie hurly-burly and gave underground music a spine. In the context of post-punk Britain, the endeavours of Scott and Travis were as beneficial and as provident as if they had been building the first roads. In the process, Scott and Travis opened the door to anyone who wished to start his own label. All he had to do was think of a catchy name and deliver a cheaply-made 45 to Rough Trade, which would – for a small percentage of the profits – despatch it to the Midlands, the north, the west, Scotland ...

Since the late 70s – the beginning of the indie label revolution in Britain – dozens of aspiring moguls had followed this procedure to the letter. Their stimuli for starting a label would vary, of course. They might be members of a young band that didn't fancy waiting to be discovered (or more probably, rebuffed) by an existing label. They might be spurred into action by an article read in a fanzine, and quite a few were. They might, like Alan Horne, covet the kudos of being the local big shot. Or they might simply realise that thanks to punk's do-it-yourself credo, things were now getting made that could never have been made before, not least money. As an *NME* writer remarked in September 1977, the first question on a young man's lips now was not 'How do I form a group?' but 'How do I set up my own record company?'

If punk had made all of this possible, the follow-on effect was a schism in the music world. On one side stood the major labels and the bands that signed to them. On the other side: the bands that released their records independently. For sure, a lot of these bands were indie by necessity – no major label wanted them. But for others, the decision to take the independent route represented an emotional rejection, based on ethics and political beliefs, of everything the major labels stood for. And nowhere were these ethics more fundamental, or more keenly discussed, than at Rough Trade.

'There were two different sets of musicians,' says Geoff Travis. 'There was one set who definitely had an agenda. They wanted a career in pop music and their aspiration was to be on a major. Being on an independent was [perceived by them to be] just mucking about. For Siouxsie Sioux, for example, or Generation X, the benefits of having an independent scene were very minimal. But the generation after – the Scritti Polittis of this world – had a different agenda.'

In the eyes of these newer bands, major labels were greedy corporations staffed by uncool straights who maltreated and undermined their artists, and thought nothing of diluting the art itself to make it commercially viable. The whole point of an indie label was that the art remained undiluted – a band could record whatever it liked. At Rough Trade, this indie-major polarisation was very much played up. Here was the righteous indie band making interesting music without compromise; and over there was the banally ambitious, morally capitulating group that had sold its soul to a major label for money. While the indies appeared to have the upper hand in the argument as far as market credibility was concerned (the influential *NME*, for instance, had firm anti-major leanings), both sides could claim to be winning a theoretical war, and each could poke fun at the other's tenets like statesmen in a political cartoon:

> *'You have hits – but at what cost?'*
> *'You have respect – but where are your hits?'*

'Obviously, lots of music that you love is on major labels,' says Travis. 'And if someone says to you: "I'll take your record and release it, and here's fifty thousand quid," that's a pretty attractive offer and quite hard to turn down, whatever your ethics. But really, it just wasn't our cup of tea. We were a new generation of people and we wanted to do things our own way. And we also wanted to deal with music whose reason to exist was nothing to do with its commerciality. All that mattered was whether or not the record gave you a thrill.'

Travis was sincere about not caring whether a record sounded commercial. The Television Personalities' EP *Where's Bill Grundy Now?*, which Rough Trade had started distributing, was musically barely competent. But it enchanted Travis, who offered the band a deal it would never have got from a major label. No royalties and half-percentages. No clauses heavily weighted in the record company's favour. 'It was an old-fashioned, spit-and-shake, 50-50 deal,' says band-member Ed Ball. 'Share the risk and share the profits.'

Re-released on Rough Trade in 1979, the *Where's Bill Grundy Now?* EP struck a mood and sold well enough – between 20,000 and 30,000 copies – to enable each of the Television Personalities to purchase a Super 8 camera and live out a pop art fantasy in the King's Road. 'Dan [Treacy] always wore white trousers *à la* David Hemmings in *Blow Up*,' says Ball. 'Sometimes I'd wear cravats, although usually I thought I was Number 6 in *The Prisoner*. Joe [Foster] thought he was Fellini. And we all thought we were Young Businessmen Of The Year 1979. We'd walk around thinking: we are famous. Which maybe for a couple of weeks we were.'

But the EP was a hit in contextual terms only. None of the tracks was played on daytime radio and despite its popularity the record did not show in the national charts. When the Television Personalities' follow-up single proved less successful, they began to resent Rough Trade's inexperience. 'We didn't really know about hit records,' admits Travis. 'That seemed like another world.'

In fact, the issue was more complicated than that. Rough Trade's ethics baulked at sending records to journalists, and the label's relationship with Radio 1 was non-existent. When Stiff Little Fingers' *Inflammable Material* took everyone by surprise by reaching number 14 in the album charts in 1979, Travis realised the company could no longer afford to be so precious.

'I came to Rough Trade in March 1979,' says Scott Piering, an American brought in by Richard Scott to introduce the concept of promotion.* 'At that point, they were asking the music press to come along to the shop and buy [the records] to review. Everybody would send over taxis. I changed all that. I gave away more copies sometimes than we sold.'

Piering stayed late every night for four months, listening to all the records in the stockroom until he was schooled in what he calls 'the philosophy of Rough Trade' – a unique ideological marriage of music, comradeship and debate. 'I got right into the ethos of it,' he says. 'There were certain things that I wanted to institute that had to go to committee meetings. We had these meetings all the time [about] whether or not to give free stock away, or pay for taking someone to lunch. There was one time when we were given a load of money and half the people wanted to give it away to worthy political causes.'

Rough Trade's committee meetings, which became notorious, were attended by everyone from Travis to the shop staff. As Richard Scott hired more people, and as the record company and the distribution department moved to new premises in Blenheim Crescent, the meetings grew in size. 'It was a majority thing where the loudest vocal factions would have influence,' says Piering. 'But I think at the end of the day Geoff had a very strong will to operate as the leader, without actually declaring himself the leader.'

As it turned out, Travis was so quietly-spoken that declarations on any subject were few and far between. 'He didn't speak a lot,' says Peter Fowler, who joined Rough Trade in the early 80s. 'He's quite a shy, awkward, self-aware guy to get on with. I'd say to him: "I think my favourite record this year is 'Shipbuilding'." And three days later he'd come back and say: "I agree with you." '

Fowler had come from a job in television, where he had worn a suit. Rough Trade was so democratic and committee-based that he assumed he had joined a workers' cooperative. Actually, it was a privately-owned company going out of its way to behave like a commune. 'Everyone was on £8,000 a year at that point,' says Fowler.

---

* Scott Piering died of cancer in 2000. The author is very grateful for his contribution to this book.

'Geoff Travis was obviously the main honcho, but ... it was very much mucking in. One minute you'd be packing boxes. The next minute you'd be dealing with Factory or 4AD or Mute [labels distributed by Rough Trade], ordering stock. And we'd all take it in turns to do the washing up.'

As Travis developed Rough Trade Records, it began to function increasingly independently of the distribution company. Soon the two were striking different types of deal. Record deals were offered to individual bands by Travis as Rough Trade Records' head of A&R, while distribution deals would be made with indie labels by Richard Scott's people, who often disagreed with Travis about which music showed potential – and what kind of potential at that.

'The record company had their own set agendas and [the] distribution [company] had their own set agendas,' says Simon Edwards, who worked in distribution. 'We were more aware of what would sell in the short term than Geoff, who was thinking about long-term A&R. The thing that held it all together was the illusion – well, the objective – of being a cooperative.' To confuse matters, Travis could – and occasionally did – sign an indie label *en bloc* to Rough Trade Records if he saw long-term potential in one or more of its acts. And this is what he was thinking of doing with Alan Horne's Postcard.

Rather than press up another 1,000 copies of 'Falling And Laughing' as Travis had advised him to do, Horne decided to put Orange Juice in a studio without delay. He had acquired another band for Postcard – Josef K from Edinburgh, who wore dark suits and played a brittle-sounding funk *noir* – and was confident that Orange Juice's next single, 'Blue Boy', would break through nationally if it were recorded well enough. Judging his principal rival in Scotland to be Bob Last's Edinburgh label Pop Aural, a disingenuous Horne asked Last to recommend a good studio in the area. Last told him about Castle Sound, just outside Edinburgh, and Horne booked an all-day session for the recording of 'Blue Boy' and the Postcard debut of Josef K.

In the meantime, Horne had come up with a slogan for Postcard – 'The Sound of Young Scotland' – which was to appear on all future releases. Lifted from Motown's 'The Sound of Young America', 'The Sound of Young Scotland' had the ring of national pride, but it dripped with sarcasm. 'There's that kind of inbred persecution complex the Scots have because of things like the Highland clearances,'* said Edwyn Collins in 1984. 'So Alan thought: right, I'll play on this middle-class guilt. He also wanted to play on Scotland as the Scottish

---

* The forced removal of Highlands crofters from their land by absentee landlords in the late eighteenth and early nineteenth centuries, which led to widespread emigration to North America.

Tourist Board would – tartans, kilts, the rest of it.' Horne – need it be said – abhorred Scotland.

Since Orange Juice had been shunned by audiences and promoters in Glasgow, Horne was determined to take the Sound of Young Scotland where it would be better appreciated: south of the border. He was relying on Travis to agree a pressing-and-distribution deal, which would remove the burdens of finance and administration from Horne's shoulders and free him up to act as a self-publicist and gadabout. A Rough Trade deal would also give the career of Orange Juice a fillip. Horne didn't worry in the slightest when Travis told him the deal was subject to 'Blue Boy' being as good as 'Falling And Laughing'.

For the recording of 'Blue Boy', Orange Juice borrowed a Vox organ from a band Collins had seen play at the Glasgow College of Technology. The five-piece Newspeak were one of a dozen groups trying to get a foothold on the regional post-punk merry-go-round, but they invariably came across as a poor xerox of early XTC. Certainly, there was little common ground between Newspeak and Orange Juice. The latter were acid-tongued fops from the west end. The former were south-siders with a reputation for being dour.

James King, who saw Newspeak play at the art school, viewed them strictly as also-rans. 'I felt kind of sorry for them,' he recalls. 'There were maybe 12 people in the place. I remember the bassist was a ginger-headed cunt, and he'd bounce up and down while he was playing.'

Following his unsuccessful audition for Simple Minds, Alan McGee had had a frustrating couple of years. At the beginning of 1978, he'd got a job as a stores clerk with British Rail, which was undemanding enough to let him concentrate on his musical career. Since then, however, he'd had nothing but bad luck.

In the spring of 1978, he had joined a band called H_2O, fronted by singer Ian Donaldson. Donaldson was an ex-punk who had noticed that alternative music was becoming less frenetic and more cerebral. H_2O was his way of acknowledging the winds of change, but he also had ambitions to become successful. The band made its public debut at an outdoor Campaign For Nuclear Disarmament festival in front of a few hundred rowdy locals, with McGee on bass. 'He had quite a note-y bass playing style,' says Donaldson. 'It was the time of Jean-Jacques Burnel where the bass was quite prominent. You had to be able to play and Alan could.'

McGee was a good deal harder for Donaldson to relate to as a person. 'He was uncomfortable with himself,' Donaldson says. 'It was partly that he was dying to do something to break out of the humdrum life and the threat of following your dad into whatever he did for a living. But I also think he was a bit uncomfortable in life. He was quite a loner and he was quite deep. He had a short fuse. He was not at ease with himself.'

When H_2O lost a guitarist after an argument, McGee brought in Andrew Innes. This line-up played four or five times before McGee began having doubts. 'It was obvious that Ian wanted to be like the Bay City Rollers instead of the Velvet Underground,' he says. McGee and Innes left, taking recently-arrived guitarist Neil Clark with them. They formed Newspeak in 1979 with a new singer, Jack Reilly, and a drummer.

Billy Sloan was the presenter of *Fast Forward*, a new wave show on Radio Clyde. The only programme of its kind on the Glasgow airwaves, it was a magnet for local bands' demo tapes. 'I was used to the pushy singer telling you that his band was the greatest thing you'd ever heard,' says Sloan. 'But McGee was the pushy bass player, and pushy in a nice way. He was naturally enthusiastic. His enthusiasm was so profound that you almost wanted it to happen for him.'

Beyond Sloan's warm-hearted patronage, however, Newspeak's options were limited. In those months before Postcard started up, there were no local record labels. McGee made 35 copies of Newspeak's demo tape and sent them to all the English record companies he could think of. None of them replied.

Newspeak fragmented. Andrew Innes wanted to move to London, and singer Jack Reilly decided to go with him. McGee had been going out with a girl who worked for British Rail, Yvonne McMurray, and was reluctant to leave her. But something made him accompany Innes and Reilly on that journey. 'It's easy to look back through the mists of time and think that I had a gameplan,' he says. 'But in reality, Andrew Innes was going to London because he was seventeen – and nuts – and I was in his band. I didn't even want to go. I went because my pals were going.' British Rail gave him a transfer to a department in London, and in June 1980 McGee, Innes and Jack Reilly left Glasgow and moved into a one-room flat in south London's Tooting Bec. Within weeks, the homesick Reilly returned to Glasgow and Newspeak broke up.

To his surprise, McGee was promoted ahead of older British Rail colleagues to the post of pay clerk. His day job, at least, was moving in the right direction. Outside work, however, he pined for his girlfriend and dreamed of an entrée into the capital's music scene. The desperate need to find a drummer was drifting through his mind when, passing a phone box in Clapham one day, he spotted two of the most outrageous-looking punks he had ever seen.

'I had bright pink hair and I think my mate had got leopardskin hair,' says Karen Bignall. 'We were off to France – that's why we were using the phone box. Alan came up and asked if I knew any drummers. I said: "I've got one sitting at home in my front room at the moment." ' McGee went back with the girls to meet Mark Jardim.

Jardim, a Portuguese raised in Croydon, agreed to be the drummer in McGee's and Innes' new trio, the Laughing Apple. In that Clapham house, the two Glaswegians had stumbled upon punk rock's dying embers. 'We unwittingly got involved in a heroin subculture,' says McGee. 'This was the first time I'd ever encountered real drug abuse. I'd never actually noticed drugs before – that's how naive I was at nineteen. And suddenly we're in a room and somebody would tie up his arm and jack up.' McGee squeamishly refused to try the drug.

'I think Alan was a little bit concerned that we might lead him astray,' concedes Bignall. 'Everyone was [taking heroin] – and not only heroin, everything.' She found McGee grumpy and hard to get along with. He recalls: 'It was quite a rough existence. I suppose you'd call it a traveller's existence now. We used to go out and nick the milk off people's doorsteps for our breakfast. This was punk in London in 1980.'

The Laughing Apple had only one useful contact, and he was in Glasgow not London. Alex Forsyth, the organiser of the CND festivals at which H_2O – and a year later, Newspeak – had performed, offered the Laughing Apple a loan of £500 to record and press up a single, in return for CND being mentioned on the sleeve. *The Ha Ha Hee Hee EP*, which the band travelled back to Scotland to record, threw an inexperienced McGee into the role of an Alan Horne or a Bob Last. Christening the band's label Autonomy (after a Buzzcocks song), he paid the first of many visits to Rough Trade's distribution department at 137 Blenheim Crescent.

Blenheim Crescent was all things to all men. The anarcho-syndicalist band Crass, whose label Rough Trade distributed, would travel in from their headquarters in Epping Forest with the latest instalment in their punk compilation series *Bullshit Detector*. Other musicians used the building as a contact address, as a hangout and as a good place to hear new records. 'There would be people coming in and flogging their instruments,' says Peter Fowler. 'The Birthday Party, who were on 4AD, always used to store their drum-kit and their guitars there. It was a very ... in a way idealistic, but completely unbusinesslike environment. It was a dream that wasn't quite happening.'

Pilfering was par for the course, and break-ins were frequent. *The Ha Ha Hee Hee EP*, however, remained unstolen and was as difficult to sell as it was to pronounce. 'The Laughing Apple were one of dozens and dozens of bands,' says Fowler. 'We had a wall the length of a restaurant, covered from floor to ceiling with boxes of 7-inches. Hundreds and hundreds of records. And I must say the Laughing Apple weren't one of the leading lights.'

McGee would pop in to ask how the EP was doing; the conversation would rarely last long. 'He would come in every week without fail,' says Fowler, 'refusing to wear his glasses – and he's absolutely blind as a bat – and he'd walk around trying to find records. He would talk passionately about music. Unfortunately, he'd talk passionately about music that no one else was passionate about.'

McGee's visits to Blenheim Crescent were more than just a matter of keeping tabs on *The Ha Ha Hee Hee EP*, however. He knew few people in London except for those on the ghoulish, opiated Clapham scene. Rough Trade offered companionship as much as anything else. 'I was ambitious,' he says. 'I wanted to be successful. And Rough Trade was the only bit of the music business that would let me in.'

Simon Edwards, in distribution, remembers McGee as a serious and rather morose person. But it was Edwards who first noticed that the Glaswegian might be a bit more intelligent than they all thought. 'He was someone who was looking and absorbing what was going on,' Edwards recalls, 'and asking what I thought were relevant and interesting questions.' Among the questions McGee asked was how many records Orange Juice and Josef K were selling. He wanted to know if the Laughing Apple might benefit from the amazing success story of Postcard and the celebrated rebirth of Scottish pop.

'We've done it,' thought Alan Horne as they left Castle Sound studios. Two singles had been recorded: 'Blue Boy' by Orange Juice in the morning, and 'Radio Drill Time' by Josef K in the evening – and both, Horne was telling anyone who would listen, were all-time classics.

As much as he liked 'Radio Drill Time', Horne's reasons for bringing Josef K to Postcard had been more tactical than musical. A label with two acts, he had noticed, was taken more seriously by the press than a label with only one. Horne was a chauvinist when it came to the crunch, and the Edinburgh-based Josef K, who were neither devastating nor quick-fire in their repartee, simply didn't excite him as much as Orange Juice did. And in 'Blue Boy', Horne believed that Orange Juice had recorded the best single of the year.

A sizzling three-minute volley of tension-and-release dynamics, 'Blue Boy' combined melodic pop with controlled punk energy. Gone was the whimsy of 'Falling And Laughing'. The jubilant outbursts and yelpingly atonal guitar solo on 'Blue Boy' showed a self-assurance that Scottish music had been missing for a decade. Horne rightly deduced that no young Scot could resist it. As Brian Hogg points out, whilst 'Anarchy In The UK' had a hugely liberating effect on the youth of England, 'it was "Blue Boy" which emancipated Scotland's pop, providing undreamed of directions and hope to new, aspiring musicians. After it, nothing could be the same again ...' Three years after the Stranglers' momentous concert at the City Hall, Glasgow had finally caught up with England. There was just one snag. The man who would be releasing 'Blue Boy' didn't like it.

Horne had made up his mind about Geoff Travis within seconds of meeting him. He had taken one look at Travis' Afro and presumed him to be an ineffectual, dyed-in-the-wool hippy. Travis, meanwhile, had clocked Horne at once as a mixture of borrowed technique and cosmetic front. ('He was a would-be Malcolm McLaren,' Travis says, 'obnoxious and snotty and insulting on purpose because he thought that was the way to behave.') In a head-to-head between the two men, the more circumspect Travis would be the favourite to prevail. But Horne was not expecting an argument – quite the reverse – when he and Collins drove down to Blenheim Crescent with the tapes from the Castle Sound session.

After listening to 'Blue Boy' and 'Radio Drill Time', Travis spoke softly and sadly, like a disappointed housemaster. He told them he wasn't as keen on 'Blue Boy' as he had been on 'Falling And Laughing'. He thought it fell between two stools: sonic sophistication at the expense of charming primitivism; but not sophisticated enough to qualify as mainstream pop. And he didn't like Josef K's single either. In fact, the whole thing was rather a letdown. Perhaps they could all aim to try harder next time?

A crestfallen Collins saw his career disappearing down the plughole. Horne was outraged. 'Alan said: "What the fuck does that disgusting, despicable hippy know anyway?" and stormed out,' says Collins. 'And he went into this partly affected, mad trance.' 'Edwyn was floored as well,' Horne remembers. 'But I don't know if Edwyn had the same expectations as me. We sat in a café and I just lost it. It wasn't madly out of character with things I'd done in the past.'

Collins reached down into the plug-hole with both hands. 'I said: "Well, if what Geoff says is true [about the relative sophistication of the production], perhaps there'll be some interest from major record companies",' he recalls. 'Alan said: "Well, *take* them to a major record company and fucking betray me, you cunt." And then he walked out into the middle of the traffic saying: "Come on, run me over." '

Collins mothered a semi-catatonic Horne back to Glasgow. In the weeks that followed, Horne declined into a drunken depression, hanging out at art-school dances and agonising over ways to get the two singles pressed up. 'He would do crazy things,' says James King. 'He'd write letters to Elton John asking him for money. Brian Taylor put on an English accent and phoned Horne pretending to be Elton John. Horne's supposed to have wet himself.'

To cut down on costs, Horne pressed up 2,000 copies of each single in a dual-purpose sleeve – one side for 'Blue Boy', the other for 'Radio Drill Time'. A few of these were posted to journalists in London, including Dave McCullough at *Sounds* who had reviewed 'Falling And Laughing' earlier in the year. Although he had got one or two things wrong in that review, McCullough was a vital and

much-cultivated figure in independent music. An Irishman, his
opinions were famously peremptory and often controversial – not
least within the offices of the publication he worked for. He wrote
almost exclusively about new bands, appearing to have little time for
established ones. 'He always had a strong image of what a band
should be in [the music business] for,' a colleague recalls, 'and that
image would survive for as long as it took for their first album to
come out. When the album arrived, it would always disappoint him.
You could literally see the suffering on his face.'

On receipt of 'Blue Boy' and 'Radio Drill Time', McCullough
arrived by train to interview Orange Juice, Josef K and Alan Horne.
His two-page article was published in *Sounds* at the end of August
and effected a wholesale turnaround in Postcard's fortunes.
McCullough called the label 'the brightest hope I have seen for a
very long time' and suggested that Scottish pop's revival in the previous six months had been 'staggering'. He added that 'a caring independent label is what Scotland has been begging for for years'. (That
was going too far. Horne cared so little about new bands that he
would refuse to listen to unsolicited demo tapes, and almost never
replied to fanmail.)

On the day *Sounds* hit the streets in London, Horne received a
phone call from Geoff Travis. He had changed his mind: Rough
Trade Records would do a pressing-and-distribution deal with
Postcard after all.

It had been an unpleasant shock for Horne to discover that Travis
was not the easy touch he'd imagined. But as he drove to London to
negotiate the deal, Horne steeled himself for retribution. He vowed
to let that hippy bastard have it with both barrels. When Horne
arrived at Blenheim Crescent, Travis spelt out the terms of the deal.
Rough Trade would undertake Postcard's pressing and distribution;
would refund Horne for the Castle Sound studio bill; and would take
care of all Postcard's promotion and marketing requirements. It was
a licensing deal in all but name, and Travis offered the standard
Rough Trade 50-50 split of the profits after costs. This was not good
enough for the piqued Scot.

'I said: "Where are you getting 50? What's your 50 for?",' recalls
Horne. 'He said, "Oh well, we're paying for the studio, and we're
doing the pressing and the promoting and the distributing." I said:
"Yeah? Well, I don't think that's worth 50." I knew he wanted us and
I just really hated him, so I said: "You'll get 15." '

Incredibly, Travis assented. After discounts, manufacturing costs
and distribution fees, the percentages were agreed as 85:15 in
Horne's favour. He was seeing to it that Rough Trade would never
make money out of Postcard.

Back in Glasgow, Horne crowed that he had put one over on the
Rough Trade hippies and negotiated the most enviable contract in

indie music. Not surprisingly, the deal was the subject of heated debate in Blenheim Crescent. 'There were a lot of doubters at Rough Trade,' says Scott Piering. 'They were like: "The guy [Edwyn Collins] can't sing, he's taking the piss." At that point Geoff said: "No, you've got to listen to this, you've got to read between the lines." And when it came time to selling the single to the assembled committee – and it's a great technique if you could put up with it – he would play a single three, four, five times in a row, just to make sure people got it. It's the ideal way that you'd love people to listen to music.'

So Travis was urging everybody to hear 'Blue Boy' five times before making a decision? The irony of that would have appealed richly to Horne.

Nineteen eighty-one was the year it became hip to be a young musician from Scotland. Edwyn Collins appeared on the front cover of the *NME* with Clare Grogan – the singer in Glasgow's Altered Images and a supporting actress in *Gregory's Girl* – and Rough Trade organised a two-night showcase for Postcard at the Venue in Victoria. Both nights were rammed to the rafters, and interest in Scottish pop grew out of all proportion. Jake Black, who had moved to London in 1980, was amazed to find his inside knowledge of Postcard getting him fêted like a Liverpudlian in mid-60s America. 'I would be in pubs with people in the music business and they would be going: "What – you *know* those people?",' he says. 'It was the hot label for about six months.'

Malcolm Dunbar was a Scot who had gone to London to work for Polydor. He compares the 1981 explosion of interest in Scottish bands to the major label feeding frenzy of the punk era, when every A&R man raced to get the signatures of any group that looked the part. 'British Airways and British Caledonian were making a fortune, as were the hotels in Scotland,' says Dunbar. 'There were just millions of bands being signed.' And the traffic was heading in both directions. Dozens of Dunbars were taking up positions with major labels in A&R, marketing and PR. 'It was like half of Scotland had moved to work in the record industry in London,' he says.

The BBC Scotland arts programme *Spectrum* made a documentary called 'Jock 'n' Roll' – presented by B.A. Robertson – which told the story of Scottish pop from Lulu to the Skids. It was inevitable that Robertson would want to meet Alan Horne and Edwyn Collins, and it was equally inevitable that the interview would be excruciating. Footage of the encounter shows Robertson squeezed between Horne and Collins on a sofa in Postcard's West Princes Street headquarters. Genial and jokey, Robertson tries to bond with his young hosts. But as Collins sniggers and double-takes, the baby-faced Horne waits to pounce on Robertson's first mistake. It is not long in arriving. Horne announces airily that he might be signing a young band called the

French Impressionists. 'They could record "Give Me Monet", I suppose,' suggests Robertson. The pun would have got a polite laugh in any other company. 'Oh yes,' says Horne, sadistically deadpan, 'that's funny.' Collins nearly falls off the sofa.

Robertson was not the only victim. Arranging an interview with Horne and Collins for a Glasgow listings magazine, Billy Sloan looked forward to a nice positive discussion about Scottish music. Instead, they poured scorn on him and on every band he dared to mention. Sloan was a burly fellow, but he admits to being completely intimidated. 'The whole Postcard camp treated everybody else, no matter what their background was, with complete and utter disdain,' he says. 'They would sneer down their noses at you. Horne was Glasgow's answer to Andy Warhol, running a whole movement, a coterie of trendy people.'

Glasgow had never had an art-school tradition. Now the traditions it did lay claim to, and was proud of – soul music, R&B, passion, working-class fire – were being thrown back in its face by contemptuous, middle-class upstarts. The streets of Glasgow teemed with new bands: the post-'Blue Boy' bands. As the Postcard scenesters lorded it over everyone they considered their intellectual inferior – from Robertson and Sloan downwards – the music of Orange Juice could be heard, with varying degrees of replication and dilution, in the songs of the Bluebells, the Jazzateers, Del Amitri, Strawberry Switchblade, Lloyd Cole and many others. The once-derided Edwyn Collins was now the single most imitated musician in the city. 'I remember being about 16 and I had "I Love Edwyn Collins" on my school jotter,' Justin Currie of Del Amitri recalled in 1998. 'You'd walk around town and you'd see him in his knee-length cavalry boots and think he's the coolest motherfucker ever seen. Couldn't sing, but it didn't matter.'

The demo tapes pressed into Billy Sloan's hands each night showed the tell-tale influence of Orange Juice. 'There were hundreds of students from the universities suddenly forming groups,' says Horne, 'or old rock people in pubs changing their sound and pretending to be camp. It was depressing. It was bad enough when the Sweet did it.'

There was even an Orange Juice-inspired band in Horne's own flat. Brian Superstar played guitar in the Pastels, formed by a gauche 19-year-old from Bearsden named Stephen McRobbie. A singer and frontman, Stephen Pastel (as McRobbie was to call himself) made Edwyn Collins sound like Robert Plant. In style and approach, the Pastels were Orange Juice in concentrated form. Quite remarkably fey, they horrified Horne. 'I wouldn't talk to them,' he says. 'I wouldn't even acknowledge them as they passed me in the hall. They were like something that Edwyn would have invented to annoy me.'

Orange Juice's third single, 'Simply Thrilled Honey', had been acclaimed by the music papers as a masterpiece. Postcard was officially the toast of London. Glasgow had leapfrogged Liverpool and Manchester to become the vanguard city for independent pop. 'It was a crazy time,' remembers Horne. 'Adam Ant would be on Radio 1 saying "Simply Thrilled" was great. The Undertones would phone up saying: "You're the best band in the world. Please come on tour with us." I realised that after all those months, we'd done it. From a punk perspective we had got quite far, and there was a sense of achievement.'

With London's A&R pack jetting regularly to Scotland, it was typical of his luck that Alan McGee had gone in the opposite direction. The Laughing Apple were snagged up in a holding pattern of bottom-rung bands trying to pick up 20-minute support slots in London clubs like the Moonlight and the Rock Garden. Karen Bignall recalls McGee bursting into the house in Clapham one night to announce that he had seen Dave Gahan, the singer of Depeche Mode, walking out of a nightclub with a girl on each arm. *That* was the pop star's life McGee aspired to ... but how to get there?

As Scottish pop proliferated and thrived in 1981, the Laughing Apple were able to take advantage only once. *The Ha Ha Hee Hee EP* found an admirer in Dave McCullough, who interviewed the band for *Sounds* in March. He hailed the EP as one of the year's three benchmark releases – the other two were Postcard singles, so this was significant praise – and promoted the Laughing Apple as a vigorous trio in the Jam tradition. In the interview, however, McGee came across as a disillusioned soul. 'They're all hippies in London,' he protested. 'Their attitudes belong to ten years ago. They really don't care about music, it's just the fashion they care about ...'

If Postcard had brought a golden dawn for music-making Scots, the Laughing Apple had the marbled pallor of late risers. McGee, an angry young man still fighting the punk wars of three years earlier, was in little doubt that progress for his band would be hard-won. He was counting on McCullough's article to start the ball rolling, but it was a vain hope. The ovations of the Irishman would go unechoed.

The *NME* journalist Charles Shaar Murray once made the observation that punk rock had created a new generation of movers and shakers – fanzine writers, promoters, indie label owners – whom he compared to the college newspaper editors and entertainments secretaries who'd come out of the progressive rock boom to land key jobs in the British record industry of the early 70s. Like prog-rock, Murray seemed to be saying, punk had signalled all-change; open sesame; opportunity knocks. By 1981, Britain was full of people like Alan McGee who proved the lie. Still standing at the conclusion of punk's round of musical chairs, these were the musicians from bands that had played far down the 1977 bills – if they had played at all – or grown up in towns and cities which had been punk backwaters. No one in a position of influence had been listening to the radio the night *their* demo tape was played.

On the face of it, McGee was a straightforward punk rock throwback. Talking to McCullough in the old language of 1977 ('hippies', 'destroy', 'revolution'), he had the tone of a forlorn warrior, an anachronism even for Clapham. But the more doors that closed in the Laughing Apple's faces – and the angrier McGee became as a result – the more he fell into step with the motley ranks of waifs, strays and stragglers experiencing similar frustration around Britain. There were, for example, two brothers from East Kilbride near Glasgow who sent a demo tape to Alan Horne in 1981. He put it to one side without even listening to it, and the destinies of Horne and Alan McGee crossed in that moment.

By the late summer of 1981, Postcard was in trouble. After their fourth single, 'Poor Old Soul', cracks had appeared in Orange Juice's relationship with Horne that could not be papered over with wit or sarcasm. Steven Daly was the first to realise that the indie route was a cul-de-sac. As the band began recording an album, Daly lobbied vociferously for the tapes to be shopped around major labels.

His words made sense. Orange Juice wanted to be in the high-street record shops – and in the Top 40 – but Rough Trade had no sales reps to put them there; such blatant commercialism was anathema at Blenheim Crescent. 'Rough Trade were ineffectual and lacked the wherewithal to get records in the charts,' says Edwyn Collins. 'And that was the whole Postcard manifesto – to get our sort of indie music in the charts.'

As Orange Juice's besotted Brian Epstein, Horne naturally wanted the best for his boys, but sending them off to a major label would spell the end of Postcard, whose *raison d'être* was to advance the career of Orange Juice. More pressingly, the band needed money. Horne, hopeless at accounting, had lost control of the finances months before. 'It was a struggle to get any money out of him,' says Collins. 'We would all go down to this café, Equi, at the foot of Sauchiehall Street. Alan would be eating knickerbocker glories and we could barely afford soup.' The joke became: Horne is spending all the money on ice-cream. But it was not funny. Collins had had his unemployment benefit stopped and was living on £3 a day.

'There was no money. I wish there was,' says Horne, who adds that indie singles do not bring in much income. 'We didn't look where the money was going. We didn't do books. How dare they think I was going to sit at home doing the books?'

As a career move, Orange Juice's smart-alecky intuition was starting to look dangerously like unworldliness. They were years behind the Top 40 bands in know-how, like schoolboys who'd fidgeted their way through lessons. 'We really had no clue how to go about it,' says Daly. 'All that language that is now familiar to every member of the public – cracking it on your third single; remixing – we had no idea about.'

Horne's hold over the group had slipped, and the line-up was breaking apart over the issue of major labels. The unpopular Daly was clutching on by his fingernails, and when Malcolm Dunbar's Polydor sent a deputation to an Orange Juice gig in Leeds, the band's lead guitarist James Kirk staged his own protest by taking the stage in an undertaker's coat and playing a guitar that wasn't plugged into his amplifier.

Josef K, of whom expectations had grown impossibly high, had recorded an album for Postcard, *Sorry For Laughing*, at Castle Sound, but shelved it when everyone from Horne to Collins expressed doubts about its production. Horne consoled himself with the thought that it was only Rough Trade's money they were wasting. Josef K's second attempt, *The Only Fun In Town*, was released in the summer of 1981 to general disappointment. By August, they had split up. Meanwhile, the only Edinburgh band that Horne had ever wanted – the dazzling, hotly-tipped Fire Engines – had signed to the enemy, Pop Aural.

Horne was exhausted. To his chagrin, Postcard's reputation in England had grown a personality all of its own – one which bore scant resemblance to the Glasgow Motown he'd had in mind. Thanks to the kilts and the tartan in the artwork, the label was widely being misrepresented as a sort of musical shortbread tin. Patronisingly, Orange Juice were cast as cuddly McMonkees with cute fringes. And Horne, the greatest misanthrope of all, was depicted as a public-spirited pop guru. Privately, he lamented the fact that Postcard's releases did not stand up to the classics. 'Whenever a Postcard single came out,' recalled Collins three years later, 'Alan would play it back to back with [the Velvet Underground's] "Pale Blue Eyes" and with tears in his eyes say: "We'll never make a record as good as that." ' One night, as he got ready to travel to a gig by Aztec Camera – the latest addition to the Postcard roster – Horne looked outside and saw that it was snowing. He spent the evening watching television instead.

Orange Juice signed to Polydor in September 1981. Steven Daly, who'd pushed hardest for the deal, would soon be out of the band, as would James Kirk. Aztec Camera moved on to Rough Trade in 1982. Orange Juice's album, *You Can't Hide Your Love Forever*, was released in February that year and drew criticism for its major label glossiness and lack of indie bite. It had actually been recorded while they were still a Postcard band, but they were playing for different stakes now.

3 The Neophyte Psychedelian

WITH THE INDEPENDENT SECTOR seemingly content to let profits take a back seat to creativity, others were only too delighted to have their cake and eat it. Flouncing forth from the night-clubs – the Blitz, the Kilt and Le Beat Route in London, and Rum Runner in Birmingham – the New Romantics not only nipped post-punk austerity in the bud but sent the clocks spinning back to the early 70s, when pop had been a world of make-believe, dressing up and self-reinvention.

New Romantic clubs were so elitist about whom they let in that Steve Strange, manager of Club For Heroes in Baker Street, even turned away his own flatmate one night. Cheerfully apolitical pea-cocks, the New Romantics were a rowdy party in the bar of a sinking ship. Shortly before Birmingham's Duran Duran broke through in 1981, one member told the *NME*: 'We're going to be rich, and when we're rich we'll buy a gymnasium and that'll keep us fit. Also when you're rich you can eat really nice food like smoked salmon 24 hours a day ..' While he spoke, four hundred Rastafarians rioted a quarter of a mile away in New Street.

The wall between performer and audience, which punk had demolished, was rebuilt. It was no surprise that the New Romantics – Duran, Spandau Ballet, Japan, Visage and others – engendered seething contempt among indie bands. Alan McGee of the Laughing Apple had two reasons for feeling insulted. Struggling to find a foothold in London life, he really didn't need to be reminded of his loneliness by the tinkling laughter from the balcony tables. And as a fan of passionate, angry songwriting, he found the New Romantic motifs of prosperity and pageantry hopelessly superficial. 'There was no sense of revolution,' he says. 'It was like punk had never happened. You couldn't align yourself to anyone bar Paul Weller and Kevin Rowland. You had no affinity with them. Whereas with the indie thing, you had an affinity with the people as human beings. Even though you might not like a lot of the bands, you met them and you believed in them.'

This was the pivotal shift for McGee, and signalled his absolute immersion in independent music. If you assumed, as he now assumed, that the agenda of the major labels was a combination of philistinism, lousy judgment and a desire to maintain the status quo at all costs, then everything started to fall into place. It explained why the real heroes were going unacclaimed – the underdogs playing in tiny clubs and releasing records on indies. 'Independents invest in human beings, majors invest in the system,' was how McGee rationalised it in an interview in 1988.

Detesting the fashion-led trends in pop which saw New Romantics and synthesizer duos dominate the charts, he started to take a keener interest in indie labels, particularly the London indie Cherry Red, which had a reputation for acquiring the hippest talent.

Cherry Red's owner Iain McNay, who was in his mid-thirties, had come from the accountancy side of the music business. In the early 70s, he had worked for the hit-making labels Bell and Magnet, and with Cherry Red he was attempting to balance a love of punk with his sober understanding of the bottom line. On a hunch, he became the first of the new breed of indie bosses to take an interest in publishing. McNay's company, Cherry Red Music, monitored hundreds of indies and snapped up any songwriter who moved, boosting its catalogue by signing unknown writers on a one-song or two-song basis for nominal advances.

One morning in December 1979, McNay woke with an idea for an independent chart. Based on accurate sales data from small record dealers, it would list Britain's 30 highest-selling indie singles and 15 highest-selling albums. There had been underground charts before – *Sounds* had printed a new wave Top 20 or Top 30 intermittently since 1977 – but these had usually been compiled from sales in a single London or regional record shop, giving a distorted picture of Britain as a whole. And they had included records on major labels, which rather defeated the exercise.

McNay took his idea to friends at the trade magazine *Record Business*, and the inaugural independent chart was published in January 1980. Among other things, the chart defined the ubiquitous word 'indie'. Though it would later be applied to everything from a musical style to a fashion sensibility, indie was neither a sound nor a look. 'To have indie status,' explained chart compiler and statistician Barry Lazell, 'a record – or the label on which it was released – had to be one which was independently distributed: produced, manufactured, marketed and put into the shops without recourse to the corporate framework of the major record companies ...' Many famous independent labels of the 70s – including Virgin, A&M, Chrysalis and Island – were distributed by majors by 1980, and were therefore ineligible for the *Record Business* chart.

In the early 80s, the indie chart (subsequently compiled by the research company MRIB) gave prestige and validity to a multitude of small labels – Cherry Red, Factory, Mute, Crass, Small Wonder, Postcard, Pop Aural and others – and, as McNay would later write, 'helped shops order records, provided information for radio stations on what was really selling, and showed record companies abroad which companies were worth talking to regarding licensing releases for their territories. For ten years, the chart served a clear purpose and for many labels was *the* chart.'

However, McNay had allowed Cherry Red Records to drift. A one-man show, it was a trashy new wave label – not fit to be seen in the modish company of Mute, Factory or Rough Trade. With the profits from the Dead Kennedys album *Fresh Fruit For Rotting Vegetables*, which had gone Top 40 in the autumn of 1980, McNay was able to invest in an A&R man. He had been taking calls from an enthusiastic young promoter in west London named Mike Alway, who managed a band McNay had never heard of. 'He'd ring up and say: "I've got this band Scissor Fits. What can I compare them to? They're as good as the Beatles",' McNay recalls. 'And he meant it. He wasn't a bullshitter, he really believed it.'

McNay passed on Scissor Fits but offered Alway a job. The newcomer took one look at Cherry Red's menagerie of three-legged punk donkeys and knew he would have to make sweeping changes. A 60s buff, Alway decided to establish Cherry Red as a credible underground label with a strong identity. He wanted melody, 60s pop flavours and psychedelic patterns, a dry sense of humour, a suggestion of darkness and as much pretentiousness as his acts could give him. Between 1980 and 1982, Alway brought to Cherry Red over a dozen bands and songwriters who – individually and collectively – made the label stand out from its contemporaries. He signed an all-girl trio (the Marine Girls), a jazz-educated singer-songwriter (Ben Watt), a darkly enigmatic, impressionist quartet from Birmingham (Felt), an arty trio from the north (the Passage), an intense post-punk duo (Eyeless In Gaza) and sardonic veterans the Monochrome Set, who yoked recherché wit to a spaghetti western guitar sound.

Under Alway's A&R direction, Cherry Red was both timeless and of its time. While his £50-a-week salary put him on one of the lowest floors of the record business infrastructure, many believed he had more style than everyone in the Warner Bros building put together. 'His press releases would be amazing,' says McNay. 'There was no truth in them whatsoever. It was just the most fantastic rubbish.' In one, Alway claimed that the Monochrome Set's singer Bid (who was of Indian descent) had been telephoned by Sunil Gavaskar, the captain of India's cricket team, and asked for his advice on how to prepare an ideal test wicket in Bangalore. 'But Mike was never good with money,' McNay adds. 'When he first came to work with me, he was homeless. He had these different girlfriends he stayed with. He was a man for the ladies.'

When the Laughing Apple supported Eyeless In Gaza at the Moonlight in 1981, Alan McGee got his first sight of the Alway aura. 'Mike was strolling about like Oscar Wilde with this sort of army-RAF bag,' he later recalled. 'He was totally charismatic. He was more charismatic than Eyeless In Gaza onstage. I didn't know much about Mike Alway ... but I knew the room was revolving around him.'

Theo Chalmers, who ran Cherry Red Music, rang to offer McGee an assignment deal for his Laughing Apple songs. The advance was far from generous – a few tenners – but it at least got McGee into the Cherry Red family. He went along to the label's offices in Bayswater. 'Entering into 53 Kensington Gardens Square was like going into a subterranean lair of creativity and inspiration,' he would later say. 'The whole of the early 80s was dominated by your chart position. And there was [Alway] who didn't give a shit about his chart position. All he wanted to do was put out these really weird art records. He created [a] whole world. If you talk about somebody who I thought: God, I aspire to be like that, it was Mike.'

However, the Laughing Apple were not invited to sign to Cherry Red Records. They had released a second single on their own Autonomy label, 'Participate', but this had put them no higher up the Rock Garden or Moonlight ranks. They'd had a change of drummer and were about to lose Andrew Innes, who returned to Glasgow to recover from hepatitis. McGee regrouped with two musicians from Lincolnshire – drummer Ken Popple and guitarist Dick Green – and started writing all the Laughing Apple's songs himself. He missed Innes' ear for a tune. '[My songs were] like a cross between Ian Curtis and Gary Numan,' McGee says. 'It was pretty abysmal.' Worse, only one person had ever been seen to enjoy a Laughing Apple concert. In an audience of seven people at the Rock Garden in January 1981, one skinny kid had danced irrepressibly from beginning to end. One fan. It wasn't much.

On 19 August, a band recently signed by Alway to Cherry Red headlined a midweek triple bill at the Venue in Victoria. The Nightingales had a rambunctious, lurching style and a droll saloon-bar poet for a vocalist, which had caused more than one journalist to describe them as Birmingham's answer to the Fall. Alan McGee would later claim that the Venue gig was the most amazing he had seen since the Clash at the Glasgow Apollo. But it wasn't the Nightingales who had amazed him. It was one of the support bands: the Television Personalities.

Prior to playing the Venue that night, the three founder members of the Television Personalities – Dan Treacy, Ed Ball and Joe Foster – had never appeared together on the same stage. At that time, there seemed to be several groups in London masquerading as the Television Personalities, such as the Times, O Level and the Gifted Children, giving the illusory dimension of a complicated in-joke. 'It was difficult to work out whose project was what,' says Clive Solomon, whose company Twist And Shout published Treacy's songs. 'The Times was Ed and the TV Personalities was Dan, but they were in each other's bands. You never quite knew who was going to turn up.'

Since the *Where's Bill Grundy Now?* EP, the Television Personalities had fallen abruptly from grace. Their lo-fidelity, character-based songs appeared trifling compared to the much more straight-faced work of Joy Division and Cabaret Voltaire, and the band had retreated into semi-retirement. By 1981, when they re-emerged as acolytes of Syd Barrett and tea-and-cakes psychedelia, the Television Personalities were stranded in no man's land. 'People could never quite get the point with us,' says Joe Foster. 'Having humour and irony was not hip. Rough Trade saw us as a comedy version of a 60s pop group, which I always vaguely resented. I thought: I'm not asking you to say we're all geniuses, but for God's sake we're not fucking clowns.'

The band's releases had dwindled to the rate of one a year. The latest 45, 'I Know Where Syd Barrett Lives', was a tribute to Treacy's reclusive hero. But their record sales had fallen off a cliff, the press rarely mentioned them and they were in complete disarray. Their gigs sometimes included poetry, painting, freeform cacophony and a revolving cast. Some nights, Treacy didn't bother showing up. The sense of anything-can-happen translated perfectly to one delighted Glaswegian in the Venue shadows.

'They sawed up a Rickenbacker guitar onstage,' McGee recalls. 'Joe Foster came on and rambled through "Part Time Punks" [from the *Where's Bill Grundy Now?* EP] like a lunatic. They had about twelve people onstage showing home movies and playing chess. It was like some kind of 60s café society'. By the end of their set, the Television Personalities were McGee's favourite band.

Until the Jam went Beatle-esque on their single 'Start' in 1980, McGee had not paid much attention to music from the 60s. The following spring, Paul Weller had written sleevenotes for a compilation by the Action, a spirited mid-60s band in the Who vein. Weller's approbation helped McGee to realise that the Swinging 60s had not simply been a self-indulgent debauch for the benefit of the middle classes. (Certainly, he could never have respected a 60s-inspired label like Cherry Red without that guarantee.) Thanks to Weller, the doors of McGee's mind swung open with a creak, and along with the Television Personalities one of the most important bands he discovered was a vintage pop art combo called the Creation.

How Does It Feel To Feel, a collection of the Creation's songs recorded between 1966 and 1968, was released in October 1982 by the British reissue label Edsel. The album was a classic in McGee's eyes. Like the Who – with whom they shared a producer, the

American Shel Talmy – the Creation were prone to unexpected explosions of feedback and distortion, and songs like 'Painter Man' and 'How Does It Feel To Feel', composed as snotty paeans to the fast-moving times, retained a punky arrogance that could stir the blood almost sixteen years later. Unlike the Who, the Creation had not had much success: 'Painter Man', in 1966, had been their only Top 40 hit. 'They were so close to making it,' wrote Julian Cope in an *NME* guide to psychedelia published in 1983. 'Because of their lack of success, Creation fans actually tend to overrate them now, so intent are they on telling us what should have been.' Alan McGee was more intent than most.

He soon found that the Creation had been a major influence on the Television Personalities. Both bands destroyed instruments onstage and spray-painted canvases during songs. To McGee, pop art seemed a living, breathing form. For example, the Creation had used vivid language that was still relevant to the early 80s punk resistance fighter. 'It's happening right now,' went one song, 'biff bang pow!' Now that was more like it.

A neophyte psychedelian, McGee bought a Regency jacket from Carnaby Street and gave it pride of place in his home. He fell in love with the imagery of the red Rickenbacker guitar, a classic 60s instrument played by Pete Townshend, Paul Weller and the Television Personalities. Listening to the songs of the Creation and Dan Treacy over and over, McGee decided that pop art-inspired music – in particular, the idea of creating while destroying – was precisely the new punk rock he had been looking for.

Jerry Thackray had his evening routine worked out to precision. Before leaving the house, he would play 'Wouldn't You?' – the B-side of 'Participate' by the Laughing Apple – which would gee him up for the concert ahead. He would queue outside the venue, head immediately towards the stage without buying a drink or speaking to anybody, and wait for the band to appear. When the musicians started playing, Thackray would begin to dance.

'It was a very peculiar dance,' he says. 'I used to expend a lot of energy. I would swing my arms from side to side – and I'd quite often be holding a plastic bag as well. I would be really frantic, too. I would keep up with the bands, however fast they played . . . I was basically a naive, friendless kid, pretty much. All my money went on records or gigs. Totally tunnel vision.'

A mathematics graduate with a dull job as a silk-screen printer, Thackray was the Laughing Apple's biggest fan. He'd read about them in *Sounds*, and although he hadn't yet spoken to them he felt a strong kinship with their music. However, when he saw them for the third time – at the Golf Club, a venue near Great Portland Street, in January 1982 – he was very disappointed. They had changed their line-up, they sounded like an uninspired New Order and their new songs were all terrible. But as he had travelled a long way from Rotherhithe in London's south east, he danced to them anyway. At the end of the concert, the singer came up and said hello to him. 'He said: "You're that kid who was dancing down the front at the Rock Garden a year ago",' Thackray remembers. 'I was like: fucking hell, a pop star's speaking to me.'

Though Thackray did not know it, McGee was on the verge of giving up. Grateful for the fan's support, the Glaswegian made an interesting suggestion. 'He was going: "We've got to write to each other",' says Thackray. 'So we started this correspondence kind of thing, writing each other really passionate letters about music.' The correspondence blossomed into a friendship. Thackray would spend several evenings a week in Tottenham where McGee lived with his wife Yvonne.

'I'd started going out with Yvonne in 1978,' McGee says. 'I met her through British Rail when she was a beautiful, 17-year-old, Italian-looking girl. I married her in December 1980 and I had some of my happiest times with her. We were very alike: we were both kind of like mongrels from our families. We were good for each other. It was quite a supportive relationship.' Thackray remembers Yvonne as 'fiery ... quite well-matched with Alan'.

When Yvonne went to bed, her husband and Thackray would continue talking. 'We would end up chatting until three or four in the morning,' Thackray says. 'No alcohol or anything like that. Just listening to records and talking, and mapping out the future of the world.' As far as Thackray was aware, McGee had no other friends in London. 'He wasn't even on his way to being established when I first met him. Not even vaguely.'

As diehard indie as they came, Thackray did not endorse McGee's growing obsession with the 60s, but he did agree that the Television Personalities and the Marine Girls were genuine pop visionaries who should be receiving all the riches and publicity afforded to chart bands like Duran Duran, Classix Nouveaux and Simple Minds. 'The first time I went round to Alan's,' says Thackray, 'he was so enthusiastic about the Marine Girls that he gave me his copy of the album. He had written his name on the label, like you do when you're a kid.'

Over the course of many late-night discussions, McGee and Thackray drew up a list of good and bad indie labels. Rough Trade was good, as was Dan Treacy's label Whaam!, which had released the Marine Girls album they loved so much. Cherry Red had been good, but was now bad. It had become too successful, was liked by the wrong sort of journalist and made too many showings in the indie charts. Thackray was terribly anti-Cherry Red, dismissing Mike Alway as a hippy. (Geoff Travis, who really had been a hippy, escaped their censure scot-free. 'We were very arbitrary,' Thackray concedes.)

Fortified by cups of tea, McGee and Thackray plotted as vindic-
tively and as helplessly as two strangers who'd forged an instant solidarity based on being refused entry to the same nightclub. They
detested the music papers, but made sure to buy their copies on the
day of publication. They despised the journalists for their cushy lives
and compromised opinions, but envied them their lives and their
means to express those opinions.

In May, McGee promoted his first concert in London. Booking a
Sunday night at the Africa Centre in Covent Garden, he telephoned
the Nightingales, who agreed to headline. But the audience was negligible and McGee lost heavily on the night. 'He was a pain the arse,
actually,' says the Nightingales' singer Robert Lloyd. ' "Oh, it's all
right for you! I've lost my shirt on this!" "Shut the fuck up for God's
sake, mate ..." '

Around the same time, McGee was introduced to Dan Treacy in a
pub on the Strand called the Coal Hole. Treacy was a man he really
wanted to get to know. Slightly in awe, he gave Treacy his usual spiel:
uncontrollable enthusiasm peppered with expletives. Treacy, a more
guarded individual, did not buy it. Still, Treacy would continue to fas-
cinate McGee for a long time to come. 'He seemed like a very eccentric, bizarre guru figure. I couldn't believe that he was so talented
and nobody knew about him.'

The previous year, Treacy and Ed Ball had co-founded Whaam!, an
indie label named after the pop art painting by Roy Lichtenstein. At
first, as they looked for ways to stamp a 60s pop identity on early 80s
London, Treacy and Ball hoped to license and release the Creation's
back catalogue (before Edsel had the same idea) and eyed up
premises in Denmark Street, the renowned Tin Pan Alley (before
rejecting them as too expensive). Forced to take the easier and more
convenient route, they negotiated a distribution deal with Rough
Trade and ran their operations from Treacy's bedroom.

'I never took Whaam! very seriously,' says Nikki Sudden, whom
Treacy and Ball had plans to record as a solo artist. 'I have this memory of Dan having the master tapes of the first two TVPs albums
leaning up against the speakers of his record player. I had to point
out to him that they'd be wiped by the magnets in the speakers. I
went back there six months later and they were in exactly the same
place.'

In Blenheim Crescent, Rough Trade Distribution had noticed
Treacy's habit of going AWOL for long periods, leaving Whaam! inac-
tive. Its releases did not sell much and Rough Trade was loath to
extend Treacy any more credit. 'Dan had taken it as far as he possibly could,' says Ball. 'He had the enthusiasm but he didn't have the
energy ... The success of the *Where's Bill Grundy Now?* EP had done
his head in. He got moodswings. He could possibly have had a minor
breakdown.'

Whaam! was in a cleft stick. It could not afford to back lost causes, but nor could it find the resources to see a band through to maturation. When Treacy was unable to finance a follow-up to the Marine Girls' album (which they had recorded in his garden shed), he lost them to Mike Alway. And when Ed Ball bailed out of Whaam! after an argument about money, Treacy's dream of an 80s pop art label began to look unviable. As well as rumours of a breakdown, Treacy had started alluding to drugs during gigs. Ed Ball found this particularly sad. 'We used to joke about drugs but we never did any,' he says. 'My closeness with Dan ended about 1982. By then, he'd seriously started to get involved in drugs.'

Just before they stopped talking altogether, however, Treacy gave Ball a word of advice. 'Dan said: "There's this guy called Alan McGee. You're going to be hearing a lot about him pretty soon." He'd been chasing Dan up to do something. Dan said something to the effect of: "He's really pushy so ... beware." '

> 'Audiences nowadays are scum. You people should be out there
> creating, not sitting around waiting. Do what you want cos this is
> a New Art School! Remember! Shake these new hippies up!!
> Infiltrate and destroy! Kneecap the enemy!' – Alan McGee
> writing in issue two of *Communication Blur* fanzine, August 1983.

McGee and Jerry Thackray had outlined many a manifesto in Tottenham, but by the summer of 1982 all they had to show for their rhetoric was a few hundred used tea bags and one poorly-attended gig by the Nightingales. McGee was still unclear about what role he wanted to play on London's indie scene: promoter, manager (of the Television Personalities, if Treacy would only let him) or label boss. But Autonomy no longer existed and its successor, Essential – which put out the third and final single by the Laughing Apple, 'Precious Feeling' – was not a serious concern.

Among the music publications McGee read avidly was *Jamming!*, a fanzine written by an eighteen-year-old Paul Weller fan named Tony Fletcher. McGee liked Fletcher's writing, often agreed with his opinions and considered *Jamming!* to be more honest and less cliquey than the far more widely read *NME*. In his summer issue of 1982, Fletcher wrote an editorial which railed at the state of post-New Romantic pop music. He concluded by urging his readers to get up off their backsides, remember punk and *do* something. McGee re-read the article many times.

Had Fletcher's assessment been purely pessimistic, McGee would probably not have been so stung by it. But although he declared the first six months of 1982 to have been 'the worst period in ages' for live music, Fletcher gave two reasons for being cheerful. In the first case, a generation of punk kids was now old enough to make its presence felt in the corridors of the music business if it so desired. Secondly, and more nebulously, Fletcher argued that music travels in cycles, producing key years for pop. This was something that McGee had himself been blinking towards since his discovery of 60s pop art and psychedelia.

Fletcher listed pop's four most momentous years as 1956 (rock 'n' roll), 1964 (Beatlemania), 1968 (rock is born) and 1976 (the evolution of punk in England). McGee swapped these four for a satisfyingly symmetrical pair of his own: 1967 (Syd Barrett, the Creation and psychedelia) and 1977 (the arrival of punk in Scotland). Sixty-seven and seventy-seven. A perfect mantra.

Fletcher also made the point that once everyone got motivated, the new uprising – whatever it might look or sound like – would not be as major label-controlled as punk had been. There was a solid indie structure in place, he insisted, which could exclude the majors from the party. This, more than anything, made McGee sit up and take notice. '[The] thing can be done ourselves, keeping control over what's going on ...' Fletcher suggested. Provided the bands were suitably organised – he imagined a 'network' of groups with similar attitudes – they could between them devise a powerful musical package to attract the kids who were growing sick of fashion-led chart pop.

McGee had never been so moved by a piece of writing. He decided to publish a fanzine of his own (in which he could develop his ingenious 1967/1977 theory) and to promote more concerts in London. He also thought seriously about starting a new independent label.

McGee's fanzine *Communication Blur* – which included contributions from Jerry Thackray – courted controversy from day one. A tirade of commands and exclamation marks ('Participate!' 'Communicate!' 'Innovate!'), it read like the work of a slightly broken Dalek. Its stapled pages heaped criticism after criticism on Cherry Red, causing Mike Alway to telephone Thackray in protest. This had two effects: it won *Communication Blur* immediate respect for hard-lining the hippies; and it persuaded McGee and Thackray to step up the abuse in their next issue.

McGee was no prose stylist, but he knew how to make optimum use of his allotted space. Besides garlanding the Television Personalities, he shrewdly advertised the Laughing Apple records gathering dust at Blenheim Crescent – a never to be repeated offer: all three singles for £2-the-lot – and he succeeded in tapping into the widespread mood of dissatisfaction among indie bands, fans and fellow fanzine writers. *Communication Blur* was by no means the only 'zine to suggest that pop music's rebirth would come from a psychedelia/punk synthesis – the Scottish fanzine *Juniper Beri Beri* made similar claims with a great deal more humour – but McGee's untrammelled syntax and illiberal stance marked him out as an incendiary new voice, and he was congratulated in print by some of his fanzine rivals. For the first time, he realised that his natural enthusiasm had the ability to inspire others. 'I felt empowered by some sort of righteousness,' he says. 'I felt as if I had a platform. And [*Communication Blur*] turned a lot of people on.'

One of its readers was Tim Vass, a 23-year-old indie fan from Luton. An ex-punk, Vass had graduated to the Postcard label in 1980, only to lose interest in Orange Juice when they signed to a major. He had since turned to 60s psychedelia, but like the writers of *Communication Blur* he was looking for a current, credible scene to connect with.

As a pop-psychedelia fan in London in 1982, Vass found he was having to look long and hard for bands worth going to see. Two of the groups he liked – the Laughing Apple and a band called Twelve Cubic Feet – led him far off the beaten track. Their gigs took place, as it were, beneath the indie scene, where only the most intrepid, or the most desperate, dared to venture. 'You got forced further and further underground looking for like-minded souls,' says Vass. 'You ended up going to gigs where there were maybe twenty people there, in the smallest, grottiest club imaginable, watching a band that was totally unknown.'

In this subterranean demi-monde, the music press was as irrelevant as the price of a bottle of champagne to a pauper. For Vass and his friends, all the information about what was effectively London's secret musical world came from the fanzines. And because the 80s were closed off to them, the fanzines held the 60s in improbably high esteem. Many a 'zine, *Communication Blur* included, illustrated articles about unsigned local bands with photos of 60s icons such as Pete Townshend, Diana Rigg or Julie Christie; or assembled collages of London buses, City of Westminster street signs and telephone boxes. It was a nice way of revealing the fanzine writer's cultural identity, while at the same time showing that he or she felt the iconography of the 80s to be vastly inferior. It was also a trick learned from the Television Personalities, who decorated their record sleeves in 60s ephemera. Despite the loss of Ed Ball and the financial troubles of Whaam!, the Television Personalities were the flagship band for this marginalised, fanzine-based, sub-indie, unnamed, out-of-time society.

'We weren't looking for 60s soundalike bands, particularly,' says Vass. 'It was more a feeling that music had lost its way. Obviously, the 60s had an effect on the way people dressed. Early on, a few of us used to wear shirts with Jackson Pollock-type action painting splashes over them. I had a shirt with a painting of Syd Barrett on it, and some of his lyrics, and my girlfriend Shirley had a shirt with "The Next Projected Sound" from the ad for "Arnold Layne", the first Pink Floyd single.'

A year before, in 1981, London's main psychedelic hangout had been the Groovy Cellar, a club in Piccadilly run by Dan Treacy's publisher Clive Solomon. Inside, teenagers in Beau Brummel clothes and granny glasses frugged to old sides by the Move and the Jefferson Airplane, or stared transfixed at the oil wheels. 'The Groovy Cellar was like walking into the club in *Blow Up*,' says Ed Ball, who went regularly. 'It really was very authentic. There seemed to be a gang of people that were into dressing up quite meticulously, dancing to records and meeting girls. There really was no place like it, where you could escape from the Duran Durans and the Spandau Ballets.'

When the newly-launched Channel 4 started repeating old episodes of *The Avengers* in November 1982 (because it was cheaper than commissioning new drama), the much-vaunted 60s revival duly kicked in. For the first time in three years, the Television Personalities, whose first album had featured Patrick Macnee as John Steed on its cover, were topical, if not exactly *dernier cri*. However, this 60s resurgence was kitschy and every bit as fashion-based as New Romantic. At second-generation psychedelic clubs like the Clinic in Dean Street, the accent was on silly behaviour and organised fun. 'People eat jelly off the floor and playfully stab each other with bananas,' reported one journalist. Tim Vass and company stayed well away.

Ed Ball's band the Times continued to carry a torch for pop art's halcyon days, but Ball was so far underground by now that he'd all but disappeared off the map. By the autumn of 1982, there was no nightspot in London to cater for the more intelligent 60s fan who wanted to hear new music as well as old. 'You didn't really have clubs any more,' says Peter Fowler. 'It was just gigs in various places. I remember thinking at the time: wouldn't it be great if we had a club like you imagine the beatniks did, where you could have a bit of poetry, drink a beer and spontaneous things would happen and it'll be crazy and wonderful?'

In October, a new Sunday night club opened in Camden Town with something like that vision in mind. The Communication Club promised music, poetry and comedy at low prices; come one, come all. The brainchild of Alan McGee, it was *Communication Blur* transposed to a live entertainment format. By definition, then, it would give exposure to the kind of unassimilated bands that no promoter in his right mind would book. Come one, come no one.

Among those who performed during the Communication Club's eight-week run were the Nightingales, the Television Personalities, Tony Fletcher's band Apocalypse, the Go-Betweens, Twelve Cubic Feet – and the Formica Tops, a group formed by a recuperated Andrew Innes. The Laughing Apple did not play. McGee and Dick Green had quietly folded the band a short time before.

If the premise of the Communication Club had been to see if there existed a genuine niche market – a 1967/1977 psychedelia/punk overlap – large enough to merit a weekly event, the size of the audiences suggested not. The club attracted fewer than 50 people a night, giving McGee another financial headache. It had closed by December.

The second issue of *Communication Blur* emerged in the summer of 1983. Inside, a cartoon showed Jerry Thackray bursting into Cherry Red with a machine-gun and shooting dead a young singer playing an acoustic guitar. This was Ben Watt, one of Mike Alway's closest friends. Alway himself was depicted in the cartoon smoking a joint. He had never taken drugs in his life. McGee's relationship with Cherry Red was over.

As before, the Laughing Apple's singles were advertised in *Communication Blur* on a two-quid-for-all-three basis. But alongside them a new record was touted: a single entitled '73 In 83'. It was credited to the Legend! and released on a label called Creation Artifact – or Creation for short.

Two things happened concurrently: a label and a new club. The idea was that one would feed the other, while both would assist sales of *Communication Blur*. By August, McGee was putting everything he had learned – from Thackray, from Tony Fletcher, from Alway and from Treacy – into practice.

Although the Communication Club had failed, McGee still firmly believed that an audience was out there. Paying for the weekly Saturday night use of an upstairs room in the Adams Arms, a pub in Conway Street underneath the Post Office Tower, he announced in the back pages of *NME* the imminent arrival of a club called the Living Room. Once again, his first phone call was to Robert Lloyd of the Nightingales.

In the headcount of characters that orbited McGee during this period, Lloyd was very much the odd man out. A hard-drinking cynic with a curdled perspective on most of what passed for independent music, Lloyd had no time for the jingly-jangly pop-psychedelia that McGee held so dear, and was too long in the tooth to share McGee's idealistic view of indie labels *per se*. The Nightingales had recorded for two of the most prestigious indies in the country – Rough Trade and Cherry Red – and watched their sales bottom out regardless. 'As far as releasing records is concerned,' said Lloyd in March 1983, 'the Nightingales are officially teetering on the waste of time.'

But Lloyd had a sneaking admiration for McGee, and *Communication Blur* was one of the few fanzines he made the effort to read. Feeling he had nothing to lose, he brought the Nightingales down to play the opening night of the Living Room on 6 August. 'I like those kinds of gigs – always have – where you're sat downstairs having a drink before you go on,' says Lloyd. 'I don't like the dressing-room, stagey kind of thing.' It was lucky he didn't.

The upstairs room of the Adams Arms was testament to the exigu-ousness of support for Alan McGee's music. 'I called it the Living Room because it was literally someone's living room,' he says. The room was already home to a weekly folk music club, Dingle's, which had set the tone of the furnishings. There were a few tables, with a candle on each one. Pictures of folk singers lined the back wall. The capacity was, if everyone breathed in, 60. McGee admitted double that amount – without moving any of the tables. 'It was incredibly dangerous,' he says. 'I was putting a hundred and twenty people in there some nights. It was a total fire hazard.'

A much smaller space to fill than the Communication Club had been, the Living Room was a packed-out success. Each Saturday – and subsequently each Friday, too – a band of the Television Personalities' or the Nightingales' calibre would headline, preceded by two unsigned groups (Twelve Cubic Feet, for example, or the Jasmine Minks, a Jam-influenced four-piece from Aberdeen), some-thing humorous involving Thackray, and a scratch combo featuring either McGee or Dick Green. 'It was a very good atmosphere, very friendly,' says Peter Fowler. 'In a room of fifty people, you'd be good friends with ten of them and on nodding terms with another ten. It became a hangout for bands and their mates.'

Tim Vass had finally found a club he could call his own. 'The rea-son the Living Room became so important,' he says, 'was because it gave a focus to all these disparate people who all vaguely knew each other. There was always a good sense of camaraderie around the Living Room. It was the place to go to get hammered every Friday or Saturday night. And it was the first time you'd felt you belonged to anything since punk four or five years earlier.'

Downstairs, the pub would fill with bands waiting for their signal to go up and play. Everyone would be asked to buy a fanzine. 'So many people in the Living Room would do fanzines,' says John Robb, the singer in a Blackpool band, the Membranes. 'There were loads of guys holding plastic bags full of them. You'd always end up doing about ten fanzine interviews in there.'

Inspired by Tony Fletcher's *Jamming!* editorial, Creation Artifact – named in honour of McGee's favourite 60s band – began life in July. McGee imagined Creation as the premier indie for new guitar music, issuing only top-of-the-range pop-psychedelia in colourful, highly collectible, hand-folded sleeves. The bands would be art-conscious – in the way that the Television Personalities and the Times were art-conscious – and the records would be summery and melodic, but with a punk edge.

There was something of a nod to both Postcard and Cherry Red in all of this, but McGee was coming at psychedelia from a more dilet-tantish angle than the cultured Mike Alway, and had none of the interest in black music of Alan Horne. The real model for Creation was a label for which each day was a struggle to survive. 'Creation was based on the identity of Whaam! McGee admits. 'That's what I wanted. I wanted to have my own record label like Dan Treacy had.'

McGee's old life was catching up with him. Ian Donaldson's latest line-up of H_2O had signed to RCA and enjoyed a summer Top 20 hit with 'Dream To Sleep', a lugubrious, well-produced ballad. In a move that appalled McGee, H_2O toured Britain supporting Kajagoogoo, a widely derided pop quintet with an adoring fanbase of pre-teenage girls. Kajagoogoo's single 'Too Shy' – a number 1 smash in February – was to McGee's ears the most dreadful song of the year. He little suspected Creation's debut was to be worse.

McGee took Jerry Thackray into a cheap studio in Shepherd's Bush to record '73 In 83', a tuneless rant Thackray had written about the music business. Thackray was going by his *nom de guerre* the Legend! – an abbreviation of the Legendary Jerry Thackray, an alias bestowed on him by McGee in a moment of madness. For the recording of '73 In 83' and its two B-side songs, McGee and the Legend! were joined by an *ad hoc* band that included Dick Green, Yvonne McGee, a bassist named Simon Downe and the former punk poet Patrik Fitzgerald. Together they came up with one of the poorest records ever released by a British label.

'73 In 83' begins with the sound of Alan McGee incompetently playing a drum-kit. A nadiresque start, but the song quickly finds a way to deteriorate. Thackray – his weak Rs reminiscent of Rik Mayall's disgruntled student in *The Young Ones* – commences a staccato terrace-chant in which he compares the music scene of 1983 to that of 1973. It is not clear whether Thackray thinks this is a good or a bad thing. Then, about a minute after it starts, it stops. Nobody ever wants to hear it again.

Robert Lloyd was among the first to be given a copy. '[McGee] was full of enthusiasm,' he recalls. 'He was like: "This is my first record!" I just thought: it's awful ... it's *awful*. I was diplomatic about it – and sort of encouraging – but fucking hell ...' Sinking like a stone, '73 In 83' sold only a few dozen copies, passing unmentioned by any music publication save for *Jamming!*, which condemned it as 'totally worthless'. The reception at the Living Room was just as hostile.

McGee was dismayed. He had assumed that everyone would go crazy for a weird single made by two groovy guys like Thackray and himself. 'I had been getting quite a lot of acclaim and I was really getting into the idea of meaning something to people,' McGee says. 'Then I put out that single and I got crucified, absolutely obliterated out of the sea. And deservedly so. And it registered.' More than six months would elapse before he dared to release another Creation single.

Journalists from the music papers started going to the Living Room in September, when an *NME* review of a gig by the Three

Johns, a band from Leeds, gave the club's profile a shot in the arm. One writer who became a Living Room regular was Danny Kelly, an *NME* freelancer whose tastes lay mostly in soul and reggae, but who had a soft spot for indie pop. A former British Rail clerk himself, Kelly related to McGee at once. 'He would look straight into your eyes and talk to you as though he'd known you all his life,' Kelly says. 'And all he wanted to do was talk about how great music was. "I've just seen this ... I've just heard that ... Have you ever heard this record?" On and on and on. It never occurred to me that Alan was making a load of money out of [the Living Room]. He was this incredibly idealistic figure.'

Throughout the second half of 1983, McGee was one of the few London promoters willing to book unsigned guitar bands. Increasingly, the guitar was being removed from mainstream pop and some commentators even feared for the instrument's future. 'There was a genuine sense that rock music was dying on its feet,' says Kelly. 'The charts were full of fop bands. Two boys, one with a keyboard, one throwing off his mental chains.* There were so few places where you could see bands wearing black trousers and playing guitars.'

By talking to Kelly and other journalists, McGee learned to relax his attitude towards the music press. Jerry Thackray, however, who still toed the hard line, was disturbed to hear of journalists getting into the Living Room without paying. Outgrowing their Tottenham debates of 1982, McGee was meeting new friends and allies who would be of infinitely more use to him than poor old Thackray. There would, for one thing, be no further issues of *Communication Blur*.

With four acts playing the club twice a week, McGee soon ran out of options and took to offering the third or fourth spot on the bill to any bright-eyed young whippersnapper who approached him with a tape. Coincidentally, one aspiring band from east London had the same name as the club. The Living Room – who would rename themselves the Loft to avoid confusion – were friends of Danny Kelly, who had met bassist Bill Prince and lead guitarist Andy Strickland on a media studies course at the Polytechnic of Central London. Prince and Strickland had started freelancing for the music papers (*Sounds* and *Record Mirror* respectively), as had the band's singer-guitarist, an occasional reviewer for *NME* named Pete Astor.

Astor intrigued McGee. He was a good-looking chap, an above-average songwriter, a below-average singer, and a bookish addition to the club's personnel. In conversation, he used the vocabulary of music theory to explain why he liked artists such as Tom Verlaine, Nick Drake and John Coltrane, dropping words like 'modal' and 'detuning'

---

* The remark refers to the lyrics of Howard Jones' single 'New Song' (1983).

into his long, carefully considered analyses. He was a bit of a dark horse. Peter Astor-Smith, to give him his full name, was of Anglo-German background. London-born, he had grown up in Colchester in Essex, returning to the capital at 17 under a new identity.

'At school, I was always Smith,' he says, 'because it was not a good idea to have a hyphenated name at my comprehensive school. Then I came to college and I thought: I'm going to reinvent myself and have a glamorous name.' He became Pete Astor, budding musician and writer. Meanwhile, Orange Juice fans Bill Prince and Andy Strickland had been looking for a singer. They found Astor in a pub in Islington playing with a band called News Of Birds. Prince recalls: 'News Of Birds were rubbish, but he had presence. Very slim. Very blond. Very good-looking. Very chiselled features. A white Telecaster and a lot of studious, I-mean-this-man stage presence.'

Astor was in his final year at Middlesex Polytechnic, where he was studying English, but spent most of his time with friends at Hornsey Art College or in the local library. He came to Prince and Strickland with a slight vapour trail of mystique. 'His tastes were interesting,' says Prince. 'You'd knock on the door and jazz would be playing. Now, he knew you were coming round at about three, so he could have slapped on Thelonious Monk's *Brilliant Corners* at five-to. But it would be playing when you got there. And he'd flip it over and say: "Listen to this. I think we can do something with this." It was slightly fatuous, but it was a good way to open your mind.'

Modelling themselves on the twin-guitar tension, poetry and poise of Television, the Loft became the Living Room's most frequent per-formers, appearing almost every other week. The more he heard them, the more McGee liked them. He saw the way the girls stared at Astor; they didn't stare like that at the other bands. Astor, for his part, regarded himself as the most talented songwriter in the club – a title traditionally the preserve of Dan Treacy. Friction between the Loft and the Television Personalities was not long in coming.

'I never got this whole thing about Dan Treacy,' says Astor. 'The TV Personalities were one microdot bigger than we were. But they were behaving like rock stars. The vibe on them that I always got was very reductive. Dan Treacy would turn up at gigs with his guitar in a plas-tic bag. It's that whole I-can't-play-the-guitar-even-though-I've-been-playing-for-twenty-years attitude. It's a bit like people in the 1970s buying pre-patched jeans.'

'There was a tiny incident downstairs in the pub,' remembers Danny Kelly, 'which got blown out of all proportion – as everything did, because of course everybody thought they were playing the Fillmore. [The Loft's drummer] Dave Morgan hit Dave Musker of the TV Personalities over the head with a drumstick in passing. It wasn't a savage attack. It was a glancing blow. And this became "the two bands are at loggerheads ..." '

McGee was becoming friendly with Joe Foster, whom he'd identified as the Television Personalities' underrated force. Treacy was not pleased. 'Joe was always being thrown out of the band or leaving,' says McGee, 'but the TV Personalities were always better when Joe was in them. Joe was the sound. He was the producer. But Dan Treacy would never acknowledge him as such. It was weird being in a room with them together.'

McGee was also starting to realise that the obscure, little-known Treacy was obscure and little-known for a very good reason. 'The reason nobody knew about Dan was that he deliberately spoked himself every bit of the way down the line,' says McGee. 'He was never going to become famous because he was completely self-destructive.' And so it proved.

In April 1984, Pink Floyd's guitarist Dave Gilmour promoted his solo album *About Face* with three concerts at Hammersmith Odeon in London, followed by one in Birmingham. An associate of Pink Floyd was asked to recommend an appropriate support band for the third and fourth of these dates. He remembered hearing 'I Know Where Syd Barrett Lives' a couple of years earlier, and thought that the TV Personalities' in-depth knowledge of Floyd lore might appeal to Gilmour's adult rock audience. The TV Personalities would be playing in front of thousands of people – a first in their history. They had their own album to promote, a painfully delivered, much-delayed collection entitled *The Painted Word*, which Joe Foster had produced. The Hammersmith Odeon would be the perfect place to start the promotional campaign.

But the band wanted to be clear about one thing. 'Around the time we were doing *The Painted Word*, we were recovering from bad drugs and getting busted,' remembers Foster. 'It was harrowing. And we all agreed there was no way we were going to go out and perform this material after all the pain we'd been through if the audience were going to go: "Ha ha ha ha." That was our attitude at Hammersmith Odeon. We thought: right, tonight no one is going to laugh.'

Within minutes of the TV Personalities starting their set, Harvey Goldsmith – Britain's most famous rock promoter – and Gilmour's manager had heard enough. The music coming from the speakers was a grinding sonic assault punctuated by bizarre, off-key singing from Treacy. Foster was right about one thing, though: nobody was laughing. A source from Gilmour's camp recalls: 'What Goldsmith and the manager got the needle [about] was, when the band launched into this twenty-minute song that they were doing, the drummer got out the *Guardian* and started to read it. I think that just tipped the balance.'

'By this time the drugs had kicked in,' says Foster. 'I was certainly not seeing an audience, I was seeing something else ... Dan decided he would read out Syd Barrett's address to the audience.' Sure enough, Treacy really did know where Syd Barrett lived. He relayed to the crowd the whereabouts of the house in Cambridge which the long-retired, schizophrenic Barrett shared with his mother. 'I suppose it was really childishly stupid to do something like that,' concedes Foster, 'but we were just kids.' Says the Gilmour source: 'Gilmour's quite a good sport, as it happens, but [reading out Barrett's address] ain't very nice. It all turned into a bit of a nightmare in the end.'

The TV Personalities were paid off and told not to bother showing up in Birmingham the following night. Back at the Living Room, they dined out on their story and accepted drinks. '[We were] convinced that we had won a famous victory on points against a rock dinosaur and a pompous big-time promoter who didn't appreciate a class act,' wrote the band's bassist Jowe Head some years later. Evidently, Barrett was not the only one who had a problem with reality.

In the late summer of 1981, Mike Alway played both matchmaker and a shrewd A&R hunch. He had signed Ben Watt to Cherry Red; and also the Marine Girls, one of whom, Tracey Thorn, had recently recorded some material on her own. By coincidence, Watt and Thorn were about to embark on courses at the same university – in Hull – in October. They had not yet met.

Alway played Thorn's songs to Watt, who liked them immensely. Alway then fired Cupid's dart in Thorn's direction. 'I said to Tracey: "You ought to meet this man",' he remembers. 'She said: "Not a bit interested." I said: "I don't know if you'll say that when you get up to Hull." And she didn't.'

Meeting in the first week of term, Watt and Thorn began to date, and also to play songs as a duo. In June 1982, their version of Cole Porter's 'Night And Day' – Thorn's voice over Watt's guitar – was released as a Cherry Red single under the name Everything But The Girl. 'It was just a bit of an experiment,' says Alway. 'For all we knew, it might have begun and ended right there.' The single was popular and rose to number 6 on the indie chart.

Returning to their solo careers, Thorn and Watt released an album each on Cherry Red, and of the two, Thorn's *A Distant Shore* in particular was a dream for Alway and Iain McNay. It cost £120 to make and ended up selling 65,000 copies, winning Thorn her first silver disc. When Everything But The Girl reunited to play a well-received concert at the ICA in January 1983, Thorn and Watt seemed to have a glittering future.

As for Cherry Red, it not only had all the credibility it could ever want but was also enjoying the sales of a large indie label. At Alway's behest, an in-house compilation album, *Pillows And Prayers*, was assembled, all the artists waiving their royalties to allow it to be sold at the discount price of 99 pence. Released in the autumn of 1982,

Pillows And Prayers showed Cherry Red in the best possible light, staying on the indie chart for almost a year, including a five-week stretch at number 1. By March 1983, it had sold over 85,000.

This had the inevitable consequence of prompting one Cherry Red artist after another to phone Alway asking moot questions. Where was the increase in promotion? Why were the recording budgets not commensurate with the label's success? Why did the bands have to slum it while Iain McNay flourished? Alway found he was spending much of his time soothing artists who felt undervalued. Caught in the crossfire, Alway began to consider his position. 'I reached a point where I thought: well, *Pillows And Prayers* is right there at number 1 and we've got seventeen other records in the indie chart,' he recalls. 'And I'm living in a flat for £50 a week with no door. I've got no shoes and the arse is falling out of my trousers. And this guy [McNay] is driving around, he's got three cars and two swimming-pools. And maybe I was beginning to resent that.'

McNay – who in fact had only one swimming-pool – offered to make Alway a co-director of Cherry Red, but it was not enough. They argued constantly. Then, in 1983, Alway had an idea that seemed the perfect solution to everyone's problems. 'I went to Iain and I said: "Iain, I really think we need another tier. We need to find a way to give these [artists] their head." What I was proposing was that Cherry Red Records would become more of a nursery to feed into a larger situation.'

Alway's idea was that he and McNay should start a new company, which they would license to a major label – while at the same time keeping Cherry Red fiercely independent. Those artists who were ready to go up a grade, such as Felt and Everything But The Girl, would be transferred to the new label, where they would reap the benefits of major label funding, increased budgets and promotion. And of course, it would still be Mike Alway handling the A&R, which would keep the bands happy.

While Alway's brainwave ran contrary to the traditional ethics of independent music – which said that you were either in or out; you either trusted the majors or you didn't – it was perfectly in tune with a new culture in which these ethics were not quite so clear-cut, if they even mattered at all. Two examples are worth noting.

In 1982, a year before Alway took his idea to McNay, Some Bizzare – an eccentrically-spelt indie label started by a no less eccentric manager-cum-impresario named Stevo – had signed a licensing deal with the major label Epic for Stevo's client Matt Johnson (a.k.a. The The). The deal secured Johnson the financial clout of a major, without him having to relinquish the discretionary power he had enjoyed on an indie. It was the start of a long relationship which twice put The The into the album chart Top 5.

A year later, Keith Armstrong, the young manager of Newcastle's

HMV record store and co-founder of a Postcard-inspired label called Kitchenware, was quick to tumble to the drawbacks of remaining strictly independent – particularly when it came to independent distribution. Kitchenware's four-band roster included one of the most ravishing acts in years: Prefab Sprout, fronted by singer-songwriter Paddy McAloon. A stylish composer and lyricist in the traditions of Jimmy Webb and Stephen Sondheim, McAloon was wasted in the indie sector. Even before the release of their second Kitchenware single in 1983, Prefab Sprout's potentially enormous appeal made them a dolphin in a goldfish bowl.

Kitchenware paid £6,000 to record the group's first album, *Swoon*. Then Armstrong started worrying. He worried that the album would not receive sufficient attention if it were released and distributed independently; and he worried that if, on the other side of the coin, he were to guarantee effective high-street distribution by licensing Kitchenware to a major label – using *Swoon* as the deal-clincher – his other three acts would be neglected by the major label's A&R department, which hadn't wanted them in the first place.

With the arrogance of youth, Armstrong had made it Kitchenware policy never to give away records free, except to one or two journalists whose prose he found entertaining. Furthermore, much of the label's attitude of defiant insularity had been learned from Alan Horne, whom Armstrong knew and admired. When two of Kitchenware's early singles – 'Roll On Summertime' by the Daintees and 'The Sun Shines Here' by Hurrah! – were praised by the music papers, CBS in London rang Armstrong requesting a copy of each. Armstrong replied that it could fucking well go and buy them. 'In a way, we probably made just about every mistake you could possibly make,' he acknowledges. 'But the only thing we had – because we didn't have any money – was credibility.'

When all four of Kitchenware's acts were featured on Channel 4's Friday evening music show *The Tube*, Armstrong's phone started to ring early on the Monday morning. He decided to ease off on the verbal abuse and see what happened. That autumn, Armstrong and his partners signed the first in a series of licensing deals for individual Kitchenware acts, placing each one with whichever major label seemed keenest to have it. 'The thinking was,' says Armstrong, 'we were twenty-two-years-old at the time and we didn't have a clue what we were doing. We weren't businessmen in any way, shape or form. We figured that we could either be an empire-building record label – and lose our acts as we went along and as they got too big for us – or do a deal where we didn't lose the acts, because no matter how big the artists got, we would benefit by taking a percentage of whatever they sold, like a management percentage.'

Kitchenware's eight-album deal with CBS for Prefab Sprout was referred to in the trade press as a licensing deal, but it was actually closer to a formal signing deal that had a lot of riders attached to it. 'We called it being a "dependent" record label instead of an independent one,' says Armstrong. 'CBS paid for the records to be made, marketed and distributed. But we would still look after all the A&R and the artwork and all the rest of it – we wrote that into the contract.'

Armstrong did a similar deal with London Records for the Kane Gang, and with the same label for the Daintees. This meant that of Kitchenware's four bands, only Hurrah! – who remained unsigned by a major – would qualify for the indie charts. But Armstrong wasn't worrying about that. In March 1984, *Swoon* stood at number 22 in the Top 40. Kitchenware had found Mike Alway's second tier.

Alway, however, was struggling to find it himself. To his frustration, Iain McNay had turned his idea down flat. Resolute on the matter, McNay told Alway he was dedicated to going his own way, and to hell with the corporations. Besides, he argued, Cherry Red was doing fine as it was. It had started employing professional pluggers (a radio promotions team) and the next Everything But The Girl single had a good chance of being a hit. McNay planned to spend what was for him an unprecedented amount – several thousand pounds – on the recording of Everything But The Girl's debut album in the autumn.

Ben Watt and Tracey Thorn were the Prefab Sprout of the Cherry Red playbill. Crouched at the starting line with a long career of successful singles and albums ahead of them, they were also politically aware, inherently 'anti-rock', and contemptuous of crass commercialism, cliché and promotional overkill – all the good old major label stand-bys, in fact. However, for their first album, Watt and Thorn wanted to use keyboards, brass instruments and session musicians, and these would cost substantially more than McNay could afford. And crucially, the loyalty of Watt and Thorn was not to Cherry Red but to their A&R man, friend and matchmaker, Mike Alway.

'We thought that the new bands like us and Felt were the only good things about the label,' Watt relates. 'We felt we had to extricate ourselves from Cherry Red mid-contract, or be destined for instant pain and obscurity.' McNay, who had told *NME* that he would not let Everything But The Girl leave Cherry Red 'for any amount of money or under any circumstances', was forced to bow to the inevitable. He settled with WEA for one per cent of the profits on Everything But The Girl's first eight albums (the last of which was released in the mid-1990s) and retained ownership of their masters for Japan. Enough to buy a second swimming-pool if he'd wanted it.

Iain McNay is perhaps the most *sui generis* record company owner to have emerged from the punk rock upsurge, as well as being a walking paradox of a human being. As Alway well knew, McNay had been making a big noise in the industry since the early 80s, and had a reputation as one of the indie sector's most outspoken radicals. In 1983, he offered himself for election to the council of the British

Phonographic Industry (BPI) – having failed in a bid the previous year – on a ticket of widescale reform and redistribution of power. He demanded the trade body start making itself useful to the indies, and called for all indies to become BPI members in a show of unity and purpose.* McNay was elected. 'Cynics might suggest that he was voted on to the ... council because he would be less trouble in than out,' speculated *Music Week*.

Few guessed that inside McNay's business mind and accountant's brain lay a restless psyche so profound and inquisitive that even his own colleagues wondered how the two halves of the man could coexist. For some years, McNay had practised Transcendental Meditation and flirted with macrobiotic diets. Within Cherry Red, where irony and persiflage ruled the roost, McNay's philosophical side was viewed with amusement. 'You couldn't take it seriously,' says Alway. 'We were like the Dudley Moore that didn't go to California, and he was like the Dudley Moore that did. We were *Bedazzled* and he was *Foul Play*.'

By 1983 – the year he took his seat on the the BPI council – McNay was thinking about matters that extended far beyond the confines of indie music. He was deliberating whether to follow his friend Morgan Fisher (the former keyboard player in Mott The Hoople) into the communal therapy and free love cult of Bhagwan Shree Rajneesh. It would involve considerable alterations to McNay's life. Initiates were required to dye their clothes orange, wear a likeness of Bhagwan around the neck, and take on a new name.

'Morgan was very attracted,' McNay says. 'He was fed up with his life, he was fed up with getting pissed. He went to India and I took him to the airport and off he goes. He comes back about six months later. I pick him up from the airport and he's all dressed in orange and he's now called Veedtharm. He said: "You know, this Rajneesh meditation is much better than TM. You must try it." '

In the summer, shortly after rejecting Alway's proposal of a second tier, McNay flew to New York to represent Cherry Red at the annual New Music Seminar. He quickly became disillusioned by the corporate deals going on around him. 'Whereas the previous year it had been much more independent, this year the majors had got in there,' he says. 'It was all too hype-y for me.' He decided to leave the seminar and visit Fisher at the Rajneesh ranch in Oregon.

'I got to Portland and flew to this little airport on the ranch,' he says, 'and when I got there Morgan had left that morning. But I met some people I'd met before and I actually had a really good time. It

---

* In January 1984, it was estimated by the Independent Labels Association, an organisation founded in 1982, that between 5,000 and 7,000 indie labels existed in the UK.

was at that point I decided to become what's called a *sannyasin*, a disciple of Bhagwan.'

McNay was given a new name: Aukash. Following a period of meditation and self-discovery in Oregon, Aukash flew back to London on an overnight flight and drove straight to Cherry Red's offices. On his desk he found something which destroyed all his new-found serenity in a second.

'It was a note from Mike Alway, who wasn't in that day,' he recalls. '[He was] resigning, and saying that he was taking with him Everything But The Girl, Felt, the Monochrome Set – basically the cream of the roster – and starting a new label with Geoff Travis.'

In August 1982, Scritti Politti, a band on Rough Trade Records, were invited to perform their latest single, 'Asylums In Jerusalem', to a national audience of millions on *Top Of The Pops*. It was easily the biggest exposure an act on Rough Trade had ever had, and it split the company's workforce down the middle. In the days leading up to the programme's recording, a high-pressure, deeply sensitive meeting was held at Blenheim Crescent. The subject of the meeting? How much of Rough Trade's money Green Gartside, Scritti Politti's singer, should be allowed to spend on a new jacket.

The chaotic nature of Rough Trade as a company – where no argument was too trivial, no meeting too spurious – goes some way towards explaining why Geoff Travis was rapidly tiring of the place, as well as indicating why Rough Trade Records had had no *Top Of The Pops* acts prior to Scritti Politti. Scritti's move to Virgin a few months later, while perceived as a betrayal of Travis and Rough Trade, was merely a question of common sense. The worry was that Aztec Camera – the golden goose Travis had signed from Postcard – would follow Scritti out the door.

In an effort to keep Aztec Camera, Rough Trade farmed out much of the distribution responsibility for their single 'Oblivious' – which badly needed to chart – to the go-getting sales force of its competitor IDS (Independent Distribution Services). On an ideological level, IDS represented everything Rough Trade despised. 'Rough Trade was like this barmy, English middle-class idea of socialism,' says Ed Ball. 'They would have brown rice there when you went in. You could help yourself to it while you waited.' The slick, mobile reps of IDS, on the other hand, dined on meat – meat! – and had blithe conversations with HMV and Virgin buyers in the provinces, discussing every subject but music for all Rough Trade knew. In a full-page advertisement in *Music & Video Week* in June 1983,* IDS illustrated exactly what it meant by 'independent' by showing a picture of a woman's

---

* *Music Week* traded as *Music & Video Week* between January 1981 and September 1983.

breasts hanging free of her bra. At politically correct Blenheim Crescent, eyes were decorously averted.

'They were a very political [company],' Edwyn Collins says of Rough Trade. 'They were very dogmatic and they had these sort of radical separatist feminists involved in their warehouse department. You couldn't have any sensible discussion about politics with them. They were very blinkered. It was like [Fay Weldon's] *Big Women*.' And despite the distribution boost from IDS, 'Oblivious' climbed no higher than number 47. When Aztec Camera signed to WEA that summer, a clear pattern had emerged. The indies were finding the talent and the majors were creaming it off.

It was a long way from 1981 to 1983. The significance of the indie charts was waning. What mattered now, as more and more bands came up with the pop hooks to merit Top 40 hits, was finding a way to adjust. And if not adjusting, finding a way to be reimbursed. When Orange Juice's *You Can't Hide Your Love Forever* – which Rough Trade had financed – was released by Polydor, the indie got back the £13,000 recording costs but Travis received nothing for his trouble. 'It was almost as if Geoff didn't want any points or overrides,' says Collins, 'because that would be seen as selling out. He had to wise up eventually, I think, that it was a competitive business.'*

The onset of competitiveness was something that disturbed the father of Rough Trade Distribution, Richard Scott. The company's all-out push for an Aztec Camera hit had not had Scott's blessing, and he was shocked to hear that Travis had told Roddy Frame he wanted to make him a star. 'Geoff, when I started at Rough Trade, was extremely political,' says Scott. 'But then suddenly he saw hits. I didn't like hits. I thought that the original intention – the original culture – of Rough Trade was to service a different area of the market.'

Things were changing. The relationship between Travis and Scott collapsed to the point where they were barely speaking. The Cartel, an alliance established by Scott in 1982 of seven regional distribution companies – with Rough Trade as its central warehouse – brought in a torrent of product so relentless that Blenheim Crescent proved unable to cope. The turnover was, as Scott Piering puts it, 'too much money for a bunch of amateurs to handle'.

Rough Trade was not losing money – or it was haemorrhaging it, depending on whom one talked to. What was indisputable was that the record label and the distribution company had different cash flow requirements, creating an unworkable situation. 'We were looking for fresh people,' says Richard Scott, 'because we were all completely zonked. We were just overworked and overstretched. We needed some good people to help us out. . . . to consolidate the Cartel

---

* A point (also known as an override) is a percentage of a record's profits. It is usually requested as a form of commission or compensation, or as a 'finder's fee', or all three.

and to put a backbone into the Rough Trade group of companies.' Geoff Travis acknowledged the logic behind it. 'The argument about "we need some expertise" seemed reasonable,' he says. 'The business was growing hugely, so there was a necessity to have a proper financial director and to have good accounts, good credit control. That all made good sense. But we got the wrong people.'

Richard Powell, a 30-year-old with no experience of the music business, came to Rough Trade from a background in DIY superstores. Employed as the company's overall administrator, he found a precarious flow of credit and debit. 'When I joined,' he says, 'there were some fairly major problems facing Rough Trade. It wouldn't have [survived] if it had carried on [the way it was going].'

Powell shook Rough Trade from its former blurred identity as a privately owned company with cooperative aspirations, and turned it into a trust. Rough Trade had been Travis' shop and record label, but it was no longer his company. There was a new power structure and a new way of talking. The buzzwords were 'the Model', 'critical path analysis' and 'spatial awareness'. Travis was disgusted.

'The critical path was treated with a great deal of satirical derision by factions [at Rough Trade],' says Scott Piering. 'It was designed to be a plan for the future, and how everybody had to reshape their behaviour and the way they interacted, to be part of a large team as opposed to being individuals. It was New Labour in action, basically. It was: "Let's be electable, let's win the game." We all made fun of it.'

Some Rough Trade workers were losing interest and looking around for a change of job. For the likes of Peter Fowler, the fear of belt-tightening threatened to undermine their love of music. And if Travis seemed powerless to act, it was because he was. 'Everyone was looking to Geoff to go: "No, no, stop!"' says Fowler. 'I mean, if it was your company, surely you'd fight a bit harder than he did.'

Travis, who retained control of Rough Trade Records' A&R, seemed to be aware of market realities in his own way. He steered clear of acts that had no commercial potential whatsoever – he'd let the Television Personalities go for that reason – and in the summer of 1983 he signed the Smiths, the most pop-orientated band Rough Trade had ever had, to a long-term contract.

The messing about had ended. Rough Trade Distribution had to learn to compete in the world of distribution companies, and Rough Trade Records had to learn to compete in the world of record labels. One meeting in early September (which Travis did not attend) included a discussion about whether the song the Smiths were considering as their second single, 'Reel Around The Fountain', was enough of a 'chart contender'.

Rob Dickins had been one of the music industry's youngest managing directors when, in 1975, he was appointed MD of Warner Bros

Music at 24. In a field where many publishers were 40-plus, Dickins was known as a forward-looker, and the two years that followed saw him make the transition to punk rock with no trouble at all. When Geoff Travis and Richard Scott had the idea of starting a publishing division of Rough Trade in the late 70s, it was Dickins they approached for advice.

A small man, Dickins did not make a strong visual impression. Once handshakes had been exchanged, however, he impressed in every other regard. Multi-talented and formidably perceptive, he could be forceful and upfront, or schmoozy and unctuous as the need arose. He enjoyed surprising people with the depth of his musical knowledge – he and Travis shared a love of the cult American singer Tim Buckley – and he had a passion for the jangling sound and aesthetically pleasing shape of the red Rickenbacker guitar. His rise to the top was simply unstoppable and he became chairman of Music Divisions UK at WEA Records and Warner Bros Music at the age of 32 in June 1983.

In the year Dickins took over, two Warner Bros acts rode particularly high. ZZ Top and Prince were intensely visual, MTV-backed artists who had crossed over from specialist markets – heavy rock and R&B, respectively – to become household names. Both had been signed by Warner Bros in America. In marketing meetings at the British company WEA, they made every one of its own signings look commercially irrelevant, with the arguable exception of the good-time, zero-credibility salsa band Modern Romance. Bluntly put, WEA was an apology for a major label.

Rolling up his sleeves, Dickins blazed through the A&R department and – as *Music & Video Week* wryly noted – kept the lights in the WEA building flickering long past the usual going-home time of six o'clock. He oversaw the signings of half a dozen artists in quick succession, including Aztec Camera, Howard Jones, It's Immaterial, Strawberry Switchblade and Black. 'I took over a company which was pretty low down the list,' he says. 'It didn't have any success. It was completely dominated by the American repertoire and it was losing money. One of the first things I said was: "We have to get this guy Geoff Travis." '

As a major company man of long standing, Dickins had no time for the indies-versus-majors stand-off, which he saw as a meaningless show of bravado and bluff. He was purely about people, relationships and doing business. And on all three counts, he and Geoff Travis clicked in the summer of 1983.

Irritated by Rough Trade's adherence to the critical path, Travis had empathised with Mike Alway when he heard about his breakdown in relations with Iain McNay. Travis had suggested to Alway that the two of them do something together. Travis pictured an independent label – to be run as a Travis-Alway collaboration – and assumed Alway was thinking likewise. But Alway surprised him. 'It transpired that what Mike wanted to do was start a label with a major,' Travis says.

Alway brought into the equation the name Michel Duval, head of the Factory-Benelux imprint in Brussels and originator of the sophisticated Les Disques Du Crepuscule. Crepuscule was a label for aficionados, and Duval was regarded as one of the key figures in European indie art-rock. But Alway also wanted access to Benoit Hennebert, Crepuscule's brilliant art director. Any label involving Alway had to have beautiful sleeves, and there were few more beautiful in the early 80s than Hennebert's.

Travis was agreeable about Duval being brought into the frame, although, as usual, he played a cautious hand. 'My frame of mind was: I'm just trying to do something with Mike. Let's see what happens,' he recalls. With Duval at the end of a phone-line in Brussels, Alway and Travis got underway.

In their approaches to A&R, the two men were very different. Though the younger by four years, Alway's ideas were informed much more by the 60s: he was interested only in records – music, artwork and label – and rarely bothered to attend concerts. Travis, however, tended to sign bands only after seeing them play a number of times. Alway, once motivated, was mercury epitomised. Travis, while he could be impulsive, was methodical with it. 'Geoff amazed me,' says Alway. 'I've never known a workaholic like him. I would go into the Rough Trade office at ten o'clock in the morning and Geoff would be sitting there, amidst a severe migraine attack, having been to six gigs the night before. He was an amazing man as far as networking and contacts were concerned. He made me feel ashamed. My idea of a working day was having one good quality meeting, planning some nice artwork and then going to the movies. Geoff was like the Frank Zappa of independent music.'

When Alway met someone he admired, he would sometimes compare him to a footballer from the 70s, the sport's artistic heyday. In Duval, Travis and himself, Alway felt sure he had assembled the perfect midfield: a couple of flair prodigies of the Tony Currie and Alan Hudson school, with Travis as wise-headed Trevor Brooking imperiously feeding the wings. In August, the *NME* gave them the piquant moniker 'the gang of three'.

The actual name of the label was Blanco y Negro, which was suggested by Bid of the Monochrome Set, one of the bands Alway intended to poach from Cherry Red. 'It had a pretentious, Iberian type of quality to it that suggested sunshine and lightness,' Alway remarks. Blanco y Negro would, he told the press, encompass pop, jazz, classical 'and every shade in between'.

Travis and Alway floated the concept of Blanco y Negro to A&M, London Records, MCA and Rob Dickins at WEA. By the autumn, it was clear that WEA was the most interested. Dickins was not one for football analogies, but he sorely needed these indie captains on his team. Already, the inexperienced Alway was baffled by the figures being mentioned, but he rubbed his hands at the thought of all the bands he could sign; all the Benoit Hennebert artwork he could commission. Blanco y Negro, he enthused, was to be the first quality indie-major of the 80s: art and commerce working together, with art – naturally – having the upper hand.

Blanco y Negro was launched as WEA's 'indie front-of-house' – a Dickins phrase – and the first act to sign was Everything But The Girl. While he was involved in the decision, Alway carelessly allowed himself to be excluded from the burgeoning relationship between Travis and Dickins. This relationship – the sub-plot to the Blanco-WEA deal – was a bit like the meeting at Hull University of Ben Watt and Tracey Thorn, magnified by a thousand. 'It was an experiment to see could we get into bed together,' says Dickins. 'It was a mixed marriage.' The guru of indie and the new face of imminent multinationalism were declared man and wife.

Back at Rough Trade, the bomb landed. Many employees lost respect for Travis there and then, seeing Blanco y Negro as a kick in the teeth. It was feared that Travis would sidestep Rough Trade and in future sign the best young bands to his paymasters at WEA. Resented for not having put up more of a fight against the critical path, Travis was now further exiled. 'It was controversial,' says Scott Piering, who tried to take Travis' side, 'but Geoff, because of the constraints and the business structure of Rough Trade, was unable to do things that he wanted to do. [Blanco y Negro] was the only outlet to do that.'

Reorganising and expanding, Rough Trade moved from west London to an old four-storey building in King's Cross in March 1984. There, Travis' separation became physical: he had his own floor. Richard Scott had almost completely lost interest. The excitement of the years 1977 to 1981, during which Rough Trade had built something good, something useful – like an altruist of indie – had pretty much evaporated for Scott, leaving little in his mind to separate Rough Trade Distribution from its rivals IDS and Pinnacle; and not much discernible difference between Rough Trade Records and the other Top 40-motivated record companies.

Rough Trade's equal pay structure had been done away with, creating a rank and file – and a division between business and music that was impossible to ignore. 'It all became a matter of stock controllers and warehouse men and fork-lift trucks,' says Peter Fowler. 'Suddenly it wasn't this funky little alternative record company. It started getting a bit like, well, if you're just going to work for a normal record company, you might as well earn shitloads more and work for EMI.'

The golden age of independent music was over.

4 A War on Pop

IMON EDWARDS, CREATION'S LABEL MANAGER at Rough Trade Distribution, had watched Alan McGee grow in stature since his nervous visits to Blenheim Crescent in 1980. He had won respect with the Living Room and seemed a man to watch. Taking the pressure off McGee's cash flow, Edwards put Creation on a Rough Trade P&D (pressing and distribution) deal in February 1984. It was a big step forward.

While the economic recession of the early 80s had not hit the indies as hard as the majors, the indie market-place had, all the same, taken a change for the worse. The high birth rate of indie labels had produced an abundance of substandard – and unwanted – product, devaluing the music's currency and making it difficult for a superior record to stand out. 'I'd started at Rough Trade in early 1981 when a Single of the Week in *NME* or *Melody Maker* meant you could sell thousands of seven-inches, not just in the UK but abroad,' says Edwards. 'By 1983, it was getting a little harder. There were an awful lot of players in a small sector of the market-place.'

Edwards tipped McGee as one player who could – as he puts it – 'make things happen'. He was getting a name for himself on the scene, and was ready to dispel the lingering bad odour of '73 In 83' and make amends for Creation's false start the previous summer with four new singles in February and March. Ginger-haired and exuberant, McGee was becoming easier to notice and difficult to forget.

At 98 Beaconsfield Road in Tottenham, the McGees' front room had been turned into Creation's base. Three of the new singles were debuts: the Jasmine Minks, Revolving Paint Dream (a duo comprising Andrew Innes and his girlfriend Christine Wanless) and McGee's and Dick Green's new band, Biff Bang Pow! The fourth was by the Pastels, the group formed in Alan Horne's Glasgow flat, who had already recorded singles for Whaam! and Rough Trade. McGee considered their move to Creation quite a coup.

Joe Foster helped him to fold all the record sleeves late into the night. An on-off member of the Television Personalities (he would leave for the final time in 1984), Foster not only shared McGee's let'stake-on-the-world outlook but also influenced his taste in music. McGee's ardour for the 60s was sincere, but his knowledge was threadbare. With Foster's vast record collection as his syllabus, he was able to fill in many of the gaps. 'Joe was the vibesmeister,' says Bill Prince of the Loft. 'Alan always deferred to what Joe was thinking or saying. I don't remember Joe being a very popular character. We didn't get on with him at all.' Like it or not, however, Foster was more than just Creation's vibesmeister, he was the producer of the records too.

'Something Going On' by the Pastels was the best of the four Creation releases by a whisker. However, all four suffered from a general lack of punch. Vocals were mixed well back; guitars were listless and dreamy-sounding. McGee's own effort – 'Fifty Years Of Fun' by Biff Bang Pow! – was a song about working for British Rail, a job he had left three months earlier to join a £40-a-week Enterprise Allowance Scheme. Lyrically, the song was bitter and gritty, but it hardly justified Biff Bang Pow!'s claim to be 'The Next Projected Sound of 1984'.

Jeff Barrett, the 21-year-old manager of Revolver record shop in Bristol, was flicking through the latest pre-releases one day in February when he came across white labels by Biff Bang Pow! and the Jasmine Minks. Unfamiliar with the names, Barrett read the accompanying handouts. He can still remember them well. 'Everyone else's sales notes went: "We are so-and-so . . . the band are from . . . this is what they do . . . this is what he does for a living, blah blah blah . . ." But these two had handwritten rants in them. They were like: "This is the sound of now! If you don't fucking like it, you're dead, you cunt." I thought: wow, what's this?' When Barrett played them, he grew genuinely excited. They were a bit Postcardesque; 60s-influenced but 'rough as fuck,' he recalls. But the roughness was part of the charm. 'They thrilled me,' he says. 'They thrilled me like I needed thrilling.'

Barrett was planning to move from Bristol to Plymouth to open an indie club. He'd read about the Living Room in the *NME*, was starting to put two and two together, and wondered if the Creation bands might like a gig in the south-west. He reached for the phone. 'This is my introduction to Creation Records,' he recalls. ' "Hullo?" "Er, yeah, hi. I've got a number off this press release for this Jasmine Minks record. My name's Jeff Barrett, I'm at Revolver in Bristol." "Yeah? *And?*" "Well, I'm going to move to Plymouth down in Devon . . ." "What do you *want?*" "Well . . . I like these records and I see this link with the Living Room and can I speak to whoever's in charge of all this?" There's me, not knowing jack shit, not knowing if I was phoning an office . . . I get these two speed-freaks who've been up all night folding sleeves and spray-painting them and putting them in bags. I'm going: "I'm opening up this club and I'd like to put your bands on." "Are you taking the piss?" "No, no, no, I'm not taking the piss." "Well, listen, man, I live in London. I've been putting bands on in these pubs. No one comes. I do a fanzine. No one buys it. I put out records. No one buys them. You are telling me that you live three hundred fucking miles away and you're interested in me? I think you're taking the piss." That was my first conversation with Alan McGee.'

'Fifty Years Of Fun' and Revolving Paint Dream's 'Flowers In The Sky' entered the indie chart at 49 and 35. 'Something Going On' by the Pastels climbed into the Top 30. 'Think!' by the Jasmine Minks failed to chart. All four singles sold around 700 copies. And Jeff Barrett received a parcel of *Communication Blur* fanzines in the post.

With an almost audible sigh of relief, the editor of *Music Week* composed his end of year report for 1983. Striking a tone midway between a 40s newsreel and an upmarket horoscope, he wrote: 'British music is once again a major force in the world markets – and there's plenty more where that came from. New ways of selling, promoting and diffusing music are already with us. The Orwellian era of 1984 should hold no fears for the music industry.'

The recession – which had seen sales of singles, LPs and cassettes plummet – was history. Figures for the second quarter of 1983 had shown the decline in LP sales arrested, cassette sales on the rise and even the single starting to breathe unaided. By the autumn, British pop was once again in rude health commercially. Yet in his quarterly report in September, John Deacon, the director general of the BPI, warned that the clouds had not quite passed. Many teenagers in Britain were becoming disenchanted with music and were being seduced by new leisure technology. 'The numbers of purchasers in the key 15–19 age group is falling,' Deacon noted, 'and growing numbers of teenagers are turning their attention to video games.'

It was not in Deacon's interests to wonder whether this exodus of teens had been hastened by the commercial predominance of Howard Jones and Kajagoogoo, next to whom the New Romantics looked avant-garde; nor to suggest that British pop might be suffering from a bad case of anaemia. But with very few exceptions, the ground-breaking, inspirational records of the period were coming from the indie sector, which seemed to have realised that the youth of Britain was there for the taking. When 'What Difference Does It Make?' by the Smiths – their third single on Rough Trade, and not an especially notable song – crashed into the Top 20 in February 1984, an indie insurrection suddenly looked feasible. The band's appearance on *Top Of The Pops* was seen as a victory for underground guitar music. That same month, at its annual ceremony, the BPI battened down the hatches, dispensing Brit Awards to one establishment team-player after another: Annie Lennox, Culture Club, Paul

Young and Spandau Ballet. The trench between the pop industry and the street had rarely been so wide.

But it was to get wider. In a remarkable show of complacency, the major record companies all but abandoned the mid-to-late teenage market and instead trained their sights on those with real money. Hailed as the salvation of the audio medium, the compact disc had been introduced in the UK in March 1983. It was pitched directly at the older music fan; Sony's launch party was attended by members of the Moody Blues and Jethro Tull. The announcement in November of WEA's 15-artist Christmas package – which included CDs from Linda Ronstadt, Chicago, Donna Summer, Shalamar and Al Jarreau – confirmed the format's irrelevance to teenagers. There followed a buoyant BPI report on the third quarter figures for 1983, revealing upward curves for LPs, cassettes and music videos. 'By grit and determination, we have come back,' said BPI chairman Maurice Oberstein in the summer of 1984. 'The British record industry is great.' They had all done very well.

In Beaconsfield Road, Alan McGee and Joe Foster had a rather different perspective. As they saw it, British pop music was not worthy of the name. In conversations at the Living Room, McGee would favour a term much used by the *NME* in 1981 and 1982: 'perfect pop'. Perfect pop had been a description applied to ABC, Dollar and Haircut 100: it suggested a certain cuteness and it had very definite Top 20 connotations. McGee stripped it of these connotations and could be heard expounding on the perfect pop of the Pastels, the Loft, the June Brides and any other band that played the Living Room. His thinking showed a siege mentality. If he was powerless to challenge for the charts, he could at least imply that the chart groups were playing an inferior version of pop; that the only reason they'd achieved success was because they were not good enough to fail.

When it came to an analysis of Creation's output so far, Clive Solomon, who published a couple of the singles, was dubious. 'If you listen to the first six Creation singles, it ain't like the first six Tamla Motown singles,' he says. 'If it hadn't been for the dynamism of Alan's own personality, Creation would have been treated as a joke. No one was going to like a track like "Flowers In The Sky", apart from Alan, myself and a few psychedelic kids.'

The more perceptive Living Room regulars guessed that McGee had been making money from the club, even if they were too cool to estimate how much. One or two, however, had discovered that behind McGee's tireless enthusiasm lay a burning ambition. 'You had to try and pick up what he was saying,' says the Membranes' John Robb. 'When he spoke, he spoke really fast and he used to spit out of his mouth because he was so excited. But one of the things he said was that he was going to become a millionaire out of the music business.'

This was not terminology Robb was used to hearing. The Membranes had ambitions, of course – to crack it in America; to become world famous – but these were daydreams. What McGee was talking about was personal wealth, the great unmentionable on the socialist indie circuit. 'Alan talked a lot in figures – of what his turnover was and what his aim was,' remembers Iain McNay. 'One time he said to me: "Iain, next year I want to do a quarter of a million pound turnover." He always had a target in mind.'

Since the defection of Mike Alway, McNay had appointed a new A&R man at Cherry Red and signed three new acts: Red Box, In Embrace and Laibach. None of them rivalled Everything But The Girl for chart potential, but the national charts had never been McNay's target anyway. 'The whole philosophy of Cherry Red,' he said in 1984, 'has always been to survive without hit singles.' He explained to McGee how this was done.

'To sustain a turnover,' McNay says, 'you need albums. I said to him: "If you're going to make [Creation] work, you've got to get albums out fast. It's no good just doing singles, because you'll be lucky to cover your costs. You must do albums." That was unusual for independent labels. They usually went the route of [releasing] a lot of singles and the occasional album ... and a lot of those labels disappeared.'

In February 1984, the Living Room was raided by police during a gig by the Television Personalities. They found over a hundred people (many holding lit cigarettes) squeezed into a space designed for half that number. The club was shut down as a fire risk. It moved to Thursday nights at the Union Tavern, a pub in Lloyd Baker Street, before relocating twice in a matter of weeks – first to the pool room of the Three Johns pub in Islington, then to the upstairs room of the Roebuck pub in Tottenham Court Road, where it would see out the summer. A compilation of live recordings from the Adams Arms was released in June as *Alive In The Living Room*, the first Creation album.

Recorded for a pittance – no studios were involved – *Alive In The Living Room* included songs by the Jasmine Minks, the Loft, the June Brides, the Pastels, the Legend! and others, all recorded on to a cassette. The sound quality was abysmal. 'For once,' wrote a *Sounds* journalist in a reference to the police raid which was heard on the disc's second side, 'I'm on the side of the law.'

Jerry Thackray was asked by McGee to write the sleevenotes. He misread the mood woefully. 'Jerry, instead of writing information, wrote vilification of every act on the album,' says Bill Prince. 'It was on a scrap of paper – handwritten very carefully with line breaks between each band – and he'd written about the Loft something like: "Bogus music journalists passing off dimly remembered imaginings of what 70s punk rock was all about. Avoid." He had basically rubbished every band on there.'

McGee was furious. 'Alan went: "Jerry! What the hell are you doing?"' says Prince, 'and just screwed it up and threw it on the floor. And Jerry was hurt. Because he thought Alan was sufficiently hip and subversive enough to go: "Wow! An album with a load of slagging-off sleevenotes!" '

Written by McGee under a pseudonym, the sleevenotes of *Alive In The Living Room* revealed the extent of his contempt for the music business, for the BPI, for Creation's rival record labels and for every other promoter in London. 'To this lost soul,' he wrote, 'the Living Room meant a place I could go ... Nothing to do with trends, fashions, haircuts or clothes ... Jasmine Minks, Three Johns, the Loft [and] the Legend! – all brilliant, all different ... Nothing to do with any cult or fashion ... The Living Room meant more in its WC1 residency than Bono Vox, Ian McCullough (*sic*), Jim Kerr ... ever will.'

Jim and William Reid, the two founder members and songwriters in the Jesus and Mary Chain, were homebody types who did not mix easily. William, the elder brother by three years, had gone slightly stir-crazy in the family home in East Kilbride, and Jim wasn't far behind him. It was not unknown for the pair to watch 14 hours of television a day.

East Kilbride was a new town developed after the Second World War, when the Abercrombie Report re-mapped the Clyde valley to alleviate overcrowding in Glasgow. Rolls Royce opened a factory in the town in 1953, and by the time the Reid family moved there at the start of the 70s, East Kilbride contained Scotland's first Olympic length swimming-pool, a cinema, a civic centre and as much concrete as anyone could ever need. 'It was one of those horrible places where everything is brand new,' says Jim Reid. 'All the houses looked exactly the same. As far as entertainment went, it was mainstream. If you wanted to go and see a movie, the choice was *Rambo* or *Rambo II*. No bands played there. There were a couple of crappy record shops, but if you wanted to buy real records you had to go into Glasgow.'

Real records, for Jim and his brother, meant punk rock, the Stooges, Dr Mix and the Remix (a French band on Rough Trade formerly known as Metal Urbain) and the Velvet Underground – music of great darkness and high anxiety that ran counter to the Reids' slow-motion lives. Even when their lives speeded up, they got no better. Jim worked for Rolls Royce for two years, bored out of his mind. William was employed in first a carpet factory and then a cheese-packing plant.

By 1979, their closest friend was fourteen-year-old Douglas Hart, a local Velvets fan and budding delinquent. The Reids' parents often remarked on the strangeness of this relationship: Hart was four years younger than Jim, and seven years younger than William. But then they found most things about their sons strange. The brothers would, for instance, go for long walks with Hart after dark, talking about music and the possibility of forming the ultimate rock group.

Unlike the punk bands of 1977, or even the new wave opportunists of 1979, the Reid brothers had severe motivation problems. Whereas other teenagers would learn a couple of chords on a guitar and be playing a gig a few weeks later, the Reids were embarrassingly unsure of how to proceed. 'We ran out and bought our first guitars in 1977,' says Jim. 'Unfortunately, they lay in a corner and gathered dust until 1982 or 1983. We were a little bit bamboozled. We wanted to be DIY. We wanted to take what people were saying in interviews, and actually do it – actually get on a stage, where you really don't know what you're doing and you're kind of bluffing it; where you're not sure whether you're going to get bottled off or people are going to say you're a genius.'

The Reids eventually stirred in the early 80s – Hart was not yet involved – and began recording songs at home on a Portastudio purchased with £400 of their father's redundancy settlement. Under the name the Poppy Seeds, they sent demo tapes to the indie labels they admired. Postcard, especially, was a label they hoped would get in touch. Alan Horne didn't even play the tape.

By 1983, Hart was on bass. If their tastes were typical of 2,000 aspiring post-punk Brits, their everyday look was not. Excited by photographs of the Beatles in Hamburg in the early 60s, they backcombed their curly hair into tall, unruly quiffs and wore leather jackets. Hart, when he put his dark glasses on, was a ringer for Stu Sutcliffe – the Beatles' then-bassist – and not just physiognomically. Like Sutcliffe, Hart found mastering the bass beyond him, even when he had removed two of the strings, a Sid Vicious trick. Hart and the Reids plastered posters of their faces all over Glasgow, wondering if anyone would notice. 'It was just before we had a name,' Hart recalls. 'The posters had a gap at the top.' A little while later, they started calling themselves the Daisy Chain.

Just as laziness had slowed their hand in learning music, something stopped the Daisy Chain from getting better at it. Hart was terrible, Jim Reid verging on novice standard. William, the principal guitarist, appeared to have no interest in the technique of other musicians, nor even in his own. Besides, William had something far more important than his guitar, namely his fuzz pedal. Bought locally second-hand, it made, when he plugged it into his Twin Reverb amplifier, a sound like a bomb going off. His hands didn't even need to touch the strings. 'The pedal was completely fucked,' William recalled in 1992, 'as I discovered when I tried to flog it to some other bloke for a tenner a few weeks later. But the noise it made was almost as if another member had joined the band.'

However, on a demo tape recorded in 1984, the anarchic sound of

William's fuzz pedal was kept at bay as the Reids concentrated on getting across the melodic qualities in their songs. Mostly, as one listens to it now, the music on the tape is murky trash-rock played to the straightforward 4/4 beat of a drum machine. The overall feel is of a grimier and more nocturnal Ramones. Submerged in echo, Jim Reid's murmured vocals suggest Nick Cave delving around the lower reaches of his register. But some characteristic Reid touches are already on display: the octave leap; the Elvis Presley 'uh-huh-huh'; the high-pitched sexual pant followed by an orgasmic groan.

The Daisy Chain sent their tape to a Glasgow promoter named Nick Lowe (no relation to the English musician), who together with Stephen Pastel ran the indie-minded Kandy Klub in the city's Lorne Hotel. Lowe didn't think much of the tape, but rather than throw it away he played the other side. Hearing the familiar sound of Syd Barrett – it was a Barrett solo album taped by Hart, whose phone number was on the cassette box – he gave it to a friend who liked psychedelia. After listening to the Barrett songs, Lowe's friend flipped the tape.

'Two weeks later, I got in from school,' Hart recalls, 'and my mum goes: "Oh, a guy phoned about your group. I asked him if he was famous but he said he wasn't." So I phoned him back and we were on the phone for about two or three hours, talking about music and films and books. To me it was amazing. We'd felt like such freaks.'

The caller was Bobby Gillespie. He had led a varied life since bowing out of Captain Scarlet and the Mysterons in 1977. In 1979, he had become a roadie for Altered Images, a band on the periphery of the Postcard circle. Edwyn Collins remembers him. 'Gillespie must have been a real late developer, because he was a tiny little guy in '79,' he says. 'He nearly always had a Greek fisherman's hat and an anorak. Of the Altered Images entourage, he was definitely the person who was most into Orange Juice and Postcard.'

Altered Images had started out as Glasgow's answer to Siouxsie and the Banshees under the guidance of their guitarist, Caesar. At the start of the 80s, Caesar left to form the Wake, a Joy Division-influenced group which signed to Factory in Manchester. Gillespie joined the Wake as a guitarist before switching to bass. Supporting the Wake on occasion was a Mount Florida teenager named Jim Beattie, a friend of Gillespie's, who sang and played guitar over pre-recorded backing tracks.

Beattie and Gillespie began to rehearse together in a local scout hall, calling themselves Primal Scream. 'We used to batter buckets and we had a two-string guitar,' Beattie says. '[The hall] had a ventilation shaft which we'd batter the fuck out of. I think Bobby enjoyed doing this white noise racket more than doing the Wake.' In an extensive interview with Michael Bonner of *Uncut* magazine in 1999, Gillespie said of the embryonic Primal Scream: 'This wasn't a real band that played real gigs. We were completely dissonant. It wasn't music, it was just fucking smashing stuff up and screaming ... It was in our heads, this band. It didn't really exist, but we did it every night for something to do.'

Gillespie left the Wake, but not before acquiring the clipped, Germanic haircut favoured by New Order's Bernard Sumner and Steven Morris. Which is what he looked like when he received the Daisy Chain's demo tape from Nick Lowe at the Kandy Klub. By night, Gillespie worked for a firm of printers. He had designed and printed both issues of *Communication Blur*, as well as the Laughing Apple's singles and those released by Creation. They were used to hearing about Gillespie at the Living Room, where McGee spoke gushingly of him as Glasgow's leading scene-maker and greatest undiscovered star. 'Bobby was this legendary figure,' says Bill Prince. 'If Joe Foster was Alan's wartime *consigliere* – to take a quote from *The Godfather* – Bobby was his peacetime *consigliere*. He was the tastemonger. Alan made him sound very cerebral.'

Gillespie and Beattie had played a couple of concerts together, one in Paisley and one in Glasgow. For the second of these experiments in sound and cacophony, they decided to take things more seriously. A bass guitarist, Robert Young, was asked to join, and it was agreed that they should look for a singer – Gillespie had no confidence as a vocalist – and a drummer. Long before Primal Scream were at full strength, McGee gave them the hard sell at the Living Room – so hard, in fact, that until Gillespie and Beattie played the club as a duo one night in 1983, people wondered if they really existed. Ed Ball, for example, found McGee's eulogies to be suspiciously over-egged. 'An idea he had straight away,' Ball remembers, 'was would I do a re-recording of a song called "If Only" from the first Times album, "... and we'll get Bobby Gillespie to play drums on it, and we'll have strings and stuff." I thought: you're taking the piss. I didn't know who Bobby Gillespie was, but this guy was talking about him as if he was Jim Morrison.'

At the end of 1983, McGee told the *NME* that Primal Scream were ready to go public, and that a single entitled 'The Orchard' would emerge in early 1984. The song was recorded with a girl singer, but Gillespie and Beattie felt it was a poor demonstration and burned the master tapes. As Primal Scream's vinyl debut was put on hold, it occurred to a few Londoners that the band might perhaps be too crazy to be released. 'We had the idea that they were complete lunatics who made a racket and shouted and screamed,' says Tim Vass. 'That was the image of them that Alan put forward.'

To the Reid brothers and Douglas Hart – who had meanwhile changed the name of their own band to the Jesus and Mary Chain – Gillespie and Beattie were a find in a million. 'Suddenly we're all together, sitting having a drink, talking about the Stooges, 13th Floor

Elevators, Velvet Underground,' says Jim Reid. Gillespie recognised their faces from the posters they had circulated in Glasgow a year or so earlier. He told them he had a friend in London who owned a record label. 'We were thoroughly impressed,' says Hart. Gillespie offered to send McGee their tape.

'The only guidance that we had was from Bobby,' recalls Joe Foster, 'who said: "This [tape] is a bit uncool." The songs were fairly fully developed but it was very Portastudio, very clean-sounding. It sounded a bit goth in some undefinable way.' McGee was keen enough to meet the Jesus and Mary Chain on a brief visit to Glasgow, but agreed with Foster that the tape was best kept under wraps. All the same, word soon reached Rough Trade. 'McGee was very tight with this tape,' says Peter Fowler. 'He wouldn't let you hear it.'

McGee intended to use a Jesus and Mary Chain track on a compilation album of unsigned bands to be entitled *Are You In Love Or Are You A Car?* In the meantime, he booked them to play at the Living Room, upstairs in the Roebuck in Tottenham Court Road, on Friday, 8 June. They would appear as the first act onstage, followed by the Loft and headliners Microdisney, a group from Cork in Ireland.

Needing a drummer, the Reids and Hart advertised in an East Kilbride record shop and found Murray Dalglish, a local teenager. The other important matter to be decided was who would sing. Jim was the shyer of the two Reids in public, but consented to be the vocalist since William was marginally the better guitar player. Jim was unhappy about fronting a band; he and Bobby Gillespie would have that much in common.

The cheapest method of public transport from East Kilbride to London was the Stagecoach double-decker bus, which the Jesus and Mary Chain boarded at midnight on 7 June with a consignment of cans of beer, stolen by Hart from a pub where he worked part-time. Arriving in London early the following morning, they were faced with several hours to kill before they were required at the Roebuck. They were not the sightseeing types; with glazed eyes and junk-food complexions, they wandered around for most of the morning, before visiting the *NME*'s offices in Carnaby Street to drum up interest in their gig.

The *NME* was on strike at the time. A dispute between its publishers IPC and the National Union of Journalists had closed the paper a couple of weeks earlier – McGee had been having trouble publicising new singles by the Jasmine Minks, the X-Men (a frantic rockabilly outfit) and Biff Bang Pow! However, the Carnaby Street offices remained open to any *NME* freelancer who cared to drop in, and one of these met the Jesus and Mary Chain in reception.

'I went out and they were just stood there with that hair they had,' David Quantick recalls, 'and a sort of dazed look. They gave me a flyer and a demo tape. The flyer was just this mess of religious photocopies and bits of typography going up and down. Embarrassingly, I'd never met anyone from East Kilbride and I couldn't understand a word they were saying. For some reason, I got it into my head that they must be a goth band. Maybe it was the hair.' Quantick agreed to see the gig.

When McGee met the Jesus and Mary Chain at the Roebuck and took them upstairs, Jim Reid's heart sank. He had been expecting a proper club – a place with a long bar, comfortable chairs and a professional-looking PA system; not some tiny, abject room with a speaker either side of the stage. After a long night's imbibing on the bus, he and the others now began to drink in earnest. Destiny hour was approaching and they all had butterflies. McGee told them they would be sound checking in an hour. They didn't know what he was talking about.

Finishing their own sound check, the Loft vacated the stage area. With them was Danny Kelly, the *NME* journalist who doubled as their unpaid roadie. He and guitarist Andy Strickland stayed to watch the East Kilbride group play its first notes on English soil. Next to them stood McGee.

Like the rock 'n' roll band that warms up with a quick run-through of 'Johnny B. Goode', the Jesus and Mary Chain began their sound check with a cover version. 'Vegetable Man' was an obscure Syd Barrett song which Pink Floyd had recorded for the Radio 1 programme *Top Gear* in 1967. Never officially released, the song loomed large in early 80s bootleg culture, and even to have knowledge of it was to impress Alan McGee. He nodded appreciatively at their good taste.

But the Jesus and Mary Chain's version of 'Vegetable Man' was no affectionate doffing of the cap to Barrett and the Floyd. In the hands of the Reids, Hart and Dalglish, it became a howling, caterwauling brute of a song. The younger Reid – drunk and struggling to hear himself over his brother's lurching guitar chords – hollered the lyric into the void of the room, growing more and more flustered as the seconds passed. William, electing to face his amplifier rather than observe the reaction of his small audience, was unwittingly producing a relentless, ear-splitting cross-current of feedback. Hart and Dalglish soon lost their places and the performance fell in on itself.

The next song to be attempted was 'Somebody To Love' by the Jefferson Airplane. Again, the feedback screeched throughout, affecting the musicians' concentration and destroying the momentum. It was a drunken débâcle, a grisly stampede. Assuming that they had cocked up their audition, the Reid brothers began to argue spitefully, almost coming to blows. At this, McGee went forward to speak to them.

'You're fucking genius,' he said. 'Do you want to make an album?'

There are fundamental laws involved in A&R – or artists & repertoire, to give it its full title – but conversely almost no foundations.

This is never truer than when it comes to signing raw, unreleased talent. Most of it is about prediction: what will an artist sound like in three or four years' time; how will the work translate to a wider audience; what sort of alterations and image tweakings will be needed, if any; and how might the finished article be sold in a way that skirts its shortcomings and accentuates its strengths? In the case of major labels in the 80s, these factors were usually conditional to an A&R executive seeing an artist perform in public – often several times – and hearing at least one professionally-recorded demo tape.

In the indie sector, A&R was less about events in the future and more about those in the present. People whose salaries do not depend on a high strike rate of commercial success are much better placed to offer recording deals to friends, local bands or anyone with a spark of talent who might sell 1,000 singles. There is infinitely less pressure on indie labels than on majors to sign the massive chart acts of tomorrow – or, to put it another way, to avoid not signing them. As the critic Simon Frith noted in a 1975 article: 'The terrible warning that hangs over every A&R man's bed concerns the Beatles: Would *You* Have Turned Them Down?'

But while the gamble, for an indie, was not so parlous in financial terms, it was in other ways just as fraught. A large proportion of indie labels – not to mention indie consumers – put considerable emphasis on hipness and cool, the perennial intangibles of the underground entertainment industry. If indies couldn't offer the most popular acts in the country, they could at least claim to have the coolest and hippest. For a regional entrepreneur such as Alan Horne or Factory's Tony Wilson, this was what set them apart from the tonnage of metropolicentric product and marked their labels out as unique and valuable. For these indies, signing a new band was tantamount to risking one's venture capital. If the band sucked, the label's reputation might never recover.

Alan McGee believed his label to be cooler than most, even if it was too small and new to have a reputation. He also felt he had an A&R instinct in his bones. But the circumstances that led him to walk the ten feet to the stage of the Roebuck and sign the Jesus and Mary Chain were a lot more complicated than a simple judgment of A&R. For one thing, he was just as interested in becoming their manager as he was in recording them. For another, it was impossible to make even a short-term prediction based on what he had heard in their versions of 'Vegetable Man' and 'Somebody To Love'. They were explosive, for sure, but they were unintentionally so; a better PA would have ironed out the feedback and exposed the hullabaloo for what it was.

Thanks to a combination of a recalcitrant PA, a lot of alcohol and their own inexperience, the Jesus and Mary Chain had made the most astonishing music McGee had ever heard. By chance, Jim Reid's genius-or-crap dice had rolled in the band's favour. 'The chaotic element really appealed to him,' Reid reckons. 'Whereas some bands used to say: "Oh, we can't really play," we *really* couldn't play. It was a case of struggling to hold down this one chord that we knew, and having arguments with each other onstage. He'd never seen anything like that before. The pure amateurishness of it.'

As fate would prove, there weren't many promoters in 1984 who would permit that degree of amateurishness, let alone pay money to hear it. The Jesus and Mary Chain had found the one man on the London scene who hated and loved pop music as much as they did, in the same measures and for the same reasons. The one man, too, who ran his record company on principles of aggression and brinkmanship, and who hoped some day to take his vendetta to the highest towers of the music business. Watching the Jesus and Mary Chain snarl and threaten one another, McGee knew they were more driven than Newspeak or the Laughing Apple had ever been. The Jesus and Mary Chain played music as though it were an outlet of expression that would be available to them only once or twice in their lives. And as far as McGee was aware, no one had played that way since the Sex Pistols and the Clash.

Andy Strickland, who had watched the sound check, was more sceptical. 'The sound was white noise, basically, with a snare drum,' he remembers. 'I said to Alan: "Fucking hell, you've gone too far this time." He's going: "Don't worry, Andy. I know what I'm doing." '

The other members of the Loft were downstairs with their girl-friends. 'Alan's enthusiasm was up a notch or two,' recalls Bill Prince. 'I had the Mary Chain described to me in very colourful language. "It's utterly extreme. It's like a bomb." Alan would always be very careful to say: "It's the most intense experience." He would never say what it consisted of.'

Prince thought little of it, but Danny Kelly soon joined them, say-ing that the sound check had intrigued him enough to want to see the Mary Chain's set, due to commence in about ten minutes. 'Normally, you'd get a beer and never go back up,' says Prince. 'But Danny was absolutely "Yep, here's my beer – oop, they're on," and he went back up to watch.' Upstairs, only four or five people saw the Mary Chain take the stage, among them Joe Foster, Dick Green and Jerry Thackray. Foster then left the room. Turning up as promised, David Quantick met him on the stairs and was told to expect a revo-lutionary performance. The next person Quantick spoke to was McGee, who told him the Mary Chain were 'the future of rock 'n' roll'.

Sean O'Hagan, the guitarist in Microdisney, had arrived down-stairs and got himself a drink. He was approached by McGee, who was trying to usher people upstairs. 'He said: "You've got to come and see this band. You won't believe it – the bass player's only got two strings",' O'Hagan recalls. McGee went back upstairs. O'Hagan stayed where he was.

Upstairs, Danny Kelly was watching. 'There weren't a dozen people in that room,' he says. 'The Mary Chain were incredibly young-looking and insect-like. They looked very small and very frail. They did their thing, blasting away there, and it was extremely loud and fuzzy.' In the pandemonium of their music, there were no references Kelly could isolate. 'Certainly, it was not a record produced in Los Angeles in 1974, sound-wise,' he says.

The Mary Chain were playing some of their own songs, but not so as anyone would know. Joe Foster, whose responsibility it was to set the PA levels, admits: 'It was pretty chaotic. I think people thought I'd turned the wrong knob or something.' As he had done at the sound check, William Reid crouched facing his amplifier. The feedback from the PA was a continuous screech that greedily ate up all the sound around it. For the elder Reid, it was less a case of being unable to control it and more a case of being unable to stop it. 'It wasn't a deliberate tactic or anything,' says McGee. 'It was a mistake. Anybody else would have stopped, but they just carried on. The feedback was the thing that made it sound totally mad.'

'It may have been, to a certain extent, the PA overreacting,' allows Foster. 'All I know is that they weren't angry about it. Far from it. They thought it was great.' So pitiless and unyielding was the feedback that no one could be certain when one song had ended and another begun. 'I could hear them downstairs,' says Bill Prince. 'All I could hear was a complete and utter maelstrom of noise.' Pete Astor decided to go upstairs and watch. There were approximately four minutes of the performance remaining.

Astor arrived to see Jim Reid smash his guitar on the stage. Like Kelly, Astor thought in a flash: God, they look so small and young. The next person on the stairs was McGee, going down once more to pick up new arrivals. Tim Vass was in the bar with his girlfriend. 'He came into the bar and said: "You must come and watch this band",' Vass remembers. 'So we dutifully trooped up the stairs. And we watched as the Mary Chain beat up their drummer onstage.'

There had already been an altercation between Murray Dalglish and Douglas Hart earlier that afternoon. Dalglish, getting ready for the gig, had put on some make-up. Trying to wipe it off, Hart had succeeded only in smearing it across the drummer's face. Now, in front of the audience, all three of his colleagues rained blows on the unfortunate Dalglish, who had his drum-kit booted in by William Reid for good measure.

Tim Vass, laughing incredulously, presumed that the Mary Chain were musical incompetents. It never crossed his mind that they might be serious. Danny Kelly, who had just about recognised 'Vegetable Man' as the final song in the set, referenced them as 60s fans and indie kids of a similar genre to other bands he'd seen on that small stage before, though much more combustible. Downstairs, he wandered over to the Loft, blowing out his cheeks in amazement. 'He said: "You guys have got to do something, man, because that was just the most extreme music",' recalls Bill Prince. 'Kind of like: "You have just been upstaged to such a degree. Don't even think about it." '

As the attention fell on those who had been too incurious to climb the stairs, McGee was a beaming mixture of radiancy and scorn. 'He was rubbishing us for not being up there,' says Prince. ' "And you fuckers ... You missed out." It had been pre-sold. It had arrived. He was vindicated in his own mind.'

There was not much *après*-gig socialising. The Mary Chain were smalltown boys, a back-combed gang of three and a drummer who seemed to be on borrowed time. Around a table in the Roebuck bar, they sat stiffly, keeping their heads down until somebody asked them a question, which one of them would answer quietly. They perfectly fitted the image of the bored, unemployed, sullen, spotty, provincial punk. That night, they went back to Tottenham with McGee and slept curled up in his back room.

Three days after the events at the Roebuck, the most eagerly anticipated British single of the year was released. Accompanied by a video featuring lookalikes of presidents Reagan and Chernenko wrestling to the death, 'Two Tribes' by Frankie Goes To Hollywood entered the chart at number 1, where it remained for the next nine weeks. As their previous single, 'Relax', remounted the Top 5 to stand guard at number 2, no one doubted that Frankie Goes To Hollywood were the most prodigious new act in the country. There was talk of their forthcoming debut album being a double; such a symbolic show of hubris, it was later agreed, exemplified mid-80s dissipation.

In August, the IPC strike was resolved. Needing copy to pad out its first few issues following the two-month recess, the *NME* commissioned David Quantick to write a belated review of the Mary Chain, which ran downpage in September. Likening their sound to 'a giant bee in a ventilation shaft', Quantick sat wittily on the fence, neither burying nor praising. Dwarfing his review in length and significance, the paper's cover story that week made no mention of the Jesus and Mary Chain but could have been – and was – interpreted by Alan McGee as a *cri de coeur* on the band's behalf. 'Into Battle', an essay by feature writer Ian Penman, was a two-page execration of the pop machine in 1984. A provocative and erudite piece, it denounced record companies, artists and Penman's fellow journalists for propagating unexciting and soft-option music founded on corner-cutting, plagiarism and sexlessness. On the front page, in lieu of a photo of one of the top bands of the day, *NME* declared in bold black type: 'War On Pop'.

As an intellectual sequel to Tony Fletcher's *Jamming!* editorial of two years before, Penman's dissertation was substantially harder to digest (at one point it quoted twelve lines of Jean Baudrillard, one of the architects of post-modernism, on the dangers of information overload) but no less gladiatorial – especially to those like McGee who were gripped by the three words on the *NME*'s cover and skimmed Penman's text.

Indeed, 'War On Pop' was a pretty flexible banner by Penman's understanding, too. This was no indies-versus-majors polemic; it was much too abstruse for that. As well as refusing to name outright the individuals he deemed guilty of 'suffocating [pop music in] banality', Penman offered only two examples of those trying to redress the balance. One was the mischievous American act Was (Not Was). Contentiously, the other – ZTT – was the record label of Frankie Goes To Hollywood, whose director of publicity was Penman's friend and *NME* colleague Paul Morley. However, this did not concern McGee. War had been declared. That was all he needed to know.

As Penman tussled with the vexed question of new technology – cheating? or a vital constituent in pop's own white heat? – so too Quantick, writing about the Mary Chain, contemplated the pitfalls of tastefully presented, cleaned-up music. Almost all *NME* journalists reviled Howard Jones and Nik Kershaw, the disinfectant duopoly of synthesizer pop; but even some punk heroes of old were now opting for ruthless professionalism and banks of state-of-the-art equipment to help them attain the sonic perfection they'd once mocked. Quantick compared the Mary Chain's meagre hi-fi apparatus at the Roebuck to the mammoth PA shipped into the Albert Hall by Siouxsie and the Banshees for a concert the previous autumn. 'The Jesus and Mary Chain are by no means a great group,' he wrote. 'If they'd thought to get a good PA, they might actually have been atrocious. But they have an appeal which is related to the fact that cheap and nasty is better than expensive and nice.' Well! He'd only gone and summed up indie in a nutshell.

While Jones and Kershaw were among the most recent perpetrators of what Penman called 'the chart's standard vocal anaesthetic' (even if he didn't identify them as such), the list of ringleaders was long, and Frankie Goes To Hollywood were as culpable as any (even if he was too subjective to see it) in shoring up the dividing wall between clean, expensively produced pop and its gutter-bound stepsister, indie music. There was a taunting refrain – heard in the voices of radio DJs; read in pop magazines like *Smash Hits* – that music was improving constantly, that the consumers of 1984 were listening to the best stuff yet. When EMI and Virgin pooled their resources on a double album of chart hits for the Christmas market, they called it *Now That's What I Call Music!* The hyperbole extended to the major labels' advertising copy, in which new MOR and pop releases were regularly described as 'stunning'.

If the noise of a giant bee in a ventilation shaft were ever to be needed, now seemed as good a time as any. Even at the *NME*, where indie acts like New Order, Nick Cave and the Cocteau Twins were promoted heavily – often on the front page – there was a sense that the years were ticking by but no progress being seen. Cave was on his fourth album, the Cocteaus on their third. Both they and New Order had been interviewed to death. The Smiths were outpacing them all as *NME*'s new favourites, thanks in part to the reader-friendly loquacity of their singer Morrissey, but there was not a pro-Smiths consensus on the paper, and several writers thought them overrated. A window of opportunity was there for a group that could satisfy these writers' more extreme tastes.

Jim Reid, a music press reader who'd been a fan of Orange Juice and Echo and the Bunnymen earlier in the decade, felt increasingly alienated by the papers, and would often make the point that the blandness of some mid-80s indie music was just as important a stimulus as synth-pop in bringing about the birth of the Mary Chain. Whatever the accidental turbulence of the Roebuck gig, he and William agreed that its roof-to-floor totality of feedback was an idea worth repeating at future concerts. It would not only cover up the fact that they couldn't play very well; it would also exaggerate the songs in a way the Reids wanted them to be exaggerated. For the brothers, feedback would not be something distinct from the music. It would be part of the music.

From reading articles and reviews, they knew a fair amount about the German group Einstürzende Neubaten, and about Nick Cave's band the Birthday Party, who had disintegrated in their native Australia the previous year. Although the Reids had not seen a concert by either, they understood that these were often extraordinary occasions equivalent to music being performed on a tightrope – in front of audiences, moreover, that couldn't get enough. The Birthday Party's fans had been a baying mob at a witch trial; a bug-eyed mêlée with the scent of blood in its nostrils. When Cave bellowed: 'Hands up who wants to die?' at the beginning of the song 'Sonny's Burning', he would be answered with a roar and a dense pink jungle of waggling palms.

Over in Berlin, Einstürzende Neubaten (the name translates as Collapsing New Buildings) had liberated their music from the traditional guitar-bass-drums formula and introduced the tools of industry – iron girders, drills and lead pipes. Neubaten's art-as-clang-ing-affray was roughly what the Mary Chain wished to emulate on their guitars. But whereas Neubaten had an intellectual agenda (according to one critic, 'They set about recording the soundtrack of entropy and the world's descent into chaos'), the Mary Chain did not.

True, in their narrow field of guitar-based rock, distortion and violence were old hat. The most unbridled songs in the genre, 'I Heard

Her Call My Name' and 'Sister Ray' by the Velvet Underground, had been recorded as long ago as 1967, and among British indie bands of the Mary Chain's generation there was near-unanimous agreement that the albums *The Velvet Underground & Nico* and *White Light/White Heat* were so timeless and so authoritative as to be unsurpassable. In envisaging a music even more abrasive than the Velvet Underground's – with flashes of the Birthday Party's comedy of incitement as a visual counterpoint – the Mary Chain were rather like the Harvard student who announces that he intends to write the Great American Novel. A laudable idea, but now comes the tricky bit. One therefore cannot overstate the role of the feedback in the Mary Chain's sound. As Quantick spotted, it may have been all that separated them from lousiness. It may, as things stood, have been their commercial suicide capsule. But it was also their hero, plot and narrative voice.

When a microphone or a guitar feeds back, it is a violation from which the listener cannot help but recoil. We flinch, grimace and quickly resume our listening level. At mainstream pop concerts in the 80s, feedback was heard only when a musician or a technician made a mistake. The piercing screech was an act of impoliteness, a social indiscretion. It was not something to be repeated. Certain punk bands, wallowing in their impoliteness, had frequently and for-mally used feedback at the end of a song as a means of wringing out the last drops of vehemence in their message before silence descended. Each one of the Sex Pistols' first four singles, for instance, had concluded with a brief, decorative squeak from Steve Jones' gui-tar. The tactic became routine for many underground groups that fol-lowed.

Of the bands the Mary Chain admired, both the Birthday Party (notably on their 1980 single 'The Friend Catcher') and Einstürzende Neubaten had raised the stakes by featuring feedback almost as a lead instrument at times. The only practicable way for the Mary Chain to outdo them was to use feedback more than either of them. But bearing in mind the increased levels of tolerance and acceptance in the indie listener of the 80s, who had had his controls reset many times, a mild feedback surcharge would only, as it were, bring the Mary Chain in line with feedback inflation. There would have to be saturation, a *deluge* of feedback, before they could claim to be more extreme than the Birthday Party, Neubaten, or for that matter the Velvet Underground.

One gig into their career, the Mary Chain already stood at a cross-roads. At the Roebuck, they had mined a sound that was both lurid and psychedelic. Sulphurous feedback had burned through the songs, making them sound hysterical and stricken, at once ruining them and hyperbolising them. It was asking a lot of an audience to withstand that noise. However, if you could get it on to vinyl, you really would be talking. McGee decided to put them in a studio when they returned to London for more dates in September.

That summer, Creation recorded a second single by the Legend! and the maiden 45 by the Loft. The Legend!'s effort, 'The Legend! Destroys The Blues' – made in a poky studio in Sydenham, south London – was, like his debut, wretched. The self-indulgent humour of Jerry Thackray was now starting to outstay its welcome. ' "The Legend! Destroys The Blues" was Jerry completely rescinding his role at Creation,' says Bill Prince. 'He had become the butt of a joke – basically a clown personality. Alan had to recruit a band to get behind him and play a faux blues rock-out pastiche. I remember thinking the Legend! couldn't destroy the blues if he tried. It was like a record Terry Scott would have made.'

The Loft were sent to the same studio a week later with Joe Foster and a non-negotiable budget of £100. Pete Astor, whose wistful composition 'Why Does The Rain' was to be the A-side, was going through a bad time personally. He was suffering from shingles – a painful skin eruption – and was applying calomine lotion every day. He was lonely, depressed and having difficulty sleeping. 'Pete was constantly either incredibly "up" about everything, and full of ideas, or else he was ill and sickly,' says Danny Kelly, who was present at the Sydenham session. 'It's unfair to call him a hypochondriac, but he was concerned about his health. If you said "How are you?" there would always be an answer.' But Prince and Strickland were too excited by the session to offer Astor any sympathy. Bad move.

Relations between Danny Kelly and Joe Foster, meanwhile, were frosty. Foster had made one or two ribald comments at the Living Room about Kelly's waistline, which the overweight Kelly did not like one bit. He was pleased when the recording session gave him a chance to score a point over Foster. 'Joe was grooving along,' he says. 'I seem to remember him going to the toilet a lot for various reasons, but anyway he's grooving along and he says: "That's it, that's the take." I was in the control room and I said: "Excuse me, there's a terrible clicking on the record." It was Bill hitting the strings with his fingers. So they had to re-record it. Give him credit, Joe had a real thing about being a minimalist. Like the way Nick Lowe used to produce records in 1976. "Right. That'll do, then." ' Later that month, when McGee put out a compilation of Creation's singles entitled *Wild Summer Wow*, the Loft were strolling to a party in north London. Bill Prince saw Kelly manhandle Foster against a wall and whisper a quiet word in his ear.

The third Creation album – released in September – was a Jasmine Minks set. *1, 2, 3, 4, 5, 6, 7, All Good Preachers Go To Heaven* received the customary Creation PR push, which consisted of McGee trying to persuade his four or five acquaintances on the music papers to review it favourably. As a publicist, McGee played the game the only way he knew how: by making extravagant claims for Creation's bands to which their music could never live up. The Loft were not simply a London band in the Television style; they were 'all the best bits of Dylan and the Velvets with a post-punk 80s edge'. Refusing to budge from the overstatement of his *Alive In The Living Room* sleevenotes, McGee was prolix yet loyal – and difficult to get off the phone. It was rather fitting that *Alive In The Living Room* had ended with a locked groove.

But despite the punk attitudes of McGee and Foster, Creation's war on pop thus far was a two-fingered gesture at the presidential motorcade by a couple of cranks at the back of the crowd. For the majority of the Creation and Living Room bands, amateurishness and lack of ambition had become self-defence mechanisms, cocooning them from the inevitable humiliation they would, like the Television Personalities, have faced in bigger-sized venues such as the Hammersmith Odeon. Some of these bands desperately wanted to be successful pop performers, yet they swam back, unwilling to risk failure. 'We all should have been contenders instead of just cowering away from it,' says John Robb of the Membranes. 'The mainstream is nothing to be scared of at all. At the time, we thought it was.'

McGee kept the bands swaddled in compliments, like a proud father seeing supermodels in his plain daughters, but who exactly was kidding whom? Creation Records was nothing more than a hobby in a hostile climate. The ineffectual music it was selling neither squared with its owner's self-image, nor looked likely to find a wider audience.

In between their Roebuck debut and their return to London in September, the Jesus and Mary Chain gave their first Glasgow performance at a goth club called Rooftops. Bobby Gillespie and Jim Beattie went along to offer support.

'They hadn't seen us [play] at that point,' says Douglas Hart. 'Again, I stole loads of booze from the pub I was working in, and we got unbelievably drunk. We were only going to play for ten minutes anyway, but I think they physically dragged us off after eight.' Beattie recalls: 'The place was empty, but there was an air of expectancy between me and Bobby. They walked on and did "Vegetable Man", but got all the lyrics wrong – so [Jim] started swearing, and then he started smashing a guitar up, and then an amp. The guy's amp that they had borrowed ran onstage and was trying to [hit] them. We all got barred from Rooftops – all of us.'

'They threw us literally out on to the street,' says Hart. 'Not even a moment's hesitation to go to the bloody dressing-room.' As the Mary Chain stood sheepishly outside the back door, Gillespie came round the corner. 'He was going: "That was fucking brilliant! That was fuck-

ing brilliant!"' Hart says. 'Which I suppose it was, because it was raw
nervousness, raw energy, not even thinking about it ...'

McGee had booked them a week of dates in London. On 13
September they played at the Rock Garden to an audience even
sparser than the one at the Roebuck. Then they played to even fewer
people at a club in Piccadilly. 'It was a joke,' says Jim Reid. 'We got
there and nobody knew that this club was on. Nobody came. We all
just sat around playing records all night.' On 15 September they
returned to the Roebuck, where some Living Room *habitués* got their
first sighting of them. 'They made me feel jealous,' recalls Phil
Wilson, the singer in the June Brides. 'They had such an arrogant
attitude towards the audience. I had always got onstage feeling
slightly embarrassed to be there. The Mary Chain came on with a
full-on Johnny Rotten attitude: this is our place – you take what we
give you – we don't give a shit if you like it or not. I had always
wanted to be like that.'

Two nights later, the Mary Chain could be found at Alice In
Wonderland, a club in Soho. Warming the stage for the American
band Green On Red, they so enraged the audience that they were
dragged off by security guards for their own safety. But the stage was
so small – and the band's movements so manic – that the Reids and
Hart became entangled in each other's leads. When a bouncer tried
to remove Jim, William and Hart came with him.

Off duty, though, they could hardly have been more different. The
Reids were dour fellows, given to inertia and long silences. McGee,
an arch-flatterer, would attempt to liven them up, to welcome them
to the Creation fold. He gave each of them copies of the label's back
catalogue. They thought it was garbage. Finally, on their last night in
London, he put them into a studio in Waterloo, which Creation had
used on several occasions for cheap all-night sessions.

Alaska Studio was situated in one of the most unsuitable locations
for recording music ever: directly beneath the railway arches of
Waterloo station. 'You had to stop every time a train went over,' says
Nikki Sudden. 'They used to go by every ten minutes and all you'd
hear on the tape would be a rumble.' The owner, Pat Collier, a former
bassist in the punk band the Vibrators, had bought Alaska in the late
70s, running it as a four-track recording studio for indie bands on
tight budgets. By 1984, it was a 24-track facility, the upgrade just
coinciding with the surge in indie labels as the McGees – who had
been inspired by the Hornes and the Treacys – were followed by
labels such as Fire (owned by Clive Solomon) and the Pink Label,
home to the June Brides. Suddenly, there was a plethora of guitar
bands that needed to record quickly and economically. Collier and
his two engineers, Noel Thompson and Iain O'Higgins, were used to
making an album in two or three days.

The Mary Chain had to record and mix two sides of a single in eight hours: the Stagecoach back to East Kilbride wouldn't wait. Against the wishes of the Reids, who had wanted to produce the record themselves, Joe Foster was in the producer's chair – and under specific instructions from McGee to capture on tape the sound of utter bedlam and bring it back to Tottenham.

Using equipment borrowed from the Jasmine Minks, the Mary Chain took several stabs at recording the single's A-side, 'Upside Down'. Foster found them affable enough. 'They were good at explaining what they wanted,' he says. 'It was like: "We know what we want. Are you going to help us do it?" ' After taping several tracks of William's guitar played through his fuzz pedal straight into the board, they added further tracks of fuzz guitar through the amplifiers, which started going berserk under the pressure. Oh, terrific, another Velvet Underground, thought Collier laconically.

The next thing he knew, one of the Reids said: 'Now we'll do the feedback.' They proceeded to fill six tracks with feedback from William's guitar. As Collier watched sceptically, Foster mixed it all together – and the band grew restless. 'They said: "This doesn't sound right",' Collier recalls. 'I said: "Look, that's what a record sounds like." They went: "No, no, no, no, no. The feedback's much too quiet." In the end I said: "Right. You sit here and push the faders up and tell me when it's right." '

As morning broke and the session drew to a close, the Mary Chain were hungover, irritable and dejected. Hearing the tapes a few hours later, McGee realised what had happened: Foster had mixed the feedback too low. McGee played it to Jerry Thackray that evening. 'He was saying: "What the fuck should I do? This is shit and Joe's my best mate",' Thackray remembers. 'I said: "Well, what you've got to do, Alan, is go back in there and remix it and not tell Joe." '

While Jim Reid, Hart and Murray Dalglish travelled back to Scotland, McGee took William into Alaska to remix 'Upside Down'. 'Show me where you've got the feedback,' McGee said. William brought up one of the feedback tracks, his finger perched over the fader. 'William took the fader from ten to nine-and-three-quarters, ten to nine-and-three-quarters, and all you could hear [on the song] was feedback,' McGee later recalled. 'It sounded amazing. I just thought: the guy is demented. I remember watching him as he was doing it and thinking: he is actually out of his mind. That was "Upside Down".'

With the feedback screaming from beginning to end, 'Upside Down' was as close to the band's live sound as a studio environment would allow. McGee was jubilant. When Jim Reid heard the new mix, he acknowledged its improvement on the original, but he was still unaccountably disappointed. McGee recalls William, too, having doubts after the fact. 'They didn't like it until I told them everybody else loved it,' McGee says. 'For the first week or two they were saying: "We're not sure about it." I was going: "Trust me." '

The Mary Chain's gig at the Roebuck on 15 September had been the final night of the Living Room. Busy to the point of distraction with Creation and his new clients from East Kilbride, McGee bowed out of the London gig scene, leaving it a good deal more vibrant than it had been a year before. To a reporter from *Sounds*, he claimed he was planning to make a film, *Waterbomb!*, in which he would ambush unsuspecting music business personages and drop a waterbomb on their head. His shortlist included Ben Watt, George Michael and the Radio 1 DJ Steve Wright. The project was soon forgotten.

At the end of the month, the Loft's 'Why Does The Rain' was released. Reviewing it cronyishly in *NME*, Danny Kelly took his hat off to his friends' achievements, twisting the knife in Joe Foster's back by criticising the 'less than thrilling production'. A more objective reviewer might have made a similar point about Astor's unimpressive vocal. Andy Strickland sent a copy of the single to Janice Long, the presenter of Radio 1's evening show. To the band's delight, Long played 'Why Does The Rain' every night that week. The 1,000 pressing run sold out, making it the biggest selling Creation single so far. 'Creation suddenly became a cool label,' says Clive Solomon. 'It was apparent that it was a cool label rather than a maverick label.'

McGee was caught on the hop. The Loft had no manager and were in sore need of an experienced PR and a booking agent. Yet McGee did not regard the Loft as a Creation priority: unlike the Mary Chain, the middle-class English quartet was too low-key to appeal to his huckstering side. As he saw it, 'Why Does The Rain' was merely a hyphen in preparation for the resounding exclamation mark of 'Upside Down'. If the Loft's corner was to be fought by anyone, it would be Janice Long.

At Christmas, she voted 'Why Does The Rain' one of her three favourite songs of the year, and it was played on Radio 1 once again. This did have an effect on McGee, but not in a way that anyone would have predicted. While almost everyone else at the Living Room agreed that Pete Astor had a wishy-washy singing voice and a standoffish stage manner, McGee's A&R eye now began to view Astor as somebody more gifted than – and quite separate to – the other members of the Loft.

Murray Dalglish was asked to leave the Mary Chain in late September. When they played at Glasgow's Venue club on 11 October, their new drummer was Bobby Gillespie. It was a busy night for him. One of the support bands was Primal Scream, now a five-piece with Gillespie as ever-reluctant frontman. He had also had a hand in the design of the tickets, which showed Malcolm McDowell holding a hand grenade in *If...*, with a warlike challenge underneath: 'Whose Side Are You On?' It was an interesting time to be asking.

'I stayed at Bobby's house that night,' says David Swift, a New

Zealand-born *NME* journalist who played drums for Biff Bang Pow!, the evening's other support band. 'His dad woke us up in the middle of the night. He was really excited because the IRA had blown up Thatcher [at the Grand Hotel in Brighton] and he insisted we all drank a glass of whisky to celebrate her death.' She survived the attack.

Bobby Gillespie had firm ideas about being the Mary Chain's drummer. A beat-keeper with no frills, he played only a snare drum and a floor tom, and stood up rather than sit on a stool. The audio-visual effect was, as he had intended, very much like Maureen Tucker of the Velvet Underground. To complete the image, Gillespie wore shades. 'It was different when Bobby joined the group,' says Hart. 'It was four focused, slightly mentally deranged people making a beautiful racket with songs underneath.'

With a German promoter named Thomas Zimmerman, McGee arranged a tour of Europe for Biff Bang Pow! and the Jasmine Minks, which the Mary Chain, though ring-rusty, consented to join. Since Gillespie lived in Glasgow and the Reids and Hart had moved to Fulham in west London, rehearsals for the tour were difficult to organise. It was decided to dispense with them altogether. On 24 October, the night before they set sail for Europe, the Mary Chain played yet another gig in London, at the Three Johns in Islington, a one-time site of the Living Room. About 40 people attended, among them two music journalists. After consuming the requisite number of pre-show beers, the band played a comparatively long set – almost 30 minutes – reaching hysteria at several points. Jim Reid lost himself in profanities not only between songs but even in the middle of titles: 'Vegetable Man' would henceforth always be sung as 'Vegetable Fucking Man'.

As usual, the songs' aftershocks were indistinguishable from the songs themselves. William's guitar was the sound of drilled metal heard from inches away. His downstrokes had the texture of a six-inch nail on a cheesegrater, and his upstrokes were a pencil being dragged up a louvre door. As the feedback eventually died away, there was a smattering of applause and a few catcalls. Most had watched in silence, a few open-mouthed.

The following day, the Mary Chain joined Biff Bang Pow! and the Jasmine Minks on the ferry to the Hook of Holland. Thomas Zimmerman met them at the other end, driving them to the first gig in Berlin. The East Kilbride boys, who had not been abroad before, were eager to live out their Beatles-in-Germany fantasy. The dream did not last long. 'As I'm sure the Beatles found out,' says Hart, 'it's fucking grim sleeping 15 to a room in the freezing cold and driving in a bus with a smashed window down the autobahn at a hundred miles an hour.' The Mary Chain's refusal to rehearse, combined with their insistence on inebriation, made for pretty extreme performances, all of them overseen by the highly strung Foster at the mixing desk. 'Some of the gigs were so bad that it was like standing there naked,' says Jim Reid. 'By the end of the gig, we'd have to be carried offstage.'

Adam Sanderson of the Jasmine Minks recalls the Mary Chain having a bad time on the tour. 'The soundmen in Europe didn't understand their sound requirements and they were not playing well,' he notes. 'Quite often Jim Reid would tell myself and [Jasmine Minks singer-guitarist] Jim Shepherd that they were ... going to pack it in when the tour was over.' Sanderson also noticed something odd happening to Foster. 'Joe began calling [the Mary Chain] "my boys" all the time, and then he began speaking in a pseudo-Scottish accent ... I don't know what got into him on that tour, but he seemed determined to separate himself and the Jesus and Mary Chain from everyone that they were working with.'

With arguments breaking out, vans breaking down and gigs being cancelled, the touring party arrived in Switzerland. 'We were put up in a hostel for junkies,' Sanderson remembers. 'We were checked for injection marks on the way in ... It had missing windows in sub-zero temperatures.' The gig in Basle was ruined by skinheads, who threw bottles at the Mary Chain as they played. Sanderson recalls incredulously: 'We spoke to the skins later. They wore Union Jack T-shirts and told us they wanted to be like London skins and drink Guinness all day.' On the drive back to Holland for the ferry, Ken Popple of Biff Bang Pow! made a sudden grab for the steering wheel of the minibus. The driver had fallen asleep on the road.

Returning home on the ferry, the Mary Chain were seasick and dog-tired. Buying a couple of music papers as they disembarked – NME and Sounds – they found two reviews of their gig at the Three Johns. These turned out to be a wonderfully symmetrical roll of the genius-or-crap dice. The Sounds write-up was relentlessly negative, dismissing the music as bluff and scolding the audience for being fooled by it. The writer concluded: 'The Jesus and Mary Chain are a pile of shit ... It was an exercise in gullibility.'

By considerable contrast, the NME review was as adulatory as if McGee and Foster had knocked it up in Beaconsfield Road. 'Not only were they good,' the journalist wrote, 'they were better than any other band I've seen live in the last eight years.' He compared them to Joy Division in power and gravitas, and contended that in excitement terms the Scots were 'the natural successors to the Pistols'.

Neil Taylor, who wrote that review, was a recent addition to the NME's pool of freelancers. A 25-year-old law graduate, he was older than McGee and all of the Mary Chain members bar William. Moreover, unlike them, he had actually seen the Sex Pistols perform – in 1976, at Barbarella's in Birmingham. Since 1983, Taylor had been present at a few Creation and Living Room nights in various London pubs, and had chatted to McGee from time to time. He didn't particularly like the music on Creation – he preferred Einstürzende Neubaten and other experimental Europeans – and he certainly hadn't been looking in Creation's direction for the next big thing. Which is why he could not believe his ears when he heard an advance copy of 'Upside Down' in October. The Three Johns gig a few days later had pushed Taylor over the edge into language which, for the *NME*, was almost taboo: one really did not compare bands to the Sex Pistols lightly.

Understandably, Taylor's review was a huge hit with McGee and the Mary Chain. It also went down well with the *NME* section editors who, to Taylor's alarm, talked of taking this exciting new band off his hands and following up the story themselves. However, he was not going to be so easily pushed aside. 'Neil was someone who seized his chance,' says David Swift, who was dubious of his colleague's motives. 'He was a smart guy who made a name for himself very quickly amongst the students of Britain who bought the *NME* every Wednesday.' If the Mary Chain really were the new Sex Pistols, they surely would not do Neil Taylor's reputation any harm at all.

'Upside Down' b/w 'Vegetable Man' – the eleventh and final single to be released by Creation in 1984 – came out in early November to a muffled fanfare, entering the indie chart at 34. The producer's credit was given to Foster, but William Reid, McGee and Pat Collier would all claim varying degrees of input. ('I was in charge of getting the sound on to tape,' says Collier. 'The band were in charge of making the noise at the other end. There wasn't a lot of leeway in the middle.') The sleeves for the first 1,000 copies were printed by Bobby Gillespie in Glasgow, and featured handwritten messages from the group. On 24 November, the single climbed 22 places in the indie chart to number 12.

Having reviewed the Mary Chain live, the next step for Neil Taylor was to meet them in person. An interview was arranged for 25 November, to take place in the hours before they played in a disused ambulance station turned indie venue in the Old Kent Road. Sean O'Hagan of Microdisney bumped into McGee in Rough Trade early that week. 'He was literally on a campaign around the floor,' O'Hagan recalls. 'He was saying: "Come to the Ambulance Station. This gig is going to blow your mind. Music's going to change." '

Sitting them down in front of a tape recorder before the show, Taylor found the Mary Chain meek and withdrawn. 'It was difficult to see where all of that angst [in their music] was coming from,' he says. 'When you met them, they weren't cynical. They weren't even sarcastic.' As he watched the venue fill with people, Taylor assumed the turnout to be a direct result of his Three Johns review. Someone in the audience even shouted extracts of the review during the show; after 'Taste The Floor' – which groaned with so much feedback that it sounded like wood protesting – the heckler chanted ironically: 'Best band in eight years! Best band in eight years!' Jim Reid leapt to the microphone. 'Listen,' he said, 'we don't want to fucking know you. We fucking hate you. We despise you. You are fucking shit. Where were you six fucking months ago, you fucking cunts?'

So surprising was Reid's outburst – even the unfriendliest audiences were never addressed so contemptuously by the singer of an up-and-coming indie group – that most people missed his very pertinent question. Where indeed had all these people been six months before? At the back of the hall, Taylor was asking himself precisely the same thing. The Mary Chain's polite caucus of fans from the Living Room was outnumbered here, and heavily so. There were newcomers several years older, in some cases well into their thirties. One or two were probably Syd Barrett completists who had been flipping their copies of 'Upside Down' to play 'Vegetable Man' on the other side. 'It wasn't a trendy audience,' says Mary Chain fan Andrew Perry, a student in his late teens. 'It was mostly old heads. The Ambulance Station was not a kids' scene.'

But nor was it a smiling psychedelic revival. Taylor, realising with a gulp that the mad-looking people shuffling around the hall did not fit his mental picture of *NME*'s student readership, instinctively checked the exits. He recognised those wild stares and knotted brows: he'd seen them in the deadbeats who came out of the woodwork at weekends to swarm around Camden Market – the frustrated, fearsome and alcoholic punks who, by the mid-80s, had abandoned formal life and slid off the edge of society. These people never went near indie concerts. Why had they started now?

Writing up his interview with the band – which ran as a news story on pages two and three – Taylor backtracked sharply from his Three Johns review. He slammed the gig, the audience and the Mary Chain as hard as he could. 'If the Jesus and Mary Chain can't take [the] pressure,' he wrote about Jim Reid's tirade, 'they should fuck off back to Scotland.' They were the words of a worried man.

Jeff Barrett had left Revolver in Bristol and moved to Plymouth, where he was soon managing a record shop – Meat Whiplash, named after a song by the Fire Engines – and an indie venue, Club Thing. He became a good servant to Creation that summer. Not only would he book the Jasmine Minks and other bands to play at Club Thing, he would even let them sleep on his floor, telling them to let themselves out when their hangovers cleared. One of the Jasmine Minks repaid him by urinating and vomiting on his carpet.

In October, McGee had invited Barrett to the Three Johns to see the Mary Chain. Blown away, Barrett booked them to play Club Thing on their return from Europe. He knew McGee would come to the gig and wanted to impress him. That afternoon, Barrett rang the local radio station. 'I said: "There's this band playing tonight called the Jesus and Mary Chain. Blasphemous or what! And they have riots at their gigs." The radio station got the local paper on to it. The BBC came down to the shop. The gig was sold out. And McGee loved that. He saw cops, he saw press ... and he was taken by it. He was like: "You're wasted down here." '

McGee had arrived in the Mary Chain's van with Stephen Edney, a 20-year-old A&R man for London Records. A Living Room regular and a Creation collector, Edney was anxious for his major label bosses to do some sort of deal with the indie livewire. 'Alan had buckets of energy and was always really funny,' he says. 'Some of it, I now know, may have been amphetamine-fuelled, but he had brilliant enthusiasm.' Edney also thought a London-Creation deal might increase his own clout at the major label.

Part of the PolyGram group, London Records' biggest commercial acts were Bananarama, Bronski Beat and the synth duo Blancmange. But while the company's A&R policy was generally cautious, managing director Roger Ames had surprised many people by tempting out of retirement Alan Horne, who had been given his own label and an office in the PolyGram building. Funded by London, Horne's label Swamplands was to be his shot at the Top 40. His acts would be given generous recording and marketing budgets: all Horne had to do was work some of his old Postcard magic and sign the right bands.

Swamplands' first release, a version of the Velvet Underground's 'Pale Blue Eyes' by Edwyn Collins and Paul Quinn, had tickled the Top 75 in August, but Ames knew Horne could do better than that. Horne had since been devoting most of his energy to an in-the-works Paul Quinn solo album. Quinn, an old schoolfriend of Collins', was a Scott Walker-like crooner with a rocker's quiff. He had already been in the Top 50 in March with the MCA-signed band Bourgie Bourgie, whom he had since left, and was seen by Horne as a potential star if his records and image were properly thought out.

Stephen Edney, desperate to sign the Mary Chain to London before other majors got wind of them, was thinking along second-tier lines. '[My idea] was to try and make London Records appear less corporate by offering a licensing deal to Creation – for the whole of Creation,' he says. Edney would have to convince Roger Ames and his head of A&R, Tracey Bennett, that McGee was the new Alan Horne, and had signed the stupendous Jesus and Mary Chain to prove it. This was difficult enough. The squalling racket of 'Upside Down' did not make it any easier. Ames and Bennett rejected Edney's idea.

However, as Edney understood it, signing the Mary Chain alone remained a possibility. A short cooling-off period might work wonders, giving Ames and Bennett time to rethink. Then again, there wasn't much time. The Mary Chain and McGee were already starting to think carefully about which of the majors – if any – they would talk to. And as much as McGee liked Edney, Bananarama's label did not figure high in his thoughts.

The word on 'Upside Down' had spread and it was now Creation's best seller. The first of many re-pressings was ordered. At Rough Trade, McGee and Foster would sit folding hundreds and hundreds of sleeves, putting singles into boxes. As each box was filled, it would be whisked away up the motorway. 'We used to hang around at Rough Trade quite a lot,' says John Robb, 'and McGee would come in and say: "I can't believe how much this record is selling. We've sold 10,000." Which to us was an incredible amount of records to sell.'

Although the Mary Chain's departure for a major label would leave a big hole in Creation, McGee had resigned himself to it. As their manager, his 20 per cent of the advance would keep Creation's head above water for most of the following year. In November, he told the *NME* he intended to release 24 albums in 1985.

In the minds of the Mary Chain, all considerations boiled down to the imminent recording of their debut LP, which Jim Reid half-suspected might be their grand finale. The intensity of the music – and of the musicians making it – put a time-limit on the band, he felt, that did not apply to normal groups. Already, people were asking the Reids what they would be doing in five years' time, as if their luck could not possibly hold. Jim pictured the album costing an absolute fortune to record.

During a routine visit to Rough Trade, McGee had introduced Jim to Geoff Travis. After initial misgivings, Creation had risen somewhat in Travis' estimation, and when he heard 'Upside Down' in the Rough Trade shop, he thought it was excellent. He'd gone to the gig at the Ambulance Station, enjoying it very much, and had popped backstage afterwards to say hello. Days later, Travis declared an interest in signing the Mary Chain, not to Rough Trade but to Blanco y Negro.

Blanco y Negro had run into serious trouble early on, most of which was being blamed on Mike Alway. Alway had since left the company, his dream of a second tier having turned into a nightmare. And still he wondered what he had done wrong.

It had been decided by Travis and Alway that in order for them to have a harmonious working relationship, they should agree on the merits of each potential Blanco y Negro project before taking it upstairs to Rob Dickins. At first, the excitable Alway did not see why this agreement should prevent him from demo-ing and recording bands – using Blanco money – provided Travis approved of the results. Then, to add to the gang of three, Alway brought in a fourth A&R brain, *Sounds* journalist Dave McCullough. It was a McCullough review in 1980 which had first alerted Alway to the unique talent of Felt. Describing Felt's debut single, 'Index' – a solo instrumental piece which their leader Lawrence had recorded alone in his bed-room – McCullough had likened it to a scene in *Fawlty Towers* where the waiter Manuel slides into the dining-room on his knees and plays a guitar in front of the guests. When Alway had stopped laughing, he signed Felt to Cherry Red.

Alway took on the day-to-day running of Blanco, which moved in the summer of 1984 from the WEA building to premises in Henniker Mews on Fulham Road. Its first releases were an album and two sin-gles by Everything But The Girl. The album (*Eden*) charted in the Top 20, proving that their decision to break contract with Iain McNay had been a good one. 'You're talking about twelve and a half grand [to record it],' says Alway. 'You could make three records on Cherry Red for that money.'

The problems started when Alway sent a string of acts into various studios around London. Of these, Felt, who were recording demos for Blanco prior to a possible signing, and Microdisney, from whom Alway commissioned an album, did not necessarily have Travis' full support. But there were others he didn't even know about. Alway had contacted the actor Kenneth Williams with a view to recording a song by the Monochrome Set. Far more problematically, he allowed Vic Godard – the former frontman of Subway Sect – to run up a bill of some £40,000 making an album at Olympic Studios in Barnes. Subway Sect's unfashionably slow music and functional grey cloth-ing had made them seem very beguiling and intelligent in 1977 to fans such as Edwyn Collins, Robert Lloyd and the Jesus and Mary Chain (who sometimes played the Subway Sect song 'Ambition' live). But a Godard LP in 1984 would have scant commercial appeal, assuming it made it past Travis to Dickins.

'What pop music was losing in the 80s, as opposed to the 60s, was intrigue,' Alway argues. 'It was becoming far too geared at people like Janice Long. It was becoming far too conservative. What I saw in people like Vic, the Monochrome Set and Sudden Sway* were people who didn't care at all about careers, who were just interested in mak-ing as much confusion as possible in a really pleasant way that was-n't going to hurt people.'

Travis was not having any of that nonsense. He played Alway some songs by a folk-pop trio called Dream Academy, whom he con-sidered ideal Blanco material. Alway hated them. 'That to me was not what the purpose of Blanco y Negro was,' he says. 'For me, the purpose of Blanco y Negro was centralising marginality. I thought Geoff was a bit of a traditionalist.' Unable to trade with Travis – your Dream Academy for my Kenneth Williams – Alway grew disillu-sioned. 'What you got,' he says, 'was two or three very opinionated, not to say arrogant people, with far too many ideas ... and chaos.'

---

* A multi-media conceptualist group from Sheffield brought to Blanco y Negro by Alway.

McCullough left as quickly as he had arrived. Blanco was once again a three-man team of Alway, Travis and Michel Duval. However, Alway operated increasingly on a go-it-alone basis. When Microdisney and Vic Godard completed their respective albums, Travis told a crestfallen Alway that neither one constituted an acceptable presentation to WEA.

If the cost of making these unwanted albums was a black mark next to Alway's name, another of his projects was much more controversial. 'I Bloodbrother Be', a song by a band called Shock Headed Peters, was – on the face of it – a loping Stray Cats shuffle. Lyrically, however, it seemed to be a homosexual anthem. Yet it contained liberal amounts of ambiguity and near-the-knuckle humour, and was sung by a man widely believed to be heterosexual. When Alway (who describes the song as 'Francis Bacon in pop form') played it to Travis, he was told not even to think about putting it out on Blanco y Negro. In response, Alway started his own indie label, él, which he ran from Blanco's offices in Henniker Mews.

Planning to pay back the cost of the recording to Blanco if he made a profit, Alway circulated copies of 'I Bloodbrother Be' – the first single on él – to the music papers and John Peel in late October. Opinion was polarised. Peel was so offended by the song that he swore at él's publicist down the phone. In the music press, 'I Bloodbrother Be' received nothing but acclaim. 'We got Single of the Week in three music papers and it crashed into the indie Top [10],' says Alway. 'So Rob [Dickins] is looking at this, thinking: why have we turned down something that's *NME* Single of the Week? Geoff phoned me up and said: "Rob Dickins is confused and shaken – *shaken* – as to why he hasn't got Shock Headed Peters. I assured him it wasn't any good really . . ." That was the last I ever spoke to Geoff.'

'I Bloodbrother Be' did not sell enough copies to make back its costs. Nor did any of the four él singles that followed, three of which had been recorded using Blanco y Negro money. 'I never made a bad record with Blanco money,' contends Alway. 'Every record was bloody remarkable. I've got nothing to be ashamed of on the musical side. On the business side, where I was perhaps a little overexcitable, it has to be said that there was nobody there to discourage me.'

The él publicist, Dave Harper, had realised something was amiss even before accepting the job. He'd been working at Rough Trade and had told a passing Travis that he was off to join Alway. 'If I were you,' Travis said, 'I wouldn't do that.' Reporting for duty at Henniker Mews, Harper found Alway seated behind an old Raj desk, surrounded by antiques, and no sign of anyone from Blanco y Negro. 'It must have been obvious to Geoff that Mike was going a bit mad with the money,' says Harper. 'Geoff was quite clever and gave Mike enough rope to hang himself with, and it didn't take him very long. Sure enough, within six weeks I was out of a job.'

When the maths had been worked out, Travis was informed of the damage. Forty thousand pounds for a Vic Godard album?! To cut back on overheads, Henniker Mews was vacated by Blanco – which moved into Travis' office in the Rough Trade building – and Alway was out of work and up shit creek. He had made himself unpopular with friends, including certain members of bands to whom he had promised the Blanco moon in happier days. He had also lost considerable face. 'I was spending all my time at home in Barnes,' he says, 'weeding the garden and listening to classical music, getting as far away from the music business as possible. I had to go through a degrading situation of going round all the people that we hadn't given Blanco to – such as Roger Ames – and offering them él for them to refuse.'

And the rejected Microdisney and Vic Godard albums? Travis put them out on Rough Trade.

Left in sole charge of Blanco y Negro after Michel Duval's predictable withdrawal, Travis found himself at the helm of something that seemed to have become an easy listening English folk-rock imprint – a bucolic habitat for Everything But The Girl and Dream Academy. What Blanco really needed was an adrenalin shot from the most extreme-sounding band in Britain.

'For me, being able to sign the Mary Chain was a rationale of why Blanco was worthwhile,' says Travis. 'I wanted to work with the Mary Chain and this was the only way it could happen.' The doubts he had been having about Blanco began to recede. In bidding for the Mary Chain, Travis was not thinking about the Sex Pistols or about Neil Taylor's panegyric, both of which he dismissed as red herrings. All he knew was that the Mary Chain had fantastic tunes buried under their feedback topsoil. This was now a much-heard refrain among the indie cognoscenti, who increasingly viewed the Reid brothers as gifted pop songwriters beneath the noise.

But although Travis hadn't taken the Sex Pistols line seriously, McGee very much had. 'Upside Down' had emphatically put Creation on the map, and the success was bringing about a change in McGee's style of management. He was now intending – with the Mary Chain's encouragement – to be a high-profile, notorious manager, a Malcolm McLaren mark two. McGee saw the Mary Chain as the battering ram with which he could wage war on pop and effect a punk-style revolution in the industry.

The Mary Chain had used McLaren-esque tactics once or twice themselves. The day after their aborted Rooftops concert in Glasgow, Jim Reid and Douglas Hart had written a dozen letters to Billy Sloan at Radio Clyde, half of them saying that the Mary Chain were the best band the correspondent had ever seen in his life, the other half saying they should be banned from ever appearing in Glasgow again.

It was an idea taken from the Sex Pistols movie *The Great Rock 'n' Roll Swindle*.

On previous showings, McGee was not in McLaren's league. The former was known locally; the latter had been feared nationally. There had been no instances of the Jasmine Minks or the Loft fleecing EMI and A&M for tens of thousands of pounds, as McLaren had done with the Pistols. Nor had there been any but the most innocuous chicanery in McGee's dealings with the press. The Glaswegian even found it difficult at times to tell lies.

'He never managed the Loft,' says Bill Prince. 'This is an important thing. "I don't want to manage you, guys. I want you to be on the label but I can't manage you." Now that's the wrong speech. He should have said: "I want you on my label, I want to manage you and I want to sign your publishing." Because other labels were doing that: Fire were doing that. I remember Alan saying to Pete very early on: "Look, if you want, I can get you publishing now. I can walk you round the corner and get you bloody publishing. But you don't need it. Don't get it till you need it." In that way he was dreadfully honest.'

While his honesty was something he set great store by – he would bristle if it were ever called into question – McGee's big plans for the Mary Chain had put a gleam in his eye, and his feet were ever so slightly starting to leave the ground. The more copies that 'Upside Down' sold, and it was now approaching 20,000, the more his vocabulary rose to the occasion. 'To me, "massive" meant the Cramps,' he says, referring to a cult American band of the time. 'But the Mary Chain was much more primal. It was *inside*, and whether they or me or anybody else wanted it to happen, it was going to go. It was one where you said: "The train's coming through. Get out of the way." '

The McLaren lessons began for real when the Mary Chain lent McGee a video tape. 'He had never seen *The Great Rock 'n' Roll Swindle* before,' says Douglas Hart. 'We brought him down a video and I think he watched it 75 times. We'd find him in Geoff Travis' office going: "You can't see the band. You can't watch the band. The only way you can get the band is to buy their record." Which is a direct quote from Malcolm.' As Hart remembers, the Mary Chain were quite happy to be McGee's shock troops in the war on pop. 'We thought it was funny,' he says. 'When Jim and I had walked about in the middle of the night in East Kilbride, that's what we talked about. "Something's got to come along ... something radical." '

Travis was less keen on McGee's mutation into McLaren, and not just because it made doing business with him a little trickier than usual. 'I'm personally always very suspicious of anyone who has Malcolm McLaren as their role model,' Travis says. 'That, to me, is 90 per cent bullshit. The negative side of Malcolm McLaren is the side that uses musicians as pawns in a game. That's the side I don't like. The idea of being a svengali, I think, is pretty laughable. What you want to do is find musicians who know what they're doing, and give them the means to get on with it.'

To Travis' mild irritation, McGee insisted that the first business meeting between Blanco y Negro and the Mary Chain take place in the front room of the McGee family home in Glasgow. A test to see if Travis was sufficiently interested to get on an aeroplane, it was also a display on McGee's part of some halcyon McLaren non-compliance. And there was even a third motive. Now that Creation was starting to enjoy success, McGee wanted to exert some power over Rough Trade's founding father, the nearest thing Creation had to a boss. Travis saw through all of these motives immediately.

Unversed in business and unwitting of their own strangeness, the Mary Chain had an inhospitable presence that seemed out of place in a Mount Florida sitting-room. Travis, not much of a hoopla man himself, remembers: 'They all sat on a sofa and didn't say a word. They just stared at the ground.' Shy and gently spoken, Travis seemed to 'get' the Mary Chain, but they could not be totally certain. 'Geoff's a weird guy,' says Jim Reid. 'You can know Geoff for ten years and not know him at all. But he said all the right things and he made all the right moves.'

He also had a reputation without equal. With his Rough Trade background of the Smiths, Orange Juice and Aztec Camera, the Blanco y Negro chief was perceived as the politic middle ground between the indie good guys and the music business *per se.* 'We believed him to be an ally,' says McGee. Well, McGee might have done. Joe Foster believed Travis to be something else entirely, and was apprehensive about the Blanco deal from the beginning. McGee forged ahead regardless, and a contract was drawn up.

It was rejected by the band at once. Jim Reid would claim the following year: 'The long-term deals they were asking of us were a joke. Like no feedback on records. Or put a little bit of feedback on just to please the fans.' Instead, the Mary Chain and WEA agreed to Travis' suggestion of a deal for one single only – with the possibility of a long-term deal if everything went smoothly. This was unheard of at WEA and at most other major labels: if the single were a hit, the band could simply walk away and sign to another company. But it seemed the only solution to the feedback problem. In the meantime, each member of the Mary Chain was given £1,000 and bought himself a pair of leather trousers.

'Upside Down' climbed from 12 to 6 on the indie chart on 1 December, the day it was announced that Bob Geldof's supergroup Band Aid would record a single, 'Do They Know It's Christmas?', to raise money for famine relief in Africa. The Mary Chain's own next single was to be 'Never Understand', a song from their demo tape which they had yet to perform live. Shortly before Christmas, they entered Island Studios in west London to record 'Never Understand' with a young producer named Stephen Street, who had been the engineer on the Smiths' album *Meat Is Murder*.

Coming fresh from Johnny Marr's diligent guitar playing, Street found it hard to acclimatise himself to the Mary Chain's unmusical approach. Gillespie had only two drums and a tambourine. Hart played a bass that was missing two strings, but was incapable of tuning either of the ones that remained. Attempting to go with the flow, Street nevertheless had an instinct to hold off on the feedback. The session ended awkwardly, and the Mary Chain returned to Alaska – without Street – to try again.

Noel Thompson, the young engineer on the Alaska session, was a veteran of many recording dates with jangly, semi-psychedelic groups, including a few sessions produced by Joe Foster earlier in 1984. Thompson found the Mary Chain in uncompromising mood after their experience with Street. 'It was unknown territory for me,' he says. 'The guitars were really, really screechy. They wanted them trebly and sharp. If it was painful, that was good. And the meters were just like . . . I mean, they would occasionally flick back off the far right-hand corner. And they were all very tense and intense people, shouting at each other.'

But Thompson could see that the Mary Chain knew what they wanted, and when 'Never Understand' was finished, it sounded just as good as – if not better than – 'Upside Down'. Impressed, McGee offered Thompson the job of mixing the Mary Chain's sound at the ICA (Institute of Contemporary Arts) on 29 December. As Foster had feared, an early development of the Blanco y Negro deal had been to oust him as the band's soundman.

The sun was over the yard arm as the Mary Chain arrived at the ICA, so, as usual, they got drunk before playing a note. While they were taking five minutes to extrapolate an actual song from the preliminary tumult of yelps, buzzes and clicks emanating from William's guitar, the audience shouted three phrases in rotation: 'anarchy', 'fuck off' and 'get on with it'. As Neil Taylor had seen at the Ambulance Station, the Mary Chain were becoming known as an act that appealed to an audience's worst instincts. Aggravated by long delays, the crowd would become restless and vociferous. The band's drunkenness and arrogance would do the rest.

'The mixing desk at the ICA was a fair way off the floor, so the audience couldn't get to you,' Noel Thompson remembers. 'It was very much like being in an ivory tower. There was me, Alan McGee and Geoff Travis up there. A couple of people clocked us and shouted at Alan: "We want our money back, this is bollocks." Alan shouted down: "How much did you pay to get in?" The guy went: "Three-fifty." Alan goes: "You're a fucking mug then, aren't you?" '

The audience included Rob Dickins and some people from WEA, who were seeing the Mary Chain for the first time. Dickins found it very entertaining. The music was incoherent, undeniably, and the show was a shambles, but not without its good points. He also noticed that the venue was full. 'I saw something was happening,' he says. 'It wasn't a question of making a value judgment on the music. Sometimes the audience just tells you.'

But what the audience was telling Dickins and what it was telling the Mary Chain were two different things. To Dickins, it was saying that the band would be good for Blanco y Negro and WEA. To the Mary Chain, as the perfomance was concluded in typically messy fashion, it was saying: 'Fucking bunch of wankers, fucking bunch of wankers, la la la la, la la la la,' over and over, until the words drifted out into the ICA's corridors in a snaking, outraged conga.

5 A Premier Concert Spoiled

THE *NME* HAD PREDICTED a barren start to 1985 following the fecund autumn and Christmas periods. Not one major tour had been announced for the early months of the year, compared to five at the same stage the year before. 'The New Year gives every indication of being as dead as a dodo,' the paper warned. 'The prospects for January ... appear abnormally gloomy.'

In Tottenham, McGee and Foster were clearing the decks for a short end-of-January tour by the Jesus and Mary Chain. Neil Taylor's reports had created a demand for the group around the country, and gigs were booked in Sheffield, Liverpool, Nottingham, Birmingham and Brighton. The releases on Creation's late winter schedule, meanwhile, were designed not to distract attention from 'Upside Down'. There was another single from the humorous X-Men, an eccentric 45 by Les Zarjaz, who sang Henry VIII minstrelsy over a baroque keyboard étude, and a debut album from McGee's Biff Bang Pow!, pop-artfully entitled *Pass the Paintbrush, Honey*.

'Upside Down' continued to head northwards in the indie chart. It was now at number 2, threatening to topple the Toy Dolls' comedy punk tune 'Nellie The Elephant' from pole position. Creation could barely cope. Foster, in between stints at Beaconsfield Road, was doing a no-fees postgraduate course at the North London Polytechnic (in return for teaching Spanish, a language in which he was fluent) and the McGees' house was cluttered with sleeves, instruments and press releases. The train appeared to be gathering speed. Rumours abounded that the Mary Chain's gigs at the Ambulance Station and the ICA had ended in violence.

On 23 January, McGee went to see Peter Reichardt, the managing director of Warner Bros Music, to discuss a publishing deal for the Reid brothers' songs. With no idea how much to ask for, McGee let the Mary Chain's reputation do his bidding. Reichardt knew of the Mary Chain and sat back to listen to a cassette. 'It was like: "Fucking hell! What the hell is *that*?"' he says. 'They were using feedback to the point of excruciating pain. I said to Alan: "You know, I've got to tell you, musically I don't get this." But I loved Alan and kids were going wild at these gigs.' Two weeks later, Reichardt offered £20,000 for the band's publishing. McGee asked him if he could make it £60,000. They settled on £40,000.

In the days before the tour, McGee made sure the Reids gave plenty of interviews, encouraging them to be outspoken and disparaging of other bands. It was a tactic that had worked for Ian McCulloch and Edwyn Collins in the past. However, the Reids spent much of their time fielding questions about their own fans. 'Most people are thick as shit,' said Jim. 'Audiences can be very sheep-like ... Most of them are basically clowns who don't deserve much and don't get it.' In another interview, he suggested: 'Probably about ten per cent of any audience would appeal to me as people.' His brother, asked by *Melody Maker* to list his ultimate ambition, replied: 'To be murdered.'

The soundman for the five-date tour was Dave Evans, an occasional Biff Bang Pow! bassist and former member of Twelve Cubic Feet. An inexperienced sound engineer, Evans was keen to help the Mary Chain cause a stir. But when he approached PA companies to hire equipment, he found that mere mention of the band's name was inspiring trepidation. Only one firm – SST in Nottingham – was willing to take the risk, on condition that all damages would be paid for.

On 29 January, the day the tour was scheduled to start, a story about the band was printed in the pop column of the *Sun*. Headlined 'Chain Gang On Rampage', it claimed that they had wreaked havoc in the offices of WEA, drawing a Hitler moustache on a photograph of Rod Stewart, scrawling obscenities on pictures of Chaka Khan and Echo and the Bunnymen, and smashing a ZZ Top display case. The Mary Chain – the *Sun* added – had been thrown out of the building by security staff. 'Our record company doesn't understand us,' it quoted Jim Reid as saying. 'They think you have to behave nicely all the time. They don't realise you can stagger around drunk and drop things.' Reid supposedly went on: 'The Sex Pistols were soft middle-class boys compared to us.'

The story had its basis in fact. There had been some misbehaviour, although no security men were involved and Reid, who had been unaware that he was speaking to a reporter from the *Sun*, had not made the comment about the Sex Pistols. Either way, a result of the story was that the first date of the tour, in Sheffield, was cancelled by local authorities. McGee was delighted by the controversy.

Because they were under-rehearsed and disinclined to learn new material, the Mary Chain were playing very short sets. This was destined to infuriate every audience on the tour. The normal duration of a gig by a band at their level was between 40 and 50 minutes; the Mary Chain planned to do only 15 – and to make it even less of a crowd-pleasing experience, they had decided to omit their indie hit 'Upside Down' from the set-list. The performance would consist of sheer malign noise, the aural equivalent of a stroboscope. Once it was over, the audience would be at cross purposes with itself: angry because the gig was terrible, and furious that there had not been more of it.

It was clear from the moment that William Reid picked a fight with a bouncer in Liverpool's Sphinx Bar that the tour was going to be swimming in bad feeling. 'Pete Wylie and Echo and the Bunnymen all came to see the Mary Chain that night,' recalls McGee. 'It was like emperor's new clothes.' If so, at least one witness judged the band to be naked. Billy Mann, a local stringer for the *NME*, sardonically listed the highlights of the concert one by one: 'It all started at 10.55pm when the band walked on and set about their self-styled form of anti-music . . . At 11.07pm the JAMC juggernaut was drawn to a halt by technical problems. A period of relative silence [followed] during which a young man in the audience decided it was time somebody told them to "fuck off you twats". It was a dissenting voice which, though soon drowned in the resumption of feedback, had succeeded in planting the seeds of discontent . . .'

To most people outside the Mary Chain's small entourage, the music would have seemed like an inept, drunken, not-even-trying cabaret – as though four students had sunk a yard of ale apiece and been egged on to provide some scratch entertainment before passing out in a heap. At one point Jim Reid, careering boozily to and fro, fell on top of Bobby Gillespie's drums. 'I've paid two bloody quid to come and watch this,' a girl in the audience was heard to complain. It was unfortunate that 'Vegetable Fucking Man', quite apart from all the swearing, included a brief passage of laughter in the vocal, seeming to confirm that the proceedings were a joke at the Liverpool crowd's expense. Before long, nationalism reared its ugly head. 'Fuck off and don't come back,' a heckler hissed. 'Wankers! You Scottish gits!'

'As they retreated to the door of their dressing-room,' wrote Mann, 'I couldn't help notice they were visibly chuffed by the whole occasion, as if they had just done three encores . . . ' Dave Evans confirms: 'They were happy to be creating such an extreme reaction. The more extreme and the more notorious, the better.'

McGee was happy enough himself. 'It wasn't a great Mary Chain gig,' he remembers, 'but if you'd read about them you wouldn't have been disappointed. It was so bad it was good. Complete and utter anarchy.' Mann reported: 'Long after they had gone, the sound of breaking glass could still be heard echoing around the room.'

At the Garage club in Nottingham the following night, the Mary Chain did two things of note. They played an acoustic song ('You Trip Me Up') and they introduced to the set a formless number called 'Jesus Suck'. In the latter, Jim Reid arbitrarily screamed the words 'Jesus', 'suck', 'fuck' and 'cunt' while the sound behind him collapsed, struggled to its feet and collapsed again. The band hoped to record the song for a B-side. The soft strains of 'You Trip Me Up', on the other hand, revealed a beguiling melody very much like 'My Boy Lollipop'.

The Mary Chain turned up in Birmingham the next day to find the gig had been cancelled by the police. Out of four dates, two had now been called off. It was, McGee reminded everyone, just like the Sex Pistols' 'Anarchy' tour in December 1976: an outlaw spree around the country. A game of tag with the establishment. A daily running of the gauntlet. John Robb, who had written the first published article about the Mary Chain – in *ZigZag* magazine – believes McGee deliberately steered the tour towards confrontation. 'He engineered the whole hype campaign,' Robb says. 'Basically, he made a couple of very shy blokes into the biggest rock 'n' roll terrors on the whole music scene. How wild were they? They used to get drunk and fall over. They weren't wild at all. They weren't Sid Vicious.'

Comparisons with the Sex Pistols had been part of the Mary Chain equation since November, and it was becoming difficult to disregard them. James King, the former Backstabber, was touring concurrently to the Mary Chain with his band the Lone Wolves, playing in some of the same venues. 'We would turn up at gigs and the club owner would say: "You guys are Scots, but you're great. Not like those arseholes",' he recalls. 'But they were winning hands down with press. They were wiping us out.' And in the press and in the provinces, the Mary Chain had a Pistols reputation whether they liked it or not.

The final concert, at the Pavilion in Brighton, began with a minute-long philippic of feedback from William while Jim, a sociopath lurching across a precinct towards a group of pedestrians, yelled the word 'fuck' until he was hoarse. The band had fans in Brighton – cheering and applause greeted each song – but when the audience realised that the seventeen-minute performance was all it was going to get, drinks and other missiles were hurled at the stage. 'It ended in total chaos,' says McGee. 'We were throwing stuff back. Jim Reid got all the money off me – it was about £300 – and was waving it at the crowd.'

Bobby Gillespie's girlfriend, Karen Parker, was struck by a glass and needed urgent treatment. Gillespie and Joe Foster took her to hospital, where they were recognised by injured fans from the gig. 'There was some student guy there with his girlfriend,' says Foster, 'and he looked as if something had been thrown at him. The girl was going berserk: "Are you happy with what you've done? You're all monsters!" It was like we had done a murder.'

To James King, who had known him in Glasgow, the change in Gillespie was a hard one to credit. 'I couldn't fathom the fact that Bobby Gillespie was part of this,' King says. 'When Bobby was an Altered Images roadie, he was totally anti-alcohol. I had a reputation as a bit of a drinker and Bobby would make jokes about it – "Are you pissed again?" – as he sat there drinking his orange juice. The next thing I know, Bobby's in a band called the Wake, playing bass in this sub-New Order thing, and he's giving you a discussion about how he thinks all bands should give up the copyright on their records. Some kind of Marxist philosophy about "free the kids". Then he disappears again, and the next time you see him he's got sunglasses on and he thinks he's Sterling Morrison, and he's playing drums in the Mary Chain. The various disguises of Bobby Gillespie. He's like *The Three Faces Of Eve*.'*

The tour consolidated the Mary Chain's standing as Britain's most wayward group and – as John Robb indicates – created a perception of them as violent and frightening people. It was a far cry from the nights of camaraderie at the Living Room, where only Joe Foster and one or two members of the Jasmine Minks had shown anything approaching aggression. Alan McGee was now seen as a somewhat menacing character, a machiavellian choreographer of fracas and fisticuffs. His name was synonymous with trouble. 'I was getting painted as this cult-of-personality manager and I was living up to it,' he recalls. 'I was living out my Malcolm McLaren fantasy.' The only fights in which he would never intervene were the frequent sibling screaming matches between the Reids.

To make the Mary Chain seem even more ingenuous and savage, McGee began to feed rumours and stories about them to the papers, guessing that the journalists would not bother to check them out. A period of complicity ensued between the Mary Chain and the media, which would last for most of the year. Gillespie's one-time membership of the uncool Wake, for instance, was an open secret, but the music papers seemed willing to hush up his youthful indiscretion. 'Alan was just a chancer in a really sweet way,' remarks Pete Astor. ' "The Mary Chain have been arrested for drugs on the bus!" And then the *NME* dutifully printed it. Every week he'd make up complete bollocks which would get printed. It was funny.'

The only person not laughing was Jerry Thackray, who was opposed to drugs and hated the Mary Chain's decadent rock 'n' roll image. Their wearing of leather trousers – such an antiquated totem, he felt – appalled him. 'I thought this was just reprehensible,' he says. 'To me, it equated with all the macho, beer-swilling bollocks.' Leather trousers and drugs were not the only things that disturbed Thackray. 'I felt McGee was surrounding himself with loads of yes-men like Joe Foster and Dick Green,' he says, 'who were not real friends and were only agreeing with him because they could see they were going to make a hefty old crust sooner or later.' Admittedly, Green and Foster had each been given ten shares in Creation by McGee, but it was

---

* A 1957 movie starring Joanne Woodward as a woman suffering from a multiple personality disorder.

unfair to draw any conclusions. McGee had divvied out the percent-ages with the insouciance of a Monopoly player, and the shares were currently worthless.

However, Thackray now formed the view that McGee was putting out certain records on Creation solely for financial reasons, and had sold out many of his original principles. In the second issue of *The Legend!*, a fanzine he published, Thackray addressed the matter with typical recklessness. He tore into McGee just as they had once done to Mike Alway. He accused his friend of being a hippy, a yuppie and a traitor. The effect was instantaneous. 'Yvonne called me up and screamed at me down the phone for two hours,' Thackray recalls. 'It was probably justified.' The McGees excommunicated Thackray as comprehensively as they had once adopted him.

But Thackray was sure he was right, and he was not alone. 'Stephen [Pastel], John [Robb] and I were a disaffected trio,' he says. 'We were the Creation outsiders once Joe Foster and Dick Green started getting on McGee's side. When I left Creation, John was up in arms about it, as was Stephen. They were like: "Oh, the soul's gone out of Creation." ' Putting his recording career on the back burner – to a few listeners' relief – Thackray threw himself into journalism. He'd been invited to submit reviews to the *NME*, which he started doing in the autumn of 1984. Having pilloried the *NME* in his fanzine for being no better than the *Sun*, he suddenly saw a golden future for the paper, with himself as its star contributor. Writing as the Legend!, he debuted with a short review of a gig by the X-Men at the Ambulance Station in September. It began: 'Like an ice-cream on a hot sticky day; the smell of grass, bodies dashing forth hitting a ball around. Your favourite T-shirt back from the house-wash, smelling all fresh and clean and soapy ...'

And there we must leave the Legend!'s review of the X-Men at the Ambulance Station in September.

Nineteen-eighty-five had been declared the United Nations' International Youth Year, during which the achievements of young people would be spotlighted and their role in society strengthened. McGee did his bit for the cause by pruning the Mary Chain's ages by 20 per cent. Suddenly, they were all teenagers. 'They make me feel like their grandfather and I'm only 24,' he told one writer conspirato-rially.

In Britain, International Youth Year struggled to get off the ground. A national petition was launched to lobby for 'a fair deal for youth', and a magazine, *Spark*, was set up. Billy Bragg named his March tour 'Jobs For Youth', explaining to the *NME*: 'The Conservatives think that youth is a disease which people go through and the sooner they're out of it the better.' Youth unemployment in Britain was at an all-time high, with more than a million people under 25 out of work. Jeffrey Archer, the deputy chairman of the Conservative Party, was quoted as saying that many young people 'are quite unwilling to put in a day's work'. The Mary Chain – serial dole-ites save for Gillespie – were doing their best to prove him right.

There was talk of Band Aid's 'Do They Know It's Christmas?' being followed by two simultaneous concerts in the summer to raise £50 million for famine relief. These events were, by necessity, a major label carve-up; no indie or underground group had the ticket power to rate even an exploratory phone-call from Live Aid's organiser Bob Geldof. In the political pop arena, for some eleven months, the support of musicians like Paul Weller, UB40 and Frankie Goes To Hollywood had been directed at the miners' strike, which ended in March. The June Brides and the Membranes had played benefit gigs for the miners, but for the most part the Creation scene, like a microcosm of British youth as a whole, had been sapped and emasculated by the Tories' victory in the general election of 1983, and the post-election blues prevailed in the indie sector well into the Government's mid-term.

'The Living Room seemed political, but it didn't seem that concerned with the finer details,' says Stephen Pastel, who studied politics at university and was a Labour Party member. 'Alan didn't strike me as someone who had a really strong grasp of politics. I think he had a good heart, but [he] said to me around '83 or '84: "It doesn't really make much difference to me if Labour or the Conservatives are in. I think I can be successful under either." '

Not that there was much sign of political realism in a Pastels show. As with many indie bands, their music was an introspective reverie. In taste, attitude and personality, they stood superciliously aloof from the moralising pro-Labour faction of Bragg and Weller. 'We didn't used to stand around at the Living Room talking about politics,' says Tim Vass. 'In our youthful naivety, we thought that making good pop records was a political gesture.' It was all a poor indie boy could do – and frankly, the Labour Party didn't need their services anyway.

Jobs or no jobs, the tunnel vision of McGee saw only the Mary Chain in 1985. 'Upside Down' had at last climbed to number 1 on the indie chart in the first week of February, and in March the band embarked on a second tour of Europe. These European dates had a different atmosphere to the British gigs. There was less evidence of antagonism between the band and the audience: people were coming to listen and watch, not to boo or threaten. Still, old habits died hard. 'Not only was I the manager and the tour manager,' recalls McGee, 'but I also sound checked the bass guitar. The Mary Chain never bothered turning up to sound checks because they said there was no point.'

Back in London, McGee's hype campaign took up where it had left off. He circulated stories that the band's honeymoon period with WEA had curdled disastrously. In reality, there were no problems whatsoever. 'Rob Dickins liked it,' McGee says. 'I made up a story that they'd been banned from the building for nicking his wallet. Rob likes the attention.' Indeed, Dickins saw the funny side – although he adds that he would not have been so easygoing if his wallet really had been stolen. The *NME* printed the story without checking, presenting Dickins as the dupe. It was all the more ironic as Dickins' father Percy had been one of the *NME*'s founders in 1952.

Dickins liked McGee a lot, but he saw through the McLarenisms every bit as easily as Geoff Travis had. In his publishing days at the height of punk, Dickins had known McLaren reasonably well, and he sensed that McGee was coming at management from another angle completely. 'Alan was a real, real fan,' he says. 'Because we were a major record company, we had Madonna, we had Rod Stewart, we had all these people, and he was always fascinated to know about stars and that kind of thing. He wasn't like: "Oh, fuck them." He was always [asking]: "What's he like?" and "What's she like?" He was really just a fan that had an entrepreneurial skill to say: "Well, maybe I'll go and do something *about* being a fan." ' Dickins took McGee seriously as a talent scout, but that was as far as it went. 'Alan was more like an artist than a manager,' he says. 'He talked music and he talked the dream.'

In February, the Mary Chain were asked to perform on the BBC2 programme *Whistle Test*. Formerly the long-running *Old Grey Whistle Test*, the show had changed its style for the 80s and was no longer an albums-led, late-night oasis of tasteful rock but an early evening rival to *The Tube*, watched by around one and a half million people. The Mary Chain were so hot that they simply had to be accommodated – but the *Whistle Test*'s producer was rightly nervous. To ensure the band did not turn up drunk, he insisted on an early morning start. 'They had to play at eleven o'clock,' says McGee, 'so I had to get them up, get them to the studio and get them drinking by half-eight. By the time they performed, they were absolutely wasted.'

The Mary Chain got back to Fulham in the afternoon, fell asleep and awoke with thick heads just in time to see their song, 'In A Hole', go out at teatime. By far the least professional outfit the programme had booked since the punk years – and arguably not even then – the Mary Chain looked young and vulnerable in front of the cameras; pale-faced and startlingly ill.

Ten days later, on 22 February, 'Never Understand' was released. Radio 1 played it on its Saturday afternoon programme and requests for interviews doubled. The single reached 47 in the national chart. McGee demanded – and was given – a fee of £1,600 from North

London Polytechnic to stage a Mary Chain gig in March. They would be earning £100 for each minute of music they played.

In January 1984, members of Einstürzende Neubaten had given a concert at the ICA entitled 'Concerto For Machinery and Voice'. Using pneumatic drills, concrete mixers and cement breakers, the musicians performed their concerto, before deciding, as a climax to the set, to drill and smash their way through the stage – apparently in the belief that tunnels underneath the road led to Buckingham Palace and Whitehall. The audience joined in, throwing parts of the PA around as staff attempted to restore order. Damage, however, was minimal. The ICA's music programmer Michael Morris reflected: 'Quite frankly I was disappointed ... It struck me as being demolition without commitment.' Gamely, he added: 'I think the audience would have liked to see the whole thing go a lot further.'

Nine months later, at the same venue, the audience got its wish. A Neubaten-style group called SPK, annoyed by precautions enforced by the ICA's fire officer, played only two pieces before leaving the stage after seven minutes. Feeling ripped off, the audience threw cans of beer, shouted for refunds and overturned leaflet stands in the foyer. The police were summoned and the *NME* ran a news story headlined 'SPK Riot At ICA'. It was written by Neil Taylor.

Since the Mary Chain's own ICA gig in December, many people around the band had been talking semi-seriously about a riot occurring at a Mary Chain show sooner or later. Some Creation artists thought it might be amusing. The Membranes, during their own gigs, would sometimes hand out metal bars to members of the audience, instructing them to bash away to their heart's content. At a show in Reading, microphones had gone flying when a crowd of metal-brandishing fans got a bit carried away. 'There is something really exciting about a riot at a rock 'n' roll show,' says John Robb. 'It's completely irresponsible and dangerous and stupid, but at the same time ... that's part of the entertainment of it all.'

Robb suspected that McGee (who had been present at the Reading gig) would be thrilled by a Mary Chain riot, and not just for the publicity it would generate. 'McGee was definitely looking for a riot,' Robb says. 'Like anybody of our age group or generation, the punk thing had been so important. We wanted those riots. We wanted to be in those riots. We wanted to instigate those riots.'

Neil Taylor's articles about the Mary Chain in the *NME* had become so distorted by Chinese whispers that a simple mention of bad vibes at the Ambulance Station had been exaggerated to the proportions of a war report. To those who had read his riot story about SPK, Taylor was something of a shadowy figure – nobody knew if his agenda was music or violence. 'All of that Neil Taylor stuff served as hype,' says Andrew Perry, who co-wrote a fanzine called *The Trumpet*

Of Truth, 'and I think [the Mary Chain] nurtured it. And it all built up towards this gig at the North London Poly.' As February gave way to March, it seemed as though everyone in London wanted to go to the polytechnic gig. There was more than a frisson of expectation. By the morning of 15 March, almost the entire audience could have said categorically – yet without really knowing why – that the evening was going to end in trouble.

Friday 15 March was, as it turned out, quite an eventful day for bands associated with McGee and the former Living Room and Glasgow scenes. The X-Men were playing in Hammersmith. James King and the Lone Wolves had a London college gig. Microdisney were doing a miners' benefit in Hackney. Elsewhere, Tina Turner was appearing at Wembley Arena supported by Bryan Adams. Neil Taylor's name was on the guest-list for the North London Polytechnic, but he had no plans to write about the concert. Access to the band was being denied, in any case, as McGee had placed an embargo on press for the immediate future. However, two interviews were conducted by the Mary Chain that afternoon: one with a television crew from Canada, and one with *The Trumpet Of Truth.*

Andrew Perry and his friend Dave Padfield were students and big Mary Chain fans. Padfield was sent to the polytechnic to wangle an interview for their fanzine. In the lobby, he introduced himself to McGee who, to his surprise, was writing 'the Mary Chain are shit' on a black and white poster. McGee refused to allow him near the band. 'He was really pissed off because the poly had got the band's name wrong on the tickets,' says Padfield. 'It said "Jesus and the Mary Chain", so to take revenge he was writing abuse all over a huge stack of posters. He gave me a pile of posters and markers, and said: "Help me vandalise these." '

After a few minutes of scribbling, McGee looked across to see Padfield writing 'Gig cancelled' on one of the posters. Laughing, McGee told him that he and Perry could interview the band for one hour. When Perry arrived at six o'clock, the Reids and Douglas Hart were talking apprehensively about the night ahead. 'The gig had been oversold massively by the students' union and the band thought they were going to get lynched,' recalls Perry. 'We were saying: "What are you doing after the gig?" and one of them said: "Getting a fast car back to Fulham." '

After the interview, the musicians headed backstage. It was seven o'clock and as Perry and Padfield chatted excitedly about their scoop, people suddenly began knocking on the front doors. They opened to reveal several hundred fans waiting outside. Within half an hour, 300 had been admitted. By the time the first band – Meat Whiplash, friends of the Mary Chain from East Kilbride – took the stage, about 800 people were milling around, or pushing impatiently to the front of the hall, and an already intense atmosphere was rapidly going downhill.

The polytechnic had been oversold by at least 300 and many of those queuing were turned away despite having valid tickets. The students' union, which later claimed euphemistically to have 'overprinted', offered on-the-spot rebates – but tempers flared, and as Hart and Gillespie kicked open the fire doors to admit between 50 and 60 fans, the police were called.

Not enjoying the ambience one bit, Perry and Padfield started going to the toilets in tandem for safety reasons. During one visit, they heard a man say he intended to throw a bottle – which he had secreted in his jacket – as soon as the Mary Chain walked onstage. 'Judging by the mood everyone was in,' says Perry, 'violence seemed a palpable inevitability. There was already a real band-audience tension thing going, without either side having met.'

Meat Whiplash were even less adept musically than the Mary Chain, and rumour had it that most of the instruments on their imminent Creation single, 'Don't Slip Up', had in fact been played by the Reids. But the young band would play a crucial role in the evening's deterioration. Rather than kowtow like a meek support act grateful for the exposure, they used their fifteen minutes exclusively to wind the audience up. The singer strutted around the stage and taunted the front rows. When a barrage of missiles was thrown at the band, the guitarist picked up an empty wine bottle and flung it into the crowd, narrowly missing heads. 'Halfway through the next song,' one band-member later recalled, 'a guy ran along the stage and punched [the bassist] Eddie in the face.' Meat Whiplash left the stage for ten minutes, unsure whether to continue. Bobby Gillespie urged them to, advising them to aggravate the audience even more by announcing that their closing song would last for twenty minutes. This they did.

The next band to play was the Jasmine Minks. 'When the Jasmines went on,' relates Adam Sanderson, one of their two frontmen, 'Jim [Shepherd] and I kept turning our backs to the audience during instrumental parts, in a synchronised way like the anti-Shadows.' This was no dance routine. Sanderson had a claw hammer in his back pocket, Shepherd a steel pipe, and they wanted the crowd to know it.

As the long wait for the Mary Chain got under way, a crush developed at the lip of the stage. 'The bar had closed because it had sold out of beer, despite it being only about quarter to ten,' Sanderson remembers. 'People had been screaming about the bar being closed for at least fifteen minutes before the Jesus and Mary Chain's appearance.' There was a sense that something historical was about to happen, although people disagreed about what. 'There seemed to be a very confused perspective – as I think there was during most of the 80s – about what people actually wanted out of indie music,' says Andrew Perry. 'People were shouting: "Give us some noise." But once the noise arrived, they took that as their cue to get incredibly violent.'

The Mary Chain came out in darkness, refusing to acknowledge an audience they thoroughly despised. After three minutes of feedback, the shape of a song eventually suggested itself. The crowd surged forward. Joe Foster stood to the side of the stage; Adam Sanderson recalls him pointing to individuals in the front rows and miming that he was going to slash their faces. A missile bombardment began.

'It seemed so liberating,' reasons Perry, who was standing near the front. 'You imagined if you went to see the Eurythmics, say, it would be an hour and forty minutes of synchronised, over-staffed bollocks exactly like their records. But here was patently a band that wasn't capable of playing even the most rudimentary music. Jim Reid had a guitar round his neck which he didn't play at all. It was just hanging there, feeding back. It was total noise and anarchy. There was absolutely no sense of there being a tune at all. Jim was just staggering around. He used to wear these big baggy black jumpers. Someone grabbed his arm as he went by and pulled him [into the audience].'

Joe Foster ran from the wings and dived into the crowd to rescue Reid. Expecting a quick punch to settle the matter, Foster looked deep into the eyes of Reid's assailant and realised immediately that the Jesus and Mary Chain were no longer an enjoyable art joke. His thoughts turned to Dave Evans, alone on the mixing desk. Reid and Foster were pulled back on to the stage and the show continued. The band played a new ballad, 'Just Like Honey', and a burst of 'Jesus Suck' before walking off, leaving the guitars wailing against the amplifiers. The audience started to clamour for an encore. The lights went up and another wait began.

'There was probably about a minute when you thought: no one's going to really do anything here,' says Perry. But the lack of an encore was pushing some members of the audience near to the edge. Some people climbed on to the stage and started to aim kicks at the PA. Others joined in. The PA began to sway perilously. 'I remember laughing throughout it,' says Peter Fowler. 'As the PA stack just sort of went over ve-e-ry slowly ... It was hilarious. Everyone, even the most timid people who would be in a back room at a Loft gig, were grabbing things and breaking things and throwing them around. It was a free-for-all. No violence was intended against individuals. Just this ... madness. Crowd lunacy. "Well, he's doing it so I'll do it." Like a western bar-room brawl.'

Adam Sanderson, a working-class Aberdonian with a fierce suspicion of middle-class students, thought it was pathetic. He remembers: 'I was there in the middle of it all, and people were laughing and giggling, the middle-class youth of England, swept along on the euphoria of doing something really wild for the first and probably last time in their lives. There was a lot of crap – absolute lies – written about the "riot."'

One of the merrymakers was Dave Padfield, who had got caught up in a crowd of people hurling cans at the empty stage. 'It was a whole mixture of people,' he says. 'There was a sort of lairy element but loads of students were getting into it.' Theft was taking place, too, as people clambered across the stage, discovered various bits of musical equipment in their path and made off with them. The police were called for a second time. 'I think Geoff [Travis] came out and got the microphone and said: "Calm down everyone",' suggests Fowler. 'Someone just threw a bottle straight at him and went: "*Fuck* off." It must have been someone who worked for Rough Trade.'

Travis was in fact backstage, where he had been consoling Meat Whiplash's assaulted bassist Eddie Connelly, whose guitar had now gone missing. The next time McGee saw him, Travis had a metal bar in his hand. 'There were people trying to climb in the dressing-room window,' says Douglas Hart. 'We locked the door and people were beating it with fire extinguishers.' Out in the hall, there was the crackling sound of wood and metal being stamped and twisted. 'People were on the stage smashing the guitars and amps up,' says Perry. 'It moved very quickly to a sort of blood-in-their-eyes destruction. It seemed like there was a large contingent of people who had crossed the line.'

A murmur went through the crowd that McGee was about to be – or had been – beaten unconscious by a man from the PA hire firm. Actually, McGee was safe, but only just. 'I had sixteen hundred pounds in my pocket,' he says. 'We were paying this guy 160 quid for the PA. This PA had been trashed and there was only one man he wanted to take it out on. He was going: "I want you to give me the sixteen hundred pounds." I was saying: "Mate, fuck off. I ain't giving you it." I thought: I'm going to get battered, because he was quite a tough guy and he had another guy with him. But they didn't beat me up and I kept the money.'

A slight feeling of anticlimax descended on the hall, where the police had now arrived. A few people looked rueful, as though regretting their loss of control. 'You could say it was a spontaneous act of rejection of what music had become by that point, but it seemed a bit senseless,' says Perry. 'I found what the band were doing musically – or unmusically – far more interesting.' The stragglers dispersed and the clean-up began. 'It wasn't as if the mob charged off down Holloway Road kicking in the windows of pubs,' Perry notes. 'People just politely went home.'

Dave Evans ventured backstage to find the Mary Chain anxious and gloomy. Padfield, speaking to Jim Reid, was puzzled by the singer's despondency, considering how provocative he had been during the gig. 'He was devastated,' Padfield recalls. 'He was saying:

"We'll never be able to play live again after this. They behaved like animals." ' Padfield tutted sympathetically.

Over the weekend, Neil Taylor worked fast. On Saturday morning, he rang an *NME* section editor at home and told him what had happened. The week's biggest story – the announcement of the all-star charity record 'We Are The World' – was truncated to a minor bulletin as, once again, Taylor was given pages two and three to compose a report about the Mary Chain.

The commonly held view of this report is that McGee wanted something very specific and explosive to appear in the *NME*, which Taylor, his close friend and puppet, was only too pleased to give him. However, that is incorrect. For a start, Taylor was careful to leave the word 'riot' out of his story; it appeared only in the headline, courtesy of an *NME* sub-editor. And for another thing, Taylor's report opted for a strangely old-fashioned description of the evening, as though he had written it for the *Daily Telegraph*. 'Last Friday night,' it began, 'amid a battlefield of destroyed equipment, missiles and mass fighting at North London Poly, what should have been a premier concert by the Jesus and Mary Chain turned into an ugly display of violence.'

Taylor did not hold the band to account, focusing instead on 'a small group of idiots' who had set out to cause mayhem. In an attempt to distance himself from such vulgarity, Taylor drew a clear dividing line between the rioters and the band's true fans. It was a nice try but – as Dave Padfield could have told him – a bit too late.

In the end, Holloway police station made no formal charges. On Monday, 18 March, the band issued a statement exonerating itself from blame. The disingenuous hand of McGee could be detected in its every syllable. 'The Jesus and Mary Chain deny all responsibility for the proceedings on Friday night,' it ran. 'Friday night proved that people are crying out for the first division excitement that the Jesus and Mary Chain provide. In an abstract way, the audience were not smashing up the hall. They were smashing up pop music.'

For Neil Taylor, the comeback was an unexpected one. Far from appeasing McGee and the Mary Chain with its restrained phrasing and its condemnation of the bad-apple minority, his report caused friction by being so dominated by violence. 'I know that Alan felt – and [the band] felt – that that piece was quite negative,' says Taylor. 'Because they felt that what that piece said was: "Oh God, here comes trouble." '

In private, however, McGee was ecstatic about the violence; he just didn't show it to the Mary Chain. Their dismay made the scenario a precise reversal of one of the most famous controversies in punk history. In the moments following the Sex Pistols' interview with Bill Grundy – punk's point of no turning back – Malcolm McLaren had been frightened and angry, even admonishing Steve

Jones for using swear-words, until he realised he might be able to turn the situation to the band's advantage. Nine years later, it was the band that needed reassuring, not the manager. The Reids were disturbed by the thought that there could be no return to normality. But however much McGee affected empathy with them, he was not upset in the slightest. 'In one sense he may have been playing a very clever game,' says Taylor. 'Alan would do that. It's not that he could be obfuscatory – and it's not that he would be deceptive – but he gave the impression very much that he could be saying one thing and doing something else.'

Taylor had written of a 'premier concert' spoiled. McGee's statement had referred to 'first division excitement'. Linguistically at least, both young men were *ad idem*; they really should have been a couple of theatre critics. But if Taylor was a convenient fall-guy in the short term, the penultimate sentence of McGee's statement suggested there would be others in due course. In a challenge that some saw as a veiled threat, he proclaimed: 'The Jesus and Mary Chain are putting excitement back into rock 'n' roll, and promoters will have to bear the consequences.'

Two weeks later, when the Mary Chain provisionally announced three major concerts for the spring – in Manchester, Birmingham and at London's Lyceum theatre – promoters were to be seen blanching at the kind of excitement this band was putting back into rock 'n' roll. A spokesman for one of the venues, referring to a pitched battle that had occurred between rival sets of football hooligans two days before the North London Polytechnic gig, told the *NME*: 'We don't want Luton versus Millwall replayed in this establishment.' None of the shows took place.

Retribution for Joe Foster was swift. When it was discovered that he had played a part in the Mary Chain concert, his postgraduate course at the polytechnic was terminated. In April, he adopted the persona of a sleazy rock 'n' roll reprobate, Slaughter Joe, and released a self-produced single on Creation, 'I'll Follow You Down'. A volcanic eruption of feedback and viola, it was absolutely marvellous.

'It was Alan's idea,' Foster remembers. 'We had the whole Mary Chain thing going on, and he felt that we could probably produce enough material to corner the market for however long the vogue lasted. We felt that, at the drop of a hat, somebody else would come along with a similar record. This is no good. We've got to show that we've got a whole bunch of stuff like this, and the Mary Chain are at the front of the pack. We've got a genre and they are the pop group.'

The teenaged Meat Whiplash (whom Neil Taylor would dub 'the most atrocious live band of the year') were sold to the music papers as Mary Chain protégés, with Slaughter Joe explained as a sort of unpleasantly talented uncle. But 'I'll Follow You Down' came with a subtle message. Foster wanted people to be aware that the sound of the Mary Chain had been as much his own invention as anybody else's. The Mary Chain were not impressed.

What was less explicable was Foster's chameleonic accent. The Londoner's bizarre slurred Scottish brogue, which he had debuted on the European tour in October, had been attributed at first to a temporary bout of cabin fever, a by-product of being cooped up in a minibus with nine Scots. Months had passed, however, and Foster was still keeping it up. (Interviewing him for the *NME* that summer, a journalist wondered if Foster might be a Geordie, before plumping for 'heavily disguised Surrey'.) His change of accent duly became accepted as normal procedure, and continues to this day.

Though the gig at North London Polytechnic had scuppered Foster's further education, it had not harmed the Mary Chain's relationship with WEA. Reading the reviews, Rob Dickins was reminded of seeing the Who at the Marquee as a teenager, when a demented Pete Townshend would destroy his guitar and amplifier. Perceiving the Mary Chain to be a group that could bring hysteria on a regular basis to a notoriously unhysterical student market, Dickins felt it was high time they were signed to a proper Blanco y Negro recording deal.

McGee, his tail up, negotiated a suitable advance for the band – excluding Bobby Gillespie, who did not want to sign the contract as he was planning to leave the Mary Chain and devote his attention to Primal Scream. When a figure for the Reids and Hart had been agreed, McGee telephoned Fulham. 'He said: "Seventy-five thousand pounds advance",' recalls Hart. 'To us ... I mean, we couldn't *spend* that much. We were all really thin at that point. We were living in bedsits with slug trails on the floor. A few weeks after we got the money, we were photographed in Hyde Park eating ice-cream, and all of us look really puffed up because we have money for once. We all lost weight again when we started buying more drugs.'

On 30 March, the Mary Chain entered Southern Studios in Wood Green to record their third single, 'You Trip Me Up'. The B-side was to be 'Jesus Suck'. Album sessions would commence at Southern when the band returned from dates in America and Scandinavia. On Good Friday, with the feedback-heavy 'You Trip Me Up' in the can, McGee took the Mary Chain to New York to play two nights at the Danceteria club. The gigs were poor and the audience seemed unconvinced, but the band and McGee, buzzing on their first lines of cocaine, felt like rock stars. 'I remember lying on my bed in New York City,' says Jim Reid, 'flicking through all the TV channels and leaning out the window thinking: wait a minute, three weeks ago I was signing on.'

But by the time they reached Copenhagen on 12 April, the lustre had worn off. William Reid threw a fit in the dressing-room and smashed all the bottles of beer. 'You were sitting there and bottles were flying past your head,' says McGee. 'His brother had the dignity to run, but me and Bobby were just stood watching him like a freak show, baffled. We were laughing at this guy having a breakdown. Me and Bobby have always shared a pretty sick sense of humour. Then William goes out onstage and starts chanting at the audience: "You bacon-eating bastards, you bacon-eating bastards." It went out live on Danish radio.'

Back in Britain, Gillespie had only a couple of days to get ready for a Primal Scream concert at ULU (University of London Union) on 16 April. Primal Scream were tipped by Creation to be its new stars – although this looked like being a close-run race with the Loft, whose second single, 'Up The Hill And Down The Slope', was about to be released. Unlike the Loft, Primal Scream remained an unknown quantity, and most people in London had yet to hear them. Sections of the ULU audience – primed by McGee – had assumed they would have a power drill sound like the Mary Chain. There was some surprise when they strolled onstage and played a series of sweetly melodic tunes.

'It was this kind of really effete singing and Byrds-y jangling,' says Tim Vass. 'It wasn't what we were expecting at all.' The musicians stood completely still while playing, putting most of the visual emphasis on the whirling tambourine of John Martin – Gillespie's front-line foil – who wore a scarf over his face like a character in *The Virginian*. The band had 60s hairdos, black clothes and pointed Chelsea boots; it seemed like a revivalist set-up all the way down the line. And few of the onlookers at ULU shared McGee's fondness for the Rizla-thin singing voice of Gillespie.

Four days later, Gillespie was back on duty with the Mary Chain when they flew to Portugal to shoot a video for 'You Trip Me Up'. In the meantime, McGee had a meeting with Geoff Travis, telling him that the Mary Chain didn't want him visiting Southern during the album recording sessions. He was to wait until the songs were ready to be mixed. The Reids were increasingly calling the shots.

But they could not control everything. On 28 April, Jim Reid took a break from Southern to see a concert by Nick Cave in Brixton. Walking through the crowd, he was recognised by some of the Mary Chain's enemies, who punched and kicked him to the floor. He was badly beaten up. Of course, in an abstract way it was not Jim Reid they were smashing up, it was pop music.

Pete Astor's 'Up The Hill And Down The Slope' was the last song the Loft played every night. The highlight of their set, it would often stretch beyond five minutes, Astor using the extra time to extemporise a hipster's rap while the band held down a busy groove. Feeling that it could be their breakthrough single, the Loft asked McGee to finance a two-day session with Felt's sometime producer John Rivers in his residential studio in Leamington Spa, at a cost of £500. McGee gave them £300 – they could pay the balance themselves, he told them, but he would not go overdrawn for the Loft or anyone else.

Despite being an indie record, 'Up The Hill And Down The Slope' took as its rhythmic backdrop two influences from the major leagues. The idea for Bill Prince's skipping bass line came from a Derek and the Dominos track, 'Why Does Love Got To Be So Sad?', on the 1970 album *Layla And Other Assorted Love Songs*. Tellingly, while this was a favourite listen among the Loft's circle, Prince would never have admitted his debt publicly. In the indie world, there was no such thing as a good Eric Clapton album.

Just as clandestine was the inspiration for the snare drum crack that opened 'Up The Hill And Down The Slope', which came from the first bars of Bruce Springsteen's 'Born In The USA'. In an era of inadequate and erratic rhythm sections, the Loft were the first Creation band to give their record a mature musical arrangement, and the first to use sources from outside the indie glossary.

Astor's lyric was more expansive still. Inspired by a day spent at the Alexandra Palace fair in north London, he turned it into a metaphor for a young musician poised at the gates of the music business. He knows it is a seedy funfair that has been travelling the same route for decades, never changing; but he looks enviously at the rides on offer and longs for a turn – if only to assuage his curiosity:

Oh, my magpie eyes are hungry for the prize
Give me the money and I'll shoot it right between the eyes
My greedy eyes, my beady eyes – they swivel and they stare
Thinking of the bright things; I might just get them there

Please ... don't say no
Once round the fair – just so I know

Year in, year out, gypsy lorries go from town to town
Ghost trains down country lanes, great big wheels by farmers' fields
Hollow sounds travel round and round; money cackles in the lucky
*   town*
Over the hill and down the slope
To the rattle of the sound I go in hope
Oh, my magpie eyes are hungry for the prize
Give me the gun and I'll shoot it right between the eyes – I'm taking aim

Stalls with prizes that once meant luxury
Tempting but not knowing how old they now seem
And those sad, tearful journeymen running on their dreams
Showing off in the rain in last year's jeans

*Lyrics reproduced by kind permission of Complete Music.

Dubious of the circus, the money-go-round and the 'sad, tearful jour-neymen', Astor is none the less powerless to resist and thirsts for entrée. The prize he craves could, he knows, be awarded to him if the very song he is singing is successful.

Janice Long promoted the record heavily, playing a white label on her show before the artwork had even been completed. She chose the Loft as her 'band to watch' on the BBC2 music programme *The Oxford Road Show*, interviewing them on Primrose Hill a few days before the show's live tranmission in Manchester. But there had been growing tension in the Loft's ranks and the interview with Long only made it worse. A casual remark by Bill Prince humiliated Astor in front of the band he purported to lead. 'Bill's going: "Me and Andy formed the band – and then we picked up *the others* along the way",' Astor recalls. 'And there's a look on my face like I'm about to be sick. I remember very clearly thinking at that moment: fuck this.'

Driving up to Manchester on 29 March to mime to 'Up The Hill And Down The Slope' on *The Oxford Road Show*, the Loft were accompanied by their friend Danny Kelly. The following day – a Saturday – Kelly went to a football match in Manchester. There he met Pete Hadfield, the manager of the Colour Field, a band led by the former Specials singer Terry Hall. When Kelly mentioned the Loft, Padfield wondered if they might be available to support the Colour Field on an upcoming UK tour.

Had the two men not met, there would have been no promotional tour for 'Up The Hill And Down The Slope' – Creation had neither the money nor the contacts to arrange one. News of the tour spread rapidly, making the Loft the subject of much envious gossip among their indie rivals, particularly as Hadfield had not requested (as some managers would have) a buy-on payment. A guitarist from the June Brides rang McGee to ask how on earth the Loft had done it. It was a prize and everyone knew it.

'Up The Hill And Down The Slope' confirmed Creation as the hip new independent label in Britain. In Pete Astor, McGee believed he had a phenomenal songwriter, and he began to talk of him as a major artist of the future. When Astor explained to him that he had a prob-lem – he was unhappy in the Loft – McGee replied that it was not necessarily a problem. He asked Astor to keep him posted.

Astor made a few changes for the Loft's tour with the Colour Field. He had a new girlfriend, a singer-songwriter named Heidi Berry. He was wearing leather trousers onstage, and he had started smoking for the first time in two years. On the tour, he roomed with Dave Morgan, the Loft's drummer. One night he asked Morgan if he thought the Weather Prophets would be a good name for a band. In the other room, Andy Strickland and Bill Prince buddied up, took lines of speed and grew further apart from their singer.

*   *   *

Creation's music policy had toughened up since the pop-psych days of 1984. The Mary Chain had opened up avenues of possibility now being explored by Slaughter Joe and Meat Whiplash. A Creation band from Cork called Five Go Down To The Sea? were raucous and jarring. An Australian group, the Moodists, were in the Birthday Party mould. After releasing singles by each of them, McGee decided he was ready to make a Membranes album. They had been on the cover of *Sounds* – and had appeared on *The Tube* – but were so full-throttle that an engineer on one of their singles had fallen victim to tinnitus and been forced to retire from the business. One review of this single had read: 'As a music lover, I find the noise borders on the unlistenable' – and that was one of the good ones.

Just as the Membranes prepared to make their album, guitarist Mark Tilton left the band. With him went the band's vague sense of melody, and the album, *Gift Of Life*, left McGee cold. 'Tilton had a pop sensibility,' he says. 'Without him, it was just John Robb going: "I am fish eye!" five hundred times.' Since the Membranes had a fan-base, McGee released the album anyway, knowing that he would recoup. But when a disappointing Jasmine Minks LP followed, there was a feeling that Creation was starting to dip.

McGee's response was to pour most of his energy into the Jesus and Mary Chain and let Creation function as a side-project. He was still capable of being hands-on when occasion demanded – he personally oversaw the mail-out of Primal Scream's single 'All Fall Down' to Radio 1 and the music press – but he regarded the Mary Chain as his supreme vocation. However, in May, he made a poor decision. He chose not to accompany the band on a tour of Scandinavia. 'They were miserable that I wasn't there,' he says. 'Suddenly, it was like their dad's not there. My relationship with the Mary Chain had become quite bizarre. Jim was my mate. Douglas quite liked me. Bobby was one of my best friends. But William had an absolute, total distrust of me.'

At WEA's suggestion, McGee relinquished the role of Mary Chain publicist to Mick Houghton, a quiet man in his thirties whose clients included Echo and the Bunnymen and Julian Cope. Houghton saw the gap widen between McGee and William Reid. 'Alan was much more drawn to Jim than he was to William,' he says. 'I remember Alan and William arguing constantly.' Douglas Hart saw it too. 'To a point, William never trusted [McGee] and to a point he couldn't take him seriously,' Hart says. 'McGee was an odd character, almost like a cartoon character. Not in any derogatory way, but like Mr Magoo or something.' By not gaining William Reid's trust, McGee was leaving a dangerous door flapping open.

In the middle of May, the release of 'You Trip Me Up' hit an unforeseen snag. Staff at WEA's pressing plant refused to handle the record, protesting that 'Jesus Suck', the B-side, was blasphemous. Geoff

Travis approached other plants, finding the same reaction. For once, Rob Dickins was negative: he thought the Mary Chain would be foolish to delay the release for something as trivial as a B-side. Consequently, the band jettisoned 'Jesus Suck', using a song from the 1984 demo ('Just Out Of Reach') instead. The potential embarrassment of the climb-down was averted by a Mary Chain statement, which read: 'This is completely typical of the state of the stale-minded music business. Jesus and Mary Chain continually try to break the music business stereotype, but this time the cliché has affected even us. The group is disgusted by it all.'

Somebody was learning fast. This piece of abstract face-saving carefully avoided criticism of WEA, and chose not to mention the last band to experience the same problem: the Sex Pistols, whose 'God Save The Queen' had been rejected by pressing plant workers in 1977. It seemed Jim and William had decreed that the Pistols references must cease.

At the root of it all lay a peculiar delusion. After months of adulation in the music papers, the Reids now anticipated 'You Trip Me Up' being their first hit single. It was little known – but becoming increasingly relevant – that they had an intense desire to appear on *Top Of The Pops*. They had loved the show as boys in the early 70s, and even in 1985 they still respected the idea of a chart-based pop programme, provided they could be on it. They were adamant that the sight and sound of 'You Trip Me Up' would transform music overnight. But there was a big difference between the *NME* holding two pages for a 'riot' story and *Top Of The Pops* agreeing to a prime-time three-minute slot. The experienced Mick Houghton knew it would not happen. 'The Mary Chain were purely a music press phenomenon,' he says. 'The problem they always had with Warners was that they never got radio play and they never got TV. They never did any TV whatsoever after the *Whistle Test*. They had a bad reputation.'

It was hard to explain this to the Reids, who were convinced they had recorded a smash hit. '"You Trip Me Up" is pure summer,' Jim said shortly before its release. 'It should be number 1 for about 42 weeks and then we'll take it to the United States and it'll be number 1 there.' The idea was all the more comical for him being perfectly serious.

'We wanted to be pop stars,' says Jim today. 'We didn't want to be part of that indie scene in London. We wanted to be like Marc Bolan, up there onstage wearing make-up and having girls screaming at us while we played all these mental feedback songs. We wanted us – and other bands like us – to be on *Top Of The Pops*. We wanted to fumigate the charts. Music like ours had been pushed underground. We wanted to break the doors open again and let people in.'

To do this, they were prepared to adapt. Houghton sensed them growing alarmed by their image as riot-inciting hoodlums, and had heard them talk of lengthening their performances and cutting down on the feedback. The problem was: what if the feedback was the only thing their audiences wanted?

Inevitably, Radio 1 did not play 'You Trip Me Up' during daylight hours. The Mary Chain may have had a major label deal but, as the station's producers reminded their plugger Scott Piering, they had not upgraded their indie sound. 'The funny thing about the Mary Chain sound – it was a wall of guitars, but it wasn't that abrasive at the end of the day,' says Piering. 'It was almost Phil Spector-esque. [But] their reputation always went against them because they appeared to be nihilistic, uncommunicative, drug-taking ... and all that stuff lessened their chances of getting assimilated by the mainstream.'

'The main obstacle was that that music didn't sell records,' says McGee. 'It really was a case of inch by inch. The big indie bands in 1985, until the Mary Chain came along, were the Cocteau Twins, the Cure* and the Smiths. Other than those bands, that music did not sell records.'

This was true. 'You Trip Me Up' did not even reach the Top 50.

When the Loft returned to London to perform at a Creation-Kitchenware night at Riverside Studios in Hammersmith on 14 May, their friends were amazed by how much they had improved on the Colour Field tour. 'Up The Hill And Down The Slope' was high in the indie chart, putting McGee in an extremely good mood. 'My mum came along [to the gig],' says Andy Strickland. 'She was talking to Alan and he was saying: "Oh, you must be very proud." "Yes, they're doing well." He said: "Yeah, but it's when they play round the corner – that's when you'll know they've made it." '

Round the corner was the celebrated Hammersmith Palais, where, sure enough, the Loft were due to support the Colour Field one more time on 24 June. In the days leading up to that gig, the Loft very politely – and exceedingly Englishly – fell to pieces.

'Andy and I were doing speed,' says Bill Prince, 'and Dave and Pete smoked [dope]. That's how we divided up. We knew we were getting better, we knew we were going down well, we knew the gigs were good. We were all filled with this sense of ego and confidence. But at the same time we all knew that this huge gulf was opening up in the band.'

In preparation for the Palais, the Loft played several shows in small clubs around Britain. On 28 May, they appeared at the Pindar of Wakefield, a pub in London. 'Before the gig, we were interviewed for a fanzine,' recalls Prince. 'At the end of the interview, the fanzine journalist said: "What question would you ask yourselves?" And I said: "Are you filling a hole or carving a niche?" Pete went: "Fucking

---

* The Cure's records were in fact distributed by the major label Polydor.

hell, that's good." And I could see him asking it of himself. His expression said: "We're just filling a hole, but my next band will be carving a niche." '

When the Loft played at Splash 1 in Glasgow – an indie club run by Primal Scream – Astor told another fanzine writer: 'The indie ethic is a joke. It's just people thinking that they're morally superior because they're not successful.' He made a point of exempting McGee from the charge, but it was obvious he was including the Loft. That evening, Astor left the stage early, not staying to finish 'Up The Hill And Down The Slope'.

McGee didn't see any more Loft shows after his conversation with Strickland's mother. Mary Chain business took him to Oslo at the end of May, and to Southern Studios for much of June. The Mary Chain enjoyed the homeliness of Southern – which was manned from a hut in the back garden. 'The hut was the control room,' says Douglas Hart, 'and if you wanted to speak to [the owner and engineer] John Loder, you had to run through the garden. Adrian Sherwood* was recording overnight with Al Jourgensen from Ministry, so they'd be up all night speeding. We would come in in the morning and there would be loads of mad people hanging about.'

The studio had been set up for the use of Crass, whose drummer Penny Rimbaud would occasionally pop by. Hart recalls: 'Penny Rimbaud came in one Friday night when [Channel 4] were repeating *Ready Steady Go!*, and he said: "You've got to watch this. I'm on it. I win this Beatles collage competition and get two LPs from John Lennon." And it was him – this guy from Crass, as a wee kid. I think he chooses a Shostakovich LP and a Charlie Mingus LP, and John Lennon's sort of looking at him like: "You weirdo." '

On 20 June, McGee was interviewed by Janice Long on Radio 1. A fan of the Loft and the Mary Chain, she was keen to know more about Creation – and about the difficulties such indie labels might face. At the time of speaking, McGee was in good health financially: he expected Creation to make a profit of £50,000 by the end of the year, and was drawing a salary of £15,000 himself. He and his wife Yvonne had been sitting tenants in Beaconsfield Road, and when the house came up for sale they were able to buy it.

For all that, however, the interview with Long revealed a restless, impatient man keen to get on in life. He took a dig at Rough Trade Distribution for failing to get his records into the shops, and sneered at major label A&R men too enamoured of their 'expense accounts' to notice the talented new bands playing around London. Both of these were old complaints. But McGee then embarked on a blatant Creation sales pitch – letting the majors know he was amenable to a

---

* A producer of reggae and post-punk acts, Sherwood is best known for his On-U-Sound label and sound system in the 90s.

licensing deal – which suggested that he knew his label was about to hit a wall.

'The problem is basically cash flow: having enough money to record up-and-coming bands,' he explained to Long. 'We just got Felt from Cherry Red – this fantastic group – and the problem is having the money to record the groups. We're releasing records that should be in the charts, not in the independent charts ... At the moment, we've got probably the strongest stable of any independent.' It could be argued he was being myopic to the strengths of Rough Trade, Mute and 4AD, but he went further: 'I mean, if you have a look at the Warners roster – apart from the Jesus and Mary Chain, they've got very little. At Creation I've got five or six bands that could definitely have hit singles. Primal Scream are a completely massive band. All of these bands are going to be discovered by the majors eventually.'

What, then, were his options? 'Well, the options are that the Cartel possibly employ a strike force, like the major record companies, i.e. people that go into record shops and say: "Do you want to buy such-and-such a record?" every single day. If that happens and we [sell] more records, sure, I'd love to stay independent ... But in reality I'm afraid [Creation] is probably going to have to go through a major some time this year.'

The day after the interview, Pete Astor was phoned at home by Bill Prince. Biting the bullet, Astor told him it was all over. He was keeping Dave Morgan – and the Loft's name – and sacking Prince and Strickland. Prince rang Strickland, who demanded Astor turn up as planned for the Hammersmith Palais concert on 24 June. 'Looking back,' says Astor, 'I don't know why I didn't say: "Well, play the fucking gig as a three-piece, pal, because I ain't doing it." '

On the morning of 24 June, Astor awoke with a funny feeling that he and Strickland were going to trade punches before the night was out. McGee, whom Astor had informed about the split, was at a gig in Plymouth with the Mary Chain. He would not make it back to London in time. The Colour Field's performance was being broadcast live on Capital Radio, which had made for a packed, sweaty Palais. Backstage, the Loft struggled to keep calm. 'Bill was doing his Hank Hill bit, avoiding the whole thing,' says Astor. 'Andy was being terribly British. It was pursed lip central. I was ready for a certain amount of confrontation – and there was none, which is almost in essence what the problem with the band was.'

In the minutes before going onstage, the Loft congregated icily in their dressing-room. 'It was this little room at the back of the Palais, and all the guitars were in a line leaning up against tables,' remembers Strickland. 'There were six guitars and Pete was standing right in front of them. I thought: I'm going to punch him as hard as I can. I don't care if all his teeth fall out and he can't sing tonight. I'm just going to punch the cunt out. And I looked – and I thought: he's standing right in front of my guitar. That's the only thing that stopped me. I was so frustrated. I just wanted to punch his smug face in.'

The Loft walked onstage and stood as far away from each other as their guitar leads would permit. In the audience, from fans in the know, abuse was levelled at Astor and a pint of lager hit the stage. More poignantly, there were shouts for them to play certain songs; it was clear the Loft had grown in popularity.

They arrived at the last number, 'Up The Hill And Down The Slope'. Before starting it, Strickland announced that the Loft were disbanding after the show. Astor, his plans to keep the band's name suddenly jeopardised, coolly took revenge. When he delivered the line about 'sad, tearful journeymen', he added comments about Strickland and Prince. 'They've no idea ...' he chided. 'Look at them, they haven't got a clue ...' Prince, who had no vocals coming through his monitor, was oblivious. Strickland, though, heard every word. 'I was looking at Pete, thinking: fucking hell, what's the matter with you, mate? Just do the gig and piss off,' he says.

Danny Kelly had not seen the Loft in some time, and was unaware that they were splitting up. 'I had no idea what was going on,' he says. 'I saw Andy mouthing things into the microphone and there seemed to be this two-way argument going on. I thought: this isn't the way the song normally goes.' 'Up The Hill And Down The Slope' came to a dramatic point. Astor looked first at Prince, then at Strickland, said 'Bad luck', and dropped his guitar on the ground. The audience watched him walk up the staircase at the back of the stage – like Sinatra – to the dressing-room. The remaining members of the band stopped playing one by one and trooped off.

When Kelly went backstage to find out what had happened, the first person he met was Dave Morgan. 'Dave had a little girlfriend at the time,' he says, 'and the two of them were laden down with big drum cases. I said: "Where the hell are you going? The van's out there." And he said: "I can't be dealing with this. I'm going home on the tube."' The other three were keeping out of each other's way. Prince was drunk and distressed; he would not speak to Astor for three years. Strickland wanted Kelly to help him ambush Astor on his way out. 'We hatched this instant plan,' Strickland remembers. 'We'll put all the gear in the van. When he comes outside, we're going to kick his head in. But he never appeared. We never saw him again.'

Kelly reviewed the gig in the *NME*, commemorating the Loft's passing with the words 'R.I.P. the Loft'. Astor now had no hope of keeping the name. Suspicions lingered that he had gone for the grand gesture, his magpie eyes on the future rock encyclopaedia entry that would read: '... swanned out of his first band onstage during a high-profile concert'.

'I've had people come up to me ever since,' declares Prince, 'and say: "I saw your band split up onstage. It was the most astonishing thing I've ever seen." Apparently, every vein on Andy's neck – the light was catching it and it looked like his head was going to blow up. I hear it was an amazing evening. Probably the blackest and most ominous day of my life.'

Joe Foster, who was in that audience, had always thought of the Loft as congenial middle-class fellows. He was stunned by the animosity of their departure. 'It's the way a band from Detroit would split up,' he says. 'I've always been a bit wary of Pete since then.' Alan McGee, however, behaved with cold matter-of-factness. Jeff Barrett, who was staying with Strickland and Prince in their house in east London, believes it was a turning-point for Creation. A well-liked band on the label – comprised of people who had been on the scene since the very beginning – had fallen apart, with ramifications for at least ten close friendships. To Barrett's unease, McGee rode the storm without even flinching.

'It was quite a shock,' says Barrett. 'Alan was immediately Pete Astor's mate and the rest of them were consigned to the bargain bin. It was very much: that was then, this is now. The whole Living Room thing became the past.'

Part Two

The Magpies

6 The Margin of Psychosis

THE FIGHTBACK OF UNDERGROUND guitar music had captured the imagination of journalists, evening disc jockeys and a handful of major label A&R men, as well as throwing up new student heroes in the Jesus and Mary Chain and the Smiths. However, it had come to an impasse. For the music to reach the consciousness of the nation, a change was required in the attitudes of daytime radio producers. The majority of indie records continued to live or die by the judgment of Janice Long and John Peel.

Scott Piering had been deadlocked with Radio 1 since 1979, unable to persuade the daytime producers to include indie singles on their play-lists. For most of that period it had been a case of two intransigent viewpoints meeting awkwardly and being repulsed. In the radio corner – as cliché had it – was a bunch of middle-aged, suntanned DJs: nest-feathering, insincere and useless. In the indie corner, a load of groups that simply weren't trying hard enough.

The latter camp, seeing the prize cordoned off, was growing paranoid and in its demands for a more democratic air space it risked becoming deluded about the very product it was selling. 'It's not that I think we should be given hours of radio play a day,' said Primal Scream's Bobby Gillespie in 1985. 'It's just that we should have access to compete on equal terms with those records that do seemingly get automatic airplay. Our songs are melodic, they're accessible – all we're asking for is a chance.'

The definition of melodic was moot, and to tackle the question of accessibility one had to take into account the context in which a song might be heard. Compared to some of the music Peel played on his 10 pm show, Primal Scream were easy listening. But compared to 'The Power Of Love' by Jennifer Rush – a chart-topping single that October – they were off-pitch and sloppy. 'If you put an indie single on during a daytime show, in amongst the over-produced material it did sound bloody odd,' says a Radio 1 producer of the time. 'The good thing about indie is that it *sounds* indie – that's its saving grace. It doesn't sound like pop, so put it in with pop and you're immediately stubbing your toe somewhere.'

Piering had heard this argument many times, and knew it was insurmountable given the nature of the music itself. 'There was this naffness – this slight crapness – that none of [the daytime producers and DJs] understood about indie music,' he says. 'The production values didn't really stand up and that's why people like Steve Wright made fun of it.' Desperate for a hit, the Mary Chain sensed a conspiracy at Broadcasting House, but the Mary Chain were actually the red herring in the scenario. Not an indie band in the true sense of the word, they nevertheless had – more than *any* indie band – the dreaded 'switch-off factor'.

For the Mary Chain, acceptance by Radio 1 was a prerequisite. Only when they were given daytime airplay could they do what the Velvet Underground had not and reach the housewives, the factory workers and the kids on their way to school – in short, effect a pop revolution not after their lifetime but during it. 'Considering that Radio 1 in that period enjoyed something like 16–17 million listeners, they could have played the Mary Chain,' says Piering. 'They had the leeway to do it.' The band's daytime debut, however, remained tantalisingly out of reach.

To the Mary Chain's and Primal Scream's further consternation, there was now a serious threat to their stranglehold over the British music press. While home-grown indie music had laboriously been joining the dots between the 60s and the 80s, frequently grasping at ideas it was not quite able to express, the American band REM had blown into London in 1983 to serve notice that the most seismic developments in 60s-influenced guitar rock were happening on the other side of the Atlantic. The sheer romance of REM's line-up – in which a flamboyantly whirling guitarist did battle with an intense, esoteric singer-lyricist – lent them a symmetry, a quintessence and a lodestar glow. Next to REM's accomplished albums *Murmur* and *Reckoning*, almost anything British seemed colloquial and underpowered.

After REM came the deluge. In what became known as the Paisley Underground movement, almost a dozen American guitar bands toured Britain on the back of albums that delighted UK rock critics. By the summer of 1985, the Long Ryders, the Dream Syndicate and the Rain Parade had not only become integrated by the British media – *Melody Maker* and *Whistle Test*, particularly – but had shot to the top of the pile, where they were promptly offered deals by UK labels.

While these bands' reference points (and record collections) were similar to those of their indie counterparts in Britain, REM, the Dream Syndicate and the Long Ryders were demonstrably streets ahead as musicians and performers. An audacious game of leapfrog was being played out, and the British groups could only watch helplessly. The standard of musicianship on the UK indie scene, with the exception of Johnny Marr and Felt's classically trained guitarist Maurice Deebank, was exposed as second-rate. For some, it was the end of the line. Eclipsed by the Californian psychedelians Rain Parade, Dan Treacy's fortunes never recovered.

Sid Griffin, the singer in the Long Ryders, was surprised at how easy Britain's live circuit had been to conquer. 'There wasn't competition, as it were, from UK bands,' he remembers. 'We were astonished that there weren't Long Ryders-type bands in Leicester, London and Bristol playing gutsy guitar music like us. And so soon after punk, too.'

At Creation, some of the Americans were liked. Their musical expertise was noted and their records were played and enjoyed. As with the Smiths – creatively so superior to the indie rank and file that they might have landed from another planet – the Americans were envied with a sigh. Many had years of experience as players and most had been liberated by punk rock in more subtle ways than their British contemporaries.

'In England, unlike America, the punks won the revolution,' says REM's Peter Buck. 'They had Top 10 records and they were famous. All the kids who listened to the Clash bought the records and thought: anyone can do this. All it takes is three chords and a guitar. But in America, punk was way underground, and most of the people who got into it had probably been playing music for years before that. I know I had. The whole thing about "we can do anything" – to [REM] – meant we could do these weird folky things and not have to be a hit band. It didn't mean "let's get some Les Pauls and play really loud and really fast".' Weird and folky or not, in the face of REM and the American cavalry, rinky-dinky British indie was a pushover.

The Reid brothers responded predictably, calling the Long Ryders and other Americans 'pathetic'. Sid Griffin thought they had a nerve. 'We had done literally hundreds of gigs to get to the point of having a hot live show that lasted over an hour,' he says. 'And here were these guys who did twenty-minute shows – and the reason they did short shows, I knew, was because (a) they couldn't play very well and (b) they were scared to death. The fact of the matter is they were incapable of an hour-and-fifteen-minute show. It was beyond them both musically and in terms of the intestinal fortitude it takes to stand in front of people and perform.'

In indie clubs, where a guitar solo could be howled down scornfully for its associations with careerism and self-aggrandisement, they would no doubt have sided with the Reids over the flashy Yanks. As Griffin was quick to perceive – and UK indie bands would not have admitted this even on pain of death – the indie scene in Britain was no less trend-obsessed and style-conscious than the chart pop it wanted to destroy. The very quality that had secured the American bands a fanbase – music, and plenty of it – was what got them sneered at by the UK indie clique. Hour-long sets! My dear, these foreigners have so much to learn!

As a result, the UK indie scene swallowed more of its tail as its parameters contracted. The newest club in London was Room At The Top in Chalk Farm – run by a semi-retired Dan Treacy and his girlfriend Emily – where the indie sounds of 1985 and 1986 were born. To Room At The Top's insular, hypercritical clientele, the Smiths were mainstream, the Mary Chain were superstars and Edwyn Collins was already an old man at 26. The most influential band in this break-off sect – the one that set the tone in sound and attitude – was Creation's neglected, near-forgotten signing of 18 months before, the Pastels. They were, claimed a member of their Edinburgh protégés the Shop Assistants, 'probably the most important band in Britain today'.

The eminence of the Pastels was based partly on a misunderstanding. Their perceived lack of competitiveness made them the cynosure for younger groups who loved the fact that the Pastels had never sold out. In truth, the Pastels had been meaning to improve as musicians, but had never quite got around to it. Strangers to proficiency, they sent out a subliminal message that making music really was as easy as it looked, and almost single-handedly inspired a rash of maladroit quartets to sing soppy love songs with heads babyishly tilted. 'You got this kind of lowest common denominator version of the Pastels,' says Stephen Pastel. 'I suppose people saw certain things in our band and multiplied them by 100.' Or subtracted by 50.

Room At The Top deserves some credit for filling the hole left by the Living Room's closure – even if (as McGee made a point of saying) Treacy and his girlfriend were copycatting rather than pioneering. But it wasn't as if toasts were being drunk to McGee's health in Chalk Farm every night. As the Glaswegian had risen in stature nationally, his popularity in London had hit a plateau. Among those he had left behind in the indie garrets, there were some who wished him well but others who were angry at being abandoned. In July, Jerry Thackray wrote, apparently without irony: 'Whatever happened to all those old punk rock groups who were so fresh and invigorating?' He wasn't talking about 1977. He was talking about 1983.

Thackray loved Room At The Top and his floor was always available for bands to sleep on. Around the country, some of these bands had clubs of their own. Big Flame ran one in Manchester. Yeah Yeah Noh did the honours in Leicester. The June Brides played mein host in Clapham. 'You would hear [a band] on the Peel show,' says Phil Wilson, 'and you'd write to them: "Are you interested in playing our club? We'd be interested in playing yours." It was people getting to know each other very informally.'

Amid these exchange schemes, some empire building was possible. 'If you bumped into somebody at a gig and got chatting,' says Jowe Head of the Television Personalities, 'you would find they were either starting their own band, or running their own club, or running their own label, or doing a fanzine. And sometimes people would be doing all four.' This was McGee's legacy. But he was not sticking around to enjoy it.

With a new nationwide indie structure came new cynicism, invariably directed from outside. Widely heard was the pejorative term 'indie kid', with its connotations of over-sensitivity and blind intolerance of other music. Within the scene itself, words such as 'cutie' and 'charming' were used to underline the infantilism of the songs and personalities. Turned off by the invasion of Smiths concerts by macho hordes, the cuties were delicate flowers, pacific and childishly attired. The favoured garment was the anorak – the clothing of primary school. 'The anorak was a style statement,' says Stephen Pastel. 'It was saying: "Everything else is fucked up and we've got to get back. Closer to the start of things. Being children." '

There were other accoutrements in the cutie's kitbag: toys, sweets, badges featuring the face of Tufty, a cartoon squirrel who had taught a generation of British kids road-safety awareness in the 70s. 'The first time I ever saw Stephen Pastel,' recalls Cerne Canning, a promoter of indie gigs in London, 'he was upstairs at Rough Trade with Joe Foster, and he was playing with an Action Man toy on a parachute. He was wearing an anorak and he looked about 13. I thought he was Joe Foster's son.'

While the stardust and golden followers of Pastel tried to get themselves back to the garden, the fanzines experienced another purple patch as the cuties recoiled from the pro-rap *NME*. In places of strong indie support – a Glasgow or a Manchester – an appropriate group could play to audiences of 800 or even 1,000. As soon as they strayed from the major cities, however, the enormity of their task would be brought home to them. In Southampton one night, the turnout for a June Brides gig was ten people – and six of them were in the band.

The Mary Chain were the *bêtes noires* of the guitar-playing underclass and, Radio 1's daytime boycott notwithstanding, were creeping overground with each instalment of their infamous story. Drugs and girls pervaded. Deliberately avoiding the pressure-cooker environment of London, they played in Nottingham and in Manchester towards the end of June.

At the Haçienda club in Manchester, members of the audience attempted to climb onstage as soon as the band appeared. 'There were four bouncers across the front of the stage for the entirety of a very shambolic 13-minute set,' says Andrew Perry, who had hitchhiked to be there. 'There were ten glasses – real glasses – in the air at every point during the set. The Haçienda has a balcony, so a lot of these glasses were coming from high up. As an 18-year-old mosher, I was well up for being down the front, but not if I was going to end up in hospital.'

As much as they were disillusioned by the violence, the Mary Chain still employed the tactics of provocation – with McGee's full endorsement, naturally. However, William Reid was pushing for proper-length sets and a more enlightened outlook from those who paid to see them. 'They were saying: "OK, we make violent music. But you don't go and see a violent movie and slash the guy next to you",' remarks Perry. 'I guess they were playing up the art terrorism side to it – and I guess they were shitting themselves too.'

Mick Houghton, the Mary Chain's link with the music press, gathered that they were in a transitional phase but it was not going to be an easy transition. 'They no longer wanted to play twelve-minute gigs,' Houghton says. 'It was like: "We can actually play [properly]." But they were probably little more than competent as musicians, so I think that was quite hard to get over.'

An *NME* report of a Mary Chain gig in Edinburgh on 5 September made it even harder. Describing how Jim Reid had fallen over in the dressing-room after drinking too much alcohol, the journalist went on: 'Once onstage, Reid renews his struggle with gravity. McGee stands at the back of the stage and assumes a catching position every time Jim sways near. The set is customarily short and messy. Out of about four songs, at least two are "You Trip Me Up" . . .'

'That gig was out of control,' remembers McGee. 'Jim was off his tits. The whole [Reid] family was on the stage with them – the mum, the dad, the granny, the lot. I think we were getting paid £750. I was getting the money and Eddie Connelly [of support band Meat Whiplash] fell through the door. I've got all the money on the table, the promoter's counting it out and Eddie's getting battered by the bouncers. So I immediately went: "Stop! This is outrageous behaviour." I got really indignant. The bouncer stopped. And as I looked out, Jim Reid had four bouncers tearing his clothes off him and battering him. I said: "Stop, stop!" I got in the middle of the bouncers. Jim Reid was standing with his shirt ripped off him. It was total Edinburgh thuggery. What had happened was, Jim was chatting up some woman, the bouncer tried to escort him out and he went: "I'm the singer in the fucking band." The bouncer grabbed him, Jim was sick over the bouncer's shoes and the bouncer kicked his head in.'

Who was in control of the Mary Chain? Was anyone? Certainly not Geoff Travis. Probably not McGee either. It was the Reids who wielded ultimate control – and ultimate veto – in the Mary Chain, and of the two brothers William's grip appeared firmer than Jim's. McGee, however, was no nearer to gaining William's trust than he had been six months earlier. 'William was more suspicious of people than Jim,' says Mick Houghton. 'I always felt Jim wanted to be more outgoing – wanted to be more friendly – but was possibly held back by William. Jim was always personable. In a weird sort of way he's very polite. But I've seen William be extremely unpleasant to people.

And when they were drunk, William was far more likely to be unpleasant-drunk than Jim.'

By extension, then, when William was drunk, nobody was in control of the Mary Chain – and William liked a drink. The train was for much of its journey driver-less as William Adam Reid sought intoxication with the passengers in the bar. And in doing so, he sealed the Mary Chain's fate. In a curious way, violence at the North London Polytechnic had been inevitable. At their next London concert, it was obligatory.

'The whole course of the evening was obvious from the moment one walked in,' wrote a reporter about the events at the Electric Ballroom on 9 September. Announced to the press in the third week of August, the gig had sold out at once. The Mary Chain had had little say in the location: the Electric Ballroom was one of the few clubs that would take them. It was in Camden Town, a tense, edgy part of London, and the atmosphere outside the venue had an unsavoury tang long before the doors opened. Danny Kelly remarked in the *NME* that the band's audience now comprised – in ascending order of volatility – 'the seekers of cheap thrills ... the easily misled and the marginally psychotic'. It was the marginally psychotic who were giving McGee and the Mary Chain pause for thought, and in some cases the margin of psychosis was by no means narrow. According to one report, 'several known gang leaders' were seen in the crowd before the Mary Chain took the stage.

'If you play with fire, you get burned,' reasons John Robb. 'Any band can have a tough reputation among their own fans. But as soon as the mad kids come in from the estates wanting a bit of a tumble, everyone starts going: "Oh no no, we don't want a *riot*." ' McGee, on the Mary Chain's instructions, had hired minders for the gigs in Nottingham, Manchester and Edinburgh. At the Electric Ballroom, these men mingled with the venue's own security staff. 'We'd started to attract a football crowd,' says McGee, 'and I didn't know that. Because I'd stopped going to the football in about 1978, I didn't know about football violence at this point. I knew you didn't get on a tube full of West Ham fans, but I didn't know how it had embraced English subculture.'

The much-loved rock movie *This Is Spinal Tap* shows a fading rock group arriving at a concert to find it has been billed beneath a puppet show. At the Electric Ballroom, the Mary Chain were effectively billed beneath their own riot. 'I went to the back of the hall,' recalls Peter Fowler, 'and overheard a group of people saying: "When's the fight starting?" ' Many in the hall could be seen – bizarrely – scrutinising their wristwatches, as though a rioting time had been pre-arranged, marked out in seconds and minutes to await the peep of a referee's whistle.

After making the audience wait for an hour, the Mary Chain took the stage to play one of the worst shows anybody had ever heard. 'It was an abortion of a gig, absolutely dreadful,' says Andrew Perry. 'Even on a visceral level, you couldn't get into it. We are talking about a severely short gig, and for the whole of the set there was a horrible buzzing noise. When they went off, there was a feeling that they'd gone to sort the sound problems out.' Cans and bottles were thrown at the empty stage. A glass, hurled high, hit one of the neon strip lights, knocking one end out of its socket and leaving it hanging over the audience, seasoning drinks with broken glass. One man mounted the stage and started to smash up the group's equipment before being removed by security. This was the cue for others to invade the stage – at which point the bouncers retreated – and there was the now-familiar sight of amplifiers being toppled and the PA pulled down.

Carrying weapons, the bouncers returned to clear the stage, where-upon a battle broke out with the rioters. This time it wasn't a question of breathless students being handbagged by ineffectual polytechnic security. These were not students and the Electric Ballroom was not a polytechnic. 'At North London Poly there had been a move forward: people were rushing to see what was going on,' says Andrew Perry. 'At the Electric Ballroom a lot of people were running back. It seemed like there were much heavier, biker-type people there.'

Some onlookers found safe places from which to witness the Pavlovian uproar play itself out. Others, however, were getting hurt – one member of the Mary Chain's security team had his head split open by an iron bar. 'I was at the mixing desk and people were trying to pull it over,' says Dave Evans. 'I know that at least one person walked out the front door with a monitor.' When Evans finally made it backstage, the band had gone.

There was no statement from the Mary Chain to the press this time, nor any post-gig comment from McGee. But earlier that after-noon he had told a *Sounds* reporter: 'We're attracting an animal ele-ment now which is very frightening and which the band don't want. We honestly didn't provoke or start the riot . . . at North London Poly. But we're suffering the consequences for it now.' When the quote was printed in *Sounds* the following week, Neil Taylor read it with raised eyebrows. He had seen McGee in his McLaren pomp – not necessar-ily provoking the trouble at the North London Poly, but certainly fan-ning the flames of the media bonfire lest it fizzle out too soon – and couldn't understand why McGee was suddenly pulling the rip cord in alarm. McGee had the shock horror headlines in the music papers. Now, surely, the red-top tabloids must follow, bringing him the renown he yearned for. Or was somebody marking his card? 'I defi-nitely feel there was an element of kowtowing to Warners,' says Taylor. 'Alan could have taken it much further. You could even make a very good argument for saying that he bottled it.'

McGee's remarks in *Sounds* did not convince Andrew Perry either, and for a different reason. 'The Joe Foster-Alan McGee scene was strange,' Perry says. 'Joe had chosen to turn up at the Electric Ballroom in his Slaughter Joe persona with McGee in tow, which involved the pair of them arriving dressed head-to-foot in black leather – with white greasepaint and black mascara – on a baking hot summer's night in one of the hottest venues in London. They stood around looking like a pair of psychos, like a couple of Alice Coopers ... McGee was loving every minute of [the violence]. He looked really drugged and drunk. As I left, he was grinning maniacally.'

Perhaps so, but McGee's hangover kicked in early. Even before the end of the night, he had recanted his McLarenisms and was a very troubled man indeed. 'We drove away in Geoff Travis' car,' he recalls, 'and we were saying: "Fucking hell ..." The Mary Chain were too smashed to know that there had been a real riot. But I was saying to Geoff: "What the hell have I stirred up? Up to now it's been the *NME* and *Melody Maker* and it's like we're all having fun together. I've shoved you at the Ambulance Station and it's a laugh. Then suddenly it's Chelsea, it's Millwall, they're coming to kill the band. It ain't funny any more." '

It had been one thing McGee wanting to be McLaren. It was another to ask the Mary Chain to be the Sex Pistols. With new girl-friends in their lives, and a longing (in William Reid most of all) to live a less frantic existence, they now needed and demanded privacy. Whatever Neil Taylor may have scented, the decision to call time on the riots was not a sop to WEA, it was an act of self-preservation.

And with that, the ride on the runaway train was over. As everyone got their breath back, laughing and coughing and spluttering, it was left to Joe Foster to spot the flaw in the strategy. 'I couldn't see a way to stop it,' he says. 'Alan may have had a plan, but I was very concerned. I couldn't see what the fuck would happen.'

Number 83 Clerkenwell Road is a red-brick Victorian building that stands opposite St Peter's Italian Church, where the restaurateurs of Soho meet in worship or to bid farewell to their dead. Just around the corner is Hatton Garden, London's jewellery mile. The first people from the indie music business to enter 83 Clerkenwell Road's fusty honeycombed corridors were Dave Harper and his partner Nicki Kefalas of Out Promotions (so called because they were always out) and they were soon joined by others. By the summer of 1985, the threadbare-carpeted rooms were filling up with new arrivals. Creation moved there in August.

From 83 Clerkenwell Road, McGee directed the affairs of both Creation and the Mary Chain. Joe Foster slipped into the role of bohemian producer-musician in residence (he had lately been depping as bass guitarist for Biff Bang Pow!) and would roll in at around lunchtime, or two hours after getting up, whichever was the later. But on Creation's schedule, the current singles – 'Singing In Braille' by Five Go Down To The Sea?, 'I'm Alright With You' by the Pastels and 'Justice And Money Too' by the Moodists – were far from electrifying.

Five Go Down To The Sea? came from Cork and had followed their friends Microdisney to London, drawn to the Living Room by reports of good music and cheap beer. McGee had put them onstage a few times. Finbarr Donnelly, their singer, snatched pints from the hands of people in the crowd and shouted surreal, Flann O'Brien-esque lyrics while his colleagues clonked out ramshackle, all-elbows rhythms. 'They were bananas,' McGee says. 'They would bite Joe's head. Joe would be walking around trying to get this little guy off his head. Donnelly would lick my ears, trying to get the wax out. But they were good to have in the club if there was ever any threat of violence to any of us. They were so mad and they were so "for us."'

A long association between Five Go Down To The Sea? and Creation was out of the question. 'The thing about Five Go Down To The Sea? is they just didn't behave like anybody else,' says Sean O'Hagan. 'Doing business with them would have been almost impossible.' By the time 'Singing In Braille' was released – selling 600 copies and no more – Five Go Down To The Sea? were living in Rotherhithe with ten builders, for whom they did the housework. 'They invited us round for tea,' recalls Peter Fowler. 'We went to their house and they brought out a tray of jelly babies. Then they turned the TV on and sat down. Me and my girlfriend were like: "This is a joke – the hamburgers will be coming out any minute." But they just sat there with a knife and fork and ate jelly babies. I've spoken to people since who've said: "No, they weren't doing that for show. That's what they did."'

The Moodists were Australians, often compared to the Birthday Party. After the break-up of the Loft, Bill Prince was offered the bassist's gig on a Moodists tour of Europe. It sounded promising: they were good drinkers, the tour took in interesting cities like Berlin and Prague, and the band's music was heading in more of a rootsy direction. Two weeks before the start of the tour, Prince cracked a wrist. 'They lived in a big tower block off Old Street,' he remembers. 'I went round there and I said: "I can't go. My doctor said if I put stress on the wrist it'll never heal." And the singer went: "You fucking poofter. My wife – the drummer – she bloody did a tour of Australia with a broken arm!"'

Prince's former friend Pete Astor had not wasted time. Three days after the Loft's finale at the Hammersmith Palais, he told McGee he was forming a band called the Weather Prophets with Dave Morgan. Astor and Morgan booked studio time at Alaska, and with McGee on bass they recorded a track called 'Worm In My Brain' (for a Creation compilation LP, *It's Different For Domeheads*) and a Robert Johnson song, 'Stones In My Passway', a sign of the band's minatory intent. Astor's education in the blues, however, was more Hornsey library than Mississippi Delta, and his pedestrian singing voice did not live up to the occasion. Searching for musicians outside the indie scene, he roped in an old friend, David Greenwood Goulding, on bass. Goulding didn't know the first thing about indie bands – he had not even heard of the Loft. Astor, Morgan and Goulding gigged as a three-piece before acquiring Oisin Little, a friend of Morgan's, on rhythm guitar. Astor made it clear to all of them that the leader, sole song-writer and principal musician in the Weather Prophets was Pete Astor. No one demurred. 'That was the thing about Pete,' says Goulding. 'He'd already been through a lot in the Loft, so he could handle everything pretty well. Or thought he could.'

It's Different For Domeheads was a smoke-and-mirrors album. It was essentially the same Creation roster as that on the 1984 compilation *Wild Summer Wow* (the Loft, the Jasmine Minks, Biff Bang Pow! and so on), but the Mary Chain, *in absentia*, had caused some reflected rock 'n' roll dazzle to light up the label, which the widespread wear-ing of leather trousers – Goulding was the latest to buy a pair – accen-tuated. Creation's old image as a psychedelians' retreat was yielding to a sexier perception of a red-blooded, no-shit-taking brotherhood of hard-drinking degenerates. It touched every band on the label, mak-ing it possible – if not exactly plausible – for the Weather Prophets to be born with a trace of danger. 'Straight away there were journalists around,' recalls Goulding. 'You could see there was a buzz about us.'

McGee agreed to be the Weather Prophets' manager, which showed how seriously he took them. 'He saw Pete as: now I'm in the door at Warners with the Mary Chain, I've now got a classic singer-songwriter with Pete Astor,' suggests Jeff Barrett. 'Pete was a funny cat. He was quite egotistical – and he wasn't A&R'd at all, that was the thing. He was just allowed to be this Pete Astor character, and I think it had gone to his head. Splitting a band onstage, man – you don't get a much bigger ego than that.'

In October, the Weather Prophets made up a travelling Creation foursome with Primal Scream, Meat Whiplash and the Bodines (a Bunnymen-styled band from Glossop in Derbyshire), playing to audiences in London, Manchester and Edinburgh. Meanwhile, three of Creation's other acts appeared at Riverside Studios in Hammersmith as part of the 'Week Of Wonders', a five-day showcase of bands associated with Rough Trade Distribution.

The promoters of 'Week Of Wonders' were Cerne Canning and Simon Esplen, two young Rough Trade staffers who'd been encour-aged by nights at Room At The Top to bid for their own pitch in the indie arena. The Creation night – Friday, 25 October – was to begin with support sets from Slaughter Joe and the Pastels. To headline, Canning and Esplen had booked the Membranes, whose *Gift Of Life* album had been in the indie Top 20. 'We turned up to find McGee and Joe Foster there in their leather trousers,' recalls John Robb. 'Now, we were all wankers. I'd turned into a wanker, McGee was a wanker and Joe Foster was a complete wanker. Our egos were out of control. We thought we were going to destroy rock 'n' roll.' To Esplen's discomfort, McGee told the Membranes that there had been a slight change of plan. The original running order had been scrapped and the three acts would draw lots to determine a new one. 'We said: "Fuck that, it's our gig",' relates Robb. 'But we drew lots and funnily enough Joe Foster ended up being the headliner. What a fucking joke.'

Foster had a scratch band – which he had barely rehearsed – and only five songs in his repertoire. Taking the stage after a singularly angry turn by the Membranes, he was roundly abused by pro-Membranes factions in the audience. 'Fuck off back up north,' he retorted. 'There must have been a lot of northerners present,' surmised a *Melody Maker* reviewer. 'The hall visibly emptied after that.'

'Mates of the Membranes threw a glass at Lindy [Morrison, the drummer],' says Foster. 'It burst just above her head. A couple of their pals backstage seemed to want to attack the girls in the group. One of these boys got the rough end of Lindy and she took her shoe off and whacked him across the face. It was all pretty unpleasant and we left as quickly as possible.'

Stephen Pastel believed, in his mild-mannered fashion, that the Membranes had been treated appallingly. On principle, he sided with Robb against Foster and McGee. He could not have made a worse mistake. 'The thing with Creation,' he says, 'was that there was a lot of egos just going out of control. It sounds ludicrous. These were bands that were selling 2,000 to 3,000 records.' As accusations flew back and forth, McGee blamed Pastel, of whose incessant whining he was now heartily sick. Robb blamed Foster. Foster blamed Pastel for being a mealy-mouthed indie shit-stirrer. Feuds hardened over the weekend. As soon as 83 Clerkenwell Road opened for business on Monday morning, the Membranes and the Pastels were kicked off Creation.

A week later, the reformation became a purge. It was reported by *NME* that the X-Men and Les Zarjaz had been dismissed by McGee (in fact, Les Zarjaz had never been intended as a long-term signing), and it soon transpired that neither Meat Whiplash nor the Moodists nor Five Go Down To The Sea? would be releasing any more records on Creation. With these eccentric outfits drummed out, Creation was stripped down to a core roster of Primal Scream, the Weather Prophets, Slaughter Joe, Biff Bang Pow!, the Jasmine Minks, the Bodines and Felt.

The Membranes resurfaced on a northern label, In Tape, as Robb began a side-career in music journalism. The Pastels found a home with the London indie Glass. Much muttering was heard on the fanzine hustings about McGee's ostracism of former allies and good guys. In the fanzine *Adventure In Bereznik*, Creation was called 'upwardly mobile' and it was not meant as a compliment. The more supportive *Hungry Beat* wrote that Creation was being 'shunned for succeeding [in a climate] where failure is a password', and pointed to the Bodines as proof that McGee had not lost his touch.

However, Creation was alienating much of the indie hardcore – the cuties; the bedroom typists; the pointy boots cadre – and some had gone looking elsewhere: to the flexidiscs given away by fanzines (an endearing alternative to the 7-inch or 12-inch single); and to smaller labels like Glass, 53rd & 3rd in Scotland and the Subway Organisation in Bristol. A lot of these people would never meet Alan McGee again.

Watching from the sidelines, Jerry Thackray thought that McGee had blown it completely. He and others on the *NME* would in time effect a full-scale backlash against Creation, disgusted by the Weather Prophets' leather-trousered arrogance and the label's increasing drugginess. 'This is something that really bugged me about the things I would read about McGee,' says Thackray. 'People always went on about what a music lover he was, what a purist. Excuse me, but if you take drugs to listen to music – if you drink to listen to music – that is not being a music purist. That is a fraud.' Creation had never been so prominent, nor so disliked.

The cuties took a leaf from more than one Bible, but if they had a supreme church it was Postcard-era Orange Juice. Edwyn Collins – uncomfortable in the role of Christ – no longer had a record deal. After their 1983 Top 10 hit 'Rip It Up', Orange Juice's soul-influenced releases had stopped selling in large quantities and Malcolm Dunbar, the band's A&R man at Polydor, had put it to Collins that he was going through a lean period. Collins responded by writing a single called 'Lean Period'. It stalled at number 74.

Dead as a commercial proposition, and seen as *passé* by the indie fans who had once adored them, Orange Juice disbanded in January 1985 amid speculation that Collins would form a duo with Paul Quinn. Quinn – Alan Horne's flatmate and the priority act on his second-tier label Swamplands – was in fact working on a much-delayed album of his own. Collins had nowhere to go but down. Polydor had paid his songwriting talents one final insult by signing his Orange Juice colleague Zeke Manyika to a solo deal. Manyika was the band's drummer.

Ensconced in the PolyGram building, Horne was spending a con-siderable amount of money, much of it on expensive lunches to which he would invite any passing secretaries who happened to feel peckish. Nobody at PolyGram knew what Swamplands' actual purpose was – least of all Horne, who had not wanted the label in the first place. The genesis of Swamplands had been a stroke of pure mischief on the part of Collins. 'In about 1983 Edwyn said to me: "All these record companies will give you money. Just walk in and say you want a car, an office and a label and they'll give you it",' Horne recalls. 'I didn't want to do it. I don't know if I was scared, but I didn't want to do it. So Edwyn phoned up London Records and impersonated me. He said: "It's Alan Horne here – I'm coming in. You can offer me what you want and I'll think about it. See you on Tuesday," and hung up. So I had to go.'

For his meeting with managing director Roger Ames, Horne had worn a long black mackintosh and eye make-up. 'I looked like a transvestite Nazi,' he says. 'I walked in, spouting off about "Before you start telling me what *you* want from *me* ..." It was a kind of art exercise. It was the only way I could approach it.' When Swamplands received the go-ahead, Horne installed a dentist's chair in his office – which allowed him to swivel up and down on a hydraulic lift – and positioned a stuffed mongoose in the corner. He and Quinn took possession of a pleasant apartment in Maida Vale, and Horne put James King and the Lone Wolves into a demo studio with John Cale, unable to resist the idea of two intimidating characters clashing head-on. 'Horne said: "I don't care what the demos sound like, I'll sign you",' King recalls. 'I think he saw us as some kind of concept. He was saying things like: "I want you to dress up in tartan waistcoats." He was threatening to bring Jayne County to our rehearsals. The first thing Cale said when he saw Horne was: "Why is that guy so nervous?" '

Jayne County, a Warhol henchman turned transsexual matron, had precisely the star quality Horne was looking for. Skimping on his brief to locate young British talent, he embroiled himself in stories of mid-70s New York, hanging out with County, the new wave chanteuse Patti Palladin and the ex-New York Dolls guitarist Johnny Thunders. Palladin and County, Horne told Ames, would release a record on Swamplands as the Savage Family, a trio completed by a live chimpanzee. 'It's Monkees, it's camp, it's family orientated,' Horne assured Ames. It didn't happen.

'I used to go round to Patti Palladin's and smoke loads of dope,' says Horne. 'She had a flat full of buffalo heads and candelabras. Jayne would come round looking crazy and she knew I loved hearing stories about Bowie and the Velvets, so she would play up. I would be sitting there stoned, lying on the couch, and she would be performing stories. It was better than any theatre, or rock, or anything.'

When none of these Horne ideas reached the recording stage, pressure was put on another project, Memphis, a pairing of ex-Orange Juice members Steven Daly and James Kirk. Lest Roger

Ames get hold of the wrong end of the stick, Horne did not predict hits. 'I've come to realise,' he told Bill Prince in *Sounds*, 'after watching everybody in this business make fools of themselves, that you have to be indulgent. To cater for anybody else is folly.' Jake Black, his old friend from Glasgow, turned up at the Swamplands office one day to find Horne appraising the artwork for Memphis' single. 'It was just this hairy Highland bullock,' says Black. 'He was going: "There y'are. Put *that* in a fucking record shop window, why don't you." Just taking the complete piss.'

With Quinn's solo album now fronting the entire operation – if and when it ever got finished – Horne stepped up the burlesque. As well as taking the secretaries out for lunch several times a week, he carried a cane, holding court like Truman Capote. As Quinn's manager, A&R man, friend, label boss and flatmate, Horne had donned at least three hats too many, and he cancelled recording session after recording session in his quest for the perfect album by his client, pal, flatmate and priority act. He tired of what he saw as trifles – bands asking for their weekly retainers; James King demanding more attention – and tedious matters such as running a record company and releasing viable product.

Swamplands looked like following Postcard into a messy collapse. Next to Quinn, whose record had repeatedly missed deadlines, Horne's hottest tip was Win, a band formed by the Fire Engines' singer Davey Henderson. Meanwhile, up to his old tricks, Horne arranged a lavish photo session for Quinn, pressing up 10,000 copies of a single before announcing that the sleeve was the wrong shade of red. 'After about a year,' says Edwyn Collins, 'Alan has a company car, substantial offices in the London Records building, he's getting a buzz in the press with Win, he's getting radio play and he decides: "Fuck this, I'm bored." After three months, Roger Ames starts noticing Alan's never in the office any more.'

Quinn's album had begun to seem more mythical than putative. Yet he and Horne were still drawing an appreciable wage. And Ames was not the only one to wonder if Horne was underperforming. In an article about Memphis in the *NME*, Danny Kelly wrote: 'Swamplands is currently in a rather volatile condition.' Towards the end of 1985, Horne received a letter from London Records' lawyer, John Kennedy, asking him if he still worked for the company. Ames requested an urgent meeting, in which Horne's motivation was called into question, and Horne departed the PolyGram building with a £25,000 settlement. It was the last anyone would hear of him for almost eight years.

Built around the monolithic drumbeat of 'Be My Baby' by the Ronettes, the fourth single by the Jesus and Mary Chain, 'Just Like Honey', was a spongy, crepuscular ballad, every last gasp of which emphasised how much ground had been made since their 1984 days of catharsis by rote. Released in October 1985, it took the heat off their controversy-dogged live activities, focusing the conjecture instead on the album they had just completed at Southern. 'There was a big, big whispering campaign going on,' remembers Neil Taylor. 'People were saying: "You know, it's going to be a lot different. You can actually listen to it." '

The Mary Chain's assumption was that Radio 1 would be won over by 'Just Like Honey'. With no feedback anywhere on it, the song was practically a courtesy gesture. Once again, though, they found the station unrelenting. Supported by evening airplay only, 'Just Like Honey' spent a mere three weeks in the Top 75, reaching number 45. As outside forces conspired – they reckoned – to deny them a proper career in pop, the Mary Chain's inner sanctum became a wigwam within an igloo. Apprehensive about the future, and anxious to confine their violent reputation to London until such time as it could be eliminated altogether, the Reid brothers made a series of comments in the press that deliberately diverged from those of their manager.

'There has never been a riot at any of our gigs, never,' said William, adding that the destruction at North London Polytechnic had been made up by Neil Taylor. 'I get the impression that our group has been completely misunderstood,' his brother told another journalist. From the inner sanctum, they appealed for answers to McGee. But it was not that sort of question.

Increasingly, the Reids believed that they might have to disappear for a long period. Such a move would almost certainly undermine their moderate fame – if not quite sending them back to square one – but it would at least save the life of the band. No other ideas came to mind. 'Looking back on it,' says Jim today, 'I'm surprised that we were surprised [by the riots]. The riots were mostly our fault. We didn't go out there with the intention of pissing people off, but none of us had ever been in bands before. Suddenly, you're living out your fantasy. Someone's coming up to you saying: "Ten minutes till you go on." And you're like: "Get to fuck. I've still got a full bottle of whisky here, man. We'll go on when we feel like going on." Not realising that there's an angry mob out there that's been waiting for an hour and a half.'

In October, white labels of the Mary Chain's album were cut. It was called *Psychocandy* and it put a spring in the step of everyone at 83 Clerkenwell Road. One immediate beneficiary was Jeff Barrett, who had moved up to London from Plymouth to work for Creation part-time. As the Mary Chain escaped to the continent for gigs in Holland, Belgium and Germany, McGee delegated Barrett to be the tour manager. Barrett, who had never been out of Britain, was eager to show McGee that he could organise a flawless tour. Faced with the surly Reids, he decided the best way to get through it was to drink as much as possible.

On this tour, there was friction with promoters and audiences wherever the Mary Chain went. Barrett panicked when the crowd at one show turned ugly, and in his urgency to get the money he punched the promoter. At a festival in Belgium, the Mary Chain wrangled with a member of the Cult, a former beau of Jim Reid's French girlfriend Laurence Verfaillie. 'After all of that, we stopped off at a roundabout on the way back to the hotel,' says Barrett. 'There was a chip van and a shout of "I want some chips". I got out and bought these chips and of course, over there, mayonnaise comes on top. William Reid goes: "I didn't want the sauce," and throws them back at me. We all agreed at that point that I wasn't going to be the tour manager for them again.'

Barrett was given a job as Creation dogsbody, helping out with PR and liaising with the company that cut the label's vinyl. In lieu of a salary, McGee lent him a sum of money to place in his bank account so that he qualified for a £40-a-week payment on the Enterprise Allowance Scheme. 'I was a "consultant",' Barrett remembers. 'There were many of us – all setting ourselves up as consultants to the music business. It was Alan's scam. A valid scam, actually.'

Test pressings of *Psychocandy* thrilled journalists. Three months in the making, the album gave body and resolution to some elliptical live favourites such as 'In A Hole', 'Taste The Floor' and 'Inside Me', and astonished even the most loyal Mary Chain fans with its heightened sense of melody. Its tunefulness became a talking-point. 'We were immensely proud of it,' says Jim Reid.

Laying the groundwork for its release, McGee blew through 83 Clerkenwell Road like a gale. He knew the music papers would hail the record as a classic – finally their lexicon would catch up with his own – and he expected the forest of positive reviews and front covers to propel the Mary Chain into a higher sales bracket. In that context, the lack of a London gig would not matter so much. 'Alan had stepped up a gear,' says Barrett. 'His thing was that it was going to be enormous. It was not "we're going to make great records". It was "we're going to be fucking huge."'

In the music papers, *Psychocandy* was easily the top news story of November. The reviews were dynamite and – a month later – it would be declared the critics' album of the year. Much of the acclaim stemmed from the fact that *Psychocandy* could be digested as a forward-looking, experimental guitar album on the one hand, and as a collection of delicious pop songs on the other. Also, it was full of cultural references – almost none of them from the 80s. In places, the flavour and the iconography were those of the 50s. One song mentioned a girl called Cindy. There was a lot of leather, and the sort of freedom-or-death motorbikes ridden by James Dean and the doomed boyfriend in the Shangri-Las' 'Leader Of The Pack'. *Psychocandy* was about anti-heroes and rebels, generation gaps and angst. When it came to rock 'n' roll's depiction of the teenage experience, the Reids knew their history well.

However, the album borrowed most heavily from the band that had inspired the Mary Chain in their cradle days. If *Psychocandy* confirmed anything, it was that for those involved in underground music in Britain, the Velvet Underground were more influential than the Beatles and the Rolling Stones combined. The New York group's legend was once again topical in the light of Victor Bockris' and Gerald Malanga's book *Uptight*, which provided new information and previously unseen photographs; and an album released in February 1985, *V.U.*, which had made public some recently unearthed performances from 1968 and 1969. It was noticed that *Psychocandy* looked more like a Velvet Underground album than *V.U.* did.

As much as *Psychocandy* looked to the past, it was recommended by critics for the opposite reason. Almost to a man, they concurred that it guaranteed the Mary Chain a future – not as a headline-grabbing live attraction but as a recording band of ability, depth and importance. The riots of March and September were old yarns now, overtaken in news value and not to be dwelt upon. But were the audiences reading the papers?

Psychocandy charted at 31, which pleased the Reids and McGee, and went on to sell 60,000 copies in Britain. The Mary Chain had established themselves as a senior, well-respected band. McGee desperately wanted them to go to America before Christmas, but Warner Bros in the States was reluctant to release *Psychocandy*, and refused to give financial support to a tour so close to the holiday. Because of the UK reviews, McGee felt them to be as bankable on the well-informed US college circuit as the Smiths (whose records Warner Bros distributed, and who had graduated to playing American theatres and ballrooms that summer), but there was debate in both the Los Angeles and New York offices of Warner Bros about whether *Psychocandy* would be too strange for the market. At last, an A&R executive in New York ratified a January 1986 release.

'Warners had agreed to put out *Psychocandy*, but it's not like the whole company was thrilled about the sound of this record,' says Steven Baker, a Warner Bros product manager in LA. 'I think as a company we failed to recognise the notoriety they had achieved in the UK. They were already building an audience [in America] based on word of mouth.' While Warners argued that a Christmas tour was pointless, as all the college students would have returned home to their families, McGee pushed and pushed, offering to manage the tour himself to save money. He could not even drive, much less arrange work permits or hire equipment. 'I phoned somebody and I found out how to do it,' he recalls. 'I never even had a credit card in those days. I said I'd bring cash.'

McGee was the only person who believed the gigs would sell out.

'Alan had a vision,' Baker says. 'He knew that there were younger fans in the United States who dug that kind of music, and he knew that they would come out to see the band no matter what the fools at the record company were saying about [it being a] bad time of year and a waste of money. Of course, every gig they did sold out.' The band even made a few thousand dollars' profit. It was McGee's finest hour of 1985.

Flying back to London on Christmas night, he heard some worrying news. At a party a few nights before, Joe Foster had got into an argument and punched an employee of Rough Trade. McGee might have been more sympathetic if Foster hadn't been driving him mad for some time. The two men had had three violent disputes (all of which McGee claims to have won and none of which Foster claims to remember) and these had started to threaten the harmony of the Creation office. 'I was not really very well,' says Foster. 'I was doing a lot of drugs. I was not so much out of control ... as in a situation where people could easily say that I *was* out of control. It was a combination of events and my own stupidity. But everybody's allowed to be stupid once or twice in their life.' McGee saw it another way. 'It was decided that at that point, for Creation to go forward, Joe had to go sideways.'

With Foster exiled – he would later move to Birmingham and start his own label – the beginning of 1986 left Creation one man down and in a fiscal bind. At least two Creation bands were unhappy about the recording budgets they were being given. The Weather Prophets were going to require a major cash injection if Pete Astor was to justify McGee's breathless descriptions of him as a genius on a par with McCartney, and Bobby Gillespie had complained to journalists about the sonic imperfections of Primal Scream's 'All Fall Down' single, and made it clear that a shortage of funds, not the band itself, had been to blame.

McGee's position was immutable. It was his policy never to go into the red to make a record, no matter what the feelings of the artist. The gap between the first two Primal Scream singles would be almost a year. Little wonder Gillespie lamented to Neil Taylor: 'We need more money and some fucker's got to give it to us.'

7 The Fifth Member Of The Mary Chain

IT LOOKED LIKE 1986 would be a make-or-break year for Creation. The state of chart pop was as bad as McGee had ever known it, a grab-bag of hi-tech, washed-out soul, mediocre rock, cover versions and reissued oldies. All the same, the best an indie group could hope for was one solitary airing of one solitary 45 on daytime Radio 1. When the June Brides' 'No Place Called Home' was played on the morning show in December, the band's plugger was, according to Phil Wilson, 'overwhelmed'.

Creation's roster boasted three strong names in Primal Scream, the Weather Prophets and Felt (whose final single for Cherry Red, 'Primitive Painters', had been a stunning six-minute epic and a much-deserved indie chart-topper). The momentum of the *Psychocandy* campaign had caused McGee to demand more effort from those at 83 Clerkenwell Road and from his bands in the studio. Hoping to double the label's annual turnover to around £120,000, he anticipated a classic debut single from the Weather Prophets to get things moving. But the band botched the recording of 'Almost Prayed', much to Pete Astor's embarrassment.

Astor suggested that rather than book another studio session, Creation should buy the rights to a version of 'Almost Prayed' which the band had recorded for the Janice Long show in October. Nobody was overjoyed by the idea. 'It was a terribly indie-schmindie thing to do,' Astor concedes. 'Buy a Janice Long session ... It was very much not what the ethos of the band was. And you'd have to have "by permission of the BBC", which was like, ooh, dear.'

Increasing the pressure on the Weather Prophets, the preparations for the record's release coincided with a wave of ill feeling in the music press against Creation and everyone associated with it. 'It's becoming more and more apparent that the best Creation can hope to achieve is to become the new Cherry Red,' Stephen Pastel told an acquiescent Neil Taylor. 'At worst, like Postcard, it will sink without a trace.' By February, McGee was being ridiculed in *NME*'s pages on a weekly basis. One journalist who had been friendly to the label in the past would soon ask apropos of nothing: 'Is there a good band on Creation?'

Creation's rock 'n' roll chic gave rise to ever greater mirth and parody. Reviewing a Weather Prophets gig, a *Sounds* journalist tittered disrespectfully at Astor's and Dave Goulding's leather trousers. 'Leather trousers . . . are a state of mind,' she wrote. 'You can't just put them on. You either are leather trousers or you're not.' Astor thought he was leather trousers – and he wore them for perfectly sound historical reasons, as he explained to the *NME*. '[Leather trousers are] not hip,' he said. 'It was fashionable in 1968, and that refers back to a whole line of things. That says to me: the Weather Prophets are not about . . . things that are only hip now. I am saying I will remain true to things that go back a long way.' In other words, it was no good being a retro-authenticist unless you walked the walk.

The Jesus and Mary Chain had scheduled a tour of Britain for late January and early February, but Bobby Gillespie did not plan to be around at the end of it. Hearing from a friend at WEA that Gillespie would soon be leaving to concentrate on Primal Scream, John Foster-Moore, a 20-year-old South Bank Polytechnic student from Reading, put his name forward. The Mary Chain asked him if he could play drums. He admitted he could not. Putting it another way, they asked him if he *wanted* to play drums. He replied that he did.

When the Mary Chain played Norwich with Gillespie on 7 February, Foster-Moore went along for the experience. He saw that they were no longer tolerating any misbehaviour from their audiences. Plastic glasses were thrown as they took the stage; Jim Reid promptly led the way back to the dressing-room. Returning a short while later, the Mary Chain played for 40 minutes without incident.

Turning up for his drumming debut in Nottingham four days later, Foster-Moore kept his head down. A Mary Chain fan, he knew enough about them to feel intimidated. 'There was this vibe about them: they're a Glaswegian gang and you can't understand a word they say,' he remarks. 'But they were pretty funny. I probably started speaking in a Scottish accent after a while.' But Foster-Moore remained wary of William Adam Reid. A man with those initials was not likely to warm to a well-spoken, middle-class student with a double-barrelled surname. When his appointment was announced to the press, John Foster-Moore had become the more proletarian John Moore.

Whatever his name, Moore was indicative of the changing face of the Mary Chain. Bigger and longer tours were being arranged, including a March tour of America, and the shows were becoming more professional. There was still a tense atmosphere whenever the Reids were in the same room – the sudden raising of voices; the telltale smash of a bottle – but the music played onstage was less dislocated than of old, and no one joked of not being able to tell the songs apart. Sound checks, once avoided, had become a fact of life. 'When John Moore appeared, it was starting to become more of a stylised, packaged thing,' says Andrew Perry. 'He was more of a looker than the others, who all had appalling skin and so on. When Moore joined, you could see the Mary Chain becoming more of a marketable commodity. It had ceased to be a wild, careering animal.'

Although he had not implemented these changes personally, McGee was mostly in favour of them if they meant the Mary Chain sold more records. Then again, he did not see why the Reids shouldn't continue to horrify, terrorise and generally cause outrage in the music industry at large. As long as they brought out their belligerent personae in interviews, he was happy. He could supply the rest himself: spread a little spurious gossip here, make up a few white lies there ...

In a busy period for Creation, McGee released a well-received Biff Bang Pow! single, 'Love's Going Out Of Fashion', and two excellent pop records in February: *Kaleidoscope World*, an album of bottom-of-the-world psychedelia from New Zealanders the Chills (which Creation had licensed from the country's indie label Flying Nun); and 'Therese', a single by the Bodines, which showed them to be a match for any guitar-toting indie band in England. In fact, 'Therese' was simply too good for Creation, for just when the Bodines needed a helping hand, the label was unable to provide one. McGee thought it much more imperative to advance the career of Primal Scream. They were, along with McGee himself, the face of Creation – but they had made no music since the spring of 1985. He gave them £2,000 to record a new single, 'Crystal Crescent', and put them in Southern with John Loder.

Neil Taylor had written the previous year that there lay 'a total contradiction' at the heart of Primal Scream: 'a sound so soft, yet as people they are bitter and hard ..' Jeff Barrett – one of the Scream's biggest fans – had been struck by that contradiction too, regarding it as central to the band's allure. An enigmatically menacing image was one of the qualities that connected Primal Scream to Love, their idols from 1960s Los Angeles, and in neither group's case was the aggression a put-on. 'People always say there's this Americana thing about Glasgow,' comments Barrett. 'You can hear that in Wet Wet Wet's would-be Memphis kind of vibe. The Primals and the Glasgow boys at that time were a bunch of Velvets-and-Love-obsessed evil bastards. They were like the East Village Motherfuckers. They were sweet melodies and switchblades, those guys.'

Primal Scream's Glasgow scene was one of hard-nosed bohemia. Rhythm guitarist Paul Harte and tambourine player John ('the Joogs') Martin lived in one of the most amazing apartments Barrett had ever seen. 'You walked into the kitchen,' Barrett says, 'and these places had really high ceilings. Hartey and Jim [Lambie, a friend of the band] had this room and there'd be like Nazi regalia on the wall. You knew they weren't [Nazis] but there'd be a P.i.L. poster with a swastika on it. Whatever. Then you walk into the kitchen – just to get a glass of water out of the tap – and there'd be this little recess with the width to hold a single mattress, and there'd be a net curtain. Suddenly, it would open and there you'd see the Joogs, and the whole fucking thing would be lined with foil. He thought he was living in the Factory. The lot of them did.'

Guitarist and founder member Jim Beattie had taken note of the Mary Chain's success and believed that Primal Scream might be on the cusp of something similar. But he also knew that their fitfulness militated against them. At one important concert in London – for which they had made an eight-and-a-half-hour journey from Glasgow on the Stagecoach – they cut their set short after only two songs. McGee was dumbfounded to see them preparing to catch the next bus home. 'He thought we were mental,' recalls Beattie. 'He said: "You're going to have been travelling for 17 hours to play for two and a half minutes!" Andy Strickland gave it a horrible review [in *Record Mirror*]: "Who do these people think they are, coming down to London and playing two songs?"' The verdict of the *NME*'s David Swift – which Gillespie found hard to dispute – was that Primal Scream were 'a lazy band'.

'Crystal Crescent' was not much of an improvement. The melody was buried in a murky mix, and when Gillespie accidentally knocked a cup of coffee over the studio desk, this was used as an excuse to ask McGee to scrap the recording. He told them they had to be kidding. ' "Crystal Crescent",' wrote David Swift succinctly, 'is a mess.' 'It's ironic,' Gillespie told him. 'We love pop music so much but we can't even get the record right.'

Primal Scream's love of music was the last word in good taste, but it was also a study in dogmatism. At their Splash 1 club – named after a song by the 13th Floor Elevators – arguments would rage about whose compilation tapes to play in the intervals. Aside from the Byrds (who had inspired the Scream's cardinal sound: Beattie's chiming twelve-string guitar) and Love (whose blurring of the sweet-evil dichotomy the Scream aspired to emulate), other turntable favourites were the Rolling Stones, Neil Young, the Beatles, the Beach Boys, the Kinks, Big Star, 70s punk, Julian Cope, and 60s garage pop and psychedelia. But the 60s bias didn't mean the Scream were permissive. When Scott McKenzie's 'San Francisco (Be Sure To Wear Some Flowers In Your Hair)' was heard at Splash 1 one night, a mortified Gillespie sprinted to the deck and wrenched the tape out.

And while they dressed in second-hand 60s garb, wore Cuban heels and wrote psychedelic lyrics, the Scream did not see themselves as revivalists – but rather as pop connoisseurs with a punk rock kick. Of two tracks recorded in Glasgow for the B-side of 'Crystal Crescent', one in particular was a skilful fusion of 1966 and 1976. Far superior to its A-side, 'Velocity Girl' began with a plangent strum of Paul Harte's Gretsch guitar, and followed with one of the most insidious – and one of the most quoted – couplets in indie pop history:

Here she comes again with vodka in her veins
Been playing with a spike – she couldn't get it right

Primal Scream had found the sweet-evil coalescence. 'Velocity Girl' lasted only 84 seconds – not even half the length of a standard commercial hit – but it would be the group's most requested song for the next four years.

Released in April, 'Crystal Crescent' climbed up the indie charts. Primal Scream made a return to ULU, this time filling it comfortably. This was more than enough to put them in the indie sector elite. Yet a more telling insight into their true significance could be found on a wall several miles away. Of the Musicians Wanted adverts pinned to the notice-board in Rough Trade's Ladbroke Grove shop, 80 per cent now listed Primal Scream as a key influence.

Quiet and amiable, Dick Green had been Alan McGee's friend and musical colleague since 1981. He had proved useful at the Living Room, standing by the door, nodding a welcome, taking the money. In Biff Bang Pow! he played decent, though not especially adventurous, guitar. He smiled and grinned under his black fringe, and was known to be a nice chap. 'Conversations with Dick were very short,' recalls Noel Thompson, who engineered some Biff Bang Pow! records. 'He was a very nervy guy, very likeable.'

Green flitted in and out of Creation in 1984 and 1985, taking occasional holidays from his job as a pensions clerk. Unlike Joe Foster, whom he would gradually supersede as McGee's assistant and sounding-board, Green was level-headed and kept his counsel. 'Alan was bold strokes, mission statement, visionary, come-on-board,' says Bill Prince. 'Dick was much quieter. Alan would go: "*This* is going to happen, *this* is going to happen, *this* is going to happen." And you'd go to Dick and say: "Is any of that going to happen? Which of all of those is going to happen? And if all of them are going to happen, in what order are they going to happen?" You often got the impression from Dick that when Alan made the big speech, it was the first time Dick had ever heard it.'

The dynamic between Green and McGee is compared by more than one Creation scenester to that of a comedy duo: McGee as the fast-talking, funny character, Green as the straight man whose well-timed feeds and reactions are crucial to the partnership. And as McGee became busier and busier in 1986, Green became more and more indispensable. Soon he too was on the Enterprise Allowance Scheme, working at Creation full-time. And when more hands were needed, Yvonne McGee left her job at British Rail to help out.

'I think Yvonne wished I would just get a normal job,' says McGee. 'By that time we had an incredibly competitive relationship. Because she was really good-looking and I was a geeky fucking weirdo, she was the one who had the power [in the relationship]. When I started getting well-known, the balance of power changed and I think it was quite hard for her to deal with that ... I wanted to be a big rock 'n' roll manager and Yvonne wanted to be a suburban housewife. I'm not being cruel, but she wanted a very normal existence. We were growing apart.'

For the Mary Chain's third and most lucrative visit to the States, in March, the entourage comprised McGee, Green and – as driver and roadie – Dave Evans. New York led to Montreal, which led to Detroit, which led to Los Angeles, where McGee refamiliarised himself with cocaine. He was feeling powerful – like a hustler. The Mary Chain were playing for half an hour at the Universal Amphitheatre and getting $30,000. McGee told himself he had the magic for certain. The only problem was fatigue: the flight back to England left him with terrible jet lag.

At 83 Clerkenwell Road, there was no let-up. McGee was tiring. He was the manager of three bands – two of which, Primal Scream and the Weather Prophets, he was hoping to sign to major labels for large advances. The indie idealist in McGee would be sorry to lose those bands to the majors; however, the realist in him knew that the money from the deals would finance Creation's next year of releases. And with McGee, realism usually had the upper hand over idealism. In any case, the selling-off of the Creation family jewels was not a matter in which he would have a great deal of choice. Primal Scream and the Weather Prophets would not stay on the label any longer than they had to; both bands were ambitious to move on and start earning money.

The Weather Prophets, whom McGee saw as a potential Top 40 albums act, had started to cause him worry. Like Primal Scream, they were only 'signed' to Creation on a handshake. But the Weather Prophets were not schoolfriends of McGee's from Glasgow. 'Alan said to me in his kitchen once: "Should I sign the Weather Prophets? Should I actually get them to sign something on a bit of paper?" ' recalls Jim Beattie. 'I said: "You probably should, Alan, because anybody could just nick them." '

Test pressings of the Weather Prophets' 'Almost Prayed' arrived at Clerkenwell in May, and its springy 'Proud Mary' groove was irresistible. It looked as though it would be the biggest-selling Creation single since 'Upside Down'. Mick Houghton, the Weather Prophets' press officer, knew from contacts at WEA that the company was interested in offering the band an album deal. 'The Weather Prophets were the next big thing,' says Jim Beattie. 'We all thought they should go to America and be like Creedence Clearwater Revival.'

McGee's fatigue had turned into a serious problem. 'I would go and get a newspaper at a quarter to nine,' he says, 'and I'd be in bed for the rest of the day. I was getting blotches on my legs.' When he stood up, he would howl in pain. He had been forced to stop wearing leather trousers as they hurt too much. 'I went to a National Health doctor and he gave me antibiotics,' he says. 'Didn't work. The pain was unbelievable. Then I went to BUPA, who diagnosed me immediately: sarcoidosis.'

McGee could not have picked a more baffling ailment. Sarcoidosis, an inflammatory disorder, can affect almost any organ in the body but is most often seen in the lung. To his horror, McGee was told that if he had gone another six weeks without being diagnosed, he would have spent the rest of his life in a wheelchair – the inflamed growths on the lung can cause permanent damage. He was prescribed a course of steroids and for the next two months Creation and the Mary Chain functioned without him.

Even by Cherry Red's standards, Lawrence had been an oddity. A poker-faced lad from a village outside Birmingham, the leader of Felt was a fussy and at times cranky autocrat, who took unusual care over every facet of his life and art. Quite a few people found his austerity unnerving. Born Lawrence Hayward, he had dropped his surname in 1980, begging journalists not to reveal it. 'A TV repair man once asked me if I was related to Justin Hayward,' he explains. 'I thought: yeah, that's what's going to happen. I'm going to be fielding Moody Blues questions for the rest of my career.' He was not mad about his Christian name either, but what were the alternatives? Lol. Loz. Laz. Larry. Hopeless ...

'Lawrence was very vain,' says Mike Alway. 'He went through a period soon after the first Felt album when he was very conscious of his weight and his receding hairline. Then the poor bugger lost his hair. I mean, I thought it was terrible that God had made that affliction on him. Eventually, he wore hats.'

Felt made four albums for Cherry Red between 1981 and 1985. These contained some of the loveliest indie music of the decade, written by Lawrence and guitarist Maurice Deebank. Classically trained, Deebank had a golden arrow sound as elegant as the Shadows and as modern as the morning. With Lawrence using his voice as a sensual instrument of gasps and sobs clustered around the same neutral Lou Reed note, Deebank pealed out lengthy, exquisite lines without a pause, as if unaware that the song was not an instrumental. They were convinced they had made a breakthrough: expressive mood-music with guitar solos people could whistle on their way to work.

As fascinating as Felt's records were, Lawrence himself was a bigger story. In his methodically arranged apartment in Moseley, his daily life was dominated by a compulsion to have order and neatness. An *NME* journalist who interviewed him in March 1984 described the apartment as 'brutally schematic', listing some of the cleaning products that Lawrence had amassed, including air fresheners, furniture polish, anti-tobacco odour aerosols and antiseptic for bathing in.

'The flat was really posh,' says Lawrence. 'It was one of the most expensive flats in Birmingham, because it was designed for rich businessmen who travelled round the country. It had two beds that came down from the wall. It had a gilt-edged mirror and built-in wardrobes. It had an entry phone so I didn't have to run down the stairs. That was unheard of in Birmingham in those days.'

When Creation released 'Why Does The Rain' in October 1984, Lawrence became a fan of the Loft, and he and Pete Astor began to talk on the phone. When Astor told him the Loft had been offered a gig in Birmingham, Lawrence invited them to sleep on his floor. They were astonished by what they found. 'He goes: "Strict rules",' recalls Bill Prince. 'We could pee but we couldn't crap in his toilet. Absolutely no way. We all drank heavily before we got there – I don't think Lawrence was very keen on that – and we all slept, the four of us, in his living room. Dave [Morgan], last thing at night, rolled himself a nice fat joint to smoke first thing in the morning. We woke up and the whole place had been hoovered and cleaned. I have never seen Dave Morgan react so quickly. He leapt up and he was ripping through the bin. Lawrence was going mad because Dave was spilling all the contents of the bin on to the kitchen floor.'

On their return to London, the Loft told their friends about the strange scenes at Lawrence's. Word got around and soon indie bands were looking for any excuse to play in Birmingham. 'Everyone wanted to get into this flat,' says Prince. 'It was just the stuff of myth at that point.' Pete Astor visited Lawrence again a few months later. 'He was very sweet,' says Astor. 'He'd taken acid and couldn't sleep. There was his great girlfriend remark. "I'd really like a girlfriend. Not to talk to. Just to walk around naked." Said without a hint of irony.' In the morning, Astor watched Lawrence tuck into an individual minipacket of Kellogg's breakfast cereal. He had a stockpile of them and would eat a different cereal every day.

Mike Alway's defection to Blanco y Negro had looked like being Felt's big break. They were one of the bands he wanted to take with him from Cherry Red, which got Lawrence very excited. But after a two-song demo had been recorded, Felt were told that Rob Dickins and Geoff Travis had scotched the deal, and they were forced to see out their contract with Iain McNay.

Their final album for Cherry Red – *Ignite The Seven Cannons* – was produced by Robin Guthrie, a bear-like Scot who played in the Cocteau Twins with his angel-voiced girlfriend Liz Fraser. Lawrence was sceptical about some of the techniques Guthrie used, which smothered Maurice Deebank's guitar in padding and dulled the bass and drums. But *Ignite The Seven Cannons* produced one song that had classic written all over it: the aforementioned 'Primitive Painters'.

'Primitive Painters' was a superior track even before Liz Fraser – at Guthrie's suggestion – overdubbed a dramatic aerial counterpoint to Lawrence's own Eeyore-ish vocal. Long and mesmerising, the song would probably have been a Top 40 hit in any other era but the mid-80s, when the electric guitar was suffering its extended lockout. Released as a 12-inch single in September 1985, it gave Felt their first indie chart number 1. 'We thought it was going to be a proper hit, actually,' says the band's drummer Gary Ainge. 'Failed miserably. It was harder in those days. We wanted to make *Rumours* – we wanted to be a massive band.' But with the disappointment came emancipation of a sort. Felt's contract with Cherry Red ended, and they moved to Creation.

When Alan McGee told Janice Long in their June interview that he had signed Felt, 'Primitive Painters' had not even been recorded. Now that it had topped the indies, he was getting the band at a good time. He was also getting them for nothing. 'There was no money in it – we weren't given any money,' says Lawrence. 'I just believed in Alan. I believed he was going to have a great label.'

The first Felt single for Creation, 'Ballad Of The Band', was partly a sly critique of Maurice Deebank – who had quit the band and emigrated to Spain – and partly a folkloric angst song written as a means of closing the door on the band's luckless past:

Where were you when I wanted to work?
You were still in bed – you're a total jerk
Oh yeah ... and I feel like giving in

'For me,' says Lawrence, 'being the leader of Felt was like dragging a sack of coal around on my back.' But now began phase two.

To McGee's surprise, the first Felt album for Creation consisted of extremely short instrumentals. Brisk and Radio 2-like, they highlighted the playful organ trills of teenage keyboard player Martin Duffy, gambolling about for 90 seconds or so, moving between movies and muzak. The entire album was 19 minutes in length. Shortly before its release, Lawrence met Bobby Gillespie at 83 Clerkenwell Road. Gillespie asked him if he had a title for it. 'It's called *Let The Snakes Crinkle Their Heads To Death,*' said Lawrence. Gillespie stared at him. 'He was going: "Crinkle? What sort of word's that?"' Lawrence recalls. 'I wish I'd listened to him.'

Two months after *Let The Snakes Crinkle Their Heads To Death* emerged to bewildered silence, Felt promoted it belatedly with a gig at Bay 63, a club in Portobello, in August. 'I had always loved Felt, but they always kept you guessing,' says Phil King, the bassist in the Servants, a support band that night. 'There was very little about them in the press and they didn't seem to do gigs very often. It made them quite mysterious.'

A convalescing McGee was in the audience at Bay 63, accompanied by Martin Costello – Felt's publisher at Complete (formerly Cherry Red) Music – and an expectant jury of A&R scouts from major labels. McGee was seeking to forge links with a major to improve his cash flow, and Costello understood that some sort of deal with Island was being lined up. The onus was on Felt to do everyone a favour by playing well. 'It was a big night for us,' says Lawrence. 'I just thought: I'm sick of people saying I'm miserable. It might be nice if I loosen up a bit. Not that I'd dance or anything – just be a bit happier.' Lawrence swallowed a tab of LSD a few minutes before going onstage.

The first the audience knew that something was troubling Lawrence was when, two songs into the set, he asked for all the lights in the club to be turned off. 'After the next song, he started saying to the audience: "Stop looking at me",' recalls Phil King. 'He was going up to [guitarist] Neil Scott and putting his hands over his guitar, trying to stop the sound from coming out.' Lawrence left the stage in a state of anxiety. Rushing backstage, McGee learned the facts from Douglas Hart and attempted to pacify a frantic Lawrence. 'He was going: "You're going to be all right, it's just the drugs talking. Get back onstage",' says Lawrence. 'I was going: "I can't." He was going: "You've got to – there's six A&R men out there." '

Lawrence was led back to the microphone and Felt began a song called 'Fortune'. Unable to ascertain when the first verse was due, or whether it had already arrived – and if so, when the second verse was coming – Lawrence gazed out over the heads of the audience and saw the rear wall of the venue start to melt. Telling everyone to ask for their money back, he left the stage for the second and last time.

McGee and Martin Costello were livid. Costello called Lawrence into his office the next day and warned him that his publishing deal was in jeopardy. 'The thing was, he kept blaming everybody else,' says Costello. ' "It wasn't me. I don't know what happened, Martin, it wasn't me." All that shit. I wouldn't have torn his contract up. I was just fucked off that he'd been so stupid.' The Island A&R department had seen quite enough. Mere months after moving to Creation, Felt's reputation lay in ruins.

Jim Beattie began to fear the worst when he heard that there was a new band called Bobby Gillespie's Haircut. He was already uncomfortable about the queues of fanzine writers that waited to interview Gillespie after every Primal Scream show in the spring of 1986. His friend's cult appeal had snowballed into idol worship. But it was not the idolisation of Gillespie that worried Beattie so much as the nature of the worshippers.

'All these kids started getting the Bobby fringe, which was just bizarre,' he says. 'I couldn't be bothered with this wee indie scene. I hated the tweeness. I mean, I'm six foot three and I'm not twee. I didn't want to be part of any clique. But Bobby didn't feel it was a clique. Bobby was the centre of attention and I think it quite appealed to his ego.'

The starmaking of Gillespie had its explanation in the sudden synthesis of three slightly contrasting movements: the ongoing 60s revivalist programme; the Stephen Pastel church of infantilism; and the bush telegraph network of indie club promoters around Britain. These movements, respectively, endorsed Gillespie as a sage, a saint and good box office. Bringing all the elements together, at the end of May 1986, was a cassette compiled and sold by the *NME*.

By the mid-80s, Britain's best-selling music paper had stopped giving indie music its unconditional support. One reason was that indie groups seldom referenced artists from the soul, hip hop or reggae genres – and would occasionally dimiss them with outright contempt, as in Morrissey's 'reggae is vile' comment of February 1985 – which sat awkwardly with the *NME*'s desire to have a broad editorial policy and maximum market reach. There were worrying indications that indie music was becoming a haven for bands and fans who did not like, or want to learn about, black music.

Despite frequent articles on hip hop, soul and jazz, however, the *NME* was still a paper read primarily by white students and teenagers. Danny Kelly, a lover of soul, hip hop and reggae who wrote mainly about white rock and pop, had tried to steer the paper in more of a guitar-rock direction, giving space to many of the new American bands in 1985. One by one, most of those bands had disappeared by the end of that year. The Long Ryders and the Rain Parade had released disappointing albums on major labels; others had lost crucial members; and still others were exposed as backmarkers. By mid-1986, only REM and Hüsker Dü continued to command respect.

Dropping the Americans like a hot brick, the *NME* looked for a new breed of guitar band and found one on its own doorstep. At Bay 63, at the Bull & Gate in Kentish Town and at the defunct but fondly remembered Room At The Top, indie guitar-pop had been playing nightly to avid audiences. Since launching 'The Music Of Sound' – a Thursday night club at Bay 63 – in February, Cerne Canning and Simon Esplen had been drawing crowds with bands that had guitars and a buzz, including the Shop Assistants, the Pastels, Primal

Scream, the Mighty Lemon Drops, the Soup Dragons, the Servants and the all-girl group We've Got A Fuzzbox And We're Gonna Use It.

'Of the people promoting [indie music], Alan McGee had been the first,' says Canning. 'What he'd done had been very significant. Then came Dan Treacy, who took it on and did loads. Then came us. And we were very naive. We weren't used to dealing with agents. We would just put on bands that we knew. One promoter threatened to have my legs broken after I approached one of his bands behind his back.' This incident apart, the bands were more than cooperative – as were the labels they in many cases owned or part-owned. Fresh and fizzy indie product was coming from the Subway Organisation and Sarah labels in Bristol, 53rd & 3rd in Scotland, the Pink Label in London, Ron Johnson in Nottinghamshire and Vindaloo (run by the Nightingales' Robert Lloyd) in Birmingham. Almost every one of these had been launched in the spirit of – even in bare-faced emulation of – Creation.

'Creation was interesting in those days,' says Canning, 'because on the one hand it was very much liked by what was deemed the anorak crowd, but on the other hand there was this rock 'n' roll ethic. You'd see these very fey kids buying a [Creation] record, but meanwhile the label was holding out to a much more classic ethic ... The other thing about Creation was how huge the guest-lists were. If you put on Primal Scream, you'd be getting a guest-list of a hundred people.'

The principal difference between indie music in the Living Room era and indie music in 1986 was speed of acceleration. As with punk, which most of the new bands had embraced as teenagers, the music was now being geared towards defining a single moment in a blinding flash of inspiration – and not hanging around to age or rust. One fanzine put it perfectly, if brutally, in a paragraph about Meat Whiplash, who had broken up after releasing two Creation singles. 'Play [them] loudly,' it exhorted, 'wallow in these two tunes' glory, then forget Meat Whiplash and move on to the next thing.'

Even so, what had made the *NME* sit up and take notice was not so much the music but the sales momentum. Primal Scream, the Shop Assistants, We've Got A Fuzzbox and the Mighty Lemon Drops were all moving up the commercial ladder, either by outselling their previous record or by kindling enthusiasm from larger labels. These did not necessarily have to be majors: the Shop Assistants' move from 53rd & 3rd to Rough Trade (in March 1986) was a giant leap in context. 'It was a very innocent time in a way,' says Canning. 'Bands would turn up with all their equipment in plastic bags. None of those bands had record companies with any money. Nowadays, to get a band to the level of playing to 300 people – and to do it without a manager and a lawyer – is unthinkable. It couldn't happen.'

The interest of the *NME* in club-level indie music (which had been virtually zero in 1983) was now sufficient to launch 22 bands in one fell swoop. With input from Canning and Esplen, a cassette entitled *C86* was compiled and offered for sale through the *NME*. The intention was to give the feel of a thriving and eclectic musical nation. It was to prove a tall order.

The main criticism of *C86* was that the balance was lopsided in favour of cheaply-recorded pop; plucky and lively, but at best semi-competent. As the *NME*'s advertisements for *C86* mentioned no particular genre, 'C86' became the genre. Instantly, the moniker had a sneering undertone: a helter-skelter, jangly racket performed by four or more pale boys with hurt feelings. By July, when Canning and Esplen promoted the cassette with a week of gigs at the ICA, *C86* – and C86 – were already being damned from all sides.

'We had no idea what a ruckus it would cause,' says the *NME*'s David Swift. 'The moment the cassette came out, there were rightful complaints about the quality of the music. A lot of the bands were lame, as it turned out. And there was quite natural resentment that the bands who were on it were getting a lot of coverage in the *NME*.' Those who stood at the top of C86's genealogical tree were among the loudest to protest. Ex-members of Orange Juice, hearing their six-year-old music played back at them through a filter of daintiness, were horror-stricken. They regarded C86 as a gross misrepresentation of their band. Here was a generation of musicians content to revisit the romantic themes of Edwyn Collins' songs, yet completely ignore the influences of soul, disco and black R&B that had been indigenous to Orange Juice's work. Steven Daly's indie drum-beat of 1980 had been the sound of an unschooled white drummer attempting to play disco patterns and getting them wrong – but at least he'd been trying to get them right. Now it was all wall-to-wall, fifth-rate Mo Tuckers, straight-armed and lumpen.

'If you had told us in 1980 or 1981 that there was going to be this thing called C86,' says Daly, 'we would have just laughed or killed ourselves. Indie was anarchic. It was amorphous. It was this, it was that. We knew what the good records were, and we'd been trying to get there. But the idea that people would just give up and say: "No, no, no, we don't want *those* influences, that's all excess to requirements. All we need is *this*, and this is going to be boiled down and it's going to be a whole type of music on its own" – that was like saying: "We don't ever want to leave home." That was horrific, you know, that was against nature.'

The opening track on the cassette – and the tune that became inextricably linked with the C86 sound – was 'Velocity Girl'. However, Primal Scream had been quick to regret their participation. Jeff Barrett, too, whose job as Creation's press officer kept him in daily contact with the *NME*, had reasons for feeling uneasy. His own indie label, Head, was represented on *C86* by the Servants, but Barrett now sided emotionally with hip hop over white indie pop.

'Suddenly, there were all these groups,' he says. 'It was good – but it was also kind of sad, because everything was "sha-la-la" and flowers. I thought it was quite dreadful that a lot of crap was being heralded as the cutting edge of music. I mean, Public Enemy versus the Pastels – come on! To me, the *NME* had been my door to this other world. And if you thought about it like that, was *C86* a door worth going through? Not really.'

But, like Danny Kelly, Barrett had bills to pay. And just as Kelly kept the *NME* on-message to its student readership, so too Barrett plugged Creation's records to Kelly. It was pure charade; each knew the other was going home and listening to black music.

For all its faults, *C86* proved popular with *NME* readers, and Rough Trade soon made it available as a vinyl LP. With the increase in attention came the interest of major label A&R men, who, seeing a ready-made movement doing well in the press, began to cherry-pick the leading bands. In the process, the major sector thawed in its attitude towards the independents.

On the other side of the fence, meanwhile, the thaw was well advanced. The proud isolationism of indie bands in 1983 and 1984 had dissipated the longer careers lasted – as, thanks to labels like Blanco y Negro, had the belief that the A&R departments of major record companies were staffed by know-nothings with big coke habits. The Smiths had been rumoured to be seeking a major label deal as early as July 1985, frustrated by the inability of the Cartel to get their singles into the Top 20. As for Creation, Alan McGee had always intended the Weather Prophets and Primal Scream to transfer to a major, not least because of the overrides and management percentages that would come his way. He would get no dissent from either band. 'If Warners or anybody offered us [a deal], we'd go for it immediately,' Bobby Gillespie said in *NME*. Of course they would.

Of the bands on *C86*, the Mighty Lemon Drops and the Shop Assistants were signed to decent-sized deals by Blue Guitar, a second-tier label financed by Chrysalis and A&R'd by Geoff Travis and the American musician-producer Mayo Thompson. Twelve months after *C86*, seven of the 22 bands had either major label deals or major distribution. For these groups, *C86* had been a successful exercise and a convenient stepping-stone to the mainland. But even for some of them – and more so for others who got left behind – *C86* would be an albatross of formidable tenacity. In years to come, their names would be forever associated with 1986. Not such a problem in 1987, but in 1988 and 1989 ...

Primal Scream would experience this problem more than any other band. Having written the keynote C86 song in 'Velocity Girl', they would find that it had put them in a no-win situation. Without a major label's recording budgets, they would never outgrow the gauche sounds of C86. With a big-budget, major label sonic smooth-over, they would risk alienating every C86 fan – and every Primal Scream fan – in the country.

The Hammersmith Palais on 8 May, 1986 was a tense gig for the Jesus and Mary Chain. Their first London appearance since the Electric Ballroom the previous September, it had been announced to the press in March by a conciliatory Mick Houghton. 'Most of last year's trouble was provoked by only playing very short sets at their gigs,' he said. 'But they're more conformist now and their act is much longer.' But there was apprehension from the Mary Chain that the violence might follow them into 1986. 'There was extra security,' remembers John Moore, 'and we were instructed: "If the bottles start flying, get off quickly." '

To their relief, the concert went without a hitch. They were all able to hear themselves onstage, and the songs' melodies rang out into the auditorium fully intact. 'We'd sort of had a chat with them,' says soundman Noel Thompson. 'Frequency-wise on their guitars, some things were really painful, so we made some halfway house [suggestions] where everyone – the band, me and the monitor engineer – was happy.'

Toning everything down brought its own problems, however. As a live attraction, the Mary Chain were not half the force they had been. 'The thing about the riots,' says Rob Dickins, 'is that when you started seeing the band play a full set and there were no riots, it was like: "Oh, this is a bit dreary. Nothing's happened." '

Both of the Reid brothers were searching for a calmer and healthier way of life. They had never been the most cheerful of men, and drinking and drug-taking had led to depression in both of them. 'We realised that if we continued the way we were going, somebody probably would have died,' says Jim. 'We actually did make a decision to slow down a bit. We'd done *Psychocandy*. We'd made our point.' A few journalists suggested the band should split up – go out on a high rather than become dull and toothless with over-familiarity. In an interview with the *NME*'s Mat Snow, Jim virtually admitted that the Mary Chain had absconded from the war on pop and were now just another band doing their thing. 'I like the idea of shaking things up,' he said. 'At one time I thought maybe we had the potential to do it, but now I don't think we have.'

For their next album, they revealed plans to ditch their trademark feedback sound and make greater use of acoustic guitars. Mat Snow wondered if this would be enough. Seeing the Reids' narrow taste in music as a fundamental problem, he theorised: 'Introducing big, booming acoustic numbers will vary the sound, but unless the Mary Chain expand their melodic, harmonic and structural vocabulary of "classic pop" sources, then the prospect of Ramonehood beckons.' In other words, year after year of imperceptible variations on an original theme, with diminishing artistic returns and decreasing sales, appealing only to a core following that would not resent the band's inability to evolve. But at least Snow wasn't suggesting the Mary Chain pack it in.

They were also very restricted by their limited musicianship. It was not as if they could snap their fingers and make a folk-rock album. At the sessions for 'Some Candy Talking' – their first single since *Psychocandy* – the simple bass guitar part left Douglas Hart scratching his head, and defeated both Jim and William too. In the end, it was played by a passing Dick Green.

'Some Candy Talking' received the biggest push yet from WEA for a Mary Chain single. Made in an expensive digital recording studio (Advision), it was then promoted with a costly video. The Reids knew it had to look and sound professional if it was to chart. 'I can't imagine what went through our minds when we thought "You Trip Me Up" was going to be a hit,' said Jim in *Smash Hits*. The more measured and moderate 'Some Candy Talking' seemed a cinch for Radio 1 airplay.

On its release in July, the Mary Chain made the crossover from music press phenomenon to commercially accepted rock group. It entered the chart at number 20, rising to 13 in the first week of August. McGee was elated. His first chart hit, 'Some Candy Talking' was a symbolic line in the sand sundering him from his hit-less mentors Treacy, Alway and Horne. But it appeared the Mary Chain would never win with the BBC. Mike Smith, Radio 1's breakfast show presenter, banned the single from his programme, claiming that its title was a reference to drugs, and *Top Of The Pops* refused to offer the band an appearance.

Deflated and incredulous, the Mary Chain insisted the BBC ban should not be top-spun by McGee, who was aching to scribble a press release about art terrorism and censorship. While the manager still held fast to a tabloid mentality, the Mary Chain were by now taking tea and biscuits with the pop magazines, and didn't want their cover blown. That summer, *Smash Hits* interviewed the Reids – amongst several other celebrities – for a feature entitled 'Should We Scrap The Royal Family?' When it was published, McGee blushed with shame. He'd presumed Jim and William would steal the headlines with a bloodcurdling statement about Buckingham Palace being razed to the ground and severed heads displayed on poles. Instead, the Reids ummed and ah'd before deciding they would like to see the royals 'dethroned' without violence. It was the Pet Shop Boys' Chris Lowe, of all people, who said what McGee had expected the Reids to say: 'They should be publicly executed.'

It was a rude awakening for McGee to learn that the Mary Chain were not even as outspoken as the keyboard player from the Pet Shop Boys. As if that were not bad enough, an interview with the

Reids in the same magazine saw them sniping at only the softest of targets: A-Ha and the Housemartins. Chart success or no chart success, McGee knew he would have to shake Jim and William up a bit.

Douglas Hart had always disliked going to McGee's house. He was allergic to cats and the McGees were friends of the felines. Instead, the regular venue for Mary Chain business meetings was a Wendy's hamburger restaurant in Oxford Street. They liked it because it was central, because it sold hamburgers and because it was quiet downstairs. Often, they and McGee would be the only people there. 'It was probably the most discreet place in the whole of London,' Hart ventures. For one particular meeting in September, however, Hart was not present. He was back in Scotland visiting his mother.

McGee was upbeat walking into Wendy's. 'Some Candy Talking' had only recently left the Top 75. His sarcoidosis was in abeyance following his intensive course of steroids – and he had met a new London band, the House Of Love, with whom he was looking forward to working. He sat down at the table and William Reid told him he was sacked.

McGee had something of a delayed reaction. Jim Reid recalls him being stoical and replying: 'I've been expecting it.' But as McGee left Wendy's and walked to the tube station, the news was already beginning to sink in, and so was a sting of injustice. 'Usually,' he points out, 'a band sacks a manager when nothing's happening at all. I'd taken those guys from £17 a week on the dole queue to £40,000 a year. I just felt, OK, I know I'm not great at getting the van there on time, but at the end of the day, I did the job.'

Primal Scream were in London that afternoon and had arranged to spend the night at McGee's house. 'By the time we got to the house, Pete Astor was sitting there and Alan's wife Yvonne,' says Jim Beattie. 'There was just this deathly silence.' McGee broke down and cried. 'It's the end,' he said. 'It's the end.' He meant the end of Creation, the label that had risen on the back of – and whose reputation was commensurate with the success of – the Jesus and Mary Chain. Who would want Creation now?

Gillespie, Beattie and Astor – the three senior artists on the label – urged him to soldier on. Each had his own motives. Beattie confesses to having been secretly pleased that McGee would be free to give more attention to Primal Scream. An inconsolable McGee picked a fight with everybody in the room. 'It was heavy duty,' says Beattie. 'I think it took him a good couple of weeks to deal with it.' When the mists cleared, McGee held three people responsible. William Reid was one. Jim Reid's girlfriend Laurence Verfaillie was another. The third was Geoff Travis.

'After McGee was out of the way, Geoff Travis assumed a far greater role,' says John Moore. '[The Reid brothers] respected Geoff –

they thought he was everything that McGee wasn't. He came across as intellectual, and they liked the fact that he'd had the Smiths and various other successes. I think they felt that with Geoff they didn't need McGee. Getting rid of McGee cut out the middle man.' Travis denies any involvement whatsoever in McGee's dismissal.

The Reids were right about one thing, though: Travis was everything McGee was not – a calm, collected personality and a sensible tactician. McGee, a catalyst and an iconoclast, arguably needed a manager more than the Mary Chain did. 'The Mary Chain blamed him for the fact that he hadn't pushed them,' says Mick Houghton. 'He hadn't pushed them into touring America at great length, or touring Europe, or promoting themselves more than they actually did. Not that they *wanted* to do those things. But they blamed him for that.'

Funnily enough, there were several points on which the Mary Chain had come to question McGee's judgment. They had found to their displeasure that they were no longer the top signings of the season. 'You would get groups coming along and being signed for £125,000,' says Douglas Hart. 'We'd been so hot in the music press – and selling records – and we kind of felt we could have got twice that. And I think we could have got twice that.'

For another thing, the Mary Chain had always disliked the bands McGee signed to Creation – with the exception of the Pastels and Primal Scream – and were scathing about the newly arrived House Of Love, a poetic and self-conscious quintet whom they derogatorily nicknamed A Flock Of Seagulls. Thirdly – and as a contributing factor, inescapable – McGee was the manager of two other bands besides the Mary Chain. 'The split with Alan came when he started to have loads of other things going on,' says Jim Reid. 'Truth be told, we felt a little jealous and neglected. We didn't understand that a manager could have loads of different interests. We rather stupidly fired him.'

The day-to-day management of the band was delegated to Laurence Verfaillie, who, according to certain people in the Mary Chain camp, was not much liked by William Reid. But unlike McGee, Verfaillie was not asking for 20 per cent. And it now became evident that the Reids had reached the conclusion McGee had not been earning his commission. 'Jim and Laurence went over the books,' he says. 'They got the books from the accountant – the accountant told me – and went through them three times to check if I was honest or not. They couldn't believe that I hadn't ripped them off. That really hurt me. Not only had they sacked me, but they'd questioned whether I was an honest person or not.'

Much of the paranoia was coming from the man who had never trusted McGee in the first place. 'William always had this idea that he was being ripped off,' says John Moore. 'If we were on tour and we'd go to a particular place to eat, he'd think it was some kind of plot – that we were going to this restaurant because someone in the organisation was getting a backhander.' Mick Houghton was a witness to a crazy incident at 83 Clerkenwell Road in the week after McGee had been dismissed. 'William walked in and tore the answering machine out of the wall and said: "That's mine. We paid for that",' Houghton remembers. 'Alan wasn't there, but Yvonne was. She and William swore at each other. He walked off with the answering machine and by all accounts dumped it in the nearest waste bin.'

John Moore noticed a gradual loss of momentum in the Mary Chain's career, which he attributes to McGee's absence. 'They had definitely been going up quite fast,' he says. 'But without McGee, I mean, nothing happened for a year and a half.' To be more precise, nothing happened that involved Moore. The brothers were at home writing the next Mary Chain album – but neither Moore nor Douglas Hart would play on it.

Just before the release of that album – *Darklands* – in September 1987, the Reids approached Chris Morrison, a 1970s stalwart who had managed Thin Lizzy and Ultravox. In Morrison the Mary Chain found the antithesis to McGee: an implementer who could also place a steadying hand on the tiller. 'We had a big talk very near the beginning of the Mary Chain,' says McGee. 'It was in this – as usual with them – burger bar. William was saying: "You'll always be with us. You're the fifth member of the Mary Chain." In my naivety, I believed him. Now, groups are like football chairmen. Whenever they tell you you're the fifth member of the band, they're about to sack you. I was 24. I trusted the guy, and he shat on me. But somebody was going to do it and it may as well have been William Reid.'

8 The Four Desperadoes

HIL KING, THE BOWL-HAIRED bassist in the Servants, had been recommended to a casting director needing extras for scenes in Diana Ross' 60s-themed video for 'Chain Reaction'. Months after filming, King was sitting in a pub with Lawrence from Felt when the video suddenly appeared on the TV screen. Lawrence was staggered. He was easily starstruck anyway – a cameo in a video for a number 1 hit was a big deal to him – and he was always envious of people with great hair. One reason he had asked Felt's bassist Marco Thomas to join the band was because, as Gary Ainge remembers, 'he had lovely, thick hair'. And no one who saw the 'Chain Reaction' video could dispute that Phil King had really stunning hair.

Since the unfortunate LSD incident at Bay 63 in August 1986, Lawrence had been keeping an even lower profile than usual. In a we-can't-follow-that gesture, Phil King's supporting Servants had actually split up after that gig, leaving King at a loose end. When Marco Thomas moved sideways to replace Neil Scott as Felt's guitarist, Lawrence did not have to look far for a bassist with quality hair. Travelling up to Birmingham for his first rehearsal, King was thrown straight into Felt's world. 'Lawrence met me at the station,' he says. 'We were standing at the bus-stop around the corner, and a pork pie dropped out of the sky from this multi-storey car park and landed on the pavement. He went: "Tsk. That just sums up Birmingham for me."' Creation had given King a white label copy of the new Felt album, *Forever Breathes The Lonely Word*, a superb piece of work that got his heart racing. 'I thought: this is fantastic. We're going to be huge.' Little did he know.

Produced by John Rivers at his studio in Leamington Spa, *Forever Breathes The Lonely Word* had a sumptuous, autumnal sound, and combined a relish for language with the historical savour of Dylan's *Blonde On Blonde*. It is to Creation's eternal detriment that it was unable to capitalise. Despite eulogistic reviews, *Forever Breathes The Lonely Word* suffered a muted commercial reception. 'The great irony with Felt,' says Mick Houghton, who was their publicist, 'was that Lawrence made a classic pop album at a point when Creation weren't geared to being a pop label. I felt very sorry for Lawrence. There were great singles on that record.'

McGee didn't really know what to do with Felt. He thought Lawrence was an unusual, gloomy man who was probably verging on the clinically depressed. As personalities they were polar opposites. McGee was always enthusiastic about the immediate future. Lawrence was resigned to it being a crushing disappointment. In one sense, this was his Midlands humour revealing itself in a unique wordless argot of tuts and sighs. Yet Lawrence did seem to have a rather glum disposition even for Birmingham. 'It was a laconic sense of humour,' says King. 'Expecting the worst all the time – and invariably it would happen. It was always: "Tsk, this could only happen to us." '

By the mid-80s, Lawrence's domestic fastidiousness had become a minor *cause célèbre*. It was not customary in indie circles to find a house-proud ascetic who hoovered with the intensity of Felix Unger in *The Odd Couple*, and who knocked on the lavatory door if his guest had been inside longer than the bare urinary minimum. Lawrence's obsession with cleanliness had given Felt their entrée into the music papers, but it was a rare journalist who didn't take the mickey.

The other members of Felt were pragmatic about their leader's condition. 'It was a phobia,' says Gary Ainge. 'He was spotless. Ever since I met him, he was always really clean. He would have two baths a day.' Lawrence also had phobias about cheese and vegetables – and King remembers him insisting on cleaning his teeth before recording a vocal. However, Lawrence was more than a hygiene and diet fanatic. In his daily life, he adhered to a set of disciplines which were not only born of his instinctive non-conformity – for example, choosing not to drink alcohol was his way of rejecting the stereotype of Midlands male culture – but also went hand-in-hand with his hopes and dreams of stardom. As bizarre as he appeared to be, Lawrence was not lacking in self-knowledge, and unlike the character in David Essex's 'Gonna Make You A Star', he understood the rock media. 'I thought my lifestyle was a great commercial selling-point,' he says, 'and I really wanted to exploit it. I always thought about the fans. I'd been let down badly by all the heroes that I'd had. I was determined not to let people down. It was a total package that you got with me – the perfect package for an angst-ridden generation.'

There is no value in a human interest story if no humans show interest. In October 1986, Lawrence's golden opportunity to address his public arrived on a platter. Gripped by *Forever Breathes The Lonely Word*, Danny Kelly sold the idea of a Felt cover story to the editor of the *NME*, and got on a train to Birmingham. He was looking forward to giving his readers a blow-by-blow account of Lawrence's peculiar antics. 'I went to his house and it was just extraordinary,' Kelly says.

'This fastidiousness thing had gone to extremes. He didn't want you to use his toilet – he would ask you to use a pub at the end of the street. He had a Manchester United shirt in his wardrobe that had belonged to George Best, he said, but he wouldn't let you see it.'

Kelly asked a couple of questions about *Forever Breathes The Lonely Word* which Lawrence seemed incapable of understanding. 'We had this bizarre conversation about music,' says Kelly, 'which ended with me asking the only question I could think of in order to get some human contact with the fellow – which was: "What do you do at Christmas?" He said: "I stay here." I said: "What do you have for Christmas dinner?" He said: "I have one of those Bernard Matthews turkey roasts." And I said: "What – with vegetables and all the trimmings?" "No. Just the Bernard Matthews turkey roast." ' Kelly and the *NME* photographer fell about laughing.

Hurrying back to London to write his article, Kelly was furious to learn that it would not be the cover story after all – a group of *NME* staffers, concerned that an indie band with average record sales of 10,000 would not be enough of a lure to the readers, had persuaded the editor to bump Felt off the front page and lead instead with an article about suicide among teenagers. 'The cover was entirely black save for the words "Youth Suicide",' says Kelly. 'It was the worst cover in the history of pop music.'

'It proved a point,' says Lawrence, who sees the *NME*'s volte-face as a critical event in Felt's career. 'It was like nobody wanted to go all the way with us. Nobody stuck their neck out and said: "This is the band." It was like, what else can we do? We just threw our arms up in the air, and then folded them and sat back. We knew what our future would be from then on.'

Kelly's well-written profile of Lawrence, which was spread across the *NME*'s centre pages, presented his life as a tragicomedy of the mundane. In self-imposed isolation, Lawrence would pass the hours by reading until evening, then by watching television until bedtime. If he wanted to kill five minutes, he would wash his hair. To hurry the clock along, he might jot down song titles for as-yet-unrecorded Felt albums. He claimed to have no girlfriend – although he did confess to a relationship of sorts with a girl in Windsor – and he spoke dispassionately of his parents and his upbringing in the village of Water Orton. 'He never talked about his dad,' recalls Phil King. 'One day I said to him: "Why don't you ever talk about your dad?" He said: "Because he's bald, the bastard." ' Lawrence had seceded from the family and – since Felt gigs were so uncommon – was close to withdrawing completely from the outside world. 'I'm trying to give up even the little bit of shopping I do ...' he told Kelly. 'If I could get all my stuff [delivered] on a Friday night ... I need never go out.'

Kelly left him in a suspended state, waiting for a day that would never come. In his anxiety to be an enigmatic pop celebrity,

Lawrence had overshot the mark by several metres. 'My take on Lawrence,' says Alan McGee, 'is that he's definitely a one-off. Having said that, there's no question that he was playing up to the myth. And then he became the myth.' Scrubbed, disinfected, uncontaminated and alone, Lawrence was a guinea pig for his own dangerous experiment.

Five years after walking into Blenheim Crescent with the Laughing Apple's *The Ha Ha Hee Hee EP*, McGee no longer had a very favourable opinion of Rough Trade. Unsatisfied with the distribution company, he was sounding out Rough Trade's main rival, Pinnacle, with a view to a transfer. The only thing standing in his way was the money Creation owed to Rough Trade, no small sum. McGee had been on a P&D arrangement since February 1984, and had regularly been advanced funds to keep Creation solvent.

The mantra about Pinnacle that Rough Trade repeated to its labels again and again went something like this. Pinnacle is a bastion of Thatcherism. The values of its chairman Steve Mason contravene every rule in the indie book. Art over wealth. Fun over survival. Good vibes over bad vibes. Music over everything. 'Rough Trade painted Steve Mason and Pinnacle as capitalists ... the absolute evil,' says McGee, who met Mason for the first time in October 1985. 'They said they were as bad as a major record company.'

The son of an insurance agent, Mason had started out in the music business in the late 60s as a bill-sticker in south London, moving into pub and club promotion at the dawn of glam-rock. He would later boast of booking David Bowie and Roxy Music into the Greyhound pub in Croydon before they were famous. In 1976, Mason became a successful exporter – his company Windsong helped hundreds of marginal labels and bands reach the international market – and in 1983 he started up two indie labels of his own, including the heavy rock imprint Music For Nations. When his labels' distributor IDS took three weeks to sell 13 copies of a Bad Brains record on Music For Nations, Mason transferred the labels to Pinnacle. However, in November 1984, Pinnacle crashed owing £2 million, disrupting many labels' cash flow and leaving some facing liquidation.

'I have to admit I really nagged Steve,' says Iain McNay, whose labels were hit for the best part of £100,000. 'I said: "Steve, this is your big chance. Why don't you go in and buy Pinnacle?" And he said: "It's not worth anything." I said: "It is worth something, because you've got the name, you've got the computer system, you've got the premises." And he went in and bought it. If he hadn't come in, we would all have disintegrated.'

Unlike Rough Trade, Pinnacle handled MOR music as well as contemporary indie rock. Richard Scott recalls Mason telling him the only reason he bought Pinnacle was because it had a contract to distribute the work of Dorothy Squires. 'Mason had a Utopian ideal of having a split between the two kinds of music,' says Dave Whitehead, Mason's general manager. 'He was a great businessman, very singular, very self-driven ... had a good financial head. I don't think he proclaimed to know anything about music as such.'

For the likes of Alan McGee, two things counted high in Mason's favour. Firstly, he was straight-talking and down-to-earth. More importantly, he was renowned for paying on the first of every month, without fail. 'He was a good guy,' says McGee. 'He made money out of music – that's what Pinnacle was all about. He wasn't as into music as the Rough Trade people, or as idealistic. But he wasn't the devil.' McGee felt a greater affinity with Mason than he did with the highbrows at Rough Trade, whom he suspected of looking down their noses at him. Mason's politics did not matter to McGee one way or the other. Rough Trade's institutionalised snobbery did.

In mid-1986, Dave Whitehead fell out with Mason, was sacked and went to work for Rough Trade, becoming head of distribution. 'Rough Trade was fairly anarchic,' he says. 'There was a spirit there, but it was pretty chaotic. I remember going down to the warehouse and saying: "Guys, it's OK to smoke dope, but can you wait until after six-thirty? When all the orders have gone out, then you can skin up." It went down like the proverbial toilet. I was almost branded as a fascist.' Whitehead was struck by how nervous Rough Trade Distribution seemed. Nervous about allowing the labels to run up debts. Nervous about what the coming years might hold. Nervous even about dealing with Rough Trade Records. 'It was a climate where people were always asking for money,' he says. 'There was a wariness at Rough Trade Distribution about pretty much every independent label that they worked with.'

Whitehead soon realised that he was going to have a problem with Creation. McGee had been bankrolled by Rough Trade through hell and high water, and the liability had once or twice touched £100,000. 'Creation was pretty much flying by its shirt-tails,' Whitehead says. 'One of the hardest things to do was bridle [McGee's] enthusiasm with some sort of fiscal sensibility.' Rough Trade would advance money to Creation against projected profit, to finance records McGee wanted to make. A release schedule would be thrashed out, but within a month McGee would be back to ask Whitehead for another £10,000. He would be bullish in his projections, but he was in danger of playing his joker once too often. His regular boasts of having found the next big thing only cut so much ice with Whitehead, who was looking restlessly at the bottom line. The departure of Creation for Pinnacle – as and when it might occur – would not be met by too many tears in King's Cross.

'The thing about Alan,' says Whitehead, 'was that there was always this feeling of undelivered promise. He was always six months away

from absolute fame or from total famine. People had heard it too
many times.'

In a triumphant mood after 'Almost Prayed', Pete Astor had been
keen to use a different – and preferably American – producer for the
Weather Prophets' second single. He chose Lenny Kaye, who had
produced James' debut album, *Stutter*, for Sire/WEA earlier that year.
Kaye plugged Astor into an heroic lineage of art, poetry and critically
lauded rock 'n' roll. An ex-music critic himself, the American had
played guitar in the Patti Smith Group and compiled the immortal
psych-garage compilation *Nuggets*. With Kaye as his producer, Astor
could time travel back to mid-70s New York and fraternise with the
hippest lecturer in the college.

Kaye convinced Astor that the perfect follow-up to 'Almost Prayed'
would be 'Naked As The Day You Were Born', a slow-burning sere-
nade with a down-in-the-dumps atmosphere. Released in October
1986 to lukewarm reviews, 'Naked As The Day You Were Born' was
snubbed by so many of the fans who'd bought 'Almost Prayed' that
Astor would still be touchy on the subject five months later. 'I feel a
bit sorry for it, like a poor child that's been rejected,' he told a journalist. 'I feel like taking it away and not letting anybody hear it again
... I thought the single should be ... something to say: "Look, we are
of substance." '

Although seen as a backwards step, 'Naked As The Day You Were
Born' did not impair the Weather Prophets' good name at WEA,
where, that same month, Rob Dickins offered McGee £75,000 for an
album by the band. McGee parlayed this into a second-tier label – to
be funded and distributed by WEA – with McGee as A&R chief, talent scout and sole employee. He would bring three or four acts to
Dickins each year, the best that Creation had at the time. The
Weather Prophets were one. The others McGee had in mind were
Primal Scream and Felt.

Were Primal Scream ready to step up to a WEA-backed label? Well,
they had a twelve-string guitar player, which made them palatable to
a Byrds lover like Dickins, and no one could deny that they had an
ardent fanbase. All the same, Dickins wasn't about to wave his
cheque-book too recklessly. He tabled a prudent £40,000 for Primal
Scream and allowed McGee to haggle him up to £55,000. McGee, who
himself made several thousand pounds from the various deals, concedes: 'The flagship band was the Weather Prophets. I think [Dickins]
took Primal Scream as an afterthought.'

Both bands were put on a weekly wage, giving up their jobs or
signing off the dole. They were quitting the indie boondocks and taking up new residence on the world stage. At least one band-member
recalls thinking in a flash: America here we come. However, as WEA
distribution would invalidate their passport to the indie charts, they

would be under considerable pressure to show up in the real ones. And to make it harder for them, both groups were to be aimed at a space in the market that nobody was even sure existed: a nationwide quorum of indie fans that wouldn't be over-offended by the groups' decision to renounce indie credibility for life in the big leagues.

This dilemma was not something that kept Pete Astor awake at nights. For the first time, he had a realistic chance of becoming famous, and he longed to leave behind what he calls 'that indie thing, that small world, that secret handshake syndrome'. Never trusted or accepted by indie grandees like Jerry Thackray and Neil Taylor, nor by the fanzine-writing reactionaries, Astor prepared to wave goodbye and go once round the fair.

Absurdly, McGee decided to call his new label Creation, apparently unaware that two imprints trading under the same name might cause confusion. When an unamused Simon Edwards told him to think again, he hit on the name Elevation. Intensifying the psychedelia affectation, the catalogue numbers of Elevation's singles were to have the prefix ACID.

The losers in the Elevation deal were Felt. Trying to come to terms with being passed over by WEA for the second time in two years, Lawrence pleaded with McGee to win Dickins over. 'In the end,' says Lawrence, 'Alan said: "Look, all they've offered is a twenty grand advance and I just can't let you do it. You're just selling yourself for nothing." I said: "I'll take it." ' But Rob Dickins simply didn't want Felt; never had and never would. It was the final nail in their coffin.

Another Elevation non-starter was Nikki Sudden, who had recorded an album called *Texas* for Creation in 1986 and yearned to take his songs to a larger listenership. The former Swell Map, now 30 years old, had been an early and important player in the indie story, but since 1980 his stock had diminished. On the disbandment of Swell Maps, he had become a rock 'n' roll balladeer-cum-gypsy in imitation of Keith Richards and Johnny Thunders. He had then co-founded the Jacobites with Birmingham native Dave Kusworth, a fellow singer-guitarist and a meticulous Richards impersonator. Kusworth and Sudden wore their influences on the sleeves of their frock coats and Granny Takes A Trip jackets, becoming so inseparable that it was not clear where Sudden ended and Kusworth began. Wedging their still-smoking cigarettes between the strings on the necks of their guitars, the Jacobites had fans in the low thousands but dreams in the high millions. Musically, if not sartorially, they were in step with Creation's mid-80s image of vagabond dissipation.

On the eve of a German tour in February 1986, Kusworth had left the Jacobites and McGee had taken on Sudden as a solo artist. *Texas* hadn't sold much, but Sudden, a walking encyclopaedia of 70s music lore, felt Creation needed him around the place to hip them to people like Neil Young, the Stones and the Faces. 'McGee didn't have a clue about any pre-punk music at all,' he says. 'When punk came along, he got swept up in this whole undercurrent which rejected anything that had come before it.' Hearing on the grapevine that McGee was searching for acts to take to Elevation, Sudden advised him to look no further. He believed he was the premier artiste on Creation's roster. And that, McGee told him gently, is what he would have to remain.

For *Texas*, Creation had given Sudden the most generous budget of his nine-year career. He now thought they were ready for an upping of the stakes. Buttonholing McGee, he told him he intended to lock himself in a studio in Oxfordshire and record 200 songs – McGee blinked at the amount, as anyone would – choosing the best ten or twelve for his next album. Nikki duly made for Woodworm Studios, a converted Baptist church in Barford St Michael, and had managed to record about 20 tracks when Yvonne McGee rang to tell him to stop immediately. Creation had run out of money again.

When Pete Astor cruised into Livingston Studios in north London's Wood Green, he specifically wanted to Make A Record: a serious, heavyweight album with much forethought and a wealth of perspicacity in the grooves. McGee was thinking in upper case too, looking forward to catalogue number ELV 1 being A Proper Rock Album. But there was the rub. Astor had become infatuated by the Lovin' Spoonful and was shifting the emphasis of the Weather Prophets to thistledown 60s pop. It was not the ideal time to be changing direction.

Lenny Kaye was retained as producer, but the album sessions saw him out-argued by the studio engineer, who thought a stainless, business-like production would suit the Weather Prophets best. For a band already playing a percentages game after the unexpected knockback of 'Naked As The Day You Were Born', a clean production seemed the safest and most obvious road to go down. They were taking the sound of C86 and blow-drying it vigorously to make it major label compatible. But this method of recording had a strict protocol. 'Up to that point, we had always made [all the musicians] record at the same time,' says McGee. 'Lenny Kaye separated all the instruments. He put down the bass, then he put down the drums, then he put down the guitars . . . So it was clinical.'

The album was finished at the end of November, and was received warmly by WEA. The consensus was that Kaye and the Weather Prophets had steered the best possible course. They had made a punchy guitar record that wasn't too heavy for radio; and arrived at an accessible sound that wasn't too sterile to scare off the indie pedants. 'I thought it was brilliant,' says Graham Carpenter, Elevation's liaison officer at WEA. 'On a purely commercial aspect, I thought this would do it. Pete Astor's songwriting was fantastic and

Lenny was definitely the right person to make the record. We all loved it.' Marketing loved it, radio promotions loved it, Rob Dickins loved it. McGee loved it, Astor loved it and the other Weather Prophets loved it too. There was not a single dissenting voice. It was called *Mayflower*, a title loved by everyone.

A fan of Primal Scream's 'Velocity Girl', Stephen Street had engineered the year's most acclaimed album, *The Queen Is Dead* by the Smiths, and was enjoying as much kudos inside the industry as Morrissey and Marr outside. One of two names short-listed to produce Primal Scream's debut album for Elevation (the other was Stephen Duffy of the Lilac Time), Street rehearsed the band for two days in Scotland before moving proceedings to Rockfield, a studio situated by the river Monmow in Wales. Rockfield was surrounded by farm land and woods, and the young producer was not to know that Primal Scream and the countryside made uneasy bedfellows. Everything that could go wrong with the Primal Scream album was to go very wrong over the next four or five weeks.

Like Lenny Kaye and almost every other rock and pop producer of the 80s, Stephen Street made records in the inverted pyramid fashion of recording the drum-kit in isolation, and adding the bass, the guitar and the vocals in that order. This spelt calamity for Primal Scream. Street could not get a steady tempo from the drums – which had to be dead-centre if any singles from the album were to be played on the radio – and grew exasperated with the band's drummer, Tam McGurk.

Street made McGurk replay every beat of the snare, every thump of the bass drum and every shuck of the hi-hat, knowing that these were the foundations for the entire album structure. In Rockfield's leisure rooms and residential cottages, the other members of the band were tiring of Street's regime, which obliged them to rise at an early hour, appear in the studio at a prearranged time, and not drink heavily on their nights off. It was a bit too much like being a soldier on parade.

'Me and McGee drove down to Rockfield after about three weeks and it was horrible,' says Graham Carpenter. 'He almost sacked [Street] on the spot. The pair of us went into the studio, sat at the desk, listened to what they'd done so far – and [McGee] just hated all the backing tracks. We drove straight back to London.'

Despite the problems with McGurk, he was not the first member of the band to be sent home. Guitarist Stuart May – who had replaced Paul Harte a few months before – was told by Gillespie and Beattie that his contributions were not up to scratch, and was sacked. But when Street offered to play May's guitar parts himself, this was seen by Beattie as a major faux pas. 'I went in one morning,' he recalls, 'and [Street] said, "I've made up a wee guitar line." I said: "That's very good. So are you going to take it away and record your own LP?" '

Beattie taped over the guitar part, which Street found completely gratuitous. There had now been a breach of trust on both sides.

'The band were arguing all the time,' says Street. 'They were in constant dispute with the drummer. Big Jim wanted twelve-string guitar on every single track, which was very hard to accommodate. Getting it in tune was driving me up the wall.' Unwilling to call in a session drummer in case this angered them even more, Street was faced with a fragmenting group suffering from too much fresh air and acting increasingly childishly. Close to despair, he sent for McGee again.

'I drove down with Yvonne and the band were fine,' McGee recalls. 'Then they stayed up all night banging things on walls and stuff like that ... They always articulated their anger at other people, but this time it was [directed] at me. I hadn't seen them for three weeks, so it was really pissing me off. I went to Bristol at seven the next morning and booked in for the day. I phoned Bobby up from the hotel and I went: "You acted like a complete arse." '

To play the rhythm guitar parts, McGee sent for Andrew Innes from Revolving Paint Dream, and the arrival of the talented Innes seemed to make a difference. But the damage had been done and the relationship between band and producer was far from cordial. 'Bobby was trying to compare Primal Scream to the classic 60s bands like Love,' says Street. 'Unfortunately, they just didn't have the musician-ship to back it up. I was used to working with Morrissey, who I regarded as a genius as far as singing was concerned. With Bobby, I just thought: you haven't got it, pal.'

Gillespie had not conquered his fear of singing 'cold' in a studio environment, and was instantly unhappy with everything he sang at Rockfield. He went out of tune; his voice sounded weak; he had to retake line after line to enable Street to compile a vocal from snip-pets of incomplete takes. Jim Beattie, who watched it all from the control room, remembers: 'We finally started dropping in a word at a time. Stephen told us that that's what Green from Scritti Politti did. I was like: "Aww, you shouldn't tell Bobby *that* ..." But that's what we did. Bobby started off with a sentence at a time. Then he would go back and listen to it and say: "That word's shite, we'll drop in there." It was a fucking nightmare.'

In a fit of frustration, Gillespie vandalised the studio. As acoustic screens were kicked over, Street turned to Beattie and a meaningful look was exchanged. That weekend, McGee returned to Rockfield with Yvonne and Andrew Innes' girlfriend Christine Wanless. The mood of the band was now like that of the dinner guests in Buñuel's *The Exterminating Angel*, who are unable to leave the house and can-not understand why. Gillespie and Beattie – who intended to call the album *Hollywood Hell* if it ever reached the stage of requiring a title – resented the visitors' encroachment; the women had come not to help but to pony-trek in the fields. Gillespie, Beattie and bassist Robert Young barricaded themselves in one of the cottages, piling mattresses against the door and filling a bucket with boiling water to drench anyone who tried to enter. 'We'd gone nuts by then,' says Beattie. 'It was too much drugs.'

By the time the McGees and Wanless left, the three men in the cottage had decided to prolong their sit-in indefinitely. Stephen Street was in turmoil over the profligacy of the sessions and the lack of even halfway decent vocals from Gillespie. When another night passed and half the band was still in hiding, a car engine was heard at daybreak. Gillespie, Beattie and Young peered through the skylight and saw Street's car positioned a few feet from the cottage. 'Jesus Christ!' Beattie exclaimed. 'He's going to ram the door!'

They watched Street get out of the car and disappear into the studio. He returned with a handful of master tapes, restarted the engine and drove slowly up the road. Silence descended once more on the Welsh countryside. 'We thought: he has fucked off with our LP,' Beattie says. 'And he had.'

The Rockfield sessions had concluded. It was five days before Christmas.

While Primal Scream, the Weather Prophets and other one-time indie bands were tackling the question of how to make artistically and commercially successful music using major league recording formulae, an important issue was going ignored. Even a clinically produced LP was not going to do much to convince the high-street record-buyers that 60s-influenced guitar bands were anything other than relics of a pre-techno age. Disco-orientated chart pop and underground rock were two very separate entities, and there appeared to be no point at which they intersected.

One of the few people at A&R level in 1986 who seemed to understand both kinds of music, and enjoy them equally, was Bill Drummond, an A&R consultant nearing the end of his three-year contract with WEA. A dry-humoured scammer-cum-dreamer, Drummond – born William Butterworth in 1953 – was the son of a minister from Galloway in Scotland. With no access to radio or television in the family home, he claimed to have first heard pop music at local fairgrounds. By 1977, Drummond was living in Liverpool and playing guitar in a punk band, Big In Japan, alongside Ian Broudie and Holly Johnson.

The following year, Drummond began a long-lasting business relationship with Dave Balfe, bass player in the Liverpool band Dalek I Love You. Launching an indie label, Zoo, at the beginning of 1979, Drummond and Balfe released singles by the city's two freshest young groups, the Teardrop Explodes and Echo and the Bunnymen, both of whom they also managed. As the Teardrops and the

Bunnymen received rave reviews in the London music weeklies, Liverpool first rivalled, then overtook Manchester as the influential city for post-punk music. Drummond and Balfe signed the Teardrops and the Bunnymen respectively to Mercury (one of the Phonogram labels) and Korova (a Warner Bros imprint fronted by a young Rob Dickins, and financed jointly by Warner Music in the UK and Sire in America). By the time these deals were done, Balfe had joined the Teardrop Explodes as a keyboard player, leaving Drummond to handle both bands' day-to-day affairs.

More than any up-and-coming manager of the period, Drummond was interested in the abstracts and subtexts of the rock 'n' roll calling, and particularly in the cabbalistic nature of genius. In private moments, he studied books about psychic energy, mythology and the cultures of ancient tribes, scrutinising the texts for concealed meanings and coincidences. These studies led Drummond far away from the earthly realities of managing two Liverpudlian pop groups, and into the realms of his formidable imagination. Among other reveries, he wondered what might happen if the Teardrop Explodes' singer Julian Cope were to be murdered by Bill Drummond.

The Teardrop Explodes broke up in November 1982, more than a year after Drummond's involvement in their career had ended. He was still managing Echo and the Bunnymen, however, when Rob Dickins became chairman of WEA in 1983. Dickins offered Drummond a job in A&R, giving him the use of an office and the freedom to sign anyone he liked. Drummond quickly found himself in a rut. 'I completely failed working within a corporate structure,' he says. 'I don't think I really signed one thing, and I was there for three years.' Actually, Drummond brought almost half a dozen acts to WEA, including Strawberry Switchblade and an upbeat dance-pop band called Brilliant, a discovery of Dave Balfe's. 'It was all looking very healthy for Brilliant,' says Balfe. 'They were trying to do the dance-rock crossover thing, and we needed [a producer] who could really pull it off.'

What Balfe and Drummond had in mind was the hyper pop-disco sound of 'You Spin Me Round (Like A Record)', a number 1 hit for Dead Or Alive in 1985. Pete Burns, Dead Or Alive's leader, was a veteran of the Liverpool punk scene, and Balfe and Drummond knew that 'You Spin Me Round (Like A Record)' was the best record he had ever made. They hooked up Brilliant with Dead Or Alive's three backroom boys: Mike Stock, Matt Aitken and Pete Waterman.

Stock, Aitken and Waterman would become the most successful writing-and-producing team in Britain during the second half of the 80s, with hits by Sinitta, Mel and Kim, Rick Astley, Kylie Minogue and others. But in 1985, their working practices were a total mystery to Dave Balfe and Bill Drummond. 'It was an enormously sort of paradigm-shifting experience,' says Balfe. 'You'd go in and be listening to the track, and then Pete Waterman would pop in, listen to it, pop out and then come back with an SOS Band 12-inch and go: "No, it should sound like this." And we'd all pop out to the pub for three hours and come back, and [the track] would have a completely different rhythm section. This is before anyone had ever worked like that. It was like music had become Lego.'

Waterman, the triumvirate's public face and subsequent media fall guy, had been a soul DJ and promoter in the 70s. A Motown fanatic, he was taking the premise of the 60s hit factory – smooth-running, high-turnover production lines; an in-house sound; no indulgence of the artist's agenda whatsoever – and was unashamedly making records for the discos and the Top 10. With the exception of Dead Or Alive's hit, which critics had loved, Stock, Aitken and Waterman productions bypassed the world of the *NME*, John Peel and the tastemakers of rock and soul. 'We make records very simply and very quickly,' explained Stock, who wrote and arranged the music with Aitken. 'We can go through fifteen ideas in an hour.'

Bill Drummond learned a lot from watching Waterman. To Waterman, pop music was just that – popular music – and was not to be confused with art or credibility or didacticism. (Stock was quoted in the *NME* as saying that groups should never make political statements in their lyrics. 'There's no place for it,' he said. 'These records are bought by young kids and I think that's sinister.') Above all, Waterman took the Alfred Hitchcock view that the finished product counted far more than the people who delivered the lines. Waterman heaped technology on to an act's sound, and if the act got in the way, he removed the act. Drummond thought this was inspired. 'I'd come from a world where bands would strum an E chord and think it was the most brilliant thing ever done,' he says. 'To Waterman, everything was dispensable. Waterman doesn't give a shit about anything other than do 12-year-old girls want to buy the record?'

Alan McGee would not have worried about Stock, Aitken and Waterman in 1986, assuming he even knew about them. High-flying dance-pop was something he viewed as strictly for musical remedials. That was exactly the sort of crap that the Weather Prophets and Primal Scream were going to blow away. And he would certainly never discuss the finer points of chart disco with Bill Drummond. 'He was of that generation that viewed the Velvet Underground as a starting-point, as the greatest band ever,' says Drummond, who was introduced to McGee at WEA in 1984. 'Because if he'd ever been into black music, he'd have had a completely different approach to how you make records. American black records can be made on a shoestring, but they're incredibly well made.'

But Drummond wasn't putting the Velvets fan down. When Max Hole – WEA's head of A&R – had played 'Upside Down' by the Jesus and Mary Chain at the weekly A&R meeting in November 1984, and let slip that the band was about to sign to Blanco y Negro, Drummond thought: these guys are fantastic. Over the next two years, Drummond and McGee would have many friendly conversations at WEA, nuanced by attempts at oneupmanship. Drummond was the droll older man trying hard not to be cynical. McGee was a yapping, excitable puppy.

'One of the major differences between us,' says Drummond, 'was Alan would think everything he was working on was brilliant – "This is the future of rock 'n' roll!" – whereas I just spent all my time thinking: oh my God, this is just the worst record ever made. How can we put this out? I'm letting the band down so much ...' Indeed, as the Stock, Aitken and Waterman sessions with Brilliant were being wrapped up in 1985, Drummond had sudden doubts about the trio's method of working, and second-guessed himself back to the drawing-board. 'I'd got to the point where I was thinking: this is so wrong,' he says. 'This is not what rock 'n' roll's about.'

Brilliant's album, *Kiss The Lips Of Life*, was released by WEA in the autumn of 1986. Unfortunately for everyone concerned, it was evident Waterman had applied his production-line ruthlessness to the wrong band. As one reviewer noted: 'Brilliant are slaves to ... the pitiless machine-beat of the modern disco floor ... Nor is songwriting among their more obvious assets.' The album flopped.

By then, Drummond was gone from WEA. Defeated by the corporation, he was at crisis point. Thirty-three years old, he vowed never to work in the music business again. As a valedictory move – and as an exorcism of the time-consuming Stock, Aitken and Waterman experience – he decided to record a solo album and retire for good. 'The whole thing was: write the songs in a week, record them in a week, next week do the album sleeve and get it out as fast as I can,' he says. Drummond asked Alan McGee if he would like to put the record out on Creation.

McGee was honoured. Drummond was practically a genius – and better still, he was offering to pay for his album himself. 'I don't think anybody else but Alan would have put out a Bill Drummond record,' says Mick Houghton. 'Especially without hearing it first.' True, McGee had never heard any of Drummond's songs before. Nor had he ever heard Bill sing. 'I think he was expecting it to be the rantings of a madman,' says Drummond. 'I don't think he thought it was actually going to be proper music.'

As McGee sanctioned Creation's most esoteric record so far – at precisely the same time he was seeking to take Primal Scream and the Weather Prophets into the national consciousness – Drummond put together a backing band containing members of the Triffids, an Australian sextet. If nothing else, thought McGee, Drummond's album might add in a small way to the sum of human happiness. What came out of the sessions was *The Man*, a surprisingly good album in a folk and country vein. Singing with a pronounced Scottish accent – like a panic-stricken Ivor Cutler – Drummond told tales of his football-mad boyhood and his fairground exposure to the music of Elvis Presley, ending the album with a poem by Robert Burns.

'The album was mad, genius,' McGee recalls. 'I really loved it, and we put it out and got great press on it. Never sold a sausage.' Says Drummond: 'By the time it was out, I couldn't remember any of the words of the songs.'

McGee did not have much respect for Max Hole, WEA's head of A&R. Hole was old-school – his career in the music business predated punk – and McGee had been revolted to discover that Hole had once managed the progressive-rock group Camel, whose concept album *The Snow Goose* McGee had avoided like the plague in the mid-70s. 'Four people ran WEA,' says Graham Carpenter. 'There was Max. There was [Paul] Conroy, head of marketing. Rob, of course. And Phil Straight; he was head of international. They were like the four desperadoes. They went everywhere together, did everything together. They decided everything that went on with every act, internationally and domestically.'

McGee would have to get used to the four desperadoes, otherwise Elevation's ride would not be smooth. But already there were signs that McGee's attitude was doing his label no favours. 'Alan was really quite slow at adapting to corporate life,' says Mick Houghton, who worked with WEA acts. 'He was quite naive when he started, and wanted to remain naive. But there comes a point when you accept that you have to ... not *become* one of these people, but at least learn to live with them.'

Bill Drummond was pessimistic about Elevation's chances, having narrowly survived the corporate tidal wave himself. 'I thought it was a huge mistake,' he says. 'A huge mistake on Alan's part and a huge mistake on the record company's part. I was aware that he was doing it because he needed the financial security for [Creation]. I thought: no matter how much he thinks these bands are brilliant, he's going to go into meetings with radio promotion departments and press departments and they won't understand where those bands are coming from. If you're working on ZZ Top, Madonna, Prince ... and the Weather Prophets, it just doesn't happen, it doesn't work.' In the meantime, McGee had to go to Max Hole and tell him Primal Scream were scrapping their album and starting again.

Tam McGurk, the drummer, was sacked in January 1987 in a Glasgow café by a nervous Jim Beattie and Alan McGee. 'He was a bit of a hard man, Tam McGurk,' says Beattie. 'Handy with his fists. I had to say: "Look Tam, it's not good enough, the drums are rubbish. We should part company." ' Just then, Bobby Gillespie and Robert Young came into the café. With remarkable lack of tact, Gillespie asked

McGurk when would be a good time to go round and collect his drum-kit. 'McGee went: "You can't take the drums off him! He was part of the group – at least give him the drums",' says Beattie. 'You know, how to kill a sensitive moment . . .'

Only one song, 'I Love You', was salvageable from the Stephen Street-produced wash-out at Rockfield. When Beattie checked, he found that £15,000 remained of the band's £55,000 advance – which the re-recording would see off easily. Primal Scream were in trouble, and WEA was becoming the enemy. Unlike the suave Astor, Beattie had difficulty relating to Rob Dickins, whose efforts to be one of the gang gave him the creeps. 'He used to do this thing with his favourite people that he'd signed,' Beattie says. 'He had a boxing glove, and if he got the boxing glove out and tapped you on the shoulder, you knew he liked you. He used to do this to me sometimes. I'd be like: "Oh no . . ." McGee and Bobby used to wind me up. "He wants to butt-fuck you . . ." And he always had these yes-men following him. I was going in one day and Dickins was coming out with his yes-men. And they were like: "Hold the doors open for him! Watch his hands, watch his hands!" It was horrible.'

Before Primal Scream set about remaking *Hollywood Hell* from scratch, they had to record a single. It had been nine unfruitful months since 'Crystal Crescent', but they had a song called 'Imperial' which McGee and Graham Carpenter thought would make a strong summer release. They put Primal Scream in the famous EMI Studios in Abbey Road with Clive Langer of the Langer-Winstanley production team that had minted hit singles and albums for Madness, the Teardrop Explodes, Dexys Midnight Runners and Elvis Costello. Langer was Top 40, not indie. Whereas Stephen Street had restrained himself from hiring a session drummer, Langer did so immediately. Primal Scream had wanted Dave Morgan, the affable Charlie Watts of the Creation family, to play on the session. Instead, they arrived at Abbey Road to find Neil Conti – the drummer from Prefab Sprout – working out rhythms on a drum-machine. Conti, who had played with David Bowie at Live Aid, wore braces and sported a suntan. He was in no way a Scream kind of guy.

'Clive was in bits during that session,' says McGee. 'He had the phone number of a taxi service that could bring you anything, what-ever . . . and alcohol was his particular whatever. At about four in the morning, Clive had done a bottle of vodka. He turned round to Bobby and he was crying – he was *crying* – and he was going: "I fucking love them, man . . . I fucking love them . . ." And Bob was going: "Who?" He went: "The Beatles. I fucking love them." I think he endeared himself forever to the Primals because of that.'

'We probably had too much of a good time,' says Langer. 'We had to kind of save [the session] at the end. It was a bugger to mix, I know that. It wasn't a great success, but it wasn't a failure either.' The release of 'Imperial' was put on hold until Primal Scream's album had been remade.

At 83 Clerkenwell Road, Jeff Barrett could see McGee's head was now in Elevation space. That's when he saw McGee's head at all. Barrett and Dick Green were often left alone in the office while McGee was afoot at WEA, where he seemed to be taking a music business crammer course. 'Alan got very into the industry,' says Barrett. 'He really felt he was a player. I remember him saying to me one day: "Barrett, I know how a contract works now. I know how to read a contract." It was a big thing for him.'

But in Rough Trade Distribution's King's Cross headquarters, the feeling was that if McGee was still serious about Creation, he had a funny way of showing it. To label manager Dave Whitehead, Elevation made a mockery of McGee's oft-made promises to keep Creation on an even keel with Rough Trade's help. Increasingly, Whitehead wondered if he was being taken for a ride. 'Elevation was kind of a hard thing to swallow,' he says. 'It was like: oh, so we're just a farming ground and all you're going to do is sign your best bands off to major record companies.' Like Blanco y Negro, in other words.

However, McGee did not have any choice. The mathematics had set the agenda. 'Last year Creation gave the Weather Prophets £3,000 to live on,' he told the *NME*. 'This year WEA, through Elevation, is giving them £100,000. Equally, if *Mayflower*, their new album, had come out on Creation it would have sold about 40,000 copies. On Elevation I reckon it'll do somewhere between 100,000 and 150,000.' It would have to. Nothing on Creation was selling.

McGee tried to impress the seriousness of the situation on his wife Yvonne, pleading with her to work harder at Clerkenwell. But their marriage was in trouble and she did not like being ordered around. 'Yvonne's idea of working at Creation was coming in at four o'clock in the afternoon and saying: "I've just spent this [amount] on the credit card",' claims McGee. 'It came to a head when I said: "We're going down the toilet. You've got to throw your weight behind me." She says: "I can't have you telling me what to do." I said: "Yeah, but … I'm going to go *bankrupt*." '

He was running out of favours. When he asked Dave Whitehead to knock a few per cent off Creation's distribution fee, the Rough Trade man had bad news for him. 'Alan had been on a standard $27\frac{1}{2}$ [per cent] deal,' says Whitehead, 'and Rough Trade had financially contributed towards Creation's growth since day one. After that, Rough Trade started to look to increase its deals to 30 per cent. There was a lot of resistance.' McGee recalls: 'I said to Dave Whitehead: "No way am I accepting this." ' But he had to.

Creation's financial burden to Rough Trade made McGee's travails with the four desperadoes seem like a day on the beach. However, his sales estimate of 100,000–150,000 for *Mayflower* – which he expected would strengthen his position with Rob Dickins, Max Hole and Paul Conroy – would prove massively over-confident.

One Saturday afternoon in the spring of 1987, McGee was overseeing a photo session in Soho for Nick Currie, the latest addition to the Creation fold. The 26-year-old songwriter – a cousin of Del Amitri's singer, Justin Currie – recorded under the name Momus, the Greek god of laughter and lampoonery. Creation's first intellectual, Nick Currie was a refined Scot with a first-class honours degree in English literature. McGee had pinched him from Mike Alway's label él – now being backed by a forgiving Iain McNay – where Currie had been part of a creative think-tank. 'Nick's motivation seemed to be to have a bit of a "go"; to have some play,' says Alway. 'Although it wasn't in vogue to be a singer-songwriter at that point, you knew there was a place in the future for that kind of character.'

If Cherry Red had been the sort of label on which David Niven might have felt at home, él was more about dissolute earls pissing their allowances up a wall. Some of the artists pretended to be members of a European royal family and the façade of luxury informed Alway's every jape. It was not unheard of for an él sleeve to cost more than the recording of the album inside it. Never less than beautifully photographed, the artwork mixed humour with the Technicolor sensuality and splendour of Powell and Pressburger's *The Red Shoes*. To those who knew about it, él was the British cult indie label *par excellence*.

'The great thing about él was that there was absolutely no commercial pressure whatsoever,' says Currie. 'There was no commercial context for it. We all saw it as a great opportunity to mess around with fantasy.' Well, maybe so. But Currie also saw what Iain McNay was beginning to see: that a lengthy involvement with él would probably leave them both destitute. Unlike Cherry Red in its 1981–3 heyday, él had no support from the press.

As Momus, Currie sang fiendishly clever, minutely detailed songs in a husky Donovan murmur, accompanying himself on an acoustic guitar, one eyebrow raised like a neoteric Jake Thackeray. The songs he wrote ignored the 1980s, preferring to focus on perverse episodes in the Old Testament or rum doings in Ancient Greece. On his album *Circus Maximus*, released by él in January 1986, Currie had set all but one of the songs in a time prior to 100 AD. Like a bored public schoolboy, he would skim through the Bible looking for dirty bits, sculpting lyrics about incest, deviation and impropriety. 'The Bible was the only book my Scottish ancestors had in the house,' he says. 'If they wanted a bit of erotic stimulation on a dark winter's night, they had to read the Song Of Solomon.'

McGee had been one of the *Circus Maximus* album's more unexpected fans. Currie was flattered, but doubted whether McGee had listened too closely to the words. Having not an ounce of rock 'n' roll in his scrawny body, Currie turned up at 83 Clerkenwell Road with a well-thumbed copy of Ovid's *Ars Amatoria* in his pocket. He found that his new boss lacked the breadth of knowledge he was used to finding in the erudite Alway. Currie and McGee couldn't talk about art, literature or films – their references were incompatible. But there were other areas in which McGee scored much higher than Alway, including wiliness, useful contacts and talking an all-action game. 'Alan seemed a lot more machiavellian than Mike,' says Currie. 'When I signed to the label,* one of the first things he said to me was: "I think we can sell you to the yuppie market." He said: "The music industry in London is run by 90 key individuals and I know 85 of them. It's all just a question of power lunches."'

Currie was amused by McGee's up-and-at-'em way of talking, but excited too. He had feared he'd been wooed to Creation to bump up the label's quota of freak exhibits – the zero sellers whom McGee accumulated like Biros. No one had ever been so bold as to tell Currie he had a *market*. Momus duly debuted on Creation with 'Murderers, The Hope Of Women', a three-song EP. For the press shots, McGee took him to an alley off Soho's Berwick Street, where a shabby doorway advertised a 'model' upstairs. McGee thought a louche image might suit the sunken-cheeked Currie; at any rate, it would be a good way of getting around his jumbo-sized IQ.

'It was about five o'clock,' remembers McGee. 'These two black kids came up. I think they thought we were the *News Of The World* trying to take pictures of the clients. I thought: we're going to get fucking battered. They went to take the camera off the guy who was taking the photos. So I said: "I'm with Warner Bros. We own the entire building." When they realised it was a record company shoot, we kept the camera and we got away.' However, McGee and Currie were left feeling jittery. To lift their spirits, McGee started talking about a concept he'd had for a Creation all-girl group. The idea, he told Currie, was to find three girls, record a single, get the front cover of the *NME* and acquire the reputation of a cunning svengali.

The take-three-girls idea was as old as pop music itself. In the mid-80s, the most ubiquitous example was Bananarama who, after a string of Top 10 singles, were about to enter an even more profitable era with Stock, Aitken and Waterman. In the indie sector, Mike Alway was prone to devising all-girl groups for él, while Robert Lloyd had unearthed and nurtured We've Got A Fuzzbox, the punky Midlands quartet, taking them to the top of the indie charts before signing them to WEA as part of a licensing deal for his Vindaloo label.

---

* Not literally. As with all Creation artists during those years, Currie's fifty-fifty deal was unwritten.

But the germ of McGee's idea had actually come from Joe Foster's long-running obsession with Kim Fowley, the notorious American producer who had masterminded the all-girl rock band the Runaways. 'In a breathtakingly blatant exercise in teenage glam-metal exploitation,' recounts *The Rough Guide To Rock*, 'the Runaways had their tender ages printed on the sleeve of their first album, a scam that launched the careers of Joan Jett and ... Lita Ford and generated more column inches than most of Fowley's [other] projects.' *Exactly*.

When McGee told Currie of his intention, Currie suggested they do it right now – go to the Virgin Megastore, a few minutes' walk away in Oxford Street, and look for the three most attractive sales girls. If journalists asked him about the girls' backgrounds, McGee could say truthfully that he had selected them for their looks alone – with no thought for their personalities or abilities – and had propelled them into the limelight like urchins up a chimney. The spuriousness of the exercise would be there for all to see. He and Currie did a quick recce of the Megastore that afternoon.

Over the next week, McGee approached the three girls individually and asked if they would like to be in a band. He didn't ask them if they could sing; that wasn't the point. Or rather it was precisely the point. Buying each one a leather jacket, he named them after a phrase he'd seen on the sleeve of an old Go-Betweens single: Baby Amphetamine. Then he sat down and wrote the lyrics for their single, 'Chernobyl Baby (Who Needs The Government)'.* 'He had a lot of fun doing it,' says Currie. 'I remember him ringing up Martin Costello and singing the lyric down the phone in this really excited way – jumping up and down on the desk singing: "Who needs the Government?" There was a real feeling of playfulness.'

Because it had to have street-level impact, McGee wanted 'Chernobyl Baby ...' to be a hip hop song. He was not completely sold on hip hop as a fan, but he respected it for being political and a means of expressing youthful dissent, and also for being an underground phenomenon – the major record companies had yet to engulf it as they had with punk. ('Alan always had this big thing: "It's happening without the permission of the music business",' remembers Danny Kelly. 'He'd say that all the time about everything, including Creation. It was probably the only thing that could ever justify Creation being what it was.') A hip hop fan named Saul was given the job of putting McGee's lyrics to music. Then McGee rang Danny Kelly to discuss the most important business of all – getting Baby Amphetamine on the cover of the *NME*.

---

* In April 1986, an accident at the Chernobyl nuclear power station in Ukraine caused widespread devastation by radiation. An area estimated at 160,000 square feet – the size of the British Isles – was contaminated.

It says something about the *NME* in 1987 that Baby Amphetamine's lack of any previous musical experience was not the obstacle Kelly had to circumvent to persuade his editor that the group merited a front-page story. Rather, it was the fact that Alan McGee was pulling the strings. The *NME* had no qualms about launching the career of an entirely fabricated band. What bothered it was the ailing reputation of Creation, a label it associated with conservative, 60s-influenced guitar music and a three-year-old single by the Jesus and Mary Chain.

But Kelly held sway, volunteering to write the Baby Amphetamine story himself. Then again, what was the story? 'I can honestly say I never heard "Chernobyl Baby ..." before I wrote the piece,' Kelly admits. 'It probably hadn't even been made yet.' The appearance of Baby Amphetamine on the cover of the *NME* – in the second week of April – smelt of intrigue and impurity, as McGee had hoped it would. Far more interesting to those outside Creation were the three girls' replies to Kelly's questions.

'McGee probably hoped we'd be really dumb,' one of the girls, Jackie, scoffed. 'Tough shit, Alan ..' One of her colleagues, Perule, elaborated: 'If we did this interview like we were told to [by McGee], we'd be saying things like: "Simon Le Bon should be given an acid bath." But all that's so old, so dated. Alan lives in a time warp ..' 'Manipulated?' mused the third girl, Jo. 'Not at all. All that's happened is that someone's thrown a bit of their money [at] us. What a mug ..' She added: 'Let's not get too serious about it – I mean, what's actually happened? We've made a record, and somebody ... has bought us a leather jacket each and been a complete wanker.'

Creation signings the House Of Love happened to be in Clerkenwell the day the *NME* came out. 'I thought: this is really weird,' says their bassist Chris Groothuizen. 'Here's a band ... and the first press they get, they're slagging off their record label. It was vitriol that should have been based on a two-year working relationship.' The House Of Love would never have dared to grouse about Creation – not in public, anyway.

The reason for Baby Amphetamine's displeasure was revealed further down the article. 'We've written some songs of our own now, but McGee's totally uninterested,' complained Perule. Indeed, in a move that McGee had not anticipated, the girls had opted to take control of their own destiny. A turning-of-the-tables had occurred, and it was intriguing to see McGee alarmed by it. It was perfectly sound Situationist procedure, it seemed, for him to treat the girls like puppets. But it appeared it was unacceptable to have strong-willed women making their own decisons on Creation's time and money.

A crude fusion of rap-metal, scatter-shot slogans and pointed digs at Bananarama, 'Chernobyl Baby ..' was a child's idea of hip hop, and Baby Amphetamine's rendition was that of a school bus threesome singing along to a radio. McGee had tired of Baby Amphetamine before the single was even released. For once, he was in the majority: everyone else was sick of them too.

'Chernobyl Baby ...' flickered briefly in the indie Top 10, but denunciations of McGee, Creation and the *NME* echoed for weeks. 'The thing went down with all hands,' says Danny Kelly. 'I took a right load of stick, some of it probably deserved, and the girls went back to working in the Virgin Megastore. But I take the positive view that it's better to have loved and lost than never to have loved at all.'

In the event, McGee emerged from the affair with honours roughly even. Whatever his tongue-lashing by the girls in the *NME*, he noticed his name had been written good and large on the front page, a sign that he could still sell papers. And who cared if Bananarama weren't remotely nettled by Baby Amphetamine, when 'Chernobyl Baby ...' had been given the thumbs-up by Bill Drummond?

'I played it to Drummond,' recalls McGee, 'and I said: "I went into a record shop and picked the three prettiest girls, bought them all leather jackets ..." And Drummond loved it. He was on the desk, punching the air! Two months later, he comes in and he goes: "I'm forming this band, the JAMMs. Do you want to do it?" I said: "What are you doing?" He said: "Sampling ABBA records." I said: "It's too mad, Bill, you'll get sued." He goes: "That's the point." '

Drummond's retirement had not lasted long. His crisis-worms sluiced by *The Man*, he was now poised to re-enter the fray, albeit from an oblique angle. With the Justified Ancients Of Mu Mu (the JAMMs), whom he had founded with the former guitarist in Brilliant, Jimmy Cauty, Drummond was shunning rock 'n' roll and going back to technology. Only this time, he was not going to listen to reason. When the JAMMs' album *1987: What The Fuck Is Going On?* was pressed up in June, immediate litigation followed from ABBA's lawyers. Drummond and Cauty were forced to withdraw the record and surrender their master tapes. The nail-biting controversy made Baby Amphetamine seem all the more prosaic.

Now label-less, Baby Amphetamine made their live debut at London's Limelight club in July. McGee was not in the audience, but he might have approved of the show. The girls left the stage after 15 minutes, having sung 'Chernobyl Baby ...' twice.

'Tired of being cynical?' taunted the double-page advert in the *NME* on 2 May. With these McGee-penned words – a return to the rash reproaches of *Communication Blur* – the major label naturalisation of the Weather Prophets was formalised in shrieking ink. Even some of McGee's closest friends found the advert's tone abhorrent. 'That was McGee's ego,' says Jeff Barrett. 'It wasn't the band's talent.'

Andy Murray, Paul Conroy's deputy in WEA marketing, had

offered McGee two full-page ads for *Mayflower* – one in the *NME* and one in either *Melody Maker* or *Sounds*. McGee had had a better idea: blow the whole budget on an *NME* spread and go for the grand statement. 'Alan was going round telling everyone: "The Weather Prophets are going to be as big as Dire Straits",' recalls Lawrence from Felt. 'He was talking about filling stadiums.' McGee and the Weather Prophets were heading for an almighty comedown.

Mayflower wasn't a deplorable album, but nor was it a very good one. It was an over-polished record, a one-dimensional tinker's curse. And slowly everyone was beginning to realise it. There was nothing on *Mayflower* to suggest that the Weather Prophets would ever find themselves in stadia, attendance of football matches aside. Pete Astor's lyrics, when heard *in toto*, had an unbargained for dreariness: six of the 12 songs mentioned rain, and the other six all sounded as though they were about to. To the band's embarrassment, the album sleeve, designed by WEA's art department, showed them posing in front of a sea-green backdrop more suited to a naval academy graduation photograph. Was this how they intended to win the student vote?

Mayflower was released a week after the Jesus and Mary Chain's sixth single 'April Skies', a Top 10 hit which earned the Reid brothers their long-awaited three minutes on *Top Of The Pops*. More inconveniently for the Weather Prophets – and for Elevation – *Mayflower* came out in the same month as Fleetwood Mac's *Tango In The Night*, and only a matter of weeks after Prince's *Sign 'O' The Times* and Simply Red's *Men And Women* – just about the three most attention-grabbing albums in WEA's calendar year. In Paul Conroy's marketing meetings, *Mayflower* did not got a look-in.

It charted at number 67, which would have been remarkable had the band been on Creation, but was no use at all to Rob Dickins. With discomfiting speed, the wheels started falling off the cart. Everybody now hated *Mayflower*. Radio promotions hated it, A&R hated it, marketing hated it, Dickins hated it. McGee also hated it and so did the band. There wasn't one single person who liked it. 'It was a very nervous, furry-walled studio album,' says Astor in retrospect. 'It didn't capture the vibe. It's that whole anal, antiseptic way of making records that's ruined millions of good albums. People not understanding how to record a rock 'n' roll band. That was a lost art for many years.'

The result for the Weather Prophets was humiliation. Defiant, McGee refused to cooperate in any way with WEA's post-mortem. It hadn't gone Top 40? The record company's problem, not his. The sales were disappointing? Served them right for not giving it a bigger push. 'I don't care if this sounds like the most pretentiously wanky statement of all time,' McGee told the *NME*. 'All right, so Alan McGee's a wanker. But I really do believe that right now it's Creation

– including Elevation – against the whole business. Creation's intent is to destroy the current standards of the music biz … And of course Elevation allows me to be a thorn in the side of that business. You don't have to be that outspoken, either. If you've got one original thing to say, or step one inch away from the company line, they think you're a bloody anarchist!'

'Alan was very uncomfortable in Warners meetings,' notes Mick Houghton, 'because he always went by gut reaction and instinct, and he couldn't believe that you'd sit in these meetings with guys that didn't like music. Well, if you work for major record companies, the last thing they know about – or care about – is music. Alan wasn't slow to grasp that. He just didn't want to.'

That was true. McGee didn't want to be corrupted by the great-record-now-how-do-we-market-it thinking of the four desperadoes, but he knew he couldn't hold out forever. 'I remember Alan coming back from some meeting,' says Nick Currie, 'and saying: "I hate that world and I hate those people, but I'm probably going to turn into one of them in a few years' time." ' However, in losing patience with WEA, McGee was letting indie-minded myopia blind him to the realities. 'I don't think they could tell the difference between the Weather Prophets and the Jesus and Mary Chain,' he says now. 'It was just that one of them sold and one of them didn't.' Surely, that *was* the difference between the Weather Prophets and the Jesus and Mary Chain?

Although he was the Weather Prophets' publicist, Mick Houghton had little liking for their music and tended to see Astor as a fair song-writer who had neither the powerful voice nor the force of personality to appeal to listeners in large numbers. Houghton suspected the same could be said of almost every band on Creation too. In a sense, the only real personality connected to Creation or Elevation was McGee himself. It wasn't much of a tribute to his groups.

Following his interview with Danny Kelly in April, however, McGee rarely spoke on the record to the music papers for the next seven years. Coming out of Baby Amphetamine and *Mayflower*, he worried people might think he was a hoaxer, a motormouth with no substance. He resolved to remind them that he was first and foremost a music lover and record maker. And at Clerkenwell, there was much work to be done.

9 R. in the I.

OMUS WAS A TALENTED songwriter but his records were going way over most people's heads. Felt were having problems in Birmingham making a new album with the American producer Mayo Thompson. The Bodines had departed for the more established label Magnet. And the House Of Love, whose debut single 'Shine On' had been released in May, were not liked by anybody at 83 Clerkenwell Road apart from Alan and Yvonne McGee. Standards and energy levels were slipping, and the widespread view was that Creation's best days had gone.

'There were comments at the time – and they weren't meant to be flattering – about Creation becoming the new Cherry Red,' says Nick Currie. 'But in a way McGee was like: "Whatever moves, sign it." ' Indeed, while McGee had always congratulated himself for not being suckered into ill-advised signings ('unlike Geoff Travis,' he would add with a smirk) he had started picking up as many acts as he could, and this was to become Creation policy as the years went by. 'The view was that the more we get out, the more cash is going to be generated,' says Dick Green. 'But we weren't thinking in terms of profit. It was literally: if we keep putting it out, it's going to keep coming back in.'

Creation's mid-1987 intake included David Westlake (ex-Servants), Jill Bryson from Strawberry Switchblade, Phil Wilson of the defunct June Brides, and a Brighton group called Blow Up. All of these acts faced a money problem, and some would have to wait months before getting their chance in a studio. And when they had made the record, they would then face a promotion problem. Jeff Barrett was good at hustling reviews in the music weeklies, but these would often constitute a Creation record's entire promotional and marketing campaign. 'We were getting Janice Long plays,' Barrett argues. 'I think we were as big as you could get for records like that. "How do we now break these bands?" – which would be an issue in any record company today – was never, ever actually addressed. There were never any meetings to say: "Right, how do we do this?" There was no fucking money. We were all still on the Enterprise Allowance

Scheme.' And when McGee did acquire an artist worth having – someone with a cachet, a name and a pedigree – he accidentally fast-tracked him on to Elevation.

The solo career of Edwyn Collins was one of the more inexplicable riddles thrown up by the music business in 1987. Unwanted by any of the major labels, and discounted by the industry at large as a troublemaker and a spent force, Collins was in the strange position of having no record deal yet still being able to fill sizeable venues every time he played concerts. 'We would have fifteen hundred people at the Town and Country Club,' he says. 'But this didn't seem to impress the A&R fraternity.* I had alienated them and made a lot of enemies.'

By chance, Collins and Grace Maxwell – his girlfriend and manager – bumped into Colin Wallace, a mutual acquaintance of theirs and McGee's. 'Colin said: "Listen, McGee's really enthusiastic and you should go with him",' recalls Collins. 'At that time Creation seemed like the last resort. But we thought: well, why not? At least somebody's enthusiastic. We phoned McGee up and we went down ... for a meeting. Grace was quite cynical about getting involved, but one thing [McGee] said seemed to make sense. He said: "You can't just trade on your past reputation." '

The news of Collins' signing was leaked in McGee's April interview with Danny Kelly. McGee, typically, named the former Orange Juice man as one of several Creation artists – Jill Bryson, Felt, Blow Up and the House Of Love were the others – whose music deserved to be in the Top 40. 'They're all making song-based music and the chart is 99 per cent rhythm-based,' he said, 'but we'll take it on.' Take it on and get nowhere, did he mean?

Collins had doubled back on his soul and funk obsessions of the early 80s and was now talking privately of rock music being the way forward. On the face of it, his reconversion made him an ideal candidate for Creation. Beneath the surface, however, it was not that simple. Collins found it hard to get attuned to what McGee was up to, and regarded the other Creation acts as lame ducks. If anything, he feared McGee was anti-rock; too locked into the 60s to appreciate the visceral kick of – for example – Keith Forsey's rattling, ultra-modern productions for Billy Idol. Collins worried that Creation might be a Luddites' ghetto.

'Don't Shilly Shally' – Collins' intended first 45 for Creation – was an unabashed 80s production and, sure enough, McGee didn't like it. Apprehensive about its commercial prospects, he also doubted it was lusty enough to effect a return to critical favour for the one-time cult hero. He told Collins he would be releasing it reluctantly. Within a

---

* Collins played the London venue twice, first in December 1986 and again six months later.

matter of days, McGee had an abrupt about-turn. 'He comes over one morning and he goes: "I've changed my mind, it's a fucking classic",' recalls Collins. 'He got so enthusiastic about it that he went up and played it to Rob Dickins. By this time we'd pressed up some copies. Dickins thought it was some kind of acetate or demo, and he said: "Yeah, we'll go with it." So it suddenly got transferred to Elevation.'

Elevation – to which Collins was promptly contracted for 'Don't Shilly Shally' and a follow-up single – was a different ball game entirely, and one in which Collins was more experienced than McGee. After three up-and-down years on Polydor, he could recognise the signs of a major label going through the motions. He guessed that Elevation was Dickins' way of humouring McGee without fully subsidising his vision.

'In Orange Juice we had this phrase "r. in the i.,"' says Collins, 'which stood for "respect in the industry". There are certain artists and individuals who have respect within the music industry. Dave Stewart is a person who comes to mind as someone who is very, very cosy with the industry. Or Kate Bush or Annie Lennox, who automatically receive Best Female Artist at the Brits. That is industry respect. Back then, McGee had zero industry respect. It's undeniable that Rob Dickins liked him and thought he had potential, but McGee had no status within the company, no influence within the company. WEA was having a little punt on the Weather Prophets and that's as far as it was going to go.'

When WEA ordered a derisory pressing-run for 'Don't Shilly Shally' (Collins insists the figure was as low as 1,000; he played to larger audiences in an evening), it looked as though Collins' comeback was destined to be a fair old *Mayflower* of a damp squib. 'Edwyn wasn't taken seriously at all because it was a singles deal only,' says Graham Carpenter. 'It's a terrible thing to say, but that's how it worked. It was a bloody fiasco.'

Collins was furious. If Dickins didn't want him, why not just say so? In the search for explanations – however irrational – Collins was disconcerted to hear that his height had been the subject of boardroom criticism. 'McGee reckoned that Rob Dickins had a Napoleon complex,' he recalls. 'Apparently he once said: "Edwyn's far too tall to ever be really successful. Look at the successful musicians: Prince, Roger Daltrey, Jagger … All my favourite artists are small." '

Of medium height and build, Pete Astor was introduced to Collins by McGee at an indie club one night in the summer of 1987. Collins had been hearing a lot about the Weather Prophets and most of it didn't add up. Even dividing by ten to make allowances for McGee's hyperbole, Collins couldn't get over the fact that the Weather Prophets were so … *ordinary*. Who'd ever imagined them as saviours of British rock? Why the big fuss about Astor? 'Pete was a nice enough guy, but a real hippy,' says Collins. 'I got talking to him about

Lenny Kaye and he said: "You know, the problem with Lenny is he doesn't have the vibe." I said: "Well, I hate that word. It's so nebulous. It doesn't mean anything." He said: "Do you not know what vibe means?" I said: "No I don't." He said: "Well, listen. You've got the vibe. I've got the vibe. But Lenny will never have the vibe." I thought: what the fuck is this boy talking about?'

The 'Don't Shilly Shally' débâcle notwithstanding, Collins, who had almost twice the audience of Primal Scream and the Weather Prophets, was the biggest concert draw on Elevation's roster. Smarting from his treatment by WEA, he was looking forward to stealing the show at the New Music Seminar in New York in July, when he and the other Elevation acts would perform in front of American executives, journalists, agents and representatives from college radio and MTV. Visas for the three acts were requested from the American embassy in London. Two would be refused.

The House Of Love made their first single, 'Shine On', at Livingston Studios. For the two-day recording, McGee took a co-producer's role with the band's singer and rhythm guitarist Guy Chadwick. As a producer, McGee knew only one trick: reverb, short for reverberation, a favourite effect of the Mary Chain. 'More reverb ... more,' McGee kept insisting, until the definition of 'Shine On' was blurred enough to appease his indie-tuned ears.

Written by Chadwick, 'Shine On' was a haunted allegory in the spirit of Blue Oyster Cult's '(Don't Fear) The Reaper'. Even with so much reverb, Chadwick's deep voice and lead guitarist Terry Bickers' tintinnabulary motifs surfaced effortlessly, interlocking four times on the cyclical, locomotive choruses. On the first evening, as everyone sat down to dinner in good humour, McGee made an announcement.

'Yvonne had cooked us lasagne,' recalls bassist Chris Groothuizen, 'and as we start to eat, Alan looks at us and goes: "I have just signed the best band in the world." And we all look at each other and think: wow, what a nice thing to say. And he goes: "They're called Blow Up." I honestly thought: you fucking twat. How can you, in the middle of our first single, just announce that you've signed the best band in the world – and it's somebody else?'

McGee's thoughtless remark is a good illustration of Creation's attitude towards the House Of Love in 1987. He was not sure that the band's style – a powerfully psychedelic noise peppered with guitar effects – was right for his label. Their songs had erotic undercurrents that hinted at bedroom politics, sado-masochism and outré reading matter, and Chadwick's intonation postured with ambiguous flicks of the tongue and metaphorically sucked in cheeks. In the normal course of events, this was not McGee's scene at all.

Nor did it rock the socks off Dick Green. A year before, he had rejected the House Of Love's demo tape, brusquely cutting Chadwick short when he rang to check on its arrival. During the same period, Jeff Barrett refused to give the band a gig at Bay 63 (where he had taken over as promoter from Cerne Canning and Simon Esplen), telling Chadwick: 'Your tape's rubbish. I don't want to talk to you.' When a second demo tape was sent to Creation some months later, it was Yvonne McGee who latched on to 'Shine On', playing it so often that her husband relented and went to see the band at the Marquee club. He phoned Chadwick a few days later and called him in for a meeting. But Chadwick was made to wait in reception while McGee finished a long conversation with Pete Astor. Emerging at last, McGee shook Chadwick's hand and asked him how old he was. Twenty-five, Chadwick replied. McGee smiled and told him he could pass for 22. Then the smile disappeared and McGee pulled the House Of Love apart piece by piece.

Your songs are far too long, he began by saying. Cut them all by at least four minutes, and while you're at it, play them faster. You wasted too much time at the Marquee; do 20-minute sets and get off quick. 'Shine On' is a good song but it's too fussy – lose a couple of the passing chords that lead up to the chorus. And your image is all over the place. Get yourself some leather jackets.

Chadwick was stunned, but he accepted the criticisms. He was impressed by the charismatic McGee, who spoke quietly and earnestly, maintaining intense eye contact and exuding a grave authority. 'It was a very strong first impression,' Chadwick remembers. 'He gave me a hundred quid to rehearse and he said: "I want to do a single. I don't do contracts." I was very aware of what that implied. I'd had a record contract and I'd been on tour and I'd had a publishing deal. But from my own point of view, Creation looked a much more exciting set-up.'

Chadwick was to learn that McGee did not like being messed around. When the House Of Love presented a song called 'Christine' as a potential debut single, McGee waved it aside, telling Chadwick it would be 'Shine On' or nothing. And he would be there for every minute of the recording and mixing. McGee had never taken such a heavy-handed tone with a band before. Whilst he had in the past made music-related suggestions to Primal Scream or to Astor, or critiqued a Creation record once it was too late to go back and change it, his handling of the House Of Love – which was unusually perceptive – saw him reach new heights as an arbiter and editor. It is important to explain the reasons for this.

McGee had not expected any significant financial comeback from most of the records he released in 1986 and 1987. A case in point was Bill Drummond's *The Man*, which had specialist appeal only. With Nikki Sudden, Felt, the Jasmine Minks, Slaughter Joe and Revolving Paint Dream, McGee could predict accurately how many records would be sold, and determine his budgets accordingly. In the House Of Love, however, he foresaw massive critical and commercial interest – enough to arrest Creation's decline and silence those who accused him of not having found a genuinely meaningful group since the Mary Chain. It was imperative for Creation to be seen to be backing a winner. The perception of the label in most corners of the media was of a nostalgio-classicist Blimp whose forays into humour – notably Baby Amphetamine – had backfired horribly; a label whose passionate love for the 60s dulled it to the present, where it had only limited relevance or influence.

The House Of Love were the first example of McGee taking a band and trying to mould it into a finished article. The indie sector's long-established practice of giving musicians a sympathetic environment in which to create with absolute freedom – a practice McGee had been proud to uphold since 1983 – went sailing out of the window. In his A&R relationship with the House Of Love, he would particularise in a way that most of his artists would have found intolerable. (In fact, some express surprise that the House Of Love allowed McGee to have *any* say in their music.) Because they were not his friends, there was no obligation on McGee to toss rose petals in the House Of Love's path. For a full year, there would be little emotion in the relationship beyond a basic rapport.

The House Of Love's studied angst and chi chi lyrics were, McGee knew, the sort of qualities that would nauseate as many people as they aroused. Some of the band's fiercest critics would come from inside Creation. The deeply sceptical Jeff Barrett would become the House Of Love's press officer, promising to get them as much publicity as he could provided he didn't ever have to say he liked them. Another detractor – Dick Green – would have to grin and bear their remarkable ascent. Over the next eighteen months, Creation would experience a renaissance in popularity and credibility, selling more records than ever before. And most of them would be sold by the House Of Love.

The 1987 Glastonbury Festival featured performances by two of Alan McGee's bands, Felt and the Weather Prophets. 'We were playing on the second stage,' recalls the latter's Dave Goulding. 'We travelled up in Oisin [Little]'s van with a lot of his mates and a PA speaker in the back playing funk massively loud until the van was wobbling. The mirror came off the front window and all weekend it never went back on. We were just constantly chopping out lines of coke.'

The Weather Prophets had been touring *Mayflower*, comforting their hurt pride by availing themselves of rock star clothes and poses. Leather trousers were mandatory. Dave Goulding had taken a leaf out of Jim Beattie's book and donned a cowboy hat. He'd also grown a beard. Up and down Britain's motorways, the Weather

Prophets watched, rewound and watched again a video of *Gimme Shelter*, the documentary about the Rolling Stones' Altamont festival in 1969. Pete Astor even wrote a song about Altamont's horrifying conclusion, the fatal stabbing of a teenager by Hell's Angels. But after the gentle rain of *Mayflower*, there were long odds on a Weather Prophets thunderstorm.

Only at Glastonbury was there a downpour, making the ground muddy underfoot and leading many to wonder how Lawrence from Felt would fare in the conditions. A cell of Creation scenesters had gathered backstage when Lawrence suddenly hove into view, glancing balefully at his dry-cleaned trousers and polished shoes. He looked utterly miserable. 'He's got mud on his shoes and he is *stricken*,' says Danny Kelly. ' "Hi, Lawrence, how are you doing?" "Not good." I said: "What do you mean?" He says: "I thought there would be cottages for the pop stars." Cottages for the pop stars!'

Lawrence had deceived the organisers into giving Felt a late-evening time slot as they were using Pink Floyd's light-show. In truth, they had one light that had once belonged to the Floyd – among many that hadn't – but although they walked onstage in romantic twilight they had been poorly miked up, rendering their first three songs inaudible to the crowd. Lawrence's first Glastonbury had been yet another career disappointment. Tsk.

To be allocated an H visa for the United States in 1987, British entertainers needed to satisfy the American Immigration and Naturalization Office that their act was of sufficient interest to the US public. Since 1985, the office had been thought to be taking a harder line on British groups wishing to tour the States. 'The bigger the name ... the easier it is to get into America,' said Musicians Union spokesman Jan Ford in 1986. 'With smaller [bands], there is naturally a greater degree of suspicion.' Edwyn Collins was given a visa to travel to the New Music Seminar in New York, but the Weather Prophets and Primal Scream failed in their applications. Collins offered to fly to the seminar and represent Elevation as a solo artist. WEA said no.

'It was sour grapes,' says Collins. 'They had paid out big advances for the Weather Prophets and Primal Scream, and yet the rank outsider in their eyes is the one that's getting interest from New York.' Worryingly for the Weather Prophets, whose album had not been released in America, Warner Bros in New York appeared to have no interest in the group whatsoever. As for Primal Scream's album ... well, there was no album yet.

Prior to re-recording *Hollywood Hell*, the Scream made a return to ULU in June. This was to be the last sighting of John 'the Joogs' Martin. Described by Danny Kelly in the *NME* as 'a tambourine-flaying skeleton in leather gloves', Martin had been victimised by his colleagues on account of having a girlfriend they disliked. 'They were always a band that would have somebody they would pick on,' says McGee, 'and he had become the target. I think he got a bit paranoid. There was this picture of Primal Scream on the dressing-room door at ULU, and I cruelly tore him out of the picture.' In the hotel that night, Jim Beattie and Bobby Gillespie played what they called 'creepy-crawl', a term used by the Manson Family to denote a sinister form of housebreaking. Beattie and Gillespie scratched on the door of Martin's room, whispering to his girlfriend: 'Fuck off, bitch ... fuck off ...' The next morning, there was no sign of the couple.

Convening at Pat Collier's new studio, Greenhouse, the diminished Primal Scream recorded their album – now retitled *Sonic Flower Groove* – with Collier as engineer and Mayo Thompson as producer. An old friend of Geoff Travis', Thompson was a bearded Texan who had sung and played guitar in the Red Crayola, a cult American band of the 60s. In the late 70s and early 80s, he had produced records for Rough Trade by Stiff Little Fingers, the Fall, the Monochrome Set and others. By the mid-80s, he was being approached by indie acts such as Felt, the Chills, the Shop Assistants and Phil Wilson, and was admired immeasurably by Alan McGee and Bobby Gillespie.

If Phil Wilson had found the Texan to have a calming presence in the studio, Lawrence deemed Thompson's production of Felt's latest album, *Poem Of The River*, so awful that he contemplated throwing the tapes off a bridge. The six tracks on *Poem Of The River* suffered from muffled sound, as though they had been recorded through a sock.

At Greenhouse, Mayo Thompson had precisely the same problems as Stephen Street when it came to recording Bobby Gillespie, who wanted to drop in his vocals line by line. 'They were fairly bonkers at the time,' says Pat Collier. 'Lovely to be with, brilliant fun. But poor Mayo had a nightmare with Bobby. I didn't envy him his job at all.' Besides taking up a lot of time, the vocal-comping process removed, as if by surgery, virtually all the feeling from Gillespie's voice. Like everything else on *Sonic Flower Groove*, the vocals sounded sterile and reheated. 'Those sessions got very bogged down towards the end,' recalled Collier two years later. 'Plus Jim – the guitarist – would say things like: "Can you make my guitar more satanic?" and I hadn't got a clue what he meant.' In short, *Sonic Flower Groove* was another *Mayflower*.

'Gentle Tuesday' was released as Primal Scream's first single on Elevation in June, followed by the Langer-produced 'Imperial' in September. As feared, the Scream's upgrade in production had no effect on sales or radio, and neither song reached the Top 75. Support for the Scream within WEA was crucially undermined. Arguably the only band with less bargaining power at the company was the Weather Prophets, whose contract came up for renegotiation in

September. 'There was money, but not an idiotic amount of money,' says Pete Astor. 'The next advance was about £70,000 and we would have gone to LA and made the record. They said: "Who do you want as producer?" so I wrote a letter saying "Pete Astor's going to be producing the next LP – this is what we want".' WEA called his bluff and dropped the Weather Prophets immediately.

Asked for a comment by the *NME*, McGee complained bitterly about the corporate thinking at WEA 'which cannot deal with sales below the level of Madonna or Prince'. Dickins let him say his piece. It was obvious that the axe would fall next on Primal Scream. On 1 October, at the end of an eight-date tour to promote 'Imperial', they played – and filled – the Town and Country club. Only Graham Carpenter was there from WEA to see it.

The Weather Prophets returned to the Creation roster, but not before McGee dragged them round a few companies to see if any were interested. After an unsuccessful meeting with IRS – which had REM and the Cramps – McGee and the leather-trousered Weather Prophets were walking past the WEA building in Kensington when they looked up to see Carpenter in the window. 'He was flicking V-signs and mouthing: "*Fuck* off . . .",' says Dave Goulding. 'It was hilarious. I love him forever for doing that.'

Sonic Flower Groove came out in October, charting at number 62. It might as well have not charted at all. When Primal Scream toured Germany the following month, the album was not being promoted and the vultures were circling overhead. 'They were at their lowest ebb,' says Nick Currie, who was the support act. 'Jim Beattie was very strange, very paranoid, sitting on a basketball and saying: "Slow down, Luke [Hayes, driver], slow down." He thought we were going to crash the van [because of] the drugs.'

On the tour, Gillespie was hanging out with James Williamson, *né* Julian Halibut, a young enthusiast of the Marquis de Sade and Aleister Crowley who had renamed himself after a Stooges guitarist of the early 70s. 'The two of them together were just like Beavis and Butthead at the back of the classroom throwing ink pellets,' says Currie. 'It was just this kind of incredibly immature "we're tremendously cool" attitude . . . But I found Bobby to be very interesting, because he's based everything on attitude and what they call subcultural capital, which is the accumulation of hipness – a rather calculated and canny understanding of hipness. He's an intellectual bully, though. If you don't like the same records that he likes, he's going to be pretty nasty.'

In October, Graham Carpenter left WEA to work for Polydor. His replacement was Malcolm Dunbar, brought in as grand vizier of A&R. As is common with major labels, Dunbar was given the freedom to ditch some of the acts he had inherited, clearing the slate for fresh faces and new relationships. Although it was a Dickins-McGee *fait accompli*, Dunbar took a close interest in Elevation – not least because one of its artists was his old Polydor oppo Edwyn Collins. 'The feeling I got,' says Dunbar, 'was that Elevation was an OK investment and an experiment on Rob's part, and where was it going? Was it going anywhere? Possibly not.'

Collins' second single for Elevation, 'My Beloved Girl', was released in November. By now, as far as Collins could establish, McGee's famous supplies of optimism and energy had almost totally run out. McGee not only hated 'My Beloved Girl' but expressed serious reservations about the photograph on the sleeve, in which Collins wore a leopardskin waistcoat and a silver shirt. 'He was appalled,' remembers Collins. 'The first thing he said was: "You're going to alienate the anoraks." Alan called them the anoraks. By that he meant the shy indie kids ... He was always saying to me, either directly or indirectly: "Don't rock the boat. Understand your market." '

When 'My Beloved Girl' failed to chart, a confrontation between McGee and Malcolm Dunbar was inevitable. They had met on several previous occasions and were, in some respects, like-minded, volatile characters. However, they were not competing on equal terms in the autumn of 1987. Dunbar had been a success at Polydor (where he had signed Lloyd Cole) and at Island (where he had supervised the company's best-selling album by a debuting group, the Christians). In comparison, Elevation was transparently an Alan McGee failure. It did not take long for the arguments to get personal.

'He took me into a room and had a real lairy go,' recalls McGee. 'He was telling me how I'd done it all wrong, and how Primal Scream would never make it. I said: "What the fuck do you know anyway? All you like is yuppie music, you cunt." It was a really intense argument.' McGee was used to being told he would never have a hit with Primal Scream – people had been saying it for the best part of three years. But after twelve months of frustration with WEA, he was close to violence. 'I was up for smacking [Dunbar],' he says. 'He knew that I wasn't beyond picking up a chair and putting it over his head.'

Edwyn Collins knew the game was up. 'Unlike McGee, Dunbar had real power at the company,' he says. 'He was in a very prestigious A&R position and one of the first things he did was to drop me.' Unsatisfied with Elevation's first-year performance – although the losses were, he concedes in retrospect, not as colossal as they seemed at the time – Rob Dickins asked McGee for names of acts to steer them through a second cycle. The first name McGee produced out of the hat was Momus. Dickins didn't wait to hear the others. In January 1988, WEA officially severed contact with Elevation. McGee returned to the independent sector without having made a dent.

Also severed was McGee's relationship with Edwyn Collins. McGee's disinclination to go in and bat for 'My Beloved Girl' had offended Collins, who declined to follow the Weather Prophets and Primal Scream back to Creation. As the swami of indie guitar-pop found himself without a record contract once again, the Creation catalogue number CRE 047, which had been assigned to 'Don't Shilly Shally' but not used, would remain abidingly blank, symbolising the mistake of his move to WEA – the mistake of Elevation.

While McGee's concentration had been elsewhere, 1987 had been a royally forgettable year for Creation. Baby Amphetamine and the House Of Love aside, the label seemed to be cornering the market in obscure, low-selling singer-songwriters – Phil Wilson, David Westlake, Heidi Berry, even Clive Langer for one 45 – some of whom McGee was more serious about than others. Wilson had been given an ample spend for his single 'Waiting For A Change', which emerged in a variety of potentially collectible formats. But there hadn't been many collectors and McGee was unwilling to risk further outgoings on a Wilson album. And then there was Westlake.

Westlake was an insular 22-year-old from Middlesex with talent to burn as a lyricist and tunesmith – the Servants' second and final single, 'The Sun, A Small Star', had been an underrated indie highlight of 1986 – but his flair was counterbalanced by an unseemly hauteur. 'Westlake was a real egomaniac,' says Lawrence. 'He thought he was bigger than his band and it wasn't true.' For a few months, McGee nurtured Westlake like a junior Astor, seeming to feel he owed him something. 'One time Alan said to someone: "Oh, I've got to make Dave a star because I told him to break his band up",' Westlake recalls. 'What could I say? "No you didn't?"'

Westlake's artless gimme-gimme-gimme-ing made him few friends at Creation – and he soon fell out with his former supporter Jeff Barrett, who refused to handle his press. When his mini-album, *Westlake*, was followed by a typical bout of Clerkenwell prevarication, Westlake took to badgering McGee by phone, demanding to know when the stardom he'd been promised would be arriving. 'When it means everything to you, it's like that Alan Partridge thing,' he says. 'He's begging the BBC Head of Light Entertainment [to give his chat-show a second series] and the guy's saying: "Look, Alan, I really don't think ..." And suddenly Partridge just comes out with: "Give me another series, you shit." And that is what you do in that situation.' McGee booted Westlake off Creation.

Clive Langer's single 'Even Though', recorded three years earlier with Elvis Costello's pianist Steve Nieve, was another in a continuing series of Creation one-offs. As a songwriter, Langer was hardly a novice – he had co-written the famous 'Shipbuilding' with Costello – so what he was doing on Creation was anybody's guess. In return for the rights to 'Even Though', he received a cash sum of £200, which he and McGee spent on champagne in the pub across the road. It was a rare instance of the high life being lived at Clerkenwell, but it was certainly not the first occasion the entire office had decamped to the Duke Of York for the day. 'The office at Clerkenwell never really seemed like a record company,' says Mick Houghton. 'There was always plenty of time to go to the pub for three hours and stay there for another three.'

'There weren't dire financial straits,' argues Dick Green, 'because there was nothing to support. Rough Trade did all the manufacturing, so we didn't have to spend money on that. We weren't paying advances to bands, so we had zero overhead. It was a lot simpler then.' In lieu of living expenses, some Creation artists would help themselves to faulty records returned by the shops, scratching off the stickers with alcohol and razor blades to make their value soar by a few extra pence. It might make the difference between a half of lager and a pint.

In November, McGee broke up with his wife. They had married young, had already separated once and had grown increasingly estranged. 'You realise that you want different things,' says McGee. 'Yvonne wanted a family and suburban life, and I wanted to take on the world.' His emotions went haywire that month and he drank fearlessly. There were a few people in his circle who reached out to him – Ed Ball of the *Times* became a close friend and drinking partner – but the best advice came from an erstwhile ally at WEA. 'I had half an idea of selling Creation,' says McGee. 'It was a fleeting moment of madness which I had occasionally for about two hours. Graham Carpenter said to me: "Don't ever sell it. That would be giving in. It's cost you loads – your health, your marriage. Don't give up now."'

Nick Roughley, the singer in Blow Up, found McGee accommodation in Brighton, where he would base himself for the next year and a half. 'Because Brighton's so gay, I ended up living with these two old gay guys, renting a flat in their house,' McGee recalls. 'I used to go out and and they'd tidy up my flat for me. It was as if you were living with your two grannies or something. They were about 60. They'd be going: "We did your washing, Mr McGee . . ."'

Although he had decided not to sell Creation, McGee was uncertain where the future lay. The House Of Love's first two singles, 'Shine On' and 'Real Animal', had sold far less than expected, and their debut album, soon to be recorded at Greenhouse, would put more pressure than ever on Creation's bank account. As much as he saw the House Of Love achieving success one day, he was hard pushed to ward off an autumnal crisis of confidence. Ed Ball visited him in Brighton towards the end of 1987, finding him in reflective mood. 'He told me: "This is what we've got coming up",' says Ball. 'He was like: "The House Of Love are going to be big. Momus is going to be big. The Weather Prophets are reinventing themselves . . ." It wasn't bluster – he wasn't banging the table. It was more like: "Things have been tough but I'm going forward again." '

Recording at Greenhouse concurrently to the House Of Love were the Weather Prophets, trying not to look too peeved about their bare minimum Creation budget of £4,000. Astor was hopeful that the group would be able to carry on as though Elevation hadn't happened; Dave Goulding worried that it might not work like that. 'The main thing was we'd alienated everybody,' Goulding says. 'I hadn't been in on the indie scene from the beginning. I didn't realise the strength of that punky ethos. We'd alienated our audience and the knives were out for us in the press. I didn't have major hopes for the next album.'

Astor was certainly a changed animal from the presidential candidate of twelve months before. Not remotely fazed by being dropped by WEA, he even spoke of his relief at being free of them. This was not the reaction of an aspiring pop star. To Lawrence, who had seen Astor very much as a contender, the change was a big surprise. 'He was going: "Oh, I'm so glad to be back on Creation",' Lawrence recalls. 'I said: "You're joking! You were on Warner Bros, aren't you bothered?" I just thought: God, he's not ambitious after all. I'd thought he was a really ambitious guy. I think he saw a bit of it, didn't like it and came back.'

Slimmed down to a trio following the departure of Oisin Little, the Weather Prophets made their album with Pat Collier, struggling to rebuild their damaged reputation with some potent and angry rock songs. Astor's guitar playing was at times exceptional, and the album – *Judges, Juries & Horsemen* – would be promoted to the press by Jeff Barrett as Britain's long-awaited answer to Big Star's underground classic *Radio City*. However, there was a large fly in the Weather Prophets' ointment.

The House Of Love – for it was they – had convinced Barrett to put them on at the Black Horse in Camden Town. From the reaction of the crowd, he could tell the band was on the verge of a breakthrough. Its five-piece line-up had been reduced to a quartet in November when one of the guitarists, Andrea Heukamp, left on the eve of dates in Holland with Echo and the Bunnymen. With Heukamp gone, the other four had toughened up and stretched out, returning to London a stunning live act. Astor was at the Black Horse to see them, critiquing with a nervous grin. 'Pete Astor was a scared man,' says Barrett. 'He saw what I saw – that the House Of Love were going to be fucking massive.' During one psychedelic-sounding number, Astor guffawed: 'They're Hawkwind! They're terrible!' Barrett nodded. 'I was thinking: yeah, but Pete ... they've fucked you, mate.'

At £12,000, the House Of Love's album cost three times as much as *Judges, Juries & Horsemen*, and the last few thousand came from McGee's own bank account. While it is true that, as Guy Chadwick remembers, 'the smart money was on Blow Up' to take Creation into 1988, the emotional currency was all on the House Of Love. Even as Chadwick fretted that their album might not be good enough, McGee was committing himself to the band 100 per cent. He started phoning Chadwick late at night from Brighton, wanting to know more about a song on the album called 'Man To Child'. McGee was fascinated by this tender ballad, playing it to the point of obsession. 'He was getting a hard time from other people on the label who were very fond of Yvonne,' says Chadwick. 'It was a close-knit label. And I was sympathetic to him because I knew what he was going through.' Chadwick had been divorced himself. Along with 'Man To Child', this was one of the factors that cemented his bond with McGee.

In November, Biff Bang Pow! toured with Felt in Europe, where McGee lost control of his drinking and consumed a bottle of vodka a day. When a promoter in Germany refused to give him any more alcohol, McGee chased him round the venue in a fury until the man locked himself in his office. 'One time we were playing,' McGee recalls, 'and I threw a bottle of vodka into the air, kept singing and forgot about it. It came down and hit me on the head, nearly knocked me out. At the end of the gig, I trashed the dressing-room. There were polystyrene walls and I was putting chairs through them. Dick stopped me and said: "What the fuck are you doing?" I said: "It's good fun." And he said: "All right," and he started doing it too.'

By February 1988 – the month that their 'She Haunts' 45 became the fiftieth single released by Creation – Biff Bang Pow! were in France on a four-week tour with Momus. Nick Currie, a Francophile, was McGee's interpreter, but the only words he had to translate were profanities as the tour lurched from one disaster to another. 'We were playing snack bars by the time we got to Toulouse,' says Currie. '[The gig was] somewhere on the outskirts of town, and 20 people turned up. The contract said Biff Bang Pow! had to play for 40 minutes, but they stopped after 35. The promoter had a big argument with Alan and Alan threw his drink in the promoter's face.'

Dick Green, who had a medical condition that made him prone to sneezing fits, was no happier. 'One gig was during the day and it was in a big gymnasium while a trades fair exhibition was going on,' he remembers. 'On one side there were people doing hairdressing demonstrations and there was us stuck in the middle.' Currie watched Biff Bang Pow! disintegrate in an alcoholic haze. 'They would do these really rocking-out encores,' he says, 'and Dick, who's this quite introverted guy, would suddenly roll around on his back on the stage. After one gig, which was in a disco in the middle of a field somewhere, he said: "We came, we saw, we fucked it up." A very unlikely rock animal.'

There is nothing like playing a string of under-attended gigs in makeshift venues on foreign soil to make a group ask profound questions of itself. Biff Bang Pow! abandoned the French tour after ten days and Currie honoured the final engagements himself. 'There was an article in *Libération* about it,' he recalls. ' "Momus, disgusted by the attitude of his boss, continues the tour alone ..." I did feel Alan was a bit rude. When he got off the ferry, he was saying: "Isn't France great? It's so civilised." But by the end of the tour he was very much a *Sun* reader.'

On returning to Britain, McGee and Green drew a line under Biff Bang Pow! The head of Creation was officially retiring from the road. This time the *NME* did not ask for a comment.

Reviews of the House Of Love's gigs were getting longer and more appreciative. To keep the engine revving, McGee persuaded Rough Trade in Germany to release a mini-album, *The House Of Love*, comprising the A-sides and B-sides of 'Shine On' and 'Real Animal'. Imported to Britain in March, it received five-star notices in the press. In April, when journalists on all the music papers had seen at least one House Of Love show worthy of superlatives, Jeff Barrett sent out white labels of their next single, 'Christine'.

Recalling the chord sequence to Roxy Music's 'Over You', 'Christine' had taken Guy Chadwick a long time to perfect. It was a thoughtfully constructed, constantly surprising song with a key change and a wide range of ambiences and guitar sounds. The second chorus alone required Terry Bickers' feet to change pedals three times. 'When we put "Christine" out, it was like: my God, do we have a shot or not?' says McGee. 'We knew the album was brilliant, but then again we'd been in that position a few times before. When "Christine" came out, instead of the House Of Love being a bit of a joke, everybody started coming to the party.'

Acclaim for 'Christine' was instant and unanimous. *Sounds* and *Melody Maker* gave the band extensive coverage, and the song was asterisked as a landmark 45 of the calibre of 'Upside Down' and the Smiths' 'This Charming Man'. The break-up of the Smiths in the summer of 1987 had left the field clear for a new challenger from the indie tribe, and much of the adulation the press had once bestowed on the Manchester band was now transferred to the House Of Love. Tipped for certain success, they would encounter no competition from their own label-mates Felt, the Weather Prophets or the underachieving Blow Up, while Primal Scream were hanging fire for a long semester of head-scratching and did not have any plans to record in 1988. All told, there was nobody on Creation with quite the commercial mind-set, to say nothing of the songwriting ammunition, of Guy Chadwick.

Although Chadwick was chuffed to be measured for the mantle of the Reid brothers and Morrissey-Marr, his real quarries were neither the Mary Chain nor the Smiths. He had his eye on something

altogether more monumental: stadium fame. Simple Minds and U2 –
the gods of Wembley overstatement – were the groups that talked
Chadwick's kind of numbers. 'I think one of the things that
impressed Alan about me was my ambition,' he believes. 'When we
were making the first single, I told him we wanted to be as big as
Simple Minds. I didn't want us to *sound* like Simple Minds ... but to
be as big as.'

The names of Simple Minds and U2 were seldom heard at
Clerkenwell, unless they were followed by a loud hawk and an
expulsion of saliva into an imaginary bucket. Chadwick, however,
had not come to Creation from an orthodox background in post-
punk, and retained very different reference points to those who had.
One or two juicy tidbits about his past had been elicited by Jeff
Barrett, who fed them to friends in the Clerkenwell circle. There
was, Barrett reported confidentially, a bit of mystery surrounding old
Chadders. For one thing, he was not in his mid-twenties, as he'd
claimed to McGee. He was 32.

Chadwick, the youngest son of a colonel in the British army, was a
Velvet Underground fan who had digressed into androgyny and per-
oxide. For two years in the early 80s, he had worn make-up and
hybridised genders as the pouting singer in a group called Kingdoms.
Third generation New Romantics, they were musically directionless
– but conceptually unilateral. Managed by Chadwick's then-wife
Beri, they were purely a starmaking vehicle for their vocalist. In
1983, Kingdoms were signed by Regard, a subsidiary of RCA.

'Guy's thing was always he had to sign to a major,' recalls his friend
Andy Jarman, who fronted the politically left-wing indie band A
Popular History Of Signs. 'We used to argue incessantly about the
merits of indie labels against ... majors.' For the type of stardom
Chadwick was pursuing in 1983, indies were never in the equation.
Only a major label deal would yield the financial rewards he needed
to prove a point to his affluent parents. 'The band had a very 80s
record company image,' says Jarman. 'Spending money on clothes
and so on. It was a commercialised view of the pop-rock of the time.'

Charles Shaar Murray, a veteran *NME* scribe and R&B musician,
had got to know Chadwick in 1981 when their respective groups
shared a rehearsal room. In 1984, Murray saw a Kingdoms gig at the
Manor House pub in north London. 'It wasn't happening,' he says.
'Guy seemed really uncomfortable and subdued. I got the impression
he didn't much like being in this band. It seemed too much like
somebody's idea of a smart move.' The promoter of the Manor House
gig, Dave Bedford, remembers the Chadwicks well. 'They turned up
like they were the Rolling Stones,' he says. 'It was: "Where's the rider?
Where's the food?" I was like: "Hang on, you're not playing Wembley,
mate." It was so unrealistic what they were demanding. The music
was very pompous and overblown, as were Guy and his wife.'

When Kingdoms' RCA/Regard single, 'Heartland', flopped in early 1984, Chadwick was put on hold for almost a year before being released from his contract. He lost his publishing deal with CBS Songs, and his marriage broke up soon afterwards. 'The group failed and it righteously deserved to fail,' says Charles Shaar Murray. 'I think if that group had been successful and Guy had been stuck with that policy and those guys, it would have killed him. One of the best things that ever happened to Guy was that group not getting over.'

As Chadwick reassessed his life and music, pondering a move away from glamour pop towards a more guitar-led approach, he was given a timely push in the right direction in September 1985, when he and his girlfriend Suzi Gibbons saw the Jesus and Mary Chain's gig at the Electric Ballroom. While he was too old to be a savant of the indie guitar scene, Chadwick was gratified to see that the Velvet Underground were back in fashion with a vengeance. He started placing adverts for Velvets-loving musicians in *Melody Maker*. 'After Kingdoms, there was a long silence,' recalls Charles Shaar Murray. 'Then I heard from Guy that he had a new group. It was like: "Oh, come and see us, we're ..." – and I'll never forget this line – "... we're really big on the Camberwell squat circuit." '

Camberwell, in south-east London, was where Chadwick found Terry Bickers, Chris Groothuizen and Andrea Heukamp. Ten years younger than him, they wore black clothes, admired bands like the Cure and the Bunnymen, and lived a life somewhere between idleness and indigence. Each of them auditioned for the House Of Love in turn, joining the band one by one. Groothuizen, a New Zealander who had moved to London in 1985, found Chadwick a disciplined leader with no patience for time-wasters. 'The brilliant thing about Guy was, from day one, you were in a band and you knew it,' Groothuizen says. 'We were always doing something. When we weren't rehearsing, we would be doing photo sessions ... You need a certain attitude to become successful. You need to be pig-headed or arrogant, or focused. No, *ruthless* is the word. And for Guy, this was his one last chance.'

Before he had even started putting the House Of Love together, Chadwick had written around a dozen outstanding songs. So rich were the pickings that the first four House Of Love singles – and even an unreleased fifth – would all be taken from this pre-written batch. 'It would be very much a case,' says Groothuizen, 'of "we need a new single; here's one I prepared earlier".' Sometimes much earlier. 'Real Animal' had been written as far back as 1981. The effect was to make Chadwick seem a dark horse to the younger members of the band. They were beginning to notice that the colonel's son played his cards very close to his chest.

An additional twist to the Chadwick agenda – and one that had a direct bearing on the House Of Love's future at Creation – was the fact that he and Suzi Gibbons had recently had a baby daughter. The House Of Love might have been a product of the Camberwell squats, but house-buying was becoming a hard necessity for their leader. 'Guy was quite a soft person,' says McGee. 'But it became obvious, as the thing rolled out of the hat, that he had a family. As soon as money reared its head he was like: "I've got a kid. I need loads of cash." '

The other rumour about Chadwick concerned drugs. During his time in Kingdoms, he was said to have burnt himself out on cocaine. This was not true, but Chadwick had had a few scrapes with amyl nitrate and amphetamine sulphate. And now that cocaine was creeping into Clerkenwell – along with LSD and the first sightings of ecstasy – McGee was worried about the effect on the inhibited, upper-middle-class Chadwick. 'We'd started working with the House Of Love in '87,' says McGee, 'when drugs weren't really a part of Creation. By the beginning of '88, it was full-on ... We were worried about Chadwick because we thought: Chadwick can't handle drugs.'

In the months since Andrea Heukamp had handed in her notice, Chadwick had been drinking excessive amounts of whisky on the road, to the anguish of lead guitarist Terry Bickers, the son of an alcoholic. 'It was like: "Right, we don't have to behave any more because there isn't a lady present",' says Bickers. 'The behaviour became more macho. That definitely contributed to Guy's demise as far as being civilised went. When he drank a lot of whisky, you could see the demons come out.'

Bickers was an outgoing individual whose wild-eyed guitarmanship often made the difference between a good House Of Love concert and an excellent one. Overlooked in the early press reports, he was now getting almost as many mentions as Chadwick himself. With Johnny Marr temporarily out of action, Bickers' coronation as the next British guitar hero seemed a probability. Within the House Of Love, however, his relationship with Chadwick was terribly confused. Chadwick wrote the lead guitar parts note for note, giving them to Bickers to play in the studio. Bickers seemed happy with the arrangement, but onstage, where he was more liberated, he would deviate from the written notes, cooking up a storm of effects-generated noise that was often akin to a one-man show. 'We would do a sound check and get all the balances right for the sound engineer,' says Groothuizen, 'and Terry would walk onstage, run his hand along the knobs and turn everything up on full, and then just go for it. His live performance had nothing to do with the records. I remember me and Guy watching a video of us playing and Guy was going: "Look what he's doing to my songs!" '

Throughout the first half of 1988, Bickers grew in confidence, approaching each gig as an opportunity to show off. 'Terry was the boy,' says McGee. 'Terry was amazing. I think Guy's ego found it hard to deal with that.' The expertise and patent whale-song sound of Bickers irritated Chadwick all the more because he knew he needed them. For some reason, those notes just didn't sound the same when he played them himself.

Whereas Bickers was sometimes so bushy-tailed as to appear an innocent, Chadwick was an adept game-player behind his blasé exterior. Both of them were humorous people, but they weren't necessarily laughing at the same joke. 'Guy had a leader's persona,' says Bickers, 'but the whole thing was too much wrapped up in settling scores. Proving to his parents that he wasn't a waster – that was a big element of his life. Guy is a very insecure person. There's a lot of fear embedded deep down within him, so he has to play people off [against] one another. It's like a control drama. There was so much negative energy in him, even though he wrote very beautiful lyrics.' Their friendship did not seem born to last.

The Greenhouse album – *The House Of Love* – came out in May.* However, it managed only moderate first-week sales and the opening dates of a UK tour were disappointingly undersubscribed. Just as the band and McGee were starting to grow anxious, a glowing testimonial arrived out of the blue from John Peel. Indifferent to the House Of Love in the past, he showered compliments on them in a review in the *Observer*. 'The House Of Love,' he wrote of the tour's first night in Leeds, 'showed within seconds that they have that inner tension that makes for a great rather than a merely good band ... There are so many moments of spooky, elusive beauty in the songs and in their playing [that] you cannot allow attention to wander for a second.'

Mick Griffiths, the House Of Love's booking agent, was reading the *Observer* as he sat down to Sunday lunch. 'I thought: bloody hell, they're going to make it,' he remembers. 'Suddenly, they got that shot in the arm. That review was the turning-point.' The House Of Love were in Glasgow that day. 'For Guy, it was fantastic,' says Andy Jarman, who had been taken on as the band's tour manager, 'because he'd been working for so long to get somewhere and finally it had happened.'

The *Observer* review changed the whole tone of the House Of Love campaign. Among other novelties, they became the first Creation band to have their album tracks played on heavy rotation on Peel's radio show, and when they recorded their fourth single, 'Destroy The Heart', on 5 June, it was in an atmosphere of unqualified self-confidence. 'That was an amazing session,' says co-producer Pat Collier. 'They were working really well and they were totally together. I bet everyone at the studio that they'd sell a million albums within a year.'

---

* This is a different album to the identically-titled German compilation that preceded it.

In the offices of Phonogram in New Bond Street, executive Dave Bates – the A&R force behind Tears For Fears, and the mastermind of Phonogram's discriminating Fontana imprint – was thinking the House Of Love could probably sell a lot more than that.

McGee had moved out of the gay couple's house and into a flat in another part of Brighton with Bobby Gillespie's younger brother Graham. The two of them lived the life of the young, free and single. 'The flat was Babylon, basically,' says McGee. 'Graham Gillespie looks like Keanu Reeves, and he was a handsome guy in 1988. We ran riot in Brighton. We were taking loads of drugs, going with lots of women and having a laugh.'

Another resident of Brighton was James Williamson, who had made himself indispensable to the Creation and Primal Scream caucus. McGee and Williamson opened an indie club in the town – called Slut – putting on the Weather Prophets, the House Of Love and other Creation bands. Bobby Gillespie and his girlfriend Karen Parker were next to seek out the seaside air, and were soon joined by Gillespie's fellow Primal Scream members Andrew Innes and Robert Young. Only Jim Beattie refused a move to Brighton, his sense of detachment compounded by a deepening bond between Gillespie and Young that threatened his co-leadership of the band. Young was present at a bad-humoured face-off following a Scream gig in Oxford in early 1988 when Beattie was accused of stealing money from the band's tour manager.

'I'd known Robert since he was a wee kid,' says Beattie, who threw the allegation back in their faces, 'but Robert was trying to get in with Bobby. In the photographs for WEA, you can actually see him getting closer to Bobby.' In a subsequent phone call, Beattie asked Gillespie to make a straight choice between him and Robert Young. He did not get the answer he was expecting.

When Beattie quit Primal Scream, he took their emblematic twelve-string guitar sound with him. Disowning the six-month-old *Sonic Flower Groove*, the remaining Scream members slashed all the guy-ropes connecting them to C86 pop. Robert Young switched from bass to guitar, making up a long-haired, front-of-stage trio with Gillespie and Innes. They began to work on a new set of songs influenced by the MC5, the New York Dolls and the Stooges. 'They got more and more involved in drugs,' says McGee, 'and their New York Dolls fixation came out. By this time, drugs had started to take a serious foothold ... They were doing loads of acid.'

Danny Kelly, writing in the *NME* in the summer of 1987, had delineated Primal Scream's vision of rock 'n' roll as 'a dodgy cocktail of myth, exaggeration, wishful thinking ... and isolated moments of incandescent music'. With the road-weary Beattie out of the picture, however, Primal Scream became less about wishful thinking and more about do-what-thou-wilt. 'We've got two Les Pauls making this amazing, raw sound,' Gillespie enthused in the *NME*. 'There's more space in the sound now. We're looser, funkier, more fun.' Their audience disagreed. It would desert the band in droves.

As Creation enjoyed a palmy summer in the music press with the House Of Love, McGee approached Ed Ball to help out. McGee put Ball in charge of answering the phone at Clerkenwell, where public relations improved overnight as a result. Ball, who was also invited to join the label's artist roster, found himself looking forward each morning to McGee's arrival. 'This is how he manages,' Ball says. 'He warms up the troops as soon as he comes in. So he'd come in and it would be like: "Ed, I had a fucking great night last night" – whatever it consisted of, whether it be women or drink or drugs. The first hour was storytelling. There was a sense that what happened last night was important.'

A decade of manning indie labels on the fringes – alone and with Dan Treacy – had taught Ball the value of the small-budget-big-dreams attitude. In the early 80s, he and Treacy had been young impresarios acting out pop fantasies in indie cloud-cuckoo-land, trying not to worry about overheads or intangibles. Even by 1988, Ball still imagined working in a record company meant wearing a cravat and sitting in a wicker chair drinking brandy from a balloon glass. A few weeks at Clerkenwell corrected his misunderstanding. 'Alan used to shout a lot,' he says. 'It was like this strange combination of having a great laugh and being afraid. The fear of going down. Always, constantly, the fear of going down.'

Almost all British indie labels in 1988 faced the possibility of imminent collapse (Mute, which had the Top 20 acts Depeche Mode and Erasure, was a rare exception), and McGee was realistic on the subject of financial doom. Since Creation was so committed to output – it had been increasing its releases by nigh on 100 per cent from year to year – there was just as onerous a responsibility on the groups to record speedily and economically as there was on Jeff Barrett to pull strings in the music weeklies. At Rough Trade Distribution, Dave Whitehead, who had realised that the House Of Love were the genuine article, as opposed to another of McGee's dubious next big things, was advising him to avoid losing the band to a major label at all costs. Did that mean Creation could have more money? McGee asked him. No, said Whitehead.

Rough Trade was not the unstable enterprise it once had been. Its distribution of the dance label Rhythm King, and of M/A/R/R/S, a collaborative dancefloor project on 4AD, had brought about a reversal of its mid-80s slump, and the company had virtually tripled its turnover in the space of two years. M/A/R/R/S' 'Pump Up The Volume', a futuristic dance track assembled from samples, had been whisked from the clubs into the Top 40. In October 1987, it rose to number 1, ousting Rick Astley's Stock, Aitken and Waterman-pro-duced 'Never Gonna Give You Up'. Six months later, S-Express' 'Theme From S-Express' – on Rhythm King – followed it to the top of the charts. These were indie records created with computers and samples, and with none of the usual constraints of the indie musi-cian's art. 'Computers brought the whole idea of "the band" into ques-tion,' wrote Matthew Collin and John Godfrey in their book *Altered State: The Story Of Ecstasy Culture And Acid House*. 'A band need no longer be four men onstage with guitars, drums, bass and a micro-phone, but something more fluid and volatile: an *ad hoc* collective of any number of people, constantly changing and redefining itself to suit new situations.' It was the beginning of the UK dance explosion.

In the offices of the *NME*, there was the sound of lips being smacked. The paper's anti-rock factions had long been pressurising deputy editor Danny Kelly to make a complete break with guitar groups and commission only articles on hip hop and dance culture. Now these journalists had a real case. In August 1986, an *NME* cover story had predicted Chicago house – a soulful electronic dance music born in that city's Warehouse and Powerplant clubs – would be the next phenomenon to hit Britain. That month, the house track 'Love Can't Turn Around' by Farley 'Jackmaster' Funk entered the UK chart at 36 on a slow climb to number 10. When Steve 'Silk' Hurley's 'Jack Your Body' went all the way to pole position the following January, house music became a legitimate commercial force and the bane of Danny Kelly's life. Coerced by pro-Chicago writers on the *NME* into giving his solemn word that 'She Comes From The Rain' by the Weather Prophets would make the Top 50 – a precondition to the band being granted an *NME* cover story – Kelly had to resort to a spot of surreptitious chart-rigging.

'I was told: "If you put them on the cover and it doesn't go Top 50, you will never get another rock group on the cover of this paper",' he recalls. 'Fine. At the repro house on Monday morning, I got hold of the charts. I took out whatever number 49 was – some dance record that nobody would ever miss – and I typed in "She Comes From The Rain". There it was in the charts. Fuck them. *Fuck* them.'

This sort of last-man-standing mentality would almost certainly have extended to Creation in 1988, since innumberable degrees of separation lay between the strummed guitars of the House Of Love and the Roland drum computers of the house of Chicago, had it not been for two unrelated facts. In the first place, Creation was turning into a drugs label, and the dance drug ecstasy had started appearing in McGee's life in April. And in the second place, two out of the four Creation full-timers had, without really knowing what they were hearing, been listening to house records with considerable interest and curiosity.

Jeff Barrett's family came from Nottingham, where he would often return at weekends to see old friends. One night in 1986, he was taken to the Garage club, where the DJ, Graeme Park, was playing house music. It was not a drugs scene – nor any scene at all as far as Barrett could ascertain – and he assumed Park was simply spinning some new electronic black music from America among his usual imports.

In Manchester, where Barrett also spent some time, it was rather different. 'Manchester had the Haç[ienda],' he says, 'which was a seven-night-a-week club. On Tuesday nights, they'd be showing Cabaret Voltaire films. On Wednesday night, it would be an indie night. It was a club where like-minded people, whether they be into black American music or tripped-out white kids into the Velvets, had a focal point. Nowhere else in this country had that.'

The connection between Barrett and Manchester was the Happy Mondays, whose first London gig he had promoted in 1986. Mike Pickering, the Haçienda's booker, who had produced the Happy Mondays' first single, had been DJing at the Haçienda since 1984, where, as Matthew Collin and John Godfrey noted, '[he] and his partner Martin Prendergast would mix electro – speedy, synthetic rap built on the innovations of Kraftwerk – hip hop, funk, techno-pop, New York dance imports, anything which moved the crowd ... a crowd that was increasingly mixed in race.' By 1986, Pickering and Prendergast were playing the early house records from Chicago.

From hearing them in Nottingham and Manchester, Barrett began to add certain house tunes to his record collection, for example 'Washing Machine' by Fingers Inc. (a pseudonym for the Chicago house DJ Larry Heard). It was a weird, repetitive piece far removed from the sort of music Barrett usually liked. But even though 'Washing Machine' has been described as the first ever acid house record, Barrett still didn't think he was listening to the future. And in London, where he ran a weekly indie club at the Falcon pub in Camden Town, Barrett's future seemed to have been marked out: another sweaty Falcon night, another indie guitar band and another black-clothed audience holding pints of beer.

One night at the Falcon in the early summer of 1988, as he ticked people off on the guest-list, Barrett was greeted by a friend named Richard Norris, who wrote for a glossy 60s psychedelia magazine, *Strange Things Are Happening*. 'I knew Richard Norris from his days working on a label called Bam Caruso,' says Barrett. 'I was sat at the door of the Falcon, Pils-ed and nosed out of my fucking balls. He said: "What are you doing later? I'm going down to the Dungeons at London Bridge – you've got to come down, there's this new thing going on, it's acid house. You've got to come and check it."'

The Falcon was a rickety, claustrophobically small venue in which – if the capacity was exceeded, which it frequently was – people would gasp for breath and drip with perspiration. On the night in question, Richard Norris was on his way to the Shoom club at Samurai Studios in south-east London where, as one witness recalled to Jane Bussman in *Once In A Lifetime: The Crazy Days Of Acid House And Afterwards*, '... there was no oxygen. We were lighting our lighter and the flames were going out.' But apart from the heat and the crush, as Norris attempted to explain to Barrett, the two clubs were incomparable. 'Both Jeff and I come from a good 60s music background,' says Norris. 'But it was an odd culture clash by the summer of '88, because I was coming down with, I suppose, the first flush of ecstasy euphoria – just totally on a mission: "Everyone must know about this, it's absolutely brilliant!" ' Barrett said he'd think about it, but ended up going straight home.

'Rude, silly and as cool as the strange kid that doesn't care what anybody thinks, acid house and the British were made for each other,' wrote Bussman. The 'acid' in acid house was never fully explained – it referred either to 'acid burning', an American DJ term for mixing; or to the psychedelic squeaks produced by the Roland 303 machine, which reminded some people of an LSD trip. Douglas Hart of the Jesus and Mary Chain raised a fair point when he admitted to an *NME* journalist: 'I'm still not sure why acid house isn't called ecstasy house. I personally could never take acid and go to a club heaving with people. You'd end up shooting them or something.'

Hart was one of the first 60s-obsessed Brits from the guitar-bass-drums cabal to feel his way into acid house by making a record of his own: the Acid Angels' 'Speed Speed Ecstassy', on which he teamed up with his old Rough Trade comrade Peter Fowler. But Richard Norris had made one even earlier. In September 1987, while the first acid house generation was still holidaying on the island of Ibiza, dancing and sweltering under the effects of ecstasy, Norris interviewed Genesis P-Orridge, leader of the shamanic underground rock group Psychic TV, for *Strange Things Are Happening*. P-Orridge was enthusing about a new form of psychedelic dance music called acid house. 'Neither of us had heard the music,' recalls Norris, 'but the concept of it sounded brilliant. Dance music that's got loads of acid in it? Sounds brilliant. And pretty much the next weekend, me and Gen said: "Right, let's go and make an album that's acid house." '

Presuming acid must mean LSD, Norris and P-Orridge took into the studio videos of 60s drug movies such as Roger Corman's *The Trip* and Richard Rush's *Psych-Out*, and also Corman's *The Wild Angels*, about a Californian biker gang. Dialogue from these films, and music from old 60s records, were sampled liberally as Norris and P-Orridge got to grips with the technology. 'We fed all this stuff into a computer and mucked about over a weekend,' says Norris. 'And we came out with *Jack The Tab*, which was an album of what we thought acid house should sound like.'

In November 1987, the holidaying Brits flew back from Ibiza and, as Bussman wrote, 'went straight into withdrawal'. Desperate to recreate the ecstasy highs of their extended summer, they found no clubs to satisfy them and were forced to start their own, playing the happy Mediterranean music they'd come to know as Balearic Beat. Shoom and Future started that month – in the south-east and West End of London respectively – and immediately became scenes of unselfconscious ecstasy dancing and Age Of Aquarius exhilaration. Room dimensions and oxygen levels aside, they were as different to London's indie clubs as one could ever imagine. The indie gig-going experience was shot through with cynicism and aloofness: only the youngest fans actually danced to music, while those who regarded themselves as mature preferred to watch, nod or, as the songwriter Robyn Hitchcock memorably put it, 'vibrate internally'. But it wasn't the disparity in dance styles that stopped the indie crowd from joining the queues for Shoom and Future. It was ignorance of their very existence.

'What happened with acid house,' says Jeff Barrett, 'was it was a specific club thing at the end of '87 that these guys knew they could do into '88. This was something that none of us were a part of. In early '88, Shoom bust [i.e. soared in popularity], but we weren't there. We didn't know about it.' The lure of Shoom was its joyful atmosphere, a mixture of sunshine music and high-speed friendships made possible by ecstasy. Adopting the logo of a Smiley face, Shoom was seducing working-class weekenders into throwing in their nine-to-five jobs and following the hedonistic creed of the club's co-runner and DJ, Danny Rampling. 'We were spreading the message of unity,' Rampling told Bussman. 'The positive energy between the people on the dancefloor was incredible.'

As Shoom raved, Norris and P-Orridge released *Jack The Tab*. Now that they had heard proper acid house records created on Roland 303s, they knew their album was an anomaly – a dark, psychedelic comedown from a party neither of them had really been to. Some fragments of their music sounded like a tormented Jimi Hendrix, and a great deal of it was hellishly unsuitable for dancing. Their timing, however, could not have been better. 'By the time it came out,' says Norris, 'a lot of people had heard of acid house and went to the acid house section in Our Price and saw our record sitting there: "Oh right, we'll have that one then." There were probably lots of very disappointed soul boys.' Norris and P-Orridge sold 40,000.

Jeff Barrett's Creation colleague Ed Ball had been trying to unravel the mysteries of Chicago house since 1987, but the records he had heard had mostly bored him. Reading a review of *Jack The Tab* in the *NME*, he ran out to get a copy. In its grooves he found psychedelic references he could relate to, and he took it down to Alan McGee in Brighton. 'I said: "Listen to this. See what they're doing with all these samples? We could do something like that",' Ball remembers.

The catalogue number of *Jack The Tab* – ACID 001 – was almost identical to that of 'She Comes From The Rain' by the Weather Prophets. This, however, was all they had in common. If ACID 1 had been a polished 80s idea of what the past had sounded like, ACID 001 was a burbling pointer to what the 90s might have in store. One of the tracks, 'Aquarius Rising' by the Loaded Angels – like all the acts, an alias for Norris and P-Orridge themselves – sampled Peter Fonda from *The Wild Angels*. 'We want to be free,' Fonda's speech began. 'We want to be free to do what we want to do .... and we want to get loaded .... and we want to have a good time. And that's what we're going to do. We're going to have a good time. We're going to have a party.'

'Alan was listening to it, going: "I don't know ..."' says Ball. 'He wasn't dismissive, but he wasn't sure.'

10 The President at the Waldorf

IN JULY 1987, TWO ENGLISHMEN met at the New Music Seminar in New York. Their conversation did not last long, was not reported at the time, yet would have immense significance for the music industry in their home country. 'Come on, Pete,' said Steve Mason of Pinnacle to Pete Waterman. 'Give us a record and I'll show you what we can do.'

Up to that point, Stock, Aitken and Waterman had been licensing their acts to individual record companies, which in turn had taken care of distributing the discs. If Mason could acquire the lot for Pinnacle, it would go a long way towards confirming him as Britain's premier indie distributor. But could Pinnacle do for the prolific dance-pop team what the majors had? At first, it appeared not. When Waterman put Mason to work on a single by Mandy Smith – the girl-friend of Rolling Stone Bill Wyman – which Waterman had produced for his own independent label PWL, the record did not even make the Top 75.

In January 1988, PWL and Pinnacle tried again. Waterman gave Mason a song by a young Australian soap actress, rejected as uncommercial by a host of UK majors, promising him that if he could get the single into the Top 30 all PWL product would be his for years to come. Kylie Minogue's 'I Should Be So Lucky' sold 900,000 copies, spending five weeks at number 1 and turning Minogue into a pop phenomenon. As good as his word, Waterman switched PWL's distribution to Pinnacle on the spot, and together the two companies took aim and fired arrow after arrow into the centre of the Gallup gold. There had not been a Top 100 since March 1986 without a Waterman-produced record in it. There would not be another one until October 1990. At Pinnacle's sales conference in 1989, a cock-a-hoop Mason would end his speech by shouting: 'Warner Bros, EMI, CBS and the rest – eat your fucking heart out.'

But even as PWL and Pinnacle blitzed the pop charts, so too did they overwhelm the indie charts. 'I Should Be So Lucky' removed

Björk and her Sugarcubes from the indie summit in February 1988, and Minogue's follow-up, 'Got To Be Certain', ended the two-week reign of New Order's remix of 'Blue Monday' in June. That year, she would have three chart-topping indie singles in all – two more than the Wedding Present and Depeche Mode, and three more than the most popular group on Creation, the House Of Love. Wholesome, prepacked and attitude-free, Kylie Minogue was the biggest indie star in Britain.

As if that were not ironic enough, Guy Chadwick, the garlanded songwriter of the House Of Love, who had emerged from the indie confluence as a broadly accessible proconsul of underground music and independence *per se*, was preparing to retrace his footsteps back to the corporate world he had left in 1984. With the House Of Love about to start a new chapter, and PWL threatening to write alternative guitar rock out of its own plot, the definition of indie had never been more subjective.

Three months after its May release, *The House Of Love* was still selling around 1,000 copies a week. By contrast, Felt's album *The Pictorial Jackson Review*, which had been released on the same day, had sold just three copies in one August week. Quite simply, Creation was being kept alive by the House Of Love – a band it had first stonewalled, then fostered and was now certain to lose.

For Chadwick to get the stadium fame he was after, the House Of Love would have to go to a major. For them to fulfil the prophecies of the press ('Really, they are the next gods of guitar rock and Guy Chadwick ... [is] its new messiah' – *NME*), the House Of Love would have to go to a major. And to sell records abroad, the House Of Love would have to go to a major. 'Creation didn't really have a foreign policy,' says Pat Fish, singer and leader of the Jazz Butcher, a Creation capture from the Glass label in 1987. 'There was nobody there who knew anything about that side of it. Even Glass, which was run by Dave Barker, one panda-like man in an office in Kilburn, had got licensing deals with major labels in America and Canada. The Jazz Butcher had already been round America once before we signed to Creation, which most people would find inconceivable.'

The House Of Love had never been further west than Exeter. While their album had won praise in the States from the influential journals *Rockpool* and *CMJ New Music Report*, it was being distributed by a US indie label (Relativity) not much wealthier than Creation itself. Even flying Chadwick over for a whistle-stop lap of meet-and-greets with college radio would have been impractical, let alone sending the whole band on a two-week tour of America's primary markets. And in any case, there was evidence that Chadwick was looking beyond *The House Of Love* to the next album, envisaging it as a money-spinner and a doorway to the international market. So bombastic was Chadwick on the matter that he looked like confounding any sensible attempts to put a true value on the band.

Cerne Canning and Simon Esplen had twice turned down offers to manage the House Of Love in 1987. Since 'Christine', they had become a good deal more interested. But when Chadwick came to their office and started outlining his goals and dreams, they knew they wouldn't be able to help him. 'When he talked about the amount of money he wanted [for signing to a major], we were like: "No way",' recalls Canning. 'It was serious money. It was three or four hundred grand an album. We were going: "If you take those advances, you're going to have incredible pressures on you." ' Chadwick came straight to the point. 'Look,' he told them, 'I want a house.'

McGee did not do contracts. He had said as much to Chadwick at their first meeting in 1986. The House Of Love had therefore nothing more than sentimental ties binding them to Creation, and McGee would not have bet on Chadwick being a sentimentalist. One day in early June, he took Chadwick on a tour of London music publishers to procure him a deal for his songs. The deal would be of no financial benefit to McGee, but it might help Chadwick to remember who his friends were. Chadwick took the largest offer, £60,000 from Steve Walters at EMI Music. It was enough for a deposit on a house, and Chadwick seemed satisfied. Three weeks later, he called McGee to a meeting and told him that the House Of Love were leaving Creation.

Considering he had been dreading the news for some time, McGee's reaction was surprising: he had a fit of self-pity. 'That's all right,' he shrugged miserably. 'Most people leave me. My wife left me last year. The Mary Chain left me the year before. What's new?' But Chadwick reassured him that he was not going to be left in the lurch. His artful handling of the negotiations with EMI Music – for instance, exploiting his solidarity with Martin Costello to fool Steve Walters into thinking that Complete Music would match any offer below £50,000 – had impressed Chadwick in a big way, especially as McGee had earned nothing from the eventual deal. Doubtless he would be an even more effective negotiator if he stood to gain 20 per cent of the bankroll. Chadwick asked McGee to take over the management of the House Of Love from himself and Suzi Gibbons, and to begin talks with major labels about a deal for the world.

'The decision to hire Alan was never discussed with me,' says Chris Groothuizen. 'I didn't necessarily think it was a bad idea. But I was never asked if I thought it was a good idea.' From Chadwick's angle, it looked terrific. He had a manager who was entertaining, foul-mouthed and arrogant, who knew where to get drugs, and who was more than capable of outplaying the music business establishment at its own game. A manager, too, who called Chadwick a genius to his face – and he didn't just say it once, he said it all the time.

The working-class, monarchy-hating McGee was now working for

a man he'd often suspected of being a reactionary Tory; a black
sheep from a privileged family who was paradoxically unable to
resist the trappings of privilege. McGee and Chadwick were the
unlikeliest of double acts – that much is irrefutable – but there was
nothing unique about their shared objective. 'It was obvious that it
was all about money,' says McGee. 'Once Chadwick sniffed the cash,
that was all he wanted.'

Two years had passed since Chadwick's first ignominious visit to
Clerkenwell. It was a rare record company that would ask him to
wait in reception now. McGee, however, was not going to let any
labels near Chadwick for the moment – and if anybody would have
to wait in reception, it would certainly not be McGee. On 14 July, he
flew to New York for the 1988 New Music Seminar, where he tipped
off Adrian Thrills, an A&R man for Phonogram, that the House Of
Love were on the market.

In Creation's advertisements for the House Of Love's 'Christine' and
the Weather Prophets' 'Hollow Heart' in May, the usual dry information about release dates and catalogue numbers had been supple-
mented by a postscript of pure facetiousness. The singles were
available on 7-inch for the bargain price of 99 pence, the adverts
explained, 'because our President still loves the kids'.

The idea of Creation being a friend to 'the kids' sniggered self-dep-
recatingly at McGee's days on the fanzine soapbox in the early 80s,
when he had not long been out of his teens and had viewed music as
the chief revolutionary force of youth. At almost 28, he could hardly
call himself a young gunslinger now: across Britain, bands were
being formed by people eleven and twelve years his junior, and some
of them would, in time, be signed by McGee to Creation. To these
new kids on the block, he was an old campaigner and a valued patri-
arch. And there were signs that he knew it.

Indeed, as Creation's advertising style got wittier and more ironic,
McGee gave every indication that he was having more fun with his
public persona than at any time since the Mary Chain tours of 1985.
As a consequence, the image of Creation was transformed. Its long-
standing reputation as a stern-faced retro label was eradicated, and it
could rightfully claim to be one of the few top-flight indies with a
sense of humour. In its self-styled President, the transmogrification
was visible. 'He was emotionally coming right out of that horrible
period that he'd been through,' says Guy Chadwick. 'He was pretty
charged. When I asked him to manage the group, the next day he
started wearing sunglasses.'

The sight of McGee in his sunglasses became common even in the
darkest clubs. His floury complexion, meanwhile, was overhung by
an ever more unruly sponge of ginger hair. To his friends, he was
manifestly on the mend. To his enemies, he was a provocative target.

'I was still quite an unpopular figure because of the Mary Chain,' he says. 'I'd be standing at House Of Love gigs and a plastic glass of beer would come flying past my head. Usually, to be fair, people would attack me first – but what I tended to do was batter them if I ever caught up with them. I wasn't a pleasant chap and my stress meter was high.'

Earlier in the year, McGee and Dick Green had met Rough Trade's Dave Whitehead and Simon Edwards to solicit ideas for a major promotion of the Creation label in the summer. Out of those meetings had come the structure for a three-pronged attack consisting of a compilation album (Creation's sixth) that would spotlight 15 artists; an all-day indoor festival in August featuring most of those artists; and several weeks of heavily increased advertising for all current releases. McGee and Green would be able to use the success of the House Of Love to further awareness of the lesser-selling groups, and perhaps generate some movement on the 30-odd Creation albums in catalogue. By keeping record and ticket prices low, McGee and Green would be forsaking short-term profits while – in theory – making long-term progress. The various strands of the July–August promotion were pulled together under the banner 'Doing It For The Kids'.

As well as being a perfect opportunity to push Creation *en bloc* to the music press during two traditionally quiet months, 'Doing It For The Kids' allowed the President to have some sport with his own celebrity. Four lifesize McGee cardboard cut-outs were manufactured and booked in for week-long appearances at major city record stores. For the all-day concert at the Town and Country Club on 7 August, he planned to swoop down on to the stage on a cable suspended from the balcony.

'The idea grew and grew into this big presentation of what Creation could be and was,' says Green. 'Looking back on it, I think we were just learning the first inklings of marketing. We were realising what we had to do to get [our records] out there.' For all but a couple of Creation's artists, the Town and Country all-dayer was to be their most prestigious gig of the year. It would also be a chance for the major labels to see the much-trumpeted House Of Love in the flesh. The guest-list soon began filling with names of A&R men.

On 4 August, the House Of Love's new single was released. A blue streak of spooked voices and squealing mini-solos, 'Destroy The Heart' was a fantastic goodbye to independence. When the House Of Love arrived at the Town and Country three days later, it was in a metaphorical fleet of limousines. 'They turned up like superstars,' recalls a watching Ed Ball, 'like the Beatles in *A Hard Day's Night*. It was very exciting.'

August 7 was an uncomfortably hot Sunday. In the humid hours before the venue opened its bars, the audience milled around in sweat-soaked clothing as minor Creation groups like Biff Bang Pow! and the Jasmine Minks blasted out unseasonal sounds already a few years out of date. Creation had come a long way from the Living Room, but the same could not be said of all of its bands. The patient audience – which was to be denied the spectacle of McGee flying through the air on cables; he had decided it would be too dangerous – would nevertheless see him appear onstage in various line-ups. Just as Bob Geldof had insisted on the Boomtown Rats playing at Live Aid, the President was loath to miss any chance of strapping on a guitar at his own festival.

Less than a year before, Primal Scream had filled the Town and Country to capacity in their own right. Ten months on, the Scream's pedestal had been reduced to matchwood and their pulling power was negligible. The rumour backstage was that they had not wanted to take part in the concert – their fellow Creation old-schoolers the Weather Prophets had declined – and were unhappy about their middle-order billing. Taking the stage with the Weather Prophets' Dave Goulding on bass, the Scream's grimy rock 'n' roll riffs, long hair and petulance moved a bewildered audience to ridicule. It was a long drop to the bottom, but it looked as if Primal Scream would be going all the way.

Much interviewed that afternoon was the Anglo-Irish quartet My Bloody Valentine, a Creation act since February. Formed in Dublin in 1984 by the American-born Kevin Shields and the Irishman Colm O'Ciosoig, My Bloody Valentine had recorded for four different indie labels by 1987, never staying long in one place. They had not had much good fortune – Shields and O'Ciosoig had moved the band to Germany in 1985, so unappreciated were they at home – and had often been criticised for unoriginality. In January 1988, Biff Bang Pow! had been asked to play a gig with My Bloody Valentine in Kent. McGee and Green were agreeable – on the strict condition that Biff Bang Pow! headlined. 'We'd seen them a couple of times with their previous singer,' recalls McGee, 'and they were pretty generic of that post-Mary Chain thing. There was a lot of spirit but they were perceived as pretty much a joke group.'

That night, McGee and Green stood at the front to watch them, trying to reconcile the indie joke band of yore with the pummelling monster howling before them. 'They were really powerful,' says McGee. 'After two songs, I turned to Dick and said: "For fuck's sake, this is like the English Hüsker Dü." I was shocked at how good they had become.' They spoke to Kevin Shields afterwards, who agreed that the band would record a one-off single for Creation. Green found them a small studio in Walthamstow, saving money by getting them to record on to videotape.

A striking-looking bunch, My Bloody Valentine were two men and two women – one of these being Shields' round-eyed, stick-thin girlfriend Bilinda Butcher. Offstage the four appeared tongue-tied and lethargic. Onstage they were anything but. One of their devices was to toy with the levels of audience comfort by using volume and distortion almost as weapons. Quite apart from being one of the loudest bands in the country, they were also one of the most difficult to record. Shields admired groups that obtained challenging and frightening guitar sounds – Sonic Youth, Big Black, Dinosaur Jr and the pain-threshold experimentalists Swans – and saw his band in the same tradition. But My Bloody Valentine were arguably more disconcerting than any of the aforementioned Americans. Amidst the ear-splitting noise from their respective guitars, the high-pitched voices of Shields and Butcher emitted siren-like purrs, creating a plaintive and otherworldly effect. 'You think you can hear things that aren't there,' Shields acknowledged in an interview. '[After one gig] someone said: "The PA was really bad. We could hear all these funny noises." ' Some of the noises were not so funny: Shields liked to use frequencies that damaged people's hearing. It was not altogether clear whether this was sonic pranksterism gone mad, or a studied act of revenge by My Bloody Valentine on a generation that had banished them.

When McGee heard the five songs they had recorded in Walthamstow, he thought they were extraordinary. Spoilt for choice of A-sides, he selected 'You Made Me Realise', a nosediving anvil of a tune with an angry, slashing rhythm and a middle section in which a grunting bass note spasmed ominously. Shields asked McGee if he was kidding; the middle section in 'You Made Me Realise' had been a spoof. McGee replied that he was perfectly serious.

Everything started to turn around for My Bloody Valentine. There were excellent reviews for the EP in the press, and when lots were drawn with the House Of Love to determine who would headline at the 'Doing It For The Kids' concert, My Bloody Valentine won. Meanwhile, Shields told journalists that the band was making its first album for Creation in a studio in rural Wales. As on previous recording sessions, he and his colleagues were going without sleep for long stretches, partly as a result of perfectionism but also with the intention of getting into unusual states of mind. 'It's very draining,' he explained of their routine. 'You're not sleeping, or not very much. You're physically tired and mentally tired from thinking 18 to 20 hours a day. The *Ecstasy* album [in 1987] we recorded in two weeks, sleeping one to one-and-a-half hours a night.' He also claimed that the cows grazing in the field opposite the studio in Wales had been so transported by the sounds from his guitar that they had run across to surround the building.

Walking on to the Town and Country's stage, My Bloody Valentine were an instant sensation. Colm O'Ciosoig rampaged around his drum-kit with flailing arms, an authentic Keith Moon for the late 80s.

Debbie Goodge, who had joined as bassist in 1985, was short-haired and very tensed up – her bass, under pressure, fell repeatedly beneath her knees as she clawed and tore at its strings. At their microphones, Shields and Butcher cooed their harmonies with impassive gazes, grinding amplified explosions from their guitars with no more than a downward stroke. It was a show-stealing performance.

If there was a major label A&R consensus regarding My Bloody Valentine, it was probably that they were much too macabre to touch. The photograph on their EP sleeve – a girl lying dead in a bed of flowers, a kitchen knife by her ear – was as uncompromising as any of the music within. Even when My Bloody Valentine won the rave write-ups in the following Tuesday's music papers, most of the chattering in the industry was about something else. 'Destroy The Heart' had failed by a hair to notch up Creation's first appearance in the Top 75, but the attention centred all the same on the House Of Love, whose ruthlessly professional set at the Town and Country had suggested they could rise to much greater occasions. The question now was how much Alan McGee would sell them for.

For the historic auction of the House Of Love, McGee decided to combine business with pleasure. In April he had started going out with a girl named Belinda White, who lived in Sheffield but often spent time in Brighton. 'She was a friend of James Williamson,' says McGee. 'He was chasing her and she was always kicking about with him.' McGee did well to get the girl. Belinda White was double-takingly attractive ... and just 18 years old. Inviting her down to London, McGee booked a suite at the Waldorf Hotel in the Strand for the last two weeks of August. If the A&R men wanted the House Of Love, they could come to him.

Phonogram, MCA, Siren, CBS and EMI were all granted early audiences at the Waldorf, the opulent surroundings of which did seem – as McGee had been hoping – to put a few of his guests off their guard. There was Elevation-related spite in his tactics, and a touch of dark comedy at his visitors' expense. What could be better, he thought to himself, than to have two weeks of enjoyable conversations with the A&R crowd about how impeccable his tastes were; what a superb talent-spotter he was; and how he had proved it not only with the Jesus and Mary Chain but again with the House Of Love? His renascent McLaren-esque glint hidden coyly behind dark glasses, McGee flicked his managerial switch to 'heavy scam'. Over fourteen days at the Waldorf, he snorted large amounts of speed and cocaine, schmoozing and jousting with the corporate foe. MCA dropped out when they heard his asking price of £80,000. The other four companies remained in the race.

A condition of any House Of Love deal, McGee and Chadwick

were adamant, was that it had to be two-albums-firm, denying the successful bidder the right to terminate the contract without complete and full payment of advances. This was in the event of the band's first album underperforming or going awry in some way – not that anyone was seriously considering any mishaps so early in the game. By the end of week one, the bids had passed £100,000. 'I was a freak-show,' says McGee. 'I was taking tons of drugs, I had a beautiful girl with me and I was asking for £100,000. But how can I go out and make money every day of my life? As a rock 'n' roll manager I can find bands and sign them to major record companies and get 20 per cent – and I can make a living out of that. And the competition is abysmal.'

By 18 August – seven days into the auction – Siren, EMI, Phonogram and CBS were still in the hat, and had been joined by Polydor and the American label Capitol. The man from Polydor was McGee's friend Graham Carpenter. 'I rang Alan and said: "Look, we have to do this. You have to give this to me",' Carpenter recalls. 'He said: "Well, the fucking money's gone through the roof. Everybody wants it." ' The offers soon exceeded £150,000, which Carpenter thought ridiculous. But he was still interested.

RCA appeared at the hotel on 20 August, the day before the UK indie music scene was revolutionised by the introduction of all-day pub drinking. On 24 August, McGee held second meetings with Siren and Polydor. The money was now hitting £200,000 and life in the suite was just about crazy enough for McGee's liking. Twenty-four hours later, the craziness reached a surreal peak. As McGee wrapped up another meeting with Capitol, the label's A&R man reached into his bag. 'We'd been talking about the album and he'd been agreeing with me how great it was,' recalls McGee. 'And he said: "I fucking love this record," and he pulled it out. It was an album by a band called House Of Freaks. He'd offered me £200,000 for the wrong band.'

When McGee checked out of the Waldorf, Graham Carpenter quickly drove down to Brighton to catch him in a more informal setting. As they went out for the evening, Carpenter tried to get a firm answer on the House Of Love. 'He went: "Yeah, yeah, definitely, you can have it. It won't be a problem",' says Carpenter. 'But Dave Bates was his next appointment.'

The head of A&R at Phonogram – and the supremo of the Phonogram affiliate label Fontana – Dave Bates had steered clear of all the hoo-ha at the Waldorf, demanding that McGee come to his offices in New Bond Street. Bates wanted the House Of Love for his Fontana roster – no ifs, no buts – and was biding his time for a dramatic entrance that would kill off the other challengers. The brash veteran of UK A&R had the nonchalance of a Soviet weightlifter waiting for his rivals to drop out of the contest one by one. Then: one lift. Gold medal for Bates. National anthem.

In the third week of August, Bates had made what appeared to be an astute move – little knowing it could easily have blown his chances sky-high. He'd gone down to Orinoco Studios in south-east London, where the House Of Love were recording a new single, 'Safe'. The single was the idea of McGee, who wanted to squeeze one last release for Creation – and a conceivable Top 50 hit at that – before the band's departure. As Bates walked into Orinoco, he was recognised with a start by the House Of Love's drummer, Pete Evans. Bassist Chris Groothuizen noticed that Bates and Evans seemed acquainted, but from where? 'He shook Pete's hand and there was a kind of weird "Oh ... hello ..."' Groothuizen remembers. 'When Bates left the room, Pete turned to us and said: "Watch him. He's trouble." '

In the business of music and in the world of A&R, Dave Bates was a genuine character. Outspoken and gregarious – particularly during his cocaine years, since curtailed – he had in twelve years at Phonogram signed bands as diverse as Def Leppard, Tears For Fears and the Teardrop Explodes. A music obsessive, he was not the kind to limit himself to a few selective genres, and he was probably the only person in Britain who liked Def Leppard and Julian Cope equally. In 1986 and 1987, he had overseen a period of pop-soul clover at Phonogram with Wet Wet Wet, Curiosity Killed The Cat, Swing Out Sister and Hipsway. It would be hard to name four bands the indie sector had despised more. It would also be correct to say that Bates could not have cared less.

Now in charge of a roster that included Dire Straits, Elton John and Status Quo, Bates also headed Fontana, the label gifted to him by his Phonogram superiors in 1986.* A bridge of sorts between the cult and the mainstream, Fontana was a specialist label with a proudly pro-artist creed. Bates had added some of his all-time favourite musicians to Fontana's books, such as Tom Verlaine, Pere Ubu and ex-members of Talking Heads (though not the one he really wanted, David Byrne). None of these had made Fontana any money, and nor would they, but another Fontana act, Was (Not Was), had had a Top 10 hit in the UK with 'Walk The Dinosaur' in 1987. And even if they never had another one, the providential signings Bates had made for Phonogram afforded him the security to do as he pleased. Tears For Fears were quadruple-platinum megastars in Britain and America, while Def Leppard's *Hysteria* album had just hit number 1 in the States after almost a year on the charts. Two gold medals for Bates. National fucking anthem.

---

* In the 60s, Fontana had been a subsidiary of the MOR label – and Phonogram precursor – Philips, owned by the Dutch electrical goods company of that name. Fontana's acts in this period included the Troggs, the Spencer Davis Group and the Herd. The label had lain dormant since the 70s.

'He wielded unique power for an A&R man in this country,' says a former colleague. 'Part of him fancied being a music mogul, an Ahmet Ertegun, an old-fashioned A&R man. But he'd also go off on these egotistical rants that had no grounding in reality. His staff were terrified of him; he could turn on the charm or he could be an obnoxious bully. But [managing director] Maurice Oberstein loved the fact that his head of A&R was a maverick lunatic and a rough diamond. You're talking about a classic Jekyll and Hyde character.'

In 1983, Bates had wandered into a recording session by a Phonogram band called the Escape. Typically forthright, he announced that the drummer was useless and told them to replace him pronto with a Fairlight computer. 'It destroyed me,' says Pete Evans. 'He was amazing at knocking any confidence out of you – if you had any to start with. Most musicians are a little bit damaged anyway, and he took advantage of that. He was just a horrible man.'

To his credit, unlike some of his A&R contemporaries at other record companies, Bates was not simply about making money. If he had been, he might have been easier to deal with. Instead, Bates was only *sometimes* about making money, a recipe for total confusion. 'I took the view that if I could get [one of my bands] to pay the rent in commercial terms,' he says, 'I should be allowed to sign three Arts Council grant projects. That was my thinking.' The £250,000 question – for that was the neighbourhood now being discussed for the signatures of the House Of Love – was did he intend them to be a rent-payer or an arts project?

Bates heard the words he wanted to hear from the lips of Alan McGee himself. Now that did come as a surprise. 'I thought [Alan and I] were going to have a real tough time getting on,' says Bates, 'because at that point in Britain there was a big thing about indie versus major. It was a very boring argument, but I thought that kind of angst might come in somehow with Alan. But he was very pragmatic, very into the idea of being successful, and his manner amused me. Amused me in the sense that I liked him. And his whole view was that he wanted the House Of Love to become – as he said – as big as U2.'

In the race to win McGee's trust, Bates would have plenty of advantages over his A&R rivals. He was hearty and refreshing. He was an encyclopaedia of popular music. He valued the sound of a record every bit as highly as the profits it might rake in; he wanted to make records he could play at home, after all. He was also notoriously prepared to spend a lot of money on recording, and time constraints were not a factor. And his favourite track – unconditionally – on *The House Of Love* was 'Man To Child'. They were an improbable pair of romantics, but Bates and McGee were betrothed in a whirl of corsets by Chadwick's poignant ballad.

Chadwick himself had a favourite label, and it was not Fontana. In the 60s, CBS had put out records by Bob Dylan. In the 70s, it had signed one of Chadwick's most cherished bands, the Only Ones. And in the late 80s, the A&R department of CBS was just as keen to get its hands on the House Of Love as Dave Bates was. On 26 August, McGee wheeled Chadwick into the CBS offices in Soho Square to talk about his music and ambitions. That evening, the House Of Love showcased for the company in a London rehearsal studio.

However, this was a black mark against CBS. The performance was stilted and the younger members of the band resented being paraded as showroom dummies. The ball bounced back to Bates.

McGee did not have a class problem with Guy Chadwick, but he certainly had one with Andy Jarman. Chadwick's oldest friend had been obliged to undergo a vetting procedure before he could be trusted with the job of tour managing the House Of Love. McGee did not like Jarman much – he was laconic, camp and a bit too intelligent for his own good. 'He used to say things like: "Well, I can see you're really honest with the money",' Jarman recalls. 'It was a bit weird. There was always this funny mixture of business and wanting to get completely off his head. He had a very posh girlfriend, too, which was a complete anachronism.'

In early September, Jarman and the House Of Love left Britain for a tour of Europe. After playing shows in Germany and Austria, they drove to Switzerland. In Lausanne, on 16 September, Chadwick and Jarman came to an understanding that Jarman would co-manage the House Of Love with McGee. An enraged Glaswegian was on the next flight from London.

'I was getting paranoid,' says McGee. 'I thought the upper-class old boys' network was ganging up on me. Me and Steve Walters [from EMI Music] were in the same hotel room, and Guy and Andy were in the next room debating while we listened at the wall. It was all about money.' Indeed, most conversations in the House Of Love that month were about money, and McGee was not encouraged by the way the conversations were going. An American manager, Tom Atencio, had expressed interest in representing the House Of Love for the States, telling McGee that he could land them a lucrative deal which would allow them to stay on Creation for the UK. It was standard indie band procedure: New Order, Depeche Mode, the Sugarcubes and others had either signed major label deals or benefited from major distribution in America, where there was none of the anti-corporate hardlining of the British press.

McGee felt it was too late for Atencio to be thinking about eleventh-hour rescue packages. Two of the biggest companies in Britain were fighting for the House Of Love tooth and nail, and more to the point, where was McGee's 20 per cent going to come from if he didn't sign them to a UK major? He stopped taking Atencio's calls.

Pete Evans was at the end of his tether. His band-mates had dismissed his warnings about Dave Bates, and Chadwick was becoming more irritating as the European tour went on. Driving into a town in France, Evans, Groothuizen and Terry Bickers were talking about their responsibilities as ambassador-musicians, agreeing that it was the House Of Love's duty to show the Europeans another side to the English football hooligan stereotype. But over dinner that night, a quarrelsome Chadwick hammed it up as a devil's advocate Little Englander. 'He was playing his usual game,' says Groothuizen, 'of winding people up to see when they would snap. Sure enough, Pete snapped.'

Evans aimed a punch at Chadwick and was held back by Jarman just long enough to give Chadwick a chance to flee the restaurant. He ran outside and hid behind a wall. 'Pete couldn't find him,' recounts Bickers, 'so to vent his anger he ran on to this dodgem track. He climbed up the pole of a dodgem car – I've never seen anything like it, he was like a monkey man – and started swinging on the bar at the top. Obviously, the guys at the dodgem track didn't take too kindly to someone trying to trash their very expensive cars, so they started running after Pete. It was like a cartoon. They were running after Pete who was running after Guy.'

Intra-group relations were prickly for the next few days. Tom Atencio, meanwhile, concerned that his calls to McGee were going unanswered, flew to Europe to make overtures to Chadwick face to face. Atencio followed the House Of Love to Rotterdam, where events rapidly took a turn for the worse.

The one thing the House Of Love did not need was any more publicity in Britain. Jeff Barrett had recently joined the press officers' 'cunt club', as he calls it, by hoodwinking the editors of the rival papers *NME* and *Melody Maker* into thinking they each had a House Of Love exclusive – when in fact neither of them did – and thereby wangling two front covers for the band in the same week. But now Barrett had flown out to Rotterdam with a writer from the third weekly, *Sounds*. The journalist, Richard Newson, who was not an especially keen follower of the House Of Love, was planning to conduct a detailed interview with Chadwick and write an in-depth profile of a man in the eye of a hurricane.

Chadwick had done dozens of interviews since 'Christine' in April – some more searching than others – and had become not only the spokesman for the House Of Love but also a reliable source of quotes about organised religion, sex and the human psyche. The subject of his own psyche, and the pressures it had lately been facing, were to dominate the interview with Newson. The conversation lasted a gruelling two hours and was, remembers Newson, 'unusually intense'.

When Chadwick re-emerged after the interview, Andy Jarman knew at once that something was wrong. For five days, Chadwick had been drinking whisky from noon till night, relying on memory to get him through the gigs. He was not in the best of health, physically or mentally. 'He started drinking whisky backstage,' says Jarman, 'and he held on to my arm and said: "You're going to have to watch me tonight." It was one interview too many. It had triggered something in his mind.'

In the minutes after the show – which had been sloppy and shapeless – Tom Atencio asked to be permitted backstage, as did Jeff Barrett and Richard Newson. They were told to wait outside in the corridor. In the dressing-room, watched by a small, horrified audience, Chadwick demolished everything he could lay his fingers on, finally throwing his naked body against the walls and screaming his head off. Bickers, thinking Chadwick was having a brain haemorrhage, started screaming too. Jarman and members of the road crew wrestled Chadwick to the floor, kneeling on his arms and legs to keep him down. 'Every so often, somebody would come out and wipe their brow,' says Newson. 'You could hear Chadwick screaming and shouting and crying.'

Chadwick was eventually pacified, but he shook off Jarman's attempts to get him to a hospital. The next morning, Jeff Barrett asked Newson to avoid mentioning the incident in his *Sounds* article. As Newson and Barrett caught a plane back to London, Chadwick was driven across Holland by a radio promotions man from a Dutch record company. He had to do an interview.

Ibiza Euro-fashion and the colours of the hippy rainbow had given the London acid house scene the look and feel of a never-ending holiday. In April, as outside curiosity grew, Future's Paul Oakenfold had opened a second club – Spectrum on Monday nights – at Richard Branson's spacious Heaven complex. Danny Rampling and his wife Jenny moved Shoom to the YMCA in Tottenham Court Road, opening on Thursdays, the same night as Future. On top of the competition between acid house DJs, there was competition between clubbers to claim the true spirit of Ibiza. And there was the inevitable dilution. House tracks by Adonis and Phuture had established themselves as acid standards, the movement's own jukebox perennials. The Ibiza veterans who had made Shoom what it was were dismayed to find their clubs infiltrated by wide-eyed sightseers – the 'acid teds', as Liverpool fanzine *The End* was to dub them – who had heard about the party and come to join it.

On 16 July, Richard Norris appeared on the cover of the *NME*, his grinning, gurning face a self-explanatory advertisement for the four pages of acid house coverage inside. 'I'd been hounding the *NME* since January,' he recalls, 'saying: "You must do this." Jack Barron and Helen Mead were the only [*NME* writers] championing the music. Eventually, Jack said: "Well, why don't I write about you and we'll put you on the cover for your record?" ' Besides Barron's articles on the Norris project MESH and on Douglas Hart's Acid Angels, the *NME*'s coverage focused attention on a club called the Trip. Opened in June, the Trip was the place where acid house went overground – or, if one was being pejorative, became commercialised. The London media reported early morning street parties as the clubbers spilled out into the open air, but could only guess at what had been happening in the club itself. For its student readers, the *NME* described an urban tableau that few would have recognised.

'A car which is blaring out acid house from a radio has been surrounded by about 20 people,' it wrote, 'who have emerged, sweating and delirious, from a night at the Trip. Some of the revellers are climbing on to the car roof while others are dancing to the freakbeats in the middle of the road, completely unaware that they are causing a massive traffic jam all the way down the street ... Welcome to the world of acid house and Balearic Beats, the music and lifestyle that's going to dominate the rest of the year!'

The home of the Trip was the Astoria, a rock club in Charing Cross Road known for its belligerent security men. It was a venue favoured by bands that had grown too big for ULU and the London School of Economics, but were not yet ready for the 2,000-capacity Kilburn National or the Town and Country. As much a bastion of the capital's rock tradition as the Marquee or Dingwall's, the Astoria was, by July, modelling an unfamiliar look thanks to the Trip: baggy T-shirts, bandannas and dungarees, and no leather jackets to be seen. 'We had fucked off to America in about May,' says Pat Fish of the Jazz Butcher. 'Came back in July and we just couldn't believe what had happened to the West End.'

With Spectrum, the Trip and the RIP club in Clink Street – close to the original premises of Shoom – all having varying degrees of influence and popularity, the 'Summer Of Love' began. The Balearic Beat at Spectrum dilated to incorporate appropriate guitar anthems by the Woodentops, the Cure and Thrashing Doves. In the autumn, Alan McGee decided he'd better check the club out.

'Oakenfold would play [the Waterboys'] "Whole Of The Moon" and "Why Does Your Love Hurt So Much?" by Carly Simon,' he says. 'I would take three Es and wander around wearing my dark glasses. You had Liam from Flowered Up there. You had Jeff Barrett there. You had Paul Oakenfold there. It was all cutting-edge people in this room with hundreds of kids dancing ... They all liked me because they thought I was a weird fucker with weird hair and big sunglasses. But I was in the hippest clubs going. Yeah, Creation was out of touch – but the entire British music business was out of touch.'

However, on Spectrum's lower floor, where the sounds were pure acid house, McGee would seldom be seen. He could not get a grip on that stuff at all, no matter how much ecstasy he took. Downstairs in

Spectrum he was a tourist, an acid ted, not confident enough to make the judgments about music that usually came so easily. All that interested him was the hugging drug that was doing for his personality what cocaine and speed never had.

McGee had taken ecstasy for the first time in April, sitting in a park in Brighton with a previous girlfriend to Belinda White. 'I did a half [tablet],' he says. 'I thought it was going to be like acid. I remember halfway through, thinking: I really like this girl ... *really* like her.' They would listen to the pleasant music of Nick Drake, or something similarly pastoral. Soon McGee was buying ecstasy on a regular basis. 'I'd be doing Es, but I hadn't equated ecstasy and acid house,' he says. 'But then nobody from our culture, which was indie culture, had actually equated them. Richard Norris was the only person who'd kind of joined the dots.'

A hot-tempered man in a pressure environment, prone to flying off the handle whenever he had business worries, McGee felt his aggression burn away on ecstasy, as football hooligans on the terraces had found the previous year. Even so, McGee's drive and appetite for success would never completely be ridden by the drug. 'Even when he was on E,' remarks a former associate, 'he would say these things like: "Next year I want to make a million pounds." Totally seriously. You'd be like: "Yeah, OK mate, whatever." He was like the Del-boy Trotter of E culture.'

The first person to feel the typhoon of McGee's ecstasy evangelism was Jeff Barrett. Ironically, Barrett had had no problem assimilating acid house music, but had never taken the drug that went with it. 'Alan turns up with pills,' he recalls. ' "Barrett, you've got to do this." And I did. But [whereas] I felt comfortable at Future and Spectrum, Alan didn't. I think he felt a bit small in this potentially big sea, when he'd got so far in his own world. Alan's always needed to be *known* – to be quite well known.'

Even as McGee was getting more involved in ecstasy, some of the original acid housers were peaking after a year of continuous use, and comedowns were being experienced. 'A lot of people who had very little experience of life prior to that, and were not mentally, intellectually or emotionally prepared, came down with a hard bump,' DJ Steve Proctor told Matthew Collin and John Godfrey in *Altered State: The Story Of Ecstasy Culture And Acid House.* 'There's still people out there in the country in homes who couldn't deal with the reality that the rest of life wasn't going to be like this.' There were others who believed – wrongly – that ecstasy was legal. And there was McGee, who got in so deeply that he couldn't get out.

In London, the word on the A&R grapevine was that Dave Bates had offered £400,000 for the House Of Love. The shock waves spread to Polydor in Hammersmith, where Graham Carpenter immediately bowed out of the race in disbelief. His own offer had been £120,000. In Kensington, where the A&R department of WEA had made tentative inquiries during McGee's fortnight at the Waldorf, Malcolm Dunbar rolled his eyes. 'Four hundred thousand was a massive amount of money,' he says. 'The House Of Love should really have been signed for £80,000 to £100,000 maximum. But [Bates] offered so much money that it was going to Fontana, end of story.'

But the story was not over. Parallel to Bates – who was not the easiest person to keep up with – CBS had tabled an offer of £600,000. This, however, required close examination. Fontana's £400,000 excluded recording costs; the £600,000 from CBS did not. Doing the deal with CBS would place the onus on the House Of Love (and on their manager) to balance their living expenses against money for making records – not a satisfactory state of affairs since it would force them to think about what their music was worth, and put an expenditure limit on what they hoped to achieve. On the other hand, it was still 600 grand.

Chadwick liked the CBS A&R executive Muff Winwood, much as McGee liked Dave Bates. What dissatisfied McGee about CBS was a visit in September to its offices in New York, which were as corporate-looking as a bank and made him feel utterly anonymous. Nonetheless, CBS was still in the running when Chadwick and McGee had an unfortunate meeting with Winwood and his managing director Paul Russell.

'Paul Russell called Alan "Andy" all the way through the meeting,' recalls Chadwick. 'And that was it, really, I think. We were in reception on the way out, and Paul Russell came charging down the stairs and virtually got on his hands and knees: "I'm really, really sorry. I'm sorry. I'm sorry." I don't think it helped.'

McGee had warmed unreservedly to Bates, whose commitment to the band seemed heartfelt and whose track record was there on the page. Bates' passionate predictions for the House Of Love – including assurances of success in America – sounded realistic, all the more so when the Bates-signed Def Leppard reached number 1 in the US singles chart in the second week of October. 'He did a big sell on how you break America,' says Chadwick. 'We'd never even been to America. But anyone who likes music is completely enamoured with America and the whole history of its music. It is *the* thing, and although it was just a hazy idea, when someone's saying: "I know exactly what you have to do ..."'

But there was a world of difference between Def Leppard, who sold millions in Britain, and the House Of Love, who had only just passed 45,000 album sales. The cold fact was that before the House Of Love could break America they first had to break the UK. Chadwick was not deluding himself here. He had told Richard Newson from *Sounds*: 'We've even had American record companies fly over to see gigs in Brighton, and it's like: *what*? It's difficult to keep your feet on the ground and say: "Hey, we're only playing in front of 300 to 500 people each night. Let's keep things in perspective." '

Bates agreed that Fontana would buy 'Safe' from Creation for future release, and also acceded to a request for Jeff Barrett to continue as the band's publicist. The House Of Love embarked on a 19-date tour of college-sized venues in Britain. Business was better than ever, almost every show selling out. Then, on 6 October, as the tour reached Oxford, EMI offered £750,000 for the House Of Love, including recording costs.

The long-time homestead of Pink Floyd, Kate Bush and Queen, EMI had ventured belatedly into indie music in 1988 by doing a deal with Dave Balfe's four-year-old label Food. By acquiring EMI funding and distribution, Balfe had forfeited his eligibility for the indie charts, but secured Food's future. The attraction of an autonomous label with major backing was enough to entice Jesus Jones and Blur to Food's door, and the hits would begin arriving in 1989. For all that, however, the deal had been a big step into the unknown. 'At the time, [EMI] had a very successful top end with Queen, Pink Floyd and the Pet Shop Boys,' Balfe told Blur's biographer Stuart Maconie, 'but they had no street-level vibe at all.'

EMI's lack of a street-level vibe nagged at McGee and Chadwick, too, and they were inclined not to take its offer of £750,000 seriously. It was too gigantic, practically an admission by the company that it had nothing to give the House Of Love but money. 'Alan's gut feeling was that EMI just weren't impressive,' says Chadwick. 'I never met anyone from EMI. But EMI were certainly used by Alan as a way of levering a better deal out of Fontana.'

On 7 October, with a Fontana deal only days away, the House Of Love played ULU. His self-belief at an absolute high, McGee celebrated by taking magic mushrooms and sitting up all night in his Notting Hill hotel, watching the television fly around the room. On 11 October, the House Of Love signed away their independence to Fontana and Dave Bates for £400,000.

That same month, after an argument about defaulting on the rent, McGee asked Graham Gillespie to move out of the flat in Brighton. To fill the vacancy, McGee approached possibly the most ill-suited cohabitant in all of the British Isles.

By 1988, Lawrence knew that Felt were never going to be pop stars, and that any album with Felt's name on it would sell the same amount as the album before. *Train Above The City*, which Creation had released in August, did not even have Lawrence on it: it had been made by keyboard player Martin Duffy and drummer Gary Ainge. Ainge had played a vibraphone belonging to ex-Felt guitarist

Neil Scott. To pay for the instrument – Scott was asking for £250 – Felt had simply recorded an album full of vibes and waited for the inevitable 10,000 people to buy it. 'It was a chance to do something that said: "There's no band like us",' says a top-spinning Lawrence. 'We can even do jazz if we want.'

For some time, Lawrence had been longing to leave Birmingham and move to London. In October, accommodation in a squat in Kilburn became available, which sounded quite nice, but just as Lawrence was packing his things and getting ready to go, the squatters were evicted and locks put on the door. Tsk. In sympathy, McGee offered Lawrence his spare room by the sea. Of course, he had heard all the phobia stories, and he fully expected Brighton's shops to start doing a roaring trade in air-fresheners, hand-towels, disinfectants and polishing cloths. With luck, Lawrence might be persuaded to let him use his own lavatory once in a while.

To McGee's amazement, although Lawrence would protest about the volume at which his flatmate liked to listen to music, and although he still refused to eat cheese or vegetables, he proved in other areas to be just as relaxed and orderless as McGee himself. 'I lived with Lawrence for six months,' he says, 'and I'm cleaner and tidier than he is. I think he'd come out of his phobia ... The anal retentive and cleaner-than-clean thing wasn't there any more.' Lawrence soon became an integral part of Creation's south coast coterie. As Primal Scream had done, he appointed Brighton the official base of Felt, and Gary Ainge moved down in due course.

Lawrence was now in full concept mode. The next Felt album was to be keyboard-based, containing a side of horror film music and a side of porno music. Lawrence was having fun thinking up titles like 'She Cried Till Her Eyes Came Out' and 'Kitty Likes It', and wanted the album to come out on 7-inch format. But after only one piece had been recorded, the idea was abandoned. Lawrence hired the producer John Leckie, who had worked with Felt on their 1984 album *The Strange Idols Pattern and Other Short Stories*, and took Martin Duffy, Rose McDowall (ex-Strawberry Switchblade) and viola player Frank Sweeney (ex-June Brides) to Livingston Studios to record a single called 'Space Blues'.

McGee had been opposed to the two-day session – even on cheap deals, Leckie and Livingston were setting Creation back a tidy sum – and Lawrence had had to argue bitterly to get them. Leckie commiserated: he was currently working on an album by a Manchester band that had the full backing of its record company, Silvertone, which was funded by the successful Zomba labels group. 'Leckie was saying: "I can't believe someone like you is having to make a record like this [on a small budget] while that band are spending so much money",' recalls Lawrence. 'It was the Stone Roses album. "The guitarist can't even tune up, the singer can't sing ..." He didn't know it was going to go ballistic. It was a fucking different story to what he said afterwards, I can tell you.'

Finding an old Yamaha synthesizer in Livingston, Martin Duffy started to make strange, spaceman-like noises on it, and Sweeney added viola and violin. With no drums or guitar, 'Space Blues' sounded lunar and excitingly fresh – as Douglas Hart pointed out when he visited Lawrence at the studio. 'He said: "God this sounds mad. I've been going to all these clubs and they're playing music like this, with mad, bubbling synths." '

The closest a Creation band had come to acid house (though its lack of a beat made it hard to dance to), 'Space Blues' became a favourite in the Clerkenwell office. Meanwhile, in Lawrence's mind, Felt's journey from 1980 had started to make a perverse sort of sense. Each record was a lifetime of a particular band, a mini-strand of Felt, and the lifetimes were getting shorter, as were the spaces between them. The temptation for Lawrence was now to complete the circle and finish the group.

'I knew that we were coming to the end,' he says. 'I knew I'd never be able to do something like "Space Blues" ever again – we were in a top studio and it had all been a favour. To do something like that on a proper scale would have cost a fortune. What had to come after [would have] had to be meticulously planned and financed properly. It's a horrible thing to say, but to make a really great record you've got to have money.' But one more Felt album would make ten. And one more year of Felt would make a decade. Lawrence said nothing to McGee for the moment.

In the flat they shared in Brighton, tasks had been demarcated good-humouredly. 'I did the housework,' says Lawrence. 'He didn't cook or anything, but he only used to eat out of a tin anyway. If he was away in Manchester or up in London, I'd be his secretary and take all his messages . . . It was a good arrangement. He'd have these great parties and play music *so* loudly. And he'd always be trying to get girls back to the flat.'

It occurred to Lawrence that McGee seemed to be relishing something he had been too serious – and too married – to enjoy the first time round: his youth.

The House Of Love's contract was typical of hard-hitting deals between major labels and ambitious, music press-backed groups at the end of the 80s. The deal was for the world but excluded South Africa, where the apartheid system had not yet been relaxed. The advance was large and non-returnable. The record company footed the bills for studios and producers. The band's royalty percentage was high. A clause prevented the record company from releasing a compilation album of the band's work without prior consultation.

Only once a record was in profit would expenses become

recoupable. If the band was dropped while still unrecouped, the debt would be wiped from the slate. Of course, nobody in the House Of Love's camp considered that for an instant.

In the case of a two-albums-firm deal, the advance is usually split into six payments, or two cycles of three. The first payment is made when the band signs, the second when it starts the recording of the album (there is no point having an artist worrying about money when he is about to make an important record). The third payment is made on either the day of the album's completion or the day of its release. The cycle is repeated for the second album, with the fourth payment being seen as a 're-signing fee', a formality in the case of a two-albums-firm agreement. The fourth payment invariably occurs four months after the third.

The first payment to the House Of Love was £66,666. McGee took 20 per cent, putting some of it into Creation and the rest of it into his body. 'It's loads of money for a guy who just loves taking drugs,' he says. Cerne Canning met McGee shortly after the contract was signed. 'I remember him telling me that the amount he got out of it was [equal to] the Creation debt at the time,' Canning says. Very much a public animal during this period, McGee was perceived by the press to be a man on top form. When he took off his sunglasses at a party, it made the gossip column of the *NME*.

Because Dave Bates was both their A&R man and the head of their label, the House Of Love would be required to make an album that appealed to the two sides of him. His ideas about music-making and record production – he had briefly been a producer in the 70s – were often expressed in the most vehement terms, and he had put the fear of God into at least one of his artists by refusing to accept that a record was finished. 'A band would come in with their new album,' recalls a former colleague, 'and he'd just say: "No, fuck off. Not good enough. Do it again." '

Stephen Hague, the American producer of the Pet Shop Boys, had worked for Bates on '(Hey You) The Rocksteady Crew' in 1983, and on a Pete Shelley album three years later. 'Dave would come in and sit down and say: "OK, let's hear it",' Hague remembers. 'And he would read the paper. That was his trip, he'd always read something. Then he'd say what he thought about [the music]. But I had a lot of respect for him because he was a real music head ... He was attentive while things were going on, but he would let you get on with it. Then you would mix it, deliver it ... and then you would start to have a huge problem.'

The House Of Love were a neurotic group of individuals needing expert, kid-glove treatment which Bates was wholly incapable of providing. Relationships within the band were on thin ice, and the increasing chumminess of Chadwick and Bates was causing tension. Groothuizen and Bickers, for example, wondered why Chadwick was invited out to dinner with Bates when they were not. Their chagrin was not voiced out loud, and so this and other grievances remained unsettled. There was a virus in the air. 'They're all intense people,' says Andy Jarman. 'Chris isn't too intense but he's very serious. Pete was a very dangerous guy. Terry was a sweet kid but obviously slightly unstable, very vulnerable. Guy's got problems ... They're all psychologically damaged to a certain extent.'

Bickers had enjoyed the recording session for 'Safe', which had been produced by the much-respected Daniel Miller, owner of the Mute label. Moreover, after having initial doubts about McGee, Bickers had come to like the idea of being on Creation. He had not wanted to sign to a large record company, and found Bates loud and overbearing. One of the things that concerned Bickers was the sheer size of the deal, which he interpreted as a veiled threat: with all the money we're spending on you, you'd better deliver.

It had not taken long for Bickers to grow disenchanted, too, with his guitar hero reputation, and the rapturous reactions of audiences now seemed to him to be rather a con. Playing with the House Of Love had become a drill – a cheering crowd, a competent band, everyone going home happy, but neither party learning anything about the other. A young man anxious to communicate, Bickers wondered if the House Of Love were communicating the right message.

Bickers was in low spirits when he attended a Fontana party in the House Of Love's honour in October. He tried to avoid Chadwick, who was drunk and babbling, but eventually they fell into conversation. Out of the blue, Chadwick said something that left Bickers badly shaken. 'You see that bloke over there?' Chadwick whispered, pointing to Dave Bates. 'He wants a death. And I'm going to give it to him.'

Part Three

Bingeing and Purging

11 The Difference Between Going There and Being There

A S JOURNALISTS TRIED TO get a handle on My Bloody Valentine, their thoughts turned inexorably to sleep. One writer called them 'soft-spoken, self-effacing, almost somnambulist'. Kevin Shields often wore what looked like a pyjama jacket over his T-shirt. In interviews, Bilinda Butcher's remarks were sometimes so quiet and distant that her voice did not record on to the journalist's cassette. 'They were absolutely parallel with that withdrawn, slacker, shutters-down approach,' says Andrew Perry, who interviewed them for *London Student* in 1988. 'They didn't say anything. They didn't let anything out. They just sort of mumbled amiably about stuff.'

Perry lived just around the corner from the large squatted house in Kentish Town's Lady Margaret Road which more than one My Bloody Valentine member called home. 'You only had to look at the conditions they lived in to see that they were pretty fucked up,' he says. 'Lady Margaret Road was a really excellent street with huge great houses with stucco pillars. But there was this throbbing cancer in the middle of the street, which was the house where Colm and his friends lived. It just festered. There was an appalling smell coming out of it. I went round there to feed their cat one Christmas, and this guy chucked me a lighter which went over my head, hit the curtain and dropped on the floor behind the couch. I reached round past all these horrible old pizza cartons, and there was this little alley of rotting cat-shit with my lighter perched in it. It was just disgusting.'

Kevin Shields would later admit that My Bloody Valentine 'don't know many happy, stable people', and gave the impression that their friends included several depressive types who periodically contemplated suicide. Shields himself was a hypochondriac suffering in squalor, with an eccentric attitude towards health and hygiene. 'He was pretty smelly,' remembers Perry. 'He had this thing that if you don't wash your hair, eventually the grease crawls out from your scalp and the whole of your hair is coated with as much grease as can actually be on it. But after that, it doesn't get either better or worse, and actually it's very healthy for your hair.' A *Melody Maker* journalist who visited the Lady Margaret Road squat described a banister rail hanging uselessly in mid-air, its rungs demolished by a recent party. The Valentines seemed oblivious to their abject surroundings.

A second Creation EP by My Bloody Valentine was released in November. Featuring four new songs, it was the equivalent of that banister rail: a broken apparatus that hadn't quite decomposed but was no real aid to anyone wanting to use the stairs. The title track, 'Feed Me With Your Kiss', was extravagantly peculiar, full of irregular beat counts, abrupt cyclones of drumming and half-buried, off-key vocals. But even this was formulaic compared to the album that followed in December. Entitled *Isn't Anything*, it saw Shields take control of the band, becoming My Bloody Valentine's producer, primary songwriter, musical navigator and uncredited bassist as well as guitarist and co-vocalist.

Producing the album, Shields went for a trebly sound that took the tick-tick-tick of Hüsker Dü's snare drum and locked the guitars and bass into a narrow tunnel. Some of the songs had the density and distortion of early singles by the Who, and a few even appeared to have been recorded in mono. 'Kevin was a real 60s popster,' says Dave Anderson, the manager of Foel Studios in Wales where the album was recorded. 'I could tell where all the songs came from – what his influences were. Every night when everyone else would finish, he'd carry on and get the next two songs sorted out for the next day. There was music coming out of his every orifice.'

Not a traditional rock album in any way, *Isn't Anything* brought Shields' soft Irish-American brogue into clear daylight – although some of the lyrics he sang were absolutely baffling – while using the voice of Bilinda Butcher as an insidious atmospheric transmitting morning terror on an erratically-behaving pill. In contrast with the preceding EPs, parts of *Isn't Anything* were sketchy and almost threadbare. 'It's weird,' comments John Robb of the Membranes, 'because it's almost as badly produced as our first album was – for completely different reasons. Kevin's head was so perfectionist. You try and get any of those sounds he got; you cannot get them.'

One of the keys to Shields' guitar sound was his tuning of two neighbouring strings to almost the same pitch, which he would then bend with the tremolo arm. But rather than give his tremolo arm an occasional twiddle in the orthodox manner, Shields would keep it permanently in his right hand – he had taped the base of the arm halfway into its socket, leaving it loose and easy to hold – and strum the strings as if he were combing a girl's long hair. Unlike Terry Bickers or William Reid, Shields used only one effect, but it was an important one. Reverse reverb, a blurring agent, conspired with his tremolo arm technique to give a mournful, churning sound like that of a drunken cello. Shields called the sound 'glide guitar' and likened it to walking through deserted parts of the City of London on Sundays: 'The sounds just seem to be there, floating around ... The thing is, the sound literally isn't all there. It's actually the opposite of rock 'n' roll. It's taking all the guts out of it. There's no guts, just the remnants, the outline.'

Shields would often complain that people mistook this sound for electronic trickery, as though My Bloody Valentine were FX junkies who simply plugged in and let their pedals do all the work. He fell short of boastfulness, but he wanted it understood that his sound had not been bought off the shelf. 'The sound is purely physical,' he said in 1992. 'It's a movement, a manual moving of the strings: the short travel of the Jazzmaster and Jag[uar] trem[olo] that gives it that characteristic sort of upwards drone to the chord.'

But as Dave Anderson recalls, a key factor in the disembodied sound of *Isn't Anything* – as opposed to the EPs – was a simple human error. Before setting out for Wales, the band had phoned ahead to ask Anderson to buy an Alesis MIDIverb, which had the reverse reverb programme Shields wanted. 'I went out and bought a MIDIverb,' says Anderson, 'not realising that there was a MIDIverb and a MIDIverb 1. I happened to buy the MIDIverb 1, which didn't have it. [The band] had all gone off to get something to eat, and I was sitting in the control room listening to the different effects [on the MIDIverb 1]. Kev came running in and said: "That's it! That's it! That's my sound." I said: "You can't use *that* – that's just the effects on the unit." He said: "No, no. This is it." There's no real guitar sounds on that album at all, it's purely the effects unit. Kev got me to erase all the actual guitars and just leave the effect. That's about as psychedelic as you're going to get.'

When McGee heard the tapes of the album, he couldn't help thinking something was missing. The concept of a guitar-less My Bloody Valentine album took some getting used to; it was a bit like having a synthesizer duo without the synthesizer. Once the album had been mixed in London, however, McGee threw his support behind it and predicted that it would become a milestone in independent music.

'My expectations for My Bloody Valentine were incredibly high,' he says. 'I thought they were the fucking revolution – the same way that I'd thought the Mary Chain were the revolution four or five years earlier. What happened to Nirvana was what I actually thought was going to happen to My Bloody Valentine. I thought they were going to be the biggest group.'

Isn't Anything drew strong reactions from everyone who heard it. ('That LP!' the *NME* quoted Jeff Barrett as saying. 'It does your head in.') While it was not a commercially successful album – it sold around 40,000 copies in Britain over a period of years – its disorientating effect would linger for a long time to come. In England alone, over a dozen bands would wonder how on earth My Bloody

Valentine had obtained their sounds, and try to replicate them through a combination of foot pedals and guesswork. This was to exasperate Shields – particularly when some of these bands signed to Creation.

Without meaning to, Shields had opened the door to a movement of indie bands that knew only the sincerest form of flattery. It made him even more determined to forge ahead. 'It must have been really weird for him,' suggests McGee. 'It was an era when the press had incredible power over pop music. Kevin was getting called the biggest genius ever by loads of people – including myself. It was quite intimidating for him to feel that so much was riding on the next release. To be called a genius by the entire independent music business was probably too much for him to deal with.'

In October, the *Sun* jumped on the acid house bandwagon with a recklessness it would later regret. Offering its readers a special acid house T-shirt for the we're-simply-robbing-ourselves price of £5.50, it also provided a glossary of the scene's catchphrases (although one or two of these appeared to have been flown in from the early 60s American surfing craze). Those were the last positive words the *Sun* would have for its readers on the subject of acid house. Already, Richard Branson had advised Spectrum's Paul Oakenfold to cool it for a while, concerned by a *Sun* investigation into drug-dealing at Heaven. And a week after its T-shirt went on sale, the paper ran a story headlined 'Evil Of Ecstasy: Danger Drug That Is Sweeping Discos And Ruining Lives'. Like Alan McGee, Britain's least libertarian tabloid was starting to put two and two together.

The most immediate side-effect of ecstasy was evangelism. As Jane Bussman wrote in *Once In A Lifetime: The Crazy Days Of Acid House And Afterwards*: 'The miracle discovery of acid house made for internal conflict: you wanted to keep it a secret but you also wanted to get the whole planet on one. In the end you were very careful and only told your few close friends. And so did two million other people.' Alan McGee was one of those spreading the word – not just because spreading the word was an ecstasy side-effect but because he was Alan McGee, a spreader of the word. And those to whom it was spread included Dick Green, Bobby Gillespie, Andrew Innes, Ed Ball and Jeff Barrett.

Barrett was running down his indie club activities in London and falling in with Happy Mondays, Manchester's musically evolving, neo-Dickensian grotesques whose second album, *Bummed*, was about to be released by the city's Factory label. In October, Barrett's name was put forward by Dave Harper, who was retiring as Factory publicist. Barrett badly wanted the job. With regard to any thought of an acid house-indie music unification – an as yet up-in-the-air concept which the thoroughly non-conceptual, asphalt-dark *Bummed* would ironically do much to realise – Factory was streets ahead of Creation. Aside from having Happy Mondays, Factory owned the Haçienda club and boasted strong historical links to New York's dancefloors in both the early 80s work of A Certain Ratio and the contemporary productions of New Order.

Barrett was invited to Manchester to meet Factory directors Tony Wilson and Alan Erasmus and general manager Tina Simmons. Wilson, the label's spokesman and public face, was not like Alan McGee in the slightest. A middle-class polymath, a north of England celebrity and a Granada Television talking head since the 70s, Wilson seemed to be able to turn his hand to anything, be it the urbane *bon mot*, the balancing of several careers at once, or the showman's entrance. 'I was shitting myself, really nervous,' says Barrett. 'I'd gone up to Manchester with Dave Harper. We went down to [the Factory office in] Palatine Road and we sat there waiting for Tony to turn up. He was three hours late. Finally, he turned up: "Sorry, darlings, *really* sorry." Then he made a spliff. "Anyway, where were we? OK, you've got the job. What next?" '

A New Order album – *Technique* – was due in January and Barrett was thrilled by the prospect of working it. Rob Gretton, New Order's witheringly to-the-point manager, was not so ecstatic. Barrett was summoned to Gretton's home to get a few things straight. 'I had long hair then,' Barrett says. 'He opened the door and said: "Fucking hell, I'll give you 20 quid to get that cut off." Those were his opening words. He had *The House Sounds Of Chicago '88* playing on his tape player, which I thought was cool. I wasn't getting any of that from Creation at all, not from the bands or from Alan. [Gretton] was constantly skinning up, getting beers out of the fridge – just talking to me about anything and everything. I said: "Look, I've got to go to London. I've got this dinner at this Russian restaurant for the House Of Love's signing to Fontana." And he said: "As long as you're not as fucking 'rock' with us as you are with them, that's all right with me." ' Barrett arrived at the restaurant as the party got going. 'It was caviar, vodka ... It was a good night. But my mind was with Rob Gretton in Manchester.'

With the blessing of Tony Wilson and Alan McGee, Barrett became a two-label publicist, representing Creation and Factory from his small back room in 83 Clerkenwell Road. He learned that the two labels operated in very different fashions. For instance, despite having a reputation as an unprofessional company, Factory would hold meetings to plan a record's promotional and marketing campaigns – meetings which anything up to 20 people would attend. There was nothing like that at Creation.

Indeed, McGee's attention was once again wandering from his label, as it had in 1985 and 1987. Nor was he spending all his nights at home. He was following the drugs and Creation was falling by the wayside. It had no hope of competing with Factory's wintertime schedule – *Bummed* was to be a year-long steady seller and critics' favourite, while *Technique* would sail to number 1 on the Gallup chart – and it looked as though McGee wasn't even going to try. In December, he went up to Manchester to combine two of his favourite pastimes: taking ecstasy and seeing New Order in concert.

The Greater Manchester Exhibition Centre, where New Order were headlining over Happy Mondays and A Certain Ratio, was awash with London media and freeloaders, but they would witness a domestic celebration, not a national one. A victorious announcement from the stage during A Certain Ratio's set summed up the nature of the occasion: 'Manchester seven, London nil'. Nine days to Christmas and the championship had apparently been decided.

Afterwards, McGee was spotted in the backstage VIP lounge by a Creation fan named Debbie Turner. Turner had, since 1985, been part of a small group of Creation-friendly Mancunians, all of them fans of the Mary Chain and Primal Scream. Backstage at G-Mex, she and her friends were lying around on the floor 'because the E was really strong,' she recalls. 'I was pretty cocky so I just went up to Alan and said: "What have you got them shades on for?" I might even have said: "Oh, I thought you were Mick Hucknall", because I knew it would wind him up. And I remember him saying: "I've got cancer of the eye." I went over to my mates and was going: "Oh my God. Alan's got cancer in his eye and I feel really [bad]." '

An after-show party was being held at the Haçienda, where McGee took more ecstasy pills. 'I almost took too many,' he says. 'At one point I was talking to this girl called Hayley, who's on the front cover of a Bodines single. I was getting on quite well with her, trying to pull her and thinking I was getting somewhere. Then her face became a green diamond. I went: "You've just become a green diamond." At which point she fucked off and left me.' He went downstairs to the dressing-room, where Factory notaries including Tony Wilson, Rob Gretton and Happy Mondays' Shaun Ryder were draped on beanbags. 'I was sitting with Dick Green and Ed Ball,' says McGee, 'and a kid that used to work at Lazy Records was giving me Es. I was lying there absolutely off my nut – I really mean destroyed on Es.'

Debbie Turner, to whom it had occurred that McGee probably did not have eye cancer, the cheeky bastard, grabbed his arm and tried to persuade him to dance with her to the acid house music. She had no luck. 'He was like: "Ooh no, I don't do that. I'm into the drugs, but I've not taken that step yet." ' Hours floated by. 'I kind of came round at about six in the morning,' McGee remembers. 'I was lying next to Debbie saying: "I think we should get married." It was that off the wall.' Turner left the dressing-room and went back into the club to dance on her own. After a while, McGee wandered up to watch her.

Like Steve Martin in *The Jerk*, his feet slowly began to move to a rhythm he'd never really understood before.

'I heard acid house music and suddenly I got it,' he says. 'Something went *click* and I went into a new world. December 17 is when I got acid house. And that's when Creation changed.'

Dave Bates rejected 'Safe' as a single, feeling that the House Of Love could do better. On 24 November, the band convened at a studio called the Chocolate Factory in London to demo the ten songs that would comprise its first album for Fontana. After two weeks, Guy Chadwick was depressed. The demos sounded awful.

As far as the public knew, however, the House Of Love's star was still rising. They were named by *The South Bank Show* as the rock band to watch in 1989, and sales of the Creation album increased. They also did well in the music papers' end-of-year polls. In December, Chadwick was interviewed by the *NME* alongside two other indie musicians who had signed to major labels: Andrea Lewis, the singer in the Darling Buds, who were on Epic; and Miles Hunt of the Wonder Stuff, signed by Graham Carpenter to Polydor a year before and just beginning to feel the pinch of corporate pressure by the end of 1988. Chadwick agreed with Hunt that record companies should be nothing more than a 'distribution service' for their bands' records. 'The artist should control everything else,' Chadwick said firmly. It was a persuasive argument to take into the new year, but it crumbled upon contact with Dave Bates.

Chadwick and McGee had found Bates' first A&R decision – the rejection of 'Safe' – puzzling. They found his next suggestion totally intolerable. He wanted them to work with the producer Chris Hughes, a former drummer in Adam and the Ants and Bates' closest friend. Sensing a conflict of interests, they requested instead Tim Friese-Greene, the producer and co-writer of Talk Talk's masterful album *Spirit Of Eden*. Friese-Greene turned them down. 'He told Guy to come back when he'd finished writing the songs,' says Chris Groothuizen.

In January, with an album release provisionally scheduled for the summer of 1989, the House Of Love started work on two songs with Tim Palmer, the 26-year-old producer of Texas' single 'I Don't Want A Lover', which Phonogram was about to release, and of the goth crossover band the Mission. And if one was talking about crossovers, a key point in Palmer's favour was that he had produced the second Mighty Lemon Drops album, *World Without End*, a number 1 hit on America's alternative charts in 1988. Backed by college radio, the one-time C86 band was averaging two American tours a year, its Billboard debut seemingly only a lucky break away. But although Tim Palmer's productions sounded good on the radio, they were not big on surprises.

For two reasons – the size of the House Of Love's advance and the level of expectancy from the media – there was pressure on their first Fontana single, which would be chosen from the Palmer sessions, to reach the Top 40. An additional consideration was *Top Of The Pops*, the usual cut-off point for which was number 40. The House Of Love would have to leapfrog the anticipated Top 50 placing of their unreleased fifth Creation single and make the quantum jump straight into the thirties, or better still the teens. Then the real business of selling the album would start. 'The problem was that Dave wanted us to make [an album] that was going to sell 20 million,' says Chadwick, 'and he had a fixed idea of what it had to sound like.' McGee concurs: 'Bates wanted a superstar number 1 album all around the world. Everyone was talking about U2 – Bates, Guy, all of them.'

At £850 a day, RAK Studios in St John's Wood was by far the most expensive – and largest – studio the House Of Love had ever recorded in, but for the first session only the drums and bass guitar were required. Palmer brought down a session drummer to tune Pete Evans' kit: if anyone in the House Of Love had thought he was still in an indie band, that was the moment the penny dropped. 'We were doing two songs, "Shine On" and "Never",' recalls Palmer. 'I'd heard the original recording of "Shine On" and found it very reverb-y and indie-sounding. I was told to make the "proper" record, in inverted commas.'

The band moved to other studios around London for Palmer to record the vocals and guitars. When Terry Bickers was needed for his solo in 'Shine On', he assembled his arsenal of pedals only to find that Palmer wanted something much less ethereal. 'He had this really melodic solo,' says Palmer, 'which was great, and he was in [the studio] playing it. He got to literally a bar before the end and said: "I can't think of anything else." I said: "It's great, Terry – just finish it off. A few notes just to resolve it a little bit and you've got it." But he couldn't do it and he was getting really frustrated with himself. And he said: "Right, I'm going home. I can't do it any more." He just gave up. He just put his guitar down and left. I had to play the last three notes of the solo myself.'

Bickers had picked a bad time to be temperamental. Chadwick soon lost patience with him and began to exclude the other members of the band from his burgeoning relationship with Palmer. 'Palmer didn't give a fuck who played on the record as long as it sounded better than the demo and Guy sang on it,' says Groothuizen. 'We were listening back to a guitar part that Terry had done and I said: "Can I hear that back?" Palmer turned round and said: "Oh, so you're the fucking producer now?" And Guy loved it. I thought: well, *you* are an arsehole, and thanks a lot Guy for sticking up for me.'

Palmer liked Bickers' guitar style. He just wished the guitarist didn't look so nervous while he was playing. 'He was frightened for his life almost,' Palmer remembers. 'You'd see him standing in the corner and he'd say: "You couldn't run me home, could you mate? It's a bit dangerous out there tonight." ' Bickers – the one man who had been opposed to the Fontana deal – was no longer sure he had what it took to be in the House Of Love. The professional studios and the Palmer-Chadwick politics were pulling a rug from under his feet. 'Terry was rather sidelined by it all,' says Groothuizen. 'Terry was the one who wanted the band to all live in the same house. He wanted us to have group hugs and be organic – basically to be a surrogate family for him.'

When McGee heard 'Never', he told Palmer the House Of Love had never sounded better. In fact, they had rarely sounded worse. The recording had the dated bluster of U2's *War* period, taking the House Of Love back to the sounds of 1983. Bates preferred 'Never' to 'Shine On' – mainly because nobody liked what Palmer had done to 'Shine On' – and chose it as a single for Easter release. By 8 February, when the recording sessions ended, the House Of Love had been to six studios in a month.

McGee had become an acid house fanatic. Having put two and two together, he was now applying the mathematics of Manchester, dancing in the Haçienda every Friday night. 'He was converted immediately,' says Dick Green. 'Everything. The whole scene. The feeling. The drugs. It was almost instantly having an effect on Creation in the way Alan was thinking – the way he was broadening his ideas of what music we should be doing.'

McGee, however, was the manager of two rock groups – the House Of Love and Primal Scream – and if Creation were to take steps to embrace acid house, neither of those bands, nor any of the other Creation acts, would be the ones to point the way. Only Ed Ball reckoned he'd like to have a go at making house music, and the clubbers at Shoom were not thought to be holding their breath.

Paul Mulreany, the drummer in the Jazz Butcher, had tried ecstasy while working at Creation as an odd jobs man. He liked ecstasy and he liked acid house. Then again, his band-leader Pat Fish much preferred alcohol to ecstasy and thought acid house was tedious. It was a typical Creation group dividing issue. 'You'd have your purists in the band who'd go: "Yeah, yeah, bleep bleep bleep",' says Mulreany. 'But having said that, I was trying to explain it as: "Well, to me, it's just good disco music." Obviously the sign of a jaded musician. But I was going: "You know, it grooves and it's all we-love-each-other. Great! Who cares what they're singing about?" ' A songwriter like Fish for one.

Dick Green was not as sold on ecstasy as McGee, even if he enjoyed it from time to time. Creation was a guitar label, Green tended to feel, and he expected it to remain one. And while Ed Ball was ever eager to understand how to operate a sampler, there was only one person in McGee's orbit who already knew which fingers went where. His thoughts turned again to Richard Norris.

Norris' project MESH – a triumvirate that also included Genesis P-Orridge and Soft Cell's Dave Ball – had recently drawn interest from WEA, where Martin Callomon ('Cally'), a co-founder of the Bam Caruso indie label which had once employed Norris, had succeeded Bill Drummond as resident mystic of the A&R department. A former manager of Julian Cope, Cally worked under Malcolm Dunbar and was searching for acts to sign to the soon-to-be-established East West, a Warners company with Max Hole as managing director. Cally, who had loved Norris and P-Orridge's *Jack The Tab*, offered MESH £12,000 to make an album in 12 days. Only P-Orridge proved resistant, so Cally signed Norris and Ball as a duo, renaming them the Grid.

Once the Grid had signed with Cally, Norris started getting calls from McGee. 'He was ringing up nightly, saying: "I want to manage you",' Norris recalls. 'He'd got on to acid house very quick. I like that revelation bit of it, because it definitely was that quick for quite a lot of people. I don't know if he was desperately trying to understand it. He just *did* understand it.' The Grid agreed to McGee management.

In their flat in Brighton, McGee was bombarding Lawrence with house music from morning to night. Lawrence knew about acid house, since he had friends in Windsor who hung around with the writers of the football-and-dance-culture fanzine *Boy's Own*. However, he had never taken up his friends' offer to come down to Windsor and check out their scene for himself, and he hated the music he was hearing from McGee. 'He'd play [A Guy Called Gerald's] "Voodoo Ray", which was good,' Lawrence recalls, 'but mostly he wasn't playing acid house, he was playing Italian house compilations. Awful. He'd got it all wrong. It was so typical of Creation to be at the fag-end of it. I just thought he'd got into it too late and he'd picked up on the wrong side of it.'

Italian house was a major-chord music of jubilation recognisable by its bellowing divas and lost-in-translation lyrics. It screamed into Britain in 1989 and sent McGee into a rhapsodising frenzy. Poor old Lawrence was a sitting duck. 'Every morning he'd get up early – after drinking a load the night before – and he'd blast out this music,' Lawrence says. 'He'd come into my room and go: "Are you into it yet? Are you into it yet?" '

Bobby Gillespie and other members of Primal Scream attended an acid house party in a Brighton warehouse in late 1988. As Lawrence remembers, Primal Scream were having bitter arguments about the merits of acid house – with guitarist Robert Young the most vociferously negative. 'We couldn't really make head nor tail of the music or the people,' Gillespie told Michael Bonner. 'It was still early days, but it was a strange, weird little underground thing. I always remember being quite fascinated by it but not quite getting it.'

'We spent ages trying to get the band involved,' Jeff Barrett told Bonner. 'They were kind of sceptical at the time ... But they were aware something was happening because they'd seen a change in me and Alan. Then they started dipping their toes in, and it took them all of about five minutes to realise what joys could be had with ecstasy.' Like McGee, the Scream were going in drugs-first.

McGee and Debbie Turner had connected on ecstasy in December. Taking her phone number, McGee began to visit Manchester more and more, often spending weekends there. 'We'd see him a lot in Manchester with his blue-and-white stripey top on,' says John Robb. 'He would always be completely off his head.' By February, McGee was considering renting a flat in the city. However, he spent much of that month on the road with My Bloody Valentine.

The Valentines seemed a very different scene to acid house. Still, there was one obvious way to make them unite. 'It was the same thing because it was the same drug,' says Debbie Turner. 'You'd go and see My Bloody Valentine or Primal Scream, and you'd want to go to a house club afterwards. It wasn't like: "We've done a gig so let's get pissed." It was: "Let's neck some drugs and go to a house club." '

In Brighton, where the Creation acid house clique remained a McGee-only show for the time being, Lawrence was having serious reservations about the doctrinal view McGee had taken. Although he had tried ecstasy, Lawrence was not so impressed by the implication that everyone ought to succumb to house music and fall into line. When Jeff Barrett came to a party in Brighton, Lawrence wondered if he'd left his free will back in London. 'I remember thinking: what the fuck has happened to Jeff?' he says. 'He was dancing all night, even in the kitchen pouring a drink. That was a period when you were supposed to dance all through the night. You were never sup-posed to stop, no matter what you were doing. You couldn't be seen to be not moving. And you had to claim to like every record going. It all just seemed fake to me.'

At any rate, McGee had made his decision – or what he believed was his decision. It would change the Creation landscape. In an *NME* article about Duncan Dhu, a rock group from Spain that McGee had picked up for one album, he insisted that Creation's horizons would widen to take in house music by the end of 1989. 'Alan was definitely losing interest [in rock],' says Lawrence. 'The House Of Love were mega but Guy was blowing it. Alan would go away for days to London and come back and tell me how Guy had stripped nude again and done something stupid.'

McGee had been on ecstasy in Chadwick's company at a Happy Mondays gig in Dingwall's in January – but had withheld the drug from Chadwick for discretionary reasons. Now they were taking ecstasy together and going out to Shoom in Kensington High Street, McGee watching irritably as Chadwick behaved like a first-time drunk. 'Guy was totally uncool,' he says. 'The coolest of the cool people in London are at Shoom, and although I run an indie label, that's cool in that sort of circle. I'm cool in the sense that I'm inspired enough to be there. But Guy would get on one and try to take his clothes off. He'd be dancing like ET or something, getting threatened by the bouncers. He was like your uncle on an E.'

However, one dissenting voice argues that whatever McGee may have imagined about being perceived as cool by the Shoom clientele, he was in some ways just as much a fish out of water as Chadwick. 'Alan McGee never got house music,' contends Jeff Barrett. 'Alan McGee got ecstasy. Alan got pilled up and excited and really into something. But he reserved judgment to a degree. He was never comfortable in London [clubs]. He felt quite comfortable in Manchester because he had Debbie with him. But Alan was not down at Shoom. He was not down at Future. He was not down at Spectrum. His face was showing every now and again, but he kept away. There's a big difference between going there and being there.'

The best-known band on Head – Barrett's mid-80s indie label – had been the noisy psychedelic outfit Loop, since departed for the Chapter 22 label. One of their guitarists, James Endeacott, had left the band and was at a loose end. He was asked if he fancied a job working for Creation. After an exploratory meeting in Clerkenwell, the offer was hastily withdrawn – Endeacott had been expecting some sort of payment – but to show there were no hard feelings, he and McGee went to the Powerhaus club in Islington to get drunk and see a Manchester band McGee had been told about.

'I said: "What are they like?"' recalls Endeacott. 'Alan said: "They've got this one song that sounds just like the [Primal] Scream." We were at the back of the bar, taking absolutely no notice of the gig at all, having a drink, and then this song came on – "Made Of Stone". Alan goes: "This is it! This is the one that sounds like Primal Scream!" And I remember looking down the Powerhaus and seeing all these kids from Manchester going mental. Alan was like: "Fucking useless." '

The Stone Roses' tour for 'Made Of Stone' – their fourth single – was a basic circuit of clubs and polytechnics, playing to a few hundred people a night. Their John Leckie-produced debut album was now finished and awaiting release on Silvertone, an indie label founded by Andrew Lauder, who had been the head of A&R at United Artists in the 70s and later a co-founder of the esoteric punk-era label Radar. Financed by the hit-making music company Zomba, the Stone Roses were beginning to turn heads in the south with their resplendent, 60s-influenced melodies, coltish lead guitar playing and sartorial street suss. In their home city, however, they were more popular by far. Though unaffiliated to the major Manchester scenes – Factory, the Haçienda and the clubs where the leading bands drank – they had a faithful following that included working-class boys, plenty of girls and, interestingly, some residual fans of the 80s band the Chameleons, who despite having a north Manchester fanbase big enough to fill 2,000 seaters had never sold many records in the rest of England.

'The Stone Roses were pretty massive in Manchester by then,' says John Robb, who had first met them in 1984. 'They would claim to be getting 1,000 people at their gigs. It was actually about 500 – but that's still quite a lot. If you got 500 people to a gig in London, you'd get a front cover of a magazine in those days. There were a couple of really important gigs that they did in late '88, early '89 when they supported James at the International 2 [in Manchester] and blew them right off the stage. That's when they started crossing over to the student audience. They were the first band for years that had united the two ends of the music scene: the students and the council estate kids.'

It had taken almost five years for the Stone Roses to be accepted unconditionally by Manchester. In 1988, Robb had heard demos of songs the band would later record with Leckie, and had tried to per-suade *Sounds* to let him write a feature. 'It was all little factors,' he says. 'Reni was an amazing drummer. John Squire's guitar playing was really good. And Ian Brown was a star – just one of those guys that's always the leader of the gang. I mean, what else do you need to be in a band that's going to get somewhere?' Even so, Robb doubted that the Stone Roses would find their rainbow so quickly. 'I was hearing the original demos of "Made Of Stone", thinking: what an amazing song this is. But I was also thinking: that sort of music's never going to be massive again. It did seem impossible for them to actually get in the charts.'

'Made Of Stone' entered the indie chart a fortnight after the Powerhaus gig, reaching number 4. It wasn't long before tapes of the Leckie album made it to Manchester, and the reaction was usually the same. 'When the cassettes started floating around, people were going: "Jesus, this is good",' says Robb. 'It went the extra yard. It was-n't just a good album. It was a great album.'

'Made Of Stone' had tickled McGee. Its chorus used almost exactly the same descending notes as Primal Scream's 'Velocity Girl' – and this was by no means a complete accident. 'The Stone Roses used to worship Creation,' says Robb. 'You'd never see them out at any gigs apart from Primal Scream gigs.' Debbie Turner was a friend of Stephen 'Cressa' Cresser, a Stone Roses roadie, and the two of them had been going to Primal Scream gigs since 1985, occasionally taking John Squire with them. 'Cressa always used to take the piss out of

Primal Scream for their leather pants,' says Turner. 'One day I was walking down the street and saw John Squire in a pair. [The Stone Roses] were totally influenced by the whole Creation thing.'

For all the similarity between 'Made Of Stone' and 'Velocity Girl', the Stone Roses were not rivals as such to Primal Scream, who had abandoned the winsome 60s elements in their music twelve months before. Bobby Gillespie, a co-writer of 'Velocity Girl', was inclined to be honourable about the resemblance. 'Bobby came up and stayed at my flat for a couple of nights,' recalls Turner, 'and we went to a Mary Chain gig at the Free Trade Hall. I was backstage and William Reid was saying to Bobby: "You should fucking *sue* the bastards." Bobby was just like: "Music's music." His thing was we're all influenced by something, which I thought was really cool.'

Lawrence had been at the Brighton date on the 'Made Of Stone' tour in February, watching with members of Primal Scream. There had been disagreement about whether the Stone Roses were any good or not. 'The Scream just stood there: "This is shit",' says Lawrence. 'But I was like: "Wow, this is great." I noticed the clothes. I'd never seen anyone wear stuff like the Stone Roses. It wasn't second-hand gear. They were wearing really expensive street clothes, leather coats. Ian Brown had new denims on – not old. I thought: God, this band are really different. And the songs were brilliant. I was going: "This is it, isn't it? It's the new thing." '

Whatever he thought of 'Made Of Stone', McGee had been right about Manchester. It was the city dictating the agenda on two fronts. The machine beat of acid house could never threaten a band like the House Of Love, but a melodic quartet with a growing reputation and limitless self-belief could. The Stone Roses were absolutely on the House Of Love's turf, with the 60s references, the virtuoso guitarist and drummer, the confident singer and the money behind them to make their songs chime all the way to London.

'I think what McGee probably meant by "fucking useless",' says John Robb, 'was "fuck, these are good. These are a bit of a challenge." People speak with forked tongues sometimes, don't they?'

Iain McNay had been having grave doubts about Rajneesh. The spiritual side of McNay – Aukash – was troubled by the arrogance in the cult's thinking, which, loosely defined, went: 'If you are a disciple of Rajneesh, you are superior to people who are not.' Moreover, McNay wondered if Rajneesh himself had crossed the line between comfortable living and ostentatious materialism.

'Rajneesh lived on a ranch in Oregon where he would speak every day, doing what's called a discourse,' he says, 'and Morgan [Fisher] would play in the band beforehand. There were some great people involved – really good people. But one thing that was always weird was, every time Rajneesh came out to speak, he would have a guy with a sub-machine-gun each side of him. He would say: "Oh, this is because I need protection from the American government." And he would drive around the ranch every day in all these Rolls Royces. There were too many things that didn't add up.'

After Rajneesh's deportation from America in 1985 for immigration violations, the Oregon commune had gradually broken up. McNay got involved in a community in northern Italy run by an Englishman named Paul Lowe, who had been Rajneesh's number two. In 1987, McNay took part in an experiment called the Six Month Project: 60 people living together in Italy with the aim of attaining enlightenment and self-realisation. McNay changed his name again – from Aukash to Roxi.

While Roxi followed his adventure in Europe, his companies in London, Cherry Red Records and Complete Music, were managed by an uncomfortable alliance of Martin Costello and James Kyllo, a Canadian friend of Mike Alway's. As McNay's sabbatical was extended to some four years, during which he did not appear in the Cherry Red offices once, Costello was entrusted with the company cheque-book and given authority over all releases, including those on Alway's mercurial, exotic, unprofitable label él.

Conceived as an antidote to the beastliness and cynicism of 80s Britain, él was a customised Alway vessel, an artefact and a caprice that allowed him to head deeper into an elaborate world of fantasy. Musically, él gave few clues that it was a mid-80s record label, seeming instead to date from a timeless epoch where the last days of British sovereignty in India overlapped with the first meeting of Roger Moore and Tony Curtis in *The Persuaders*. Since the departure of Momus, most of the artists on él's roster were either pseudonymous or figments of Alway's imagination. 'He would think up the names of the acts,' says McNay. 'He would think up the names of the songs. He wasn't credited for writing lyrics for songs, but I suspect he did.'

If there was one man in 1987 who antithesised both yuppie greed and generic indie label drabness, it was Alway. In 1981 he had not looked at his chart positions. Six years on, he wasn't even looking at the indie chart. 'I think Iain allowed me to indulge myself with él because he thought that I'd find another Everything But The Girl,' he says. 'I found lots of good people with él, but it was too off-beam ... out of kilter. Maybe I shouldn't have been so cavalier.' Alway was a fantasist, sure, but he was not unaware of the realities. And if he ever forgot them, the music press would remind him. The *NME* came up with a nasty – but in a way fitting – motto for él: 'We make it, no one buys it.'

Even before embarking on his travels, McNay had become a little more selective in acceding to the hyperactive Alway's requests for money. Alway's reaction was to make él even less accountable, deliberately distancing it from the jeering media. And now, with McNay no longer in England, Alway had neither patronage nor guidance. 'Iain pissed off to northern Italy to faff around with his fucking guru, never coming into the office, never giving any leadership,' he says. 'It was a ridiculous situation. The likes of Martin Costello would play records by [él acts] Bad Dream Fancy Dress and the Would-Be-Goods – records with character rather than musical accomplishment, if you like – and I can remember the humiliation of sitting there while some elements in the office were laughing and taking the piss.'

One upshot was that Alway's friend James Kyllo left Cherry Red in 1988, unwilling to spend another minute in Costello's company. Kyllo took a job with Record & Tape Exchange, and worked there for several months before being approached by Alan McGee and Dick Green. 'We were trying to learn business techniques,' says Green, 'because none of us had any business training or acumen. Alan was still doing royalties by hand. We had no financial control particularly, apart from adding up the cheque stubs. James had the knowledge. He'd worked at Cherry Red and he knew how to work computers.'

Kyllo joined Creation in January 1989 as business manager. His first job was to find new office space, as 83 Clerkenwell Road was not big enough for a five-man workforce. Kyllo drove around London, looking at places in affordable areas and drawing up a short-list of four. He took McGee to the first of them, an office above a sweatshop in Westgate Street, Hackney. Ribbons of black fabric littered the stairs to the top floor, where another staircase – this one spiral – led on to a glass roof and a balcony. 'He said: "We'll take it",' recalls Kyllo. 'He didn't even look at the others on the list.'

Paul Mulreany took charge of the move from Clerkenwell. 'Me and my mate Steve moved all the stuff in a hire van,' he says, 'and McGee paid us in returned copies of *Doing It For The Kids*. "There you are – just take those down to Record & Tape Exchange." We had about three or four hundred of them. The minute Creation moved in, the office just started falling to pieces.' Jeff Barrett arrived with his assistant Emma Anderson to be told there was nowhere for them to sit. 'We didn't even have a desk,' recalls Anderson. 'I was sitting on the floor with a phone, a piece of paper and a pen.' After a week, she and Barrett moved their PR operation to his flat in Shepherd's Bush.

'There was a different perspective on things at Hackney,' says Dick Green. 'It was starting to become a company. There was staff being paid wages, and we started to pay advances to bands.' Kyllo and Ed Ball became the first paid Creation employees. My Bloody Valentine were signed to a proper contract, which not only fended off the other UK labels but gave Creation worldwide rights to the band's music. (This was important: McGee and Green hoped to license My Bloody Valentine to the American company Sire for a windfall sum.) 'There was so much structural change that had to be done [at Creation],' says Kyllo. 'The real thing that I was brought in to do was take it from being essentially a hobby – where Rough Trade did all the work and all the business – and take it in-house. So we took over our own manufacturing and international.' Creation came off its P&D deal and moved on to a much less prohibitive Rough Trade distribution deal. 'I remember Alan saying: "You can't believe how much more money you can make by doing your own production",' says Chris Groothuizen. True; those Rough Trade percentages had been creeping up and up.

The lack of a nearby tube station made Westgate Street less accessible than the more central Clerkenwell, which seemed to confirm that the intention of McGee and Green was to become more businesslike. Nick Currie recalls: 'There was a certain point at which Alan decided that all these people hanging round the office shouldn't be encouraged. There would always be somebody in leather trousers lying on the floor when you went into the Clerkenwell Road office. When they moved to Hackney, although there was a presidential suite where Primal Scream were allowed to lie on the floor in leather trousers, it wasn't encouraged so much.' The mirrored presidential suite was the lair of the President himself, and McGee's semi-comical nickname would now stick.

Creation's cash flow was still heavily dependent on the House Of Love, whose album continued to sell tens of thousands of copies months after their signing to Fontana. The next biggest seller was Momus, but his profits were not on a large scale. While there was still no evidence that Creation would achieve success with any of its acts, the feeling that Hackney represented a new start was the signal for the company's capital to be redistributed. Yvonne McGee's shares were returned to Creation as part of her divorce settlement, and Joe Foster was bought out. Alan McGee was left with 68 shares, Dick Green 27 and McGee's father five.

The behaviour of Terry Bickers was becoming more and more irregular. He was giving away his money at an alarming rate, and he was binge-eating. His fluctuations in weight were frightening. When the House Of Love played a gig in Sunderland in February, Bickers told Pete Evans he was worried about being fat. Evans told him not to be ridiculous – he was as thin as a rake. A week later, Bickers looked like he'd put on four stone. 'He told me how he would go to lunch three times,' says Chris Groothuizen. 'He found himself going into a curry house and having lunch, and then just going on and having another ... It was phenomenal. He would just balloon. For some reason he could actually eat that amount of food.'

Bickers' inability to come to terms with the money the band had received from Fontana should have been an indication that he was unhappy with the Fontana deal full-stop. But as the relationship between himself and Chadwick deteriorated, it was Bickers who was increasingly seen as the sinner. And Groothuizen found himself agreeing with Chadwick. 'Terry would buy you dinner,' says the bassist. ' "Oh, it's on me, no problem." But then he'd come to you three days later and say: "You know that dinner I bought you? I could really do with the money now." And he wouldn't understand why people thought he was a wanker for doing that.'

The unravelling of Bickers was not relayed to the outside world, since the House Of Love played few gigs during these months and closed ranks when they were in the presence of journalists. But this wasn't simply to protect Bickers. 'It was very difficult to know how to deal with it,' says Chadwick, 'because his behaviour was so unreasonable. Unreasonable isn't the right word. It was *indescribable*. To try to describe it to anyone would have been a betrayal. He was just fucking completely mad.'

Clearly, Bickers' enthusiasm for playing music with the House Of Love was now minimal. The stability he had found in the band's early years was under threat from a variety of sources – Fontana; the upgrade to cold and clinical recording studios and processes; Chadwick's habit of cold-shouldering him out of new friendships with producers – and each injury triggered off anger, fear and vulnerability that had been suppressed since his childhood. 'We knew he was unhappy,' says Groothuizen. 'But . . . it's a terrible thing to say, but when he manifests his sadness in a way that's annoying, you can only take it for so long. I had him crying on my shoulder, and [I was] giving him advice – trying to help – and then having it all thrown in my face. And I was thinking: well, how much more can I put up with this?'

McGee had no previous experience of mental illness or breakdowns. The most serious incidents he'd ever had to witness as a manager were the screaming matches between the Reid brothers in the mid-80s. Misunderstanding Bickers' cries for help, McGee felt the guitarist was throwing drug-induced tantrums. There was certainly no way Bickers' conduct could be tolerated much longer: McGee and Bates had booked Stephen Hague to produce a six-week recording session beginning in April, by which time 'Never' would be released and would require promotion. No one, least of all Bickers, knew the seriousness of his condition. 'You better believe me when I say we weren't being callous,' says Groothuizen. 'I do feel bad that we didn't do more – but at the time there was no more we could do.'

After two dates in Ireland at the end of February, the House Of Love began a short tour of England. Groothuizen was now ignoring Bickers if he was in the room. In Canterbury on 4 March, Chadwick collared Bickers and told him it was time for a man-to-man talk. 'Give me an hour,' said Bickers. Puzzled looks were exchanged in the band.

Why did Bickers need an hour in Canterbury? Eventually reappearing, he was driven back to Chadwick's house in south London. Communication broke down at once and a furious Chadwick threw a glass at a wall. As it smashed, Bickers laughed uproariously.

On 6 March, Bickers paid the first of several visits to a psychologist, Dr Keith Stoll, in Upper Harley Street at Fontana's expense. For these consultations, McGee deputised the genial Ed Ball – who adored Bickers – to ferry the guitarist from Camberwell to Stoll's door. The consultations went on for a couple of months, twice a week. En route, Ball would attempt to gee Bickers up, telling him how talented he was, how fortunate to be in a band that was going places. He found Bickers 'fatalistic . . . very dark. I saw someone who was pretty gentle, a really gentle sort of fellow.'

Bickers was diagnosed as clinically depressed and prescribed tranquillisers. To McGee and the House Of Love, who worked in a business that repeatedly overstates depression, the diagnosis was far from helpful. After a few more visits to Upper Harley Street, Bickers started hiding from Ball whenever he came to collect him.

In Camberwell, Bickers hung around with fly-by-night friends from the squat scene who befriended him for a few days, accepted his generosity and vanished. His clothes would turn up on the backs of people walking around south London; it did not do much for his self-image. At Easter, following an unsuccessful intervention by McGee, Bickers slashed his wrists in his flatmate's bed. He then left the house and went out into the night.

Groothuizen got a call from Chadwick at ten o'clock the next morning. While Chadwick rang everyone he knew to establish Bickers' whereabouts, Groothuizen walked around Camberwell trying to find him. 'I remember the day vividly,' says Groothuizen. 'I knocked on 20 people's doors, saying: "Have you seen Terry?" "Why, what's wrong?" "Oh, nothing's wrong. I'm just up at ten o'clock wondering where Terry is." ' Groothuizen had no luck, nor did Chadwick on the phone. At five o'clock in the afternoon, Bickers turned up on Chadwick's doorstep with his mother and stepfather.

The guitarist had checked himself into the Maudsley psychiatric hospital in Camberwell, but had been allowed to leave. He sat in Chadwick's kitchen, incommunicado, as Chadwick sobbed helplessly. 'I felt terrible for his mother,' Chadwick says. 'She was in agony, watching her son in this situation. It was horrendous – you cannot describe it.'

The following day, the House Of Love recorded a performance in Brixton for the TV programme *Big World Café*. Watching the distracted Bickers going through the motions, Andy Jarman had to admit the damn thing was getting too scary.

12 Viaticum

MCGEE WAS SPENDING SO much time in Manchester that he decided to rent some property there. In March, he moved some of his possessions into a two-bedroom flat in Palatine Road, above the offices of Factory. He offered the other room to Debbie Turner.

Down in Brighton, where he continued to surface from time to time, McGee attempted to illuminate acid house for Bobby Gillespie's benefit, sure that a conversion would follow. He played Gillespie a record by A Guy Called Gerald, raising his eyebrows hopefully. Gillespie retorted that it did not have much of a tune. But Gillespie was genuinely interested in McGee's descriptions of hedonistic club life in London. By April, McGee, Gillespie and James Williamson – whom McGee had put in charge of Creation's new publishing arm, Creation Press – were making up a clubbing threesome.

Gillespie wouldn't dance in the clubs, but at least he was in them. Primal Scream's rock 'n' roll-loving guitarist Robert 'Throb' Young refused even to set foot inside. 'Throb wouldn't talk to me one night because I had a baggy T-shirt,' remembers McGee. 'He thought I was a traitor.' Martin Duffy, who was now playing keyboards for Primal Scream as well as Felt, seemed to concur with Young. Andrew Innes was not so intransigent. It all made for interesting musical politics in Brighton. 'Alan would have these parties,' says Lawrence. 'There was always the Scream at one end, and Alan championing house music and playing it to them. Then Bobby would put on *Goats Head Soup* and all the Scream would go mad. Then Alan would take it off and put some more house on. This was going on all the time. There was a lot of debate about whether this new culture was going to be embraced by Creation or not.'

Robert Young's reluctance was understandable. Controversial or not, the two-guitar rock 'n' roll direction that Primal Scream had taken since splitting with Jim Beattie had been good for team spirit, and they were preparing to record an album – their first since 1987 – in that style. All over the land, guitar bands were making snap judgments on house music, for or against – one or two, such as the

Shamen and the Beloved, even dropping the guitar and changing their sound completely. But why hurry? Just because McGee was proselytising didn't mean he was right. Hadn't the Scream had bad experiences of musical trends before?

Most of McGee's judgments and decisions were in any case drug-influenced. If New Order played anywhere in Britain, he would take ecstasy and get on a train. Reflecting his increasingly carefree behaviour, he started sleeping rough in the Hackney office, a practice he would maintain on and off for nearly eight months. On 21 April, he took Chadwick and Groothuizen to a meeting at Daniel Miller's home to discuss an upcoming recording session for the House Of Love. 'We got a taxi back,' McGee recalls. 'Chadwick phoned me up later and said: "I've just got to tell you this as your friend. You smell." And I said: "Well, I haven't had a bath for ten days – does it show?" He said: "When you got out of the taxi, the air got better." '

That night, Creation threw an office-warming party in Hackney, inviting all its bands and management clients, a selection of friends and a handful of journalists. Among those in attendance were My Bloody Valentine, the House Of Love, Primal Scream, Pete Astor and *NME* deputy editor Danny Kelly. 'I remember this record – Alyson Williams' "Sleep Talk", a brilliant soul ballad on Def Jam – that they played over and over again,' says Kelly.

'There was a spiral staircase up and down between two floors. Guy was there and took all his clothes off in the heat. He looked like Gollum out of the film of *Lord Of The Rings*. I remember thinking: cor, that's weird.'

Kelly left Hackney feeling that changes were afoot at Creation. For the first time, he had seen white indie rock musicians dancing to soul and house music. 'All of that rock classicism on which Creation was based fell apart there and then,' he says. 'Suddenly, all doors were open. Because they weren't dancing to some piece of 60s rock music. It was "Sleep Talk".'

None of the members of the House Of Love listened to much acid house, even if Terry Bickers, typically, was interested in its consequences of dancefloor democracy and come-as-you-are open-heartedness. As for Guy Chadwick, he took the drugs but his musical spine remained Lou Reed rigid. 'The House Of Love were squares,' says McGee. 'Guy just wanted to rewrite songs from the 60s.'

Ecstasy makes people like one another, though it is only a synthetic and temporary liking. The House Of Love were taking a fair amount of ecstasy by April, but they were not taking it together. Only once was Chadwick moved to embrace Bickers in a loving hug – at a Creation party – but the bond did not survive the morning. The view in the House Of Love camp of Bickers' wrist-slitting episode, meanwhile, was that it had not been a serious suicide attempt.

The day after the *Big World Café* recording was transmitted, 'Never' was released. Reviews and sales were disappointing, and it charted at 41, one agonising position outside the catchment zone for *Top Of The Pops*. Since they were a major label band, there were no mitigating circumstances. 'Around the time of "Destroy The Heart",' says Cerne Canning, 'they were on the cusp of being a band completely in control of their own territory like the Smiths. But with "Never" it very much felt like huge A&R boots came wading in. That's when a few of us lost interest.' McGee agrees: 'What Creation gave the House Of Love – that indie thing – made them sexy. The minute you put them on Fontana, they were just a band on Fontana.'

The House Of Love had been signed by Fontana because they were the best in their market. 'Never' had diluted their music in an effort to appeal to the greater market, and it had not worked. But it was too late to back out of the deal, and nobody wanted to. An ambitious plan was taking shape for the recording of their album, which would either propel the House Of Love into multi-million-sales heaven or send all the budgets haywire, depending on how things landed.

Tim Palmer was in the doghouse, but all the same, 'Never' was an album definite and 'Shine On' a probable. McGee, Bates and Chadwick were going to farm out the other ten-to-fifteen songs to different producers – each one working on a couple of tracks – in order for the album to give a panoramic view of the House Of Love rather than a snapshot.

With so many producers being used, the album could not possibly be made in a linear fashion. As many as three studios might be running simultaneously, and additional sessions in cheaper studios would have to be slotted in to record songs for B-sides. Were the House Of Love to play the popular game of multi-formatting – maximising sales potential by flooding the shops with 7-inches, 12-inches, cassettes, CDs, gatefolds and picture discs – anything up to eight B-sides might be needed per A-side. 'Never' had been only bi-formatted. Perhaps that was why it hadn't done better?

A 36-year-old American, Stephen Hague had produced New Order's single 'True Faith' – their Billboard chart breakthrough – and worked with them on *Technique*, a recent favourite on the House Of Love's tour bus. Having started out as a producer of guitar bands, Hague had secured his reputation with synth-pop productions such as the Pet Shop Boys' re-recording of 'West End Girls' (a number 1 hit in 1985) and its parent album *Please*. When the House Of Love hired him, Hague was coming off the back of *Nine*, by John Lydon's PiL, a creatively successful union of guitars and technology. He expected a lot more than vibe, feel or any of the other nebulous words in the indie dictionary. And he was used to music being made on machines.

'I was on a hot streak,' he says. 'I was in the middle of having a bunch of Top 10s in a row, so I was feeling pretty cocky. And Bates was feeling pretty cocky. He was basking in the Tears For Fears, superhot-kind-of-A&R-guy thing.' The House Of Love were not feeling quite so cocky as they walked into Advision, a 24-track recording studio, on 25 April. At £1,200 a day, it was one of the most expensive places in London, but Hague needed Advision for its new Sony digital tape machines. Hague had gone digital in 1987 with 'True Faith': this was another modulation the analog House Of Love would be expected to make.

For his two songs, Hague had chosen the atmospheric but not terribly enthralling 'Shake And Crawl' from the Chocolate Factory demos, and 'I Don't Know Why I Love You', a storming rock track debuted on *Big World Café*. A dry, even-tempered man, Hague soon detected an odd nuance – then an actual complication – in the responses of Terry Bickers. Advision had a roof that could be accessed in warm weather, and the guitarist had gone up there when he was needed downstairs to play.

'I sent one of the assistants to look for him,' recalls Hague, 'and he was up on the roof pacing and chain-smoking. Then somebody else in the band went up there and didn't come back. Then somebody else went up and they didn't come back either. There was this kind of vortex forming on the roof of the building. And then [Bickers] finally came down, pottered around for a while and went straight home. So nothing happened that day. Next day, he came in and he was like a different person.'

Hague knew nothing of the tense dynamic between Bickers and the others. He was just trying to keep all four members of the band off the roof. Dave Bates, who had started hearing 'strange stories' from Advision, paid a visit in the first week of May. Accounts of Bickers' moroseness worried him; though he had little affinity with Bickers as a person, he knew how important his musicianship was. 'No one was really saying what was going on,' Bates remembers, 'other than that he was doing a lot of drugs.'

Bates's attitude towards drugs was ambivalent. He had cleaned up in 1985, and knew how deceptive the relationship between cocaine – in particular – and creativity could be. That said, he was not a puritan like Rob Dickins, who would occasionally advise his young artists to stay drug-free. About ecstasy, however, Bates knew nothing at all. And the House Of Love were not a cocaine band brimming with overconfidence and conceit; they were an E band trying to balance disorientating emotions with even more disorientating hangovers.

Such a band was ill-suited to Stephen Hague's obsession with perfect timekeeping. His digital comping-and-stitching marathons were a nightmare for the House Of Love's rhythm section, and he admits he had difficulty adjusting from tried and tested machine-derived accuracy to Pete Evans' innovative drum patterns. 'Hague had a very weird way of working,' says Groothuizen, 'which he explained to us when we sat down. He talked about sync-ing everything up and getting us to play a hundred times to get [the timing] perfect. We kind of sat there going: "Yeah, yeah – but then we'll just come in and play the songs, won't we?" But no. We went in and we played everything 17 times and he sat there with two digital tape machines and sync-ed it all up. It was excruciatingly boring.'

'I Don't Know Why I Love You' was supposed to be released as the follow-up to 'Never' in the summer, but the sessions dragged on to the end of May and still it was unfinished. The musicians felt Hague's methods spoilt the fun of recording and were an enemy to inspiration. It certainly seemed an ingenious way of going about things: he was effectively using a rock band like a sequencer. On the other hand, the House Of Love weren't much of a band. They were a magpie-eyed leader, a mystified bassist, a perplexed drummer and a guy on the roof who had to be persuaded to come down to play his guitar.

The parties continued in Hackney, becoming almost a weekly occurrence. McGee and Jeff Barrett would make up acid house tapes to play for the ecstasy-charged dancers. When it all got too much for Primal Scream, Bobby Gillespie would amble over and put on the New York Dolls. Then the Dolls would be pulled out and the house would go back on. And so forth. Get it off; leave it playing.

The parties were not celebrating anything but the existence of the party. Creation was not a label in clover, and none of the groups had a major record out. They were drugs and music parties, but none of the music was Creation music. Nick Currie would sometimes be the only person who had not taken ecstasy. 'I was probably having a more weird experience than they were,' he says. 'When you're straight and everybody's in a rugby scrum with everybody else, it's incredible to witness.'

My Bloody Valentine were not as religious about rock music as the House Of Love. The Valentines had sampled a hip hop rhythm track from a Public Enemy record for their eerie 'Instrumental', released on a 7-inch given away with copies of Isn't Anything; Kevin Shields admitted he had conceived 'Instrumental' as an acid house track. All eyes were on Shields to take My Bloody Valentine further into dance culture on their next album. If Shields was truly in tune with house, as he seemed to McGee to be, Creation's parties might soon echo to one of its own records.

By making journalists welcome at the parties, the label strengthened its links to the music papers, and to the NME above all. Danny Kelly had not been the only NME staffer to see that tastes were changing, and in the remaining months of 1989 the bias of the paper would creep closer towards the Manchester quartet of the Stone Roses, Inspiral Carpets, Happy Mondays and New Order – the last two of which had Creation's own Jeff Barrett as their publicist. With Barrett and McGee both regular fixtures at New Order and Happy Mondays gigs, and with McGee living half his life in Manchester, it was sometimes difficult to remember that Creation was a London-based label founded on a love of traditional guitar pop. The hipness of Manchester and the intercommunion of the east London parties gave Creation the appearance of being up-to-speed with developments in both cities, when in fact the perception was purely journalistic. McGee had merely realised what everyone else was realising: that indie fans could like dance music, and vice versa.

'Was it cynical [to invite journalists to the parties]? I'm not sure it was,' says Dick Green. 'Alan was preaching – he was converting people to the cause. Unless that's me being naive. I suppose it was: this is the new punk. Everyone's got to know about this – and we'll be at the forefront of it.' Judging by the Nikki Sudden and Jasmine Minks albums Creation released in 1989, they would be lucky to be at the tail-end of it.

Chris Groothuizen stopped going to the Creation parties when Guy Chadwick became too much of an embarrassment. His perpetual nudity was no one's idea of a spectator sport, and the long-running enmity between the House Of Love and Primal Scream had led to an altercation between Chadwick's girlfriend Suzi Gibbons and Robert 'Throb' Young. 'Throb was a serial womaniser,' says McGee. 'He was sitting with his girlfriend of the time, and Suzi was pissed and just shouting at him. The funniest thing was her shouting: "You've probably got a one-inch dick." Throb is known as Throb because he's got an extended fucking family down his trousers. We were all waiting for him to whip it out.' According to Groothuizen, the House Of Love's standing at Creation went down that night and stayed down.

However, there were two areas in which – all rivalry aside – the House Of Love were grinding Primal Scream into the dirt. In a display of squandermania that even Terry Bickers found enjoyable, the House Of Love travelled everywhere by taxi on their Fontana account. Although they all lived a short walk from each other in Camberwell, they would leave Advision in separate cabs, and for Bickers this had become an art. He would call a cab to the studio, keep it waiting for twenty minutes while he went back to finish his game of pool, fetch a guitar, put it in the cab, go back into the studio, return to the cab with a guitar pedal, take out the guitar, go back into the studio, get another guitar . . . When Bickers ran up an £89 fare for a journey that included a stop-off at a drug dealer's and a leisurely browse around a record shop, the House Of Love were told to stop taking liberties. They had a higher taxi bill than Def Leppard.

And whereas Primal Scream had scrapped only one recording session in making their Elevation album, the House Of Love were about to junk their second. The Stephen Hague recordings had yielded nothing that anyone was too elated about, and a stint with Daniel Miller in Orinoco Studio in May had pushed Bickers once again over the edge. He smashed his amplifier, threw his guitar around and broke a boom microphone stand. No music from the session was usable.

'No one in Manchester was surprised. People were willing them to be massive because there was so much pride in them. People really did realise that it was a special record ... All that summer, you would hear it everywhere: all round Affleck's Palace,* coming out of people's bedsits and people's houses.'

John Robb's recollection of the effect on Manchester of the Stone Roses' album dovetails neatly with a quote in *NME* in June 1989 by the band's bassist Mani. 'The E scene is just going to explode this summer,' he said. 'People in the media just don't realise how massive it's getting in the provinces.' The Stone Roses' taste for ecstasy was no secret. In almost every photograph of the band, the faces of Mani and Ian Brown would have the blown-out cheeks of an E rush. But in the south, the album 'limped out unannounced', as *Mojo* journalist Pat Gilbert would recall a decade later, 'initially to widespread indifference. Its growing cachet during the early summer of 1989 was merely a function of the populace realising, via TV appearances and radio play, that the album was rammed with the kind of magnificently understated indie-psychedelia that Primal Scream, the Soup Dragons and the La's had been threatening to cut for nearly two years but had not yet managed to deliver'.

The chart life of *The Stone Roses* was simply astonishing. Entering at 32 in May, it made five re-entries over the next year, peaking at 19. In July 1989, only four months after their small-scale tour for 'Made Of Stone', the Stone Roses were performing before a sold-out 4,000 audience at the Empress Ballroom in Blackpool. A week later, they were reported to be looking for a London venue big enough to hold 10,000.

The contrast with their former heroes Primal Scream was stark indeed. When the album *Primal Scream* – a turgid set of biker-rock hand-me-downs – arrived at Creation, not even superfans McGee and Jeff Barrett thought much of it. 'The LP had one great moment on it, "I'm Losing More Than I'll Ever Have",' says McGee. 'We put "Ivy Ivy Ivy" out as a single [in July] and nothing happened. Primal Scream media-wise were a fucking joke.'

Specifically, the music papers wondered why the Scream insisted

---

* A clothes market on the site of the old department store Affleck & Brown.

on paraphrasing the MC5 and the New York Dolls, bands for whom they were not a match. More generally, their twin Les Pauls, long hair and arrogant posturing made it hard to associate Primal Scream with any other time but the pre-punk early 70s, an era almost unanimously derided by the media in the late 80s. Jeff Barrett, chiselling *Primal Scream* into the last oh-by-the-way moments of conversations with editors about Happy Mondays, held McGee partly to blame for not offering the band constructive criticism like a good A&R man. 'You can't talk Primal Scream *out* of stuff,' Barrett says from experience, 'but you can talk to them *about* stuff. There wasn't consultation. But I think I can speak for a lot of fans – it wasn't the record I expected them to make.'

As all routes for Primal Scream appeared to lead backwards, the forward path was sighted not by McGee, but by one of the band's two guitarists in conjunction with a quondam bricklayer from Slough. What was to happen between July 1989 and February 1990 would be nothing like as seamless as the key players would later claim, but it would put Primal Scream where no one had ever imagined they could be: in the vanguard of a commercially successful synthesis of rock and dance.

If the proletarian cuddle of house culture meant that no one at Shoom or the Trip cared about the history of indie labels like Creation, it was ironic that one of the favourite bands of Andrew Weatherall was the Jesus and Mary Chain. A bricklayer turned DJ, Weatherall was a guitar rock fan who had been known to spin records at the Trip wearing a Wonder Stuff T-shirt. Like his friend Terry Farley, a fellow founder of *Boy's Own*, Weatherall had made the jump from influential fanzine journalism to influential DJing and was renowned for playing much more than just house music. He claimed to be unable to decide whether he was 'a soul boy or a punk'.

'What Andrew used to do was play records that weren't expected to be played, upstairs at Shoom,' says Jeff Barrett. 'He'd play African Headcharge records. He'd play Matt Johnson records. He'd play "Everything's Gone Green" [by New Order]. Everyone booked Andrew because he'd play these odd things.' Barrett had been told about Weatherall by Richard Norris, who couldn't believe they didn't know each other. Keen to meet one of the brains behind *Boy's Own* – which he calls 'the hippest magazine ever' – Barrett introduced himself to Weatherall at the next opportunity. They got on well.

Bobby Gillespie and McGee had already encountered Weatherall at a Shoom summer rave in a field outside Brighton. 'He had long curly hair and a New Order T-shirt on,' McGee told Michael Bonner. 'It was one of those great nights. We'd driven around Brighton for hours looking for this place, walked miles through this field, and when we got there we found Flowered Up, the KLF, Richard Norris, Weatherall and [the producer] Youth in a tent. These were our people. Nobody

Top: Geoff Travis at Rough Trade, 1979. His indie label and distribution company operated on a knife-edge balance of commerce and benevolence. 'A barmy, English middle-class idea of socialism,' as one bandmember puts it.

Right: Edwyn Collins of Orange Juice. Their 1980 single 'Blue Boy' 'emancipated Scottish pop. Nothing could be the same again'.

Top: The Laughing Apple, March 1981. From left: Alan McGee, Mark Jardim, Andrew Innes.

Above: Alan McGee and Bobby Gillespie, Glasgow, 1982. 'We were intense friends… almost like brothers.' Gillespie's Primal Scream formed the following year.

FANZINES...

Once upon a time fanzines werea vital part of an underground vibrant pop scene,
always one step ahead of the music papers by spotting the good group before
anyone else and exposing the lies laid before you by The Record Industry because
basically fanzines were in general run by people who were young idealistic and
not relying on C.B.S. full page adverts to pay the rent.But what happened?
Seven years on from "Sniffin Glue",fanzines are now considered a sort of Post-
Punk anachranism.Fanzines - like good group are non-existant. Most of the fanzines
that still exist are PATHETIC and that's the long word for them.No enthusiasm and
all of them very rarely challenge anything at all.Fanzines now seem to come out
regularly,more out of force of habit rather than any urge to express an opinion.
So why do they still cotinue? Now I'm sure thathalf the fanzines in Britain will
now write to me saying what right do I have to criticise them and how all fanzines
should stick together etc.etc. Well to you I reply this.... I have every right
to criticise you as much as I have every right to be criticised by you, because
you compile a fanzine it does not give you direct entry to some exclusive little
circle. We should be trying to get better instead of forming little sewing bees,
exchanging patterns etc.
There are exeptions to the GeneralRule, take a bow Groovy Black Shades,Juniper
Beri Beri,Action Times and who knows, there may be more.At least these fanzines are
trying.But there should be more, hunderds and hundreds more. Fresh young people
with fresh ideas. Fanzines should challenge! It is no place for fence sitters,
something unfortunatly that the dreg ends of punkhave forgotten........
Above all when you read a fanzine it should Inspire. A promise.. If we ever get
complacent we will give up! Sermon ended...... Amen.

BR
PoF
/S

Two MINS BEFORE WE GO TO PRINT — JUST HEARD MICRODISNE
SINGLE "PINK SKINNED MAN" - B

THE LEGEND!

Pretty Girls, Pretty Boys have you ever heard your

Mummy say noise annoys! Go! The Legend! Big headed

Bastard imagine calling yourself that! Well believe

it or not The Legend gets prescribed at this kids

Post Punk Doctors surgery as a cure for growing

your hair and listening to Aztec Camera. The Legend !

Means irony!Everything and everyone is poked. This

month sees the release of his E.P 73 in 83 on Crea—

tion Records. What's the difference 10 years! Positive

Punk or The Legend the choice is yours!

Snap, Crackle, Noise! Go!

McGee's vitriol-peppered fanzine *Communication Blur*, Issue 2, 1983. The Legend! (Jerry
Thackray) had recorded the first Creation single, '73 in 83', a few weeks before.

The chemical brothers: Jim (forefront) and William Reid of the Jesus and Mary Chain. In 1985 their shambolic, feedback-saturated performances incited audiences to riot. But was it spontaneous pandemonium or cynically orchestrated hype? 'Alan McGee made a couple of very shy blokes into the biggest rock 'n' roll terrors on the whole music scene,' says one contemporary.

Top: Jim Reid is accosted by a member of support band Raw Herbs, whose amplifier he has damaged. Three Johns pub, Islington, October 1984.

Above: When the Mary Chain returned to Creation in 1998, McGee believed they could help the label recapture its punk values. It was to be a forlorn hope.

The Weather Prophets: they left the Loft and aimed for the stadium, only to face humiliation. From left: David Greenwood Goulding, Dave Morgan, Pete Astor, Oisin Little.

Lawrence of Felt: 'the perfect package for an angst-ridden generation'. He surrounded himself with air-fresheners and polishing cloths, bathed twice a day and ate no cheese or vegetables. The stardom he craved would prove elusive.

Looking towards Brighton: Primal Scream's *Sonic Flower Groove* line-up, 1987. From left: Bobby Gillespie, Robert 'Throb' Young, Andrew Innes, Jim Beattie. Within months Beattie had gone and the others had disowned the album.

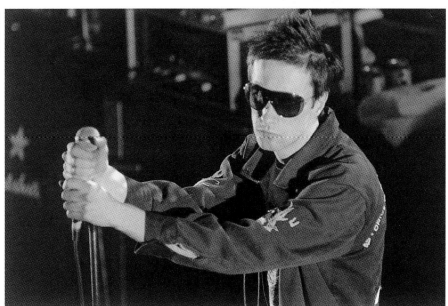

Top: Bobby Gillespie, self-conscious rock 'n' roll animal, 1989. 'I think I can speak for a lot of fans – *Primal Scream* wasn't the record I expected,' said their publicist Jeff Barrett.

Above: A transformed and vindicated Gillespie onstage in London, 2000. Primal Scream's *Exterminator* album was the best of their career.

Top left: Biff Bang Pow! in 1988. From left: Phil King, Ken Popple, Dick Green, Alan McGee. They retired from the road that year following a disastrous tour of France.

Top right: Terry Bickers (left) and Guy Chadwick of the House Of Love: an alliance as doomed as it was magical.

Right: 'I asked Alan to manage the House Of Love. The next day he started wearing sunglasses.'

Top left: My Bloody Valentine prepare to steal the show at 'Doing It For The Kids'. From left: Kevin Shields, Colm O'Ciosoig, Bilinda Butcher, Debbie Goodge. Town & Country Club, London, August 1988.

Top right: Shields used 19 studios to record the *Loveless* album, almost bankrupting Creation. 'What is it to be beyond your means?'.

Above: My Bloody Valentine onstage in Gourock, Scotland, spring 1990. Their *Glider* EP was 'mind-blowing… a sound which seemed to come from nobody else.'

Top: Teenage Fanclub personified Creation's early-90s swing from acid house to American rock. 'Kurt Cobain was going round every radio station saying Teenage Fanclub were the best band in the world.'

Above: 'I will now do the deal with the devil.' Creation gets into bed with Sony, August 1992. From left: Jeremy Pearce, Alan McGee, Paul Russell, Dick Green.

Top: Shoe-gazers to the rescue: Slowdive, fronted by Rachel Goswell. One journalist described them as 'the My Bloody Valentine Creation can afford'.

Above: The Boo Radleys pre-Britpop. From left: Rob Cieka, Martin Carr, Sice, Tim Brown.

Top: A rare photo of McGee convalescing after his nervous breakdown. Rotherhithe, 1994. The toddler is the son of the Orb's Thrash.

Above: Oasis upstage Ride and the Boo Radleys at press conference for 'Undrugged', May 1994. 'It was obvious what Creation was going to be from then on: Oasis' record label.'

Top: Ride perform at 'Undrugged' with the Creation, the 60s pop art band that gave McGee's label its name.

Centre: The Creative Industries Task Force. Seated, from left: Lord Puttnam, Richard Branson, Paul Smith, Alan McGee.

Above: Kate Holmes, Liam Gallagher and Alan McGee at a friend's wedding, Italy, 1999. Holmes and McGee had got married in the Caribbean shortly after Christmas 1997.

Top: The Creation Workers Mutiny (1). Mishka on stage. 'Everybody in the office thought it was a complete joke.'

Above: The Creation Workers Mutiny (2). The outrageous comeback of Kevin Rowland. 'People just began to see him as a sad old git.'

shut doors in those days – there was no closed shop in dance music.' Nevertheless, the *NME* journalist Jack Barron would write of his surprise at seeing Gillespie – 'the figurehead of arguably the quintessential British indie rock band' – at the event. Debbie Turner, who was also there, recalls: 'Bobby still had his long fringe and his winklepickers on, but he was dancing away in front of the speakers. That's what the house scene was about. It sounds cheesy but anyone could go. It didn't matter what anyone looked like, or projected themselves as. Get into the music and dance. That was it.' The rave ended at eleven o'clock in the morning, at which point Weatherall wandered over to Gillespie and McGee and said hello.

'I'd seen them about at clubs,' Weatherall later recalled, 'but when I met them the first words Bobby Gillespie said to me were: "Is that a perm or is your hair really that curly?" They're a tight-knit bunch and the fact that [my] hair was a bit Marc Bolan-esque broke the ice.' Weeks later, Weatherall called round to Jeff Barrett's for a beer and a chat. Barrett gave him a copy of *Primal Scream*. 'He said: "Oh, that's good timing. We're just about to do the new *Boy's Own* and I need some records to review." ' Barrett didn't know it, but he was about to get his first positive reaction. 'Andrew rang me the next day saying: "Fucking hell, the ballads on this album!" Now, nobody in the world had said anything about that record – and I'd sent it everywhere. Everybody had said: "Shite." '

Barrett made a point of passing on Weatherall's comments to Gillespie and Andrew Innes, who were flattered. Perhaps they noticed Barrett looking relieved. 'I couldn't get [publicity for] that second Primals album to save my life,' he admits. 'It had got so bad that Innes had said to me: "Can you not even get us in the guitar papers?" '

The House Of Love had taken their name from an erotic novel. The tale had since turned into a thriller and had lately become a cross between a penny dreadful and a shaggy-dog story. 'Terry was a nightmare at Orinoco,' says Chris Groothuizen. 'That was when we thought it was time – not to replace him; and there was no question of sacking him – but we needed someone else to take over his role and let him just be Terry. He was not up to the task of playing the guitar parts that Guy wrote.'

At the back of their minds was the Reading festival in August, for which Mick Griffiths had bargained hard to book them a prime slot. With a well-rehearsed auxiliary guitarist in the line-up, Bickers might savour his elbow-room on the big stage, perhaps even playing himself out of his depression. Feelers were sent out, bringing back the name Bill Carey. An American, he played in a band called Crash who were known to Groothuizen. It was decided to ease Carey in over the summer.

In the meantime, Bickers had been seeing a therapist and had learned to meditate. 'I went on this course that tried to help people who had low self-esteem,' he says. 'It was a bit late in the day by then, for the state I was in. But I went to meet this group of people called the Bellin Partnership, who did a course called the Turning-Point – a sort of crash course in emotional therapy, almost like a Yogi thing. It was people trying to lose some of their demons, if you like.'

As far as Mick Griffiths knew, Bickers' depression was no significant obstacle to booking dates. In June, Griffiths went for the adventurous touch. The House Of Love played a week of shows at the ICA, using a large PA and a lavish light-show. The gigs sold out quickly, indicating that the House Of Love were still a major draw. It was true, however, that the quality of the shows rose and fell according to Bickers' mood from night to night – and as Pete Evans remembers, there was more ecstasy around that week than usual. 'We weren't really in control,' says Groothuizen. 'I think people watching it probably thought we'd cracked it and now we were just showing off.'

On the final night, Chadwick arrived at the ICA to find Bickers in the dressing-room writing out the set-list, looking happier than he'd been for some time. That evening, Groothuizen had his first proper conversation with Bickers in months. 'It took us all by surprise,' he says. 'We thought: hang on, Terry's normal – this is great. It did seem like a weight lifted.'

Bickers' recovery had a lot do with Jeff Barrett's PR assistant Emma Anderson. Destined to succeed where a psychologist, a therapist and a course of tranquillisers had failed, Anderson had become Bickers' girlfriend in May. 'When I started going out with him, I didn't really know the problems that he had,' she says. 'He was manic depressive but I didn't actually know what that was. I was only about 20 and I was a bit naive to it all. It soon became apparent that this was no normal relationship. He was very depressed. He was living in Camberwell in a really nice house, but he didn't know the people. They were three girls who had nothing to do with the music business. He was eating too much, staying in bed most of the time and walking around in a daze.' Anderson moved Bickers into her own flat in White City, where he began to show an improvement. 'That was the real turning-point,' he says. 'She was a friend – an angel, really. Everybody else was like: "Ooh no, keep back, Terry's on the nutty warpath." But she stood by me and I'll be forever indebted to her.'

The House Of Love's album was some way behind schedule. Mick Griffiths had booked three-nighters in Leeds and Edinburgh for the middle of June, but was asked to move them back to August to enable the band to record at Marcus Studios in Fulham with Stephen Hague's engineer Dave Meegan. Producing two songs, Meegan got good results, and 'Someone's Got To Love You' and 'Blind' joined Tim

Palmer's 'Never' in the album-definite pile. The remaining songs were to be recorded with the producer Paul O'Duffy at Abbey Road.

After one of the ICA gigs, Chadwick had assured Danny Kelly that the album would be out in September, but even he had lost count of the number of producers – he told Kelly they'd used six. Rumours were rife about the album's mounting costs and bewildering delays, most of the rumours having a tone midway between fatalism and ridicule. And nowhere did the album sessions get more fatalistic or more ridiculous than at Abbey Road.

As the producer of Swing Out Sister in the mid-80s, Paul O'Duffy seemed a bizarre choice for the House Of Love. Dave Meegan knew him quite well. 'It's not such a bizarre choice when you think of Dave Bates,' he says. 'Bates wanted the radio-friendliness and the pop-ness of that kind of stuff, while somehow trying to hold on to the indie sense as well – [but] that's an odd line to hold sometimes.' During their six weeks at Abbey Road – in Studio 2, where the Beatles had made their records – the House Of Love recorded ten songs with O'Duffy, barely caring what any of them sounded like.

'Abbey Road was about going back to school,' says Groothuizen. 'Being told that there's all these rules about when you can drink and when you had to have lunch – and you have to keep the noise down. And we just reacted like schoolchildren. Guy had this thing of throwing bits of food up on to the exterior window because it looks down on to the studio, and watching all the sandwiches rot over a period of days until the poor caretaker had to get up on his ladder.'

The Leeds and Edinburgh dates were postponed again, and a festival appearance in Sweden was cancelled. Phonogram had given the House Of Love a bar tab at Abbey Road, so they would start drinking at lunchtime, returning to Studio 2 in the evening to mess around on a few improvised chords. 'I was going down there a few days a week,' says Bill Carey, who was learning the songs prior to joining the line-up for Reading warm-up dates in Holland. 'My personal feeling was that I couldn't see any correlation between the producer and the band. He didn't have much of an affinity with their music. There was him and Guy having all these power trip games, in a real public school sort of way.'

Throughout the Abbey Road period, the House Of Love were virtually unmanaged. McGee's relationship with Dave Bates was distant, and he was unsympathetic to the band – he believed the House Of Love were paying the consequences for chasing the money. Since January, they had spent £10,000 on taxi fares alone – almost the total cost of their Creation album. If that entered their heads, it was only as a source of amusement. Chadwick now had a nanny and a cleaner. There was even a rumour that he had employed a valet. McGee was close to giving up on them lest Chadwick hire a cellar-man and an ostler.

But Dave Bates was not giving up. As Groothuizen points out: 'Having signed Tears For Fears and made a fortune out of very expensive recordings, Bates believed that you spent as much as it cost.' But were the House Of Love making *Songs From The Big Chair?* It didn't look like it to Bill Carey. 'I didn't see lots and lots of music being made,' he says. 'Takes were done and things were put on tape, and obviously it was proceeding. But it wasn't like: "This is the best thing we could be doing in the whole world." ' And when McGee did materialise – to jam with the band on a version of Neil Young's 'Like A Hurricane' – the orchestra in the next studio sent an engineer to ask them not to make such a bloody racket. His eyes met Chadwick, leering drunkenly, trousers around his ankles.

'Alan was only into the flamboyant side of being a manager,' says Groothuizen. 'Not the gritty, they-really-need-to-make-this-album-or-their-career's-over side of it.' It scarcely mattered what McGee was into. Six weeks had been wasted and the House Of Love had completely lost sight of their album.

'One afternoon we were down the office,' recalls the Jazz Butcher's Pat Fish. 'We'd done Europe, we'd done America – we'd sold out right across America and Canada. And we're shuffling about: there's Kizzy [O'Callaghan, guitarist] in his dirty jumper and me and Mulreany looking like a pair of third-hand hooligans milling about in the street. And around the corner come the Scream, who are doing absolutely fuck all. It's Throb and Innes and Bobby, and fuck me do they look like a band. They look like the Ramones. And it's funny, because they haven't done anything for six months. But they just look like the business. Even at their moment of apparent nothingness, they're still the Scream.'

A devil-may-care wind blew inside and outside of Primal Scream. The UK tour to promote their second album had begun in August, staggered over three legs leading into November. Creation had booked them almost a hundred gigs. 'They didn't seem to be going anywhere at that point,' says Dick Green. 'They were enjoying themselves, but there was little interest press-wise or public-wise. They were jumping in the back of transit vans, out on the road touring. It was real back-to-basics stuff and it didn't seem to be gathering any momentum.'

On the tour, new songs from *Primal Scream* alienated fans of 'Velocity Girl' – still the most requested Scream tune. 'Word was that the Scream had rocked out,' Jeff Barrett recalled to Michael Bonner. 'People were literally saying it to each other: "Have you heard? The Scream have *rocked out.*" It was like something dirty had happened. All these fucking sad anoraks – these fanzine writers – got really upset. People weren't having it.'

'The drug of choice at this point was speed,' McGee told Bonner. 'I mean *real* amounts of speed – and the vitriol in the band was amazing. Bobby Gillespie is probably one of the closest people in the world to me, but I would get in the van and I would get such a major caning. It'd be like: "This guy hates my guts. What's his problem?" But it was just speed psychosis – they were all basically speeding off their tits.'

The album had come out in September and not charted – as if anyone was surprised. 'I think [Gillespie] was near to breaking the band up,' says McGee. 'I'd put them out on a six-month *(sic)* tour to try and get a fanbase, like I did with the House Of Love. It wasn't happening. He was still playing to 200 people a night.' But one gig in September – in Exeter – was reviewed for the *NME* by Andrew Weatherall.

Weatherall had started writing reviews under the pseudonym Audrey Witherspoon, and he/she appeared to enjoy a good night out. The events in Devon were described in the style of a young ne'er-do-well going in search of drink, girls and debauchery (' ... we stormed out into the Exeter afternoon in search of action'), which was almost hilarious given the area's well-known dearth of pizzazz. Weatherall found Primal Scream to be rather a downbeat bunch drinking orange juice and halves of lager. But things perked up. 'It was a fun night,' he later recalled. 'We all went on to a discotheque and ran out because a fight started when the DJ played "Lip Up Fatty" by Bad Manners. Halcyon days.'

Weatherall's review of the Scream's performance was brisk, even dismissive, and the kindest thing he could say about them was that they 'pay homage to their heroes'. There was no mention of dance culture at all. In fact, Gillespie himself, in an interview that summer, had scoffed at the very idea of Primal Scream using dance rhythms or commissioning remixes. 'We're not that stupid,' he said. 'We couldn't do it if we tried. When white people make dance records they just turn the snare up.' Gillespie liked dance music, but of the old school: Sly Stone, Parliament and Funkadelic.

As journalists and fans deserted Primal Scream, Jeff Barrett worried about the band's future. Neither the Scream nor their audience seemed sure where to go – or whether it was worth going anywhere. By reacting so much against C86 and the fanzines, Barrett wondered if Primal Scream were even being true to the spirit of Primal Scream. Arguably the person least concerned by this thought was one of their two guitarists, Andrew Innes.

In the 12 years that they had known each other, McGee and Innes had come through several sticky patches, including bouts of illness and one or two serious fallings-out. A shy man with a piercing wit, Innes had never pushed himself forward in Primal Scream and people tended to view the long-serving Robert Young as the more important musician. Because Innes never did interviews, it was not widely known that he was well-educated and had studied chemistry at university. It was certainly widely known by Primal Scream, however. 'Innes can tell you what the drugs do to you,' says McGee. 'The joke in Primal Scream is that when it all ends, Innes will go and open a chemist's shop. Legally, he could do it.'

'Innes had never been shy of drugs,' Jeff Barrett told Bonner. 'He was a speed king, a 24 hour guy. But what E did was open everybody up to experiment ... It was like a blank piece of paper.' And it was Innes who had the idea of Andrew Weatherall remixing a Primal Scream track – the ballad 'I'm Losing More Than I'll Ever Have', about which he'd been so complimentary – to make it suitable for dancing to.

There were few DJs more hip than Weatherall, but he had never made a record before and his only experience of studios was watching Paul Oakenfold do a mix of a Happy Mondays track. That was not a problem: Primal Scream weren't asking for Weatherall's CV. 'It was purely experimental,' explained Gillespie. 'We gave Andy the tapes and suggested some ideas of our own.' Weatherall liked the way he was approached. 'If they had just turned up out of the blue asking for a dance remix,' he said, 'I would have told them where to go!'

Described by one music encyclopaedia as 'more a revolution than a remix', Weatherall's makeover of 'I'm Losing More Than I'll Ever Have' was created at Bark, the Walthamstow studio where My Bloody Valentine had recorded 'You Made Me Realise'. Weatherall's remix was to be a no less envelope-pushing track. Giving Primal Scream's original ballad credit for being 'well structured', he kept its bass line, piano, horns and some percussion. He built a loping rhythm track from a breakbeat on an Italian bootleg mix of a Soul II Soul collaboration with Edie Brickell – on 'Circle', from her album *Shooting Rubberbands At The Stars*. Weatherall derived a similar feel to 'Sympathy For The Devil' by the Rolling Stones.

For the intro, Weatherall sampled an extract of speech from a cult movie that seemed appropriate to the anti-acid house hysteria of the tabloids. 'It's a naff old film,' he later said, 'but basically [those are] the sentiments of a lot of people in Britain right now, what with the Government and [the police] trying to crack down on the scene.' It was the self-same plea for liberty expressed by Peter Fonda in *The Wild Angels* and used by Richard Norris and Genesis P-Orridge on *Jack The Tab* over a year earlier. 'We want to be free .... We want to be free to do what we want to do ... and we want to get loaded ... and we want to have a good time. And that's what we're going to do. We're going to have a good time. We're going to have a party.'

Fonda's words gave the Weatherall remix its title: 'Loaded'.

In August, Paul O'Duffy mixed the songs from the House Of Love's Abbey Road session. They were presented to Dave Bates more in hope than expectation, and he was not slow in coming to the point. 'He said: "None of this is any good",' recalls Chris Groothuizen. 'He had no problems with just chucking tapes out of windows.' Only one song, 'The Hedonist', was deemed good enough to go on the album.

Psychologically addicted to ecstasy, McGee was in no fit state to argue the case for the defence. Nor was Chadwick. After eight months of recording, the House Of Love had only four releasable songs – six, if 'Shine On' and 'I Don't Know Why I Love You' could be mixed to theirs and Bates' satisfaction. The album was a disaster.

It was a miracle if Bates, McGee and the House Of Love agreed on anything in the summer of 1989. But one thing they all agreed on was the sterling work the band had done in June with Stephen Hague's engineer Dave Meegan. A Dubliner, Meegan had been getting hints from his manager that the O'Duffy sessions had been unproductive, and that Meegan might be needed to tweak some of the tracks into shape. He didn't realise how many.

Joining the House Of Love for festival dates in Holland, guitarist Bill Carey saw a much more cheerful Terry Bickers than the one at Abbey Road. Bickers had bicycled his way back to fitness, and was playing well. Too well, as it turned out, because McGee decided there was no longer any need for Carey to be in the band. The House Of Love would play Reading as a four-piece. 'Terry was back,' McGee reasons. 'Guy had tried to throw him out of the band but I wouldn't have it. I knew I had a world-beating band with Terry Bickers in the line-up. Three times Guy came to me and said: "We should kick him out." And I always said: "He's too good to be kicked out. You don't get another one of these."'

Although it is common for bands to perform at festivals when they have no new product in the shops, the fact remains that the House Of Love's album should have been on sale by late August. Yet there was not even a single ready for release. It was almost 13 months since Pat Collier had wagered his colleagues at Greenhouse that the House Of Love would sell a million records within the year. Had he predicted they would spend £1 million in a year, he would have been nearer the mark.

The year 1989 was a momentous one in the history of outdoor rock music in Britain. For the first time, the three-day Reading festival was promoted by the Mean Fiddler Organisation – owner of several popular clubs across London – and the bias of the event changed dramatically. 'In the last two or three years of the previous set-up,' says the House Of Love's booking agent Mick Griffiths, 'it had degenerated into a heavy metal festival of the worst kind. Every band was getting bottles of piss and mud thrown at them. It was like a sport.'

The Mean Fiddler Organisation came in with a simple plan – to strip away the heavy metal old guard and present indie and underground guitar bands as the new establishment. Something of a dream bill was assembled of credible, medium-profile acts, including New Order, the Pogues, the Sugarcubes, the House Of Love and My Bloody Valentine. The result was the largest number of UK indie music fans ever gathered in one place. 'It was the first time anybody had tried to put bands of that level on at a big festival,' says Mick Griffiths. 'It was a massive gamble.'

And it paid off. With well-behaved crowds and positive reviews from the press, Reading opened the door to a new festival age that put the emphasis of the indie sector's commercial year on August, encouraged keen competition between bands and agents, and made it possible for fans and commentators to determine precisely when a band had broken through or, alternatively, turned a corner.

It had taken a lot of negotiating for Griffiths to place the House Of Love third on Friday's opening-day bill. He had meanwhile acquired a new client only the night before: Lush, a band in which Emma Anderson played guitar. Terry Bickers had moved out of her flat while she was on holiday, and when she returned he was back in Camberwell and acting like a different person. 'He was in the manic state,' she says. 'He was really up ... He was hyperactive, and he was going on about how he was going to change the world. I was like: "What's happening? He's changed completely." He was out of control.' The couple broke up a week before Reading.

But Bickers was back in the land of the living and about to have one of the most profound weekends of his life. Watching the other Friday bands perform, he felt secure and purposeful within the music cocoon. 'The Swans played before we did,' he says, 'and I remember seeing [singer] Michael Gira in bare feet. It was almost as if there was some sacred space up there that day. And little things like during our set – and I've never been the greatest of footballers – someone threw a ball up onstage, and I booted it back and a big cheer went up. That sticks in my mind because I could never score goals at school.'

Warmed by the House Of Love's terrific reception, Bickers took some ecstasy and stood at the side of the stage to watch New Order, the evening's headliners. The drug was soon making him highly emotional. Near to tears and almost collapsing, he was helped down from the stage by the plugger Nicki Kefalas, who told him he was experiencing a rebirth. An excited Bickers went to tell the rest of the House Of Love, but they could not decipher what he was saying. He was screaming in Pete Evans' face. Evans made a discreet getaway.

McGee was backstage with Guy Chadwick and a girl called Hannah, Creation's cleaner. She introduced McGee to her boyfriend Noel, a small-ish man who spoke with a Manchester accent. McGee didn't ask for his surname. As everyone headed back to London, Bickers elected to remain at the festival for the duration, going out into the crowd to look for cosmic camp-fires and face-painters. He would be 24 in a fortnight, and believed the next phase of his life had begun. On the final day, as he was leaving the site with no destination in mind, he was introduced to Sallie Johnson, a music business PR in London. She became his girlfriend.

The House Of Love returned to Advision, this time with Dave Meegan as their producer. Listening to the O'Duffy tapes, Meegan proposed that the vast majority of the songs should be recorded again. Over the course of seven weeks he would become the project's driving force, producing the lion's share of the music, re-recording the Stephen Hague tracks, revisiting two songs from the Chocolate Factory demos and providing a satisfying conclusion to the longest-running saga in recent guitar rock history. That the music would appear unbroken was a tribute to Meegan: one song, 'Se Dest', was a patchwork quilt of Chocolate Factory, new recordings and four bars of O'Duffy.

'Dave Meegan rescued that album,' says Bickers. 'He was a sound bloke with a nice, happy disposition, and he did the usual thing that good engineers and producers do: he had the same meal every night. "What do you want tonight, Dave?" "Lemon chicken and a pint of milk." Every night. It's the sign of a good producer.'

The appreciation was mutual, but within reason. Meegan was content to accommodate the unfathomable Bickers provided he did not wander too far from Advision. Resorting to friendly threats, he told Bickers he would wipe one of his guitar parts if he was not at the studio on time the following day. 'He phoned the next morning,' recalls Meegan, 'must have been about eleven o'clock. He'd just woken up on the beach in Brighton. I said: "Right, Terry, it's gone." '

On 29 August, the much-loved Irish band the Undertones were supposed to get back together again for a surprise appearance at the Subterania club – formerly Bay 63 – to celebrate the fiftieth birthday of John Peel. But a death in the family prevented the reunion from taking place, and the House Of Love played instead. In the audience, McGee was approached by James Brown, the features editor of the *NME*, who insulted him. McGee hit him in the face with a plastic beer glass. Brown replied with a direct punch in the mouth, and the two men were pulled apart. Had they not been, Brown would have won.

McGee's fighting days were drawing to a close: he was preparing to move to Birmingham where his girlfriend Belinda was at college. He was anxious to clean up his act. The flat he shared with Debbie Turner in Manchester was relinquished and his macho behaviour curtailed. In October, he and Belinda moved into a flat in Birmingham and a period of domesticity followed.

For the past few months, McGee had been managing the Grid, whose music of altered states had been ideally suited to his lifestyle in the first half of the year. The arrangement, however, was approaching termination even before the Grid's East West debut single was released. 'It wasn't really working out,' says Richard Norris, 'because he'd had Elevation [at WEA] before, and it was all company politics there.'

On 6 October, McGee had a meeting at East West with the Grid's A&R man Cally. Both men had been – and were – fans of guitar music, psychedelia and exciting new talent. Indeed, McGee had been looking for a young, noisy band to fill the breach while My Bloody Valentine worked on their second album for Creation. The trouble was, he lamented to Cally, there were no good groups out there. Cally said: 'Well, what about this?' and cued up a track by a band he had been demo-ing. Entitled 'Drive Blind', the song sounded extremely promising, a mixture of the House Of Love's keening guitars and My Bloody Valentine's pounding noise.

A quartet from the university city of Oxford, Ride were composed of three foundation art students and a young employee of a local record shop, and they had been playing together for less than a year. Their sound was heavy on mournful delay effects, distortion, descending harmonies and whirlwind drumming. 'Drive Blind' was not their only knockout song – they had another just as good, 'Chelsea Girl'. 'We were playing through really crappy gear,' recalls lead guitarist Andy Bell. 'I think we arrived at the band's sound, really, not through amps but through will power.'

Ride were not thinking too far into the future. The most popular band in Oxford at the time, the Stooges-influenced Shake Appeal, would play to only 50 people or so in the bar of the polytechnic. And the Oxford guitar bands before Shake Appeal had not lasted long, only Talulah Gosh – a cutie group on the 53rd & 3rd label – having graduated from releasing singles to making an album. Still, Ride had already made a sizeable splash locally: a demo tape recorded in April had been sold around Oxford and its songs had been praised by the newsletter *Gig*, co-written by a promoter at the indie-minded Jericho Tavern named Dave Newton. In the summer, a copy of *Gig* was seen by Ben Wardle, an East West A&R scout, who tipped off Cally and a publisher at MCA Music, Mike Smith. Wardle and Smith got the train to Oxford, saw Ride play at the polytechnic and agreed they were brilliant.

Wardle and Smith were young guys with only 18 months' experience of the music business between them. Both wanted to investigate Ride further, but Smith was already worrying about how he would pitch them to MCA Music. 'It was hard to have a reference point for a guitar band like that in terms of selling it to your bosses,' he says. 'Coming back and saying: "I've just seen this incredible band, they're like My Bloody Valentine" would have got you fired. Ben and I were both essentially looking to do something ourselves.

We went back again to see [Ride] at the Jericho Tavern – just to check to see if they were good – and they were fantastic. They were a real jaw-dropper.' Wardle spotted something else, too. 'They *looked* really good, particularly [singer-guitarist] Mark Gardener,' he says. 'It has to be said that's part of the A&R man's motivation – to get a group that sounds and looks great.'

A direct signing to East West was not on the cards for the moment. Ride had the typical indie fans' suspicion of major labels, and Wardle's and Cally's A&R superior seemed unlikely to green-light such an aggressive sound. 'Malcolm Dunbar was head of A&R, but Malcolm's taste in music was very much the Lloyd Cole kind of intelligent, articulate 80s pop,' says Smith. 'He was enjoying a big hit with Tanita Tikaram and something like Ride was much more alternative, much more rock – which is where Cally came in.'

Cally was not much like the usual major label A&R man. Working from an office lit by a single light bulb over which he had draped a black silk shade, he had, Smith believes, 'guru status' at the company on account of having managed Julian Cope and co-founded the baroque indie label Bam Caruso. Cally was working for a company that had learned from bitter experience with Elevation that indie and major ways of thinking did not necessarily mix. Like its conservative other half WEA, East West stuck to what it was good at, launching only those acts that had commercial potential.

'There was a really heavy doctrine at the company about who they would sign,' says Cally. 'Rob Dickins was being almost draconian in his signing policy. Ben in particular was finding bands that wouldn't stand a chance under that kind of iron fist. You wanted a bit of room to manoeuvre and make it up as you went along, as most bands and A&R men do. We had, over a long period, kept hammering at Malcolm's door, [saying] that we wanted to be able to sign something that didn't fall under such an intense microscope. When Ben gave me a cassette of Ride in an A&R meeting, it was almost out of exasperation. It was like: "Well, there's absolutely no point in us listening to this, then." '

Playing the tape that weekend, Cally was just as bowled over as Wardle had been. Between them, they wondered how they might circumvent the Dunbar problem. 'Ben and I had these conversations about "well, let's face it, however great we think it is ..."' Cally remembers. 'I think Ben called it "a cathedral of sound". I was more gung-ho about the whole thing. I couldn't believe that anything that great could sit around and not be noticed.'

As they discussed possible ways to bring Ride on board without frightening them off by a sudden move, Wardle sighed that it was a pity East West couldn't finance and release a couple of Ride singles independently – on an indie label covertly funded by East West, for example – and maybe raise the subject of a formal contract a year or so down the line. The band would be happy, Cally and Wardle would be happy, and the indie diehards on the *NME* and other music papers need never be any the wiser. In Cally's darkened office, a vision of the music business in the 1990s had just been hesitantly illuminated.

Cally had a friend called Pete Flanagan who ran an indie label, Zippo, from his record shop of the same name. Zippo had been particularly active in the mid-80s as an alma mater of the Paisley Underground scene, putting out strong-selling albums by the Rain Parade and the Long Ryders. There was also a Zippo sister label – One Big Guitar – on which Flanagan had released two singles by Underneath What, a rock band Cally was keeping A&R tabs on. A label with no connection to East West other than the Flanagan-Cally friendship, One Big Guitar was adjudged perfect for releasing a single by Ride, financed by East West's demo fund. Chicanery would be involved, admittedly, but it would be righteous chicanery. By keeping East West's name off the record sleeves, music press goodwill would follow, helping Ride to skirt the backlash against major label signings like the Darling Buds and the Wedding Present and avoid the baleful reviews of the House Of Love's 'Never'.

Working behind Malcolm Dunbar's back, Cally gave Ride £1,000 to record a few songs in an Oxford studio in July. They came out with three mini-classics. 'I was just awestruck at how good the music was,' says Cally. 'The band had a fantastic understatement about everything they did. They worshipped My Bloody Valentine, which I couldn't understand. I thought they were so much better than them.'

Taking the version of 'Drive Blind' from the original demo in April, Cally now had four songs to release as an EP on One Big Guitar. But he then made two mistakes in quick succession. He played 'Drive Blind' to Alan McGee; and he told him Ride were already signed when in fact they weren't. In a flash, all Cally's careful efforts to allay Ride's suspicions of major labels had been undone. 'We switched off at that point,' says Andy Bell. 'Cally became a bad guy.'

'I wouldn't say that was a bad thing for Cally to have done,' reflects Ben Wardle, 'although it did backfire. Ride were exceptionally obsessed with the indie ethic.' Which placed one obvious candidate in the frame. Within minutes of learning that Ride were unsigned, McGee rang Cally. 'He was very honourable about the whole thing,' Cally remembers. 'He phoned me up and said: "Would you mind if I pursued this?" But he went at it like a hooligan.'

McGee got Dick Green to ring Dave Newton, who was now Ride's manager. 'We had got to the point of doing the artwork for this One Big Guitar release,' says Newton. 'Then our agent, Ben Winchester, got us the support slot on a Soup Dragons tour starting at the beginning of November. Alan McGee turned up at the first date in Sheffield. And he turned up at every gig after that for about a week.'

McGee's reputation preceded him. Newton and Ride's bass guitarist Steve Queralt had worked in Oxford's Our Price record shop and knew a lot about indie labels. Queralt was a 4AD fanatic, but Creation came a close second. The House Of Love and My Bloody Valentine were major influences on Ride, and all four members had seen McGee interviewed on the BBC2 music programme *Rapido* in November 1988. 'It was that Pavlov's dog thing,' says drummer Loz Colbert, 'where you see the Creation label and you get excited.'

On 1 November, at Sheffield Polytechnic, McGee bought chips for the four Ride boys and sat them round a table. 'Once he met the band,' says Mike Smith, 'he was glaringly obviously the right man to be putting out their records.' Tempering Ride's excitement, however, was a nagging feeling that – as Queralt puts it – 'Creation were good at discovering bands but not very good at holding on to them'. They found McGee to be friendly, almost entirely unintelligible and a touch eccentric. Rather than talk about record contracts, he asked all of them in turn what their favourite Neil Young album was.

Having seen Cally's laidback gait unwittingly detonate the landmine, McGee played it very cool, never lingering too long on the subject of business. 'That was what was so persuasive about him – the fact that he wasn't trying to persuade,' says Dave Newton. 'We had Fire Records turn up at a gig, and they were talking about a six-album deal and this sort of thing. It was like, *hang* on. These guys were 17 and 18; no one was thinking beyond the next few weeks.' McGee uncled Andy Bell and Mark Gardener to a House Of Love show in November, where he and Gardener began to bond. Days later, Cally's artwork for the One Big Guitar EP was amended. It now displayed the logo of Creation instead.

The prescience and ingenuity of Cally and Wardle had seen them go unrewarded. In January, Mike Smith at MCA Music, too, would emerge from negotiations with Ride empty-handed. The karma boomerang, meanwhile, would give McGee a resounding whack on its return journey.

13 The Road Less Travelled: Wales Visitation

THE END FOR THE Weather Prophets came with a song called 'Crashing Wave'. Recorded for consideration as a single, it reunited Pete Astor with the Warwickshire studio owner and producer John Rivers, whose pin-sharp recording of the Loft's 'Up The Hill And Down The Slope' in 1985 had given a young Astor the keys to the fairground. The magic proved elusive the second time around, however, and 'Crashing Wave' was rejected by McGee. For want of a better idea, the Weather Prophets decided to split up. 'The fun had gone out of it,' says Dave Goulding, 'and there wasn't much money in it.' McGee asked them to stay together for appearances' sake – Creation was about to issue a compilation of their B-sides and out-takes – but the charade did nothing much to enhance sales and the farewell gigs were bad-tempered and unpublicised.

In the summer of 1989, Astor contributed backing vocals to another swansong: Felt's final album *Me And A Monkey On The Moon*. Lawrence had used his south coast connections to good effect, roping in Robert Young on bass and finding a studio in Eastbourne that didn't ask for too much money. Produced by Adrian Borland, ex-leader of the post-punk group the Sound, *Me And A Monkey On The Moon* was recorded efficiently but soon fell into financial hot water. '[The studio] wouldn't let us take the tapes away because Alan hadn't paid the bill,' recalls Lawrence. 'I said: "What's happening, Alan?" He said: "We just haven't got any money. I can't do anything." '

Lawrence suspected it went deeper; that McGee had become bored with Felt and the other Creation guitar bands of the mid-80s. He hadn't even asked to hear Lawrence's demos, and was unaware that many of the songs were nakedly autobiographical. Making a clean break with ambiguity and rococo poetry, the lyrics on *Me And A Monkey On The Moon* looked back to Lawrence's childhood in the early 70s, and touched on some of the insecurities that had followed him into his late twenties. The sense of a circle being completed in his life harmonised felicitously with his desire to bring down the curtain on Felt's career, leaving a score-sheet of perfect tens – ten years, ten singles, ten albums. For symmetry to be realised, however, he needed to get the tenth album out of the studio in Eastbourne and into the shops before the end of December. Impossible on cash-strapped Creation, but what about taking it to él?

Much as he loved Lawrence, Mike Alway would never in a blue moon have allowed Felt to be on él. They were a group of real human beings, after all, not one of Alway's idiomatic exercises in hypotheti-cal identities. An album by Felt would undermine él's verisimilitude as graphically as if one of the nuns in *Black Narcissus* were to have whipped out a Walkman. But Alway could not veto the Felt album's release, because Alway was not at él any more.

The final straw for Martin Costello and the hidebound Cherry Red cheque-book had been Alway's decision to record a band called Hunky Dory. Based in the Sussex town of Lewes, Hunky Dory were children who sang songs written by their father. You couldn't make it up – or in Alway's case, you could, which was the problem. One day in 1989, Iain McNay's spiritual quest in Europe was interrupted by an urgent phone call from Costello in London.

The plug was pulled on Alway, but él was not closed down. It released a couple more records, setting Alway's teeth on edge by signing a derivative indie guitar band, the James Dean Driving Experience. But although this appendix to él appalled Alway, senti-mentality was – just once – to be Costello's forte. He listened to Lawrence explain his ten-years-of-Felt brainchild, and agreed to come to the aid of the concept. Knowing there could never be a fol-low-up, he bought *Me And A Monkey On The Moon* from Creation, sprang the master tapes from their Eastbourne prison and financed some mixdown time in London. Felt were back where they had begun – in the bosom of the Cherry Red group – but the changes in the interim years had made strangers of them all: Lawrence, Costello, the banished Alway and the peripatetic McNay. There was no more appropriate time to be growing apart.

At the beginning and end of 1989 respectively, two long-serving independent distributors and Cartel members – Red Rhino in Yorkshire and Fast Forward in Scotland – went out of business. In an unrelated move, Rough Trade Distribution's managing director Richard Powell left the company in April, followed in December by Dave Whitehead and Simon Edwards. These were the first public inklings that Rough Trade and the Cartel might face a survival strug-gle in the early 90s. At the annual Umbrella seminar of indie labels and distributors in June 1990, the outlook was unusually gloomy: despite superficial impressions of vitality and abundance, indie record shops, squeezed by the megastores and hit by low sales, were closing down at the rate of one a day, and the prospects for those that remained were even bleaker than they had been in the recession-hit early 80s. Already, widescale reassessment at Rough Trade had led to the appointment of a new managing director – George Kimpton-Howe, previously Steve Mason's understudy at Pinnacle – as well as designs for an administrative overhaul, a move to larger premises and the introduction of full computerisation. 'In general it will be a new beginning,' Kimpton-Howe told *Music Week*. In point of fact, it would be a slow death.

Meanwhile in 1989, two famous independent labels of the 60s and 70s had been bought by the PolyGram corporation – 75 per cent owned by the Dutch electronics company Philips – which paid a reported £300 million for Island in August and the same amount for A&M in September. When the statistics for 1989 were tabulated, PolyGram had become the predominant record company in the UK, distributing via its many imprints more than 26 per cent of all singles and 27 per cent of all albums. Further investments that year saw EMI acquire 50 per cent of two smaller labels – Chrysalis and Enigma – and the Japanese company Fujisankei procure a 25 per cent stake in the record division of Virgin. Arguably the most telling development from the indies' point of view, however, came in June when Polydor bought half of the independent dance label Big Life.

'When I returned [to London in May 1991],' wrote Iain McNay several years later, 'both the music and the structure of the music industry were rapidly changing. It seemed that the huge multinational corporations had decided that the way to ... break new acts in the UK was through the indie network. The independent charts which I had helped to initiate way back in 1980 had become invaded by records released by labels that were either financed by – or, even worse, owned by – the multinational corporations. The word "indie" had become a marketing word that ... had absolutely nothing to do with either the original intention of the chart or even the meaning of the word.' And McNay went on: 'The attitude of the acts was also fast changing. No longer were they willing to build their careers over time, over two or three albums. Success – both creative and financial – was wanted fast.'

Mike Alway, who in 1983 had tried to fly with a major label and crashed like Icarus, would not be granted a second chance in such a power-political, results-based climate. Nor would he enjoy another heyday in the independents, for the 90s would demand compromises that he was not able to make. Of the four key influential figures in the early career of Alan McGee – Horne, Treacy, Alway and Travis – Alway became the third to disappear from view. He says today: 'I'm disappointed that I let go a massive opportunity. I could be like one of those yuppies living up on Richmond Hill, or like Mickie Most ... Not that I miss any of that. What I miss is the power to make records. That's my frustration. My wife says that I strike her as somebody with incredibly bad karma, because I've just done nothing – or nothing compared with what it should have been. Maybe she's right.'

It was Dave Bates' idea that the House Of Love should do a long tour. Upset by the music papers' mauling of 'Never', which he blamed for its failure to make the Top 40, he suggested to Mick Griffiths that he should book gigs in as many towns and cities as possible. Happy Mondays and the Stone Roses had both overtaken the House Of Love in different ways – the former were ever-presents in the weeklies, while the latter had announced a 7,000 capacity spectacular at London's Alexandra Palace for mid-November – but the ground could be made up, Bates believed, if the House Of Love's tour digressed from the usual major city circuit. A three- or four-month journey down the road less travelled – taking in towns such as Bridlington, Cleethorpes, Tonbridge and Hemel Hempstead – could conceivably win the House Of Love tens of thousands of new fans.

Then McGee had a devilish notion. He argued that the itinerary should favour towns that contained a chart return shop – the retail outlets whose sales influence the compiling of the Top 75. Officially, the whereabouts of these shops are a mystery. Off the record, a list was easy to come by. 'You'd be surprised at their locations,' says Griffiths. 'Some really obscure small towns have two or three chart return shops.' McGee, Griffiths and Bates imagined the House Of Love reaping a glorious Gallup harvest come the releases of their next single and long-awaited album.

'I really went to town on it,' says Griffiths. 'I got them gigs absolutely everywhere. My personal motivation was let's book more gigs than any band has ever done in the UK.' Soon he had booked 50, and then 60 – and then finally 70 dates in Britain and Ireland, stretching from the end of October 1989 to the end of March 1990. Fontana shaped its campaign around the tour: a single ('I Don't Know Why I Love You') in November; another ('Shine On') in January; the album in late February; and one more single in March to coincide with the tour's last lap. It was anticipated by Bates that at least two of those singles – if not all three – would be Top 20 hits.

The album was finished on 22 October, nine days before the first gig in Leeds. While Dave Meegan would not get his full share of the credit – the record sleeves, which had been printed months before, listed the various producers in alphabetical order – he could congratulate himself for doing what few had thought possible: suturing the gaping inconsistencies of ten months' recording, finding a happy medium between alternative and mainstream rock, and coming up with a 50-minute album that had the House Of Love, McGee and Bates nodding their heads in unison.

The overall cost of the album is put by most insiders at around £500,000, but by one source at nearer to £800,000. Both estimates include studio bills, producers' fees and advance payments from the record company to the band. The more exorbitant estimate includes 50 per cent of the cost of videos for the album's singles – which would continue to rise, amid much controversy, until the final single in March – as well as additional expenses such as the hiring of Jeff Barrett as publicist, taxis and bar tabs.

In short, the House Of Love were massively in debt to Fontana. For the record company to break even, it would need to sell around 600,000 copies of the album – an increase of some half a million on its Creation predecessor. Even promoted by a 70-gig tour, this was almost certainly out of the question. Assuming sales were a more realistic 200,000, the recording of the next album would start with a high six-figure debt already established, and three instalments of the House Of Love's £400,000 advance still to be paid. It is not unknown in such cases for the record company to pay up and drop the unre-couped band before it can do more damage. However, Mike Smith, who was to become the House Of Love's publisher a few years later, believes Fontana would not have been contemplating anything so drastic. 'There is a very different equation between a band recouping and the record company making its money back,' says Smith. 'Record companies don't really want bands to recoup. They always look for opportunities to keep the band unrecouped. I'm a publisher, so I have a slightly cynical view on this, but I don't think record compa-nies really want to start paying bands royalties. They would rather try and keep them in debt.' And as a rule of thumb, a band in debt is much less inclined to be dictatorial and much more likely to do exactly what its record company wants. Which is, of course, exactly what the record company wants.

'I Don't Know Why I Love You' was as powerful and FM-friendly a rock single as any recorded by a British group in 1989. It was play-listed by Radio 1 and released in November on six formats – 7-inch, gatefold 7-inch, cassette, 12-inch, CD and a 12-inch with alternative B-sides – all of them chart-eligible. The aggregate sales were expected to be more than sufficient for a Top 40 placing. It was quite a shock, therefore, when 'I Don't Know Why I Love You' charted at 41 – no higher than 'Never'; no chance of a re-count; no *Top Of The Pops*.

'It made no sense,' says Dave Bates. 'It was a huge body-blow.' There was talk around London of a jinx on the House Of Love – some kind of sinister payback for them snatching so greedily at the major label dollar. Bates, though, was unshakeable in his belief that even darker forces were at work. A man who lacked McGee's knowledge of how the late-80s music press worked, and who had no truck with the ongoing indie-versus-major polemic, Bates could not understand why the press was now turning away from the House Of Love. For someone as high-placed as Bates, incomprehension was not an enjoyable feeling.

One week after the disappointment of 'I Don't Know Why I Love You', the Stone Roses' double-sided single 'Fool's Gold'/'What The World Is Waiting For' charted at a conspicuously high 13, with Happy Mondays' *Madchester Rave On* EP at a more than respectable 30. Both bands were invited to perform on *Top Of The Pops*, and when the programme was aired – on 30 November – their show of strength was interpreted by many commentators, including Alan McGee, as the most subversive and ground-breaking event in music television since the days of punk. McGee would henceforth make a point of releasing two Creation singles on the same day, hoping desperately for a similar TV landmark.

The House Of Love, who were on tour in Aberystwyth when *Top Of The Pops* went out, became obsolete in the time it took to smoke a cigarette. No longer the golden boys of the future, nor the most talked about band of the present, they travelled to Swansea on 1 December, and then to a polytechnic in Treforest for the last night of their Wales visitation.

Since being sacked by the Jesus and Mary Chain in 1986, McGee had missed having Jim Reid as a friend. Reid evidently felt the same way, for a reconciliation took place in 1989. 'They hooked up at a party,' recalls Reid's then-girlfriend Laurence Verfaillie, 'and like good old Scottish people they had a few drinks and were very jolly. It was water under the bridge very, very quickly.'

For their part, the Mary Chain had, since their *Darklands* album in 1987, singularly failed to be the revolution McGee had predicted. They had their place in the scheme of things, much as Nick Cave or the Sisters Of Mercy did, attracting black-clad audiences that looked rather like the members of the band. Journalists gradually tired of the Mary Chain's gigs, often wishing in print that they could inspire terror and mayhem once again. According to Mick Houghton, the Reid brothers detested these reviews more than any. Yet they continued to be written. Exactly what the *NME*'s Mat Snow had feared in 1986 had come to pass: the Mary Chain had lost their impact and become toothless.

'They had a sleeve for "April Skies",' recalls Rob Dickins, 'and it was a picture of someone on a cross holding a revolver. They came in [to WEA] and they went to the head of marketing, and he went: "Oh, you can't have this. This is going to upset everyone." They came out of his office and I said: "Oh, I love the sleeve – it's fantastic." They went: "Well … we've just decided not to use it." I said: "What's wrong with you?" That [sleeve] was the *point* of what they were. It was that shock value – it *had* to be there. And I think the problem was when the shock value went. They were good pop writers … and it's not enough.'

John Moore, who had switched from drums to rhythm guitar, felt the Reids had become too insular in the way they recorded. Like Douglas Hart, Moore had not played a note on *Darklands*, and he found it strange that the Reids, who were not enamoured of much contemporary dance music, preferred to programme drum machines, with all their tinny shortcomings, than use a real drummer. Moore left the Mary Chain acrimoniously in 1987 when a review in *Sounds* of a show in Nottingham infuriated the Reids by referring to Moore as the band's 'visual linchpin', printing a photo of him slashing at his guitar for good measure.

Hart, meanwhile, had refused to scale down his drug-taking, had become passionate about acid house and was increasingly surplus to requirements. Only once – on their much-admired 1988 single 'Sidewalking' – had the Mary Chain sounded comfortable with the idea of marrying guitars to a dance pulse, but that had been more by fluke than design, and had had nothing to do with Hart. During periods of Mary Chain inactivity, he had recorded with Peter Fowler in the Acid Angels – and started a video company, Momentum, making promos for indie bands. 'I have to say the golden years of the Mary Chain were over for me,' he says. 'When I'd turn round onstage and see John Moore or James Pinker [on drums], I'd get a slight deflation.'

Never prolific, the Mary Chain released their third studio album, *Automatic*, in October 1989. Almost a Top 10 hit, it nevertheless left them with little choice but to retrace their footsteps touring the same old concert halls, inviting the same mildly disappointed reviews from the same despised journalists. 'Even before *Darklands*, they thought they were getting short-changed by the press,' says Laurence Verfaillie. 'The press was used to hype them, but they never liked the press. They never befriended any journalists, which is rare.'

Although she shared her boyfriend's mistrust of journalists, Verfaillie had decided to look for a job as a record company publicist. In December 1989, after sending out her résumé without reply, she heard from McGee that a post had just opened up in Hackney. Jeff Barrett had been relieved of his responsibilities as Creation's PR.

'The Mary Chain sacked McGee in a Wendy Burger?' says Barrett. 'Well, he sacked me in a pizza place at the corner of Oxford Street and Tottenham Court Road. I said to him: "Can I carry on doing the Valentines and the Primals?" He said no – but he never told the Primals that I asked that.' Barrett had become one of the most sought-after publicists in the music business, juggling his three principal commitments – Creation, Factory and the House Of Love – like so many oranges, and seldom seeing a month pass without one of his acts appearing on the front page of a music paper. Overstretched and refreshingly unadulterated (he would refuse, for instance, to nominate himself for the annual *Music Week* PR award, and disdained his rivals for festooning their office walls with framed front covers),

Barrett was easy to blame when something went awry. Something like 'I Don't Know Why I Love You' only getting to number 41.

'Chadwick was actually quite a gentleman,' he says, 'because he was very, very appreciative of what we did. The House Of Love were nice fellows, and they did used to say thank you. You don't get that nod very often in this game. Chadwick had the balls to say: "Your heart's not in this now, is it?" ' Barrett wasn't sorry to be losing the House Of Love. But he was mortified to be ousted from doing Primal Scream.

For certain lower-profile Creation artists, a change in publicists had its benefits. Momus had always written his own press releases, handing them over to be re-typed with the obligatory eight or nine spelling and punctuation mistakes. To mark the release of his single 'The Hairstyle Of The Devil' – a surprise Top 100 entry in April – Barrett had arranged a press call in a hairdressing salon in Covent Garden. Wires got crossed: journalists thought they would be required to have their hair cut by Momus, and none turned up.

Nikki Sudden, meanwhile, who had released an album called *Groove* in 1989, asked one day if he could see his Creation press files. Expecting a Securicor van to bring round dozens of bulging folders containing hundreds of clippings, reviews and thoughtfully composed essays about his work, Sudden was instead handed a single piece of paper with two sentences handwritten on it. They read: 'Nikki Sudden was formerly the guitarist in the Swell Maps & after leaving this band formed his own group "Nikki Sudden & the French Revolution" & signed to Creation. Since then he has released a number of LPs & singles & considers himself a rock poet in the style of Johnny Thunders & Kieth *(sic)* Richards.'

As he stood forlornly re-reading this mess of skimpy information and hurried ampersands, Sudden grew indignant. There seemed few things more upsetting or humiliating than a 12-year career condensed into 55 words – with the most important word of them all spelt wrong. 'That was possibly the moment, I seem to remember, that despite Alan's protestations that he was willing to release my albums forever, it was probably time for me to be moving on,' Sudden relates.

Laurence Verfaillie was interviewed for the job of Creation publicist by McGee and Ed Ball in the mirrored presidential suite in Hackney. 'I more or less said: "I've got no experience, I don't speak very good English and I don't particularly like journalists",' she recalls. 'Alan goes: "Great, that's exactly what I want." ' She was given Ride as her first project, installed in the back office and left to get on with it.

It had not been a bountiful year for Creation. Only eight singles had been released, none of them earth-shattering. Of 17 albums, not one had caught the imagination of either the public or the media.

They included compilations of the Loft and the Weather Prophets, albums licensed from abroad – Duncan Dhu from Spain; the Sneetches from California – and two CDs that had been shrinkwrapped to assist sales of an Edgar Allen Poe anthology published by Creation Press. Launched back in February, Creation's publishing arm had debuted with a James Williamson book, *Raism*, inspired by the fifteenth-century French Satanist and child murderer Gilles de Rais. Williamson, writing under the name James Havoc, had described the experience of reading *Raism* as 'a mind rape'. Not many book-lovers had been tempted to see if he was right, and the ailing Creation Press was shortly to be abandoned.

As for McGee, he had received more attention in 1989 as the manager of the House Of Love, and as a drug-taker, than as the head of a record label. 'Creation were not the coolest label on the planet,' says Verfaillie. 'Factory had been getting really big. Alan knew we weren't seen as being as cool, and he wanted to get a really tight team around him that were totally dedicated. I knew that financially things were pretty low, but it wasn't an issue that was being discussed. And I very quickly realised that Creation were about to come back with very cool stuff.'

One release in the pipeline – though hopes of it charting were slim – was Primal Scream's 'I'm Losing More Than I'll Ever Have', scheduled for February. At certain points on their autumn tour, the Scream had revealed that the B-side would be a dance remix. Andrew Weatherall had been fine-tuning 'Loaded', under the watchful eye of Andrew Innes, and tapes had started drifting over to Hackney. Those who heard them could not believe the changes in Primal Scream. For one thing, Bobby Gillespie was not on the track.

McGee was as intrigued by 'Loaded' as anyone, but like Gillespie he needed time to adjust to the innovations. 'We'd make comments like: "Can we please have Bobby on it?" ' he recalls. 'It got sent back about three times for tinkering with. I said to Bobby: "I want you to have some vocal on it." He said: "No, McGee, I just don't want to be on it." ' Pat Collier, who had delivered a more orthodox remix of 'I'm Losing More Than I'll Ever Have' for release as the A-side, presumed that Weatherall's B-side mix would be opportunist and tacky: Primal Scream had never struck Collier as acid house fans.

On 6 December, a cold Wednesday night just prior to the music industry's Christmas party season, Primal Scream played at Subterania in west London. It was six days after the Stone Roses and Happy Mondays had appeared on *Top Of The Pops*, and Sunday's chart had confirmed that Manchester's influence was spreading. The city's dance quartet 808 State had joined the Stone Roses in the Top 10, and Happy Mondays had climbed to 19. Aside from a downward-sliding single by Morrissey, there was no other indie guitar-based or otherwise *NME*-sponsored music in the Top 40.

It was not a week to feel good about being a Primal Scream fan. Dick Green, citing exhaustion, missed the Subterania show. Judging by the meagre attendance, virtually the whole of London followed suit. 'Creation as we knew it died the night Primal Scream played Subterania,' says Lawrence from Felt. 'Hardly anybody was there. They were doing their rock 'n' roll thing to almost no audience, and Weatherall was DJing. I stood there thinking: it's all finished. It's over.' Having won his race against time with days to spare – *Me And A Monkey On The Moon* had come out on él in December, and Felt played their last gig in Birmingham on the nineteenth – Lawrence packed up and moved to New York.

DJing for Primal Scream at Subterania, Weatherall had not had much of an audience to warm up. But on 14 December, when he returned to the venue to DJ at a dance event called Sub Club, the floor was fuller and livelier. Always a man to be relied upon to play something from left field, he treated the dancers to 'Loaded', now remixed to completion. Andrew Innes, who was there to watch the reactions, phoned Bobby Gillespie at four o'clock in the morning to tell him that the Sub Club had gone nuts.

Nobody had given very much thought to whether a 70-date tour was a wise undertaking for someone of Terry Bickers' state of mind. After the House Of Love's appearance at the Reading festival in August, it had been assumed that Bickers was over the worst of his depression. He had settled down with his new love Sallie Johnson, and seemed contented and optimistic. Setting up the tour, Mick Griffiths had been more concerned about Guy Chadwick, and had tried not to overburden the singer's voice with too many shows on successive nights. However, by November, Chadwick had smashed a guitar at a sound check in Sunderland after an ugly scene with Bickers, and as old wounds reopened McGee was summoned and warned of serious ructions.

'Guy was not at all sympathetic to what I'd been through,' says Bickers. 'I remember once he pinned me down on the floor, knelt over me and slapped my face. I was lying there thinking: what *are* you doing? He was saying: "Why did you do this to me? Why did you do this to me?" I was like: "Sorry. I'll try and time my nervous breakdowns a bit better next time. Try and fit them into your schedule." '

As usual, Bickers was unhappy about money. He had been learning more about house culture from Grant Fleming, the House Of Love's on-the-road T-shirt seller, and what Fleming had told him – that people were coming together in clubs; that barriers were crumbling; that inhibitions were being discarded – sounded far preferable to the financial agenda Bickers sensed in the House Of Love.

Under the effects of hallucinogenics – the band's drug of choice at the time was magic mushrooms – Bickers was feeling musically accomplished and highly creative, yet little suspected that his band-mates were finding him more unbearable than ever. 'He had become a bit of a Brian Jones figure,' says Andy Jarman. 'He wouldn't turn up at sound checks when everybody else turned up, and he was eating a lot of mushrooms. The band were beginning to tell me not to give him money.'

As the tour moved to Wales at the end of November, McGee and Dave Bates flew to America with tapes of the House Of Love's new album. They met up with executives from Phonogram's US company Mercury on both coasts. McGee, emerging from a long period of debauchery, was making strenuous efforts to behave in a normal fashion. Bates had been clean of drugs for some years. 'Bates hires this penthouse suite to play the House Of Love to all these top record guys desperate to do charlie,' McGee recalls. 'Me and Bates are sitting there, and they're looking at me – this guy with red hair, drugged out from a year and a half of abuse, with sunglasses on. And Bates is teetotal, just going: "TheHouseOfLovetheHouseOfLovetheHouseOfLove ..." They must have thought: who the fuck are these two guys?'

In Bangor, where the House Of Love played a university gig on 29 November, Terry Bickers asked a student if he could get him some mushrooms. They arrived in a carrier bag. 'Everything went fucking pear-shaped,' says Dave Francolini, the drummer in support band Something Pretty Beautiful. 'I'll never forget me and Terry walking up a hill in Bangor with linen tied round our heads, holding snooker cues, and him saying he was Jesus Christ and I was John the Baptist.'

Treforest, the next destination, was a polytechnic gig, the House Of Love's fourth and last night in Wales, and their eighth show in as many days. Bickers was now a wholly and completely separate entity from the rest of his band. Before taking the stage, he demanded £200 in cash from Andy Jarman, who told him he couldn't have it. Furious, Bickers deliberately sang his backing vocals off-key during the gig, chanting the first words that came into his head. Attempting to drown out Chadwick by shouting the words from an old Sham 69 song, Bickers finally went too far and Jarman turned his microphone off.

After the show, Bickers had a bad night on mushrooms. He was not the only one. 'The hotel was a late nineteenth-century house in the middle of nowhere,' says Jarman. 'You could imagine weird, black magicky things going on there. We all took mushrooms and I literally had to hide under the blankets. Every time I tried to watch the TV, there was a horror film on. All I could hear was this shouting and screaming and banging.' Jarman wondered if he was dreaming it. In fact, what he was hearing was Bickers smashing up his room in a fright after seeing a spaceship from his window.

Walking to the van the next morning – a day off – Bickers was met by a frosty scene. Even the roadies were now refusing to look him in the eye. Again he demanded money from Jarman. Again Jarman said no. The House Of Love's van filled up with people: Chadwick and Gibbons; Jarman and his girlfriend; Bickers and Sallie Johnson; Pete Evans; and Dave Francolini, whom they were taking to the M32 so that he could thumb a lift to his native Bristol. The van would then proceed to London. Groothuizen elected to travel in another van with two members of the crew.

In the group's van, Bickers waited until they were outside Cardiff before beginning to shout some dialogue from *The Exorcist*. To Bickers' right, Chadwick slowly reached down under his seat and put his hand on the end of his snooker cue. The van was approaching Aust services at Severn Bridge, where Jarman had suggested a stop-off to buy provisions. 'Guy said: "We've got to talk",' remembers Bickers. 'I said: "You're fucking right we've got to talk." '

There was silence for a few minutes. Bored with *The Exorcist*, Bickers did something quite unexpected. He picked on Pete Evans, with whom he had always been on good terms, criticising the quiet drummer for not donating enough of his income to charity. By way of underlining the allegation, which was laughable, Bickers produced a banknote – he remembers it being a tenner; Dave Francolini, seated behind him, says it was a fifty – and set fire to it.

'I was sort of shrinking in my seat,' says Francolini. 'He was going: "Dave could live for a week on this." I'm thinking: well, hand it over then. It was rather a contradiction in terms, I thought.' The van pulled into the services at Aust. Saying not a word, Pete Evans clambered out, reached back inside for his bag, placed it on the ground, climbed back in and punched Bickers half a dozen times in the face. Bickers did not feel any of the blows land.

By coincidence, the other van had stopped at Aust to get petrol and was parked about 200 yards away. Seeing Evans striding past with his bag, Groothuizen called out to him and was met by a stream of abuse. Grant Fleming got out to see what had happened. He found Chadwick and Gibbons in the cafeteria and was told that Evans had left the House Of Love. With magnificent presence of mind under the circumstances, Jarman, working out the subtleties of the situation like a man asked to ferry two alligators and three kittens from one riverbank to the other in a small rowing-boat, offered to drop Bickers and Johnson (who were arguing bitterly) and Francolini at a train station in Bristol, and come back for everyone else. Evans was talked into retaking his seat in the group's van on the understanding that Bickers would be getting out. 'It was very cinematic,' Bickers says. 'It was like exchanging prisoners in a spy movie.'

'It did seem very surreal,' agrees Groothuizen, 'but after three days of doing mushrooms myself, nothing seemed impossible.' Not until later that day would he be absolutely certain who was leaving the House Of Love and who was staying.

At the Chateau Marmont hotel in Los Angeles, the phone rang. It was Chadwick for McGee. Some minutes later, a phone rang in Camberwell. It was McGee for Groothuizen. 'What have you done?' he said simply.

Terry Bickers had been sacked from the House Of Love – whether he knew it or not – and Pete Evans reinstated. Chadwick and Groothuizen had already contacted a replacement guitarist to help them finish the tour. McGee seethed and swore, but was powerless. Still, it didn't stop him trying. Ordering Groothuizen to do whatever it took to get Bickers back in the band, he succeeded only in causing offence. 'He was going: "But don't you understand, without Terry you're *nothing* . . .!" ' Groothuizen recalls. 'This is our manager talking, you know.'

If there is a line between virtuosity and musical intellectualism, Simon Fernsby had crossed it a long time before Groothuizen came knocking on his door muttering something about a gig in Portsmouth. A friend of the House Of Love since their earliest concerts in 1986, Fernsby was particularly close to Bickers – which is exactly why the scheming Chadwick wanted him in the band. No other guitarist would freak out Bickers more.

Fernsby, a jazz lover whose stage name was Simon Walker, had not been following the House Of Love's career closely. Friends were friends, he reasoned, but the House Of Love were pretty boring. 'I was 25 and I'd been playing in a band which had a jokey self-image of a surrealist Booker T. & the M.G.s*,' he recalls. 'I'd got to the point where I thought rock stars – and people who wanted to be rock stars – were completely ridiculous. I was being asked by people in the [House Of Love]: "Do you want to be in the biggest band in the world?" There was no *way* it was going to be the biggest band in the world.'

Walker had no time to rehearse for Portsmouth. Chadwick taught him the songs in the van. At the venue – another polytechnic – it was mooted that a sign be placed by the front entrance explaining that Bickers had left the band. Last-minute confidence set in, however, and no such information was given.

Almost a week elapsed before the press discovered that Bickers had gone. An official statement from the band claimed that he was suffering from 'mental and physical exhaustion' due to the House Of Love's hectic schedule, and was merely taking a breather prior to a future reappearance. Portsmouth had been kind to Walker, but the

---

* The band was called the Dave Howard Singers.

itinerary for March was full of major cities where Bickers' absence would not be so easily glossed over, and where music papers were bound to send their most cynical reviewers. Chadwick knew that no one in the band – the studious, head-down Walker included – had a fraction of Bickers' electrifying stage presence.

As a personality, Walker was much less of a variable than Bickers. Yet he could be just as forthright as Bickers about anything he deemed worthy of comment. Intense and argumentative, he was also capable of marathon feats of conversation. He sneered at the simple riffs Chadwick composed, and scoffed that Chadwick could not keep time. Though a full member of the band from January 1990 onwards, he refused to sign a contract; he didn't see why he should put his name to a huge debt that he had not helped to run up. Bill Carey, who played guitar in Something Pretty Beautiful, wondered if Chadwick had chosen the right man to fill Bickers' shoes. 'It was kind of like, out of the frying pan and into a different frying pan,' Carey says.

With the press now taking the view that the House Of Love were no-hopers without Bickers, Mick Houghton, who had been the band's PR for a few months in 1987, was brought back to settle everything down and reaffirm the mission statement. And if he could get a few front covers while he was at it, so much the better.

The *NME*'s coverage of Manchester's swirling psychedelic colours and bowl-haired stars had seen its weekly circulation increase from 92,667 to 105,630 in the second half of 1989. The paper had less and less time for the unfashionable frowns and downbeat student rock of the House Of Love. Chadwick's policy of steering clear of anything to do with dance music – excepting the six-week wash-out with the metronomic Stephen Hague – was all well and good, but what if the band's student audience had changed its allegiances?

And while the House Of Love did spend a lot of time and money on a remix, the song being remixed was 'Shine On', and it was merely speeded up a shade to get on a Radio 1 play-list. It charted at 22 in February, rising to 20 after a *Top Of The Pops* performance. 'Of course I was scared when [Bickers] left,' said Chadwick at the time. 'But I think ... in a few months' time we should be better than ever.'

The House Of Love were at their most successful commercially between February and March 1990, without Bickers. In the short term at least, the hole left by his sacking was not reflected in sales of records and tickets. The album – untitled but usually referred to as 'Fontana' or 'The Butterfly Album' – had a midweek chart position of 2, entering a few days later at 8. An Albert Hall concert sold out effortlessly. Even in Manchester, playing to fans in Joe Bloggs jeans and baggy tops, the House Of Love were well received. 'The last leg of the big tour was their peak,' says Mick Griffiths. 'I went to quite a few of those gigs and they were going down the same way the Smiths had gone down – it was like a football crowd type of reaction. And I thought: well, they've got away with it.'

Andy Jarman was less sure. He had left at the start of the year, dismayed that the hard-drinking road crew was effectively controlling the band. 'I thought they'd lost the plot completely,' he says. 'They tried to become *lads*. That's not what the band was about. The band was about being slightly fey, English, faggy ... They were trying to adopt something that was nothing to do with them.'

14 Removing The Unwanted Associations

IN FEBRUARY, A COUPLE of months before Creation's move to Hackney, McGee had put My Bloody Valentine into Blackwing Recording Studios in Southwark to record an EP. Their first new music since *Isn't Anything*, it was keenly awaited to say the least. Five days into the session – which was to be followed by an extensive UK tour – a journalist went down to the studio to interview the band for the indie sector's trade magazine *The Catalogue*. He was told that Shields had arrived at Blackwing with no songs written, and that recording had only recently got under way. The band seemed fraught. Poltergeistian occurrences had seen one of the studio's speakers fall off a wall, narrowly missing Shields, and windows rattle at inopportune moments.

During the interview, Shields was called away to speak to McGee on the phone. When he returned, he said McGee had been shocked to hear that, five days into the session, only the drums had been recorded. When McGee and Green rolled up a few days later, they got an unpleasant surprise. 'We were doing an overnight mixing session with Kevin and Colm,' McGee recalls. 'We were trying to get Kevin to make decisions on tracks, and there was just no way we could. It was like there was an immovable thing in his head that we couldn't get past.' The session was abandoned and the EP never came out.

It was September before My Bloody Valentine returned to a studio. This time they went to Elephant in Wapping, a 24-track, £25-an-hour basement with an in-house engineer, Nick Robbins. 'The record company had an idea that they wanted the band to make an album that was a bit more of a *band* record,' says Robbins. 'Up till then, it was clearly pretty much Kevin's brainchild from start to finish. What was wanted was a record that reflected what they sounded like live.' McGee had told Robbins about the aborted session at Blackwing, and advised him that My Bloody Valentine might be grateful for his suggestions. He couldn't have been more wrong.

'On the first day in the studio it became clear that Creation's ideas were not what Kevin had in mind,' Robbins says. 'One of the very first things he said to me was that he didn't want my opinion on anything, and that I was just there to press the buttons. He really endeared himself to me by saying that ... The next thing that happened was the drummer arrived with all the gear. I told him what the record company had said about making a live-sounding album, and he laughed at me. He said: "Well, that's not going to happen because the girls don't come in the studio anyway." I never saw the girls except when they would bring some equipment and take it away. They never appeared in the studio for any other purpose.'

Robbins realised that Creation simply had no idea how My Bloody Valentine went about making records. Neither McGee nor Green had been a witness to the *Isn't Anything* sessions in Wales, and Shields was pretty insistent that he didn't want either of them hanging around at Elephant. As far as Robbins could gather, the reason for this was that Shields was paralysed by nerves. 'He had no material,' says Robbins. 'He had nothing. He'd got four weeks booked in the studio and he had absolutely not a note of music.'

The closest thing to a strategy that Shields had was to modify the role of the brilliant but erratic Colm O'Ciosoig by recording his drums into a sequencer, so that various beats could be triggered at a later date. While Robbins and O'Ciosoig recorded the drum-kit – and it took them weeks – Shields repaired to the studio's pool room to write music on his guitar. When this didn't work out, he decided to write at home instead. 'Colm and I would come into the studio around midday,' says Robbins, 'and Kevin wouldn't even turn up until seven o'clock in the evening because he was supposedly at home writing. He'd come in – and he would clearly have not written anything at all – and then he'd disappear off to the pool room again and we wouldn't see him until midnight. Then he'd come out at midnight and go home. And this was day after day after day.'

Unbeknown to Robbins, O'Ciosoig was falling ill. A drug-and-squatting lifestyle had pushed the quiet drummer towards a breakdown, and he would soon be unable to play drums with any conviction. 'At the beginning of [the] album I was essentially homeless,' he later explained. 'After every day in the studio, I'd walk down the streets until I'd find an empty house to live in. It was just too much.'

Having fielded Dick Green's inquiries for a month, Robbins decided to be straight with him. Green let Shields convince him that there was a reason for working so slowly, and the studio was re-booked for another month. Meanwhile, Robbins had come to the conclusion that Shields was a charlatan.

By the end of October, Shields and O'Ciosoig had compiled 22 tracks of drums. Robbins was bored out of his mind. 'If you haven't got a song to go on top of it, what's the point?' he says. 'I just thought:

this is a fucking waste of time – I'm out of here.' A colleague of Robbins', Harold Burgon, was brought in as an engineer, and the studio was booked for a third month. It was obvious that there would not be a finished album at the end of it. 'Kevin needed a studio where he could feel totally free to come in at whatever time of day he wanted,' says Elephant's then-owner and manager Graham Sharpe. 'He needed a studio with a lot of flexibility, and an engineer with a lot of flexibility too. I think Kevin would try most people's patience. I know he tired Harold out after a while.'

For a change of ambience, a 26-day session was booked at Woodcray, a residential studio in Berkshire. Shields spent all 26 days on rhythm guitar parts. After four months of work on the album, the musical contributions of Debbie Goodge and Bilinda Butcher were nil, and Shields didn't appear to have a clue what he was doing.

In January 1990, Ride signed a £20,000 publishing deal with Steve Walters at EMI Music. Their recording deal with Creation – which released the four-song *Ride* EP that month – was an unwritten agreement, meaning that Ride were technically free agents, but McGee was in no hurry to reach for a pen. The advance from EMI Music had made the Oxford lads financially self-sufficient for the moment, and a verbal understanding between them and Creation seemed to be enough. As their manager Dave Newton kept reminding people, Ride were still at an early stage in their career. Indeed, when he heard that Creation had pressed up 4,000 copies of the EP, Newton worried that McGee might be moving too fast. 'We'll never sell that many,' he protested. The EP sold out in three days.

Suddenly, Ride were the most acclaimed young band in the country. Fans and journalists who had fretted in 1989 about the state of indie guitar music considered Ride much more than just a hot new group – they were a restoration of faith. Moreover, the EP was seen as a roaring return to form by Creation after a year of fitful releases and druggy carousing. 'The bands that had been hailed, like the House Of Love and My Bloody Valentine, hadn't really taken off in any way,' says Newton. 'Both of them looked like hitting serious problems in 1990, and they weren't young either. And here were Ride waving the flag.'

Within days of their EP coming out, Ride had plugged the gap in Creation's roster left by the House Of Love. On the Wednesday, Laurence Verfaillie inquired of James Kyllo if the EP had a midweek chart position. It was the first time that a Creation employee had ever asked such a question. On Sunday, the EP entered the chart at 72 – Creation's Top 75 debut.

'This was all stuff we weren't really expecting,' says bassist Steve Queralt. 'We thought you put out an indie single, it got into the indie charts in the *NME* or *Melody Maker* and you got on with your next single maybe a year later. And you still had your day job. This is what indie bands did. So all of a sudden it wasn't like being in an indie band, it was like being in a proper pop band. We had to think about videos, we had to think about our next single. It was an amazing time – really, really exciting.'

Ride were the first band from the south of England to be championed by the music papers since the embracing of Manchester the autumn before. With only an EP to their name, the Oxfordians posed no commercial threat to the Stone Roses or Happy Mondays just yet, but they spoke for a demographic that Manchester's stars tended to ignore: the southern-based indie fans who hadn't picked up on the dance scene and didn't want to. Indie fans like Ride themselves, in fact. 'I didn't really understand dance music at all,' says Queralt. 'I'd completely missed all the '89 E-mania, and acid house didn't mean anything to me. It was a time when if you were into indie music, that was it. You had your blinkers on and that's all you listened to.'

Blinkered though they may have been, Ride talked a language that indie fans could relate to. In an interview with the *NME*, Queralt criticised Rough Trade's high-flying waifs the Sundays for playing in large-sized venues before they had 'paid their dues' in smaller ones. The journalist and broadcaster Steve Lamacq would comment: 'When you buy a Ride record, you're buying into a pale, determined, insecure guitar-pop dream – a band who symbolise a fragile, vulnerable stage of youth.' If Lamacq was right, Ride were close to being the ultimate middle-class teenagers' panacea. And even if he was wrong, Ride's growing popularity suggested that Manchester, for all its bright colours, confidence and boisterous party spirit, had not sounded the death knell for noisy pop from the Thames Valley, and never would.

'Manchester helped Ride a lot,' says Dave Newton, 'given that there was some other movement that we could almost be the alternative to. It gave us a bit more space to exist. And another factor was that it was the end of the 80s and the start of the 90s. Putting your single out two weeks into a new decade, and being 18 years old, and being signed to a blossoming independent label ... It really was like a new start.' With the Roses-Mondays *Top Of The Pops* still fresh in the memory, Newton was not alone in feeling that indie music's decade-long struggle for mainstream radio and television coverage had ended in victory, and that the good-looking Ride would be more able than most to take advantage.

On 31 January, Ride played a gig at Royal Holloway College in Surrey. Watching were Seymour Stein of Sire Records and his A&R man Joe McEwen, who had flown in from New York after being briefed about the band by McGee. 'Everyone was just petrified of them,' says Newton. '[McEwen] seemed about twelve foot tall. They both wore big, long coats and they just started talking about all the bands they had signed.' The most famous artist on the Warner Bros-owned Sire was Madonna, a favourite of Steve Queralt's, but Sire had also been known since the 70s as a label that collected cult bands from Britain and Ireland: the Rezillos, the Undertones, Echo and the Bunnymen, the Smiths and James. McGee had been talking to Stein and McEwen about a North American signing for My Bloody Valentine, to whom Creation had the worldwide rights.

By January 1990, a North American deal between Sire and My Bloody Valentine had been sanctioned bar the formalities. (It would be made public in August.) But Ride were a quite separate issue. Legally unsigned anywhere in the world, they were McGee's emotional property in the UK, but they certainly didn't need him to strike their deals for other markets. By notifying Stein and McEwen, McGee had made a critical error of judgment.

Sire could do what it had done with My Bloody Valentine and make an offer for Ride's North American rights. Or it could do something else entirely: sign Ride to a deal for the world excluding the UK, with the result that Creation would not profit from any record sales abroad. To a label that needed as much money as it could get, this would be some loss.

Although Alan McGee, Ed Ball and Jeff Barrett could all claim to have been on the dance scene in 1988, acid house and dance culture had had no influence on Creation's musical output either that year or the next. The first dance record to be made by a Creation artist was a mini-album by Ed Ball – entitled *Tones* and credited to Love Corporation – which the ever-indulged, multi-pseudonymous Ball recorded in the second half of 1989 and released in January 1990.

'I was recording it at the same time as I was making [the Times' album] *E For Edward*,' Ball recalls. 'I was doing *E For Edward* in a studio at one end of Shorrold's Road in Fulham, and at the other end I was making the Love Corporation album in some guy's house that had all this computer equipment.'

Prior to release, white labels of *Tones* were distributed to DJs, among them Shoom's Danny Rampling. Ball was delighted when Rampling agreed to remix a track from the album, 'Palatial'. '[*Tones*] was well received,' says Ball. 'It wasn't like putting out a Times album and hearing people groan: "Oh fuck, it's that cunt again with another Times album." It was fresher than that. Rampling had been one of the founder members of the dance thing in Britain, so people were quite open-minded. "Palatial" was played [on Radio 1] by Annie Nightingale – in fact, she still plays it periodically.'

Meanwhile, promo copies of Primal Scream's Weatherall-remixed 'Loaded' had been played at raves and clubs in London and the south-east. This plea for emancipation with a floor-filling groove had picked up a buzz as the anthem of the moment. 'Within two or three weeks,' says McGee, ' "I'm Losing More Than I'll Ever Have" went from being the A-side to a double A-side, and "Loaded" was the [priority].' At Phuture record shop in London, DJs asked for 'Loaded' weeks in advance. Creation received 7,500 orders before its February release.*

Primal Scream were on tour in Europe, where they had already sacked one sound engineer, hired a replacement and then sacked him too. Dave Evans was flown out to Barcelona, with the just-finished video of 'Loaded' in his luggage, to take over as soundman for the rest of the tour. The Scream were in what he calls 'their Thin Lizzy days', but it wouldn't be for much longer. 'I did the sound for two gigs,' says Evans. 'Then they decided they didn't want to do any more – they'd had enough – and flew home.' Home to an ovation, as it turned out.

Laurence Verfaillie had joined Creation in December, when Primal Scream's media profile had been at an all-time low. She was now seeking publicity in the music press for a Scream record which, in sound and listener-impact, bore no relation to their ill-fated second album. Verfaillie was fortunate: the *NME* employed several veterans of the Creation acid house parties and was – better still – a paper for which Andrew Weatherall himself wrote. But the *NME* was not the only publication to swoon over 'Loaded'. 'I was a bit scared of having to work it,' Verfaillie admits, 'but it was incredible. I was phoning the likes of *Blitz* and *The Face* to ask if they'd got the record, and hearing the track being played in the background. It was overwhelming.'

Primal Scream's reputation began a rapid vertical ascent. Journalists started phoning Verfaillie, rather than the other way round. Bobby Gillespie was suddenly in demand for interviews again. 'The vision that people had of Primal Scream as rock 'n' roll has-beens just disappeared,' Verfaillie says. 'Anyone who introduced an element of acid house into their music, but still kept loyal to their thing – because "Ramblin' Rose" was on the B-side, of course – suddenly was the ultimate in cool.'

Gillespie, once a king of guitar pop, took the opportunity to put as much distance between 'Loaded' and British indie music as possible. In two sentences he declared the jangle-guitar genre well and truly kaput. 'If the Sundays are the best that scene can come up with, then it's definitely dead,' he said. 'Anybody who calls their album *Reading Writing And Arithmetic* has severe problems.'

---

* The wave of interest in 'Loaded' took Creation by surprise. Because it would have cost too much to remaster the CDs – on which 'Loaded' had been positioned third after 'I'm Losing More Than I'll Ever Have' and a live version of the MC5's 'Ramblin' Rose' – the order of the songs was amended on the sleeve only. For some time afterwards, Creation would receive returned CDs of 'Loaded' because the printed track-listing did not correspond to the sequence of the songs on the disc.

For various reasons – because a mental picture of the remixing process did not come easily; because Weatherall had remixed a song that was not widely known in the first place – 'Loaded' resisted attempts to place it in musical context. Since it combined a dance groove and an upbeat message, it was compared initially to the Beloved's contemporary single 'Hello', an ecstastic salute to a cata- logue of quirky household celebrities. The comparison, however, had less to do with conceptual similarity and more to do with the short supply of rock-dance crossover records at the time. Weatherall was quick to stress that 'Loaded' was made of tougher material. The best way to enjoy it, he said, was to play it at a party when the police were just about to kick down the door.

But although 'Loaded' had proven popular with the London cognoscenti, any hope of national success depended on Radio 1. Had plugger Scott Piering taken a Creation track called 'Loaded' to Broadcasting House in 1986, they would have listened no further than the title. Now, with producer-perestroika emerging thanks to Manchester and umpteen turn-of-the-decade house tracks, Radio 1 added 'Loaded' to its daytime schedules. The last piece of the jigsaw had fallen into place. 'This wasn't something we were very used to at all,' says Dick Green. 'Once it started getting played on radio during the day, you realised: my God ... it's going to be a hit.'

But 'Loaded' was not an immediate smash. In its first week of release, it missed the Top 40 – while the Stone Roses shot in at num- ber 8 with 'Elephant Stone', a reissued single from 1988. Seven nerve-racking days in Hackney followed before 'Loaded' entered the Top 40 at 32 on 10 March. There was an explosion of relief. 'We were at Dover,' recalls Paul Mulreany of the Jazz Butcher, 'on our way back from a tour of Europe. We put the radio on in the van and "Loaded" was in the charts. We were all like: "Yes!" That was a really good feel- ing. "Nice one. Well done, chaps." '

A week later, 'Loaded' climbed to 24 where it was expected to peak. But it wasn't finished yet. On 24 March – a day which McGee spent with the House Of Love in Birmingham – 'Loaded' finally entered the Top 20 at 16. As McGee poured the champagne, Chris Groothuizen and Guy Chadwick were torn between pleasure and envy. 'I was just a little bit put out,' recalls Groothuizen. 'I was like: "Well, *we* got into the Top 20, Alan." Guy had to say to me: "Yes, but this is a *Creation* band." "Oh ... yeah, right, OK." ' McGee was not impressed by their attitude. When the champagne bottle was empty, he didn't buy another.

'Loaded' was not only big for Primal Scream, it was also big for McGee. It flicked the nose of anyone who'd believed that Creation would never crack the upper half of the charts. It showed that the label was capable of making much more than guitar music. And it won the long-running argument that McGee had had with WEA about Primal Scream's importance. As their manager, friend and most loyal supporter, McGee was utterly vindicated.

Conceived as a bit of extra-curricular fun, 'Loaded' had become the most successful record in Creation's history. 'If Ride put Creation back on the map,' says Laurence Verfaillie, ' "Loaded" gave it a pioneering dimension that was missing. That real cutting-edge thing. Coming up with a good guitar band like Ride – you know, Food and other labels were doing it too. But coming up with "Loaded" was something extra. The first indie dance act, as far as I'm concerned, was Primal Scream. They were pioneering a mixture of acid house and rock 'n' roll.'

But as 'Loaded' slipped out of the Top 40 in mid-April, it was still not publicly – or even privately – clear if it had been a one-off venture, or something Primal Scream intended to repeat. Even among those who had liked it, there was a tendency to view 'Loaded' as a record in which the Scream themselves had taken little part. Norman Cook, the former Housemartin who spearheaded the dance group Beats International, remarked in the *NME*: 'Suffice to say that if I'd done all the work Weatherall obviously has on this record, I'd assume it was my song, not theirs.' It was not the last time Primal Scream would hear that.

By February, My Bloody Valentine had been to six recording studios and were working so clandestinely that Creation could only guess at their activities. McGee and Green had been discouraged from visiting any of the studios. No official ban had been imposed, but they would be kept waiting in pool rooms and television rooms, and would not be allowed to hear or discuss music with Kevin Shields. 'We became the enemy pretty early on,' says McGee. 'We would hang with the band – we would be invited to their parties or whatever – but the studio thing was something completely separate.'

All the same, McGee cajoled Shields into letting him hear one of the songs. It was a piece that had neither a vocal nor a melody as yet, but it had enough to convince McGee that it would be very special. 'It was Stooges guitar over Happy Mondays beats,' he recalls. 'It was total genius. Straight away I went: "That's a single." ' With an album overdue, he told Shields to concentrate on making an EP.

The new engineer on the project was Alan Moulder, a freelance who had worked with the Jesus and Mary Chain on their *Automatic* album. Laidback and versatile, Moulder had been one of the few technicians to get on well with the Reid brothers. McGee pointed him at My Bloody Valentine and crossed his fingers. 'I was going to do the EP,' says Moulder, 'and then work with them and help them finish the album. I was told when I got involved that the album would take another three to four weeks.'

At Trident 2, a studio in Victoria, Moulder engineered a mix of

'Soon' – the song Shields had played to McGee, and to which vocals and keyboards had now been added – so that it could lead off the EP in April. A stunning blend of hip hop rhythms, rock guitars and aerated keyboard patterns reminiscent of Philip Glass, 'Soon' gripped Moulder in the few seconds it took him to push the faders up on the desk. He then made the mistake of complimenting Shields on it. 'I said to Kevin: "I really like the track, it's pretty psychedelic", he recalls. 'Kevin said: "Hmm ... I never thought of it like that, but I suppose it is." That's when I realised that Kevin was pretty choosy about the type of input he wanted. He didn't like you saying anything about a song – even if it was positive – in case it differed from what he thought and threw him off course.'

Moulder's assistant at the studio, Adrian Bushby, was just as awestruck by 'Soon'. He remembers: 'It was a bit of a shock at first. I hadn't really heard anything like it before. It was quite complex in the amount of sound that was going on.' Orchestral and hypnotic, 'Soon' seemed to have about 15 guitars playing on it. It was a typical Shields illusion: actually, there were only two or three. 'It was an all-night session,' adds Bushby. 'We had done a guitar overdub, and I was unplugging the gear and tidying up as the other session was coming in for the next day.'

To complete and mix three other songs for the EP, Shields and Moulder moved to Falconer, a studio in Chalk Farm, and then to two more studios in a matter of weeks. In April, Shields would tell the *NME* that he had around 30 songs recorded – his and Bilinda Butcher's vocals apart – and was attempting to decide which were the best ones. In truth, however, while Shields had 22 pieces of music in progress, at least 20 had progressed no further than basic backing tracks. 'None of the other songs had anything but drums and guitar,' says Moulder. 'The first thing we attacked after the EP was bass.' He and Shields went to Falconer's second studio in Kentish Town, where Shields amazed him by briskly adding bass lines to the backing tracks without consulting reference tapes or notes. A partial dyslexic, Shields had memorised the details of the songs rather than write them down and risk not being able to read them back.

Moulder had committed himself to another project in the spring – a Shakespears Sister album – and would also be called away in the summer by Ride. To engineer during the periods when he was unavailable, Creation approached Anjali Dutt, who lacked Moulder's experience but was prepared to work with My Bloody Valentine on all-night shifts. She spent her first week with them at Falconer in Kentish Town. 'They didn't work very fast,' she says. 'They were also very, very vague. You didn't ask a lot of questions – they were a little bit frowned upon. There was a bit of paranoia going on there. I don't remember anything happening at Falconer other than them looking at the video for "Soon" over and over and over.'

The EP was named *Glider*. Its title track, an instrumental built around a recurring loop of Shields' guitar feeding back, made startling use of the tremolo arm to give a profoundly giddy sensation as the feedback see-sawed, squealed and surged. When Laurence Verfaillie heard the song playing in the Creation office, she presumed that the vinyl was warped and wondered why no one had got up to take it off the hi-fi. Then she remembered that the vinyl hadn't been cut yet – they were listening to a cassette. The warp was deliberate.

'The *Glider* EP was an absolute monster,' she says. 'It was very strange, but it was worth waiting for and it gave a lot of hope for the future.' Verfaillie knew My Bloody Valentine socially – she and Jim Reid lived just around the corner from Lady Margaret Road. She was aware that Shields had missed his album deadline, and would probably miss others, and that it was becoming a painful process for all concerned. 'Everybody was biting their nails at Creation,' she says, 'but they were very supportive. Going to Kevin and telling him to hurry up would have been the wrong thing to do.' It would also have been impossible to do: Shields had appointed his sister Ann Marie as the band's manager, with specific instructions to keep McGee and Green at arm's length.

Bottom line, Creation needed an album from Shields, not an EP. Despite the success of 'Loaded', money was so scarce at Hackney that Verfaillie was becoming embarrassed. 'I was putting together some trips to take journalists to Manchester for live reviews, working on really tight budgets,' she recalls, 'and Dick Green was being Mr Money. I'd found a really cheap deal with one of the hotels in Manchester – something like thirty quid a night for these horrible rooms with no windows – and Dick was saying: "Can't you find something cheaper like a bed-and-breakfast?" I remember leaving his office screaming: "For Christ's sake, why don't we get tents and put [the journalists] in the bloody park?" '

After showing a midweek chart position of 28, *Glider* fell just outside the Top 40. Shields, however, was as oblivious to the charts as he was to the frustration he was causing in Hackney. He told the *NME* that the new album would be 'bang up to date ... uncompromising and difficult'. Certainly, the music on *Glider* had been greeted by gasps of astonishment from Shields' label-mates. ' "Soon" was completely mind-blowing,' says Andy Bell from Ride. 'We recognised that as being incredible right from when we first heard it.' Bobby Gillespie concurred: ' "Soon" was the first time they came up with a sound which seemed to come from nobody else, that was purely them.' But the more time and money Shields spent in the studio, the more it was rumoured that he was reaching for a new form of music that would make even 'Soon' sound pusillanimous – music unlike any ever heard.

On 25 April, My Bloody Valentine began a short tour of the UK and Ireland. Noel Thompson was hired to mix the sound, and was immediately struck by the Valentines' attritional attitude towards their audience. 'They were like: "It's got to be really loud",' he says. 'All right, fair enough. I got this big Nexo sound system, very powerful. But we sort of fell out a bit because they wanted people throwing up or something. They wanted the audience to be in pain. That's what they were into.'

All the members of My Bloody Valentine wore earplugs onstage, and Shields recommended the audience do the same. For My Bloody Valentine's shows in February 1989, Shields had stationed McGee at the mixing desk to make sure that the sound engineer didn't reduce the volume when no one was looking. McGee had had a whale of a time. 'I seem to remember I used to blow people's eardrums out or blow the PA up,' he says. 'Kevin was crazy enough to let me do it.'

When Shields was asked by an *NME* writer in 1990 why My Bloody Valentine felt the need to play at such ear-splitting volume, he replied: '[It's] because we know that once you get above one hundred decibels, that causes a physical change in people. Endorphins get released into the system because the body can sense imminent danger.' The only thing Noel Thompson sensed was some kind of ghoulish art statement that he didn't like one bit. He recalls: 'At one point Colm said to me: "We're doing these shows at ULU – two nights – and what I'd like is trays of amyl nitrate on the front of the stage and [electric] fans blowing it into the audience." That was when I said: "I think you better get someone else, mate." '

Like most journalists, McGee imagined that Shields' ideas about sound and volume had been learned from the Mary Chain, Hüsker Dü and Sonic Youth. Thompson, who watched Shields take 90 minutes to tune a guitar at one sound check on the tour, preferred to think of him as a kind of inanimate oddball. Alan Moulder – who does not hesitate to call Shields a genius – has a totally different perspective. 'I remember taking my dog into the studio once,' he says, 'and seeing Kevin do experiments on how the dog responded to certain frequencies. That's his angle on things. This is a guy who, at four years old, used to sit his sister facing him on the other side of the kitchen, and they used to hum notes. And then he'd slightly take it out of tune so that the notes would modulate and drive his parents crazy. That was at *four*.'

But Shields' obsession with sound caused major problems in the studio. He could hear telephones ringing a quarter of a mile away; one of the reasons he liked to work at night was because the receptionists had all gone home. When several weeks' recording time was booked in Terminal – a studio off Walworth Road in south-east London – Shields left after only a few days, complaining that currents from the railway line running between Elephant & Castle and Loughborough Junction were interfering with his Fender guitars.

As the cost of the sessions rose, McGee and Green grew alarmed. Having reckoned on a £30,000–£40,000 spend back in September, they now had to face the likelihood of this figure tripling or even quadrupling. 'It was always "the studio" that was at fault,' says Green. 'They never seemed to be able to settle at a place. Kevin would go down and see [the studios] before we booked them. Then it somehow wouldn't happen.'

The only studio where Shields felt comfortable was Protocol in Holloway, where 248 nights of recording would take place in 1990 and 1991. 'The joke at Creation at the time,' remarks James Kyllo, 'was that it would have been cheaper to buy the place.' In May, work began at Protocol on a second stopgap EP – but this one would not be delivered as promptly as *Glider*. It would in fact take the best part of seven months. Anjali Dutt remembers: 'There was one point at Protocol where three weeks were spent recording a tambourine for one song ... It went on and on and on. There was an awful lot of doing nothing. We would come in at eight [in the evening]. Then we'd eat. Then it would be about eleven, and we'd watch some telly until about twelve. Talk until about two. Then we'd get started.'

Assisting Dutt at Protocol was Guy Fixsen, an in-house engineer. Like her, he soon got accustomed to working nocturnally. 'You get to a certain time of night and your mind thinks in a more lateral way,' he says. 'I remember talking to Kevin about it. There is this whole thing whereby sleep is what makes your mind more ordered. During the day, you have all these associations build up, and sleep and dreaming are all about going through those associations and removing the unwanted ones, the illogical ones. So just before you go to sleep, you have a lot of these unwanted, illogical, lateral leaps in your mind and you're more capable of – essentially – creativity. I'm sure Kevin was trying to exploit that.'

Shields later told a journalist that he went for 'two or three months' in 1990 without seeing any daylight.

When the tour to promote the *Ride* EP finished at the London School of Economics on 9 March, a tour to promote their second EP, *Play*, began almost at once. As a key London date at ULU approached, the band's drummer Loz Colbert happened to mention in an interview that it would be nice if people brought daffodils – the flower featured on the sleeve of the *Play* EP – to the venue. That night, the entire front-of-stage was swamped in yellow. 'It was very Smithsian,' recalls Dave Newton. 'People were taking them home as souvenirs.'

The *Play* EP entered the Top 40 in the same week that 'Loaded' left it. On 18 April, Ride played the first of three dates in Europe supporting the House Of Love. Chris Groothuizen remembers Guy

Chadwick being 'absolutely petrified' of Ride, who were younger, louder, hipper – and blatantly trying to blow the House Of Love off-stage. 'Guy was standing behind our soundman,' says Andy Bell, 'trying to physically turn the sound down. He had a really paranoid vibe.' The House Of Love hoped that McGee might have a word with Ride about their lack of discretion, but he refused. 'We were supposed to be Alan's darlings,' points out Groothuizen. 'It was like: "Are you our manager or not?" "Well, no, I'm actually the head of Creation and here's my new band." '

The *Play* EP had not been expected to chart in the Top 40. McGee had tried to persuade Ride and Newton to agree to a 7-inch release (in addition to the usual 12-inch and CD) to increase sales, but they had resisted, adamant that they would not compete in a Gallup commercial race and that each song on the EP should be seen to have equal billing – to the extent of linking the four song titles in a circle rather than listing them vertically, so that no 'A-side' would be apparent. 'It was a very simplistic indie ethos,' says Newton. 'But part of the reason we were on Creation was that we wanted to do things our way. Of course, the House Of Love had gone from Creation to Fontana, and their single came out in eleven formats.'

Taken from the House Of Love's 'Butterfly' album, 'Beatles And The Stones' was actually released in 12 formats, staggered over three weeks. The ploy was slammed as a desperate measure from a band and record company increasingly prone to doing whatever it took to have hit singles. 'That [formatting] was a cynical cash-in,' concedes Groothuizen. 'We never really understood what we were letting ourselves in for.'

The controversy over multi-formatting was nothing, however, compared to the torrid arguments within the House Of Love on the subject of the 'Beatles And The Stones' video. Here, there was one aim only: to get on to MTV's heavy rotation play-list, giving Fontana's counterparts at the American label Mercury some leverage when they took the single to commercial radio. But when Groothuizen and guitarist Simon Walker learned that the video would cost £80,000 – and be filmed in Los Angeles for no apparent reason – their mouths fell open. Walker, who had a Marxist overview of all things financial, protested to Chadwick, McGee and Bates that it was an obscene waste of money.

'We had seen what [the director] had written and it was insulting,' says Walker. 'It was walrus suits and people dressed up as the Beatles and the Stones.' To his further unease, Walker discovered that he had been marked down to play the part of Brian Jones, the Stones' deceased guitarist. 'Simon, bless his heart, said: "This video is not going to do anything for the band – if anything, it's going to destroy it",' recalls Groothuizen. 'Guy and Alan were in LA doing the press rounds and hanging out with the major executives. They'd be like:

"Dave Bates has put his job on the line for this. If we don't do it, he'll lose his job and our career's over." '

Groothuizen, Walker and Pete Evans refused to fly to LA for the video. 'I was ringing Guy and Alan saying: "Forget it",' Groothuizen remembers. 'This was a *five day* conversation. I'd be in Steve Walters' office at EMI Music – who was letting me use his phone because he agreed with us wholeheartedly. But [we were told]: "You are coming to LA because that's what the record company wants, and we will spend £80,000 on the video because that's what it takes to get you on MTV." ' Groothuizen, Walker and Evans flew to LA and made the video. 'And did it get us on MTV?' says Groothuizen. 'Did it fuck.'

When 'Beatles And The Stones' charted at 40 in Britain, eight places lower than Ride's EP, Chadwick's nervousness about Ride seemed all the more justified. The last thing he needed was to be upstaged by the younger band in front of the European media. In Brussels on 19 April, when the latest midweeks were phoned through, it was clear that 'Beatles And The Stones', despite its limited edition monogrammed CD slip-cases, hand-woven horsehair cassette pouches and iridium-plated vinyl in three tasty fruit flavours, was not selling well enough to make the Top 30. Chadwick panicked. 'We were talking backstage in Brussels,' says Dave Newton, 'and the House Of Love's tour manager came over and said: "I'm sorry, lads, but you can't play tomorrow night in Paris. Guy doesn't want you to play." '

But Chadwick's power had lost its punch. Ride turned up in Paris and played the show as though nothing had happened. 'Beatles And The Stones' dropped out of the Top 40 a week later. And the House Of Love never made it in America.

With two Top 40 hits in two months, Creation basked in its double whammy. 'People were overwhelmed by the fact that, wow, we're releasing records we think are really cool and people *agree* with us,' says Laurence Verfaillie. 'Remember, we were struggling for day-to-day survival. We were happy to get the units out there and make some money. There was no proper marketing plot sorted out at that point. It was still very DIY. It was improvised all along.'

It was almost too good to be true. Commercially clueless in 1989, Creation was now in the vanguard of the rock-dance crossover – and leading the return of the classic indie guitar band to boot. To the surprise and amusement of some of the label's other artists, there emerged a new 'hit' mentality in Hackney. The Jazz Butcher, whose tuneful albums invariably walked a fine line between ironic classicism and exclusionist whimsy, were used to making a virtue of the fact that their records did not really interest the British population: they were simply too weird and witty, mate. The right amount of guitars and clever melodies, for sure, but the wrong amount of humour.

Let's face it, lads, on the serious indie scene, any amount of humour was the wrong amount. Laugh? You couldn't even play an honest joke on Dick Green any more.

'I had a funny conversation with Dick when we were making our album *Cult Of The Basement*,' Pat Fish recalls. 'He phones up – and they'd just started having the first hits at the beginning of 1990 – and Dick's on the blower saying: "Pat, how's the album going?" "Oh, we're having a rare old time." He goes: "Any hit records on it?" I said to him: "Dick, this is our commercial suicide LP. It's going to sell eight copies." He put the phone down on me.' No hits on a Creation album? Fish had to be joking.

Cult Of The Basement was released later that year, but whereas in 1988 and 1989 the Jazz Butcher had shared Creation schedule-space with other guitar groups, they now shared it with the dance acts Hypnotone, Sheer Taft, Fluke and Danny Rampling's Sound Of Shoom. 'We'd been looking into dance for some time,' Dick Green would later explain. 'Initially, our idea was to set up a sister label specifically for dance. But then we realised that Creation has always been all-encompassing, so we changed nothing. The fact that we can have Danny Rampling and My Bloody Valentine on the same label is just brilliant.'

As with Creation's guitar bands, the dance acts were a case of McGee's friends bringing along other friends. Sheer Taft was a pal of Primal Scream's from Scotland. The idolised Rampling was an acquaintance of Ed Ball – and of Grant Fleming, the House Of Love's T-shirt seller, whom McGee had asked to keep an eye out for potential club hits. By the end of 1990, Creation's discography had a new vocabulary: the release of a single called 'Nena De Ibiza' by Crazy Eddie and Q.Q. Freestyle showed how much things had changed.

'Grant Fleming came in and effectively manned the dance division,' says Ed Ball. 'He used to do all the white labels – he'd make sure all the clubs got the records – and he hunted out things like Fluke and Crazy Eddie. Unfortunately, a lot of these people started to be more like bread-heads than any of the indie crowd used to be. The general vibe was that all these people who were making dance records felt they only had one or two records in them; that the whole thing was going to disappear in days. So they were asking for silly money.' In the race to appear current, mistakes would sometimes be made. A single by a group called Pressure Zone had to be withdrawn by Creation when it was found that another label had already released it.

Even the Jazz Butcher made a dance record. In Hackney, Paul Mulreany was introduced to Steve Proctor, a DJ and record producer. Proctor was on the lookout for a band to record a dance version of 'We Love You', a Rolling Stones single from 1967. 'We'll have a crack at that,' Mulreany volunteered. As it happened, none of the members of the Jazz Butcher had worked with a programmer before, nor had any concept of how dance tunes were made. 'It was like being in Bananarama,' says Pat Fish. 'Me, Paul and Laurence [O'Keefe] went in the booth and sang together. I put a bit of guitar on, Laurence put a bit of bass on – but it's Steve's record. Before it was released, they oozed it out into the clubs and Alan and Ed were coming back saying: "Pat, you won't believe it – 400 kids on the floor punching the air to your record!" I thought: yeah, *right.*'

Cynics accused Creation and the Jazz Butcher of trying to pull a similar stunt to the Soup Dragons, the Scots C86-ers who had sniffed the wind of change and reached the Top 5 with an indie-dance version of the Stones' 'I'm Free'. However, McGee insists that 'We Love You' was made with no ulterior motive in mind. 'We loved going to clubs and hearing our records,' he says. '["We Love You"] wasn't a great record, but it was still a better record than most people were putting out.' A few days before the single was released, Ed Ball rang Pat Fish to ask him what he was going to wear on *Top Of The Pops*. 'They actually got us half-psyched into thinking this might happen,' says Fish. 'Of course, it came out and like all dance records from then to now, it sold 4,000 copies.'

Until 1992, when a specialist dance label was set up by McGee and Green, Creation led a strange double life, issuing by turns the guitar music for which it had become celebrated and the dance music for which it hoped to become more respected. 'Somehow it still felt that there was a real unity to the label,' says Laurence Verfaillie. 'For me, working Ride wasn't miles away from working "Loaded" or working Sheer Taft. Even if musically we were going in two directions, at the end of the day there was an A&R logic to it – which was Alan's personality.' Or as Pat Fish puts it: 'In 1990, yes, the dance thing was all kicking off – but at the same time that was the year everybody started name-dropping Alex Chilton. So there were two sides to it. You could go out and listen to Sheer Taft, or you could climb under the table and listen to "Dream Lover".'

In a post-'Loaded' climate of indie-dancing and genre cross-pollination, Creation hardly had the field to itself. Flowered Up, a north London band influenced by Happy Mondays and the house scene, stole the music press headlines in July, and were followed in September by the Farm, veteran Liverpudlians who soared to number 6 with their 'Loaded'-inspired 'Groovy Train'. 'The Farm stole our thunder,' admits McGee. 'They got their album out and sold 500,000 copies. And the Soup Dragons stole our thunder as well. But Primal Scream were the real deal. They had basically invented a genre of music. They were the dons and [the Farm and the Soup Dragons] were a bunch of chancers.'

But indie-dance was not something that could be copyrighted, and the role of figurehead was anyone's to grab. When Factory director

Tony Wilson and Happy Mondays' manager Nathan McGough addressed the New Music Seminar in New York that summer – sitting on a discussion panel provocatively titled 'Wake Up America, You're Dead' – Wilson made the point that dance music had so influenced the UK that any band playing in a non-dance style might as well split up. 'There are groups which American A&R men go berserk over – the Sundays, House Of Love – who in England are now so marginalised that they are irrelevant,' he said.

The exception that proved the rule was Ride, who were going from strength to strength. Although major labels in Britain were leaving the Oxford boys alone, apparently on the incorrect assumption that they had a contract with Creation, the picture was different in the US where several labels were interested. Seymour Stein and Joe McEwen at Sire were leading the pack, with Columbia and Capitol not far behind. In June, while Ride were recording their debut album, Dave Newton was flown out to the States and wined and dined in New York and LA. It was the first time he had ever been abroad. 'He came back with a load of notes written on each [company],' recalls Steve Queralt. ' "Capitol took me out and gave me loads of Beatles CDs ..." But he was really taken with Sire/Warners.'

Columbia and Capitol wanted Ride's North American rights only. Sire/Warners were more ambitious: they wanted to sign Ride for the world excluding the UK. Newton took advice from the band's lawyer, George Babbington, who pushed through a deal in August that gave Sire/Warners worldwide rights to Ride outside the UK (at a price of $350,000 per album, one of the largest advances ever agreed by an American label for a British band) and enabled Ride to own and license their music to Creation in the UK. 'We were in a very strong position,' says Newton. 'Creation needed everything that we could give them.'

'I didn't even find Ride,' says McGee, 'so the karma that I deserved probably ultimately came back to me ... I went in good faith to Joe and Seymour. Seymour then put a deal to them that was huge – and I couldn't match it. So I ended up being the A&R man and getting [UK] rights only. I learned a big lesson.'

Ride now had the best of both worlds. In America and around the world, they were a major label act with Warner Bros' marketing and promotions teams at their disposal. In the UK, they were as credible an indie band as one could wish for – on a 50:50 profit-share arrangement, moreover, that could conceivably make them millionaires if their commercial success held. While the difference in the agendas of Ride and the House Of Love seemed a massive one in the summer of 1990, it was all a question of perception. And as is often the case with perception, an indie band could smell of roses even when the ground was squelchy underfoot. Steve Queralt remembers a conversation with McGee about hyping singles. 'He said: "Oh, we'll chuck loads of free singles into Our Price",' Queralt recalls. 'I said: "No! That's not what we're about. You can't do that." He turned round and said: "Well, how do you think the first EP sold?" It was a real awakening.'

For almost four years, McGee had been dissatisfied with the service Creation had been getting from Rough Trade Distribution. RTD had helped put 'Loaded' in the Top 20, but it would be one of the last Creation records it distributed. 'Alan had got fed up with the mentality of Rough Trade, which was very much indie-er than thou,' says Dick Green. 'He was never that way inclined. He was never indie for indie's sake. When people used to call us indie, he'd say: "No, we're independent, we're not a fucking indie." '

Since breaking through with the House Of Love and My Bloody Valentine in 1988, Creation had been selling records in greater quantities, and its status in the industry had risen. McGee and Green had signed a lucrative publishing agreement with EMI Music, giving them a percentage for every artist they sent EMI's way. Now that Creation was finally having hits, the tables had turned in its business relationship with Rough Trade Distribution. The latter often owed Creation money. 'We'd been with them too long – six years,' says McGee. 'We were part of the furniture. Out of 50 labels that they had, we'd been number five or six. Then we started having hits. But they never acknowledged the fact that the tide was changing, and that it was us and One Little Indian* that were going to come through.'

Under its new managing director, ex-Pinnacle man George Kimpton-Howe, and with a turnover exceeding £22 million, Rough Trade Distribution had made a decision near the end of 1989 to fight Pinnacle tooth and nail for the crown of top UK indie distributor. The following July, Rough Trade Distribution and Rough Trade Records moved from King's Cross to a 31,000 square foot warehouse and five-storey office building in Finsbury Park.

Computerised sales equipment costing £750,000 was installed, and plans were announced to increase RTD's number of indie label clients from around 55 to 70. There were serious implications for the overloaded Cartel. Probe, a distributor in Liverpool, had left the Cartel earlier in 1990, and Fast Forward (the Cartel's Scottish arm) had gone out of business. Nine Mile – the Midlands arm – had been reduced to a one-man operation. In July 1990, the Cartel was disbanded altogether, with RTD declaring an intention to take over the national indie distribution network itself.

'After the big management change, we never used to hear from them,' says McGee. 'We used to put records out and we wouldn't

---

* An indie label whose roster included the Sugarcubes, the Shamen and – briefly – They Might Be Giants.

speak to [anyone at RTD]. There was nobody holding it together. The new guy that came in [Kimpton-Howe] – it wasn't his fault. The whole thing had fallen down a hole ... They were treating us like shit, not taking it seriously. They owed me £72,000 which was three weeks overdue. We were about to go out of contract with them, so we said: "We're walking unless you give us the money." ' The sum was paid two days later.

'Walking' – switching distribution to Pinnacle, in other words – had been at the back of McGee's mind since his first meeting with Steve Mason in 1985. 'Pinnacle were much more businesslike and much more organised [than Rough Trade],' says James Kyllo, who had dealt with Pinnacle when he worked at Cherry Red. 'It was less indie in the traditional, imaginary way – but it was less likely to lose the stock and more likely to pay us at the end of the month.'

Fantastically successful, Pinnacle had a roster that included chart-busters and esoteric acts alike – from Pete Waterman and Kylie Minogue to Frank Zappa and Keith Jarrett – and it distributed all the important music from Manchester on Factory (New Order, Happy Mondays), Rham! (A Guy Called Gerald) and Silvertone (the Stone Roses). 'If you were an independent label five years ago,' said Mason in January 1990, 'the probability is you had tatty distribution, you were constantly worried about the financial stability of the distribu-tor and you were never taken seriously by radio, particularly Radio 1 ... Pinnacle has changed the whole face of the independents. We have dragged independent distribution into the twentieth century ... Today, there is nothing a major can do that we can't.' Interviewed by Tony Wilson at a *Music Week* awards lunch in March, Mason – a man frequently accused by Rough Trade of not liking music – described Pinnacle in terms that were almost McGee-esque. 'We are there with the kids,' he said. 'The majors are in their ivory towers. In Orpington [the town in Kent where Pinnacle had its offices], space is £2 a square foot. *That's* where music comes from.'

Although Mason was not looking for new labels to distribute ('We're full,' he told *Music Week*), he had met McGee again in November 1989 and was agreeable to taking Creation on board. For one thing, there was a principle involved. 'When I was negotiating the new deals,' says Kyllo, 'there was a bidding war between Steve Mason and George Kimpton. I think Steve felt a bit betrayed that George had left Pinnacle, and George was sort of showing that he was his own man. It put us in a really strong position because they both had something to prove to each other.'

In the bidding war, there was only one possible winner – and it was not RTD. Kyllo and McGee played one company off the other for a while, obtaining a substantial reduction on their distribution per-centage. 'We got it down to such a low percentage – eight or nine per cent knocked off what we were paying to Rough Trade – and they both said: "We can't go any lower",' recalls McGee. 'I had to go away that weekend and think about it. And I thought: do you know something? I just fucking hate Rough Trade.'

In July 1990, Creation signed a three-year contract with Pinnacle, removed its stock from Rough Trade's warehouse and transferred it to Orpington. It was what music industry commentators would subsequently refer to as a narrow escape.

15 American Kamikaze

U P TO AND INCLUDING the March–April chart run of 'Loaded', Primal Scream's deal with Creation had been on a handshake basis only. Not wishing to risk another Ride scenario, McGee and Green formally signed the Scream for £15,000. The house-gospel anthem 'Come Together' – the second single in Primal Scream's new crossover style – was released in August. The *Primal Scream* LP, though less than a year old, had been quietly forgotten about; it was obvious that the band's next album would not owe much to Thin Lizzy or the MC5.

Recorded by Andrew Weatherall and issued as a double A-side comprising back-to-back mixes by himself and Terry Farley, 'Come Together' showed Scream agnostics that there was plenty more where 'Loaded' had come from. Some of those who had been sceptical about 'Loaded' from the outset now revised their opinion. 'Like a lot of people, I thought "Loaded" was a gimmick record,' says Andy Bell. 'I didn't see the genius of it until I heard the Terry Farley version of "Come Together". With hindsight I realised it was actually an exciting thing to be happening.'

But 'Come Together' had not had a painless birth. Two of Primal Scream's three principal members had flounced out of the studio, needing some convincing that the band was on the right track. '"Come Together" was a total fucker to mix,' says McGee. 'Primal Scream had tried to make a dance record with a real drummer. Then they took him out and put on a drum machine. Then Terry Farley couldn't get a mix of it. We got Andy Weatherall to do [an instrumental] mix, and Weatherall's mix was genius. I phoned up Bobby going: "Unless we can get the Terry Farley mix better, we're going to have to go with the Weatherall." This would have been two records that Bobby wasn't on. Throb had already walked out of the session because his guitars weren't on the Weatherall mix. Then Bobby walked out of the studio.'

When McGee spoke to Gillespie on the phone, his friend was downhearted. 'He was going: "Well, there's no point in me being in the band",' McGee recalls. 'I said: "Look, we'll go back and we'll get the Farley mix right." He was going to me: "McGee ... no way." He had real, total self-doubt. I said: "Whatever happens, you are the singer in this band. We're putting out a record with you singing." I knew that to everybody in the world, Primal Scream was Bobby Gillespie. I had to have him singing on the fucking track.'

In public, of course, Gillespie did not allow any of these doubts to surface. Responding to a journalist's suggestion that 'Come Together' was more Farley's and Weatherall's record than Primal Scream's, Gillespie riposted: 'But it is our record ... It's us that arranged it, arranged the gospel singers. That's our tune they're singing. OK, we hand the tapes over to Andy and he comes up with something completely different, but that's the whole point of it. We don't want it to be a slightly different version. We want him to take it somewhere else completely out of this world.'

The extent of the Scream's input into 'Loaded' was still being questioned by the media. At Creation, nobody doubted the involvement of Primal Scream in the record for a second – not because they knew for a fact that the Scream *had* been involved, but because nobody at Creation ever doubted Primal Scream. Merely to think of doing so would have been a sackable offence. 'I was absolutely infatuated with Primal Scream's music, utterly passionate,' says Laurence Verfaillie, and she was not the only one. 'That's why McGee gave us all a job. Because we would go head-on.'

Farley finally pulled a terrific mix of 'Come Together' out of the hat. At that, McGee saw a transformation in Gillespie. 'Two days later [he] was like: "Ta-da!",' McGee remembers. 'A warrior. A reinvented warrior.' The *NME* photographed and interviewed the reinvented warrior for its front cover, on which Gillespie wore a white sweatshirt, white jeans and a haircut styled to mod specifications. The only connection to his past were his black winkle-pickers. The interviews took place in London and in Brighton, where Gillespie, who was certain that dance music was the most rebellious social movement since punk rock, had been accepted and welcomed by the dance community at the town's Zap Club.

The *NME* cover story was timely. As well as being Gillespie's first, it communicated a subliminal message to the paper's readership that Creation was poised to pull ahead of Factory as the country's most fashionable record label. 'At that point,' says Verfaillie, 'I thought: that's it, we've got it, we're out there. Everybody had been going on about New Order, but now everybody was really looking at Primal Scream, going: "Bloody hell, this is different." And with Primal Scream I had angles all over the place: rough edges, rock 'n' roll attitude ...'

On the day that Gillespie and the *NME* journalist met, Margaret Thatcher's home secretary, David Waddington, declared his support for moves giving police new powers to crack down on acid house parties, which Waddington called 'havens for drug dealers'. As a piece of music, Primal Scream's 'Come Together' was drugged to the eyeballs, tripping, leering and insatiable. Asked to explain his position on the drugs issue, Gillespie suggested that Primal Scream represented a bohemian libertarianism that nodded back to the Rolling Stones' outlaw reputation in the 60s and looked forward to anti-police demonstrations in the future. 'I would definitely proselytise for drugs any time,' he said, 'because people who use drugs wrongly – you know, that's their problem. If you've got a brain, then you're OK with drugs really. It's like a motor car. You can kill yourself with a car if you drive wrongly. Give people the choice, that's what I say. Don't infringe on anybody's personal liberties.'

Hitherto, Primal Scream's use of drugs had been expressed more in innuendo than by any full-scale inventory. Talking to the *NME* about an upcoming tour of America – where the Scream had just signed to Seymour Stein and Joe McEwen at Sire – Gillespie became amusingly coy. 'I'd quite like to see what America does to some of the people in our band,' he said. 'I'd like to see how people cope with that, and I include myself ... It appeals to my sense of humour. Basically, someone's not going to come back from America ... There'll be some good stories to tell.'

'Come Together' was a Top 30 hit in late summer, staying in the Top 75 for six weeks. But there was disappointment at Creation that it had not risen higher than its initial entry position of 26. Weren't Primal Scream singles supposed to keep going up? Hadn't they pioneered this sort of music in the first place?

My Bloody Valentine were still at Protocol when Alan Moulder returned to the project in August. He was surprised how little they had achieved in the interim. Kevin Shields was visibly fatigued, and motivation was not coming easy. Much of the work Shields and Moulder did after August was devoted to one song, an apparently formless piece which Shields was interlarding with confounding undulations of guitar feedback recorded into a sampler. There was still a long way to go.

'The songs didn't have names,' says Andy Wilkinson, who worked at Protocol as a rookie engineer. 'They were numbered. There were at least 21 of them and it was hard to keep track of which was which. They'd say: "Oh, we'll work on Song 4 now, then Song 17." But none of them had vocals, and although it was obvious that they weren't finished, you didn't know to what extent they weren't finished.'

Songs 8, 10 and 21 were being developed for My Bloody Valentine's next EP, which was allowing Shields to put the album on hold for the moment. He and the other members of the band had run out of explanations for its late arrival. 'I would bump into them all the time,' says Andrew Perry. 'Colm would be fine, but Kevin would be incredibly evasive and avoid eye contact. "Don't ask me about the record." Increasingly, it became obvious that he was getting pretty obsessed by it.'

The pressure on Shields was unrelenting. Not only was there each new deadline to confront, but he was also a martyr to malfunctioning equipment. Darkening his horizon at every turn were a lack of money, a lack of empathy from his record company and – lest he forget – the huge sense of expectancy that this mild-mannered Brian Wilson of indie pop would deliver the greatest album of the decade, whichever decade he happened to deliver it in.

'The way it came across to me, rightly or wrongly, was that this was a record that he was going to take to any lengths it needed to go to,' says Moulder. 'I didn't think he was struggling for perfection – just what he considered acceptable. Sometimes you felt he was uncomfortable with the "genius" tag. When we used to go to gigs, he wouldn't wear his glasses because he thought it was playing the scientific boffin a little bit too far.'

McGee had become used to Ann Marie Shields relaying her brother's latest complaints, asking for more money and trying to buy time. But with Creation remaining solvent only by the skin of its teeth, Ann Marie Shields proved remarkably adept at picking the wrong moment. 'She wasn't very tactful,' says McGee. 'She was new to the music business and she was coming in with, "You will do this." We were like: "Fuck off, we're rock 'n' roll." ' The relationship between My Bloody Valentine and McGee was in danger of deteriorating to nothing. 'Kevin was feeling very frustrated,' says Laurence Verfaillie, 'because he knew exactly what he wanted and he didn't want time and money to be an issue ... But even if no one was daring to say anything to him, the pressure was there. Everybody was getting increasingly: "When the hell is it going to happen?" '

Shields' delays and steady increases in expenditure were threatening to have a knock-on effect on other Creation artists who were in production at the time. For all their occasional moments of efficiency, Primal Scream had adventurous plans for their next album and would require patience and financial backing. And Ride, who ordinarily gave McGee and Green few sleepless nights, caused a minor scare in the summer by handing in a poorly-recorded debut album, which had to be remixed completely by Moulder.

Shields, on the other hand, was making great music but was troubled by inexplicable technical problems everywhere he went. Even in Protocol, his supposed home from home, he encountered gremlins the like of which engineer Andy Wilkinson has never experienced before or since. 'We had this electrical static, crackling sound that would come over the speakers when anybody walked round the room,' he says. 'I've never known that happen in any studio. They seemed to be plagued with these obscure, out-of-the-ordinary faults that nobody understood.'

Wilkinson's colleague Guy Fixsen remembers the faults well, but takes a more phlegmatic view. 'You can say: "Oh, they were a bit jinxed", he comments, 'but the thing is [Shields] was getting into the real detail of things and he wanted an answer, and he was coming up against problems that most people don't even notice are there. But they did seem to be bizarrely unlucky. It was like: "Why is that channel on the desk not working? Why is there that strange noise?" '

Ever nomadic, Shields tried his luck in other studios, working his way around the map of London like a hand on a clock-face. 'He would always come back to Protocol saying: "Oh God, you won't believe what's happened at this other place", recalls Wilkinson. The studios Creation hired for Shields tended to be in the mid-price range, often with questionable maintenance. By working to a slow pace, Shields inevitably spent more and more time in such places. Caught in a vortex of inferior studios, he was obliged to work more and more slowly. His biggest fear during this period, he later said, was that he would die of boredom.

One day, word filtered back to Dick Green that Shields had put up a tent inside Protocol. Green had an immediate attack of the jitters. 'I'm sure there were perfectly sound, logical sonic reasons for doing that,' he says. 'But they didn't seem very sound or logical at the time.' The tent – which was to become the symbol of the album's descent into tragicomedy – had been erected for the purpose of recording a guitar. 'What he wanted was a very large, claustrophobic sound with no ambience,' says Anjali Dutt. 'So it would be a case where the sound was big but it wasn't made bigger by reflection. This is going to sound really silly, but you know how the Wizard of Oz was a little man with a voice that was amplified? Now that is different to an *actual* very large voice from a large person. Kevin wanted to be like a large person, as opposed to a small person megaphoned up.'

However, Shields had not investigated the tent idea in detail. 'Lots of other problems start up when you do that,' says Dutt. 'I've got a degree in electronics, and one of the things that happens is if you start taking reflections away, all you do is make other reflections more apparent. So this became more and more of an obsession. He'd say: "I can hear something that's making the sound not quite right." So you'd have to get rid of that reflection, and by doing so another reflection would become obvious. You have to create a completely dead environment quite scientifically. If you do it the trial-and-error way, you can actually take a very, very long time. And he did take a very, very long time.'

Songs 8, 10 and 21 – now entitled 'To Here Knows When', 'Swallow' and 'Honey Power' – were completed for the EP along with a fourth track, 'Moon Song', and sent to McGee in November. 'I was in

Birmingham when I got the tape,' he says. 'It was not a particularly great tape – it was like a Woolworth's tape, or something that Dick would have got from his newsagent – and I put it on, and I remember phoning Kevin and saying: "There's something wrong with the tape." And he went: "No, that's the record." I said: "No, there's definitely something wrong." And we got into this bizarre argument. It's the only time I ever questioned Kevin's vision. For about five minutes I was going: "Kevin – there's something wrong with the tape." He just blew up, saying: "I can't deal with this." '

It was the sound of 'To Here Knows When', a song so elasticised and overheated that it sounded as if a sickness had violated its house. When McGee realised that the effect was intentional, he wondered what in God's name record-buyers would think. As he scheduled the EP's release for early 1991, his estimated time of arrival for the album slipped back to February. 'We were hoping,' he says. 'We had no idea we were about to go through sheer pain.'

Dave Newton did not have years of experience as a manager to draw on. Like Ride, he was learning as he went along. He was only three or four years older than they were, and was so much at the hub of their closely united friendship that he was paid 20 per cent of their publishing income. In Hackney, where artists were held in high regard and managers were seldom seen, Newton's vested interest in Ride's financial affairs was seen as overstepping a boundary.

But McGee and Green underestimated Newton. They thought he was a provincial promoter on a lucky streak – the kind of well-meaning but uncool hick who draws crotchets and quavers on concert posters to show everyone that there's live music tonite. They couldn't take him seriously. McGee would poke fun at his fur-hat hairstyle, which dangled at the back like a raccoon's tail. 'I would take phone calls from Joe McEwen and Seymour Stein on a daily basis about Ride,' says McGee. 'They looked at Dave Newton ... I think they described him as "the man with three haircuts". He had a mullet, a wedge and a pony-tail all on the one head. The bottom line is they never trusted him.'

Yet Dave Newton, for all his inexperience and overprotectiveness, had shown himself to be the most indispensable manager the indie sector had seen since Joe Moss in the early days of the Smiths. What he lacked in age and physical stature Newton easily made up for in his determination not to be outgunned by the wily McGee. And whether he said the word 'no' with a smile or not, Newton's style was emphatic. 'He became a pariah at Creation,' says Andy Bell. 'He was the most hated person within the Creation office. McGee would always be bitching about him.'

Each sight of Newton's face – and his hair, for that matter – was a painful reminder to McGee that he had let the worldwide rights to

Ride slip from his grasp. Equally, each step up the ladder for Ride seemed only to confirm that Newton's take-it-nice-and-easy style of management was far more effective than McGee's alternately crazed and neglectful handling of the House Of Love. 'Since the Ride times, I've really come to appreciate what Dave Newton did for us,' says Bell. 'We'd have a meeting in Oxford and say: "This is the way it should be." He'd go: "Fine." And the next day, he would go to Creation and that's the way it would be. You've got to trust somebody, and he decided to put his faith in us rather than Creation.' The result for Ride was creative freedom, and that freedom was total.

To many people – and McGee was one of them – Ride appeared to have a clear leader, Mark Gardener. One of two singer-guitarists in the band, he was the one who stood centre-stage and sang most of the lead vocals. 'We knew that Mark had the charisma,' says Bell. 'We're talking about unspoken things here, just feelings. We weren't a big band for talking about things. But it was obvious that Mark was a charismatic person, very charming ... a nice person to be around.' McGee felt it wouldn't hurt to make greater use of Gardener's cute looks, but he was touching a sensitive nerve. The principal songwriter in the band was not Gardener but Bell. A fan of 60s pop, folk-rock and psychedelia, Bell had added the important element of vocal harmony when Ride recorded their first demos, transforming the way the band sounded. And whether he was buying the latest guitar pedals or writing out the Ride fans' news-sheet by hand, Bell was the group's most energetic member.

Bell, however, was a self-conscious 19-year-old with a short attention span, and he had almost no knowledge of how the music business worked. Ten months after signing the EMI publishing deal, for instance, he remained unaware that the deal related to the band's songs. Like his colleagues, he had no burning desire to be famous or recognised in his own right. Ride's records – the most recent was a third EP, *Fall*, in September – had no photos of the band-members on the sleeve, as they were determined that they should be viewed as an ego-free, selfless unit. 'It was a bit like the Party in Communist China,' says Bell. 'The Party is the important thing and you're very happy to sacrifice everything you do for the greater good. There was something really pure about the early days of Ride, and it was a beautiful thing.' So unmercenary was their *modus operandi* that not even Dave Newton knew how many of the songs were Bell's. 'It didn't really cross my mind to ask,' he says. 'In an early interview with *Local Support*, an Oxford paper that I ran, they were asked who wrote the stuff and Andy was quite vociferous as to the fact that it didn't matter.'

Neither Bell nor Gardener came across as forthright individuals in interviews, tending to appear dippy and torpid on the page. Laurence Verfaillie could see this becoming a handicap. 'They were straight from Oxford, still living with their mums and dads, very polite,' she says. 'Press-wise, it was tough. Their speech was: "The music speaks for itself." ' It had to: Ride had nothing else to say about it.

To make them seem more interesting, the music papers tried to generate a scene around them, since they were now too familiar to be presented as young pretenders to the House Of Love's throne. Ride were placed at the head of a small movement of guitar bands from the Thames Valley – Swervedriver from Oxford; Slowdive and Chapterhouse from Reading – all of which numbered Creation acts as influences. In the event, Ride had as little to say about these groups as about their own. The more the press jousted, the more Ride clammed up. When their debut album, *Nowhere*, was released in October, it didn't even have the name of the band on the cover. 'We did everything we possibly could to make it difficult to sell,' admits Newton. 'It was the opposite of marketing.'

As a plan of campaign, such understatement was advantageous – until it wasn't. Three EPs down the line, there had been only borderline support for Ride from radio and TV. Gardener had a weak singing voice – a common enough indie failing but a bugger if you were programming a breakfast show – and although a song from the *Fall* EP, 'Taste', had been played by Radio 1's afternoon DJ Steve Wright, and the video shown over the closing credits of *Top Of The Pops*, the EP had charted at a disappointing 34, leaving Creation and Newton wondering where they had gone wrong. McGee again suggested promoting Gardener as a pin-up.

'McGee really did go a bundle on trying to push Mark as the front-man,' says Newton. 'The two of them got on very well socially. And Mark really was very sociable. If you can imagine him at school, he would have been the one with the mates and the car as soon as he was 17.' Gardener was put in an awkward position when the chance of an *NME* cover came up in October. He was already losing interest in the promotional side of Ride's career. 'I felt very wary about the fact that we hadn't been a band that long,' he says. 'Suddenly I could have spent most of the day talking to journalists rather than making music. The world was trying to get into our world before we'd even worked out what our world was.'

Reluctantly, he agreed to be photographed by the *NME* stripped to the waist and assuming a submissive pose. Lipstick marks were applied to his chest and neck by an embarrassed Laurence Verfaillie. But when Gardener did not appear on the cover the following week, the four members of Ride vowed that they would never again be photographed separately.

Some of their anxieties drained away when *Nowhere* debuted at number 11, Creation's highest charting album by far. As part of a national tour that autumn, Ride played a homecoming show at the

1,600-capacity Oxford Apollo; a year before, they had been watched by 40 people in a tiny club in Harlow. Steve Lamacq, who saw both gigs, wrote of Ride in the *NME*: '[They have] achieved in one prolific year what most independent bands fail to do in five.'

A knowledgeable follower of the indie scene, Lamacq had been around the block enough times to see young groups wilt under the strain of media scrutiny and constant touring. While he was pleased to see Ride doing so well, he sounded a note of caution. 'My only fears for Ride – catapulted into the mainstream with the accompanying pressures of higher expectations – are that they'll lose their way like the House Of Love,' he wrote. 'That the sudden success will mess up their heads and they'll forget why they started a band in the first place.'

As he watched the reports of the Gulf War on television, Kevin Shields felt small and insignificant. Between starting the album in September 1989 and finishing work on the new *Tremolo* EP in January 1991, he had sat in front of many television screens, seeing the Berlin Wall dismantled, Communist regimes deposed in Hungary, Poland, Czechoslovakia, Bulgaria and Romania, and the reunification of East and West Germany. It was agonising for McGee to think that the Iron Curtain had to topple before Shields was satisfied with the sounds he was getting on tape.

'There were periods of apparent inactivity,' concedes Guy Fixsen, 'but some things had happened very quickly. For example, the [sampled] flute part on "Swallow" – Kevin played it in one take. He sat down at the keyboard and played this totally evocative flute part that really used the whole nuance of the sample. Me and Anjali sat there going: "Wow. Can't believe he just did that." '

Tremolo was an exceptional EP, and not just because the music broke new ground. Including 'Swallow' and 'To Here Knows When', it had seven pieces of music on it. To comply with Gallup regulations, which stipulated that an EP should have a maximum of four songs, three were not given titles. But even the songs with names were weird and uncommercial. 'I remember walking to the studio,' says Fixsen, 'which took me about an hour and a half because there was really heavy snow that year, so that I could edit "To Here Knows When" as it was possibly going to get played on *Top Of The Pops*. That would have been a total trip. "What's this bizarre white noise coming out of my TV?!" '

Emerging from nine months of hibernation, a pernickety Shields harried Creation relentlessly in the period before the EP's release. He wore down Laurence Verfaillie by asking to hear the promotional cassettes before she sent them to the music papers. 'He made an absolute fuss,' she says, 'because he didn't think the quality of the sound on the tape was good enough. I was trying to explain to him that they'd be played on crap little hi-fi systems and it wouldn't make any difference.' It made a big difference to Shields, who insisted on listening to them one by one. The man with the superhuman hearing was taking no chances.

Tremolo charted at 29 in February, giving My Bloody Valentine their first Top 30 hit. Shields now returned to the album, which was still a long way from completion. Interviews he had given for *Tremolo* were pored over at Creation to see if they provided any clues to a delivery date. They didn't. Instead, Shields offered a warning. 'There is a semi-kamikaze attitude within the band,' he said in the *NME*, 'in the sense that we'll just go in whatever direction we want, which could really fuck us up ... What we're attempting to do is to keep other people's opinions completely meaningless. There's only one rule for us and that's simply to do what we feel is good.'

Shields was an intelligent and articulate man, and his lucid responses gave the lie to industry rumours that he had lost sight of his target. By never admitting that he was at fault, he would leave his interrogators in no doubt that everything was proceeding according to plan. Even Nick Robbins, who had found him intolerable at Elephant, concedes the Irish-American could be 'very convincing'. McGee, however, was being driven to delirium. Scanning the song-titles on the EPs – 'Soon', 'Don't Ask Why', 'To Here Knows When' – he had the irrational notion that Shields was trying to unhinge him by sniggering at his impatience.

Close to tears one morning, McGee phoned Moulder at home, begging him to gee Shields along. But Moulder could only do so much. 'I knew that I couldn't lean on Kevin any more than I was doing,' he says, 'because Kevin was so stressed that he couldn't deal with another person on his back. I had to be seen as support. I couldn't betray that position.' McGee remembers Dick Green twice urging him to pull the plug on the album (Green denies this), but such a move would have been to everyone's detriment. 'The trouble was there was so much invested in it already,' says James Kyllo. 'We did always believe that they would finish soon.' That much was true at any rate. My Bloody Valentine had finished 'Soon'.

Alan Moulder finally left the project for good in March. He had been in the frame to help Shields mix the album at some future time unspecified, but had meanwhile received a request from the Jesus and Mary Chain to engineer their next record, which they were making in their own studio, the Drugstore, in south-east London.

Events were overtaking Shields. The Drugstore had formerly been Terminal, where Shields had been hexed by technical headaches the previous year. And when he and Moulder had revisited Trident 2 with a view to remixing 'Soon', they found the studio had been knocked down and rebuilt. Eastern Europe and the

London studio landscape had changed; My Bloody Valentine still hadn't finished.

The Brit Awards for 1991 showed a sea change. The BPI ignored the old guard for once, and the Happy Mondays, the Stone Roses and the Charlatans were all nominated for trophies. Awards organiser Jonathan King arranged a weekend of BPI-sponsored concerts at Wembley Arena, where Ride – who were not in line for an award – played on the same bill as the Cure. With the singles and albums charts now seemingly open to all, the industry was moving to embrace the music of independence.

The first two Ride EPs had been released in America by Sire/Warner Bros as a long-player, *Smile*, in the autumn of 1990. The *Nowhere* album came out there in March, whereupon Mark Gardener and Loz Colbert flew out to do a week of press. They were starting at square one and they knew it. 'It was hard to get as excited about America as the UK,' says Dave Newton. 'If you go into the Top 10 in Britain, you know what it means. But if you're number 17 on the modern rock tracks chart in the States, you don't really know what that means. It wasn't a case of making the US a priority. We were going wherever anyone wanted us.'

McGee had been pressing the band to release a song from *Nowhere*, 'Vapour Trail', as a single in the UK to keep the momentum going. The only song on the album sung by Andy Bell, it had a breezy tune and McGee expected Radio 1 to play-list it. 'We'd done a video for the States because it was a single over there,' says Newton. 'It was begging to be released [in the UK]. But the band had more songs ready and wanted there to be a final chapter in the story of early Ride.' Andy Bell remembers the conversation being even shorter. 'Fancy releasing "Vapour Trail"?' 'No.' 'Fine.'

An all-new Ride EP, *Today Forever*, came out in March and charted at 14. Invited to mime to one of the songs – 'Unfamiliar' – on *Top Of The Pops*, they didn't hide their resentment of the programme's lack of support for them in the past, nor of their continuing failure to strike lucky with daytime radio. At the *Top Of The Pops* studio, the show's presenter Simon Mayo said to Gardener: 'It's a fanbase thing with you lot, I take it?' Gardener replied that it was a good job they had one. *Today Forever* fell to 25 the following week, confirming that only ardent Ride fans had bought it.

Having turned down the chance of opening for the Cure on an arena tour of America – because they would have been onstage for only 20 minutes a night – Ride set out on their first US tour as co-headliners with the 4AD band Lush, playing to audiences in the mid-hundreds. 'Ride and My Bloody Valentine were well-received [in America],' says Joe McEwen. 'It was at a time when KROQ in LA, for example, would champion English bands. KROQ really loved Ride. It was pre-Nirvana, pre that explosion which wiped English music off American radio. "Loaded" was sort of an underground hit, as well as "Come Together". None of [the bands] ever exploded but they all had fanbases.' The British acts Jesus Jones and EMF would enjoy major Billboard hits in the summer – but these were rhythm-based pop-dance tracks, very different to the dreamy guitar wash of Ride and Lush.

'We'd done a mini-tour of the States about three months before,' recalls Lush's guitarist Emma Anderson. 'We did all right over there. We never sold a million records or anything, but we always sold around the 100,000 mark. But bands who were doing really well [in Britain] were going to the States and expecting the same reception, the same size of venues and the same press, and not getting it and coming back saying: "Oh, it was bloody awful." '

Aside from what Loz Colbert calls 'little sparkles of development', none of the Thames Valley or Creation heroes would make much headway in commercial America, their statuesque performances and pedestrian vocals invariably failing to connect with any but the most Anglophile audiences. 'The fans in America were college kids and they were all obsessed with England,' says Steve Queralt. 'You didn't get the feeling that you were reaching the American people. You were just playing to English people abroad.'

Ride returned to Britain to find that the 'Loaded' vogue was showing stamina. Far from blowing over or becoming discredited, the indie-dance sound was inspiring more and more bands to adopt a groove-based style using rhythm loops and skipping beats. The latest indie-dance smash was 'There's No Other Way' by Blur, a Top 10 hit which synchronised teenage suburban lassitude to a snare sound as loud as a school playground at lunchtime. Indie-dance was doing what major labels had tried and mostly failed to do in the 80s: pluck raw bands out of the gig circuit; commercialise them by harnessing their melodies to a radio-approved rhythm template; and then sign another band just like them. Result: three lemons on the A&R fruit machine.

Since 'Loaded', Andrew Weatherall had been in heavy demand as a remixer and producer. Drummers were taking novels or computer games to the studio, anticipating prolonged sessions of inaction. The Q magazine competitor *Select* was relaunched in April to give coverage to indie-dance almost exclusively, which the *NME* and *Melody Maker* had been doing for months. Indie venues and student discos resounded to Blur, the Farm, 'Loaded' and the Charlatans' year-old 'The Only One I Know'.

By keeping dance rhythms out of their music, Ride were playing an unfashionable game. Even Chapterhouse, whom most indie fans would have considered technological slowpokes, looped a dance base-frame from a sample of Led Zeppelin's John Bonham for their crossover single 'Pearl'. Though fans and friends of many of the aforementioned groups, Ride rebuffed all suggestions that they meet indie-dance halfway. Above all, they refused to even hear of letting their songs be dance-remixed.

Creation had turned down Blur after hearing an early demo tape, so it could hardly complain when the Food label began to dominate indie-dance with Blur and Jesus Jones. Nor had McGee liked Chapterhouse, who signed to Dedicated, a label financed by BMG, one of the 'big six' majors. Strangely, given that Creation had a history of signing soundalike bands, McGee did not look for any that sounded like Primal Scream. He looked instead for those that reminded him of Ride and My Bloody Valentine.

Slowdive, a young five-piece from Reading, had released a self-titled EP on Creation in November 1990. Its sensual, celestial music – made up of mood-altering guitar pedals and chorister-like voices – enchanted journalists and sold well enough to justify a second EP, *Morningrise*, the following year. This one was even better: the sound of an undefiled and affordable My Bloody Valentine. Fronted by the pale, Mona Lisa-like Rachel Goswell, Slowdive were becoming an important group to Creation both as an alternative to the indie-dance conventionalists and as short-order stand-ins for senior Creation bands temporarily in suspension. 'There was a certain continuity with the Ride project,' says Laurence Verfaillie, 'and maybe a certain starvation for My Bloody Valentine. If My Bloody Valentine had come up with an album at that point, I think Slowdive probably would not have signed to Creation.'

Like the slightly older Ride, Slowdive came with no manifesto. With an average age of 20, they admitted to being 'vaguely middle-class' and showed no traces of the melancholia that waterlogged their music. Indexed editorially as apolitical rich kids – a judgment also made at various times of Chapterhouse, Ride and Blur – Slowdive were architects of a Thames Valley offshoot sound that was christened 'shoe-gazing' for the musicians' tendency to look downward while playing. If Creation was unwilling to stake more of a claim on indie-dance, it certainly attempted to colonise shoe-gazing.

Shoe-gazing appealed to the south only, an impediment that faced pretty much every non-indie-dance newcomer featured in the music weeklies. A double-bill of Moose and the Cranberries – both much-publicised by *Melody Maker*, the former on the cover – drew only 28 people to a concert in Leicester. Even in their own catchment area, Chapterhouse were forced to cancel a second night at London's Town and Country Club in October due to poor ticket sales. The same band's 'Mesmerise' single, unluckily released to coincide with a shoe-gazing backlash, died on its feet at number 60.

A group often linked with the shoe-gazing family, but so much more assertive that it merited comparison with some of the leading

American grunge bands, was Swervedriver from Oxford. Under the name Shake Appeal, they had been Oxford's biggest band prior to Ride. Now ratty-haired and unkempt, these fans of Hunter S. Thompson sang auto-romantic songs perfect for freeway journeys. Fittingly, McGee had first heard them in Los Angeles. 'I was driving in a limousine with Guy Chadwick along Sunset Boulevard,' he recalls. 'Mark Gardener had sent me a tape of Swervedriver and said: "Please listen to this." And me and Chadwick were listening to it, going: "This is fucking all right." And Chadwick goes: "You should sign it." I went: "I'll do it." '

Two Swervedriver singles were released on Creation in 1990: 'Son Of Mustang Ford' and 'Rave Down'. Onstage, the band was wilder and more spontaneous than any shoe-gazers would dare to be, and press support was coming not only from the weeklies but from heavy metal magazines. Swervedriver's potent Americana enabled McGee to kill two birds with one stone. He licensed their North American rights to A&M for a $250,000 advance, and threw Creation's cash flow a life-jacket just when it needed one.

Paul Mulreany arrived home from a Jazz Butcher tour to be given the job of looking after Creation's export department. He saw it as a wonderful opportunity to be paid cash-in-hand for doing very little. 'I started work in the warehouse, which was on an industrial estate over the road,' he says, 'and I was doing all the exports – Europe, Ireland, Australia – until Graham Gillespie was brought in full-time. Me and him were cynical as anything. We'd be like: "No fucking way, someone's just bought a Momus album." It was a way of passing the day.'

Homeless at the time, Mulreany was allowed to sleep in the Creation office as his boss had once done. 'I was living in the reception area,' he says, 'with a sleeping bag and a big lump of wood – because it was forever getting broken into. It had a shower in there as well, for some strange reason. Many a morning James Kyllo would come in and I'd stick my head out of the shower and shout: "Morning, James!", at which he would look quite disapproving.'

A friend of Mulreany's was asked to build Dick Green a room of his own: office life in Westgate Street had become too anarchic for Green's liking. 'It was a cupboard,' remembers Mulreany. 'It had no windows in it. Dick was like: "I need my own space." We were laughing, going: "Dick, you're going to go insane in there, mate." He said: "It's better than out there." '

The pressure didn't ease up for Green, even when McGee was on the other side of the Atlantic. McGee was a veritable mobile office and a phone-aholic. 'When those phone calls started at nine o'clock in the morning, they didn't stop all day,' Green says. 'And you'd better have done what he'd asked of you. There were some severe tirades.' The phone call would pass around the office like a shiver. 'Sometimes when I was really running out of energy,' says Laurence Verfaillie, 'a phone call from Alan would get me going for a month. But he started travelling quite a lot. I was missing him very badly, because there was such a positive vibe when he was around.'

McGee almost always spent part of the week in America. If he was not doing business on Creation's behalf, he was at least a sandwich-board for its music and hedonistic lifestyle. The Swervedriver deal with A&M had cancelled out some of Creation's debts and McGee now looked to do similar deals for other acts. However, Sire and A&M were satisfied with the bands they already had, and neither was likely to dump hundreds of thousands of dollars in McGee's lap for the pleasure of licensing Pete Astor or the Times. 'As his relationships with the various A&R people blew hot and cold, their interests cooled as well,' says James Kyllo. 'And also – as always with the international licensees – they're waiting for you to have a hit in the UK. They're not going to try and break groups for you.'

Creation's next generation of bands – Moonshake from London, the Telescopes from the Midlands – would not be as easy to trade to America as Primal Scream, My Bloody Valentine and Swervedriver had been. Still, McGee had to try. 'Unfortunately, we became absolutely reliant on [money from America] because we weren't selling enough in the UK,' Green later recalled. 'So he was literally forced to go out there and sell ... the bands to American labels – license the bands to American labels – to make the money. We were like: "Right, you need to sell one by *that* date, because we're going to need that much money ..." '

One of the key American deals of 1991 involved the Glasgow quartet Teenage Fanclub. But it did not make money for Creation, however much McGee might have liked it to. Teenage Fanclub had put out an album entitled *A Catholic Education* on the London indie Paperhouse, a division of Clive Solomon's Fire mini-empire, which was A&R'd by Dave Barker, one-time owner of the Glass label. McGee had known Norman Blake and Raymond McGinley – two of Teenage Fanclub's three singer-songwriters – since their days in a Glasgow band called the Boy Hairdressers, and through their friendship with Bobby Gillespie. A good-time, non-showbizzy outfit with strong American influences and a self-deprecating sense of humour, Teenage Fanclub were exuberant onstage and had a natural rapport with audiences. But they weren't just a great live band. Their June 1990 single 'Everything Flows', taken from *A Catholic Education*, was superlative.

In the States, Teenage Fanclub had signed a two-album deal with the indie label Matador, which released *A Catholic Education* to underground acclaim. Based in New York, Matador was more or less in the same ethical and philosophical neigbourhood as Dave Barker and the pre-Elevation Alan McGee: uncompromisingly pro-music and anti-marketing. The Matador name had helped to give Teenage Fanclub a reasonable profile in America, and the label's values tallied with the group's Glasgow post-punk ethics. 'We grew up in the shadow of the Pastels,' says bassist and songwriter Gerry Love. 'There's a certain self-consciousness. You feel that you're accountable to people in Glasgow. You tend to shy away from marketing ploys.'

'Everything Flows' was followed by an appearance at the 1990 New Music Seminar that made Teenage Fanclub one of the most talked about bands of the 350 playing that week. 'I was sort of representing them because they didn't have a manager at the time,' says Dave Barker. 'My phone was ringing constantly with American A&R men. A lot of those calls you take with a pinch of salt. But I guess it was pretty serious because I can recall Gary Gersh, who was the big man at Geffen who'd signed Nirvana, coming over to see the Fanclub play at the Old Trout in Windsor.'

McGee ran into Teenage Fanclub at Euston station near the end of 1990, shortly after their latest single, 'God Knows It's True', had been a hit with evening radio in Britain. They didn't owe Paperhouse any more albums, and word had come back via Bobby Gillespie that they would be interested in signing to Creation. But just as McGee was getting dollar signs in his eyes, he was told not to expect a worldwide deal. The Fanclub were still under contract to Matador for one more album, and were then going to see what the US major labels had to offer.

'Norman and Raymond were both very smart guys and they were on the case in terms of the potential in America,' says Chas Banks, who would become Teenage Fanclub's manager in 1992. 'Raymond had sold all his furniture and literally slept on the floor for seven months to raise the money to take the band over there. They had a presence in America that was quite remarkable. Kurt Cobain was going round every radio station saying that the best band in the world was Teenage Fanclub.'

When the Fanclub went to New York to do the rounds of the companies, their air-fares were paid by one major label, their *per diem* allowances by another and their hotel bills by a third. What the band hadn't revealed was that there were many more companies eager to sign them, and the Fanclub intended to meet every one. 'Columbia Records paid the hotel bill,' says Raymond McGinley, 'and when we arrived at the hotel the phone rang. It was the A&R guy from Columbia, freaking out. He was like: "I know you're seeing Warner Bros and Geffen. But I've just found out you're seeing ten other major labels." He cancelled the hotel.'

They were taken to lunch and dinner by record companies for ten days. Geffen had to fly in from Los Angeles because the Fanclub didn't fancy going to meet them on home ground. 'There were so many suitors that the Creation deal was almost an afterthought,' says Chas Banks. 'It was the Americans who were hot to trot.' The Fanclub were able to negotiate a split-territory deal, signing for three albums with Creation for the UK and Europe, and for five albums with Geffen for the rest of the world. 'We thought: what would an American company know about France?' says McGinley. 'Let's just split it down the middle.'

The first Fanclub album to be released by Creation was *The King*. Recorded in a day, it was a collection of unpolished instrumentals and was not seen as a serious work. Certainly not by Matador, anyway: the label refused to accept it as the second album on the Fanclub's contract. 'Matador thought we were taking the piss,' says McGinley. 'We had to buy our way out of the deal.' But when Creation put out *The King* in the UK, it almost charted.

By the summer of 1991, McGee calculated that Creation would need an injection of £750,000 if it were to survive into 1992. 'We were nearly bankrupt,' he says. 'My Bloody Valentine were bankrupting us. Primal Scream weren't bankrupting us, but we needed to get their record out. We had the Fanclub, we had Saint Etienne ...* I was just trying to get the albums out – in between saying: "Do you want another line of charlie?" '

Output was essential. Best ofs; worst ofs; albums by Dick Green's side-project Sand; collector-friendly long-players rounding up deleted singles from 1983–7. Anything to fill an otherwise empty month; anything that would sell 5,000 copies and make revenue. Ed Ball was told to make as many records as he liked. He made four a year.

'We were growing,' says James Kyllo. 'The turnover was growing quite a lot – which is a dangerous cash flow bubble – but because the amounts are going up, you can keep on paying the creditors as they come due without ever really being very solid financially. We just needed to keep on putting out records to have the money to pay the debts from months before.' Creation's album output grew from 17 in 1990 to 39 in 1991. More than a third of them featured previously released material. As long as they sold a few thousand, it didn't matter. 'It was getting serious,' says Pat Fish, who put out three albums that year. 'No one could afford to eat because of Kevin Shields. There were Friday nights when [Creation] couldn't pay the wages bill. Kevin had had it all.'

---

* Though signed to Creation, Saint Etienne released their records through Jeff Barrett's label Heavenly. The profit share worked out as 50 per cent to Saint Etienne and 25 each to Creation and Heavenly.

One of Fish's albums, credited to the Black Eg, showed how reckless McGee was willing to get. It consisted of Fish producing sounds from his guitar's delay pedal. 'It was made on my four-track,' he says. 'Somehow Alan got to hear of it and he said: "Pat, Pat – put it out." I'm going: "No, it's unreleasable." I had to fuck off to LA to sing with the Blue Aeroplanes, and just before I left I dropped off a cassette of some mixes on Alan's desk, with a note saying: "There you go. Unreleasable, isn't it?" When I got back from LA, Creation had *cut the record*. Because it was free! Anything that could raise them another fifty quid to keep Kevin in the studio, they would do.'

McGee's belief that he could always pull something out of the hat drove him back to America time and again. ('Alan still has a bit of a reputation in the States for coming and yelling and pounding on people's desks,' Rachel Felder, an A&R at Columbia, said in 1998.) However, by extracting from US labels considerable advances that would immediately be swallowed up by Creation before it was even clear if the band was going to recoup or not, McGee was swimming in dangerous waters.

'If one of our records had sold internationally, I would have been bankrupt,' he says, 'because I would have had to pay the band a load of money. I would take probably three quarters of a million [across three albums] off A&M on behalf of Swervedriver ... which would go into the Creation pot. Now in fact, Swervedriver managed to sell a total of 50,000 records in America. If they had ever sold a million records, I'd have suddenly had to pay them £1 million. This is how most indie labels go bankrupt. They've got a great businessman that can go and take money off everybody. Then suddenly he has a hit and he owes £1 million, and he's going: "Fucking hell, I've just spent it." '

One part Malcolm McLaren to two parts Zero Mostel in *The Producers*, McGee knew that he would need to do the mother of all deals that autumn to tide Creation over. My Bloody Valentine's album had been allocated the catalogue number CRE 060 at the start of 1991. Six months later, Creation had put CRE 076 – the new Primal Scream album, *Screamadelica* – on the schedule and removed CRE 060 from it once again. 'I'd be flying to America and the diary would say week 14,' McGee later recalled, 'and I knew *Screamadelica* was coming out in week 34 and I had no idea whether we'd make it that far.'

In the UK, money had come back to Creation from Ride – the *Today Forever* EP had sold 80,000 copies, boosting the sales of *Nowhere* in the process – but *Screamadelica* would not be out until September, and profit from Primal Scream's singles was being neutralised by the cost of the videos. Flouting etiquette, McGee went to Protocol for an urgent talk with Kevin Shields. 'They had a bit of a chat,' Guy Fixsen remembers, 'and [McGee] said: "Look, you're going to have to hurry up or else there won't even be a label for you to put [the album] out on." The pace quickened quite considerably after that.'

Creation's parlous state had affected Ride, who were now seeing the downside of signing to a hip indie label with a perfectionist-genius and diminishing resources. While Creation had been subsidising Shields, Ride were owed almost £75,000 in royalties for *Nowhere*. 'We hadn't really noticed the problems up to that point,' says Dave Newton. 'We'd done *Today Forever* down in Black Barn Studios in Surrey in January 1991. Then we went back in about May and started working on a new album. The studio owner came up to me and said: "Creation's cheque has just bounced for the third time. You're going to have to leave." I had to write him out a cheque there and then to keep the band in the studio.'

Ride had been a charm to Creation, not least because their sudden take-off meant they required minimum ongoing promotion. And although McGee bitterly regretted not being able to license them to an American label for a few hundred thousand dollars, the fact was that had they not recently collected their second advance from Sire/Warners, their Black Barn album would not have been released on Creation. 'We could have walked from our deal,' Newton points out. 'They couldn't pay us our money. We renegotiated the deal while we were in the studio – and we took on the payment of recording costs ourselves – but what we didn't do was walk from the deal. And at that point we would have been worth a lot of money to any number of labels.'

Before signing their new contract with Creation, Ride had a key man clause inserted, stating that if either McGee or Green ceased to be involved in Creation the contract would be closed. An additional clause gave Ride the right to terminate the contract should McGee and Green sell more than 50 per cent of Creation to an outside party.

CRE 076 – *Screamadelica* by Primal Scream – was nothing like either of their previous albums. Organically grown and speculative, it juxtaposed house music, rock 'n' roll, dub, psychedelia, California sunshine symphonies, space rock and gospel.

Produced largely by Andrew Weatherall and his assistant Hugo Nicolson, *Screamadelica* also included contributions from Hypnotone, the Orb, bassist Jah Wobble and the American Jimmy Miller, producer of the Rolling Stones' run of classic albums from *Beggars Banquet* in 1968 to *Goat's Head Soup* in 1973. McGee had met Miller in a New York hotel room in the late 80s when the Scream were metamorphosing into a rock 'n' roll group. The tracks on *Screamadelica* which Miller produced and mixed with Andrew Innes in America were spiced with maracas and shakers, as though airlifted from side three of *Exile On Main Street*. However, the majority of Primal Scream's album had been made in insalubrious north London.

'We were in a place called Jam Studios ... which was the old Decca Studios up Crouch End–Finsbury Park,' Bobby Gillespie told Michael Bonner. 'Mostly it was done in there with tape ops ... We had a nice time in Jam Studios, I remember it was a good time. There was a good lot of ideas. I remember [Martin] Duffy, when we were doing "Inner Flight", he was tripping on acid. I remember him jumping on the mixing desk going: "Bob, Bob, I'm pissing on the sky, I'm pissing on the sky ..." '

One critic wrote that Weatherall 'taught Primal Scream to breathe out'. Gillespie put it differently, observing that they had been 'deconstructed' as a band. 'Instead of having two guitars, bass, drums, vocal, we destroyed that,' he told Bonner. 'It was ... anything goes – synth, tabla, drum machine, no vocals, instrumentals, gospel singers, sitars. The whole range of anything-goes noises. And suddenly the band were freed. It was a much looser approach to making music. And then getting people like Andy and Hugo, and Alex Paterson and Thrash from the Orb, Jimmy Miller, Wobble, you know – these people, messing with our music, taking it somewhere else, making it more interstellar, as far out as ... It was incredible. The greatest time.'

An album that profited from so much collaboration inevitably made it hard to apportion credit. Jeff Barrett, who managed Weatherall, comments: 'People go: "Oh, Andrew Weatherall made that record." Bullshit. Andrew made that record what it *was*, but he didn't make that record. [Primal Scream] made the fucking record. Bottom line? Andrew Innes made that record. Innes said what went on that record. Innes had the final say.'

Then again, Barrett also claims that he himself played a substantial role in *Screamadelica* by opening Primal Scream's eyes to ecstasy and acid house, while McGee counters that it was he more than anybody who guided them in the right direction. 'I think Alan was very instrumental in the album,' says Andy Bell. 'When we were getting signed, he was talking about "Oh, I've got to get this thing sorted out for Primal Scream – they want to try and get the drums to a click [track] and they don't know how to do it. I've got to find an engineer for them," and that kind of thing. They were reaching for something that they couldn't quite get, and he was able to help them.'

Is that A&R? Barrett doesn't think so. 'Nobody A&R'd *Screamadelica*,' he says. 'They just made it.' McGee's recollection is that the album was fairly straightforward to assemble, but only because he made it so. 'I would get the Orb to do a mix,' he says, 'and "Higher Than The Sun" came out amazing so I went: "That's the single." And it just fell into line.'

Featuring Jah Wobble on bass (Primal Scream had no full-time bassist, but used Henry Olsen, an ex-backing musician for Nico, on live dates) 'Higher Than The Sun' actually took a few listens before McGee was convinced that it was an appropriate follow-up to 'Come Together'. A projected single in the autumn of 1990, 'Don't Fight It, Feel It', had been pulled by McGee because Gillespie did not sing on it. 'Higher Than The Sun' did have a vocal by Gillespie, but the song was a weightless, liquescent prayer with no tempo for the first 50 seconds. It was guaranteed to be a *Screamadelica* high point, but it was hard to imagine it on the radio. Gillespie himself saw it as 'a sad track, like someone drifting off into death'.

To McGee it suggested the opposite, however, and he decided to run with it. 'That is a hymn to hedonism, that song,' he says. 'I phoned Gillespie up and said: "It's the best single since 'Anarchy In The UK'." And he went: "Would you please say that in the press?" ' (Gillespie later suggested that the conversation had happened the other way round.) Soon the entire Creation office was mad about 'Higher Than The Sun'. Dick Green and Laurence Verfaillie believed it was the best single Creation had ever released. It came out in mid June.

'I was in Kent with my parents sightseeing,' recalls Verfaillie, 'and I went to the only phone box in the village. I heard the midweek: it wasn't Top 40. I was devastated.' Between Wednesday and Saturday, 'Higher Than The Sun' put on a modest sales spurt and managed to chart at 40. It was scant compensation. 'Everybody put on a brave face,' says Verfaillie. 'I think at the end of the day we knew we had the album. We knew we had something very special and if people were not getting it – fuck it, it was a beautiful piece of art.' The following week, 'Higher Than The Sun' dropped out of the Top 40. A week later, it vanished from the Top 75.

The release of a fourth pre-*Screamadelica* single – the restored 'Don't Fight It, Feel It', a soul-influenced house track sung by the black singer Denise Johnson – was brought forward to August. In late July, Primal Scream began a British tour, their first since 1989, with Andrew Weatherall and the Orb as DJs. Denise Johnson joined the line-up, and the Scream's entourage included Douglas Hart – who was videoing events for a documentary film – and the booking agent Alex Nightingale, son of Radio 1's Annie, who had become friendly with the band in Brighton. Verfaillie took journalists from *Melody Maker* to the Manchester show on 24 July. 'No one could understand how it could actually work,' she says. 'There were these two conflicting elements in the music – how do you do that live? But that gig was phenomenal. Everything [fit] into place so well. When the computer programming broke down, they just went and did acoustic songs. I was crying.'

In the hours before and after the concert, Gillespie was hospitable and seemed to enjoy the journalists' questions about the more colourful characters on the tour. About Alex Nightingale, who had been hospitalised that afternoon after cracking his head open following a blackout, Gillespie enthused: 'It's a crazy life he's had. Like, three months ago he did six Es, a bottle of Jack Daniel's and some champagne and came down to my house at quarter to eight to wake me up to do a video shoot. We went along and they started freebasing coke, and Nightingale collapsed and started having a fit ... So he lives quite an excessive lifestyle. He was a heroin addict for ten years.'

Warming to his topic, Gillespie admitted that Primal Scream's own drug-taking could give Nightingale's a run for its money. 'Whether we're on tour or not, it's always fairly excessive,' he said. 'There is a lot of drug-taking. I know that if we weren't in this group we'd still be the same.' His thoughts turning to the heavy-drinking keyboard player Martin Duffy, Gillespie confided: 'A lot of people look at him and say: "Well, he's going to die pretty soon." I mean, even Nightingale has told me Duffy's days are numbered, that sooner or later he'd going to walk under a bus. But that's the way Duffy lives his life. If he walks under a bus, he walks under a bus. But he wouldn't be Duffy if there wasn't a chance of him walking under a bus.'

On 24 August, 'Don't Fight It, Feel It' entered the charts at 41 – and now there was dread at Creation regarding *Screamadelica*. It had cost around £80,000, which was not wildly expensive, but in lieu of a finished My Bloody Valentine album *Screamadelica* had the future of Creation riding on it. That future looked increasingly threatened. 'Their singles had progressively [sold] worse,' says Dick Green. 'We got stuck at 41. Everything was 41 at the time. It hadn't taken off the way we had thought. There was no reason to think that the album – the majority of which was singles we had already released – was going to kick in. I certainly wouldn't have expected it to sell more than 50,000.'

16 More Like Torture Than Entertainment: My Bloody Valentine Say Goodbye

D AVE WHITEHEAD AND SIMON EDWARDS left Rough Trade in December 1989 to start a media promotions company, Real Time. Whitehead, these days based in New York, is thinking back to his last year as managing director of Rough Trade Distribution. 'It was a lucrative time for distribution, but you could see the way things were going,' he says. 'I don't think anybody realised how fine a margin distributors worked on. The way most labels looked to save money was to cut their distribution deal by a couple of per cent if they could. And of course they all did that ... but still required the same level of funding and service from their distributors. People demanded cheaper deals. People compared their independent distribution deals to deals they could get from a major record company.'

A year after the departure of Whitehead and Edwards, Rough Trade Distribution had lost control of its overhead. The elopement of Creation in July 1990 had been followed by mass desertion – first Sleeping Bag, a New York dance label that had experienced what UK manager Mervyn Anthony Lyn described as 'a torrid and disappointing 18 months' with Rough Trade; then another dance label, Gee Street, and – in December – all the labels distributed by Rough Trade's long-time partner and Cartel co-founder Revolver, which promptly linked up with Pinnacle. Rough Trade's business was reduced by ten per cent at a stroke.

A week before, 40 staff had been laid off – bringing the total to 70 in three weeks – after months of complaints from retailers about Rough Trade's computerised sales system, which was running ominously slow. Indeed, it was rumoured that only one person knew how the computer worked. Rough Trade sources told *Music Week* that some workers, angry at being made redundant, had vandalised property and daubed graffiti in the warehouse. The *NME* reported that the company had hired extra security after managing director George Kimpton-Howe was sent excrement in the post. It was becoming apparent to the industry that there were serious problems in Finsbury Park.

A former warehouse worker quoted by the *NME* revealed that orders which should have been processed in a matter of hours were taking up to four days. 'At the moment they are eight hundred orders behind,' he said. 'That means eight hundred shops – a lot of them chart return shops – just can't get the records as quickly as they need them. They've got a computer system worth a quarter of a million pounds and it just isn't working – and that was before they sacked seventy people. They think they'll be able to get through the bad patch and carry on as normal next year. They must be joking.'

A video company, Parkfield, had crashed in the summer owing Rough Trade almost £500,000. Rough Trade's own debts included rent due on the King's Cross premises it had left in July. In October, the folk label Cooking Vinyl laid off 50 per cent of its staff, managing director Pete Lawrence blaming delays by Rough Trade in getting records to the shops. His sales were almost two-thirds down on projected estimates.

Rough Trade had survived financial scares before, but not in a climate where indie stores were closing at the rate of one a day. In February 1991, a month in which Rough Trade paid no bills whatsoever, Kimpton-Howe received several phone calls asking if the company was in receivership. 'We are not in danger of going under,' he said, although he admitted the situation was worrying. Rough Trade had been losing money every week for the last year. 'We are currently waiting to finalise a very big financial deal,' Kimpton-Howe added, referring to negotations with Geffen in the States, which hinged on the combined value of Rough Trade's two key assets: the Sundays and the back catalogue of the Smiths.

Mid-February saw another 40 Rough Trade staff out of a job. Accountants KPMG Peat Marwick McLintock were called in to install a new management team and save the Rough Trade group from collapse. 'It is their diversity which has proved their downfall,' said Steve Mason, brushing away a tear. The only thing keeping Rough Trade afloat was the support of labels such as Mute – owed a high six-figure sum – and Big Life. 'We are going to make sure Rough Trade is not going to the wall,' said Big Life's Jazz Summers. 'The future of the music industry depends on the independents.'

Summers may have had a point, but then again he had sold half his label to Polydor in 1989. Smaller labels than his were sticking it out with Rough Trade on the understanding that £3 million was protected in a ring-fenced escrow account, and that all of them would be paid in time. These smaller labels included Fire, a recent arrival from Pinnacle. Clive Solomon's move to Rough Trade looked like being his worst business decision since passing up an invitation to manage Wham! in 1982.

In April, after a meeting of 70 labels to put together a cost-cutting package, Rough Trade began fighting for its life. Two-thirds of the Rough Trade Records workforce was made redundant, and plans were drawn up to find cheaper premises for the group. Immediately, Martin Heath, the owner of Rhythm King, pulled his two biggest acts – S'Express and Betty Boo – out of Rough Trade Distribution, shocking Geoff Travis who was last to hear the news. Travis had been absent from recent meetings, irritated that his warnings of meltdown had not been heeded.

George Kimpton-Howe resigned at the end of April, just as the Rough Trade group prepared to seal a series of future-securing deals. Jazz Summers, owed £312,000, chose this as his moment to bail out altogether. One of Rough Trade's staunchest backers in the past, he now began distributing his new releases through PolyGram. Within two weeks, it was announced that Rough Trade Distribution would cease trading.

The company's only hope of survival lay in a new plan – backed by ten major creditors including Mute, 4AD, Situation Two, KLF Communications and Rough Trade Records – to sell off the Smiths' back catalogue and Rough Trade America to cover the group's £3 million debt. But as acting group managing director David Murrell of KPMG later lamented, the accounts were so muddled that it was unclear whether Rough Trade Distribution owed Rough Trade Records £1 million or vice versa. In the event, the rescue plan failed when Rough Trade America collapsed – becoming worthless overnight – and the value of the Smiths' catalogue took an unexplained dive. There was nothing to offer, nothing to sell. The end came with a 17 May High Court administration order.

Rob Dickins, who has continued to work with Travis on acts signed to Blanco y Negro, spent time with him on the day Rough Trade died. 'I was almost in tears,' Dickins remembers. 'This was his dream. The funny thing was, a lot of those indie labels who hated him because he went down and owed them money – and it *was* their existence – but without him, and without what he started ...'

In July, Daniel Miller was asked by a reporter from *Music Week* if he could define 'independence'. Thirteen years after the birth of Mute, Miller put it like this: 'It means that no mystery figure in Tokyo or Hamburg tells us what to do. It also means we constantly fight off companies who want to buy us, steal our bands or attack us at a weak point.' The death of Rough Trade Distribution had left the major labels better placed than ever to exploit the financial instability of the indie sector. Brenda Kelly, a former editor of the indie trade magazine the *Catalogue* and a co-producer of the music programme *Snub TV*, commented acerbically: 'Being independent right now seems to mean being financially beleaguered. Independent labels are not major multinational corporations with diverse holdings in everything from leisure industry interests to hardware and armaments, so they're vulnerable. Most independent labels are still in the market-place primarily to release music that means something on their – and their artists' – own terms.'

Alan McGee, whose label fell slap in the middle of that category, was safe for the moment under the aegis of Steve Mason at Pinnacle. As McGee recalls, Mason 'did me bigger favours than Rough Trade ever did. Rough Trade may have started me up, but I actually did go a few times to Steve Mason and say: "I'm so much in the shit, you need to give me a quarter of a million." And he would write me the cheque. The guy was a geezer.'

By September 1991, when Mason bought Rough Trade Germany, Pinnacle not only dominated independent distribution at home but had a network covering Germany, Austria, Switzerland and Benelux. Speaking at a sales conference in Croydon, Mason claimed that it was now the majors, not the indies, who were Pinnacle's rivals. Even when he lost the PWL contract in November, Mason was far from heartbroken. 'If it had happened two years earlier, it would have been a big blow,' he said, 'because they were 40 per cent of our turnover – as opposed to five per cent when they left.'

A tall, bearded, bespectacled millionaire – and a reformed smoker who had banned cigarettes from Pinnacle's headquarters – Mason, at 42, owned a house in stockbroker Kent and had two young children at private school. But when *Music Week* went to Orpington to profile him, there was no trip to a fancy restaurant for a leisurely lunch on expenses. Mason tucked into a sandwich wrapped in greaseproof paper, and directed the reporter to a hot dog trailer across the road. '[He] is an unlikely figure to be the saviour of the UK's independent record industry,' the journalist wrote, 'but that's what many people consider him to be.'

When he had stood for election to the BPI council in 1987, Mason had been of the Iain McNay ilk – an indies-versus-majors thorn in the flesh. In the years since, Mason had continually stressed his allegiance to the indie cause. 'But indie to Mason is a business philosophy, not a musical one,' the man from *Music Week* cautioned. 'In ten years, the indie sector has grown from a musical ideal into an efficiently run, multimillion pound business. Mason had led the way ... In a part of the industry created by and for mavericks, it is Mason's conservatism, allied to his no-nonsense deal-making, which has triumphed in the end.'

By the end of 1991, Pinnacle distributed eight per cent of all records sold in the UK.

The House Of Love's sacking of Terry Bickers had taken minutes to implement but almost a year to fully execute. The process cost the band thousands of pounds in legal and accountancy fees, added to which Bickers remained on a £100 weekly retainer – which he would collect from Creation's bank in Holborn – until he was finally bought out in early 1991. He and Dave Francolini had formed a new group, Levitation. In a televised interview for *Rapido*, Bickers demonstrated his abiding flair for causing trouble by describing Guy Chadwick as one of the creepiest people he had ever met in his life. Vengeance was Terry's, and he was repaying.

Bickers wasn't too pleased with McGee either. He accused his ex-manager of trying to delay his severance settlement, and boasted to journalists that Levitation were the musical and spiritual antithesis to the market-geared House Of Love. But it depended on which day you got him: he was apt to be a weathercock. 'When we were cutting [Levitation's] *Coppelia* EP at Blackwing, Alan rang up,' recalls Francolini. 'Terry was screaming down the phone: "This is going to be a fucking hit!" and holding the phone up to the monitors. He was still talking in the language of the financial pressures of the music business.'

Levitation were hot for most of that year. While Bickers was reciting his side of the House Of Love story into journalists' cassette recorders, his old friends Groothuizen, Evans and Walker were awaiting the call from Chadwick, who was writing the band's next album in EMI Music's demo studio. Dave Bates, however, was rejecting most of what Chadwick presented to him. 'Basically, Guy spent a year trying to write ten songs and going fucking mad,' says Groothuizen.

McGee was finding Chadwick obnoxious and dreaded their meetings. Chadwick in turn felt neglected by McGee, who seemed to have absolutely no interest in the career or welfare of the band. 'Our relationship with Alan was just appalling,' says Groothuizen. 'The whole thing was that Alan was supposed to be managing *us*, not anybody he could get 20 per cent off. We invited him down to the studio so that Guy could give him a dressing down. Alan turned up and we started this kind of "well, you know, Alan ..." And he said: "Well, actually I just don't think I want to manage you any more." So any ideas of Guy giving him a hard time about not managing us very well went out the window, and Guy started trying to convince him to stay.'

McGee wanted the House Of Love out of his hair more than they knew. He had scarcely listened to the 'Butterfly' album, and had no wish to hang around for the follow-up. He regarded them as hippies, bread-heads and bores. 'They had done everybody's head in,' he says. 'They were so far up their own arses it was unbelievable.' McGee and Chadwick did not speak for another two months. Finally, Chadwick picked up the phone and told McGee he was sacked. Replacing the receiver, McGee exhaled a sigh of relief.

'Some of the best fun I've ever had in my life has been with Guy

Chadwick,' he said a few years later. 'The guy has got one of the best senses of humour. He is basically a good guy. And unfortunately I think he just got fucking corrupted by the money ... It's when you get to the airport and expect the limousine. Whenever people send limousines, I've always just laughed. You just don't take it seriously. Whereas the House Of Love got to the point where they turned up at the airport and expected the limo.'

In July 1991, acting on an idea of Mick Griffiths', the House Of Love announced their return to the London stage to play three shows in one night. As a story to get them back in the news pages, it had its merits: the audience would be taken from venue to venue by bus, and the location of the third gig would remain a secret until the last minute. But as if to mock the House Of Love's declining fortunes, Status Quo promptly revealed their intention to perform four concerts in four major cities in one day, travelling from arena to arena by helicopter. The House Of Love were in the *NME* – but Quo were in the *Guinness Book Of Records*.

'After that, of course, every gig we did had to have a gimmick to it,' says Groothuizen. 'One suggestion was that we do a gig on a boat. This is just after the *Marchioness* disaster, when no one – especially me – wants to go and pack a boat full of people on the Thames.* It's just an appalling idea. And they wanted to do the Royal Albert Hall again – but do it in the round, because it had never been done before. It always seemed to be: "How can we make this seem like we're an interesting band?" '

The third House Of Love album, *Babe Rainbow*, had been demoed in a rehearsal studio by a well-drilled band enjoying its own company for once – only to outdo the 'Butterfly' album, if such a thing were possible, in the amount of anguish it caused and the number of rethinks it required. 'The whole thing was going to be really simple,' says Chadwick. 'We didn't want to make a fussy, overproduced album. The songs didn't need that. And then the same thing happened. Dave Bates was like: "Where the fuck are all the guitars?" It ended up as four months' extra work.'

Songs that had been learned backwards and forwards were suddenly questioned. Were they finished? Could more work be done to them? Was that a powerful enough chorus? Would Bates prefer a minor chord here? 'It was like dealing with a madman,' says Chadwick. 'He was irrational and completely insensitive. I found this a lot when I was at RCA – with major record companies you get people like that. They are exposed to people like Elton John and Bob Geldof and Jon Bon Jovi, and all these heavyweights, and they think that is the way to behave: to make people's lives a complete misery.'

---

* On August 20, 1989, the *Marchioness* riverboat sank after colliding with a dredger on the Thames at Southwark. Fifty-one people died.

But Simon Walker remembers that the House Of Love used to joke about a conversation between Chadwick and Bates after a concert in Paris. Chadwick had been telling Bates that he thought he would make a good A&R man. 'No you wouldn't,' replied Bates. 'You're not enough of a cunt.' Chadwick looked offended. 'But I *am*,' he protested. 'I *am* enough of a cunt.'

For Walker, the album sessions were too much to bear. Mind games were being played in the studio, not helped by Chadwick's new-found taste for smoking grass. 'Guy said to me: "I don't want you to come to the studio any more",' Walker recalls. 'I turned up the next day and he said: "I told you I didn't want you here." So I took a holiday. A month later I got a call from Guy saying: "You're not showing a lot of commitment." ' On the first day of rehearsals for a tour, Walker left the band.

The third single from *Babe Rainbow*, 'You Don't Understand', was the signal for an extraordinary visit to the *NME* offices by Chadwick and his publicist Mick Houghton. Chadwick had come to ask Danny Kelly – *NME* editor and long-time House Of Love fan – to put the band on the cover one more time. Houghton was uncomfortable about this: he and Kelly both knew that the House Of Love's day had passed. Chadwick resorted to pleading. He told Kelly he was prepared to do anything – *anything* – in the photographs. Wear a dress ... a Nazi uniform ... strip naked ... you name it.

Kelly thought about it for a while. Then he came up with a solution. The House Of Love could have their cover, he told Chadwick, provided they shared it with Levitation – and Chadwick and Terry Bickers would stand back to back, holding duelling pistols. 'Anything ... except that,' said Chadwick. He never appeared on the cover of the *NME* again.

The vocals for My Bloody Valentine's album were recorded at Protocol and Britannia Row studios between May and June 1991. It was the first time that Bilinda Butcher had been involved in the record to any great extent, and she and Kevin Shields made it an unforgettable experience for the engineers. 'We weren't allowed to listen while either of them were doing a vocal,' recalls Guy Fixsen. 'You'd have to watch the meters on the tape machine to see if anyone was singing. If it stopped, you knew you had to stop the tape and take it back to the top. We were pretty much flying on instruments.'

In Britannia Row, Shields and Butcher hung curtains over the window between the studio and the control room. When they thought they had done a good take, they would open the curtains and wave. Nobody was shown any lyrics at any point. Anjali Dutt remembers: 'Kevin would sing the track, and then Bilinda would get the tape and write down words that she thought he might have sung.'

Now that an end was in sight, Creation moved quickly to accommodate Shields. He was placed in a new studio, Eastcoate, where he seemed confident he could finish the album. But it transpired that Britannia Row's bill had not been paid by Creation, and the studio would not release the band's equipment. '[Britannia Row had] bent over sideways for us,' notes Dutt, 'and I don't know what excuse Kevin gave them for leaving. He had to raise the money himself to get the gear out.' After giving Eastcoate the thumbs-up, Shields soon complained that it was not up to standard, and left after eight days.

Dick Green thinks that it was around then that he had a break-down. Anjali Dutt remembers being 'desperate to leave' and was grateful when another band offered her an engineering job. As the bodies fell, McGee took the wheel. 'I had basically put every single penny I had in my own personal bank account into finishing the album,' he says. 'It was two years into the album and I phoned [Shields] up in tears. I was going: "You have to deliver me this record." To be honest, I think I emotionally blackmailed Kevin into delivering the record. But it still took another five months after that phone call.'

Dutt's place in the control room was taken by an Irish engineer, Dick Meaney, and the tapes were brought to the Church, a studio in Crouch End owned by Dave Stewart of the Eurythmics. It was the nineteenth studio Shields had used since September 1989. He was now ready to mix the songs and compile the record he would call *Loveless*. McGee shuddered when he heard the title.

The bad news for Creation was that Shields had lately been afflicted by tinnitus, a hearing impairment. He and Butcher were martyrs to their ears: she had once suffered a punctured eardrum during a My Bloody Valentine gig. Shields attributed his tinnitus not to the band's live act, but to too many nights listening to loud mixes on headphones. He dismissed accusations that My Bloody Valentine played at gratuitous volume levels as 'ill-informed hysteria'.

Laurence Verfaillie was sympathetic to Shields, but she was more concerned about Dick Green, whose hair had gone grey. He was 30 years old. 'Dick was the one every morning who was opening the post *shaking*,' says Verfaillie. 'Alan was still full-on, positive about everything, but Dick was taking the everyday pressure. I still think about it a lot when I see him. He would not have grey hair if it was not for that album.'

When Shields had finished the mixing, another crisis loomed. He was unable to get the tapes out of the Church because the studio was demanding a bill of £22,000. His own bank account drained, McGee did something he had never done before. 'I borrowed the money off my dad,' he says. 'My dad's a panel-beater; he's not a businessman or anything like that. And I'll tell you why that really got to me. It was the insurance money my dad had got from my mum's death. I bor-rowed it to finish a record.'

In September, *Melody Maker* printed a rumour that Creation had been put up for sale due to irrevocable cash flow problems. It was just that – a rumour – but the cash flow problems were real enough. 'It wasn't so much a question of money being quickly swallowed up,' says James Kyllo, 'as it arriving to fill the big hole that was already there. We weren't ever ahead of the game. There was one Sunday that Alan, Dick and I met in the office to look at the finances. I remember I was playing cricket and had to leave halfway through. We figured out that we had to find £50,000 in the next week or that was *it*. On that occasion, they went and got an advance on a French distribution deal and got enough money to keep going.'

The *Melody Maker* story also quoted a figure of £250,000 as My Bloody Valentine's studio bill to date. According to McGee and Green, this erred on the low side by £20,000. 'Once you'd even got it recorded and mixed, the very act of compiling, EQ-ing, etcetera took weeks on its own,' says Green. 'Everything had to be put in order. There were pieces of connecting music that needed exact timings for all the complex cross-fades, so he had to find the absolute best technology at the time, the best form of mastering, the best form of pressing.'

The editing was done on a computer system that had previously been used for film dialogue. The computer threw the entire album out of phase. Shields was later heard to marvel that in the history of computerised album editing, this complication had happened to only one other artist: Cliff Richard. As for the mastering, it was a procedure that normally took one or two days' work. Shields took 13. During this time, McGee heard that Shields had detected a serious flaw in the recording and was threatening to remix the whole album from top to bottom.

Ride would not be releasing another album until 1992. To keep themselves in the public eye, they played second on the bill to the Pixies at an outdoor event in Crystal Palace in June 1991. Ride were tour-weary, and the number of weeks they could anticipate spending in studios that year was barely in double figures. They had become a band that wrote songs on the road about being on the road, and this would become a theme of their new album. 'I felt a growing sense of anxiety at the amount of time we were chasing around like monkeys,' says Mark Gardener.

Ride's schedule sent them out on the European festival circuit in the summer of 1991. At Hultsfred, an annual three-dayer in Sweden, Bell was reunited with Idha Ovelius, a girl he had met in Stockholm and Uppsala on the band's first European tour the previous autumn. Bell was clearly taken by her: in Uppsala he had, as Gardener puts it, 'turned into Jimmy Page for the night', throwing his best rock 'n' roll shapes for Ovelius' benefit. They spent the duration of the Hultsfred festival together. 'There was obviously some serious chemistry going down,' says Gardener. 'It was bizarre because Idha was engaged at the time. I'd even met her fiancé. I was staggering around Hultsfred, hitting the drink, and suddenly I walk into this guy and he's saying: "Where's Idha? Where's Idha?" ' Gardener knew very well where Idha was, but it wasn't the sort of thing he could announce to her fiancé.

The girlfriends of Gardener and Steve Queralt had been on the scene since the earliest days of the band. Bell had been going out with the sister of Queralt's girlfriend, but had not seen much of her since Ride had started touring internationally. Idha Ovelius was the first girlfriend to come from outside. Crucially, Bell now had someone to whom he could confide some of his doubts about the state of play within the group.

In an imperial gesture intended to vault them far ahead of their shoe-gazing challengers, Ride headlined their own outdoor show at Slough in Berkshire, playing to 7,000 people. Coming on top of sold-out concerts at the National Ballroom in Kilburn and – twice – at the Town and Country Club, Ride had now been seen by more than 20,000 people in and around London since March. Free time in August and September was the cue for everyone but Gardener to buy a house in Oxford with their *Nowhere* royalties. Idha Ovelius came over to live with Bell, working initially as an au pair. By October, Ride were recording their second album in Chipping Norton, Oxfordshire with Alan Moulder.

Bell was behind a move to drop some of the band's reverb and delay effects and opt for a drier, tighter, more controlled sound. 'I felt like we were the Floyd,' he says, 'and that we'd come out with a gimmicky sound that would date. This is something I don't think any more. We were feeling that we'd got to where we were by having quiet bits followed by noise. We began to get too self-conscious about it, feeling that we had to move forward for the sake of it.'

The most progressive and important-feeling of the new songs was 'Leave Them All Behind', a near-heavy rock epic that palpitated around a Gardener lyric about travel and an arpeggio figure obtained by Bell holding down keys on a Hammond organ, using a gate triggered by a click track to recreate the premonitory staccato of the opening passage on the Who's 'Won't Get Fooled Again'. Stretching beyond eight minutes – with no singing for the first two – 'Leave Them All Behind' hardly had comeback single written all over it, which is precisely why Ride wanted it to be released as one. Many a judicious A&R man would have advised them to think again. Not Alan McGee. 'We played him "Leave Them All Behind" and he went mental,' recalls Bell. 'He started playing air guitar and jumping around the room.'

McGee was excited by the screw-you subtext of putting out an eight-minute single – just as Ride were proud of the implication in the song's title that they were looking down on the indie cortège from on high. 'We were all feeling that there were a lot of mediocre bands that were beginning to jump on the bandwagon,' says Gardener. '"Leave Them All Behind" was a statement of intent. I'd felt good that we had been a bit of a charge on [other bands], but as time went on I felt a bit distressed because a lot of these bands were not very good.' Gardener is too discreet to name names, but it's safe to say he had one or two Creation acts in mind.

Having got off to such a fine start, Ride's album was completed in good time. McGee and Green gave it a March 1992 release date, with 'Leave Them All Behind' as a February taster. Just as recording ended, Andy Bell swallowed hard and asked Dave Newton for a minute in private. 'That was probably the most fearful moment of my life,' Bell remembers. 'To go cap in hand to Dave and say: "I've been thinking ..." I've never felt so alone and so small.'

Bell wanted to know if Ride could depart from convention on the new album and credit the songs to their individual writers. He had five songs on the record and thought it would be fair if his name was in brackets after each one. Newton replied that it was too big an adjustment. Would Bell be satisfied if only the lyrics were credited, rather than the whole composition? Meekly, Bell said yes.

By the autumn of 1991, the number of acts on Creation's roster was approaching 25. Admittedly, Ed Ball was at least four of them – but even so, there were more demands on McGee and Green than at any time in Creation's existence. Most of the artists wished to make records, a few of them required management and almost all of them needed money. 'You just had to try and give them as much contact as you could,' says Green. 'Alan would be on the phone to bands day and night – whoever needed it at the time. And mostly we'd spend money on them regardless. Even when we didn't have it, we would get the money somehow.'

The release of *Screamadelica* in September was not foreseen by either McGee or Green as bringing much succour to the overdraft. Whilst the 65-minute album's status as an epochal masterpiece was never for one instant in doubt at Hackney, Green was sufficiently cautious to order a pressing of only 50,000. The first indication that this might not be enough came with a phone call to McGee from Norman Blake of Teenage Fanclub. He had just been to three parties in Glasgow, and *Screamadelica* had been playing at all of them.

'There was much more demand for that album than we thought,' says McGee. 'We'd run out [of stock] by the Thursday. We had never had a record that had done that kind of business before.' Creation re-pressed for all it was worth. *Screamadelica* hit number 8 on the album chart, and landed with such force in the music press that critics voted it record of the year. So extensive were the hallelujahs, and so exalted Primal Scream's once star-crossed name, that the commercial dead duck of two years before was now reckoned to be bivouacked at the intersection of all contemporary music and art, beating its chest like King Kong.

Actually, *Screamadelica* was not the retail walk-over that the accolades suggested* – but if it wasn't quite battleships to Creation's rescue, nor was it the killing fields of Kevin Shields' Last Stand. As folklore had it, one WEA marketing meeting in 1987 to discuss a Primal Scream release on Elevation had been brought to a standstill by McGee spluttering: 'Listen ... Primal Scream are at the pineapple of their career!' With *Screamadelica* in the Top 10, malapropism became fact. And when the Scream toured in October, they were the must-see show of the season.

'What happened with *Screamadelica* was a lot of the dance people wanted Primal Scream as their rock 'n' roll band,' says Jeff Barrett. 'And at certain gigs they got them. Everybody had bought the album, so you'd get a lot of these dance guys going: "Wow ... genius," and you'd get the indie kids going: "Ah! This is what's possible ..." '

Since going back on the road in July, the Scream had added several cover versions to their repertoire, including John Lennon's 'Cold Turkey', the New York Dolls' 'Personality Crisis' and Sly and the Family Stone's 'Don't Call Me Nigger, Whitey'. This last choice alone – which Bobby Gillespie and Denise Johnson delivered as a call-and-response war cry – showed the scale of the band's ambition. However, what intrigued people just as much were the scenes backstage. Primal Scream were one of the few bands with an 80s indie music background to behave consistently – so whisper had it – in the outrageous, Dionysian traditions of behemoth rock acts of the 60s and 70s. The presence on the tour of Douglas Hart and his video camera invited speculation that the Scream proposed to put together a document that would compare with the Rolling Stones' 1972 pornographic road movie *Cocksucker Blues*.

'The *Screamadelica* tour was an insane tour,' remembers McGee. 'There's footage around ... and it's probably more extreme than *Cocksucker Blues*. Loads of people taking drugs and having sex. Not me personally ... That tour was an insane tour.' Andy Weatherall struck a philosophical tone with Michael Bonner: 'What can I say? Some men didn't come out the other side. I remember certain members of the band disappearing for the whole day, and literally walking onstage as the first chord was due to be played.'

But Hart's footage would – like *Cocksucker Blues* – be denied a public release, for Primal Scream were about to change their attitude to

---

* *Screamadelica* finally earned a platinum disc in 1998 for UK sales of 300,000.

backstage reportage and journalism in general. An article in Q magazine, written around a concert in Glasgow, seemed no more revela-
tory on first glance than the *Melody Maker* interview in which
Gillespie had talked about drugs, Alex Nightingale and the unlikeli-
hood of Martin Duffy reaching 30 – an interview, incidentally, which
Gillespie had enjoyed reading. However, there were a couple of
small but important differences between the *Melody Maker* and Q
articles. The Q journalist was female, which made Gillespie drop his
guard; and in a moment of weakness he told her: 'If you look at our
band and you look at the drug usage involved, it's not just as simple
as ecstasy. It's basically everything you can think of. How could I put
it? A lot of what we do is quite . . . quite . . . quite strung-out and quite
heroin-y.'

The first published mention of heroin in connection with Primal
Scream's personnel, it led to them pulling up a drawbridge. No more
reporters would be ushered into the dressing-room to watch the
drugs being doled out (a ritual that had made for a particularly scenic
passage in the Q feature) and not until the end of the decade would
Gillespie admit publicly that certain members of his band had turned
to heroin in the wake of *Screamadelica*.

'We had all sort of become professional drug takers at that point,'
says McGee. 'It was a good laugh, but that's when it started becoming
more serious. Methadone . . . heroin . . . ecstasy . . . amphetamines . . .
cocaine . . . speedballs . . . crack. I naively thought they were always
coming back alive, but there were a few times they nearly didn't.'

In the late 80s, Mike Mena worked in the alternative music radio
department of A&M in New York. With projects including Iggy Pop,
Robyn Hitchcock and the Feelies, he had built up good relationships
with most – if not all – of the important alternative radio programmers in America. He was also a regular sight at music business con-
ventions, where he had made the acquaintance of Daniel Glass, a
senior promotions man at Chrysalis. One day in 1989, a mutual
friend told Mena he should 'call Daniel about SBK'. Mena replied:
'What's SBK?'

SBK stood for Swid, Koppelman and Bandier, three names rich with
experience in investment, A&R and publishing. SBK was the newest
record label on the block, launched as a multimillion-dollar joint venture with EMI. Daniel Glass had already signed up as senior vice-
president of promotion, and he doubled Mena's salary to bring him
on board as director of alternative radio promotion. 'Daniel is a true
American record promotion person,' says Mena. 'High energy.
Everything is "awesome" and "great". Depending on your perspective,
it either comes across as wonderful and empowering . . . or full of shit.
Personally I think the world of Daniel, and he told me that SBK was
the most exciting company to happen to the record industry in years.'

In 1990, its first full year of trading, SBK enjoyed the sort of prosperity that music executives dream about – chart-topping singles and albums across the globe – with the kind of acts that music lovers have nightmares about: Vanilla Ice, Wilson Phillips and the Teenage Mutant Ninja Turtles. In fact, it was such a bubblegum operation that Mike Mena became frustrated: he was in charge of alternative radio promotion, yet there were no alternative bands to promote. He expressed this concern to Glass, who told him to stop moaning and go and look for some bands himself.

Neither of Mena's first two quarries – Screaming Trees and Nick Cave – made it past the wishful thinking stage. But then Mena chanced upon Jesus Jones. Unknown in the States, they were available to SBK because their UK label Food had an option to release records in America on any EMI-affiliated label. Mena chipped away at SBK's chairman Charles Koppelman, telling him Jesus Jones would be a perfect way to broaden the company's musical horizons and get the alternative kids interested. 'Quite frankly, I think he said yes to shut me up,' Mena recalls.

In October 1990, Jesus Jones had a setback in the UK. After a Top 20 placing earlier in the year for their fourth single 'Real Real Real', their infectious fifth, 'Right Here, Right Now', fell just outside the Top 30. This did not worry SBK unduly, as it was planning to wait for the band's second album, *Doubt*, to come out in February 1991 before giving 'Right Here, Right Now' an American release in the spring. However, on 19 January, these plans were thrown into confusion when Jesus Jones performed at Wembley Arena with Ride and the Cure. A party of US radio programmers flown over by Elektra (the Cure's record label in America) went wild on the spot for 'Right Here, Right Now', raced out to buy copies in London and started playing them on the air back home. A baffled Mike Mena phoned the stations, thanking them for their support but asking if they could hold off until the single was actually on sale.

'They said: "Fine, we'll take it off",' he recalls. 'Then about a week later, I got a phone call from a major programmer at Live 105 in San Francisco. He said: "Mike, I took it off and I started getting complaints from listeners saying how come you're not playing that song any more? So I'm putting it back on the radio and you guys better hurry up and put it out." It was literally an unstoppable hit.'

As SBK brought the release date forward, 'Right Here, Right Now' was adopted as an anthem by American forces fighting the Gulf War, and picked up free advertising every night as background music on news reports from Kuwait. At last it peaked at number 2 on the Billboard charts in July, and was followed by a Top 5 smash for 'Real Real Real' and a platinum disc for *Doubt*. Suddenly, Charles Koppelman was interested in everything Mike Mena had to say.

Mena persuaded Koppelman to take up the option on a second

Food act, Blur. Koppelman assented. But Blur would not be as easy a ride for SBK as Jesus Jones, because for one thing, although they shared a UK label, the two bands were chalk and cheese as personalities. Jesus Jones' leader Mike Edwards was the last word in good manners and English formality. Blur, by contrast, were disobedient, arrogant and almost never sober. Their four years on SBK were to be disastrous. 'When they signed Blur,' recalls Jim Merlis, SBK's alternative music publicist in the early 90s, 'the guys went into Charles Koppelman's office and he said: "We've spent a lot of money for you guys – *so don't fuck up*." That started the bad vibes between that band and the record label. It was a terrible, terrible relationship and it happened literally day one.'

Jim Merlis was on $8 an hour, had hair down to his shoulders, played in a grunge band and stuck out at SBK like a sore thumb. He describes the company as 'incredibly corporate. There was a cult of personality around Charles Koppelman. Everyone dressed like Charles did: red [braces] and really expensive suits'. Mike Mena remembers Koppelman having 'gleaming cuff-links, big Cuban cigars, a huge office, a real air of authority . . . very much the epitome of the American record executive'.

Koppelman set great store by his pop-trained ears – Vanilla Ice had been his own pet project – but was not so sure-footed when it came to alternative rock. 'Charles was very song-driven,' says Mena. 'To him, the song was more important than the artist. It's a philosophy that he and I clashed on fairly frequently. The philosophy of SBK was to take a hit and wring it out for all it was worth. Some of the things they did really accelerated the overkill process to the point where people got sick of the acts.' Or, in the case of Blur, the act got sick of the label. Says Jim Merlis: 'The thing about SBK was they never got to know the bands. They would always make these flip statements like: "Well, we did it with Jesus Jones so we can do it with you." '

Certain that Jesus Jones' success could be repeated at will, SBK spent a lot of money targeting Top 40 radio willy-nilly, pointlessly advertising its alternative acts in tip-sheets at $40,000 a time. Mike Mena knew this was no way to create a buzz. An Anglophile, he had an empathy with UK indie music – he had been in the A&R race for Ride in 1990 – and he knew that T-shirts, teaser ads and, of course, alternative radio were the far better route to take. And losing Ride to Joe McEwen had in no way diminished Mena's immense admiration for the label he considered the UK's best: Creation.

To Alan McGee, SBK meant Vanilla Ice and four ridiculous toy turtles. There were few labels straighter or more dreadful, he believed. That said, McGee was simply desperate to do another profitable deal with an American company. He contracted an attorney, Bob Flax of Grubman Indursky Schindler, to notify the leading US labels that

Creation was willing to do business. One of the people Flax called was Charles Koppelman. 'Charles said: "Mike – Creation Records. Does that mean anything to you?"' recalls Mena. 'I said: "Yes! We *have* to get this deal." I pursued it as aggressively as I've ever pursued anything.'

McGee had already met Mena – at EMI Music in London – and found him easier to like and less gushing than the usual American music promo men. Not that Mena was incapable of gushing: he was such a fan of Creation that he had gone to EMI Music that day specifically because he knew McGee would be there. 'There were other labels keen on doing [the deal with Creation],' Mena says. 'Columbia Records was quite keen on doing it, and a few others were in the running. But I remember Alan was quoted as saying: "Other labels were chasing us, but Mike Mena was relentless"'

McGee flew to New York to meet Koppelman. But when he stepped into the SBK building, his heart sank. 'You walk into Barclay's Bank and you see some vaguely groovy people. You walked into SBK and everybody was in suits and ties. I thought I was going into a financial institution.' His next stop was Koppelman's office, where his heart sank even lower. 'I love all the old-school characters – always will do. But you walk into his office and the guy has got a fucking oval table about 60 foot long. You walk in the door and you're at one end of the table. It's really awkward – it's like a total power play. And he sits and smokes eight-inch cigars. It was an unbelievable place.'

McGee faxed the contract back to Dick Green, who remembers everything being done 'in very rapid fashion'. Sealed in November 1991, the three-year deal gave SBK first option on North American rights to any Creation bands not already placed with other labels. SBK agreed to take a minimum of three acts per year (starting with Slowdive), paying Creation $300,000 for each album released. McGee and Green would have expected to make $900,000 in at least two of those three years, and probably a few million in all. But as Mike Mena says, hindsight is a wonderful thing.

My Bloody Valentine's *Loveless* was – like one or two of the invoices Creation had received during its protracted gestation – outstanding. Days after being rapturously reviewed in the press, it appeared in the shops on 11 November. 'It was just such a beautiful record,' says James Kyllo, 'and it was wonderful to have it. But it didn't sound like a record that was going to recoup all the money that had been spent on it.'

Reactions in Hackney varied. McGee listened to the album, liked it and put it to one side. Laurence Verfaillie played it on a loop in her office. Dick Green did not play it in his. 'Strange times,' he says. 'To have achieved it. And to know that you couldn't really carry on.'

Admired and respected by industry luminaries from Rob Dickins to Seymour Stein for their perseverance and personal commitment to a project that had almost crippled them, McGee and Green had poignantly decided to let My Bloody Valentine go. And James Kyllo agreed with them. 'It was quite clear that we couldn't bear the idea of going through that again,' he says, 'because there was just nothing to say that [Shields] wouldn't do exactly the same thing again. It was a wonderful album. That's enough. Let's step back.'

Promoting *Loveless* in an interview with the *NME*, Shields, who was unaware that the decision to offload the band had been taken, made it clear he was in no mood to be painted as Creation's loose cannon. In a comment that hurt McGee and Green badly, he said: 'We know more about how the record industry works than our record company half the time. We do. I'm not joking.' He also claimed that My Bloody Valentine had spent 'ten times less than other bands. A chunk here, a chunk there ... We spent ages doing things that never worked, and that's where the stupid money went'.

Shields returned to this theme in a 1994 interview. 'I don't think people realise just how much juggling of figures went on,' he said. 'I don't think people fully appreciate just how much money went through the label and how much was made back ... There used to be all this talk in the press about us spending £250,000 making *Loveless* ... We spent a lot of money, maybe £140,000. What is it to be beyond your means? Maybe it's good to stretch yourself, to put yourself in a situation where you're just about to go under but actually achieving what you want to achieve. The general atmosphere at Creation was that money was there to be used.' (That same year, McGee conceded that Creation's financial control in 1990–1 had been 'fucking shocking'.)

Mark Dennis was Creation's internal label manager in 1991, responsible for marketing, coordination and product manufacturing. 'Later on, a lot of real figures started to appear with regard to *Loveless* and whether it actually did cost a quarter of a million,' he says. 'I think there was an element of the industry – the press – which liked to *think* that it did. I know it cost a lot of money. It is possible. But our accounting was not the best in the world, that's for sure.'

My Bloody Valentine toured *Loveless* around Britain in December, for which Creation stumped up some financial support. The band had not made *Loveless* easy to sell: there would be no singles taken from it and one had to squint hard to spot the band's name on the cerise, out-of-focus sleeve. Meanwhile, McGee was anxious to get rid of the Shieldses before they ran up any more tour expenses in Europe. 'I wanted Kevin out of my hair and I wanted Ann Marie out of my hair,' he says. 'I thought: I went to the wall for you. If this record bombs, I've stolen my father's money. And they were so ... not understanding of anybody else's position. They were so selfish at that point that I just went: "That's the end of the relationship." '

When Ann Marie phoned to ask him if he would be attending any of the British dates, McGee hung up on her.

My Bloody Valentine's tour of December 1991 was and remains a unique chapter in live music. Best remembered as an exercise in punishing volume, it is also famous for what has become known as the 'holocaust' – an extended section during 'You Made Me Realise' in which the sound first plunged like an elevator with a snapped cable, then maintained the same violently rumbling chord for nine or ten minutes on end. It was My Bloody Valentine's favourite part of the show, often sending them into a trance.

The *NME*'s Danny Kelly saw the third gig on the tour – at the Corn Exchange in Cambridge – and knew at once that it was not going to be a normal concert. 'I was up in the balcony and I had a half pint of lager – a pint glass, half full,' he says. 'They hit their first note and it was so loud that it sent the glass hurtling. The beer didn't shake – the glass flew off.' To play the upper register melodies from *Loveless* that had been obtained on a sampler, the Valentines were using a young American flautist, Anna Quimby. Walking out on to the stage, she seemed deceptively unthreatening. 'She looked just like the girls in the Living Room five or six years before,' recalls Kelly. 'She had a little skirt on, black tights ... She was a little indie girl. But when she blew into the flute, it was like fucking Woodstock.' Describing the show in his *NME* review as 'more like torture than entertainment', Kelly revealed that he had been unable to sleep on returning to London that night, 'such is the pain in my chest from the pounding it's taken'. Most of that pounding was taken during the holocaust.

The experience of hearing and watching the holocaust was laid out in detail by the US critic Mark Kemp in *Options* magazine when My Bloody Valentine took the show to America the following year. Kemp wrote: 'After about thirty seconds, the adrenalin sets in; people are screaming and shaking their fists. After a minute, you wonder what's going on. Strobe lights are going mad and you begin to feel the throb in your chest. After another minute, it's total confusion. People's faces take on a look of bewilderment. The noise starts hurting. The strobes start hurting. The noise continues. After three minutes, you begin to take deep breaths. Some people in the audience stoop down into the crowd and cover their ears and eyes. Anger takes over. A few people leave the room. After about four minutes, a calm takes over. The noise continues. After five minutes, a feeling of utter peace takes over ...'

Shields and Butcher would stare at faces in the front rows, monitoring the gradual changes. Shields was amused by the idea that the audience was afraid the ceiling was about to collapse. Danny Kelly observed that Shields' right hand appeared to make the male masturbatory gesture as it stroked the holocaustal chord. And as a point of interest, when the concert was over Shields did not say good night. He said 'goodbye'.

Part Four

The Prize

17 Forty-Nine Per Cent Of An Insolvent Rock 'N' Roll Label

TEENAGE FANCLUB'S EBULLIENT LIVE SHOW, terrific singles and beer monster reputation had won them the backing of the music papers in Britain, and they were being put forward as a major band of the 90s. Their second Creation album, *Bandwagonesque*, had been released in November 1991 and excelled in two regards. In the first place, it was an appealing set of songs examining romance and friendship with dry humour, making listeners glad that they had listened. In the second place, it was a musical tribute to some of the Fanclub's favourite artists, chiefly the early 70s Memphis band Big Star.

Big Star and their singer-guitarist Alex Chilton had become the key names to drop among Creation-ites. McGee positively worshipped Big Star, and Primal Scream spoke highly of their disconsolate third album, alternately known as *Third* and *Sister Lovers*. Teenage Fanclub preferred the warmer timbres of the first two, *No. 1 Record* and *Radio City*, and got deucedly close to reproducing them in some songs on *Bandwagonesque*. Most critics, and even Alex Chilton himself, took the homage in the spirit in which it was intended. A few, however, accused the Fanclub of musical tailgating. 'We did an interview for "God Knows It's True" and the guy was asking us what kind of music we were listening to,' recalls bassist Gerry Love, 'and we said Big Star. He didn't know who they were. We said: "You know, Alex Chilton." Still blank. Then he reviews *Bandwagonesque* and says we're just ripping off Big Star.'

Teenage Fanclub came to personify Creation's musical programme in the years following the acid house revolution. McGee had stopped going to clubs, complaining that the quality of ecstasy had deteriorated, and liked to host late-night listening sessions and cocaine parties at home. He would spin records by Big Star, Neil Young, the Faces and Tom Petty, pathologically stopping them after 90 seconds and substituting another, even better disc. If a song seemed too good to confine to his apartment's four walls, he might call up a Creation friend and play it down the phone. Andy Bell recalls: 'A typical thing would be you would arrive home and press the answerphone, and it would be Alan ranting about some track. "Wait, I'll play it!" Hear the needle going on, then this deafening racket coming out.'

Creation had emerged from its brush with house culture carrying blazing torches for American rock, soul and R&B. In tandem with his extroverted marketing consultant and cocaine partner Tim Abbot, McGee was consciously restyling Creation as a label of unimpeachable scholarship and panache. Abbot had sold Northern Soul records at the age of 14 in the early 70s, working for a chain of record shops. Knowledgeable about rock, punk, soul and street culture – Richard Allen's *Suedehead*, football terrace fashion, clubland – he was a self-styled 'educated hooligan' from Walsall in the West Midlands who had met McGee by chance in Birmingham, where he ran a house club called the Better Way.

'My younger brother Chris worked for Jeff Barrett,' says Abbot, 'and Jeff and Alan had come up to Birmingham to see the Manic Street Preachers supporting Saint Etienne at Burberrys in 1990. After the gig I invited everybody back to my house in Sutton Coldfield. The party's in full swing, it's two o'clock in the morning and there's a knock on the door. It's Alan McGee and Bobby Gillespie ... I'd got this long wall with maybe a couple of thousand vinyl [albums]. I kept clocking Alan and Bob going through the vinyl all night. Bob goes: "Great records." Alan came over to me and said: "Unbelievable, man. I've never seen somebody have Miles Davis and Patti Smith next to each other. What do you do?" '

Abbot had studied marketing at college and had worked as a rep for Pernod Ricard for four years, around the country and in Europe. McGee, who was semi-based in Birmingham with Belinda White at the time, asked Abbot if he could stay in touch. Of course, said Abbot: why don't you and your girlfriend come to the Better Way one night?

'There was a fuck-up with the guest-list and I was told there was some bloke at the door with red hair, foamed off his nut,' recalls Abbot. 'He had steam on the inside of his glasses and this beautiful, incongruous-looking bird with him. I took him into the back room and he was totally triple-fried-bananas. People are going: "Who the fuck's that? Is he Drugs Squad?" I'm going: "No, look, he's really cool." But anybody that's coming up and being introduced to him, he's going: "Do you want an E?" And you know the daft karma of clubland – everybody wants some gear but it's like: "Hold it down, hold it *down* ..." He was making people paranoid.'

* * *

During McGee's time in Birmingham, he and Abbot went out for dinner, partied at the Better Way and at Venus in Nottingham, and became friends. 'In '86–87, I'd been doing quite heavy HRD – human resource development – for a consultancy down in Bristol, sitting in boardrooms presenting employee improvement suggestion schemes,' says Abbot. 'But when I met Alan, I was living this double life. I was hitting 30, coming through the parallax of ecstasy and the hump of ecstasy ... We got deeper and deeper into what's-it-all-about, aspirations, daft drug talk, and McGee said: "Well, look. If you're a management consultant, come down and see us." I put on a pair of grey slacks, a double-breasted blazer, shirt and tie, briefcase, and went down in a totally straight capacity to look at Alan's company.'

Abbot undertook an internal audit of Creation, going through the books, analysing strengths and weaknesses, and suggesting some strategic planning. 'Nobody signed in – it was all flexitime,' he says. 'The office was a rabbit warren. Dick had this massive old Amstrad printer which rattled all day. They had over £250,000 of artwork going through three different graphics companies. [Courier] bikes alone came to something like £12–15,000. I said: "OK, here's a concept: desk-top publishing." '

As Creation invested £15,000 in a computer system and recruited an in-house art director, Abbot moved down to London, living in a large house in Wandsworth owned by his friend Andy Taylor, the former guitarist in Duran Duran. Prepared to make himself unpopular with the Creation troops, Abbot concentrated on telling McGee what he thought he wanted to hear. My Bloody Valentine are causing you grief? Get shot of them. The Creation employees are your trusted friends? Then they should be there on time every morning. 'Everybody deemed me as a threat,' says Abbot. 'I came from an alien world. But there's a thing in management, which is you don't have to be loved by everybody.' By the beginning of 1992, Tim Abbot was McGee's marketing manager, afterhours companion and foot lieutenant.

He was also his confidant – more so than Dick Green. All of McGee's reservations about the Creation workforce, Green included, were divulged to Abbot. And there were plenty of reservations. 'Alan bred an incredible loyalty,' says Abbot. 'To quote Alan, we were all misfit geniuses. We didn't fit in in normal business, so we chose to live our lives as we did. But a lot of that loyalty was about making people believe that they were working solely because of him – and wouldn't get a job anywhere else.' But while Abbot brought marketing know-how, he was more rock 'n' roll than those at Creation he professed to outrank. His two golden rules were never to drink alcohol during the day, and not to take drugs while he was working. However, some days Abbot finished work at two in the afternoon.

Creation had never costed its marketing budgets upfront. When a single or album was ready to be released, McGee would announce that he wanted advertisements in the music papers and street posters, but the details would come off the top of his head. For all his vast vinyl collection, Abbot viewed records rather more pragmatically than McGee – as fast-moving consumer goods jostling for position in the market – and he saw little point in throwing money around for the sake of it. He also took a salesman's overview of what Creation had to offer. 'One of the first things I did was present the records to Pinnacle's sales force every month,' he says. 'We used to have these jokey-jokey Creation presentations. Sometimes me and Alan would have been up all night and they would *roar* when we came in off our nuts. But Alan didn't want to do it. He hated the music business, he hated all the trade establishments; he thought they were all ganging up on him. I've gone: "Alan, it's a win-win if we get these people on our side." He's gone: "You do it." He wanted to keep his allure and his mystique.'

Abbot did not buy into the cult of Alex Chilton and Big Star – and he had once silenced a room by extolling the virtues of Led Zeppelin – but where he and McGee concurred was in their love of the swaggering overstatement and enduring aesthetic magnetism of the sporting and cultural celebrities of the 1970s. The five-foot-eight-inch Abbot liked to describe himself as 'small in stature, big in reputation', while McGee was being hardened by cocaine into a character not so much gregarious as aggressively unceremonious.

'Belinda was smartening him up,' says Abbot. 'He started to dress of-the-time. He was changed during that period into "lad", or his definition of "lad". There was a definite move away from the old indie-core of shoe-gazing into what became the Primal Scream movement and that excess vibe. The Scream loved Axl Rose. They loved the lifestyle of Guns N' Roses. And of course, post-ecstasy, the excess vibe was the thing.'

Andy Saunders joined Creation in 1992 as assistant press officer to Laurence Verfaillie. He recalls: 'Tim, Alan and Dick all worked in a downstairs room that was known as the "bunker". It was a windowless cellar plastered with various things that Alan and Tim had cut out of newspapers and magazines: models, icons, George Best, boxers. Classic rock 'n' roll iconography all over the walls. Various scrawled obscenities. The bunker was very much like stepping into some kind of subterranean club.' Verfaillie, who did not much like

Abbot and hated cocaine, remarks nevertheless: 'All of us at Creation – the people who were going out in public – were epitomising the Creation attitude. We had a reputation of being party animals. I think we were probably very arrogant.'

For those who were quieter, such as Dick Green and James Kyllo, the brashness and uncouthness of Creation under Tim Abbot's influence were changes they would never be comfortable with. Even Verfaillie, who was powerful within Hackney, drew the line at sexism: some of the pin-ups on the walls of the bunker made her queasy. If Dick Green had an opinion, he was keeping it to himself. 'Dick dealt with a massive part of that company that I never knew about,' says Abbot. 'We used to go for a drink after work and I would say to him some nights: "Fucking hell, Alan's beaten you up, dude." We'd get pissed – Dick could drink like a tin leg – but he was very tightly wrapped. He had his rucksack which he used to come in with, take off and take back home again, and the world was in that rucksack.'

With Green at the far end of the room with his noisy Amstrad, the agenda in the bunker was dictated by the cocaine-snorting and icon-fixated McGee and Abbot. (Andy Saunders remembers Green taking him for a drink at the end of his first day in the office. Unaware that Green had any status at the label, Saunders asked him who he was and what he did. 'I'm Dick Green,' came the reply. 'I co-own the company you're working for.') One Creation artist witnessed a perfect tableau of bunker life in the early 90s: Abbot on the phone, boasting about some bill that Creation had yet to settle, while Green frantically signalled to him to shut up.

'We were always skint, always overdrawn, always financially mismanaged,' says Abbot, 'and we all knew about it. That was the great thing about it. We were the three merry fools in the bunker. It was like "writs for the day", or the bailiff-o-gram. There was lots of heading [the ball] off the line all the time.' The soccer analogy was apt for a company that McGee and Abbot increasingly saw as the music industry's equivalent of George Best: dangerous, sexy, a law unto itself.

In the same month that Teenage Fanclub's *Bandwagonesque* was released, Primal Scream headed out to Ardent Studios in Memphis, where Big Star had worked in the 70s, to record tracks for an EP. But whereas Teenage Fanclub used the brightest colours in the Alex Chilton paintbox, Primal Scream were after something darker. While the press in Britain continued to hail *Screamadelica* as an exultant album, the Scream were searching for a sadder, more soulful and devout music of the American south. Bobby Gillespie had done his homework; and what he didn't already know he learned from his friend Tim Tooher.

Tooher was a willowy ghost of a man who worked at Creation as an A&R assistant. A fount of musical minutiae, he was the company's nearest thing to Paul Gambaccini – with a fighting weight closer to that of an anorexic. 'Tim was a kid who would go in a record shop and read the backs of the records,' says Tim Abbot. 'He could quote the engineer off a 70s session by anybody. He was into the depth of the Alex Chilton Memphis plot, and the Muscle Shoals/Stax vibe ... Timmy Tooher was instrumental in the whole Creation-Primal Scream American vibe.'

Tooher was part of the Primal Scream entourage that flew to Memphis on 19 November 1991. In Ardent Studios, the Scream returned to the rock 'n' roll balladry that had been one of the many dimensions of *Screamadelica*. They used Willie Nelson's pedal steel player on two songs, and were introduced to Jim Dickinson, a producer-musician who had worked with Big Star and contributed piano to the Rolling Stones' 'Wild Horses'. Primal Scream's own pianist Martin Duffy wrote in a diary published by the *NME*: 'Blues, country, gospel and soul, we must have bought and heard a thousand of them between us in two weeks over here – 75 per cent of these songs were down to women, the other 25 per cent are left to Jesus ... The day we went to Graceland, the home of Elvis, it rained from morning to night. We all knew what that meant – it was the King crying.'

Bobby Gillespie later told Michael Bonner that the Memphis trip had been 'an adventure. I think music should be an adventure. I think that's why you get involved in it: to get out of your environment, to get out in the world and have adventures. Just experiment, see what happens. That's what Primal Scream's always been about ... We all lived together in this wooden house beside Ardent Studios. Sun Records was just up the road.' And Shoom and Spectrum were a million miles in the other direction.

With Teenage Fanclub and an Americanised Primal Scream as its star turns, Creation was potentially a bigger player internationally than ever before. *Bandwagonesque*, a record dipped in British irony and sung by Scots in emulation of Americans influenced by English pop singles of the 60s, was absorptive on a broad scale, leading some to theorise that Creation's consensus on classic rock – even if McGee denied there was any such consensus – would do a lot more good for its American profile and interests than the mild-mannered, Anglo-jargonistic Ride ever had. McGee had been as puzzled as anyone when the Stone Roses failed to take off in the States. Now he was optimistic that Creation could have a real effect there.

By early 1992, Creation had released more than 100 albums and 100 singles. End-of-year plaudits for the autumn triptych of *Screamadelica*, *Loveless* and *Bandwagonesque* had reinforced the view that the label was hitting sensational form, but in fact, as McGee freely admitted, it could have gone bankrupt on any one of 1991's

365 days. '*Screamadelica* and *Bandwagonesque* made a big difference,' says James Kyllo. 'We started to sell some records internationally and we were able to get bigger advances based on the fact that we were having hits in the UK. Our turnover was growing and growing – almost doubling year on year – and that kept us able to keep trading all the time, even though the economic base of it was still profit-share deals.'

The profit-share deals had not been probed by Tim Abbot's Creation audit, but they had been a concern of Kyllo's for some time. As much as they made Creation seem inviting to an artist such as Nick Currie, who was able to live well on proceeds from relatively low-selling albums, they were detrimental in the long run to the label, which had recording costs and overheads to consider and could ill afford to keep giving high profit percentages to the bands. What had seemed like splendid socialism in 1984 had become unworkable practice by 1992. 'In general our contracts were 50:50 in the UK, 70:30 in the band's favour [outside the] UK,' says Kyllo. 'That in itself is enough reason for the label to be financially insecure even without recording My Bloody Valentine albums.'

McGee had woken up to this fact himself, and knew he would have to start signing bands to a more standard royalty deal that gave Creation a realistic portion – roughly two-thirds – of the profit. Attending the first significant A&R event of 1992, an *NME*-promoted January showcase of unsigned bands at the Venue in south London, McGee alighted on the young group that would inaugurate the new royalty-based Creation culture. While other A&R men at the Venue were getting worked up about Suede, a four-piece whose demo tape had sat unheard on a desk at Creation for two months, McGee dismissed them as tiresome show-offs and instead made a surprise offer for the lowest band on the bill.

From Coventry, where they had met as university students, Adorable were a second-wave shoe-gazing band with a twist. In place of the usual mouselike front-line of mop-top haircuts, they had an unmistakable focal point in singer Piotr Fijalkowski. Surrey-born of Polish parents, Fijalkowski was an Ian McCulloch fan who aspired to whip up a storm with a rent-a-quote big mouth offstage and a mike-stand-fondling self-conceit on it. Adorable had not taken their name in jest.

'We had been around for about a year,' Fijalkowski remembers. 'Every gig we'd played was to 30 or 40 people at most. We realised that if we didn't get a deal at [the Venue] gig, then that was probably it. So we all just went a bit mad onstage. In some ways it was almost like the first real Adorable gig.' The following day, McGee phoned their manager, Eddie Connelly, the former bassist in Meat Whiplash. Using his links with SBK as part of his pitch to persuade them to choose Creation ahead of two other interested labels, McGee signed

Adorable for £60,000, and began to talk up Fijalkowski as a future superstar.

When SBK's first-look deal with Creation had been reported in November, it had been Mike Mena's intention to release Slowdive's album *Just For A Day* in January. In love with the band, whom he saw as a modern-day Pink Floyd, Mena got the ball rolling by stencilling Slowdive's name on pavements outside MTV and various radio stations – and even on the shaved heads of members of the audience at the band's New York debut. If this made McGee laugh incredulously, it left SBK publicist Jim Merlis squirming: Mena had pinched the idea from Merlis' band Honus Wagner, who had stencilled their name on every block throughout the Lower East Side. 'We were a New York band, so it made sense,' says Merlis. 'Slowdive didn't make any sense at all. They were a fey English band that New York had never heard of.'

Merlis had done well to get Slowdive a story in the *New York Times*, which would coincide – so he thought – with SBK's release of *Just For A Day*. 'I showed it to a guy in the marketing department,' Merlis recalls, 'and he said: "Oh ... we pushed the record back three months. Can you push the story back?" I was like: "No! It's out. And why didn't you *tell* me this?" ' With the publicity campaign out of sync with the release date, *Just For A Day* sold only 35,000 copies in America. SBK chairman Charles Koppelman rejected the next three Creation bands that Mike Mena brought him.

'Pretty much everything Alan gave me I thought was high quality,' says Mena. 'After a series of "no"s from Charles, I went to see Alan at the Chelsea Hotel in New York City, and he took out a cassette and said: "Mike, it seems like they're saying 'no' an awful lot." I said: "I know, it's frustrating." He goes: "Well, I have something here – and he *has* to say 'yes' to this one." He played it to me and I said: "Oh my God." I listened to it over and over again.'

The song was 'Sunshine Smile', the first single by Adorable, which Creation was going to release in April. Mena did indeed get Koppelman's approval on the band and started spreading the news that Fijalkowski was a genius. What Mena had no way of knowing was that, over the ocean in Hackney, the feelings about Fijalkowski and Adorable were almost all negative. The £60,000 advance represented a serious commitment on Creation's part, so Fijalkowski's big-mouth interviews would have to be backed up by decent sales. However, many people wondered if they were quite the important band McGee imagined. The group he had passed over at the Venue – Suede – was roaring ahead in the press, and ended April on the cover of *Melody Maker* before even releasing a record.

For Fijalkowski, the onward and upward movement of Suede was doubly unfortunate. It was he who had tipped off the *Melody Maker* that they were a band worth investigating. He should have kept his mouth shut.

In February 1992, Paul Russell was walking through the departure lounge at Heathrow airport when he spotted a familar red-haired figure. Russell, the chairman of Sony Music, walked over to Alan McGee and said hello. 'He was looking really miserable,' Russell recalls. 'I mean really miserable. I chatted to him and he started to pour his heart out about how he felt that Creation's releases hadn't been worked properly internationally. He was in his chops. He was really upset about it.'

A more topical reason for McGee's displeasure was the week's UK chart entry positions for Primal Scream's Memphis EP *Dixie-Narco* and Teenage Fanclub's single 'What You Do To Me'. Both were lower than McGee had anticipated; *Dixie-Narco*, he had told people, would be Creation's first Top 10 hit. Instead, it had gone in at 12. McGee was blaming the Pinnacle sales force.

Russell was interested to hear all of this: McGee was a man who had his respect. 'I said: "Well, we should talk about this some more. Maybe you want to think about coming over to us?",' Russell remembers. As they separated to board their flights, McGee said he'd phone him when he got back. But it would be three months before he made the call.

McGee had been fielding inquiries from UK major labels since 1990, but had refused to consider doing a deal. His intractability was now qualified by his belief that Creation was not producing remotely adequate sales abroad. Outside the UK, Creation worked with a patchwork of third-party licensees, taking pot luck with foreign release schedules and press departments. 'The bands were suffering,' Dick Green later explained, 'because we couldn't harmonise release dates and straightforward exercises such as promotional tours.' McGee complained in 1994: 'Overseas licensees could deal with Depeche Mode, but nobody worked our product effectively.' That same year he fumed: 'I got fed up with selling 200,000 Primal Scream records in England and 18,000 in Germany. I got tired of selling only 3,000 *Bandwagonesque* there. It's all about distribution. If you're signed to some shit fucking indie, no matter what it does for your credibility, it does nothing to promote your group.'

Creation had been talking with Beggars Banquet and Mute about forging an international alliance that would see the three labels work together on European licensing. 'The idea was that the three of us would be such a strong front that we could get better advances and survive,' says James Kyllo. 'Mute were very strong with Depeche Mode and Erasure at that time, and Beggars had a very big catalogue. We would have been the smallest label of the three.' The alliance did not materialise, but in the meantime Creation succeeded in getting a higher-than-usual royalty rate from Intercord, Mute's licensee in Germany.

The economic climate had worsened greatly since the cloudless days of August 1988 when McGee had talked to Paul Russell about the House Of Love. With the music industry declining in the face of the worst recession in a decade, sales of singles had fallen to their lowest figure since 1972, and vulnerable record labels were disintegrating or being engulfed. The eight-year-old Siren had folded in November 1991, the same month that EMI paid £16.9 million to complete its takeover of Chrysalis – a drop of £30 million on what it had spent to acquire 50 per cent of the same label two years earlier. 'Chrysalis now has a knockdown fucking steamrolling company behind it,' EMI president Jim Fifield said. 'That is the future of the company.' The first thing the steamroller did was lay off 20 Chrysalis staff. And when EMI bought Richard Branson's Virgin Music Group for £560 million in March 1992, the last of the pre-punk indies disappeared into the corporate maw. Three months later, EMI merged the Virgin and Circa labels and 80 workers were steamrollered out of a job.

Of the post-punk indies, Factory was in crisis due to thriftless outlay on new albums by the Happy Mondays and New Order, and would soon have to sell a stake to London Records to stay alive. Rhythm King, hit hard by the recession, halved its staff and pared its roster from 60 acts to 14 in the space of six months. 'The general slump in record sales has hit the indies hardest of all,' wrote one commentator, 'because they have neither the back catalogue box sets nor the straightforward advertising [and] promotion muscle of the majors to fall back on.' In addition, the stringent stocking policies of Our Price and other retail outlets were handcuffing the indies, making them less able to operate on their normal ten-misses-for-every-hit ratio.

McGee's answer was to launch three new labels, seemingly in defiance of Creation's financial unsoundness. To Tim Abbot, McGee's reasoning fell somewhere between a stroke of genius and the showmanship of a lunatic. 'Considering that Alan had no business training – he didn't take the *FT* or anything – he was a raw entrepreneur,' says Abbot. 'The idea was that we would go into niche markets. I'd looked at a lot of figures for the smaller acts like Swervedriver and said: "Look, we've got to make decisions based on what we're actually selling. You add it up and Swervedriver sell 12,000 albums. Our problem is we spend about £4.50 in marketing costs per album, instead of £1 or £1.50. If you put a video in there, that's £30,000. Poster campaign: £2,000 – £1 to stick them up, £1 to print the fuckers – and before you know it, it's 35 grand." The overhead was going up, but Alan was never-say-die. Backed into a corner – and this is part of his greatness – he was like: "Fuck them.

Instead of consolidating, slashing down and dropping, I'm going to be even more aggressive." '

Joe Foster was brought back to front a reissues label, Rev-Ola. Chris Abbot, Tim's younger brother, was given his own techno imprint, Infonet. Finally, Dave Barker was headhunted from Fire to run a guitar label called August. A 38-year-old from Essex with a cigarette permanently wedged in his fingers, Barker was a minor hero of McGee's and had signed three acts – the Jazz Butcher and Nikki Sudden to Glass, and Teenage Fanclub to Paperhouse – which had later transferred to Creation. But McGee believed that Barker's greatest signings were still to come. 'Alan's quote was: "Dave Barker, man, he's always missed the big one", says Abbot. 'It was like: Dave Barker, come on down. Come and miss the next big one.'

By McGee's and Abbot's calculatations, August, Infonet and Rev-Ola could sell in the low thousands on small marketing budgets and still make their existence worthwhile. While Chris Abbot and Joe Foster were put on retainers, Dave Barker went on the payroll: the press department was instructed not to treat him lightly. 'It was explained to me that Dave was a genius', says Andy Saunders, 'and that Alan always wanted to work with genius, and respected and bounced off genius, and that if you have a genius in the office it breeds genius. Alan sold it in very hard as Dave being this mad professor that would magic up great bands – because essentially his taste was the same as Alan's. And that's Alan's definition of a genius a lot of the time.'

Barker will not easily forget the day he arrived at the Creation office. 'I'll tell you the first thing McGee said. I walked in and he said: "Dave Barker . . . I'm going to make you a fucking millionaire." ' The first month Barker started, the wages were late.

In the same February week that Andy Bell and Idha Ovelius married quietly in Oxford, 'Leave Them All Behind' by Ride charted at number 9 as Primal Scream's *Dixie-Narco* climbed from 12 to 11. Ahead of 'Leave Them All Behind' were eight dance, soul and MOR singles, all of which had had their sales boosted by regular radio-play. Having been furious at missing the Top 10 with *Dixie-Narco* a week before, McGee was now triumphant – for nestled between Ride and the Scream at number 10 was 'Reverence' by the Jesus and Mary Chain, completing a cluster of Alan McGee discoveries and projects.

'When Ride and the Mary Chain were in the Top 10, it felt like a victory', says Alan Moulder, the engineer on both singles. 'The great thing about that time was you were hoping [the records you made] would turn up on daytime radio and you knew they didn't belong there. That's why McGee felt so fantastic. We had the same opinion of getting one over, if you like – getting something on there that didn't belong. Kind of childish, but fun.'

To Tim Abbot, there was nothing childish about it: getting on to the radio and into the Top 40 were supremely important objectives. With this in mind, Creation had started using a new plugger, Garry Blackburn, who had scored good results with the Beautiful South and Beats International. 'The producers were becoming more and more sophisticated at Radio 1,' says Abbot. 'The dance thing had gone out. People were looking for an alternative ... Because I was sales and marketing-orientated, for me the metaphor was we were a stable, with a trainer, a horse, a saddle-man, there'd be forms – and each week there was a race. And you'd got to finish in the 40.'

McGee's taste in music was no longer debatably popular, but indisputably so. Exactly eight years after releasing debut singles by Revolving Paint Dream and Biff Bang Pow!, Creation was in the first division. For three days, 'Leave Them All Behind' had even had a higher midweek than the new single by Michael Jackson.

With their *Going Blank Again* album due in March, Ride and manager Dave Newton geared themselves for a ticker-tape reception. According to Abbot, *Going Blank Again* was expected to sell '100,000 and the rest – it was a watershed album'. Mike Smith, who had succeeded Steve Walters as Ride's publisher at EMI Music, remarks: 'Dave Newton perceived the band as being ready to make a crossover on a level with the Cure. He felt that by the autumn of 1992 Ride would be playing Wembley Arena.'

The confidence of Newton, Abbot and McGee rubbed off on Creation's label manager Mark Dennis, who pressed up *Going Blank Again* on the assumption that it would be a high seller for about six weeks. 'Part of the problem,' says James Kyllo, 'was that Alan was a pretty frightening proposition in those days, particularly when we would run out of records the week they were in the charts. Alan, as is his way, was talking about the phenomenal numbers [of *Going Blank Again*] that we were going to sell. And Mark pressed them.' Abbot sympathises with Dennis. 'He was only working on what the sales force and everybody else were telling him. He got carried away by peer group pressure. Poor cunt, he couldn't win.'

The reviews of *Going Blank Again* were mostly unfavourable. A few suggested that Ride had lost their early charm and become self-indulgent. Others found the album dull next to American grunge rock. Ride had watched the video of 'Smells Like Teen Spirit' many times while recording in Chipping Norton; now they were about to feel the chill wind of a Nirvana-changed world. American groups proliferated in the UK press: with the exception of Suede, indie bands at home were being ignored in favour of copious and unrestrained coverage for Nirvana, Sonic Youth, Belly, Faith No More and Pavement. 'It was the worst possible time to be working in British music,' says Mike Smith. 'It was my first year at EMI Music and it was a fiasco.' Only one of the UK-based acts Smith signed that year –

Eugenius, from Glasgow – would make any money back, ironically by virtue of having songs written by their leader, Eugene Kelly, recorded by Nirvana. 'It's interesting looking back at the deals that could have been done that year if you were a publisher,' says Smith. 'You could have signed Radiohead. You could have signed the Cranberries. You could have signed Pulp. You could have signed Therapy? There were deals to be done, but none of those acts actually did anything in '92. It was a terrible year.'

For Ride, becoming an established force in the UK indie sector had brought both pluses and minuses. They were free to introduce ambitious ideas into their music without worrying that they might be deviating from an indie formula. By doing so, however, they stood even less chance of winning peak-time airplay. The more albums they sold and the closer they got to realising Dave Newton's Wembley Arena dream, the more they risked alienating the press and their grass roots support – yet if they did not reach new buyers in greater numbers, Radio 1 could counter that they were merely a fanbase act and the inevitable result would be that they would go unheard by most of the population. Sure enough, *Going Blank Again* did not make the vital breakthrough. With first-week sales of only 45,000, Creation was left with tens of thousands of unshipped copies.

Wembley Arena did not happen. None the less, Ride's itinerary for the rest of 1992 was formidable: two British tours, two stints in Europe and second visits to America and Japan. Before the first of the British legs, Andy Bell asked Newton if his wife Idha could come on tour to keep him company. He was told it was out of the question. And Bell was not the only one who had to bite his tongue. In discussions about the next single from *Going Blank Again*, Ride yielded to pressure from Creation and agreed to a tactical release – 'Twisterella', a 60s-influenced pop track which McGee, Tim Abbot and Garry Blackburn felt was a serious contender for Radio 1's playlists.

'Twisterella' was one of five singles played to the listeners of the breakfast show, who were asked to vote for the one they would like to hear every day for a week. Dave Newton reckons he personally made 180 calls to Radio 1 that morning – a mobile in one hand; his home telephone in the other – to ensure that 'Twisterella' beat Kylie Minogue's 'Finer Feelings'. If Radio 1 wouldn't fight fair, nor would Newton. Even so, 'Twisterella' only just scraped into the Top 40.

'What everybody misjudged was that people in the student market bought albums, not singles,' says Tim Abbot. 'But there was also a fine line with Creation which nobody quite worked out. There was the concept of trying to imitate the majors, but there was also the thing about not wanting to rip the fans off. It was one of the brand equities of the label: we don't rinse the punter out.'

The low chart position for 'Twisterella' undermined *Going Blank*

Again and augured ill for Ride's year-long tour. It also cancelled out the possibility of releasing a third single from the album; it might have struggled even to reach the Top 75. 'For the first time, the band weren't as hot as they had been before,' says Newton. 'The album was only in the charts for three weeks, then it was gone. And the shops wouldn't commit to the single while they still had stock of the album.'

Ride would arrive in America to find *Going Blank Again* underpromoted, and would come home to Oxford shattered and divided. 'The balance was tipped very quickly,' says Mark Gardener. 'The spirit of the band eroded gradually. It was starting to feel like hard work.'

One of Ride's fellow Creation acts had something else to worry about. Heroin was in Primal Scream. 'They were doing bad drugs,' says Jeff Barrett. 'Not my kind of drugs. I didn't want to know. I wanted to know *them* – but they had their mates around them and it was a personal thing. It was a smack thing.'

McGee remembers turning up at a date on the *Screamadelica* tour and not recognising anybody in the dressing-room. 'It was full of these new mates that were all drug dealers,' he says. 'I went: "Who are these people?" to Bobby and Throb, and Throb had invited ... these two cocaine dealers to go on tour with them. I said: "But your first stop's Amsterdam. Why are you taking these cocaine dealers?" They went: "Well, you can't get good stuff in Amsterdam. They cut it." That's how off their nut they were. Obviously, everything comes *in* from Amsterdam, and they were taking their own coke dealers from England so that the stuff they bought in Amsterdam wasn't cut! Their lack of understanding about how the fucking thing worked was bananas.'

Gillespie later told Michael Bonner that the Paris gig was 'like a drug dealers' convention' and recalled McGee urging the band to get some bodyguards. The Scream toured America for four weeks in February. 'Things changed after that February tour,' Gillespie told Bonner. 'Things were going ... getting darker.' He went on: 'Then the band kind of fell apart after that. Fell to pieces.'

McGee had been Primal Scream's manager – mostly unpaid – since 1984. Conflicting interests had recently made his position untenable. He was their manager and label boss, was involved in their publishing deal and was Gillespie's best friend. 'It was messy,' McGee says. 'The lines were getting blurred and I had to pull back out of their business. Bobby was complaining that Dick hadn't paid some invoice on some tour. He was really caning Dick, and I said: "You know, we're not your managers, we're your record company." This was a band that was getting big publishing advances and selling 500,000 records. We weren't taking 20 per cent – *and* we were getting complained about. It was time for it to go on to a more professional footing.'

So McGee handed the reins to Primal Scream's booking agent, Alex Nightingale. The question was: was a former addict the best man to manage such a difficult band? Dick Green believed not. Even McGee was unsure; he remembered Nightingale phoning him 23 times one night in Brighton, and being unable to make sense on any of the calls. Laurence Verfaillie, however, was one person who thought Nightingale was born for the manager's job. 'Big mouth, big attitude, interesting character,' she recalls. 'He had already had his fair share of exposure as a wild kid. There might have been some doubts about his ability, but everybody was willing to give him a chance. Who can keep complete nutters in shape better than a complete nutter himself?'

On 9 April, Nightingale accompanied Gillespie and his girlfriend Emily Hughes to a club in Victoria where Flowered Up were playing. They met the singer Kevin Rowland, who took a taxi with them to the gates of Downing Street. A crowd had gathered: it was general election night. Nightingale asked a policeman who had won. 'Tories,' he replied. 'Tory landslide.' John Major's Government had been re-elected against all predictions.

In Hackney, Dick Green opened his post one morning to find a flyer from an accountancy firm, Casson Beckman. It read: 'Have you got cash flow problems?' Funny they should ask. Green hired the firm and found out for the first time how much money Creation had been losing: it was approximately £1.3 million in debt. Green resigned himself to the fact that the label had come to the end of the line. He and his wife began to make plans: she would go back to work while he stayed at home to look after the children.

Tim Abbot started to discern a change of mood in the bunker. Since joining Creation full-time, he had assumed the company's management to be a triumvirate of McGee, Green and himself. He had also assumed that he would one day be offered the shares to make it official. When he overheard McGee and Green having urgent conversations about their own shares, Abbot wondered what was up. He noticed that McGee and Green were suddenly great friends again, all differences forgotten. Abbot began to suspect that something was about to happen that might not include him.

A former managing director of A&M in the UK, Derek Green had set up China Records in 1984. After successive three-year distribution deals with Chrysalis and Polydor, and hits by the Art Of Noise and Labi Siffre, Green decided China was strong enough not to need the majors, and in early 1991 he signed his distribution over to Pinnacle. A year after that, he started talking to Brian Lane, the manager of Yes. 'We were observing the UK record industry,' says Green, 'and I was looking at the chances I might have to grow China very dynamically. Brian said: "How would you do that?" I said: "One of the ways is you buy someone else." And Brian said: "Who would you target?" I said: "Well, the best independent I know is Creation." '

Lane knew Creation's accountant at Casson Beckman, and rang Derek Green a week later to say he believed the label might be for sale. In May, Green and Lane became business partners for the purpose of effecting a partial Creation buy-out. It would be an unusual deal for the industry – a high-profile indie being bought by a much less prominent one – but stranger things had happened. Green hoped that Alan McGee might A&R both labels, stewarding a run of success for their combined rosters.

'Me and Dick went down to China Records,' says McGee, 'and we were in their big sort of war-room for about three or four hours. Our first impression of Derek Green was that we quite liked him. Then Derek and Brian Lane came over to Hackney. The office was freaking their heads out. It was a pretty freaky place, I must admit.'

Now McGee made his long-promised call to Paul Russell, telling him about the China development. Russell and his Sony colleague Jeremy Pearce met McGee at the Groucho, a West End media club. An experienced lawyer and publisher, Pearce headed Sony's Licensed Repertoire Division, a department controlling the company's licences with third-party labels in Britain and Europe. Sony LRD had struck a deal with the Farm's label Produce, and was training its sights on other indies such as Saul Galpern's Nude, which had a two-singles agreement with Suede.

'Sony traditionally had been pretty bad on independent-type repertoire,' says Pearce. 'Apart from the Clash, which was sort of a fluke, they had always specialised in big, charismatic artists like Alison Moyet, Paul Young, Sade and George Michael. Their band roster was pretty thin. They just weren't signing Teenage Fanclub, Ride, Primal Scream and stuff. When LRD was established, Paul Russell had in his mind that Creation would be a good deal to do.'

Russell and Pearce explained to McGee that Sony LRD could supply Creation with funding and international licensing, leaving it as much creative discretion in the UK as McGee desired. 'We wanted the repertoire,' says Pearce. 'You could either try and beat the independents or join them, and Sony had failed to beat the independents for years.' Russell and Pearce came away from the Groucho feeling the talks had gone well.

McGee had never heard the expression 'to break bread' until Derek Green used it. With Dick Green in tow, McGee went out for dinner with the China boss one evening. China was not McGee's idea of a cool label – its foremost act was the Levellers, a politicised folk band – but he was impressed by Derek Green's house: this was a man who had done well out of music. 'Alan told me that Derek's house was rammed full of antiques,' says Tim Abbot. 'He was going: "It's fucking amazing, man." Never mind your right-on, Alan lives and breathes dosh. He went: "That's serious money, man. Supertramp and all that. It's great." '

Old punk that he was, McGee could respect Green for selling millions of Supertramp records at A&M. McGee had not actually bought any Supertramp records himself, but he had seen them at the Glasgow Apollo in 1975 and quite enjoyed them. Moreover, he had to admire any band that had made it big in America, which Supertramp certainly had. So had Brian Lane's Yes: six US Top 10 albums in the 70s, all on Atlantic, one of the greatest record labels of them all. Getting into bed with Lane and Green might not be too traumatic at all, McGee thought.

Then, over dinner, Derek Green told a story that made McGee lose confidence in him completely. McGee had always known that the Sex Pistols had been thrown off A&M in 1977 – just as he knew they had been thrown off EMI two months earlier. He now realised he was breaking bread with the A&M managing director who had made the decision. Green had dropped the Pistols after his friend Bob Harris, the presenter of the *Old Grey Whistle Test*, had been threatened in a club by Sid Vicious. For McGee, there could be no excuse.

'What I did at the time, I did for a combination of reasons,' says Derek Green. 'I was in the music business; I wasn't in the social attitudes business. When the Sex Pistols tape came my way, my interest was only the music. What a tape! Bloody fantastic. You couldn't like music if you didn't like that tape. But when I spent three months dealing with McLaren and their lawyers to find that they felt it was everything *but* the music ... get out of my life. It took me three months to sign the Sex Pistols and four days to drop them.' And it took only one meal for McGee to think that Creation would be better off with Sony.

In the early 90s, the all-important indie charts, used by retailers as a guide to ordering stock, had been swamped by the bleeping bane of the guitar label: one-off dance singles. Feared and despised, these cheaply-made records were pushing the conventional four-piece indie combo further and further down the rankings and out into the cold. The indie singles chart for one week in July 1992 was so top-heavy with dance product that no guitar tune appeared higher than number 13. The peeved bosses of guitar labels protested they were not being given a sporting chance, and put pressure on chart compilers CIN to introduce new legislation that would redefine the word indie by making musical genre, not method of distribution, the criterion for chart inclusion.

A body called Entertainment Research and Analysis announced that it would employ musicologists to determine whether a song was 'indie' or not. It was expected that major label-signed or -funded bands such as Blur, Curve and the Manic Street Preachers would soon join the likes of Ride, Primal Scream, the Pixies and Teenage Fanclub in a new 'alternative' chart. Long-established indie acts Erasure, New Order and Depeche Mode – whose music favoured electronics and keyboards rather than guitars – did not appear to have much of an alternative chart future. Borderline cases like Primal Scream might, it was thought, qualify with certain records but not with others. 'The one-instinctively-knows-what-is-alternative approach depends ultimately on the cabal of experts being hip to the ever-shifting definitions and distractions of the volatile alternative scene,' noted a *Guardian* writer.

The situation descended into farce when Strange Fruit, a label so independent of corporate control that it was run from its owner's garden shed, was told it no longer qualified for the indie chart because it had left Pinnacle to use a distributor linked to PolyGram. Equally contentious was the chart eligibility of Hut and Dedicated, two labels distributed by independents but owned by majors. Dubbed 'mandies', these ersatz indies were 'financed by corporations but distributed by plucky lads on mopeds', as the *NME* put it.*

As the polemic reached a crescendo that summer, the journalist Steve Lamacq made a clever observation. Since the 80s, he had been teased for being an indie true believer, an apologist for left-handed guitar pop that sold neglible amounts. But now major labels were courting indie credibility overtly – whether by launching their own mandies or by seeking to join forces with indies like Creation and Nude – in recognition of the failure of their own A&R departments to find new talent in a recessionary climate and nurture it through their labyrinthine internal structures. Hence Lamacq's point. 'What I find interesting,' he said, 'is that [indie has] gone from being a derogatory term to a term of praise.' It was a turnaround Lamacq could not have foreseen in 1986.

Alan McGee's terse comment in July – that all definitions of indie were redundant – was understandable given that he was on the verge of selling half of Creation. But to whom? China and Sony had agreed similar ballpark figures of around £2.5 million. 'We'd decided that we probably wanted to go with Sony,' says McGee, 'but Derek Green was still in the race. But I was thinking: I can't sign to a guy that dropped the Sex Pistols at the height of them being the greatest band in the world. We're talking about ideology here.'

Uncertain which way he should jump, McGee phoned Rob Dickins and Seymour Stein. Both of them advised him to go with Sony. But the wired and fractious Glaswegian was seeing bear-traps and webs of intrigue wherever he looked. And at that moment, every indie label's worst case scenario happened to Creation when

---

* The compromise was reached that the CIN indie charts would keep the distribution ruling, but that hardcore dance records would be excluded.

it was put on stop by Mayking, the company that manufactured its records.

For the first six months of 1992, McGee and Green had been surviving on cash flow and an advance from Pinnacle, and had been pushing back the bills as far as they could. Their main creditor, Mayking's managing director Brian Bonnar, was owed a six-figure sum and was refusing to press any more Creation records until it was paid. 'Any new projects were placed with other manufacturers like Nimbus,' says Mark Dennis, 'but the problem ... was that Brian held all the masters of the catalogue. He basically held all the cards.'

McGee had first met Brian Bonnar in 1981 when he used his company to manufacture the Laughing Apple's records. He had taken a dislike to Bonnar's condescending manner and had done his best to avoid him ever since. 'As far as Bonnar was concerned, I was this enigma who took loads of drugs,' says McGee. 'We used to send Dick because Dick soaked it up.' (Tim Abbot recalls Green, who was on medication for a stomach ulcer, steeling himself for one encounter with Bonnar by taking a gigantic gulp from his bottle of kaolin and morphine.)

Bonnar had learned from Casson Beckman that Creation was effectively up for sale, and had been asked if he could be more flexible in the credit department. He could not. Another of his debtors had gone down owing a fortune – not all of which had been covered by Mayking's insurance – and Bonnar was in any case extremely sceptical about the way Creation managed its accounts. 'What I had always been trying to elicit from Dick Green was some plan as to how they would salvage the situation,' he says. 'And on that particular occasion there wasn't one. There wasn't enough leadership in the business for them to come round and say: "Look, here's a payment schedule. It's six months or nine months long, but we feel we can adhere to this." ... Creation offered no positive arrangement for repaying the debt, other than [that] perhaps they might be sold.'

Jeremy Pearce was taking it nice and steady. He knew Derek Green and Brian Lane had a head start on Sony, but he also knew that Creation would be perfect for LRD. The name being mentioned most was Primal Scream: the thought that LRD could have their next album for the international market got Pearce's lips smacking. 'McGee said: "At least Jeremy's honest. At least he's offering a straight-up deal",' recalls Tim Abbot. Dick Green thought the LRD deal 'seemed acceptable: the key to it was they left us alone in the UK, so it was basically an international licence, which was what we wanted'.

Because of the deals already in place for Primal Scream and Teenage Fanclub, LRD would have no claim to those bands in America – which Pearce admits was an irritation – and it would have no rights to Ride anywhere in the world. Then there was Creation's marriage of convenience with SBK, inconveniently giving Charles Koppelman first dibs on new blood. Creation also had licensing deals running in Japan, France and Germany. 'The French one was a problem,' says Pearce, 'because there was quite a long retention period. But the American was by far the most problematical, being such an important market.'

Paul Russell had been more or less aware of the size of the Creation debt since running into McGee at Heathrow. 'We knew what we were getting into,' he says. 'We knew Creation was in difficulties.' Negotiations proceeded carefully throughout June and into July. 'One of the difficult things about it was that it was not the sort of deal that we had previously done,' says Russell. 'There was a lot of internal discussion at Sony about how we were going to structure it. It took a long time to get going ... But when everybody wants to make a deal, you know, the deal gets made.'

Derek Birkett, the managing director of One Little Indian, unexpectedly requested a Friday morning meeting in Hackney to discuss buying Creation. Seething with anger, McGee agreed to see him. Birkett owned 40 per cent of One Little Indian. The other 60 per cent was owned by Brian Bonnar. 'There was no way that Brian could make a formal approach to Alan, because Alan wouldn't talk to him in a million years,' says a source. 'Alan interpreted [from] Derek's meeting that Brian was involved.'

He certainly was. Bonnar and Birkett had hit on £400,000 as the amount Birkett would offer to McGee for 100 per cent of Creation. 'Derek made an offer for a company that was technically insolvent,' says Bonnar. 'In our terms, as a small indie label, it was a pretty full offer.' McGee laughed Birkett out of his office. 'He said: "Why would I want to sell to another indie?" ' Birkett recalls. 'Then he told me to sling my hook.'

Neither Bonnar nor Birkett had known that Sony and China were thinking in the millions; in fact, neither of them had known that Sony was even at the table. Had he been notified of that, Bonnar says he would not have put Creation's manufacturing on stop. 'Dick Green did not volunteer the information that a sale to Sony was going to happen,' says Bonnar. 'When I'd asked them how they planned to recover the situation with us, they just said that they didn't have any ideas.'

The notion of being owned by One Little Indian filled McGee with so much horror that, as he told Dick Green and Tim Abbot, he would rather have liquidated Creation and gone on the dole. 'I was fuelled by total Colombia [cocaine],' McGee says, 'and these people dared to come into my gaff and try and buy my record company. Derek Birkett said something like: "Well, everybody just thinks you're mad and you're off your head on drugs." I said: "Derek, you're a fucking embarassment." '

Bonnar had always found McGee elusive. He would soon find him vengeful when Creation withdrew all its business from Mayking. 'Alan McGee read what he read into it,' says Bonnar. 'The fact is that Creation had been with us for a long time, they'd been a good account and we had supported them over the years to quite some degree.' Mark Dennis, who left Creation for One Little Indian in August, remarks that an Alan McGee–Brian Bonnar coalition would have been 'a relationship made in hell'.

Creation's lawyer was John Kennedy, a 39-year-old star of the music industry. Awarded an OBE for his work on Live Aid, he had received national attention in 1991 as the lawyer who extricated the Stone Roses from their contract with Silvertone Records and Zomba Music, having argued successfully in the High Court that the band had been a victim of bad legal advice prior to signing in 1988. In the early 90s, Kennedy was listed by a magazine as one of the 20 most powerful people in the music business.

'Kennedy was beyond genius,' says McGee. 'He's one of my heroes. If Bill Drummond is the biggest genius I've ever met in the music business – with the KLF and having four (sic) number 1 hits, and making Tammy Wynette sing "we're justified, we're ancient and we drive an ice-cream van" – John Kennedy was unbeatable in the Sony negotiations. At the last minute he'd go: "We want another quarter of a million." He was unbelievable.' But even as the talks with Sony were nearing a satisfactory conclusion, Kennedy urged McGee to let China perform a due diligence exercise as a precaution in case Sony fell through.

As he was not a shareholder in Creation, Tim Abbot was absent from the meetings with Kennedy and Sony. Kept abreast of events by McGee, Abbot played cheerleader within the office, reassuring those who had little more than an outline of the situation. 'I'd had this holiday booked on the Norfolk Broads,' says Andy Saunders, 'and I didn't know if I was going to have a job when I came back. Tim had said to me: "Listen, if anything goes down I'll let you know – but if we don't do this deal it's going to be a bit tricky. Why don't you give me a call halfway through your holiday?" So I rang up Tim from a payphone in a supermarket in Oulton Broad, and he said: "It's going to be fine." '

China's accountants were still trawling through documents in the Creation office when McGee and Green agreed the deal with Sony. 'You lot – get the fuck out,' said McGee, bounding up to them. For £2.5 million, Sony acquired a 49 per cent shareholding in Creation and the right to distribute its records internationally through Licensed Repertoire Division. (Creation acts licensed elsewhere would switch to Sony for the rest of the world when their various American and European arrangements expired.) The deal, which made McGee a millionaire overnight, also included an additional £1 million to Creation in loans and advances.

Andy Saunders returned from his holiday in Norfolk in time for a Creation party that compared with the ecstasy nights of 1989. It was paid for by Biff Bang Pow!, who – by an extraordinary coincidence – had just received a large royalty cheque from Alan McGee and Dick Green at Creation Records.

SBK's obsession with Top 40 radio and fear of missing a trick were driving more than one band up the wall. Blur almost broke up during a 1992 tour of the States on which SBK gave them only two days off in 44. They were promoting an SBK remix of an old single, 'Bang', that they hadn't even been told about. 'They had no sense of aesthetics, these people,' bassist Alex James told the band's biographer Stuart Maconie. 'They were just after a fast buck. You know how if there's a cool, fashionable pair of trousers you can buy in good shops, then Carnaby Street will sell you a shit version of it six months later? That's what SBK were like. They just counterfeited the good stuff.'

Mike Mena was having terrible problems getting SBK to understand the musical subtleties of Slowdive, who were adrift in the herring pond of low sales and reduced company interest. 'There was a point in time where the head of A&R came to me and said: "You know, I could remix this song and make it sound like Blue Oyster Cult",' Mena recalls. 'I was like: "Over my dead body." ' The relationship with Creation had been damaged by SBK's rejection of three bands – the Boo Radleys, Silverfish and the Telescopes – and therefore three albums that would have netted Creation $900,000. McGee's subsequent deals with Columbia for the Boo Radleys and Silverfish, while useful, were not to produce anything much in record sales. And although SBK had taken Adorable, McGee was now trying to walk out of the contract, feeling that developments on both sides – personnel changes in New York caused by an SBK-EMI merger; the Creation deal with Sony LRD – had rendered the 1991 pact invalid. But as much as he screamed and yelled, the deal was solid.

McGee wasn't just taking British music to America; he was bringing US acts to Britain. Creation had licensed one or two American projects since 1989 – the Sneetches from Alias Records in San Francisco, and later the Poster Children from Limited Potential in Illinois – and had in 1991 signed Velvet Crush, a Rhode Island band in the Teenage Fanclub-Big Star style. These were pop-flavoured outfits unlikely to turn the heads of all the UK Nirvana-and-grunge fans. For another Creation-licensed artist, however, the prize was there to be taken.

Had he not been such an intense and dark man, the international explosion of Nirvana might have afforded Bob Mould a satisfied grin. Kurt Cobain had been a big fan of Mould's first band Hüsker Dü in the 80s, as had Nirvana's other principal influence the Pixies. Now in his early 30s, Mould was a godfather to the grunge generation – he had been suggested as a possible producer of *Nevermind* by his then-managers – and was arguably more comprehensively gifted than those he had inspired. Yet despite having had major label backing and the support of the press since the mid-80s, Mould had not had commercial success either in Hüsker Dü or as a solo artist. Self-managed and self-published, he was perceived as a difficult person to work with.

Mould talked to friends in the States and heard the same name again and again: Alan McGee. An innovative user of guitar sounds, Mould was a My Bloody Valentine fan and also knew of Swervedriver. When a solo tour brought him to London in December 1991, Mould went to see McGee in Hackney and was impressed by the cramped offices. 'Everybody was in everybody's face and had posters of their favourite bands up, whether they were on the label or not,' he recalls. 'It was such a refreshing thing compared to the stale, neo-industrial Virgin Hollywood office. I was like: "This is the way it's supposed to be." '

Taking a modest advance, Mould licensed his music to Creation for the UK and cut a similar deal with Rykodisc in America. In the summer of 1992, he let McGee hear an album he had made with bassist David Barbe and drummer Malcolm Travis. 'At that point he sold 7,000 around Europe,' says McGee. 'But when he gave me *Copper Blue*, I immediately knew it was an important album.'

Calling themselves Sugar, Mould and his two colleagues had all the power and volume of Nirvana, an album as good as *Nevermind*, and much of the follow-up already recorded. If Mould expected anything, it was that press coverage for Sugar in the UK might awaken interest in Sugar back in the States. A July cover story in the *NME*, published before the paper had even received a copy of *Copper Blue*, showed his hunch to be a shrewd one.

Though ostensibly very different in temperament – the American was a recovering alcoholic who lived a frugal life – McGee and Mould had corresponding chips on their shoulder which made Creation an ideal billet for Sugar's thermonuclear music. Mould explained to the *NME*: 'There's some people I want to show that they were wrong, people that I don't think should be in the music business. Some of them aren't any more, luckily, and some of them won't be very shortly ... I've got a real fuck-you attitude right now.'

The closure of *Sounds* in April 1991 had left two weekly music papers, the *NME* and *Melody Maker*, competing for readers and stories. It was common for interviews with British bands on tour in America to be offered to one or the other paper, in return for a cover. It was also common for journalists to exaggerate the band's importance across the Atlantic, and to skirt around the fact that the tour was a tame affair playing mostly to Anglophile audiences in clubs of 200–300 capacity.

A few acts, however, appeared to have a better shot in America than most, and two of them were Teenage Fanclub and Swervedriver. In May, ex-Orange Juice drummer Steven Daly, now a journalist based in New York, composed an article for the *NME* in which he graded Teenage Fanclub as the best British indie rock band to tour the States in recent times. 'Though fellow Glaswegians Primal Scream dominate the press,' he wrote, 'their record sales [in America] seem to move in inverse proportion to critical acclaim. If Creation is ever going to see the return of any of that My Bloody Valentine budget, it will most likely be through the US sales of *Bandwagonesque*.'

Teenage Fanclub's Los Angeles show was attended by rock celebrities Kurt Cobain, his wife Courtney Love and Perry Farrell. MTV had been featuring the Fanclub's videos, and KROQ radio was sponsoring the concert. 'It's almost like after Nirvana they don't know what's going to happen next,' Norman Blake told Daly. Dave Barker, who flew out to LA with McGee and Dick Green, recalls: 'It was looking fantastic for the Fanclub. They did *Saturday Night Live* on that trip, with Mike Myers doing the Scottish accent and all that. And they did another show, Dennis Miller, in LA. They were staying at the Hyatt [hotel], and the night they did the show they moved to the St James across the street – that flash place that's in *The Player* – because all Dennis Miller's guests *had* to be put up at the St James.'

But the Fanclub were starting to have a few doubts. Gary Gersh at Geffen had been keen for them to make professional videos that MTV could play regularly. However, 'The Concept', a humorous track from *Bandwagonesque*, was ill-served by a video showing a girl trying to touch the band-members, who were playing on a TV screen. Geffen then pulled the video off MTV and replaced it with 'What You Do To Me', shot artistically in 35mm black and white. This picked up fewer plays and made Teenage Fanclub, who had been dressed and primped for the occasion, look affected.

Bandwagonesque had reached 150,000 American sales very quickly, but soon eased up and stopped a long way short of the psychologically important half a million mark. 'It didn't do quite as well as everybody thought,' says the band's manager Chas Banks. 'At the slightest sign of any failure in America, people disassociate themselves from you at a rapid speed. It's something that's in the national psyche. There are no grey areas. It's winners and losers, I'm afraid.'

Swervedriver were in LA at the same time as the Fanclub. Ground down by an arduous criss-cross tour of the country supporting their A&M label-mates Soundgarden, Swervedriver were finding the Hunter S. Thompson road odyssey not to be so romantic after all, and had taken to joking cynically about Soundgarden's po-faced singer Chris Cornell during their set. Laurence Verfaillie, who was coordinating music press interviews, recalls: 'There was only medium interest in Swervedriver from the crowd. It was at the Palladium, a big show. My status as Creation press officer was friend of the rich and famous, so I was hanging out with people from Hole. But ... I have to say working at Creation was taking its toll on me. I was running out of steam.'

And so was Teenage Fanclub's American conquest when their Geffen champion Gary Gersh left to work for Capitol.

Creation had always been a press-led record label. The publicising of its new releases, bands and general attitude took place in the retail music papers and magazines. Prior to 1992, there had been no interest in Creation from the trade journal *Music Week*, nor vice versa. Unlike 4AD's Ivo Watts-Russell or Mute's Daniel Miller, McGee was never available for comment, wasn't one for music industry forums or debates and felt himself to be outside the *Music Week* world.

The dramatic events of August put a reluctant McGee centre-stage. Just as news of the Sony deal broke, the short list was announced for the first annual Mercury Music Prize, to be awarded to the best UK album of the preceding twelve months. Three of the ten albums on the list had a Creation or McGee connection: *Screamadelica*, Saint Etienne's *Foxbase Alpha* and the Jesus and Mary Chain's *Honey's Dead*. There might even have been a fourth had McGee not refused to nominate My Bloody Valentine's *Loveless* as a petty dig at the Shieldses.

But while the Mercury short list confirmed McGee as an immensely influential figure in the British music industry, he was, as usual, being choosy about whom he talked to. Not one word passed his lips on the subject of the Sony deal: the feeling that he had bowed before the storm nagged at him, no matter how much he told himself that Sony would have no real control over Creation.

'It wasn't with any optimism that I entered into the Sony deal,' says McGee. 'It was like: "I've sold the name to SBK. I now need to sell my soul. I will now do the deal with the devil." ' Drinking in the Camden Palace nightclub with Tim Abbot, McGee was spat at by an indie fan upset that Creation had sold out to the majors. 'I went and knocked the bloke out,' says Abbot. 'But Alan was freaked out by it. He only stopped for one drink and then he said he had to go.'

Because it was still distributed by Pinnacle, and would still appear in the indie charts, Creation could claim under the existing ruling to be an independent label despite being half-owned by Sony. In terms of how Creation would be perceived in the period after the deal – and perception was paramount to indie fans and to the excitable music weeklies – the key issue was control. The crucial statistic, as McGee saw it, was that Sony had bought 49 per cent of Creation rather than 50. This allowed Creation's press department to contend that the label was more independent than not, an argument that journalists seemed happy to buy. 'I expected there to be a massive music biz backlash about the whole thing,' says Andy Saunders. 'But there wasn't really. Once it was explained that we were going to run things in the UK, and the deal was essentially an ex-UK licence, everybody was fine.'

It came down to perception again. As Jeremy Pearce recalls, Sony could have bought 50 per cent of Creation if it had wanted to. 'The fact is we were happy with 49 because shareholdings aren't that important,' he says. 'We had safeguards in the contract. We had the foreign rights. We were protected against things going badly wrong. We had ample control. We had everything we needed.'

One of Sony's safeguards was to get rid of the key man clauses that three Creation bands had written into their contract, which would effectively have given McGee the power to hold Sony to ransom by threatening to leave and take the bands with him. Sony pressured Adorable and Swervedriver into dropping the clause, but one band held firm. The band that made a habit of saying no: Ride.

'The Sony deal horrified us,' says Steve Queralt. 'We had a clause in our contract to prevent them going all the way. Creation got really shitty with us about that.' Signed to Sire/Warner Bros for every territory outside the UK, Ride fell outside Sony LRD's jurisdiction and weren't interested in what Jeremy Pearce wanted. They were much more concerned about how the Sony deal might change Creation. 'It may even have taken some of the excitement out of it, knowing the label wasn't going to go bust any more,' says Queralt, indie kid to the last. 'But having said that, that whole indie snobbery had gone anyway. There was almost a yuppie attitude by now. We could make good money. We *were* making good money.'

However, one fact about the Sony deal was not made public. Nor would it be for another four years. There was a clause in the contract that gave Sony the right to buy the remaining 51 shares in Creation at the end of the deal's four-year term. This had nothing to do with perception – this was a real and sincere threat to Creation's long-term existence. And at least one long-serving Creation employee presumed that Sony would exercise its option to buy when the time came. 'I thought that the term of that deal would be all there was in the life of Creation,' says James Kyllo, 'and that we would then get folded into Sony.'

No wonder Jeremy Pearce felt Sony had everything it needed. And no wonder McGee was worried about who exactly controlled whom. Come the summer of 1996, Sony would hold McGee's and Creation's fate in its hands. And all talk of independence – and who retained it, and who did not – would surely then be silenced for good.

18 Maximum Life Expectancy

RIMAL SCREAM WON THE Mercury Music Prize, having been the bookmakers' clear favourite, and collected their £20,000 cheque at the Savoy Hotel in September. Within hours the cheque had been mislaid by Alex Nightingale, who had to phone for a replacement the following day. Adding to the sense of confusion, retailers were unable to take advantage of sudden demand for *Screamadelica* – because the famously efficient Pinnacle had been caught on the back foot and run out of CDs.

When the problem was sorted out, the Mercury Music Prize put an extra 25,000 on sales of the album. It also built up hopes and expectations for the follow-up, on which Primal Scream started work that month in north London's Roundhouse Studios. 'All of a sudden, from being on the floor, Creation was saved,' says Tim Abbot. 'And the [next] Primal Scream album was going to be the jewel in the crown.'

McGee would have been more than content with *Screamadelica* part two. Yet it was already apparent that the drugs some of the bandmembers were taking ruled out any possibility of another hands-in-the-air record. 'We had a lot of heroin addiction in the band, a lot of cocaine,' Bobby Gillespie told the *NME* years later. 'We were fucked up and we wanted to make a different record.' Jeff Barrett recalls that the Scream were infuriated by people's tendency to credit Andrew Weatherall as the mastermind of *Screamadelica*, and wanted to deliver an album that was clearly all their own work.

The recording sessions, however, were a shambles. 'We tried to record the album down there in the Roundhouse in September-October 1992, and nothing really came of it,' Gillespie told Michael Bonner, 'just all-night jams and people getting fucking far out, strung out and collapsing and really fucking mad shit and nothing. The band really was falling apart ... Everybody was too fucked up to make a proper record and we had to cancel the sessions. Jimmy Miller was going to work on it. Shortly afterwards, Jimmy died. That time was ... near-deaths, deaths and mental illness. All sorts of fucking bad things happened to us or our friends.' McGee later described the Roundhouse sessions as '47 grand's worth of cover versions'.

McGee had never taken heroin, and regarded it as a gruesome drug used by weak people. Not that he was the embodiment of clean living himself: newly made a millionaire, he was taking more cocaine than ever before, much of it in the company of Tim Abbot and some of it in the Creation bunker. 'It was nasty in the office,' says Laurence Verfaillie. 'I don't like cocaine. I can smell people who are on cocaine. It turns them into a monster ... The main characters were *all* on cocaine. When we had the Sony party, there was a lot of champagne and I remember waking up with a 50 quid note in my pocket, full of dust. I hated it so much. It creates a lot of artificial connections between people.'

Andy Saunders found himself on the end of one of McGee's cocaine screaming fits in September. Saunders had been asked by Bob Mould to recommend a support act for Sugar's first UK tour. He innocently suggested a band called the Venus Beads. There was nothing controversial about them, except that they were not a Creation act. At ten o'clock in the morning, Saunders was asked down to the bunker.

'I didn't know that there was this procedure where you try to put your own bloody bands forward,' he explains. 'I thought I had been doing Bob Mould a favour. In the bunker, Alan freaked out at me like nobody has ever freaked out at me before. He was literally frothing at the mouth, screaming that I was a disloyal cunt and if I didn't like it I could fuck off. He hadn't even pre-empted the screaming with anything – he'd just gone from zero to freak-out mode. "How *dare* you fucking usurp me? How *dare* you fucking undermine me?" I was shocked, absolutely shocked.'

Tim Abbot witnessed many a similar freak-out in the bunker, particularly when McGee started arriving back from trips to America laden down with over-the-counter speed. 'He would be eating these, like, Dr Bongo's ephedrine cough tablets,' says Abbot, 'and by about three hours into that he would be foaming. And whoever happened to walk in would get the knee-jerk.' Most of the tirades would contain McGee's favourite phrase of the period: 'This is not a *democracy*. This is a *fascist dictatorship*.' The recipient of the tirade would be well-advised not to laugh.

'He was doing that to a lot of people at that time, this whole fascist dictatorship thing,' notes Saunders. ' "What I say goes. Nobody else has any input whatsoever." I think a lot of that was down to the fact that he was losing a bit of control to Sony. He was trying to grab all his control back the only way he knew how.' Tim Abbot, who almost had a fist-fight with McGee on one occasion when his brother Chris was screamed at, recalls: 'Alan had this thing that everybody was stealing off him. He was security bonkers. If he thought that somebody had nicked £8.10 worth of envelopes, he would go fucking mad. But then he would offer largesse to the same person a week later: "Go and get some drugs, man. Do you want 50 quid?" '

Laurence Verfaillie felt uncomfortable as a woman in the boorish Hackney environment. To those who took cocaine, however, Verfaillie was becoming a real drag to be around. Only a year before, McGee's music taste had been close to her heart; she had been thrilled to see Teenage Fanclub and the Boo Radleys come to the label. But lately McGee had been signing bands that Verfaillie could not see the point of – Adorable and Silverfish being two – and she wondered if cocaine was having an adverse effect on his judgment. 'The prospects for bands like Adorable and Silverfish were quite minimal,' she says, 'and Creation had reached a level where you couldn't disappoint people. There was a lot of pressure from the media.'

McGee viewed this sort of talk as treasonous and had dismayed Verfaillie by giving the autumn's key project – Sugar's *Copper Blue* – to Andy Saunders. 'That was a real blow to Laurence's power base,' says Tim Abbot. 'When Sugar took off, it was Andy Saunders' coming of age.' Indeed, a flood of Saunders-generated Sugar publicity was followed by a number 10 album chart entry for *Copper Blue* that surprised and delighted McGee. He decided to see the Manchester date of the Sugar tour on 8 October.

At the Manchester Boardwalk, McGee met his friend Debbie Turner, who took him downstairs after the gig to smoke a joint. Turner was the rhythm guitarist and singer in a band called Sister Lovers who used the basement of the Boardwalk to rehearse. McGee had been down there in the summer with the Creation band Medalark 11, and had watched them get into an argument about football with another band, Oasis.

As he and Turner entered the basement, McGee saw a drum-kit and a Union Jack montage on the wall behind it. Bashing around on the kit, he asked Turner who was responsible for the Union Jack. Oasis, she replied, adding that Sister Lovers thought it was stupid and usually tried to pull it down when they rehearsed. 'I went: "Are they mods or are they fucking National Front?" ' McGee recalls. 'And she goes: "They're National Front." I went: "*Are* they?" . . . This was her just basically saying it so that I wouldn't be interested in them. She knew that if she'd said they were mods, I would start asking questions, because I'd always had this thing about the Jam.'

McGee promptly forgot all about Oasis. Sister Lovers, however, continued to share the Boardwalk basement with them, and one day Turner noticed that they were sounding much improved. 'When we first started sharing with them, they had quite U2 guitar lines and the voice wasn't up to much,' she remembers. 'Then they worked with the Real People* and they did really change. They wrote songs after

---

* A briefly popular Liverpool guitar band with whom Oasis recorded some demos in early 1993.

that. I remember saying to my friend Lorraine: "God, their guitars sound brilliant. That's how we've got to get our guitars sounding." '

With so much hope riding on the next Primal Scream album, McGee held clear-the-air talks with the band and Alex Nightingale in February 1993. Three of the six musicians had drug problems which looked like jeopardising the band's future, and McGee felt he was the only person who could impress on them the seriousness of the situation. 'We had a crisis meeting at a place called the Square in WC1,' he recalls. 'Nightingale had cleaned up about six months earlier and I said [to them]: "You know this is the end of the band if you can't get this sorted out in your heads. You've got to come off the gear." '

The relationship between Creation and LRD was meanwhile seeing its first signs of tension. To Jeremy Pearce's surprise, McGee and Dick Green had asked for more money not long after the deal had gone through in August, and had seldom stopped asking since. With each new loan, the importance of the Primal Scream album grew exponentially: Sony was looking to the band to produce a million-seller at the very least.

'As soon as the deal was done, it became clear that [Creation] had ongoing cash problems,' says Pearce. 'We didn't have a lot of choice in a way. It's like spending money on repairing a house. You can't just stop, because the thing will fall down.' Pearce had realised what others had known for years: Creation could not manage its affairs to save its life.

The decision was taken that Primal Scream should go abroad to record their album, owing to the availability of heroin in London. New York, Los Angeles, Miami and Berlin were non-starters for similar reasons, as was Barbados, where members of Happy Mondays had been sucked into crack addiction the previous year, a contributing agent in the November collapse of the Factory label. The best solution seemed to be to send Primal Scream back to Memphis. 'Really, it just turned from getting them off heroin to "let's get a serious cocaine problem", unfortunately,' says McGee. 'But at least they were off heroin.'

To produce the album, the band approached Tom Dowd. An American in his mid-sixties, he had a peerless portfolio of production and engineering credits dating back to the 50s, including records by Aretha Franklin, Otis Redding, Wilson Pickett, John Coltrane, Cream and Rod Stewart. 'He was chosen by Bobby because of all that Stax and Atlantic thing,' says McGee. 'The whole Memphis Horns thing; that whole era of music. But he was also chosen because he was 65, 66, and he could actually turn round to them and go: "Shut your fucking mouth. Get in and do your guitar solo." They wouldn't take that off anybody else.'

Selected on the basis of records he had made 25 years earlier,

Dowd unquestionably deliberated before consenting to work with Primal Scream in 1993. When they sent him *Screamadelica*, he didn't know what to make of it. Four demos from the Roundhouse were more to his taste, but could hardly be called finished songs. Choosing to accept his mission in March, Dowd sent the bassist and drummer from the Muscle Shoals house band of the late 60s – David Hood and Roger Hawkins – to rehearse with Primal Scream in London. A week later, Dowd followed them over. In late April the Scream, Dowd, Hood and Hawkins flew to Muscle Shoals, Alabama, to commence pre-production on an album that had still not completely been written. In May, recording began in Ardent Studios, Memphis.

Jeff Barrett had not worked for Primal Scream in any official capacity since being relieved of his publicist's duties by McGee at the end of 1989. While the Scream were in Memphis, McGee asked Barrett if he would be prepared to A&R them. 'The answer – any day, any year, any time of my fucking life – was yes,' says Barrett. 'At that point in time, it was actually a good move on Alan's count. Alan and Bobby and Andrew [Innes], their communications had broken down. Alan knew that I could communicate with the record company *and* the group. I could deal with the politics side of it.'

Barrett went down to Memphis to see how the sessions were going. 'What a fucking mess,' he recalls. 'It sounded great, but it was a mess. They were all pretty out of it ... They knew what they wanted. They wanted southern, swampy, a Keith [Richards] kind of vibe. But all the way through, when he was doing a session, Dowd kept saying: "I've got to give the singer some lessons." I think they did have this vision of a southern soul record, but between them and Tom the songs weren't communicated quite as well as they could have been recorded. It ain't Dowd's fault, it's the band's fault.'

When the Ardent sessions finished in July, most of the songs Primal Scream had recorded with Dowd were ballads, and none of them sounded like hit singles to McGee.

The *NME* had made *Copper Blue* its album of the year at Christmas 1992, causing KROQ and MTV to listen with fresh ears to 'If I Can't Change Your Mind', a Sugar single released in the new year. One by one, Bob Mould's predictions were coming true. 'All Rykodisc had to do was make sure the records were in the store,' he says. 'It was all UK-based momentum that translated to LA radio, which was dictating MTV.'

Sugar had already recorded their next record, a scalding, martyr-themed mini-album entitled *Beaster*, which Mould had played on the tour bus to his support band the Boo Radleys. They'd got very excited about it and so had Creation. Sensing it would do well in Britain, Mould argued for an April release; *Beaster* duly entered the album chart at number 3, two places behind the debut album by Suede.

Unknown a year before, Sugar were now Creation's leading commercial force.

The Boo Radleys had released two albums – *Ichabod And I* on a small northern indie; *Everything's Alright Forever* on Creation – and had ambitions that went far beyond the Merseyside shoe gazers rep utation that circumstances had given them. Influenced by Lennon and McCartney as much as by Kevin Shields, the Boo Radleys' guitarist and songwriter Martin Carr wanted to make albums that served as aural journeys, ejecting the exhausted passengers several ports ahead of their point of embarkation.

'We didn't think there were any bands on Creation that were nearly as good as us,' says Carr. 'The Valentines had left. Primal Scream – we didn't expect them ever to make a record again, for some reason. After *Screamadelica* I couldn't imagine what they would do. And as regards Ride, I thought "Leave Them All Behind" was terrible one-note rubbish.'

Seeking a complicated mixture of success, respect and self-gratification, the Boo Radleys had put out an artistic breakthrough single, 'Lazarus', in November 1992, winning many admirers at Creation but getting no higher than 76 in the charts. They now planned to record a masterpiece. *Giant Steps* would push back the boundaries as *Screamadelica* had, using the studio as a laboratory and crashing from genre to genre as though the band was making its very own 'White Album'. As far as Dick Green and Andy Saunders were concerned, *Giant Steps* was to be the key album of Creation's year.

'I went down to the studio and heard that record and I thought: this is a work of genius,' says Saunders. 'Alan had really liked "Lazarus" – he'd said: "This is the record that this band have been threatening to make" – but its chart position had been terrible. With *Giant Steps*, me and Dick were the only ones who got it. We were saying to Tim Abbot: "Chuck everything at it, Tim, this is a great record." ' The only one not jumping up and down was McGee.

His doubts about *Giant Steps*, which centred around the fact that some of the material was too avant-garde for him, did not worry Martin Carr too much, since McGee had taken almost five months to appreciate its 1992 predecessor, *Everything's Alright Forever*. Delayed reaction was a well-known McGee trait. As Nick Currie observes: 'Alan's way, if he likes a record, is to call you into the office and play you your own record. It's quite funny, you're sitting there saying: "Well, I've heard this, Alan." But he's just heard it three months after it's come out, and he says: "This is a great album – we should release all these songs as singles." '

Carr was at least grateful that McGee wasn't telling him to have *Giant Steps* remixed by a professional, as some label bosses might have. 'He was keen and he understood that it was something a bit different,' says Carr. 'But he would sit us down in the office and say: "It's going to be Swervedriver's year. You're going to have to take a back seat." Their record [*Mezcal Head*] was really well produced and he thought it could be big in the States.'

Giant Steps was released in July, the same month that Creation reached – though not celebrated – the tenth anniversary of its first ever single. Excellent reviews helped *Giant Steps* to 17 in the charts, whereupon an extensive advertising campaign got under way to keep sales bubbling. It was then that Andy Saunders took Carr aside and told him that the public face of the band – Carr and vocalist Simon 'Sice' Rowbottom – was something that needed to be looked at. Uppermost in Saunders' mind was the fact that Creation had missed having a perfectionist craftsman and genius since Kevin Shields had left the label in early 1992.

'Andy was convinced that people were looking for a Brian Wilson,' says Carr. 'This is what he kept telling me. He pulled me in the office and said: "You've got to make a choice. You can either sit there and do interviews as a band, and have two people sitting there doing nothing. Or you can start taking it on your own shoulders." And I thought: fair enough.'

The press would henceforth be ushered past the singer and rhythm section and left alone with Carr, an entertaining and intelligent 24-year-old who could sermonise on the future of popular music while drinking journalists under the table. Too personable to be mistaken for a tortured auteur, he left no one in any doubt that he could make pop records as well as critics' records if he wanted to. And he wanted to. 'I felt that everything was moving towards this big pop thing,' he says. 'Loads of bands – young bands with guitars – were getting in the charts. Blur were getting there. Suede were having hits. We didn't sell that many records with *Giant Steps*, but everyone was dying to see what we were going to do next.'

Adorable were not coming through. As the profile of Suede snowballed in Britain, Adorable's shrank to nothing. The two groups had kept pace in one sense only: neither of them released an album until at least three singles had come out. But whereas each Suede single had shot them further up the charts, Adorable's fell outside the Top 75 every time. And while *Suede* had become the fastest-selling debut album in the UK since Frankie Goes To Hollywood's *Welcome To The Pleasuredome*, Adorable's *Against Perfection* had barely charted.

'After the first single, things went completely wrong with us and the press,' says Piotr Fijalkowski. 'We never got another interview in the *NME* or *Melody Maker*. On McGee's suggestion, we took out an advert when *Against Perfection* went Top 75. There was a feeling that we had maybe turned a corner, although in retrospect I think it was the beginning of the end. McGee's suggestion was that we place an ad saying: "Adorable – the band you love to hate", as a fuck-you to the press. I can just imagine all the journalists reading that and feeling *really* chastened.'

Realising they had no future in Britain, Adorable were eager to tour America. However, incensed by Creation's deal with Sony, SBK was not exactly preparing an Adorable welcoming committee. 'We went out to the States in '93,' says Fijalkowski, 'and although our tour support was very modest – we were slumming it in a minibus for five weeks – they refused to pay the £10,000 we needed. They said they would only pay half of it and we didn't know if they were bluffing. With three weeks to go [before the tour started], our nerve cracked and we ended up paying half the amount ourselves.'

SBK's anger at Creation was reciprocated, and McGee was critical of the American company's sluggishness in capitalising on west coast radio support for Adorable's 'Sunshine Smile'. But as James Kyllo points out: 'It was Suede, the Auteurs and Adorable kind of all at the same time. Adorable came limping in third in that race in the UK, so they weren't that exciting a prospect to the Americans. I think SBK felt they'd got left holding the baby.'

It was not an argument that convinced McGee. Andy Saunders recalls him stomping around Hackney, kicking chairs and photocopiers, raging about SBK. 'It wasn't helped by the fact that Superstar had signed to them,' says Saunders. 'Alan was very pissed off about that, because we'd released [their 1992 album] *Greatest Hits Vol. 1* and he'd offered them a deal. They'd been one of the very few bands to turn him down. He wasn't used to being turned down by people – and then they'd gone and signed directly to his mortal enemy.'

Adorable still had a loyal supporter at SBK in Mike Mena, but Mena's influence had been undermined by a personnel shuffle and he was in any case up to his eyeballs with a new Blur album. Adorable got passed around from department to department. 'Some of the people at the label were absolutely dreadful,' says Fijalkowski. 'There was one guy who wanted us to storm into Charles Koppelman's office unannounced, jump up on the table and play a song for him. We were completely horrified.'

Worse was to follow when Adorable trekked around America to find hundreds of posters with the 'band you love to hate' slogan adorning the walls of the venues. They would spend fifteen minutes tearing down the posters before even unpacking their instruments. Finally, just as it was looking possible that the tour might be extended to include a second concert in the band's key support base of San Francisco, Adorable were told they were going home. Home to the only man apart from Mike Mena who had any confidence in them, Alan McGee.

'We mistakenly thought: well, McGee *is* Creation, so as long as we get on with him what's the problem?' says Fijalkowski. 'But Alan would be talking about how in the next video we should all be skydiving in Rio De Janeiro – aeroplanes, big yachts – and Dick would look up from his calculator and say: "We've only got £5,000." McGee would go: "Oh, all right, we'll just have you in a room, playing some guitars." '

With their key man clause waived, Adorable had no defence against a changed office. Andy Saunders, who hadn't been employed when they were signed, had careered past Laurence Verfaillie to become Creation's main link with the media. His view of Adorable was that they were 'big-mouthed gits who never followed it up with the music'. If that was discouraging, so was the look of the office whenever Adorable came calling. 'One of the reasons we'd signed to Creation was because the office was like our bedrooms,' says Fijalkowski. 'It was a warren with all these pictures of Creation artists pinned and Blu-Tak'd to the walls. But it was noticeable that there were never any Adorable pictures among them.'

It had become the fashion in the early 90s for record companies to have their own dance labels. A&M's Breakout imprint and Chrysalis' offshoot Cooltempo had taken off, encouraging even the folk-and-world music label Cookin' Vinyl to experiment with the dance-orientated Kickin' Vinyl. Creation's own dance label, Infonet, had forged its own identity with a series of 12-inches by the techno act Bandulu. However, not all of Infonet's records were well-regarded by McGee.

'The biggest fans of Infonet were the Abbots,' he says. 'They just kept telling me how big and important Infonet was. Then you'd get the record sales and they were about 800 copies.' McGee decided the best thing for Chris Abbot to do would be to sign the 20-year-old techno wunderkind Richard James, a.k.a. the Aphex Twin, who had a growing profile in the music press. Chris Abbot told McGee that he been in touch with James' representative Rob Mitchell and arranged a meeting.

Thinking they had been approached to do an Aphex Twin remix for some Creation band, James and Mitchell showed up in Hackney and were taken down to the bunker. 'I want to sign you,' McGee told James, expecting that he and Mitchell would then get down to business. Puzzled, Mitchell pointed out that James was already signed – to the dance label Warp, of which Mitchell was the owner. McGee, caught red-handed trying to poach another label's star act, was excruciatingly embarrassed. 'To his credit, he recovered pretty quickly,' says Mitchell. 'It was quite a sociable meeting after that. But walking in that room, I thought there was no way his intention was to try and sign the Aphex Twin.'

As Infonet's releases became more and more sporadic, the Abbots resented what they saw as restrictions placed on them by McGee, and argued that Dave Barker's August label was getting preferential treatment. They had a point. Barker was bringing to August the most indie of indie groups, not one of which was selling in large amounts. He had divided the office – roughly 90 per cent against and ten in favour – by signing Shonen Knife, a girl trio from Japan whose primitive pop punk sounded like cats brawling in a dustbin; and an act from Glasgow, 18 Wheeler, that seemed to be a throwback to early 80s indie endeavour-over-aptitude.

'August was the spoilt label because it was a closer genre to Alan,' says Tim Abbot. 'It had a Postcard sensibility and it had links with Norman [Blake] and the Glasgow art-school mafia. Dave would go: "Oi, McGee, Shonen Knife – this is fucking great." Dave could sell his argument in. He could stand up to Alan in his own right. The dichotomy with Dave is I loved him as a person, but August was like the little indie joke. Dave was in the back office so it was like indie and super-indie. It was Creation past.'

The August label was symptomatic of Creation's inability to consolidate the success of 1991 and 1992 and establish a consistent track record. Laurence Verfaillie had made a private joke about Barker signing anyone from Glasgow who could hold a guitar. She wasn't far wrong: one band that he picked up – Boyfriend – included ex-members of the Teenage Fanclub road crew. 'Dave Barker was not as motivated as McGee,' says the Fanclub's Gerry Love. 'He's a massive fan of music and he's not interested in power or financial success. He liked where he was. He didn't have any ambition to own a mansion.' But if Barker had McGee's backing, it would not be forever. Andy Saunders was once challenged by McGee to name one lousy band that Creation had signed. Saunders named three. 'Not Creation bands,' said McGee triumphantly. 'Dave Barker signed them.'

The third of the affiliated labels, Joe Foster's Rev-Ola, had been launched with a Fire Engines compilation in 1992, followed by a crazy poetry-and-psychedelia album recorded by the actor William Shatner in the 60s, *The Transformed Man*. Foster then began bidding for the rights to ten albums made by Shatner's *Star Trek* colleague Leonard Nimoy, as well as titles by the Modern Lovers, the American power-pop band Shoes and Maureen Tucker.

'Joe is the dude of dudes,' says Tim Abbot. 'Poor old Joe, he was on a grand [a month] and he had no A&R expenses. But Rev-Ola broke even. Joe would deliver – month in, month out. He knew his market space and he would go: "I've researched this. We'll do fourteen hundred." And it would sell thirteen hundred and ninety every time.' (In an interview in 1994, McGee described Rev-Ola's fanbase as 'loonies'.)

It was asking a lot of McGee to relinquish complete A&R control to Dave Barker and Chris Abbot, even if this was precisely what he had promised them. Left to his own devices, Barker was never going to sign a band that would change the company's fortunes. He would be more likely to spend money on acts that McGee would have rejected as not being good enough for Creation. Jeremy Pearce at Sony LRD was anxious for McGee to cut Creation back to the bare essentials and stop wasting time and money on trifles. And Pearce wasn't just talking about the August acts. Nine months into the relationship, he was far from convinced of the wisdom of the Sony-Creation deal. Take away Sugar and the whole thing looked like an expensive mistake. Where was the much-vaunted Primal Scream album? What were these worrying reports of the new Teenage Fanclub record being a disappointment? And who the hell were the BMX Bandits?

'We realised that they had too many no-hopers,' says Pearce. 'We never made Alan do anything. In fact, technically I doubt if we could. But it was getting bad. Very bad.'

So many rumours and half-truths have been told about the events of 31 May 1993 that it's no wonder Alan McGee has never been able to get his account straight. He has explained his reasons for dropping in at King Tut's Wah Wah Hut, a club in Glasgow on the premises of the old Saints and Sinners pub, as a desire to see if the Dave Barker-signed 18 Wheeler – the top band on the night's bill – were as good a live band as Barker said they were. He has also claimed that he went to King Tut's to meet a good-looking girlfriend of his sister Susan, whom he'd been assured was going to be there. Thirdly, McGee has revealed that he wanted to surprise and startle Debbie Turner, whose Sister Lovers were on the bill, by arriving at King Tut's unannounced. There is some truth in all of these explanations, but what is certain is that McGee entered the club with few expectations beyond getting drunk, hearing some music and whiling away a few hours before returning to London the following morning.

In the bar of King Tut's he met Gerry Love, whose friend Mark Coyle, a former Teenage Fanclub monitor man, was handling the sound for the three bands billed. But Love was hearing that there might be a fourth band playing. 'I knew a lot of the people at King Tut's,' he says. 'I turned up at nine o'clock and was told that all these guys had arrived from Manchester in a bus and entered the building. There was a bit of excitement because they were refusing to leave unless they were allowed to play.'

Oasis had been invited on to the bill by Sister Lovers, who had forgotten to tell the King Tut's promoter. 'There was a sort of rivalry between the two bands,' says Debbie Turner. 'It was like boys against girls. There were three girls in our band and they were a total lad band. We'd been showing off to them, going: "We've got this gig in Glasgow." And then we said: "Why don't you lot come up and do it?" '

Oasis had brought a number of friends down in their bus, intending to make a night of it. Told that there would be no time for them to play a set, Oasis protested strongly. Sister Lovers offered to pull out in sympathy. A third band, Boyfriend, did the same. Alan McGee was meanwhile staring at one of the youths in the Oasis party. He had a Paul Weller haircut, wore a smart Adidas top and gave off an air of nonchalant menace. If there was going to be a fight with the King Tut's management, this youth would not be a bystander. A member of Boyfriend came into the bar, confiding to McGee that trouble was about to break out.

'He was going: "It's going to go off, it's going to go off",' McGee recalls. 'I went upstairs to have a look at what was happening and make sure that 18 Wheeler didn't get mixed up in a fight. I knew the bouncers and I was going to say: "Cut it out, they're good kids." ' The next thing McGee knew, Oasis had persuaded the promoter to let them play four songs. Buying another Jack Daniel's and Coke, McGee went inside to watch them and was surprised to see the boy with the Paul Weller haircut walk onstage and pick up the microphone.

'You thought: that kid's got something,' McGee later said. 'Onstage he was giving it totally like – there were 12 people there and he was just giving it to everybody.' The arrogance of the singer mesmerised McGee, but he had plenty of opportunity to check out the other Oasis members. They had a balding rhythm guitarist who played mostly barré chords, a curly-haired drummer who kept his head low over his hi-hat cymbal, a bassist who looked like he was waiting for a bus and a lead guitarist who sounded like Steve Jones and had a facial resemblance to the singer.

'They did their first song, which I think was "Bring It On Down",' says McGee, 'and I went: "This is great." But I was thinking: a fluke. Then they did another song – I think it was "Up In The Sky" – and it was *great*. And I thought: fuck. I said to Susan: "I think I might do it." The third song they played – I can't remember what it was – was fucking brilliant. And I went: "I'm signing them."*

'When I say it was brilliant,' McGee goes on, 'I mean it was pretty flawless. But at the same time I thought: I can have this, and I can maybe sell half a million round the world. That's what I thought the maximum life expectancy was of this band.'

Had he attended the Manchester music seminar In The City the previous September, McGee would have seen Oasis play to a venue full of A&R men, none of whom was stirred by what he saw or heard. Factory Records, in the months before its closure, had been in possession of an Oasis demo tape but had not made any approach to the band. Other than the occasional trip to Liverpool or Oldham, Oasis tended to stick to Manchester, playing to between 20 and 50 people.

---

* The actual order of the songs Oasis played was: 'Rock 'n' Roll Star', 'Bring It On Down', 'Up In The Sky' and a version of the Beatles' 'I Am The Walrus'.

They would say not a word to the audience, and would refrain from making any movements onstage.

'They were just another band,' says Debbie Turner. 'It wasn't any big thing in Manchester. You knew Liam looked great and stuff, but to other people his whole stance [made them say]: "Well . . . is that all he's going to do?" That's how other people saw it.' Indeed, Turner remembers Mancunians being cynical about Oasis' similarities in attitude and demeanour to the Manchester stars of the late 80s. 'To those of us who'd grown up with the Stone Roses, it was like: "Come on, we've done that one",' she says. 'The music papers were getting into Suede or whatever and it was all going a bit more art-school, rather than baggy jumpers and just standing there looking aggressive.'

Creation did not have any bands that looked aggressive, save perhaps for Primal Scream, and its closest thing to a frontman with an attitude was Piotr Fijalkowski. But when you matched Fijalkowski's flowery poses and indie baritone against the belligerent charisma and raucous bark of Oasis' singer, it didn't seem to McGee to be much of a fair contest. To him, the Oasis boy was a natural pop star. Seeing Mark Coyle behind the mixing desk, McGee said hello and asked who was in charge of Oasis. They did not have a manager, but Coyle told him to talk to the lead guitarist, a one-time Inspiral Carpets roadie named Noel Gallagher. McGee found him with the rest of the band in the bar.

McGee did not realise that he had met Gallagher briefly at the Reading festival in 1989. Gallagher was rather taken aback by how much McGee had changed in the meantime: he was overweight and had lost a lot of hair. 'Do you want to hear a tape?' Gallagher asked him. McGee said: 'No, you're real. I'll sign you.' Gallagher gave him a tape anyway. 'He was very amenable, brilliantly bright, knew tons about music,' says McGee. 'He also knew a lot about the music industry. He had seen the pitfalls with Inspiral Carpets and he knew why they had failed.'

Gerry Love had stayed in the bar while Oasis played. He had heard them booming out, but there had been nothing that sounded particularly interesting to him, nor any different to the other bands he saw most nights of the week. He was a bit surprised that McGee was so impressed by them. But it made more sense to Debbie Turner, who knew how passionate McGee had been about the Stone Roses and Happy Mondays. 'Here was another band from Manchester, with this amazing-looking singer,' she says. 'Alan had had sort of lad bands before, but not like Oasis. You're talking about Primal Scream or the House Of Love. Primal Scream weren't a lad band; they liked to put on satin shirts and go for it. They weren't street.'

John Robb, who would soon be tipping Oasis as the band of the future, has another theory about why McGee was so attracted to them: Reid brothers déjà vu. 'Because they were the band that launched his label, he's always been looking for another Mary Chain,' says Robb. 'That's what Oasis are: four of them in a row across the stage, a surly singer and his brother who he fights with all the time. A big barrage of guitar sound with pop songs underneath. When McGee was seeing Oasis, he was seeing them as the Mary Chain.'

The next morning – a Tuesday – McGee phoned Dick Green at the office and told him that all their troubles were over. 'It was a totally ecstatic rant,' Green remembers. 'I'd had them before, but this was even more . . . This was like, he had found fucking stars – in the middle of nowhere. "We've got to get to them as quickly as possible. Bring them down in a couple of days . . ." '

19 Jacuzzi Rock

FOUR DAYS AFTER OASIS' GIG at King Tut's, Liam and Noel Gallagher and rhythm guitarist Paul 'Bonehead' Arthurs travelled down from Manchester to visit the Creation offices. Walking in, the first thing they saw was a cryptic message in black marker pen which Tim Abbot had scrawled on the ceiling of the reception area the night before. It read: 'Northern Ignorance'. The Mancunians were nonplussed.

'They went: "Fucking hell, that's bonkers – what does that mean?" ' Abbot recalls. 'I said: "Er ... oh, well, all northerners are ignorant. Heh heh. Aren't we?" ' A few heads turned as the Gallaghers strolled around. Their exaggerated gait, rolling shoulders and bobbing heads made them look like a cross between boxers and puppets. 'Noel was your total Manc kid,' says Abbot. 'Liam had got this green kagoule on, zipped right up. He looked really young, like a little mouse with a feathercut. But if ever there was a definable face of the time, he looked it.'

The Gallaghers and Arthurs were introduced by McGee to selected members of staff as the future of rock 'n' roll. Nobody had ever heard of Oasis before. 'I didn't know who the fuck they were,' says Andy Saunders. 'I shook their hands politely, made a football joke and that was it. I took no notice of them whatsoever. It didn't strike me as being anything other than the usual Alan McGee hype.'

The gregariousness of the Abbot brothers and the football-natured chit-chat made Creation an attractive proposition to the Gallaghers, as did the lines of cocaine chopped out for them in the bunker. Deal-less or not, Oasis had already developed a taste for the high life. McGee reiterated his desire to sign Oasis to Creation and extracted an assurance from Noel Gallagher that no other labels were in the running.

'What's that?' someone asked, pointing to the swirling Union Jack design on the band's demo cassette box. 'It's the greatest flag in the world,' replied Liam Gallagher, shoulders rolling. 'It's going down the shitter, and we're here to do something about it.' He paced around, critiquing the posters on the bunker walls. Tim Abbot couldn't take his eyes off him.

Noel Gallagher was quieter than his brother but – as songwriter and band leader – strikingly self-confident. Laurence Verfaillie remembers everyone swarming around this funny, slightly furtive little man with darting eyes. McGee was certain that it would be Noel's decision whether or not Oasis signed to Creation.

'The thing about Oasis,' McGee would say years later, 'is that they share my ambition. Noel definitely does. So does Liam in his heart of hearts, although he pretends he doesn't give a toss. See, for me, it's always been about being the best, the biggest. No offence to any of the other groups I've worked with over the years, but they didn't have the hunger for success that Oasis have. The Jesus and Mary Chain didn't have it. Primal Scream don't have it. But as Liam says, Oasis are mad for it – the same way that U2 were mad for it. It's taken me a long time to find a group that want to go all the way.'

Within days, McGee was preparing the ground for Oasis' arrival. Verfaillie was not going to do the band's PR: that job was being given to Johnny Hopkins, a publicist-cum-A&R man who had the physique of a jockey and was of equally small stature within the company. But Hopkins had been quicker than Verfaillie to see the potential value of Oasis; he noticed it as soon as they walked through the door. 'The conviction that they had was incredible,' he says. 'It was absolutely rooted in ability, not arrogance. Liam had the voice. Noel had the songs. It was going to happen.'

Verfaillie took the blow badly. Depressed and disillusioned, she had seen her authority challenged by Andy Saunders, who was now hoping to repeat the success of his Sugar campaign with Teenage Fanclub, an erstwhile project of Verfaillie's. With McGee regularly abroad on business, Verfaillie answered in theory to the company's new managing director, Tim Abbot. In practice, she answered to no one.

'Tim started putting the knife into Laurence very early,' says Saunders, an Abbot supporter at the time. 'Alan had been loyal to Laurence above and beyond the call of duty. Laurence was not making a lot of friends at the company. She was very domineering, very overpowering ... and acting in a bizarre fashion in a lot of ways. She was totally beyond the control of Tim.'

Seizing the initiative, Saunders had organised reams of press for Teenage Fanclub, who were holed up in a Cheshire studio some seven months into the recording of their new album. They had started it in Glasgow the previous year, expecting to be finished in six weeks. 'It was one of those things,' says Gerry Love. 'The bigger the budget, the longer it'll take you to do it. The discipline wasn't really there. I think we were all too close to our own beds.' Raymond McGinley admits the Fanclub were 'knackered' and had embarked on the record too soon after touring.

Before taking journalists to the studio in Cheadle Hulme, Saunders was warned that the Fanclub, whom he had yet to meet, were diffi-cult to work with and did not take easily to southerners. Unlike other Glaswegian bands, they had continued to base themselves in Glasgow rather than move to London, and were known to be stub-born opponents of marketing and hype. Saunders, who had pictured them as a friendly gang of beer-quaffing wits, was disconcerted to find them stretched out into the four corners of the studio, barely communicating.

Saunders liked what he heard of the album, but Dick Green was less sure. Creation needed another *Bandwagonesque*, but it was widely felt that the new record was not in that class. 'There was this big element of secrecy,' says Saunders. 'I could take [journalists] up to the studio, but they weren't allowed to listen to the record. Max Bell was going to do a piece for *Vox* magazine and I remember saying to him: "You can't hear the record." He said: "That's absolutely outra-geous. Who the fuck do you think you are?" and slammed the phone down on me.'

Stripped of Teenage Fanclub and passed over on Oasis, Laurence Verfaillie took a train with Tim Abbot one day in July. During the journey, she articulated her unhappiness and her fears for the way Creation was going. All those A&R misjudgments of McGee's ... those silly August acts ... and she had to be honest, the Oasis demo tape did not strike her as the work of an important band. Did Alan not realise that the image of the label was suffering?

Verfaillie had just talked herself out of a job. 'Very shortly after that, I was called into the bunker,' she says. 'Alan was very sharp. He said: "You don't believe in me. You don't believe in my company. You've got nothing to do here." ' Andy Saunders was appointed head of press within days of Verfaillie's sacking.

A straight talker with no time for sensitive egos or pseudo-artistic bullshit – the press nicknamed him DI Saunders because he reminded them of a policeman – Saunders was trusted by McGee in ways that Tim Abbot was not. Saunders was the man McGee took aside and told about a deeply worrying event that had happened to him recently at Heathrow. Taking his seat on a flight to Glasgow, McGee had been gripped by a suspected heart attack and had made the crew take the plane off the runway. He had then checked into a nearby hotel and summoned a doctor. The diagnosis was severe hyperventilation.

'Alan was scared by that incident,' says Saunders. 'It was not some-thing he wanted to boast about. He may have boasted about it to Tim and his other drug buddies, but to me he wanted to relay what a shocking and saddening episode it was. He didn't want me to see the humour in it. He was horrified that he'd been pushed through the airport by a pregnant woman. He was horrified that he'd been sitting on his bed in the hotel and he'd made the bellboy hold his hand until the doctor arrived.'

McGee's panic attack was known about by senior Creation staff members; however, few knew that there had been several such attacks before. On at least five occasions, McGee had blacked out on cocaine, but he was unable to stop taking the drug. 'I didn't realise the extent of it,' says James Kyllo. 'Although it was clear there was an awful lot of cocaine around, I didn't know that it had become such a problem.'

McGee's use of cocaine had escalated in the period following the Sony deal, and he was throwing himself frequently into three- or four-day binges. 'When I first became a millionaire, it started to send me out of my head,' he told a journalist in 1997. 'After the money started coming in, I would just start buying seven grams of coke rather than one.' The Sony deal had opened doors to him, and he now moved in very different circles to the McGee of the 80s. He had attended the launch of Madonna's book *Sex* in New York, and had been introduced to Michael Jackson backstage at a concert in Tokyo. He had also been a guest of Sony at Bob Dylan's star-packed thirtieth anniversary celebration in Madison Square Garden.

McGee's girlfriend Belinda White had virtually given up on him, disgusted by his cocaine addiction. McGee himself had long passed the point of enjoying the drug. Ride, who were ready to record another album and were looking around for producers, were getting no clear ideas or direction from McGee, both of which they needed badly. They would arrive for meetings to find Tim Abbot in charge, and would be left to guess where the President might be.

Tim Abbot had always been amazed by McGee's ability to party recklessly, have a few hours' sleep and function perfectly the next morning. Abbot, who had come across many eccentric management techniques in his time, had never seen one as simple and effective as McGee's. He kept his desk in the bunker completely untouched, working instead from a sheet of paper on which he had listed his phone calls for the day. As each one was made, he would score the name out with a pen. 'To this day, it's probably one of the best management systems ever,' says Abbot. 'If any management guru could tap that – and model what made that guy tick – it was that system. Biro, piece of paper, list. One knee pumping up and down while he made his calls.'

James Kyllo remembers 'constant nagging' whenever McGee was away from the office. 'He was on your case all the time, ringing up all day long. You would hear the scratching at the other end of the phone, which was him scribbling things out on his list of paper.' Says Paul Mulreany: 'He would go days without sleep. He'd say: "Go home, Paul, you look fucked." And I'd be like: "What are you doing, you going home?" "No, I'm all right." He was a fucking trouper. I'd get to sleep it off and eat some healthy food, and he'd still be at work.'

By mid-1993, Creation employees and bands alike were wondering how long McGee could keep it up.

McGee wasn't the only person who had decided that Oasis were the band he had always been looking for. Marcus Russell, a manager with a chequered history in the music business, had been taken to an Oasis gig in Manchester by his long-time client Johnny Marr. Russell told Noel Gallagher's girlfriend that Oasis reminded him of every band he had loved in the past 20 years. Driving back to London, he made up his mind to manage them.

A Welshman, Russell had been a promoter in the 70s before becoming a secondary school teacher. In the 80s he had started a management company, Ignition, taking on the soul band Latin Quarter and the Chrysalis-signed pop act the Bible. Through Johnny Marr, whom he had represented since the break-up of the Smiths, Russell met and managed Matt Johnson of The The for a time, and in the early 90s he placed a young band called SKAW with WEA without any success. Russell's up-and-down fortunes had left him with a profound longing to meet a band that had the capability to work hard to sell millions on an international scale. He took on Oasis after one meeting with Noel Gallagher – and before even hearing a tape.

Russell and McGee met for the first time on 2 July. At that point, Gallagher was all for signing to Creation provided he was granted total creative control. McGee was quite happy to yield to Gallagher in the UK, but was less able to guarantee what might happen in America. The problems really began when McGee advised Russell that Creation's arrangement with SBK still had some 16 months to run.

'The SBK deal was a pain in the arse,' says Jeremy Pearce, 'because everything on Creation had to go to SBK first – and SBK were completely hopeless, I must say. Any act we signed wanted to know what was going to happen in America, and when they heard it was SBK they thought of Vanilla Ice or whoever, and didn't want to sign.' Marcus Russell made it clear that under no circumstances would Oasis sign to Creation if there was a possibility of SBK acquiring the band.

The SBK deal was worrying Pearce, too. As a Sony man, the last thing he wanted was to keep giving Creation bands to SBK's owner – and Sony's rival – EMI. But as a lawyer, Pearce knew the contract was watertight. 'We desperately sought a way where we could avoid giving Oasis to SBK,' he says. 'I was absolutely not prepared to let EMI have the band.' Pearce racked his brains for a solution.

Outside Creation, McGee had been keeping Oasis under his hat. He had listened to the demo tape with growing astonishment as songs came and went, almost all of them sounding to him like potential hits. However, he had not run to Sony LRD immediately. 'I never had the impression at that point that this was the obvious, absolute winner,' says Pearce. 'Alan had never said: "This is going to be the biggest band in the world." He may have thought that, but it would have been unlike him not to have said it.'

There was one thing that neither McGee nor Pearce needed to say: Creation was once again critically short of money. As their income from worldwide licensees had dried up, McGee and Green had been forced to put in money of their own and to borrow more from Sony. McGee confesses that Creation was governed by a shoebox-under-the-bed mentality. 'Me and Dick were terrible with the money,' he says. 'I was a fucking coke addict and Dick was the guitarist in Biff Bang Pow! – and we were running a record company.' Creation had lately exceeded its funding arrangements with Sony. For Creation to sign Oasis for a five-figure advance would require Paul Russell to lobby his bosses in New York. This would take time; time during which Marcus Russell could approach any other labels that took his fancy. 'There was a huge danger of us not getting the band,' McGee admits.

Acclaim and middling sales for Teenage Fanclub apart, McGee had yet to deliver a band that America embraced. Whereas Mute had cracked the States with Depeche Mode – and 4AD would soon with the Breeders' album *Last Splash* – Creation was struggling to improve on the 200,000 sales of *Bandwagonesque*. True, Primal Scream were making an album that McGee and Sony hoped would do in excess of a million, but it wasn't going to happen with a bunch of Tom Dowd-produced ballads. McGee wanted George Drakoulias, the producer of the Black Crowes, to toughen up two tracks for release as singles. Aching for success in America, McGee was even thinking about relocating Creation to Los Angeles. 'He came in one day very excited because he heard that Ivo Watts-Russell had upped sticks and gone to America,' recalls Jeremy Pearce. 'He talked to me about how cool that would be. As I remember, there was a woman involved.' McGee was talked out of it.

Confirmation that McGee was respected as a player by the Americans – if not as a hitmaker – arrived in July when he was honoured at the New Music Seminar with the Weber Prize for excellence in business and music. This coming-out-of-the-cold award for a notorious wild card and black sheep was reported widely by the press in Britain: McGee was only the third person from the UK to receive a Weber, after Daniel Miller and Island's Chris Blackwell. Other previous recipients included Seymour Stein and McGee's hero Ahmet Ertegun of Atlantic. The award recognised McGee's role as 'a visionary in discovering new talent and an accomplished entrepreneur'. 'It's a great honour,' his interestingly-worded advance statement read, 'to accept this award on behalf of myself, Creation Records and the UK independent record scene.'

A super-obnoxious McGee gave a rare, eve-of-ceremony interview to the *Glasgow Herald*, in which he claimed that the award meant nothing to him and sneered at the managing directors of UK major labels. Referring to a lowly Scottish football club, he likened his competitors to 'Stenhousemuir, but not as exciting'. He talked of his south London riverside penthouse flat, with its swimming-pool and jacuzzi: '[That's] where we have end-of-tour parties-stroke-orgies and get wasted . . . I believe in that funny rock 'n' roll thing: if you're going to get a flat, get one with a swimming-pool . . . I want to be 65 and worth £40 million, with houses all over the world and superstars on my label.' Spinning off into fantasy, he went on: 'With Sony's money we can sign anybody. We put in a £1 million bid for New Order. No one is beyond our cheque-book.' No one except possibly Oasis.

Flying to New York with his father to receive the Weber, McGee took so much cocaine that his behaviour became Napoleonic. He threatened to beat up the concierge in his hotel when the plastic door-key to his room didn't work (until he realised he was on the wrong floor). At the ceremony in Manhattan, he sat stiffly between Boy George and Sylvia Rhodes, the chairman of East West, who was receiving an award herself. In an emotional speech, Rhodes spoke of music's responsibility to family values before bursting into tears. When his name was announced, McGee strode up to the rostrum, said 'Thanks a lot' into the microphone and walked straight off. There were audible gasps.

Primal Scream were in disarray. Tom Dowd's mix of the album was not rock 'n' roll enough for anyone's liking. Martin Duffy had reportedly been stabbed in New York – it later turned out that he had got drunk at a party and fallen on to broken glass, narrowly missing a kidney. The Scream had since decamped to the Chateau Marmont in LA for talks with prospective US management.

'At that point with the Sony deal, we were nearly over the first year,' says McGee. 'Sony were going: "Where's your Primal Scream record?" I needed a flagship. We were a big noise in the indie world, but now we were in the world of Jamiroquai and Pearl Jam. We needed some real juice. About £350,000 into the album, we didn't have a hit.'

Members of Ride were also in LA, keen to meet George Drakoulias and convince him to work on their album. Since the signing of the Sony deal, Ride's autonomy had been chipped away and they had gone from being one of the most important bands on Creation to one of the least. They had been working on material in an Oxfordshire studio and were banking on Drakoulias to marshal them into shape and get them singing more aggressively. The indie band of yore was listening to Americana these days: the Black Crowes, Little Feat, Gram Parsons and the Steve Miller Band.

That week in LA, McGee played the Oasis tape to death. From his 100-mile-an-hour rants, Andy Bell picked up bits of information here and there – Johnny Marr, Manchester – and agreed with McGee that the tape had something special about it. 'It was very summery,' Bell recalls. 'It was not noisy. It had about ten songs on it and Alan was just caning the tape.'

McGee had been confident that Oasis were The One, but not so certain that he hadn't solicited the views of others within the Creation family. Three months after King Tut's, however, he became certain – as certain as one human being could ever be – when he heard a new song they had recorded, 'Live Forever'. He took it with him on holiday to Honolulu and put the word around his other artists. From then on, Oasis had a firm fan in Martin Carr, who was playing 'Live Forever' to almost everyone he met.

Attempting to describe Oasis to people, McGee would sometimes mention the Kinks, the Stone Roses and the Who, and declare that Oasis were a perfect blend of the three. At other times he would speak of the Beatles, the Sex Pistols, the Jam and T. Rex, and claim that Oasis were as good as all four. In a meeting with the plugger Garry Blackburn in July, McGee said: 'Garry, you're at Wembley. It's a penalty. The goalkeeper's been sent off. It's the eighty-ninth minute. It's nil-nil. All you've got to do is kick the ball straight in and it's a goal.' Blackburn was persuaded – but Oasis still hadn't signed to Creation.

Marcus Russell returned from America impressed with the Sony label Epic, whose A&R executive Dave Massey had reacted positively to the Oasis demo tape. With Epic looking the likeliest US label to sign the band, Russell's American campaign was slotting into place; it was the UK that was a bloody mess. If Oasis went with Creation – as Russell, Noel Gallagher and Alan McGee all wanted them to – Epic would instantly be squeezed out of the picture in America by SBK. 'I told Alan that I wanted Oasis,' says Mike Mena, to whom McGee had played the tape as a friend. 'I told him I'd like to use this band to repair the relationship, and to prove to the company that the Creation deal is a special deal. This was why we did the deal – to get a band of this calibre. Alan came right out and said: "I'm not going to let you touch this." '

In September, Oasis performed for the second time at Manchester's annual In The City seminar. The attendance for their gig in the Canal Café Bar was moderate, for the buzz at the seminar centred on several other groups including the London-based Elastica and Tiny Monroe, and a band from Scotland called Whiteout. With around 70 unsigned acts on show, the *NME* elected not to review the Oasis gig, and subsequently made no mention of them in its three-page In The City coverage.

Jeremy Pearce, who had not seen Oasis play before, was at the

Canal Café Bar with his Sony LRD colleague Mark Tattershall and people from Sony Music Publishing. 'Mark and I both thought Oasis were absolutely fantastic,' says Pearce, 'partly because I assumed Liam had written the songs. I remember thinking he was the new Bob Dylan ... His presence was so extraordinary you couldn't stop looking at him. But I must say it was a very muted reception from the other Sony guys.'

Following Oasis' appearance at In The City, Marcus Russell received inquiries from Go! Discs and the Mother label, the latter a joint venture between PolyGram and U2. Mother's A&R man Richard Brown had played the Oasis tape to his boss Malcolm Dunbar, who was dazzled by Liam Gallagher's voice. 'Marcus was clever,' says McGee. 'He knew Noel wanted to sign to us, but he was also talking to Mother and Andy Macdonald at Go! Discs. He was seeing what the options were. And the option ultimately was: "I'll tell you what. We'll sign to Sony, we'll go with Epic for America and we'll license Oasis to Creation for the UK. Do you want to be involved?" Oh yes we do ...'

Licensing Oasis to Creation – as opposed to signing to the label directly – neatly removed SBK from the equation. Moreover, since the Oasis contract was with Sony LRD, Paul Russell wouldn't have to press for more money from New York to cover the band's advance. 'I was pretty sure that we wouldn't have too much trouble getting approval,' Russell says, 'but the very quick solution – as Alan was desperate to get this thing signed, like, tonight – was simply to sign them to Sony, where we didn't need anybody's approval.'

There was a flicker of worry that SBK might sue. Jeremy Pearce was prepared for a battle. 'People were saying: "It'll never work, it's a sham",' he recalls. 'I was saying: "Well, actually it's not a sham. This is what we're actually going to do." ' Mike Mena remembers that SBK considered legal action 'for a moment' but backed down. 'It was like: "We could fight this. It's in our deal",' he says. 'But another term of the deal was that we were also supposed to release three records per year, and we hadn't been. It was better not to fight it. There was no way to fight it.'

On 22 October, Oasis signed to Sony LRD, which immediately licensed the group to Creation for the UK only. The advance was £40,000 – £20,000 less than what Creation had paid for Adorable. Epic in America acquired the band under Sony's inter-company agreement.

The terms of the deal in the UK, which gave Oasis the financial security of Sony and the credibility of Creation, were kept from the music press. Oasis did not want people to know they were signed to Sony, and nor, for pride reasons, did Creation. The press in Britain took Oasis at face value as a Creation-signed act, a vital factor in the torrent of publicity that followed the next year. 'We didn't go broadcasting the fact that Oasis weren't signed to us,' says Dick Green. 'We didn't *lie* about it . . . but why tell anyone?' Why indeed. The early 90s were littered with examples of major label acts – Rain, the Real People, the Mock Turtles, Ocean Colour Scene – that had suffered in the media by virtue of having the wrong credentials. These were not examples that Marcus Russell and Noel Gallagher intended to emulate.

As for the SBK-Creation deal, it was officially dissolved in 1994. McGee's one-time friend Mike Mena had been fired a couple of months earlier.

'Who's the square guy in the corner?' Andy Saunders asked Tim Abbot one day in October 1993. Abbot named the suited, bespectacled newcomer as Mark Taylor, who had just joined Creation from Sony as financial controller. At 29, Taylor was not much older than Saunders, but he was an accountant who had come to do a job, not to hang out or be admired for his dress sense. 'The company was in a dreadful state,' he recalls. 'I was asked to go in on a fairly short-term basis to try and put some fiscal shape into it . . . Creation had borrowed heavily off Sony and Sony were understandably nervous about giving more cash until I'd stabilised the situation.'

Taylor was greeted with wariness by some of his new colleagues. Was he a spy in the camp? Whose payroll was he on? 'In terms of reporting back [to Sony], I produced monthly figures which obviously everybody saw,' he says. 'But in terms of me being there to give some inside information, that was never asked or expected of me. I was working for Creation. Everybody wanted a company that was stable and successful commercially.' Jeremy Pearce was particularly uneasy as Creation's record sales were down on the previous year, and McGee later lamented that not one of his 1993 releases had alleviated the label's financial burden. 'Albums like *Giant Steps* – classic fucking albums – would only sell 150,000 copies around the world,' he said. 'This was before the mainstream connected with this kind of music.'

Creation's infatuation with *Giant Steps* ensured that advertisements ran until the end of the year and beyond, and further tracks from the album were released as singles in the hope of a Top 40 place and a *Top Of The Pops* invite. Nevertheless, when the campaign was wound down, only 60,000 copies of *Giant Steps* had been sold in Britain. Meanwhile, Teenage Fanclub's *Thirteen* came out in October to indifferent reviews, performed half-heartedly over the counter and was criticised in interviews by the very people who had made it. 'Chas [Banks] and a number of other people told us we were stupid,' says Norman Blake. 'I suppose we were. We didn't realise that if you tell people your record's crap they might believe you.'

The accent was suddenly on retrenchment. From a commercial

perspective, there was no sense in proceeding with August and Infonet, and the end for both labels was on the cards once Mark Taylor looked at the books. Estimated to have lost Creation £400,000 between them, August and Infonet would be closed early the following year. Taylor, despite finding McGee an intimidating character, would continue to suggest cutbacks in roster size and reductions in marketing spends.

George Drakoulias had rehearsed Ride for a week in Oxford with a view to producing their album in the autumn. Seeking ways to streamline their sometimes open-ended music, he got them to play tightly-structured versions of the Creation's 'How Does It Feel To Feel' and the old standard 'Windmills Of Your Mind'. 'It was almost like a songwriting workshop,' says Andy Bell. 'He was great at taking a song that was five minutes long and making it three-and-a-half, without losing any of the punch. "You've got to go to the middle-eight here. You haven't got a middle-eight? Well, *write* a middle-eight." '

However, when the band was ready to make the record, Drakoulias was unavailable to do it. Ride had lost the one man who could have taken them in an American rock direction. 'I think he saw us as just too English,' says Steve Queralt. 'There was no way we were going to sound like the Black Crowes.'

The antithesis to Drakoulias' ball-busting biker personality, the reserved Englishman John Leckie had just given up on the Stone Roses' second album and had a window free before he was due to begin a Radiohead project. Leckie and Ride moved into Sawmills studio in Cornwall during the snowy winter of 1993. Access to the studio, which stood on an inlet on a river, was via a boat. Egress seemed only a matter of time.

'I nearly left the band,' recalls Queralt. 'It was a case of being homesick and being stuck in the middle of nowhere with no escape. If you're not getting on with people in the band, Sawmills is just hell. I felt like a session bassist and Andy was starting to dictate too much how things should go. I remember him standing by Loz for ages, telling him what beats to play. You didn't get any praise for what you did any more. You'd do a bass line and no one would say anything.'

With Ride's rhythm section seeming increasingly functional, and as apathy set in right across the personnel, Christmas saw a change of location to the Manor in Oxfordshire. The sound of the album changed, too – to psuedo-majestic, hallucinogenic anthems tinged with tambouras and the Louisiana swamps of Dr John. What had been planned as an immediate-sounding, American-produced live rock album was turning into the most embellished – and at £150,000, most expensive – record Ride had ever made.

By the time George Drakoulias got to remix two tracks by Primal Scream in November, four other songs from their Tom Dowd sessions in Memphis had been re-worked in Detroit and London respectively by George Clinton, the leader of Funkadelic, and Paul Weller's co-producer Brendan Lynch. All four songs made for good album material, but McGee still hadn't heard his hit. 'George Drakoulias saved their arse,' he says. 'Until Drakoulias put that big, dumb drum beat on "Rocks", we were going to sell no amount of records whatsoever.'

The stomping, cavalier 'Rocks' – a deliberate play on the Rolling Stones' 'Rocks Off' – was played down the phone to McGee by Drakoulias and Andrew Innes from Oceanway Studios in Los Angeles. He bounced around the room. 'I knew at the very worst that we were going to get our money back,' he says. When Drakoulias and Innes played him a second uptempo track, 'Jailbird', a few days later, he deemed it another certain smash.

'I thought it was the best album they'd ever made, and so did Alan,' says Andy Saunders. 'He gathered everybody together in the bunker and played "Rocks" and "Jailbird" back to back, jumping on the desk, punching the air. The *NME* got a tape of "Rocks" at Christmas and [editor] Steve Sutherland was holding up the phone and saying: "Listen! We're all dancing to it in the office ..." '

Most of the Creation staff had still not seen Oasis play live. It was a key component of Marcus Russell's gameplan that the band should delay making its London debut until the new year, and Oasis' October tour with the BMX Bandits and 18 Wheeler had played to the regions only. On 4 November, however, a private showcase was held at London's Powerhaus for the benefit of Creation, Sony and Epic employees. There was a hung jury.

'I had heard the tape before that and thought: it's just too derivative, there's no way anybody's going to want this. That song's all right, but it's just stolen from T. Rex,' says James Kyllo. 'I was very dubious about the wisdom of it, and I wasn't further encouraged at the Powerhaus. Strange, funny-looking guys with big eyebrows who didn't ever take their coats off. And the whole set sounded awfully derivative.'

Kyllo was not alone. In general, Creation staffers were sceptical about Oasis, partly due to Noel Gallagher's custom of juxtaposing other people's melodies with his own, and partly due to their lack of animation onstage. 'I thought they were shit,' says Andy Saunders, who saw them play Wolverhampton in December. 'I thought they needed a stylist. "I Am The Walrus" was awesome, but I couldn't give two shits for the rest of their songs. I didn't get it at all.'

Dick Green was also at the Wolverhampton gig. 'I didn't think it was amazing,' he says. 'There were parts of it that were. You could see there was a presence there, but I don't think it immediately said to me: "World-conquering".' That same week, the *NME* gave Oasis a terrible review for a show in Birmingham, judging them 'too well versed in old records to do anything new'.

At Creation, only McGee, the Abbots and Johnny Hopkins praised Oasis unreservedly. An Oasis faction was taking shape that would harden over the next five years, adding new members and losing others. The faction, having divided the company, would go on to drive it. Hopkins, all but inconsequential a year before, would soon become one of the most indispensable people at the label. But Andy Saunders' personality clashes with Hopkins made his wrangles with Laurence Verfaillie seem like lovers' tiffs.

'Live Forever' had been a standout track for McGee, and the one he'd envisaged as Oasis' debut single. But Marcus Russell didn't want a single released until the band had a nationwide following – and either way it wouldn't be 'Live Forever'. Meetings were held between Russell, McGee and Tim Abbot to decide how best to approach Radio 1 in the run-up to Christmas. In the meantime, McGee changed his mind about 'Live Forever' and pushed for the first single to be the jet-propelled 'Bring It On Down'. 'I thought they were the revolution,' McGee says. 'They were incendiaries. I mean, they didn't give a fuck – and I wanted to come out with a song like that. "You're the outcast, you're the underclass, but you don't care because you're living fast ... You're the uninvited guest who stays till the end ..." '

It was a nice idea, but in fact Noel Gallagher chose the debut single himself: a recently-written tune called 'Supersonic'. With a release looking unlikely before March, an Oasis taster was offered to Radio 1 in the form of a white label of 'Columbia', a track from the demo tape with a mood of growing psychedelic turmoil. Once 'Columbia' had been premiered on Radio 1's *Evening Session*, Christine Boar, a producer at the station, took it to a play-list meeting on 16 December. The result was that 'Columbia' was aired a further 19 times in the ensuing two weeks – the first instance of a place on the play-list being given to a record that was not for sale. At once, Creation knew that Oasis were going to be a major act.

All the same, there was not exactly an Oasis groundswell in the music press. Tipping its bands-to-watch-in-1994, *Select* magazine wrote presciently that a rock 'n' roll revival was looming, but gave its vote to Whiteout without mentioning Oasis. The writer of the article was Andrew Perry, erstwhile student and Jesus and Mary Chain fan, now *Select* reviews editor. 'I'd got a "Columbia" white label, but it was seen from the press point of view as quite a half-hearted push,' Perry says. 'The push wasn't like: "This is the best band you're ever going to hear." For me, it didn't sound like something out of the ordinary. You know, they used distorted guitars – like all the other fucking indie bands. Jeff Barrett was the guy who kept going on about them to me, but it was purely about their characters. No one was really talking about the music.'

By the end of the year, McGee was getting ready to talk about Oasis' music and character to somewhere between 15 and 20 journalists. Andy Saunders, who had convinced him that there were would be good commercial sense in celebrating Creation's tenth anniversary – even if belatedly – was booking interviews with McGee for January and February, including an *NME* cover story to run in two parts and be based around his next trip to Los Angeles. Saunders, Dick Green and Tim Abbot were also looking ahead to a Creation indoor festival in the summer, intended to be the culmination of a six-month promo campaign.

Knowing that 1994 was to be an intensive year for him, McGee's way of dealing with the pressure was to numb himself with drugs, taking cocaine and slimming pills for energy and drinking Night Nurse to ward off insomnia. 'Alan was withdrawing more and more,' says Saunders. 'He was seriously fucked up. I had set all these interviews up with no guarantee that he would do them. There was a sense that Alan was doing me a really big favour.' Saunders was fully prepared for McGee to give three or four interviews and cancel the rest.

Three days before Christmas, McGee and Tim Abbot were given some MDMA powder that turned out to be a lot more powerful than they were used to. It sent them crazy. 'People were supposed to have a line of it – a couple of centimetres,' says Abbot, 'but Alan and somebody else had got hold of a [gram] and did this MDMA powder in one go. It really tucked him up.' McGee was confined to bed for ten days.

Abbot flew to LA for the cutting of the Primal Scream album, which Andrew Innes was overseeing, and stayed until January. 'Alan was supposed to fly out with me,' Abbot says, 'to get over Belinda and everything else. But as it is, he went fucking doolally and disappeared. I got to Los Angeles and it was the normal Chateau Marmont super-drug-abuse going on. Alan phoned up a couple of times, off his nut, on Christmas Eve. He's gone: "Fucking hell, man, I'm in bits. This fucking stuff's sending me over the edge." I was chatting with him, going: "Look, you've got to slow up. You're like a bull at a gate with stuff like this." ' But when *NME* journalist Keith Cameron interviewed McGee in LA a few weeks later, the thing he noticed most of all was the frightening amounts of cocaine that were on the table.

The morning after Cameron flew back to London, McGee and Abbot partied late, getting back to their rooms at the Mondrian at around four o'clock in the morning. Less than an hour later, Los Angeles was hit by an earthquake measuring 6.6 on the Richter scale.

'I was on the tenth floor and Alan was on the third,' says Abbot. 'I legged it with a rap band who were staying there, all running down the ten floors of the service well. But Alan stopped in his room. He went introverted. I couldn't find him in the car park. There was a black dude trying to find his girlfriend, so we blagged this torch off somebody and went back into the hotel. I went down to Alan's door in the dark and he was very shocked. We said: "What do we do?" We were still off our nuts. And as the sunrise came up, they put the cable TV back on at six. You realised how devastating it was: this wasn't just a local incident, it was a national disaster.'

Abbot and McGee lay together on the bed, shaking in time with the after-effects of the quake. At around eleven, George Drakoulias drove over to the Mondrian in his twelve-seater Land Rover and picked them up. 'He went: "Shall we go out wreckage-watching?" ' Abbot recalls. 'I said: "Yeah, come on, let's go and have a look around." But Alan went: "No, I don't think it's like that, Abbot. You don't get it." '

As soon as he and Abbot were safely back in London, McGee flew out to Japan for meetings with Sony. 'I always say that that was when I said *goodbye* to Alan,' declares Abbot. 'He phoned me a few times from Japan, saying: "I'm going out of my mind here. I can't talk to anybody because of the language. They don't know who I am. I've met the number two at Sony who thinks I manage the Clash. He keeps asking me about Joe Strummer and Mick Jones." '

Abbot believes that the earthquake had affected McGee in a profoundly serious way. The pre-earthquake McGee, he feels, never resurfaced. 'I came back as a verballer,' Abbot says. 'I still can live off that story and get goose-pimples from recounting a near-death experience. If you talk to anybody who's in a post-trauma [state], you have to get it out of your system and actualise it. But Alan didn't. I think it was a definite contributor to what happened next.'

20 On Bended Knee

THE ATMOSPHERE AT ABBEY ROAD was tense. Andy Bell and Mark Gardener addressed each other economically and without humour, like a married couple that has agreed to stay together for the sake of the children. The kids – Steve Queralt and Loz Colbert – wondered if a quick divorce might be a better idea.

It was January 1994. Ride were mixing their album, which it had become painfully clear was over-long and rather too self-important. McGee told the *NME* he heard 'five hit singles' on it. That was five more than anyone else heard. Andy Saunders remarks: 'I had huge misgivings when Alan came bursting in and went: " 'Birdman' – it's the first single. We come back with a difficult record that makes people think." We were going: "What's your thinking behind this, Alan?" He's going: "It's an epic! It'll confuse people!" '

Sire in New York was taking a close interest in the album. Joe McEwen sat in on a meeting to decide the track-listing and argued the case for a collection of ten punchy songs. Unfortunately, ten punchy songs were not something Ride had. McEwen told them to do more work on the Creation's 'How Does It Feel To Feel' and put it on the album, or Sire would not be releasing it. The last of the self-governing indie bands of the early 90s gave in to the A&R man's ultimatum without a protest.

During the mixing stage, Noel Gallagher had been a frequent visitor to Abbey Road. The Gallaghers were Ride fans – Liam had once had a burst of 'OX4', from *Going Blank Again*, greeting callers on his answering machine – and Ride were just as interested to hear the latest news from the Mancunians' camp. 'Noel was welcome,' says Loz Colbert. 'There was a brilliant sense of joviality and cheerfulness from him, and an excellent approach to the whole surroundings and trappings of music. He was a complete gem while he was sat there in Abbey Road, and a brilliant antidote to everything that was going on around us.'

Andy Bell had always had a tendency to get dizzily excited about the new thing in guitar music – the House Of Love, My Bloody Valentine, the Stone Roses – but Oasis held him in a near-religious spell. It was hard for him to feel inspired by his own album when tapes of 'Live Forever' were being passed around. 'Noel was like a shoulder for me to cry on,' he says. 'I'd talk to him about things I didn't feel right talking about with the band guys. He basically said: "Take pride in what you're doing. What you do is really valuable to this band. You've got a right to say something if you don't feel happy with things." That rubbed off. Around that time, I went to the band – with a bit more confidence – and said that I wanted to put the full writing credits on the album. Not just the words but the whole song.'

Sole authorship was something Noel Gallagher planned to claim on Oasis' records in no uncertain terms. The issue remained, however, a bone of contention in Ride. 'There was always an indistinctness about the roles me and Mark played,' says Bell. 'The attraction of Oasis in some ways was that it was very much like: "*He* does this. *He* does that. *They* do that. And it works." Noel's got a very straightforward way of looking at things.'

Gallagher had brought to Abbey Road a tape of Oasis' debut album, which they had been recording in Wales. He wasn't happy with it at all: his impulsive decision to work with the former Inspiral Carpets sound mixer Dave Batchelor – who had produced albums by the Skids and the Sensational Alex Harvey Band in the 70s – had backfired when Batchelor insisted on recording all the instruments separately, sluicing the coarseness from the Oasis sound. 'We were losing the spirit of the demos,' says McGee. 'We scrapped it at £50,000. I went off and told Jeremy Pearce. To be fair to Jeremy, he took it on the chin.' Oasis started again at Sawmills, with Mark Coyle producing and Anjali Dutt mixing, and this time they recorded together as a group.

McGee had raved about Oasis in his January interviews, calling them 'potentially Creation's biggest ever band'. They gave their first official London performance on 27 January at the Water Rats club in King's Cross, by which time Marcus Russell's waiting game had created a genuine sense of anticipation. 'When you saw them live, they made sense,' says Andrew Perry. 'The place was absolutely mobbed, and a buzz circulated from there amongst the media.'

The *NME*, like *Select*, had wondered what exactly it was supposed to make of the 'Columbia' white label. One or two journalists aside, the paper was cautious about supporting a band that seemed to be retracing the footsteps of the five-year-old Madchester movement. 'We were very noncommittal,' recalls John Harris, an *NME* writer of the time. 'People had been taken to see them, and [Steve] Sutherland had been wined and dined a little bit, but no one was very sure if they were anything more than an all right Happy Mondays.'

Oasis picked up live reviews here and there. In February, Johnny Hopkins sent a photographer to shoot a session in Amsterdam, where the band was to play its first gig outside Britain. The trip turned into a news story when drunken misbehaviour on the ferry ended in arrests – though not for Noel Gallagher, who had been asleep in his cabin and missed the whole thing – and Oasis were sent back to England without a note being played. 'Johnny came up and said: "Oh my God",' remembers Andy Saunders. 'I said: "Great fucking press." Johnny was going: "Yeah, great press but what a nightmare." We were thinking: Christ, it's over.' Marcus Russell was livid, as was Noel Gallagher, but the undertones of danger and chaos in the *NME* news story gave Oasis a clear edge over other, less unpredictable bands such as Whiteout, 18 Wheeler and Shed Seven. Two or three months of spadework had effortlessly – and quite accidentally – been circumvented.

A second track from Oasis' demo tape, 'Cigarettes And Alcohol', was given free to *NME* readers as part of a five-song Creation cassette that same month. 'Again, no one was too sure,' says John Harris. 'It was a very different version [to the one they later recorded]: the riff was completely backwards and Liam sings in this weird, reedy, thin voice. I thought it sounded like a bad version of "The Concept" by Teenage Fanclub. Sort of knowing, gonzo rock – without the "knowing" bit.'

The *NME* cassette was organised by Andy Saunders as part of Creation's tenth anniversary marketing campaign. Other promotional items were arranged, including a ten-track CD sold via the *NME*, and there was a significant retail push on new releases and back catalogue at Virgin and Our Price. Two in-house pluggers, Anita Heryet and Aude Prieur, were handling regional and college radio, and Saunders' press department had taken on an ex-publicist for East West, Matthew Rumbold. All activities were geared towards an anniversary concert at the Albert Hall in June – an all-acoustic performance by Creation artists which Tim Abbot, as a pun on MTV's series *Unplugged*, had entitled 'Undrugged'.

'Bear in mind that there wasn't really any long-term strategy at Creation,' says Saunders. 'It was a very organic company. A lot of it was down to: "Oh, you're the girlfriend of one of the bands. We better give you a job." It was funny reading in interviews Alan saying that the company needed to be scaled back, because he was really the last person who had realised that. Everybody else was saying: "What's going on here? Who are these people?" The whole employing-girlfriends-of-bands thing went on well into the late 90s.'

McGee had indeed been promising journalists that Creation's oversized roster would be chopped down to a more manageable ten or twelve acts, and that only the best would be allowed to stay. 'It's not a charity,' he told Q. As an illustration of how it might have been construed as one, Creation had released around 140 albums in ten years; in the same period, its contemporary Food had put out just nine. As James Kyllo points out: 'Alan may have said that he was going to cut down the roster, but he was still signing two new groups for each one that he got rid of.'

However, Creation would sign no new acts between February 1994 and April 1995. The President had more pressing matters to contend with. 'On 20 February, 1994, I got on a plane to Los Angeles,' says McGee. 'I got taken off at the other end by paramedics, and two days later I was being given oxygen in Cedars-Sinai hospital. I was out of the game and on my back.'

McGee had flown to Los Angeles with his sister Susan after spending two nights taking cocaine and speed with Primal Scream in a Bermondsey rehearsal studio. He'd left them at nine in the morning and made it to Heathrow with Susan just in time to catch a midday plane. Four hours into the twelve-hour flight, McGee was hit by a panic attack which he later compared to being on very strong acid. Susan got the flight crew to telephone ahead for an ambulance, and her brother spent the next eight hours hallucinating at 30,000 feet, dropping in and out of consciousness.

When the plane landed, he was met by paramedics who examined him and told him he had nervous exhaustion. McGee didn't think this sounded too serious. He and Susan checked into the Mondrian where he started on an alcohol bender lasting some 36 hours. 'It was like that line from Bowie's "Diamond Dogs",' he said later. ' "When they pulled you out of the oxygen tent, you asked for the latest party." '

His bender took him to a Swervedriver show at the Roxy, where he proceeded to drink almost a bottle of Jack Daniel's. Returning to the Mondrian in the early hours of the morning, he was begged by Susan not to take drugs. After agreeing that he wouldn't, he went into the bathroom and swallowed a handful of diet pills.

The next day, he was driven out to Burbank for a meeting with Mo Ostin and Lenny Waronker at Warner Bros. McGee's toes were curling up in his socks and he felt as though he had a metal pole in his back. In the Warners building, the desks seemed to rise and fall like waves before his eyes. Not wanting to make a fool of himself in front of Ostin and Waronker, he got a cab straight back to Hollywood. Feeling hot and uncomfortable, he asked the driver to stop at a store and bought a bottle of water to pour over his head.

In his room at the Mondrian, he took his clothes off and had a shower which failed to relax him. He thought he might be having a heart attack. Lying naked on the bed, he saw the blinds on his window start to move, at which point he went downstairs and told the people on reception that he was going to need medical assistance. The paramedics were summoned; McGee remembers 17 of them arriving. His blood pressure was high and the paramedics feared he might not make it to the ambulance. He was put in a wheelchair, given oxygen and told not to move. Walkie-talkies crackled and people stared in concern as he was wheeled through the lobby.

'There's a point at which most people who survive drugs snap,' McGee later wrote. 'That's enough. There's no further to go. That's the point I had reached.' He was taken to the Cedars-Sinai hospital, a famous resting-place for Hollywood's drug-addicted actors and musicians, where he was pumped with Valium and discharged later that night. Each day for the next ten days, he was visited at the Mondrian by a doctor who injected him rectally with medication. In that ten-day period, McGee remarkably found the time and energy to attend a Jesus and Mary Chain video shoot and have an affair with a local girl.

Ed Ball was on tour in Tokyo, playing keyboards with the Boo Radleys, when McGee's PA Kle Boutis rang. She told him that McGee needed him in Los Angeles. 'I had fallen to pieces,' McGee says. 'To get from the bed to the toilet was like running up a hill. My brain wasn't accessing the energy in my body. I didn't have the strength to get my bags and go to the airport.'

Flying to Los Angeles via London, Ball found a McGee he barely recognised. 'He was fragile, very fragile, like someone who had lost his bearings,' Ball later remembered. 'It was weird because in all the years I'd known him, he had been this confident, impulsive, obsessive character, and suddenly it was like he was a shell.' Ball and McGee stayed in LA for a couple of days before returning to London.

As the Creation staff arrived for work, they were told by Dick Green that McGee had had some sort of vague incident and been flown home. Andy Saunders recalls Green telling him to cancel some last-minute interviews with McGee for the anniversary campaign. 'Dick said: "Alan's going to take some time off",' Saunders remembers. 'That was his euphemism. I didn't have any sense of how serious it was.'

McGee spent a week at his flat in Rotherhithe being cared for by his father and Ed Ball. Tim Abbot, who had received a rambling call from Los Angeles a few days earlier, went down to Rotherhithe and was alarmed by what he saw. 'I went for a walk with Alan and ... he could literally only walk for about ten or fifteen minutes before he was out of breath,' Abbot says. 'He couldn't make the congruence between his head and his body. But he wasn't recognising that he was ill. He was like: "I've had a setback. I'm going to convalesce for four weeks and I'll be back on the skip again." '

McGee's father suggested his son move back to the family home in Glasgow. He lived there for several weeks, remaining in contact with Kle Boutis and Dick Green and also with Colin Brewer, a London psychiatrist who specialised in cases of drug abuse. 'The drugs hadn't cleared out of my head,' McGee says. 'Before the doctors could do proper therapy, I had to balance. They didn't think I was balanced enough to deal with all the emotional shit that was going down.'

Like snapshots from a bad dream, the interviews McGee had given for the anniversary campaign were now being published, many of them romanticising his lifestyle and signing off with a grating, here's-to-the-next-ten-years-of-degeneracy-Alan wisecrack. With lamentable timing, Jim Reid, asked by the *NME* how McGee should celebrate the anniversary, had replied: 'Buy loads of drugs and get wasted.'

A dazed McGee was seen on the streets of Glasgow by Jim Beattie. The former guitarist in Primal Scream had gone on to form his own band, Spirea X, releasing an album on 4AD in 1991. 'He could hardly walk,' Beattie recalls. 'I met him crossing the road. He said: "You and Bobby were my best pals, and it stuck in my throat that you never came to me with Spirea X." I said: "Alan, I tried to get hold of you but Dick Green wouldn't put me through ..." He was really ill.' Days later, McGee moved back to Rotherhithe.

Nobody at Creation bar Boutis, Ball, Green and Tim Abbot had spoken to McGee since February. He was living on his own, going for walks and experiencing a surreal form of double vision: he realised he owned two copies of many of his favourite records and books, and couldn't understand why he had bought duplicates. 'We didn't know how long he would be gone for,' says James Kyllo. 'In some ways it seemed that it might be a good thing for Creation, to help settle it down. Having a month or two of relative peace – to be able to calm things down and get things running sensibly – didn't seem like such a bad thing.'

The public was unaware that McGee had had a crisis, and the few journalists who heard rumours of something amiss were stonewalled by Andy Saunders' press department. 'There was this great hope that he was going to make an appearance at "Undrugged",' says Tim Abbot. 'Even if it was just a Queen Mother salute from the box. Then it all grew that it was getting too much for him.'

A depressed and beaten McGee was vowing to cut his ties with Creation and the music business. 'I was very bitter,' he later said, 'because before that everything I'd done was to please other people. Everyone wanted Alan McGee to be out of control, whether it's my friends or people who wanted me to keep up the legend. The only person who got fucked up was me.'

It became accepted within Creation that McGee would not be at the Albert Hall for 'Undrugged' in June. What he might do after that was anyone's guess.

Bobby Gillespie had given Primal Scream's album the title *Give Out But Don't Give Up*. Pre-publicised heavily by the music press, it appeared to have every chance of becoming one of the major records of the spring and early summer – and retailers and accountants alike had been pleased to see 'Rocks', the first single, head straight for the Top 10. Great things were expected of *Give Out But Don't Give Up* not only in Britain but in America, where the band had agreed to tour intensively as a support act.

Above all, *Give Out But Don't Give Up* was to be the album that made sense of the Sony deal, racking up international sales that would cancel out the £2 million that Creation had borrowed from Sony since 1992. But when the album was released at the end of March, a first-week UK chart position of number 2 was followed by a rapid tail-off in interest and sales right across the board. 'Sony had talked it all up,' says Tim Abbot, 'and it performed as any Creation album would have performed. We creamed the fanbase properly. In the UK it wasn't deemed a flop. It's only in retrospect that people say: "Well, that was the dummy album." But really they were an *NME* band trying to have a crossover pop hit.'

Gillespie later complained that Primal Scream's 22-week world tour was like clocking in and out of a factory. The American leg – supporting Depeche Mode – saw the Scream play their southern-influenced rock 'n' roll in amphitheatres to mystified audiences made up, as Gillespie put it, of 'middle-class goth girls'. American sales of *Give Out But Don't Give Up* did not even total 100,000.

'A guy called Steve Rennie was appointed their manager in America against Alex Nightingale's better judgment,' says Abbot, 'and Rennie was all-time Captain Rock: "Heyyy, guys, you're fuckin' great ..." We were in Las Vegas on that Depeche tour and he'd brought a guy from President, a merchandising company. They've gone: "Got some great T-shirt designs for you." And one of them was an *elephant*. On a Primal Scream T-shirt. I'll never forget it. They caned Rennie out of the room. They were like: "Get us off this fucking tour." '

Give Out But Don't Give Up sold around 600,000 worldwide, a fraction of what Sony had hoped for. Jeremy Pearce found dealing with the Scream difficult, and suspected they simply weren't equipped for the amount of conscientious promotion and strict punctuality that go into breaking an album internationally. 'What we found ... was that although they fancied selling a few more records in theory, they just weren't ready for the heavy marketing approach,' Pearce says. 'There was a huge weight of expectation on them because the deal had been made for them. As is so often the case, of course, it turned out that they weren't the most important act any more.'

The friendship between Bobby Gillespie and Alan McGee had been in trouble long before the latter had fallen ill. It was not to improve. 'Primal Scream had had contact with me a couple of times up to May,' McGee says. 'Then they did the Depeche Mode tour and didn't contact me for three or four months. By that point my attitude was: "Well, if you haven't contacted me for four months, fuck you." '

But if McGee was angry that some of his oldest friends were not by his side in his hour of need, Primal Scream were helpless without their number one confederate and tower of strength. 'When Alan went poorly, the Primals needed him so badly,' says Jeff Barrett. 'They really needed him and he really needed them, and neither of them were there for each other ... I was in New York with Bobby, sitting in a hotel room doing an interview. Alan had just been took fucking daft. [Bobby] had been on the phone with him and they were both *lost*. But neither of them knew how lost they were.'

The brunt of the Scream album's comparative failure was borne by Creation, and by the much-pressurised intermediaries at Sony LRD. Jeremy Pearce was in an especially invidious position, having put his shirt on *Give Out But Don't Give Up* while at the same time building up LRD as an enterprise quite separate to Paul Russell's Sony Music Entertainment. Now Pearce had to take the criticism from all sides. 'Paul Russell thought Alan was faking his illness because he couldn't face the position he was in,' Pearce says. 'Russell wanted to make me pull him into the office for a dressing down. Actually, we protected Alan amazingly against that. Dick couldn't do anything – he was totally relying on our goodwill to keep the thing going.'

Sony LRD owed its existence to deals with emerging labels and Creation had been its kingpin. With Creation in peril, the obvious follow-on question was what was the point of LRD? 'Dick was at one end of the chain,' says Stuart Middleton, LRD's finance director. 'Paul Russell was at the other. And we were stuck in the middle. Russell was putting us through shit.'

While he feels it would be wrong to blame *Give Out But Don't Give Up* for Creation's predicament, Mark Taylor concedes that unexpectedly low record sales were disastrous for a company that frequently spent too much on marketing, had a high headcount and lacked the financial stability to make expensive albums. 'Sony were looking at what the monthly figures were telling them, and seeing that the roster was large and needing cutting,' Taylor says. 'It was a combination of too many bands, too many staff and records not selling well enough. Those were the constant issues that we were discussing with Sony.'

One band not yet seen as crucial by Sony was Oasis. They began phase three of their album in May, giving the Mark Coyle and Anjali Dutt tapes to Owen Morris, a protégé of Marcus Russell's from Wales, to undertake a thorough remix. It was now almost a year since Alan McGee had discovered the band. However, Oasis had in a relatively short space of time become the music critics' idea of what an exciting rock 'n' roll group should be. On 7 April, Noel and Liam Gallagher had given the *NME* one of the most notorious interviews of the decade.

Performing at the six-day Sound City '94 festival in Glasgow, supporting the Boo Radleys, the Gallaghers had been introduced to *NME* journalist John Harris by Martin Carr. 'He was in awe of them,' Carr recalls. 'Liam says to him: "How's it going?" John says: "OK, yeah." Liam goes: "Not good enough," and walks off. John's like: "*Wow* ... that's really rude!" ' Carr had spent a strange night with the Gallaghers, during which they had exploded one by one all his preconceptions about them. Although the Boo Radleys and Oasis were effectively label-mates, they were from different planets. 'I was quite into meeting journalists and having intellectual discussions about music,' Carr says. 'But the Gallaghers were just into drinking, shagging and being in a band. We stayed up all night talking about music, and we didn't agree on anything. I was into the Beatles as a progressive band, but they were just like: "No. Beatles. Mad for it." That was the most you could get out of them.'

In their interview with Harris, the Gallaghers squabbled about the incident on the ferry to Holland – about which Noel was still furious – before threatening each other with a beating. Harris printed their outbursts verbatim and in doing so sealed their reputation. The article began with Liam shouting at Noel: 'Let's fucking go then, you dick! Let's have a fucking fight.' The *NME* had never known anything like it.*

'Fantastic,' says Andy Saunders. 'It was all building brilliantly. We weren't used to having bands that did this kind of shit. This was proper rock 'n' roll shit. This wasn't playing at it. This was fucking pianos in the swimming-pool.' Johnny Hopkins, who had been in the room when the argument erupted, later called Harris' article 'one of the great rock 'n' roll interviews'. Two weeks after it ran, Oasis' debut single 'Supersonic' charted at 31. Those who had assumed Oasis were another Adorable – Steve Queralt of Ride, for example – were caught by surprise. Dave Newton had earlier asked Liam Gallagher if Oasis would like to support Ride on their next UK tour. 'Yeah, brilliant,' Gallagher had replied. Suddenly, it wasn't so clear which of them was the bigger band.

After their own sell-out tour for 'Supersonic', Oasis continued to play around the country in May, immediately beginning a third tour at the start of June. Meanwhile, Owen Morris and Noel Gallagher had completed the final mix of the album that Tim Abbot was already predicting would be a *Never Mind The Bollocks ...* for the 90s.

'Me and my brother were social friends with them,' says Abbot. 'We went out every night, seven days a week. They were like no other band. Wherever they were – if they were at a party or round some-

---

* Extracts from the interview were released in 1995 by the indie label Fierce Panda as a single, 'Wibbling Rivalry (Interviews With Noel and Liam Gallagher)', credited to Oas*s.

body's house – they would have a tape of [Oasis] with them, and whatever was playing, be it house or whatever, they would fuck it off and go: "Listen to this." They would *play their own music*. Unbelievable. I've never seen any other band so blatantly or unashamedly do that. None of this "I'm an artist and I'll wait my turn". They would go: "Fuck that off. This is us." The *front* of those people.'

'The whole Swinging London … was a myth anyway, but all eyes were on us. If we can get just a little bit of that back, some of our pride, then it's all worthwhile.' These are the words of the bassist in the Direct Hits, a Dan Treacy-sponsored 60s revivalist group that played Alan McGee's Communication Club in the early 80s. The bassist was speaking to a fanzine in 1985, when pride in British pop was anything but fashionable.

In an interview prior to his breakdown, McGee had talked of his longing 'for good British music to sell in America'. It was particularly relevant given that guitar rock and pop – the music on whose behalf McGee had been fighting since the days of the Communication Club – was finally starting to sell in substantial quantities in Britain. Leading the charge was Blur, a band Creation had rejected.

In 1993, having had some initial chart success only to fall away badly, Blur had released their second album, *Modern Life Is Rubbish*. Written in America on a punishingly long tour organised by SBK, the songs pined for a traditional England of greasy spoons and Sunday roasts. Arguably the first record in the genre that was to become known as Britpop, *Modern Life Is Rubbish* reacted strongly against not only American life but American music – not least the grunge movement that had been partly responsible for Blur's commercial decline. Promotional photographs for their single 'For Tomorrow' showed Blur wearing Fred Perry shirts and Doc Martens, standing under the graffito 'British Image 1'. A proposed title for their album had been *England V. America*.

But although Blur achieved a modicum of success with *Modern Life Is Rubbish*, it was Suede who had won most plaudits in 1993 with their modernised, melancholic take on glam-rock. The two bands offered very different slants on British (or English) pop and ran a fascinating race for most of that year – Suede topping the charts and receiving the Mercury Music Prize for their debut album; Blur jumping back into contention with a critically exalted set at the Reading festival – which was made all the more piquant by the fact that Justine Frischmann, the ex-girlfriend of Suede's singer Brett Anderson, had left him for Damon Albarn.

Both Anderson and Albarn would soon claim that the idea of referencing British or English imagery and musical trademarks had occurred to them first. Where Blur had an advantage over Suede was in their use of humour, inspired by Ray Davies of the Kinks, which evoked a bittersweet Britain not quite nostalgic and not quite futuristic. It was, by the autumn of 1993, the sound of London. 'There was a general growing sense of confidence and vibrancy in the whole music biz,' publisher Mike Smith recalled to Blur's biographer Stuart Maconie, 'and it was in lots of ways generated by Blur and the kind of things they were trying to do, and the scene they moved in in Camden. After years of this slacker culture and everyone wearing flannel shirts and jeans and taking their musical cues from the States, there was a lot of talk of the influence of British music.'

Martin Carr of the Boo Radleys had told journalists around the time of *Giant Steps* that the band's next album would contain ten or twelve 'pop songs'. From watching other bands' careers, Carr knew that commercial success and radio-play were not the pipedreams they would have been in 1992. Unlike Albarn, Carr wasn't batting for England necessarily – a Scot with a Scouse accent, Carr was not the type to care about territorial oneupmanship. 'I liked Blur a lot,' he says, 'but where they lost me was the patriotic stuff. I must have missed a nationalist meeting.'

As Carr and others started writing songs with radio and the charts in mind, *Music Week* pointed out that they'd better come up with something special: the market-place was not as convinced by alternative, indie or Brit-revivalist bands as the London-based music press might have thought. Even the indie charts were hard to get into. 'With the covers of *NME* and *Melody Maker* almost exclusively dominated by the likes of new chart-toppers Suede and Björk,' wrote *Music Week* in March 1994, 'one could be forgiven for thinking that it was they who would dominate the independent singles chart. But ... 1993 was the year that dance totally overran the singles market.' The year's three highest-selling indie singles were by Urban Cookie Collective, Capella and Sub Sub, and they didn't have a guitar or a bittersweet English lyric between them. Sensing defeat at the hands of dance, Dave Balfe negotiated with EMI to sell his shares in Food on the eve of release of Blur's third album, *Parklife*. 'He felt guitar music was over,' Mike Smith told Maconie. 'That was the big reason why he called it a day ... He didn't see that a huge renaissance was just around the corner.'

Had Balfe looked closer at Radio 1, he might just have thought twice. A new controller, Matthew Bannister, had instigated what *Select* magazine called 'one of the most extreme overhauls in [the station's] history', making sweeping changes to the daytime schedules and encouraging the evening presenters Steve Lamacq, Jo Whiley and Mark Radcliffe to introduce more new bands. Bannister's inspiration came in part from the London BBC station GLR (Greater London Radio), which he himself had rebuilt from the carcass of Radio London in the late 80s and early 90s; and also from the unlicensed indie station XFM, which had been on air for trial periods in the capital and had delighted its small listenership with Nick Cave at breakfast and the Boo Radleys for elevenses. Impressed by the friendly, knowledgeable style of XFM's presenters, Bannister took a sword to Radio 1's veteran clowns and egomaniacs, guaranteeing experimentation and an end to rigid play-lists. 'Columbia' by Oasis had already been one beneficiary.

Blur's single 'Girls And Boys', released in March 1994, zipped and beeped with a holiday mood that alternative music had, with the exception of the Wonder Stuff's 'Size Of A Cow', almost never experienced before. 'It was catchy and original,' Blur's producer Stephen Street told Maconie, 'and it was witty and humorous in a way Suede never were.' The song charted at a remarkably high number 5. *Parklife* was released the following month, with seemingly the entire country eager to hear it. It entered the album chart at number 1 and sold to a vast number of people who had not been part of the band's fanbase.

'*Parklife* changed the perceptions of the UK music industry,' Food's managing director Andy Ross claimed to Maconie. 'There was the status quo, which included ... the indie sector, and *Parklife* moved the goalposts almost without us knowing. It didn't just sell a shed-load of records, it invited a lot of people back to music as a hobby. A lot of 30-year-olds decided they liked music again.'

The re-entry to record stores of these guitar music fans was more than simply the kiss of life for an endangered genre. It was the beginning of the Britpop boom that would make millionaires of Albarn and Blur, alter the bias of the music business from dance to guitar pop, and lead ultimately to Creation becoming one of the most successful record companies in Britain.

Control of Creation had not been handed over to Dick Green in any formal sense by McGee. Green manned the fort as an administrator, working closely with Sony LRD, but more than one source has alleged that McGee in the post-breakdown period felt as bitter towards Green as he did towards everyone else. 'Alan was anti-everyone: the bands, the Creation employees,' the source remembers. 'He wanted nothing to do with the business. His breakdown was so severe that he couldn't stand any contact with the business. It was quite stunning.'

The credit for steering the ship in McGee's absence is claimed by almost everyone in a position of influence at either Creation or Sony. Most vociferous of all is LRD's Jeremy Pearce, who remarks: 'We were dealing with Dick on cash. Dick was important because he was actually the one who was within the company running it, but ... Dick was nothing to Sony. They didn't care about Dick. [Paul] Russell used to call him Fatty Green. He had complete contempt for Dick. At least Alan was the guy who signed the bands, but Dick was just the guy who didn't know what the fuck he was doing, as far as Sony was concerned.'

Mark Taylor does not concur with Pearce's account. 'I think we all were [keeping Creation alive],' he says. 'I'm very aware that an awful lot of people put an awful lot of effort in. As to one person taking credit – if anybody could, I think Dick could. As far as I was concerned, it was just: get your hands dirty and let's try and keep this baby afloat.'

Andy Saunders' recollection is that he and Green ran Creation as a team, with assistance from Tim Abbot whenever he was in the office. Johnny Hopkins counters: 'Tim was very important. Andy likes to think he was. He was busy doing his politicking. A circle formed around Dick – not of Dick's making, but people trying to edge into control ... Dick's not the natural leader that Alan is, but he's honest and genuine and intelligent. Dick really held it together.'

Many of Abbot's skills as a motivator overlapped with McGee's, and he had proved invaluable to Primal Scream and Oasis in ways both abstract and concrete. 'He was the main cheerleader,' says Saunders. 'He had taken the role of Alan, which was to be the maverick boss – the one who went in and said: "It's OK, I'm the grown-up, I'm paying for everything." '

Abbot sees his contribution to Creation at that time as being a mixture of A&R leadership and what he calls qualitative control. 'I ran the outward communication side,' he says, 'and Dick dealt very much with the legalities and the finances and the bootstrapping of keeping that organisation together.' Abbot's relationship with Green was as close as Green would allow, but all around them schisms were beginning to show. Abbot and Andy Saunders, who had been allies a year before, were drifting apart the more time Abbot spent outside the office. 'Tim was basically locking in his supporters – Johnny, Christine [Wanless, label manager], the ones who were working directly with Oasis and Primal Scream – and there was me and Dick on the other side,' says Saunders. 'Tim was basically saying: "I'm on the glory train here. I've got a few people with me. The rest of you are shit." '

Some months before McGee's fateful flight to Los Angeles, he, Abbot and Green had come out of a tempestuous meeting at Sony feeling that the two companies were mortally incompatible and would be unlikely to see out their 1992 deal. 'We got in the lift,' says Abbot, 'and Alan said: "Right, this is it. It's us three against those fuckers. I want you, Tim, to come equals with [me and Dick] on what's left of the company." '

Abbot, seeing his long-dreamed-of shares in Creation appear out of thin air, spent the following weeks chivvying Green to make it happen. The legal firm Lee and Thompson was instructed by Abbot to get the necessary paperwork out of Creation, whose solicitors assured him that the matter was being taken care of. 'It wasn't like: "Oh, we've got 20 million to carve up",' says Abbot. 'It was: "It's the three of us now. I want you to be looked after." And Alan would often say: "Has Dick got that deal together yet?" I told him it was all being looked after. Then Alan had a breakdown.'

McGee's breakdown hadn't made him and Abbot fall out as friends, so Abbot didn't see why he shouldn't pursue the question of shares from time to time in their phone conversations. One night Abbot was at home with Christine Wanless and Paul Mulreany when McGee called up from Rotherhithe in a state of high anxiety. 'He was going: "Tim, I'm ill. You shouldn't talk about business when we talk." This went on for about four or five phone calls, with me saying: "Look, Alan, I'm sorry to bring it up. But if this is going to come on top and we might get taken over by Sony or whatever, I want to complete on these shares." In the following phone calls [he said]: "Fucking hell, man, that really gets me going. Is that all you're interested in when I'm ill?" "No, no, no, Alan. You know I love you." Blah blah blah. This carried on till about two o'clock. Then there was a phone call at three, just when I'd gone to bed, and I was like: "Alan, you're driving me up the fucking wall. Please – this is crazy. This is eight, nine phone calls now. You're winding yourself up over [nothing]. Just chill out. Relax, my man. You know I love you. I can't do any more for you. I'm running your fucking label as I see it, I'm dealing with Primal Scream . . . These are tough times for everybody. Just relax." '

Abbot arrived for work the next morning to be met by an apprehensive-looking Dick Green, who asked him what the hell he'd said to McGee. McGee had phoned Green and told him he would never work with Tim Abbot again. 'I went: "Oh, that's fucking nice, isn't it? I'll call him this afternoon",' Abbot recalls. But when he asked Kle Boutis to place a call to Rotherhithe, she replied that McGee had forbidden Abbot to contact him. 'For about two or three weeks after that, I would ask Kle to put calls in,' Abbot says. 'And she'd go: "He's not taking any calls off you at all." '

One of the things that had made the McGee-Abbot bond seem so exclusive to other people was their 24-hour 'open line', whereby one would ring the other to chat, plan campaigns or play music down the phone. With the open line rescinded, Abbot was in limbo. 'It all went horribly wrong for Tim,' says Andy Saunders. 'Alan felt he was exploiting his illness – which I think is exactly what Dick wanted to happen.'

Saunders had often been bewildered by the extent to which Green permitted Creation to be controlled by the McGee-Abbot axis. Repeatedly ridiculed and undermined – a put-upon Private Pike to Abbot's streetwise Private Walker – Green had shied away from any confrontation with Abbot and had instead, Saunders now believes, played a clever political game. 'Dick had kept a very dignified silence during the whole reign of Tim Abbot,' Saunders says. 'That was a really interesting thing for him to do. I think he was playing a shrewd long-term strategy and he watched Tim fuck himself up in the pursuit of glory with Oasis and Primal Scream, and then make the fatal mistake of being . . . disloyal to Alan by trying to force his advantage.'

Abbot never got close to McGee again. But nor did he leave Creation Records. He went to Green and offered to stay for the sake of the label's relationships with Primal Scream and Oasis. Green had no choice but to agree.

When he heard *Parklife*, Steve Queralt knew it was all over for Ride. Next to Damon Albarn's bubbly self-confidence, they had the look of a woolly mammoth in an amusement arcade. The average age of Ride was 25, but it might as well have been 40. 'The mood of the nation was happy,' says Queralt, 'and it seemed like all our songs were just too slow and too dreary.'

Ride were still popular with the music papers up to a point, though, and *Melody Maker* had planned to feature the band on its cover. After overseeing an interview and photo session in Los Angeles, Andy Saunders got a call from the paper's features editor a few days before the story was due to run. 'He goes: "I've got some terrible news. Kurt Cobain's died",' Saunders recalls. 'I'm like: "Have I still got my cover?" He goes: "No, you don't understand – I've got some *terrible news* . . ." '

Being bumped from the *Melody Maker* cover was, says Saunders, 'a real portent. It had all been set up really nicely. Suddenly, we couldn't give it away.' Relations between Ride and Creation soon hit an all-time low when an *NME* journalist quoted an unnamed person at the label as saying that the group would probably split up in the near future. The source was later revealed as Dick Green.

And it seemed that Green might be right when 'Birdman', the first single to be released from the new album, charted at a startlingly low 38. 'It was like: oh, is that it?' says Dave Newton. 'Last time we released a new single off an album, we got to number 9. Is this the last time we're in the Top 40?' The answer was yes.

As Ride were losing friends at the label, Oasis were gaining them. The widespread feeling towards the Mancunians from Creation acts was congratulatory rather than resentful, and there was much speculation about how far they could go. On 5 May, members of Oasis, Ride and the Boo Radleys faced a room full of *NME* readers at a conference to promote June's 'Undrugged' concert at the Albert Hall. 'I couldn't believe it,' says Steve Queralt. 'Liam and Noel were just so charismatic and friendly.' Martin Carr, who was representing the Boo Radleys with Sice, remembers: 'We had no chance. Every question, nearly, was towards Liam and Noel. I think Ride got two questions and we got one, and our question was about Oasis.'

One comical exchange from the Gallaghers was almost worthy of the Beatles' early press conferences in America. Liam: 'You've got to progress. But it doesn't mean to say you've got to go forward.' Noel: 'Eh?' Liam: 'You can progress sideways. Or backwards. I'm right. Tell me I'm not.' Noel: ' ... Progression is going forwards. Going backwards is regression. Going sideways is just gression.'

'That press conference told me quite a lot,' says Dave Newton. 'I sat there thinking: they're in their element here. They were a brilliant double act. Mark and Steve, who had done a lot of press, weren't a patch on Liam and Noel. From then onwards, it was pretty obvious what Creation was going to be. It was Oasis' record label.'

Although he had no intention of taking part in 'Undrugged', Alan McGee found it impossible to put the event to the back of his mind. Ed Ball, his near-constant companion, was to be the evening's emcee and McGee was curious to hear what introductions he had written for the acts. Ball told him he hadn't written them yet. 'He says: "For fuck's sake, Ed, have you not worked out what you're going to say?",' Ball recalls. 'I said: "No, I'll just busk it." He says: "You can't *busk* something like that. Let's do it now." Then he says: "Fucking hell, I'm under stress and I'm here scripting the stuff with you." It was his first sort of step back into the business.'

McGee's illness was no longer a closely guarded secret. In his review of 'Undrugged', *NME* editor Steve Sutherland wrote clumsily: 'Rumour has it he's in retreat from living the dream too high and fast.' Friends had tried to tempt McGee along to the Albert Hall, not realising that he had developed a fear of crowds and loud noise. Instead he passed instructions down the phone to Dick Green. 'He rang up to say he wanted John Coltrane's *A Love Supreme* played during the breaks, and that the whole night should be dedicated to Curtis Mayfield,' says Andy Saunders. ' "... and I want [KROQ DJ] Rodney Bingenheimer to introduce so-and-so." These messages would come through Dick. "I've been speaking to Alan. He says Rodney Bingenheimer's got to ..." I'm like: "Who the fuck is Rodney Bingenheimer?" Even from his so-called sickbed, he was sending out these annoying interferences.'

'Undrugged' on 4 June was notable only for its absentees: McGee, Primal Scream, Teenage Fanclub and many others besides. A dull evening of acoustic guitars and time-consuming changeovers, its subtext was pure hubris: Creation was presented as a songwriters' academy whose graduates merely had to strum three woody chords and murmur into a microphone to merit comparison with Bob Dylan and Neil Young. Proving the fallacy, the best performance came from Arthur Lee, a man not even signed to the label.

'It was a really badly organised night,' recalls Andy Bell. 'We hadn't realised that the Scream weren't booked for it. They were the natural headliners. Bob Mould came on and headlined, and to everyone – to me, anyway – he just wasn't appropriate to headline a celebration of ten years of Creation. The way I imagined it was going to be was so different. I thought they'd get the House Of Love to reform, and the Mary Chain would turn up, and the Valentines of course.'

Primal Scream, who were touring in America, appeared on a video screen speaking from Los Angeles. 'Tim Abbot had gone on this road odyssey with them,' says Andy Saunders. 'He wanted to do Gracelands, he wanted to do all this American-iconography-cocaine-road-trip and to live out this bizarre dream that he had. I'd told him to take a video camera out there and record a message from the Scream, which he did really badly. We had a terrible video of them going: "Uhh ... you're all there ... and we're all here ..." I'm like: "Cheers." ' The video had to have subtitles added to make it intelligible.

Bob Mould's headlining slot was preceded by short sets from William Reid, Pat Fish, Pete Astor, Idha Ovelius, Velvet Crush, Noel Gallagher and Bonehead from Oasis, and Stephen Duffy, leader of the early 90s Creation act the Lilac Time. 'Stephen Duffy said the best line by anyone all night,' recalls Dave Barker, 'which was: "Now we know how many plus-ones it takes to fill the Albert Hall." ' But even before Bob Mould had finished playing, journalists and other guest-list freeloaders were spilling out into Kensington Gore to hail taxis to the Forum in Kentish Town, where the after-show party was being held.

The third album by Mould's Sugar had been a fraught and confidence-sapping exercise in how not to make a record. Co-producing with bassist David Barbe, Mould had put a brave face on things but eventually called Kle Boutis and told her the album was being re-recorded from scratch. 'The tide was turning against us, and rightfully so,' Mould says. 'Britpop was speaking to the British kids much more than we could. I'd heard Oasis – and Alan had been talking them up and down – and I had a sense that they were going to be huge.'

Mould still expected Sugar's album to make its September release, but when tapes arrived at Creation they were greeted with disappointment. 'I sat down with Mark Bowen, who had joined the company [as an A&R man],' says Andy Saunders, 'and me and Mark were the biggest Hüsker Dü and Sugar fans in the world. We were sitting there listening to it, really wanting it to be brilliant. Get to the end of the record and we're going: "This isn't very good, is it?" Dick came in and said: "This is shit." The company had a downer on it.'

With Sugar's supremacy at Creation now just a memory, Oasis were about to become the unchallenged stars of the label. During their set at the Glastonbury festival on 26 June, which saw them play to 30,000 people, Jeremy Pearce leaned over and kissed Marcus Russell in delight. Five days later, Oasis' second single 'Shakermaker' flew into the charts at number 11.

When Ride's new album *Carnival Of Light* was released in June, the track-listing spelt out in black and white that whatever the difference in agenda of Mark Gardener and Andy Bell, it had gone past the point of being a healthy rivalry. All of Gardener's songs were on one side, all of Bell's on the other.

Carnival Of Light sold only 10,000 in its first week, with no hope of recouping its recording costs. A second single, 'How Does It Feel To Feel', bombed. Dave Newton's idea for Ride to play ten shows in America fell through when Sire pulled the tour. 'There were all these things happening over the summer,' says Newton. 'There was never really any good news.'

For Creation, the only good news was coming from Oasis. By mid-June, its loans from Sony having exceeded £2 million, Creation was in serious trouble and the situation was growing more tense by the day. 'It was all about trying to staunch the losses,' says Jeremy Pearce. 'There was a lot of pressure from Paul Russell to put a general manager in [the Creation office], who he thought was much better than Fatty Green. We resisted it. It was anathema to Creation and we didn't want it either.'

On 17 June, Creation came within an inch of being shut down. Dick Green was away from the office that day, but had been made aware by Pearce and LRD's finance director Stuart Middleton that Paul Russell had his finger over the button. 'We were worried,' says Pearce. 'I'd gone to a health farm – I don't know if it was because of the extreme tension of the situation. Stuart and our colleague Sylvia [Coleman], who's a lawyer, were trying to keep it alive but Paul Russell was saying: "You can tell fucking Alan McGee that we're going to close the company and he and Dick can work out of their bedrooms as A&R men if they want." It was that close to Russell just saying to Dick: "It's over. No more money." '

In Pearce's absence, Middleton tried to convince Russell to put more money into Creation, using Oasis as his collateral. 'Dick Green was on his way to his mother's in Lincolnshire and he didn't have a mobile phone,' Middleton says. 'He must have stopped at every phone box on the A1, or whatever it was, to call me to see whether there was any news from Russell.'

The outcome was a reprieve for Creation on condition that it laid off some of its 21 members of staff and cut more than half a dozen acts from its roster. In August, an emergency meeting was held at Green's home in Essex where it was announced that five people would be made redundant. 'We went through the list: "Which five people?" ' remembers Andy Saunders. 'It was a big deal … a big crisis.' Among those who lost their jobs were press officer Matthew Rumbold – he had not even been there a year – and the regional plugger Aude Prieur. 'We were winging it,' says Johnny Hopkins. 'It was close to the edge.'

Jeremy Pearce, who had been holidaying in Mauritius when the meeting at Green's house took place, returned and began drawing up a list of Creation artists, putting them into three categories: definites, possibles and probably nots. The label dropped several bands including Adorable (who immediately disbanded), the Telescopes, Dreadzone and Medalark 11. 'Dick, at this stage, was on his knees,' says Pearce. 'Alan was nowhere. I'd been foolish enough to send him a fax on the day after the Albert Hall concert – to tell him it had all gone well and that we'd missed him – and I got a furious reply telling me "never to fucking do anything like that again" or words to that effect ... The situation was looking desperate, I must say. No one at Sony was saying – except LRD – that Oasis was a big band. And we weren't saying *big*. We were just saying: "Don't give up on this label yet." '

One result of Creation's £2 million debt to Sony was that Tim Abbot had been allocated only £60,000 to spend on marketing the Oasis debut album, *Definitely Maybe*, in the UK. That £60,000 – based on a shipment of 95,000 copies to the shops – had to cover press advertising, in-store displays, street posters, database promotion (sending cut-out-and-fill-in cards out with CDs) and buying rack-space with key accounts in the high streets. This last was seen as a prerequisite for a successful album.

'We were fucked,' says Abbot. 'We didn't have any money to do anything. We had credit from our media agency, so [I was relying on us] being billed for a big chunk of the advertising about 90 days later. There was none of this "let's go out and blanket it". It was: "We have to make our communications lethal." This was Creation's last chance.'

The important changes in the musical climate – *Parklife*; a return to favour for guitar music; and the new regime at Radio 1 – had coincided with the launch of an aspirational magazine aimed at politically incorrect young males, *Loaded*, and a football renaissance centred around fanzines and Nick Hornby's tragicomic account of his life as an Arsenal supporter, *Fever Pitch*. Tim Abbot was a football lover, as were Oasis, and saw an opportunity to position the band at several strata of working-class and middle-class magazine readers at once. Using the music press as only one of many cogs in the overall wheel, Abbot advertised *Definitely Maybe* in the football publications *Shoot*, *90 Minutes*, *Match Weekly* and *When Saturday Comes* and in match programmes sold at league grounds; and in the style and fashion magazines *Loaded*, *The Face*, *i-D*, *Dazed And Confused*, *Arena* and *GQ*.

But it wasn't only football fans, fashion followers and rock-and-indie kids who were targeted. Unlike Blur, who were blazing a trail for the end of the dance music cycle and the rebirth of the song-based guitar band, Oasis were liked by ravers and ex-ravers for their work-hard-play-hard image and their working-class roots. Tim Abbot had first noticed this the previous year when he took a Birmingham house DJ to see Oasis play in Wolverhampton.

'This dance kid was in on their whole persona and everything else which came with it,' says Abbot. 'He's going: "Fucking hell ... this is rock 'n' roll!" And a couple of other lads told me: "As soon as people leave clubs, they're playing Oasis in their cars. Not Blur. They play Oasis." That was one of the marketing *coups de grâce*, because all of a sudden it was like: "Let's change the demographic of who we're trying to speak to." ' Abbot placed ads for *Definitely Maybe* in the dance titles *Mixmag*, *Jockey Slut* and *Herb Garden*.

The most significant review in the campaign in terms of effecting a crossover would come from *Mixmag*. 'It broke it wide open,' says Abbot. '*Mixmag* gave the album five [stars].' Parts of the review were later used in a pivotal Oasis press advert, beneath a photograph of them taken at a train station in Nagoya, Japan. 'One of them is holding a football,' says Abbot. 'The whole inference of it is it looks like a firm of hoolies on an away-day.'

'Live Forever', which Noel Gallagher had been dedicating to McGee during Oasis' gigs, was released as a single in August. The shipment figure for their singles had risen by over 100 per cent – 45,000 for 'Live Forever' compared to 20,000 for 'Shakermaker' – as Creation and Marcus Russell stepped up their expectations of Gallup, as opposed to indie chart, success. Having played in clubs to 200 people in January, Oasis were now selling out 1,800-capacity venues like the Astoria, and looking for 5,000-seaters to play in the autumn.

Riding the crest of a media-wide submission to Liam Gallagher's voice and Noel Gallagher's melody, 'Live Forever' entered the Gallup chart at number 10. Pre-release excitement about *Definitely Maybe* was already great enough for Creation and Sony LRD to begin thinking of a possible number 1 album. 'The trajectory was going up and up and up,' says Johnny Hopkins. 'You absolutely knew – because Noel had the talent, the songs, and Liam had the personality onstage – that they were going to be a world-beating band. Sooner or later they would be absolutely huge.'

The album with which *Definitely Maybe* was competing for a chart-topping position was *The Three Tenors In Concert 1994* by Jose Carreras, Placido Domingo and Luciano Pavarotti, globally recognised superstars whose concert had been broadcast to billions before the World Cup final in July. *The Three Tenors ...*, a follow-up to a thirteen million seller by the same trio, was a Teldec release through Warner Classics, and the £950,000 marketing spend represented Warners' biggest-ever UK campaign. The company expected the album to sell 2.3 million copies all told, at least one million of them by December. And just in case anyone had forgotten the World Cup concert so soon, £700,000 worth of TV advertising, spread across all ITV regions and Sky for a fortnight, would help to refresh their memory.

In Creation's in-house memos and in faxes to Marcus Russell at Ignition, the opposition was routinely referred to as 'the three fat bastards'. The minutes of a Creation meeting on 31 August reported the latest shipment of 10,000 copies of *Definitely Maybe* by Vital – the company that had succeeded Pinnacle as Creation's distributor – before concluding: 'Outselling three fat bastards, well done everyone, so far so good.' In a watered-down version of the phrase, Andy Saunders was quoted in the press that week as saying: 'Three fat blokes shouting is no match for Oasis.'

The midweek chart positions indicated that Oasis would have the number 1 slot on Sunday. *Definitely Maybe* was selling strongly in the Midlands, in Yorkshire and in Lancashire, and fantastically well in Scotland. Here was proof that Oasis were in a different echelon to the usual metropolicentric, *NME*-backed bands; and proof, too, of the wisdom of Marcus Russell's strategy of getting Oasis to tour the country three times rather than focus on London. Carreras, Domingo and Pavarotti – never a big band in Hull or Dundee – were being thoroughly out-fanbased and out-marketed.

Certified gold after only four days on sale, *Definitely Maybe* was on its way to becoming the fastest-selling debut album the UK had ever seen. Creation's first number 1 album, it had sold over 50 per cent more than *The Three Tenors* ... stunning retailers and distributors alike. With some pride, Tim Abbot says: 'My budget was £60,000 – and I fucking did *The Three Tenors* ... I look back now and think: how the fuck did we do it?'

The reasons why Creation and Oasis did it are manifold. Noel Gallagher's well-reported supply of present and future singles – to which he kept adding by the week – was unusually effective in giving the impression of an unstoppable creative brain behind the otherwise random-acting Oasis machine. Liam Gallagher's brawn and integrity, his yearning, Cobain-esque singing voice and his tearaway good looks made him an exquisitely viable northern black sheep to counterbalance Damon Albarn's blond Essex boy-next-door and Brett Anderson's effete West End existentialist. The warring sibling dynamic of the Gallaghers, not seen on the British pop stage since the heyday of Ray and Dave Davies, was a fraternal-fratricidal powder-keg that unquestionably struck a public nerve.

Oasis were the first band of the decade that appeared to come – as their biographer Paolo Hewitt later wrote – 'directly from the football terraces.' Their 'mad for it' catchphrase, the origins of which dated back to acid house, seeped through the rock 'n' roll underbelly until it eventually entered common usage and became the title of a children's TV show. 'They just kept coming out with amazing songs,' says Steve Queralt. 'I thought after "Live Forever" they would never do anything as good as that again. But they *did*. Then they invented laddism, which was a breath of fresh air for loads of pent-up indie kids who were suddenly allowed to go out, like football and drink beer. It was the beginning of a new era. The country was starting to feel happy, and going out and partying.'

Britain still had a Conservative government – and would for the duration of the Britpop movement – so if there was a party mood in the country, it was not because of political change. Nor was there any galvanising achievement that year by British footballers; none of the home nations had even qualified for the World Cup. Nevertheless there were glimpses – for those in the know – of 'a new reality', as Tim Abbot puts it.

'I had conversations with Noel about this,' he says. 'The people who had come out of acid house were the tools of Thatcher's black economy. They were people who had learned to put on raves or [sell] Es or do this and that, and they've gone: "Do you know what? We can use these entrepreneurial skills and make a living. We can actually become part of society again." The vilification of everything Tory and yuppie had passed. There was a sense that the whole Tory environment was on its last legs.'

Abbot and Andy Saunders had gone to lunch with Steve Sutherland of the *NME* and listened to him enthuse about Britain being on the up; Suede and Blur were, Sutherland felt, besting everything American music had to offer. The suicide of Kurt Cobain had frozen the march of grunge rock, rendering songs of angst, solipsism and dysfunction unfashionable overnight. For at least a year after Cobain's death, these and other themes – self-disgust, misery – were regarded by Britain's rock media as being in bad taste and a reminder of something unpleasant. Liam Gallagher's callous and widely quoted remark about Cobain being 'a sad cunt who couldn't handle the fame' was more than just the anti-American knee-jerk of an avowed grunge-hater; it verbalised the head-in-the-sand hedonism that was starting to course through British life and culture.

Tim Abbot had been a Nirvana fan, and he detested any criticism of Cobain. But the rise of Oasis was for Abbot kismet, a career zenith and the time of his life all rolled into one. Like most true phenomena, Oasis were a reaction to what had gone before and a hint of the pleasures still to come. And as Britpop spread through the north and south, Creation bathed in reflected glory and became – for the first time in its history – the most famous record label in the country.

Alan McGee had a small coterie of friends and well-wishers around him in Rotherhithe, including Andy Bell and his wife Idha, and

Richard Gordon, the manager of 18 Wheeler. They would join him on walks or sit with him in his penthouse, listening to music. McGee was depressed and had recently entered a suicidal frame of mind.

In June, he had tried Narcotics Anonymous but stopped after two meetings, unable to talk openly in front of strangers or listen to them talk about themselves. 'I could relate to their drug addictions but not to the horrendousness of their stories,' he says. 'My story was fucked up, but I wasn't murdering people or raping people. I was basically a kid who'd read too many Rolling Stones books and fallen off the track.'

One day in Rotherhithe, McGee spent an hour and a half walking around a large pond nine times. No longer sure what was real and what was imaginary, he telephoned Ed Ball. 'I said: "Ed, I think I've lost it again",' he recalls. 'Ed said: "OK, meet me halfway." He lived in Mill Hill [in north-west London], so we met at the rose gardens in Regent's Park. He was really worried about me. He phoned my dad and said: "You're going to have to come and get him." '

McGee was having a nervous breakdown, but didn't know it at the time. His father took him back to Glasgow, where rather than live in the family home he stayed with his father's fiancée, Heather Johnson, in her council house. 'Heather was a lovely person,' he says. 'She moved her daughter out and me in. It was a heavy two months – July, August – a heavy, heavy time. But Heather and my dad were getting married and I talked to Dr Brewer and said: "What do I do? I've got nobody to take care of me." And Brewer went: "I think you're ready now for proper therapy." '

McGee would later say that he owed his life to Colin Brewer for helping him through months of alcohol and cocaine withdrawal. The road had not been smooth: in addition to his fleeting thoughts of suicide, McGee had gone to church for the first time in twenty years to see if religion could help him. Arriving back from church, he had played his answering machine and found a message from Dick Green telling him that *Definitely Maybe* was at number 1. 'About the hundred-and-ninety-fourth priority in my life at that point was their chart position,' McGee remarks.

He was placed in the rehabilitation unit of a north London clinic, the Charter Nightingale, where he would spend the next six weeks. On alternate days he was seen by Colin Brewer and by Keith Stoll, the Harley Street psychologist who had treated Terry Bickers in 1989. Having seen very few visitors in the Charter Nightingale, only months later would McGee reveal that he had been there. He was quite ashamed to admit it.

'These places are like mental institutions for rich people,' he says. 'It was an eye-opener because you had everybody in there from stressed-out, middle-aged business people to heroin addicts to bulimics to people in car accidents with brain damage. The whole gamut of damage was in that hospital, and it sort of made me realise: you might be fucked up, you might be damaged, but fucking hell, you're not as damaged as most of the other people in here.'

McGee emerged from the Charter Nightingale feeling tired but mended. He had been weaned off Valium and was now taking no medication at all. In Glasgow that summer, he had rediscovered his adolescent passion for football and had seen a match or two with his father, a Rangers supporter. Football was to replace drugs in the coming months as McGee's comfort zone.

'I moved back into my place in Rotherhithe,' he says, 'but it was soulless. I was just sitting in this mad penthouse that had two of everything. I was on my own and I lasted about two days before I started feeling terrible again.' Passing the palatial Landmark Hotel in Marylebone on one of his marathon walks, McGee decided it looked like a nice place to stay. He lived there for the next two months at £200 a night.

Jeremy Pearce and Marcus Russell were talking about Blur. Pearce was saying how wonderful it would be if *Definitely Maybe* could depart from Creation convention and stay in the Top 10 not just for one week but for five or six months. The only British guitar pop album to do so in 1994 had been *Parklife*. Pearce pressed what he assumed would be the right button with Russell. 'I was a bit disparaging about Blur,' he admits. 'I said to Marcus: "Surely they're pretty average?" And he said: "If we could ever be as big as Blur, we'd be doing pretty damn well." He was a very cautious, realistic manager.'

Following its week at number 1, *Definitely Maybe* stayed in the Top 10 for a further four weeks. It was at number 6 when Jeremy Pearce and Stuart Middleton took a flight to New York for a meeting on 3 October that would decide whether or not Creation had a future. Dick Green had shrugged off rumours that Sony was poised to take complete control of the label, telling *Music Week*: 'It's rubbish. I've lost count of the times this rumour has appeared.' However, what Green couldn't shrug off was the possibility that Sony would refuse to give Creation any more short-term funding and thereby allow it to die.

'Oasis was still only an English phenomenon,' says Pearce. 'We'd already had big English success with Suede, which hadn't translated internationally at all. It does seem remarkable in retrospect, but it was really touch-and-go to keep Creation going.' The first income from *Definitely Maybe* was due to reach Creation in early November, and the cash flow projections being drawn up by Mark Taylor were showing a positive trend. 'But although it was looking good,' says Pearce, 'Creation could have run out of time – and it couldn't borrow anywhere else. And it owed Sony a ton of money already.'

It would have been cruelly ironic if Sony had called time on Creation just after it had had a number 1 album. But there was a chance that the executives in New York might cut out the middle-man by putting Oasis on Sony for the UK (since they were signed to Sony in the first place) and abandoning Creation as a dead loss. 'It would have misfired terribly on Sony,' points out Pearce. 'They would have been perceived to have stolen the act.'

Pearce and Middleton were middle-men too: employees of Sony who liaised between Paul Russell and Creation – and wanted to do the best for both sides – yet knew that losing Oasis would finish LRD. But as they boarded the plane to New York, they feared that they might not have a choice. 'The Sony bosses in New York definitely thought that Creation was Alan,' says Middleton. 'Without Alan, was there really a Creation? It was another factor in whatever decision they were trying to come to. It wasn't just about whether Creation could manage to stand on their own two feet in the future. It was about whether we would ever earn back all the money (a) we had paid for the shares and (b) the loans that had gone into the company.'

The meeting in New York was chaired by Bob Bowlin, the head of Sony Music International. Bowlin knew that McGee was ill (but not that he was in rehab) and was aware that it was a sensitive issue. 'Jeremy and I begged for more money for Creation,' recalls Middleton. 'The meeting went on and on and on. They wouldn't make their minds up. Bob Bowlin's secretary came in and said: "Bob, your next meeting's arrived." And he just stood up and said: "Nice to meet you, guys." We said: "Wait a minute. What's the decision?" And he just said: "Oh . . . OK then." '

As a result of the Bowlin meeting, more funding was put into Creation to tide it over until the end of the year. Alan McGee, who generally has a tough job giving Jeremy Pearce credit for anything, admits that 'Jeremy, through the dark days of '94, probably kept it alive'. Pearce himself says: 'We absolutely saved Creation at that point. God, it was enough to give us a nervous breakdown.'

After that scare in October, things levelled off. The sales of *Definitely Maybe* provided cash and stability, and Creation coped as best it could with the growing Oasis-mania. 'We had done the fire-fighting,' says Mark Taylor. 'We'd got ourselves back up and running again. Now we could take this cash and reinvest it back into the business. We could repay all the promises that we'd made to suppliers who very graciously gave us extended credit. We were fully functioning again.'

But there was still trepidation – and this really was justified. Early one morning in late September, Tim Abbot had received a transatlantic call from Noel Gallagher, telling him that he had left Oasis less than a week into an American tour. The trouble had started when, finding themselves with a day off in Los Angeles, a few members of the band got hold of some crystal meth – intensely strong speed – and partied all night. The following evening's show at the Whiskey had been shoddy and bad-tempered, reaching a low point when Liam, who was snorting crystal meth from a position behind the amplifiers, angrily struck Noel with his tambourine. Enraged by their unprofessionalism at such an important gig, Noel had walked out of Oasis and skipped town.

As a fearful Abbot flew to Los Angeles, the rest of Oasis waited for their leader to phone in. After two days of no contact, they asked to see the phone bill for his hotel room, which revealed a number in San Francisco. It was answered by an evasive-sounding girl, who put Noel on to Abbot. They agreed to meet in San Francisco the following day.

'I thought: fucking hell, how can someone have a number 1 album, have all this at their fucking feet and throw it all away?' Abbot recalled to Paolo Hewitt in *Getting High: The Adventures Of Oasis*. 'Everything had been achieved. The album was the biggest, fastest-ever-selling debut album. Number 1. Beatlemania in Japan. What else do you want?'

Abbot and Gallagher spent two days working their way through a bag of cocaine in San Francisco, before flying to Las Vegas on a whim. All the while, Abbot kept Marcus Russell abreast of their movements. In a casino, Abbot tried to persuade Gallagher to meet up with the rest of Oasis in Austin, Texas, to record B-sides for a future single. Gallagher slept on it before giving his agreement to the session. The following day, he decided to rejoin the band permanently and continue the tour in Minneapolis on 14 October. Not a word of any of this was reported back to the British press.

'You had to be careful with Oasis and America,' says Abbot. 'Fortunately, Richard Griffiths and David Massey at Epic were English guys who knew the temperament of the band. I presented Oasis to the Epic team at a conference call and I said: "Look, they're not being temperamental – but half the vibe here is the backstage and everything else which goes with it. These are not the guys to be hugging and kissing the radio station controller's wife." Normally, that's the kiss of death. But contrary to popular opinion, Oasis worked their asses off doing promotion over there. They would do 22 phoners [interviews] a day.'

Still, there would always be the fear at Creation that Oasis were so volatile that they could come apart at any minute – wherever they were in the world. It didn't make Dick Green any less of a nervous man.

21 A Corporate Virus: The Marketing Revolution

T HE PHOTOGRAPH FOR THE sleeve of Oasis' fourth single, 'Cigarettes and Alcohol', was taken in a suite at the Halcyon Hotel in Holland Park, and featured the Gallaghers, Bonehead and a few friends cavorting decadently on and around a bed. When the artwork arrived at Creation, eyes were raised to the ceiling. In the foreground of the photo, punching the air as though he had just scored the winner at Wembley, was Tim Abbot.

'It caused massive friction in the office,' he recalls. 'By this time it was common knowledge that the Abbot-McGee thing had gone down. I'd started saying: "Well, that's it then. It ain't going to work." I was more Oasis than Creation by that stage ... Noel chose the shot for the cover. I just think it was his way of saying thanks for Las Vegas.'

As a kiss-off to Creation, Abbot could scarcely have made his point any clearer. His days as managing director of Alan McGee's company were over, and at the end of 1994 he became a freelance marketing consultant to Oasis. In December, he and McGee met awkwardly at a recording for the BBC TV programme *Later With Jools Holland*. 'How do you blow it with somebody when you've been so close?' Abbot wonders. 'All of a sudden he's got the most successful band in the world *(sic)* and he's going to come back, but he wasn't around for any of [the success]. It wasn't for me to piss on his party. I never played that game.'

Denied further contact with McGee, Abbot was *persona non grata* at Hackney and moved into his own offices in Baker Street. 'Tim was the man that nobody talked about,' says John Andrews, who was appointed marketing manager by Dick Green in November. 'I didn't realise why he'd gone. He still turned up at marketing meetings for Oasis ... There was a lot of jealousy and bitterness because he'd got close to Oasis, because he was a very charismatic person, because he was successful without compromising.'

There was, of course, another reason why Abbot had to go. Whilst he had stopped drinking alcohol, he remained a chronic cocaine user. Drug-taking at Creation had become less acceptable in the light of McGee's illness, and in preparation for his return the worst offenders were being asked to leave.

By the end of 1994, *Definitely Maybe* had sold 440,000 copies in the UK. The cost of marketing and promoting Oasis in the four months since September totalled £205,000. On a spend-divided-by-sales ratio, presenting *Definitely Maybe* to the public had cost Creation only 46 pence per unit. Statistical analysis was yet another area where *Definitely Maybe* had triumphed. But perhaps the truest measure of Tim Abbot's importance in the Creation and Oasis stories can be seen in the messages Noel Gallagher inscribed on CDs of *Definitely Maybe* when Abbot was nominated for a *Music Week* marketing award. Circulated among the judges, they read: 'Vote Abbot. I did.'

John Andrews came from Virgin Retail. A diligent and rather taciturn man, he talked of records as 'product' and saw the product as being the egg from which the four Ps of the marketing campaign – packaging, pricing, positioning and promotion – had to hatch. The difference between Andrews and Tim Abbot was that Abbot had marketed Creation in his own image while Andrews had come to sell records purely and simply. The success of *Definitely Maybe* had given cause for glee, but it was in no way being seen as a one-off. '[Creation was] under pressure from Sony to deliver more chart acts,' says Andrews. 'The two acts I was briefed to bring commercial success to were Teenage Fanclub and the Boo Radleys.'

Martin Carr was introduced to Andrews in a pub in Hackney and saw immediately that Creation was about to change. 'Instead of trying to give me drugs or show me pictures of shops with our record sleeves in them, he was scaring me with all this talk about marketing,' Carr says. 'It was the first time we'd ever been asked to participate alongside marketing and take an interest in it.' Teenage Fanclub, too, knew that Creation had never had anyone like Andrews before. 'Everything had been kind of busked,' says Raymond McGinley. 'John was very much like: "This is a job." He would actually tell you to your face what he thought, which is a fairly rare thing when you're dealing with people at record companies.'

Andrews had arrived at a convenient moment. Carr's Boo Radleys were making an album that looked like it might intertwine perfectly with a marketing strategy, and be easier to sell than the dense, multifaceted *Giant Steps*. One new song in particular, 'Wake Up Boo!', was a hayfever-catchy pop tune that had been written almost specifically to get the Boo Radleys into the Top 20. In looking for some of the immediacy of *Parklife*, Carr seemed to have recognised that his band's hour was approaching. Recording that autumn, he received a postcard from Alan McGee telling him to 'use every trick in the book – even if it's a dirty one'. Carr kept the card on the mixing desk.

Andrews' other clients Teenage Fanclub were not looking for hits *per se*, but there was, none the less, a let's-shape-up mood in the band – and a new face behind the drum-kit, Paul Quinn.* 'The group had split up in a way,' says Gerry Love. 'Brendan [O'Hare] had left and that changed things quite dramatically. We'd been a unit for the first four or five years, experiencing all the moments together, and there had been a bond there. It was like starting again. There was a motivation . . . an attempt at redemption.'

The Fanclub recorded a new album concurrently with the Boo Radleys – the former in Oxfordshire, the latter in Wales – and had a much happier and more fruitful time than during the eight-month pregnancy of *Thirteen*. The new album was mixed in Los Angeles, partly because their American producer David Bianco lived there, but also because Chas Banks felt it would make sense to set up camp within a cab ride of the Geffen offices. Unlike Creation, however, which was showing real excitement about the album, Geffen's people appeared indifferent. 'For the most part, they couldn't even be arsed to come to the studio,' says Banks. 'Of course, they had this huge thing going on that we didn't know about. David Geffen was off to do DreamWorks, they were focusing in a different area and Geffen was losing its momentum without a shadow of a doubt. Once David Geffen's personality left that company, it was a downward spiral.'

The irony was that Teenage Fanclub's *Grand Prix* was a superb British-American rock album. It had all the qualities needed to effect a complete rehabilitation for the group in the eyes of fair-weather fans and critics. The only potential hurdles would be radio (as usual) and promotion: what was there left for journalists to write about the Fanclub that hadn't been written in 1991, 1992 and 1993?

As Dick Green shored up the company, a Creation management team was put in place that included Andrews, Mark Taylor – now operating in a de facto managing director's role – and Andy Saunders. Saunders was becoming a close ally of Alan McGee, much to the envy of the departed Tim Abbot. And it was Saunders whom McGee phoned near the end of 1994 and asked: 'How do I handle coming back?'

McGee began his comeback by going into the Creation office once a week. He would not be involved in marketing meetings, but would merely listen to upcoming releases and express an opinion about which tracks should be singles. Sometimes he was listened to. Sometimes – with Oasis' singles, for example, which Noel Gallagher selected himself – he was not.

---

* This Paul Quinn is no relation to the Paul Quinn who sang with Edwyn Collins and was managed by Alan Horne.

After spending Christmas in Scotland, McGee checked out of the
Landmark Hotel and took a flat in nearby Dorset House, feeling safe
as long as he stayed in the Marylebone Road area. On match days he
would venture farther afield, accompanying lifelong Chelsea fans
Andy Saunders and Ed Ball to Stamford Bridge. 'Alan became very
interested in football very quickly,' says Saunders. 'He's an obsessive,
compulsive guy. Once he gets his hooks into something, that's it –
and football became very important to him. It's a good thing. Better
than drugs.' It took no time for McGee to become a lifelong Chelsea
fan himself.

Thirty-four years old and single, the new McGee was softer and
quieter than anyone remembered. Having been obnoxious to people
pretty much since discovering cocaine in the 80s, he began a process
of showing kindness and remorse. 'He wasn't the old McGee hiding
out in the bunker and running Creation like in the past,' Saunders
says. 'It was a slow process coming back. There was a real sense that
we should wait for him to talk to us rather than go to him with our
problems.'

McGee had not drunk alcohol or taken non-prescription drugs
since being flown home by Ed Ball from Los Angeles, and would
instead sip peppermint tea and eat health food. His lifestyle had
become more Nick Currie than Andrew Innes and he got used to
excusing himself from the room when drugs appeared. 'I've had to
reconstruct my lifestyle, think about who I hang with,' he later said.
'I used to hang 24 hours a day with Primal Scream. To be honest, now
the only way I can see them is to spend half an hour once a month
with them in a coffee shop.'

His workload changed with his diet. As great swathes of his former
way of life were placed off-limits – after-show parties, backstage
areas, nightclubs and hotel bars – he began to care more about the
technical considerations of running a record company, such as
choosing a good producer or liaising closely with a manager. 'In a
way, sobering up took a lot of the fun out of rock 'n' roll,' he admits.
'But it was essential to actually become a human being and to have a
life outside Creation Records.'

Anthony 'Tones' Sansom, who had been taken on as an assistant to
the press department in August 1994, had to wait months before
meeting McGee in person. Their first conversation neatly delineated
the old ways and the new. 'He goes: "Do you want some chewing-
gum, Tones?" ' Sansom recalls. 'I'm like: "Yeah." He goes: "Ah! See,
wrong era. A year ago it would have been an E!" '

In February 1995, Laurence Verfaillie, to whom McGee had finally
been reconciled, introduced him at a party to a woman he had long
admired from afar. Kate Holmes had been the flautist in the pop
band Frazier Chorus in the late 80s and early 90s. McGee, tactless as
ever, had once or twice commented on her beauty to Belinda White

when Frazier Chorus' videos appeared on TV. 'I had always fancied Kate,' McGee says. 'I'd say to Belinda: "God, I really think she's good-looking." Belinda would go: "She's an ugly cow." Belinda was a bit like that with other women. When I saw Kate at the party I waved to her, and she waved back. Then she came over and we started talking.' Two months later they began dating.

With Holmes providing the stability his life had needed, McGee accepted Andy Saunders' advice that he should be honest about his breakdown – both to the Creation staff and to the media. McGee would discuss his illness whenever journalists asked, usually sounding halfway between rueful and relieved. The only time he lost his temper on the subject was when a writer from *Esquire* began an interview with the question: 'Why did you take a nine-month sabbatical in 1994?' Shocked by the lack of preamble, McGee threw him out of his office. 'The old Alan rose to the surface and he was absolutely blazing,' says Saunders. 'He was like: "Get that fucking cunt out of here!" ' Saunders calmed McGee down and the interview resumed an hour later.

James Kyllo, the longest-serving member of Creation staff after Dick Green, remarks that McGee's old-style obsession with detail would have ill-suited a company that had coped – just about – in the period without him. This was one reason why McGee no longer felt the need to pace the floor or stand over everyone's shoulder. But there was another way of looking at it: no one wanted him to. 'The company had gone through a fucking revolution while he was away,' says Andy Saunders. 'The company was actually doing pretty well. The fact of the matter is we had this band [Oasis] starting a motor big-time, and it was running itself. Suddenly, everybody's job got a lot easier, a lot more defined.'

McGee would later talk of his surprise at learning that Creation had introduced a marketing department while he was away. Yet marketing was becoming just as imperative to the company as he himself had been, perhaps more so. The revenues from *Definitely Maybe* gave Creation the leeway to spend more money on its campaigns, thereby increasing the importance not only of marketing's pragmatic disciplines but also of anyone who worked in the marketing department. For McGee, it was as much of a culture shock as having to drink tea instead of Jack Daniel's. For the press department, it was the end of an unofficial six-year stranglehold. For Creation as a label, it was, as McGee would later say, 'the beginning of the end – or the start of the future'.

On 29 December, two days before their fifth single, 'Whatever', made the week's highest new chart entry at number 3, Oasis played the 6,000 capacity Brighton Centre. Appearing as last-minute special guests were Ride.

Ride had suffered a tough few months financially and had been grateful for a backdated payment from EMI Music. The final single from their dark, pretentious album *Carnival Of Light* – now referred to within the group as 'Carnival Of Shite' – had been Andy Bell's 'I Don't Know Where It Comes From', a non-hit at number 46 in October. Although a gig before 6,000 people was not to be sneezed at, Steve Queralt thought it a dreadful idea and said as much. 'That was us admitting that we're not as big as Oasis,' he says, 'and Oasis have been around for five minutes. That won't look good to anybody.' No one listened to him. Ride had headlined the Brighton Centre the previous year; now the indications were plain of their new place in the scheme of things.

Ride warmed up Oasis' crowd with a 45-minute set of their most popular songs. No one realised it but it was the last British concert they would ever play. Beginning work on their fourth album on 2 January, they knew it would have to be a lot different to their third. 'We'd worked for a long time on *Carnival Of Light* and it had come out and sounded really out of touch with what was going on,' says Andy Bell. 'We had a conversation where I was going: "We should try and get [an album] out really quickly. Prince can do it. Why can't we?" It was the only option. It was that or split up.'

On Bell's insistence, none of the songs on the new album was rehearsed or demoed. The plan soon presented pitfalls: the other three members of the band were unfamiliar with the material Bell was bringing in, and his songs weren't too fantastic to begin with. The recording sessions were notable only for the presence of McGee, who told everyone he was A&R-ing the album. In actual fact, there were few decisions that had not already been taken by Bell.

'Alan had seen that there were obvious problems within the set-up and was trying to do his best, as we all were, to get it back on track,' says Mark Gardener. 'But personally, I didn't really want to be in the studio. I wasn't liking what I was hearing. I couldn't even tell you the tracklisting of that album.' His cage rattled once too often by Bell, Gardener began to make other arrangements.

Martin Carr had left Oasis' gig at the Brighton Centre in the company of Mike Smith. He recalls the publisher asking casually if the Boo Radleys would like to be as famous as Oasis were getting. Carr replied that they would indeed. 'But you have to understand,' Smith stressed to him, 'that that would involve playing to the very people who tormented you at school – the bullies, the football kids, the wankers.' Carr smiled back at him and said: 'Bring on the wankers.'

In November, a delegation from Creation had turned up at the Church in north London to hear finished mixes of the Boo Radleys' new album, *Wake Up!* As the music played, Carr and Andy Saunders watched old-school Creation tussle with the modern version. Carr and Saunders wanted 'Wake Up Boo!' to be the first single from the album – that's why it had been written, after all – but the indie values of stalwarts like Dick Green died hard. Green lobbied for a less commercial number, 'It's Lulu'.

'This is the way Creation used to think,' says an exasperated Saunders. 'It was like: "Don't release an obvious single, because people will think you've sold out. What you do is release 'It's Lulu' – and then you bring in 'Wake Up Boo!' when you've got your credibility sorted out ..." There were four people standing on one side of the room, and me and Martin on the other side saying: "You are *insane*. This is a smash." '

Saunders and Carr were right. Bursting into life with a jaunty trumpet reveille, 'Wake Up Boo!' flew into the Top 10, spending two months in the Top 75 before floating off into the world of classic pop radio programming, where golden oldies like Katrina and the Waves' 'Walking On Sunshine' and Bill Withers' 'Lovely Day' hibernate on library shelves, awaiting the summer solstice. Carr had not just written a pop song – he had written a seasonal anthem. And despite never liking the term, the Boo Radleys had made one of the definitive Britpop records.

As one of marketing's four Ps, pricing was a key element in John Andrews' campaign for 'Wake Up Boo!' By general consent among major labels, CD singles were discounted at £1.99 in their first week of release, moving up to the normal £3.99 thereafter. These price wars were a game Creation simply had to play. But again there was disagreement between the old and new schools of thought. 'There were massive ructions about what the price should be,' recalls Andrews. 'Dick and James Kyllo were reluctant for singles to be undersold. But price was a tool that affected where you went into the charts.'

A few days after 'Wake Up Boo!' came out, Andy Saunders and Chas Banks met for a coffee in Bayswater. Saunders was piecing together his campaign for Teenage Fanclub, and Banks was particularly anxious to know where the band stood with the *NME*. Was there, for instance, any chance of a cover? As they were talking, Saunders' mobile phone rang. He was told the midweek chart position for 'Wake Up Boo!' – it was number 7 – and asked Banks to bear with him while he rang Steve Sutherland. In less than a minute, Saunders had sealed an *NME* cover for the Boo Radleys. Sorry, Chas, you were saying? Any chance of a what?

'About two weeks later,' says Banks, 'I was doing this workshop called the Ten Day Weekend in Glasgow. They asked me to sit on a panel with [former Simple Minds manager] Bruce Findlay and a couple of other people. Someone said to me: "If your band is not getting played on the radio, how do you go forward? Is the press the answer?" And I said: "Well, I saw something two weeks ago that makes me think there's going to be a big change in the press. A paper like the *NME* used to be a trend-setter. But if the parameters for getting on the front cover of the *NME* are that you've got a midweek of number 7, you're going down a road that there's no coming back from. The days of the Jesus and Mary Chain are *over*. I absolutely guarantee you that within 18 months, you'll have Take That on the front cover of the *NME*." Everyone laughed, but of course 18 months later the *NME* had the Spice Girls on the cover.'

There was nothing on Teenage Fanclub's album *Grand Prix* that sounded like it might have a Top 10 midweek. But that didn't stop John Andrews from doing his best to sell the product. He told the band he wanted the album artwork and singles artwork to share a visual theme; good packaging and positioning sense. 'John got heavily involved in the album sleeve,' says Norman Blake. 'We had this idea that it would be good to have a Formula 1 car with our logo as the livery. John totally went for it. He got in touch with Simtek and persuaded them to deliver a Formula 1 car. We had it spray-painted. John did a great job.'

But not all of Andrews' marketing strategies appealed to the band. The three singles from *Grand Prix* – 'Mellow Doubt', 'Sparky's Dream' and 'Neil Jung' – were each released on two CD formats, inviting fans to buy both and bump up the chart position. This was something that Oasis had refused to do (although not the Boo Radleys) and the members of Teenage Fanclub were dubious about the tactic. 'We did it but I hated it,' says Gerry Love. 'Buy one and buy the next one the next week. I really thought that was a rip-off.'

None of the three singles made the Top 30. Feeling compromised, Teenage Fanclub now had a deep suspicion of Creation's new marketing approach. And whilst it never reached the stage of a stand-up row, the feeling in the band was that it knew more about the quirks of the record industry than its label did. The next Fanclub release would be a deliberately scrappy-looking EP with the cynical title *Teenage Fanclub Have Lost It*.

'Record companies have tended to perceive us as not being ambitious enough,' says Raymond McGinley. 'But having been a musician for a few years, you realise that you can make as much effort as you want, but ultimately if people want to buy your records they'll buy them. And if radio stations want to play your record they'll play it, even if you've fucking shat all over them in the past. If you're going to do anything in music that's attractive to other people, it's best to just relax and get on with it. If you don't, you're going to make unattractive music.'

However, the Boo Radleys were proving that the market was there to be seduced. 'Wake Up Boo!' had been the second most played record on Radio 1 in the first quarter of 1995. When the *Wake Up!*

album was released in March, it went straight to number 1. It was no more or less than New Creation had been expecting.

Towards the end of 1994, Mike Smith had given Andy Saunders a tape of a new band formed by ex-members of Whirlpool, an unsuccessful Food act during the indie-dance era. The new group was called Heavy Stereo and Smith and Saunders were impressed by their song 'Sleep Freak'. Saunders played the tape to Creation's A&R man Mark Bowen. 'I really like it,' said Bowen. 'It sounds like "Instant Karma" by John Lennon. Let's play it to Alan.'

Saunders met McGee at the Landmark Hotel, where he was watching a football match on television, and slipped the cassette on to the ghetto-blaster at half-time. McGee liked 'Sleep Freak' too, and said he wanted to see the band's next gig. When Heavy Stereo played at the Square in Harlow, Creation arrived mob-handed. The label had not signed a new group in over a year.

'We were the only people in the venue,' recalls Saunders. 'We were quite excited – loads of us made the trek out to Harlow on a wet Tuesday night. It was quite an event because we hadn't ever gone out as a company before to make a judgment en masse.'

Heavy Stereo put pen to paper on 1 April 1995, signing to Creation for a £70,000 advance, and were launched to the media with a showcase gig at the Africa Centre in Covent Garden. 'We invited every single person we knew,' says Saunders. 'We had the whole industry down there. They played the gig ... and it didn't really go as well as we thought it would. The feedback we got from the industry was fairly negative.'

McGee's prediction was that Heavy Stereo would be Creation's second Oasis: a rock 'n' roll band with musical and songwriting influences from the days of glam-rock, football scarves and Rod Stewart tartan. But as Heavy Stereo started to record an album with Mark Bowen A&R-ing, there were already signs that neither Sony LRD nor Garry Blackburn's Anglo Plugging was convinced by McGee's enthusiasm. Nor, for that matter, were many of the other Creation bands. 'Mark said he signed them with his head, not his heart,' recalls Martin Carr. 'That was the way it was with Creation at that point. It wasn't: "Who's good?" It was: "Who's going to be famous?" '

The signing of Heavy Stereo was followed later in April by Creation's move from Hackney to new premises in Primrose Hill. Among some of the staff, this was rumoured to have been engineered by McGee as part of his recovery and gradual shunning of people and places that might bring back painful memories. The real reason for leaving Hackney, however, had nothing to do with McGee. 'We were tired of getting burgled,' says Mark Taylor. 'I was fed up with replacing the computers every month. The final straw was when somebody took our front door off with a sledgehammer.'

Primrose Hill was close to Camden Town – Britpop's centre of gravity, where the Food label and Suede's publicists Savidge and Best were based – and within walking distance of Britpop watering holes such as the Good Mixer in Inverness Street and the Saturday night easy-listening-and-60s-soundtracks club at the Laurel Tree in Bayham Street. The new Creation offices at 109X Regent's Park Road had been converted from parts of the Old Primrose Hill School chapel; there was nothing about the low-slung building and semi-hidden front door that suggested the careers of Oasis, Primal Scream and the Boo Radleys were being plotted from inside.

Though smaller than the Hackney premises, the new offices had an important advantage for New Creation: they were open-plan. The personnel could now see each other (and in the case of Johnny Hopkins saying 'do you know what I mean?' every twenty seconds, hear each other). The press department took the ground floor; marketing, the mezzanine. The siege mentality of the Hackney days had gone. One journalist noticed another change: 'Despite Creation's resolutely anti-corporate stance, there are now gold records on the company walls.'

Its gold disc notwithstanding (it would eventually sell 140,000 copies in the UK), *Wake Up!* had made an unhappy camper of at least one member of the Boo Radleys. Sice, the shaven-headed singer, disliked being regarded as the cheery bald chap who sang 'wake up, it's a beautiful morning', and was the first to become disillusioned by endless touring and promotion. 'They were being asked to do the kind of media they'd never done before,' says Andy Saunders, 'like Disney programmes in France, [ITV's *This Morning* with] Richard and Judy – real mainstream media stuff. They had always positioned themselves as a left-field band. I know Martin had been making noises about wanting to be a pop star, but in his heart of hearts he was an *NME* kid, and he couldn't understand the shallow media stuff of having your photo taken and then being told to fuck off.'

The Boo Radleys used the expression 'custard pie' to denote the children's TV and housewives' programmes where pop bands were expected to muck in, play the fool and chop some coriander. 'I think Sice felt the pressure a lot,' says Carr. 'I was quite driven, so I was doing just about anything I was asked to do whether I liked it or not.' This included an interview with *Sky* magazine. When Sice refused to take his hat off for the photos, he and Saunders had a furious argument which ended with both of them in tears and Saunders being sacked as the group's publicist.

A more subtle problem came with the release of 'Find The Answer Within', the follow-up to 'Wake Up Boo!'. The new single was put on Radio 1's play-list, but 'Wake Up Boo!' was not taken off. Indeed, the latter song's chorus hook – 'wake up, it's a beautiful morning' – made it ideal for summer-long airplay. The programmers obviously hadn't heard the first two words of the lyric: 'summer's gone ...'

'I remember being on holiday in Scotland with [my girlfriend] Rebecca,' says Carr, 'and we were listening to the radio in the car. And the guy said: "The new single from the Boo Radleys is out today, 'Find The Answer Within'. Here's 'Wake Up Boo!'"' Alarm bells there ...'

When Noel Gallagher was punched onstage by a member of the audience at a gig in Newcastle, it had two results. Marcus Russell demanded bodyguards for Oasis, and the red-top tabloids pricked up their ears. The Newcastle show had been in August 1994 and the tabloids' showbiz writers had been keeping tabs ever since on these wanton Mancunians with a taste for trouble.

Coverage in the populist papers was unknown territory for Creation, but it wasn't completely unknown for Johnny Hopkins, who had been working at One Little Indian when the Shamen's chart-topping ecstasy apologia 'Ebeneezer Goode' caused a minor media furore. 'I was well aware of how that whole scenario could go,' Hopkins says. Tim Abbot thought the tabloids could be useful if they were handled correctly. He had made a point of getting to know a columnist from the *Sun*, Andy Coulson. 'Oasis were slowly becoming hot news in tabloid land,' Abbot says. '[The papers] were being blanked and blanked and blanked by Johnny, and there were always going to be negative stories. Ignition wanted the tabloids totally locked down because they were terrified of getting stitched up. But I would speak with Coulson and he'd be going: "I will do anything – anything – to get them on-side." I would try and play this game: "One day we will get on board with you. And it will be you, not the *Mirror*." '

Clearly, however, Oasis would not be able to pick and choose – they were becoming one of the biggest groups in the country. In April, they broke the 10,000 barrier by playing to 12,000 at the Sheffield Arena. Less than eighteen months earlier, they had been the support band for a gig at the local university. And a fortnight after Sheffield Arena, their swaggering new single 'Some Might Say' debuted at number 1.

'Everything was going at a hundred miles an hour,' says Tones Sansom. 'Creation was a nice place to be. When "Some Might Say" went to number 1, we had a spectacular party in Covent Garden and everyone was on cloud nine ... The exciting part was watching this out-and-out rock 'n' roll band slowly getting soaked up into the culture. There'd be Kate Moss' agent calling up asking if Kate could come along. The exciting time was the transition: the stepping from one world into another.'

Rock 'n' roll band or not, the rise of Oasis reflected and accentuated the commercial takeover of Britpop. The Boo Radleys and Elastica had both had number 1 albums, while Blur had collected a remarkable four Brit Awards in February. New Britpop anthems were coming out at the rate of around one a month: 'Inbetweener' by Sleeper, 'Waking Up' by Elastica, 'Wake Up Boo!' by the Boo Radleys, 'Some Might Say' by Oasis, 'Yes' by McAlmont and Butler, 'Common People' by Pulp, 'Staying Out For The Summer' by Dodgy and 'Alright' by Supergrass each charted in the Top 20 between January and July.

One of the principal selling-points of Britpop was that it gave teenagers of the mid-90s an accurate feel of what it must have been like to live through the years 1965–7, when the Beatles, the Rolling Stones, the Beach Boys and the Who challenged and inspired one another to greater creative heights. However, the reality of Britpop was that Blur, Oasis and Suede went out of their way to claim that they did not listen to their peers. Furthermore, it was a Britpop truism that nobody ever admitted to being Britpop. As a musical movement, it was Spartacus reversed.

'It was one of the things I was most disappointed with,' says Martin Carr. 'I thought being in a band would mean meeting people with the same interests, sitting around having a smoke and talking about music. I've hardly met anyone from another band that I like being with. A lot of them are very stupid – and for a lot of them it was just a career. Pre-Britpop, no one was taking very much interest in marketing. A year later, people like Menswear, that was all they knew about.'

The word Britpop may never have appeared in a Creation press release – Hopkins dismisses it as ' a tacky, simplistic term ... far too parochial a concept for an international rock 'n' roll band' – but then those press releases weren't being written by John Andrews. Appreciating Britpop for its commercial power, Andrews decided to cooperate with a nationwide retail campaign in Virgin and Our Price. The campaign included albums by Blur, Elastica and the Boo Radleys, and Andrews was happy to commit 20,000 units of the ten-month-old *Definitely Maybe* to Virgin and Our Price shops. Marcus Russell hit the roof.

'Marcus Russell proved himself without doubt to be one of the shrewdest managers in Britain by choosing not to align Oasis with Britpop,' says Andy Saunders. 'He was saying: "I don't want to be in the Britpop campaigns. I want the band to be called a rock 'n' roll band. I don't want them aligned with Blur or Pulp or any of the other bands coming through." I remember thinking: do the campaign! They're asking you to put another 20,000 units in – do it! But he was going: "No, this is going to be short-term. This is a flash in the pan." '

An embarrassed Andrews withdrew *Definitely Maybe* from the Virgin/Our Price campaign, protesting that Russell's deputy at

Ignition, Alec McKinlay, had been fully aware of his intention to include it. What aggravated Andrews, apart from McKinlay denying they had spoken, was that he had been made to feel unreasonable for wanting to sell records. 'My job was to sell as many units as we could and give Creation a level of control so that Sony wouldn't interfere with us,' says Andrews. 'The more records we sold, the less control Sony would have. It was as simple as that.' But selling records for Creation was not the same as selling records for Oasis. And giving Creation a foothold over Sony was not one of Marcus Russell's priorities.

Britpop's second wave washed through the pages of the music papers and the lower reaches of the charts, bringing trawlers full of post-*Parklife* bands. The Bluetones, a Hounslow quartet McGee and Saunders had watched but not thought much of; Cast from Liverpool, a tuneful bunch of 60s-loving potheads; the female-fronted Echobelly, rated highly by Morrissey among others; the Camden-based Menswear, disciples of Blur with not an ounce of their talent; Dubstar, a blonde girl's take on Pet Shop Boys ennui; Gene, a Smiths copycat band that even Morrissey thought was going too far; Ash, punk-powered A-level students from Northern Ireland; all these and more would join the fray that summer. In a year when guitar pop damn near had dance music and MOR on the run, even Edwyn Collins, 35 years old and out of the charts since 1984, had a Top 5 hit with 'A Girl Like You'. Suggs – the singer in Britpop forerunners Madness – killed two birds by saluting Britpop's nerve-centre and his own neck of the woods with his Top 20 single 'Camden Town'. Britpop godfathers from Paul Weller and Squeeze to Rod Stewart and David Bowie were roped in and asked for their views on the new generation.

After receiving little support from radio, however, Heavy Stereo's single 'Sleep Freak' missed out on the Britpop bonanza and skidded only to number 46. The official comment from the Creation press department pointed out that 46 was the label's second-highest placing ever for a debut single; but so much had happened to both Creation and the market-place in the fifteen months since 'Supersonic' that the attempt at spin did not convince. Having failed to chart even as high as Menswear, Heavy Stereo were already playing catch-up before they had released an album. To be doomed so early was cruel, but theirs would not be the only high-speed career of the Britpop epoch. As ex-members of Fluffy, Powder, Embassy and Pimlico can bear witness, some were even shorter.

Noel Gallagher's girlfriend Meg Matthews was out of work. Her DJ booking agency, Flavor, had crashed and Gallagher was worried that she had nothing to fill her days. McGee suggested she come and work at Creation. 'It was announced by Alan that Meg would be joining the company,' recalls Andy Saunders. 'Everybody sort of went: "Are you sure?" And he was like: "Well, I don't think I have an option." We said: "In what role?" He said: "I don't know. One will appear." '

A vivacious socialite and networker, Matthews was equally comfortable in clubland, media salons and tour-buses. Displaying none of her boyfriend's shyness, she had introduced both him and his brother to a new set of friends in the capital. 'Meg was incredibly well-connected, no two ways about it,' says Tim Abbot. 'She brought an element of glitter and superstar-isms to two pretty unkempt-looking characters. She put a West End spin on Oasis.'

When Matthews joined Creation as artist liaison manager, she was initially regarded with extreme caution. 'There was a hell of a lot of opposition to her coming,' remembers Johnny Hopkins. Andy Saunders raised the point that life could become awkward if people were not able to speak openly about Oasis. McGee replied that they would cross that bridge when they came to it.

Matthews' artist liaison job entailed organizing Creation events and parties. Creation's idea of a party was to start at a pub and then go to another pub, but Matthews was much more imaginative: she took Creation into Soho and Kensington. 'To her total credit,' says Saunders, 'she was fucking good at it. She was a real asset. A lot of people who had a problem with her when she came in – because she was Noel's bird – really came to respect her. She was fantastic at liaising with bands and giving the company a bit of glamour that it had never had before.'

Matthews arrived just as Creation was preparing to release a new single and album by Oasis. *(What's The Story) Morning Glory?* had been recorded at Rockfield with Owen Morris, taking its title from a song in the Broadway musical *Bye Bye Birdie*. With a new drummer in their line-up, Alan White, Oasis had started confidently at Rockfield and worked fast. But a heavy-drinking Liam Gallagher threw a tantrum when Noel chose to sing one song – 'Don't Look Back In Anger' – on his own, and returned from the local pub in a murderous mood. He attempted to enter the studio to smash his brother's guitars, but was prevented by locked doors and iron bars on the windows. In the resulting mêlée, punches were thrown between Liam and Bonehead, and Noel hit Liam several times with a cricket bat. Noel drove away from Rockfield with Alan White, telling the drummer that he was leaving the band and going solo. Marcus Russell phoned Rockfield the next day to instruct the other members of Oasis to pack up and go home. Noel Gallagher would not be completing the album.

More than a week elapsed before Gallagher had a change of heart. Fingernails at Creation were in the meantime bitten down to the quick. The album sessions soon restarted, but in June the *NME* interviewed a pensive Noel, who conceded that the band would probably only make one more album. The comment, which was immediately picked up by other publications, terrified the life out of Creation.

The only man who revelled in the brittleness of the Gallaghers was Alan McGee, who often found it hilarious. 'What I like about Noel,' he told a journalist in July 1997, '[is] while he's dealing with some *NME* hack or Sony bigwig or some bollocks award ceremony, he doesn't meet them halfway. He insists on respect. It is a working-class thing. It's about pride in your achievements and not forgetting where you came from, and not letting anyone think they can patronise you or take the piss. That's what Oasis are about and that's what I'm about.'

Partly by virtue of their working-class pride, there was bad blood between Oasis and the middle-class Blur, which had grown more serious as both bands became more successful. Blur's guitarist Graham Coxon detected a nasty atmosphere between their adjacent tables at the Brits, with most of the intimidation coming from Liam Gallagher. And although on one of his four visits to the stage Damon Albarn announced that Oasis deserved the Best New Band award as much as Blur did, the olive branch was not accepted. 'Oasis were not a threat,' Mike Smith told Blur's biographer Stuart Maconie, 'and Blur genuinely wanted to encourage this British pop renaissance. They felt anyone with a guitar was on the same side.'

This was something that Tim Abbot believed too. The first singles from the respective Oasis and Blur albums were due to be released within a week of each other in August, both virtually guaranteed to top the charts. 'My thinking was,' says Abbot, 'isn't it better that we have two number 1s for Britpop guitar music – one after the other – to show that this is the genre that kids are listening to? As opposed to pop or whatever else was about? And it was all fine until Damon decided to throw the gauntlet down.'

Unwilling to let Oasis put out their single 'Roll With It' before Blur's 'Country House', Albarn told Food and its owner EMI/Parlophone that he wanted a same-day release. 'Country House' was brought forward to 14 August so that the two singles clashed. 'In the end I just said: "Fuck it, let's go head-to-head. If they want a confrontation, let's do it properly",' Albarn told Maconie. He little realised what a can of worms he was opening.

In Primrose Hill, Albarn's move was interpreted as sheer provocation. At a Creation management meeting, it was mooted that 'Roll With It' should be pulled forward to 7 August: for all Oasis' strengths, there was still some trepidation about squaring up to Britpop's top dogs. 'In the end, there was a belligerent "fuck it – we'll leave it where it is",' says Andy Saunders. 'Which was very Creation.'

The two bands began to trade musical insults. The Oasis camp compared Blur's knockabout 'Country House' to the cockney duo

Chas 'n' Dave, while Blur retorted that Oasis sounded like Status Quo. Interviewed on Radio 1, Albarn sang along sarcastically to 'Roll With It', breaking into the ' ... and I like it, I like it, I la-la-like it' refrain from 'Rockin' All Over The World'. As the story grew, it was turned by the media into a face-off between north and south; football and art-school; working-class and middle-class. BBC and Channel 4 news programmes dispatched reporters to the record stores to see which single was out-performing the other. The story was followed up by CNN, by most broadsheets and tabloids and even by the press in Europe.

Food's managing director Andy Ross told the *NME* that he had bumped into Alan McGee a few nights before. 'We couldn't remember the last time there was this much interest in two singles coming out,' said Ross. 'It harks back to the 60s with the Beatles and the Stones ...' McGee seemed to agree, telling the same paper: 'This is the most important time in British music since punk. Groups like Blur, Supergrass and Pulp are in the charts – they are the mainstream. Finally, kids are embracing these bands again.'

That may have been true. But when Albarn hosted a BBC2 special, *Britpop Now*, in the days leading up to the chart rundown, Oasis were conspicuous by their absence. And even though Creation employed more middle-class than working-class people, it was felt by many at Primrose Hill that Albarn was too conceited and too enamoured of publicity to see what they had seen: that Oasis were not in the business of wordplay or leg-pulls. 'Alan's quote was: "The thing with Blur is they think that taunting Oasis is good media fun. The problem is you've got five kids off a council estate in Burnage who want to kill them for it",' says Andy Saunders. 'I thought that was quite a nice little bomb to throw in.'

Coming at the height of the silly season – the summer weeks when news is hard to come by – the enmity between Oasis and Blur brought a staggering amount of attention. As the story was pushed further and further up the news bulletins, Creation struggled to cope. 'There was a real sense that things were moving completely out of our control,' says Saunders. 'I remember saying at the time: "This makes absolutely no sense. We're in the middle of a hurricane." '

Creation saw itself as the underdog, the giant-killer, which was not an easy thing to justify when certain journalists started reporting the sub-plot to the rivalry between the bands, namely the rivalry between the major record companies EMI and Sony. Alan McGee was determined that this misconception should be nipped smartly in the bud. In a letter to the *NME*, he wrote: 'What people are not acknowledging is the David v Goliath situation between the companies. Creation has nineteen employees. EMI has 1,500. Sony do not sell, manufacture or distribute Creation. On paper we shouldn't stand a chance ... It's the equivalent of Brentford v Manchester United.'

In Primrose Hill, the Blur single was felt to have the commercial advantage as it was available on two CD formats – fans of Blur would need to buy both to hear all the B-sides – and sold at a discounted £1.99. The fight, however, was not being conceded just yet; according to John Andrews, Creation matched EMI's advertising spend – how things had changed since Tim Abbot's skirmish with *The Three Tenors* – and offered deals to retailers where it could. 'Where EMI would have trumped us,' says Andrews, 'is they would have given away more product at the stores than us. I don't think our deals were anything like as generous.'

More potentially harmful to Oasis' chances was a barcode error on copies of 'Roll With It', which was discovered only on the Wednesday before release. 'Microdot had designed the sleeves,' says Andrews, 'and on the CD they had designed a box for the barcode to go in. The lines of the box were so thick that the two ends of the box read as additional bar code lines. A load of stickers were done. There was a sales conference going on at [Creation's distributor] Vital, and all the label managers spent the night in the warehouse labelling Oasis singles.'

The barcode panic brought tension between Ignition and Andrews to a head. But it could easily have been avoided, as Tim Abbot explains. 'Creation were so fucking tight. Christine Wanless had said countless times – because it wasn't the first time we'd had barcode problems – that you could buy a software program for 300 quid and generate your own barcodes and have them cross-referenced by CIN. They had never got round to it and the rest is history. Everyone went: "Well, I'm fucked if I'm taking the blame for it. Who should have checked it?" And John Andrews gets the blame. Simple.'

On the Sunday afternoon, EMI threw a party for Blur at a West End club. Their victory in the duel was by now assured and the chart rundown on Radio 1 was a formality. 'Country House' had outsold 'Roll With It' by 274,000 to 216,000 to debut at number 1 to the latter's number 2. 'Everyone was gutted that we hadn't gone to number 1,' says Johnny Hopkins, 'but it almost didn't matter in the long run. Oasis were growing at such a pace that it wasn't about the singles – it was about the album.'

Having told the *NME* a week before that 'it's not about chart positions', Marcus Russell requested that John Andrews be removed from all Oasis assignments, and that Creation take on a former employee of WEA, Emma Greengrass, as marketing manager working on Oasis exclusively. It was a request which Alan McGee and Dick Green were powerless to decline.

Because Oasis had their own A&R man – his name was Noel Gallagher – McGee had had not one iota of input into *(What's The Story) Morning Glory?*. When he heard the finished music, and particularly when he heard Gallagher's song about Meg Matthews, 'Wonderwall', he was able to listen with fresh ears. In spite of Ignition's pleas that he play the tapes to nobody, he invited Andy Saunders round to his flat for a listening session. They both felt the album could be huge.

It was not as brash a record as *Definitely Maybe*, being something of a comedown from the band's year-long party of 1994. But Jeremy Pearce shared McGee's view and decided to pre-empt the renegotiation of Oasis' royalty deal with Sony, which was still some way off. 'It wasn't a foregone conclusion but we thought there was a good chance the album was going to do very well,' Pearce says. 'It's always been a thing of mine that if you know you're going to get hit with a renegotiation, it's quite disarming for the other side if you offer more. So we went to the band and offered them a bigger royalty. Which I think so astonished them that they said: "Fine, all right, thanks a lot." They hadn't even asked for it, you know. It was just a gesture which they appreciated quite a bit. I remember getting roundly criticised by Paul Russell for it. He thought it was a stupid thing to do. But it was a modest increase given what happened.'

Licking their wounds in the aftermath of the singles battle, Oasis and Ignition had on 28 August announced a concert at the Earls Court arena in November – a 20,000 capacity venue that the press quickly noted held 3,000 more than the Mile End Stadium where Blur had played in June. Now that the fuss over 'Roll With It' and 'Country House' was dying down, there wasn't much to choose between the two groups in terms of popularity, and losing the race to be number 1 had dented no more than Oasis' pride.

However, as everyone who knew him said time and time again, Marcus Russell was an extraordinarily cautious manager. While McGee expected *(What's The Story) Morning Glory?* to annihilate Blur's *The Great Escape* in sales and reputation, Russell doused all wild predictions with cold water. 'People recalled marketing meetings before I joined,' says Emma Greengrass, 'where Marcus was apparently quoted as saying: "I think we're all getting a bit carried away here. This album isn't necessarily as good as *Definitely Maybe*. We should all calm down a bit."'

The Great Escape was lavished with praise by the music press, had plenty of possible hits on it and seemed set fair for a long spell at number 1. For ... *Morning Glory?* to freeze at 2 would be disheartening for Creation and Ignition, but far from implausible. 'The war with Blur had moved Oasis into the households,' says James Kyllo. 'But we still weren't sure of getting a number 1 record.' The belief of some journalists who had heard advance cassettes was that Oasis would be lucky if the album were even released: a track called 'Step Out' was so similar to an old Stevie Wonder single as to be potentially actionable.*

---

* 'Step Out' was taken off the album at the last minute.

In September, two weeks before ... *Morning Glory?* came out, Noel Gallagher blurted a poisonous message to Damon Albarn and his bassist Alex James, telling the *Observer* he hoped they would both die of AIDS. As his words were condemned far and wide, he issued an apologetic press release. Gallagher's AIDS outburst was seen as evidence that the pressure was getting to Oasis – and when the reviews of ... *Morning Glory?* rolled in, almost all of them critical, the pressure mounted. 'The Friday night before it came out, Alec McKinlay said on the phone to me that it would do half of what *Definitely Maybe* had done,' recalls John Andrews.

Like the final scenes of *Carry On Up The Khyber*, in which the Raj is battered by insurrection as the English brass hats enjoy a genteel dinner party, the Oasis album was launched amid surreal scenes of upper-class grandeur. Meg Matthews organised a Sunday get-together in a Kensington house, where ... *Morning Glory?* was performed in its entirety by a string quartet as waiters hovered discreetly with plates of devilled kidneys. 'It was a Meg Matthews masterpiece,' says Andy Saunders, who took his young children. 'Instead of doing a club launch on a Saturday night with loads of Es, they did an aristocratic brunch. It was one of the best things the company ever did.'

In *Getting High: The Adventures Of Oasis*, Marcus Russell recalled to Paolo Hewitt: 'There was hardly any daylight between the *Definitely Maybe* campaign and the ... *Morning Glory?* campaign ... That was part of the whole thing, to get across that this band was a phenomenon and not just some band putting albums out now and again.' In October 1995, Oasis became that phenomenon. When Emma Greengrass took her desk beside John Andrews as co-manager of marketing, ... *Morning Glory?* had just entered the charts. 'The day I started, it was number 1 with flying colours,' she says. 'And it was a rollercoaster from then on.'

Selling over 350,000 copies in its first week, ... *Morning Glory?* ranked with Michael Jackson's 1987 album *Bad* for sheer velocity out of the traps. The charge levelled by journalists that Oasis had started to become derivative not only of other bands but of themselves represents one of the decisive moments in rock history when critical and public opinion diverged. Record-buyers cared not a jot that several songs on ... *Morning Glory?* resembled classic tunes from the past. What became apparent the more copies were sold was that Oasis' configuration of familiar and unfamiliar ingredients made for a musical package that accessed people from one end of the social spectrum to the other. It was a monster of a record.

'Oasis were going to *happen* at that point,' says John Andrews. 'It was about one generation's need for role models and another generation's need for nostalgia – and the possibility that the 60s weren't dead. Here's a band who weren't killed by acid house and who still love all those great 60s values. They've got wonderful haircuts. They've got Rickenbackers. They spanned two generations and that's why they sold a lot of records.'

Much more of a people's band than Blur had been at their commercial apex, Oasis had borne out a quote from Noel Gallagher to *Mojo* magazine at the end of 1994. Talking about why people liked Oasis, he reasoned: 'They've got the band they always wanted.' In the sleevenotes to *The Beatles Anthology 1*, the journalist and archivist Mark Lewisohn wrote of the Fab Four's televised appearance at the 1963 Royal Command Performance, which was watched by almost 40 per cent of the population: 'Not on this scale, not by anyone or anything, neither before nor since, has Britain allowed herself to be so happily consumed as she was in those jolly winter months of 1963/64 when the Beatles were rampant.' One of the effects of the ... *Morning Glory?* explosion was that Lewisohn's tribute now required the codicil ' ... until Oasis'.

When 'Wonderwall' was released as a single in November, the album campaign entered another dimension. The slow, plaintive love song overwhelmed the radio stations, which played it round the clock. '"Wonderwall" was the key thing that broke ...*Morning Glory?*,' says John Andrews. 'We had sold a lot of records up until that point, but "Wonderwall" drove it. Huge amount of radio-play; massive song. You'd hear it in every pub, on every radio, walking down the street.' While it wasn't a number 1 hit – the MOR vocal duo Robson and Jerome's double A-side 'I Believe'/'Up On The Roof' was selling to a middle-aged female demographic not even Oasis could reach – 'Wonderwall' became only the eleventh single of the 90s to stay in the Top 75 for 20 weeks unbroken. Had it not charted at all, Oasis would still have surpassed Celine Dion as the act spending most weeks in the Top 75 in 1995 – the first British group since Frankie Goes To Hollywood to head that list.

In less than three months, ... *Morning Glory?* became the year's second most successful album behind Robson and Jerome. Among those it outsold were Celine Dion's *The Colour Of My Love*, Simply Red's *Life*, Queen's *Made In Heaven* and Michael Jackson's *HIStory – Past Present And Future Book 1*. Blur's *The Great Escape* only narrowly made the highest-sellers' Top 10. As one journalist put it, ... *Morning Glory?* was 'entirely overshadowing British music'.

'It was a social change,' says John Andrews, echoing most people who have attempted to explain it. 'We were seeing the growth of lad culture, and that's what Oasis spearheaded. It was the backlash against the politically correct hangover of the 80s. It swept all of that away. It was almost like the rebirth of the permissive society.'

Creation was understaffed and barely able to deal with the demand. Johnny Hopkins and Emma Greengrass were each fulfilling the workloads of two or three people. 'It was manic,' says

Greengrass, 'but once you're in that situation it's like being in a bunker, and you just get on with it. You put your head down and you don't really think about what's going on around you. I was thinking very much in my little area at the time.' Andy Saunders remembers: 'It was all crisis control. Johnny was battling the whole of the UK press on his own. Nobody had time to stop and reflect, or strategise for the future.'

The success was on an international scale. Stuart Middleton recalls Sony LRD being unable to move for statistics. 'There were emails coming in from all over the world: the album's gone gold here, platinum there . . .' he says. 'It was massive all around Sony.' In America the album sold 250,000 in a week, eventually reaching the Top 5. 'They were legendary times,' says Johnny Hopkins. 'It's what you want to see happen. It was a golden period in British music.'

Among other things, ... *Morning Glory?* knocked the career of Blur completely off its axis. Chiefly a product of Essex comprehensive schools, Blur were re-cast nevertheless in the role of public-school dilettantes whose songs took a condescending view of the working classes. The truth was that Damon Albarn's lyrics directed the vast majority of their scorn at the comfortable suburban middle-class lifestyles their writer had taken great pains to avoid, but perception – so often the key to a band's downfall – overrode the truth. *The Great Escape* sold well in excess of half a million, but it had begun to be described in the music press as an artistic and commercial disaster. Blur's reign as kings of Britpop had ended in their metaphorical beheading.

Andy Saunders was the only person at Creation who knew Blur socially – he and Mike Smith would often hang out with Damon Albarn and Alex James. 'I was getting really bizarre signals from Blur around that time,' says Saunders. 'Damon was almost in a deep depression. He had such a competitive edge, and here were Oasis going supernova, just insane, taking off.' To add to Albarn's humiliation, Alan McGee started telling journalists that he would have liked to have signed Blur to Creation – because he thought they were quite a good singles band.

It would be impossible to quantify to what extent McGee and Creation helped to shape the ... *Morning Glory?* phenomenon. Even with Emma Greengrass on board, the band's marketing and promotional campaigns originated from outside, ordained by Marcus Russell and carried out by his acolytes Greengrass and Hopkins. Tim Abbot recalls Russell being 'derisive' of Creation as a record company – especially compared to the polished salesmen of Epic in America – and trying to deal with as few people in Primrose Hill as possible.

But the album's success had created an abundance of glory to go round, and much of it would go to Creation and Alan McGee. The entertainment industry is inclined to see its stars as long-jumpers, judging them on their greatest and most recent triumph, and over-looking the ignominious occasions they tripped and fell head first into the sand. In nearly all of his subsequent press profiles, McGee would be given the cinematic soubriquet 'The Man Who Discovered Oasis'; it had a far glossier cachet than 'The Man Who Signed Adorable'. Perhaps, as James Kyllo says, it was merely the case that McGee had the foresight to 'see the diamond in the pebble', and make a move for Oasis when no one else wanted them.

(What's The Story) Morning Glory? made McGee a multi-millionaire and put him in a different echelon to every one of his contempo-raries and erstwhile idols. He would say about Malcolm McLaren less than 18 months later: 'Ultimately, he was an idiot because he blew it. The Pistols could have been the biggest band in the world. Oasis *are* the biggest band in the world.' By overseeing a marketing revolution rather than a musical one, McGee had achieved vindica-tion and riches beyond his dreams. Cash-merry and riding high on a £12 million turnover, he said in the autumn of 1995: 'Now that we're the biggest indie, the aim is to get as big as Virgin. The target is £35 million in five years' time – real corporate size.'

For those who weren't part of the Oasis/Ignition inner sanctum, the records being broken by ... *Morning Glory?* brought mixed feelings. Andy Saunders and John Andrews were heads – or joint heads – of department, yet they could not escape the realisation that Creation was slipping away from them. 'It was bittersweet,' says Saunders. 'You felt that you were part of it and not part of it at the same time. You saw quite starkly that a real division was opening up within Creation, and that Creation's whole culture was changing as a result. Whereas before, bands would fit into the Creation culture, now what was happening was that Creation was fitting into Oasis' culture. There wasn't a label identity as such any more, because it was all geared towards making Oasis a success. Any kind of indie philoso-phy – or any of the good bits of the indie philosophy, such as the no-rules aspect of it – had gone out of the window.'

The division changed the politics of the company, bringing power to those who worked on Oasis and wresting it from everyone else. Johnny Hopkins was now the most important publicist in Britain, something that Saunders found intolerable. But Saunders felt uncom-fortable talking about Oasis to the press himself in case he 'set off a mine by giving away even the most basic piece of information. Any loaded question from a journalist that I answered in the wrong tone could have set off a domino effect.' Saunders thought Hopkins could use some assistance from his superior. Hopkins thought Saunders could go fuck himself.

Like the division between Hopkins and Saunders, the division between the Oasis faction and some of the other staff-members was personal as well as political. While Oasis campers Tones Sansom and his press department colleague Vanessa Cotton were well-liked, Hopkins and Emma Greengrass each had their detractors and were further isolated by their close bond with Ignition. 'I had so much shit flung at me,' says Hopkins, 'and so much snideness done to me by a couple of people. Things like not being paid as much as Andy when I'd put in the work ... It's important to be acknowledged for what you do.'

Had Hopkins and Saunders been able to share a conciliatory bottle of wine and a chat, they would have concurred on one point at least: Creation was not the funky little record label it had been. Hopkins believes the thin end of the wedge was the sacking of Laurence Verfaillie in 1993. 'Starting with Laurence,' he says, 'there was an exit of true believers in Creation: people that were utter characters, utterly lay-down-and-die-for-Creation, loved the music ... All those people either got sacked or got fucked off with the way it was. Laurence. Tim Abbot. Christine Wanless left of her own accord. Those people were Creation through and through.'

Andy Saunders feels equally strongly that much of the spontaneity of Creation was lost when John Andrews was joined in the marketing department by Emma Greengrass. 'Marketing started to establish more power,' says Saunders. 'They started to pull everything in towards them and make themselves the sun that everything orbited around ... Before, marketing was way down the list of disciplines. It was always A&R that was important – find a band, start a revolution – followed by media promotion and marketing. Now *everything* was led from marketing: A&R, press, radio promotion. Everything stemmed from a marketing-centralised plot.'

Saunders was no fan of marketing, as he felt it took product as its starting-point instead of heeding the requirements and emotions of the artists. Recent years had seen the death of the 'Norm ovation' – the *Cheers* moment when a beloved eccentric walks through the door and is greeted warmly. More than one long-serving Creation artist tells a story of going to Primrose Hill and recognising few of the personnel, or worse, not being recognised himself. 'As the label began to roll,' says the Jazz Butcher's Pat Fish, 'the time-servers and the pen-pushers and the bean-counters started to clog the office up. One time I went in to see Alan and the girl answering the phone looked at me and said: "Postman?" I said: "No. Butcher." '

'Before McGee's breakdown,' says Andy Bell, 'Creation was the opposite to how it was afterwards. It was a very, very positive label ... Creation would make things happen the way you wanted. No one would pressure you about things; they'd try and develop *your* ideas. The bad side of it, obviously, was that the organisation side of it was terrible and the cash flow problems were terrible. Then, while

McGee was having his breakdown, Oasis was happening. [Creation] had to bring in a lot more people – and that's when it changed. It became very anonymous and corporate.'

The question of Creation having a corporate climate is where the views of Andy Bell, Pat Fish and Andy Saunders tally. 'Let's not get it wrong,' says Saunders. 'John Andrews and Emma Greengrass are both very skilled at what they do. But the problem is ... we brought these two people in from a corporate culture – Virgin and Warners – who brought with them a corporate virus that infected the company. And they changed the whole vibe of Creation completely.'

This appeared to have gone unnoticed by Alan McGee. Indeed, Andy Bell wonders if McGee even suspected what had happened to Creation in his absence. 'He's come back and he's feeling the same as he always felt,' says Bell. 'But the clout that he used to have is gone ... The whole balance of power shifted.'

With *(What's The Story) Morning Glory?* at one million UK sales and rising, McGee had a lot more to occupy his mind than worrying whether the troops were happy with the war effort. But some Creation employees were asking themselves why they weren't seeing any of the money that the company had made over the past few months. One of the first to go to McGee and Dick Green to ask for a pay rise was Andy Saunders. They took him out on to Primrose Hill to continue the conversation on a park bench. The politics at Creation had become so delicate that no discussion about money could be held in the office – even behind closed doors – for fear of starting the wrong kind of revolution.

22 The Unstoppable Juggernaut

For most of 1995, Jeremy Pearce had been minded to preserve the terms of the Sony-Creation deal when the contract came up for renegotiation in 1996, rather than have Sony purchase the remaining 51 per cent of the shares. 'The ideal situation was to just go on,' Pearce says. 'We weren't bothered by the shares because it was working nicely. I always said to Alan that I wanted him to be our Seymour Stein, and as long as it was working I'd be very happy for him to stay independent.'

One of the reasons why Pearce felt this way was because the shares were worthless for most of 1995. 'The date was coming towards us when we would have a difficult decision to make: whether we bought them for zero or whether we just left them with Dick and Alan,' he says. 'Suddenly, the scale of the Oasis success meant that the shares were going to become worth something. I remember saying to Alan: "Look, you don't want us to buy your shares. We'll give you some money and we'll buy *some* of them, and you can keep the rest." I think he felt that I was trying to get his shares cheap. Actually, it was the last thing I wanted to do.'

McGee had been hoping to have a serious conversation with Pearce about the renegotiation since early 1995, and his thinking had little to do with affairs of business. 'I'd come out of rehab,' he says, 'and all I wanted was to re-sign a deal as confirmation that I had a worthwhile aspect to my personality. You've got to understand, my ego was shot to pieces. Jeremy Pearce was laying it on me on the level of "well, we don't know if you're better" – that sort of vibe – and I wanted somebody to say: "Here's a three-year contract. You found Oasis. We believe in you, and well done for coming off drugs." We had no idea about … *Morning Glory?* – I hadn't even heard "Wonderwall" by this point. I was on £50,000 a year and I thought: maybe I'll get a five-year deal at £200,000 a year and that'll be great. That was my expectation. And nobody would do that.'

McGee continued to believe long into 1995 that Pearce doubted the success of his rehabilitation. He recalls telling Pearce on two occasions that he and Green would love to sign a new contract. 'Jeremy would just go: "Well, let's see if you pull through",' McGee says. 'It was kind of like: "Well, let's see if you stay off drugs." '

For his part, Pearce worried that LRD might lose Creation if Sony effected a buy-out the following year. There was nothing to stop Sony giving Creation to one of its other labels – such as Epic, with which Marcus Russell had an excellent relationship. And this became more of a worry for Pearce the more units *(What's The Story) Morning Glory?* sold. 'Up until then, Creation had been a basket case so there wasn't anything to get worried about,' Pearce says. 'It wasn't worth anything; it was just a problem. But then people started to become aware of life after the deal.'

Pearce was meanwhile becoming aware of life after LRD. On holiday in Turkey that summer, he had read in his newspaper that Richard Branson's four-year restriction period – a condition of his sale of Virgin to EMI in 1992 – had elapsed, leaving him free to start another music company. Pearce phoned Branson's office (to be told that Branson was in a balloon) and made an appointment to see him. The two men began talking soon afterwards.

While Pearce sounded out Branson, McGee let slip to the press in October that he had received an offer of £2.5 million to accept a job with an unnamed Sony rival. This was Roger Ames at PolyGram, who was interested in acquiring McGee and Green when their present contract ended. By January 1996, McGee was deeply concerned that Sony had yet to discuss the renegotiation with him, and he worried about what the silence might mean. As it turned out, one of the things it meant was that Jeremy Pearce did not expect to remain at Sony any longer than he had to.

(What's The Story) Morning Glory? had now sold more than one and a half million copies in the UK and had topped the charts in seven territories around the world. As one writer succinctly put it: 'Even people who don't buy CDs bought that one.' McGee took her point, admitting to another journalist: 'I'm sure that most of these people have never heard of the Boo Radleys or Primal Scream.' As ... *Morning Glory?* struck oil and sales of *Definitely Maybe* put on a spurt (selling 520,000 in the UK in 1995, to add to the 440,000 it had sold the year before), the label's other autumn releases were rendered, as Andy Saunders says, 'totally irrelevant'.

Heavy Stereo were especially unlucky to have their second single, 'Smiler', released in the shadow of ... *Morning Glory?*. A 'sub-glam-rock track', in the words of John Andrews, it stalled at number 46 just like their debut. Andrews takes the view that McGee lost his enthusiasm for Heavy Stereo there and then. Two months later, McGee and Green presented Noel Gallagher with a Christmas gift of a Rolls Royce – to thank him for all the money he had made for them

– in a ceremony at a Holland Park hotel that Andy Saunders remarks wryly was 'for the Oasis interior ministers only'.

With the end of the first Britpop annum came the knowledge that 1996 would be sorely different. Blur were to release only two singles that year, and Oasis and Pulp a mere one. The dearth of new product from those bands already looked like leaving a big hole in the British music scene. 'There doesn't seem to be anybody immediately in their slipstream in terms of talent,' a spokesman for the HMV chain said in February. 'You have to drop down about six notches before you get to the next lot. The Bluetones are all right, but they haven't got anything like the star quality and talent that bands like Pulp, Blur and Oasis have. The same goes for Cast, Ash and Northern Uproar. Unfortunately, they're a little bit too anonymous and run-of-the-mill. They all have this element of being crushingly OK.' It was a faultless analysis; there would be no Britpop surprises in '96.

As commentators looked to other musical frontiers, the Bristol-based trip-hop movement was expected to have another bountiful year and the glam-grunge trio Placebo were tipped for stardom. Wales was seen as having the makings of a new Manchester, with a string of bands including 60 Foot Dolls, Gorky's Zygotic Mynci, Catatonia and Super Furry Animals. 'I think this year we're going to feel the Britpop backlash,' Mark Bowen, who was himself Welsh, said in the *Independent On Sunday*, 'with people doing slightly more inter-esting things ... Everyone's sick to death of smiley Britpop. People will think more about innovation rather than worrying about chart positions. Hopefully, people will take their cue from musicians like Tricky rather than Echobelly.'

If Bowen's comment about chart positions set him at odds with his company's marketing department, his love of Super Furry Animals saw Creation unite behind him. He and Andy Saunders thought the band sounded like Teenage Fanclub and would be an ideal act for the label. Super Furry Animals had issued two singles on Ankst, a Welsh indie label, in 1995 and had served a long apprenticeship on the Welsh language circuit before that. '[The] Welsh language circuit extended beyond just Wales,' revealed group member Gruff Rhys in the *NME*. 'It went right through Europe into other countries with minority cultures, Celtic countries, Basque countries ... We did that for years. Eventually, we stopped and thought: we have the songs, we have the technology, we have the capability. Let's attack the European mainstream media and get to some more people.'

In fact, Alan McGee wanted to sign two Welsh bands: Super Furry Animals and 60 Foot Dolls. The latter, however, chose to go with Ben Wardle's BMG-funded mandy Indolent. McGee settled for the Super Furries, whom he watched one night with Mark Bowen. After they had played, McGee pointed out to them that their songs would sound even better if they were sung in English. They looked at him curiously. 'They were in English,' one of them replied.

Nine of the twelve tracks on Ride's fourth album, *Tarantula*, had been written by Andy Bell. Left with only a morsel of involvement in the record, Mark Gardener flew to America to record his vocals, so reluctant was he to stay in the London studio where Ride were working. During his trip to America, it dawned on Gardener that if the band were to promote the album with a tour, he would be no more than a rhythm guitarist and backing singer.

But Ride's itinerary was not exactly chock-a-block with concert dates. In the space of two years, they had become demoralised and unwanted, and were down to the last £1.11 in their bank account. 'There was this incredible pressure to finish and release the album,' says Bell, 'so that we could break even.' As Bell saw it, *Tarantula* might not be a Top 10 contender but it would at least be current and fresh. To recapture lost momentum, he was quite prepared to swallow his pride and go back to playing smaller venues. However, the band's finances – and the way their income was distributed – had begun to gnaw at him. He had no desire to surrender his songs to Dave Newton's new publishing company.

It was obvious which band had stolen Bell's heart. When he mixed *Tarantula*, it sounded like a sorry attempt to emulate *Definitely Maybe*. 'It wasn't like a wall of noise,' says Newton. 'It was like a curtain of noise.' Once the album had been remixed, a meeting was called at Newton's house – attended by their lawyer George Babbington – to wade through complex deals for North America and the world. As contracts were handed round, Mark Gardener interrupted Babbington to say that he was leaving the band. 'They'd reached the end of the road,' says Newton. 'It was largely pointless. It was like: "Look, if we met now, we wouldn't be in a band together".'

'I remember walking back with Loz after we'd suddenly realised that we'd split up,' says Steve Queralt. 'We went straight to the pub and had a drink. It was almost a feeling of relief that we didn't have to go through any more shit, any more treading on eggshells, watching what you said in front of Andy or trying not to upset Mark. It was like: this is the first day of the rest of my life. I have so many opportunities. I can go to college. I can join another band. But at the same time it was like: my God, what the hell am I going to do now?' Queralt's question was all the more moot given that Gardener had taken Loz Colbert to one side and asked him if he wanted to be in his next band. The invitation was not extended to Queralt.

Ride were obliged to keep their disbandment a secret for six months while Newton finalised an American deal with Elektra, of which Seymour Stein was now vice-president. 'I had the pleasure of flying out to New York that December [1995] and sitting in a big meeting with Elektra to discuss the marketing plan for the album,' Newton recalls. 'Seymour knew what had happened, but he said: "Let's have the meeting as if it's all going to be OK." I said: "Look, it *won't* be OK." I had to sit through an hour-long meeting discussing marketing and potential touring for an album that just wasn't going to be worked that way.'

At home the *NME* reported that Ride had broken up, which Newton hotly denied. In February, a blistering Bell track, 'Black Nite Crash', was released as a single, followed by *Tarantula* in March. Copies of the album were sent to journalists with handwritten messages from Alan McGee. Preposterously, he wrote that *Tarantula* was a classic and would put Ride back on course. It was deleted after only a week.

'The album should never have come out,' says Bell. 'The album wasn't finished. There was no album. It was just a bunch of tracks we'd recorded – and then there was no band.' As a protest against Newton, Bell refused to take a penny in publishing from an album he had written most of. His 20 per cent share of the money remains uncollected to this day.

As Marcus Russell looked towards another Oasis tour of America, due to start in February 1996, *(What's The Story) Morning Glory?* and 'Wonderwall' won Brit Awards for Best Album and Best Video. Oasis also took the award for Best Band – with just as much industry-baiting churlishness as they accepted the others. Noel Gallagher told the press that the trophies meant nothing to him; the only awards he respected were those voted for by the public. Alan McGee was amused and proud.

(What's The Story) Morning Glory? had sold almost four million worldwide, and the assumption in Primrose Hill was that it would break ten million by the end of the year. 'It was number 1 forever and after a while you took it for granted,' says Emma Greengrass. 'Now I look back at it and think: fuck! How could I have taken that for granted? That was *genius*. What a great time. Why wasn't I lapping up every minute of it?'

With the exploits of the Gallaghers rarely out of the British tabloids, Oasis concentrated for a time on the States, where the album had entered the Top 5. A full-scale British Invasion – there had been none since 1983-84 – was expected to ensue, but one thing was for sure: Oasis' battle with Blur would not be re-enacted for the Americans' benefit. *The Great Escape* was nowhere on the Billboard chart. As McGee said in February: 'Blur isn't the competition now. It's U2.'

By the time Oasis returned from America in mid-March, they had scored number 1 hits in sixteen countries and sold around six and a half million copies of ... *Morning Glory?* throughout the world.

Creation's guesstimate of ten million was far ahead of schedule. 'It wasn't about hashing statistics, particularly,' says Greengrass. 'It was just about keeping control of the whole situation. It was about keeping track of sales to a degree, but also trying to put across the right messages to the media. Pretty damn hard when they were creating stories out of thin air.'

'Johnny would be the doctor on call,' says Tones Sansom about the sequence of events that preceded and followed many an Oasis story in the papers. 'He'd hear about it some time in the night normally. He'd have an idea about how to respond to it, but then it had to go through Ignition who would have their own ideas. The daily press obviously turns over very quickly, and often we would be in a situation where Ignition would take so long getting back to us, or we would have our hands tied, that the moment had passed.'

Hopkins contends that there was no such thing as a typical tabloid story about Oasis. Some would be known about in advance. Others would not. Some would be leaked to the papers by people in the Oasis bubble. Others would come from nowhere. 'There was a hell of a lot of stuff that never appeared,' says Hopkins. 'I'd say maybe 75 per cent, 80 per cent of the stuff never appeared. [The threat of an injunction] was something that was used at different times ... Quite often I spoke to the person and said: "This didn't happen – and you know the scenario if you get it wrong." '

Oasis dates in Cardiff and Dublin had been squeezed in for March, prior to a stint in Europe and another US tour in April. The two Dublin shows coincided with rumours in the tabloids that Liam Gallagher and his actress girlfriend Patsy Kensit were about to break up. However, a far more serious tabloid intrusion was about to manifest itself.

'It was completely normal fare for how some of those journalists work,' says Hopkins of the sinister stunt engineered in Dublin by the *News Of The World*, 'but it was absolutely shocking. The thing that pissed me off was that the security knew that he was there, but they didn't think to tell me.' Thomas Gallagher had been an abusive father and husband, and following years of violence his wife Peggy had moved herself and the young kids out of the family home. Liam and Noel Gallagher had had no contact with their father since. 'The dad was booked into the hotel by the *News Of The World*,' says Hopkins, 'and he phoned up Liam's room. That obviously upset Liam, and by extension it upset Noel – and Peggy was there as well. That night they played a blinding gig under the shadow of all that was going on, and got back to the hotel. Everybody was sitting around having a drink, celebrating. Suddenly, in the corner of the bar someone spotted Tommy Gallagher with this woman from the *News Of The World*.'

With heavy sarcasm, Hopkins goes on: 'Of course, it was all done in the light of "we want to reunite the family". Come on ... That wasn't right. That was really not right at all.' *Select* writer Andrew Perry, who was present, says: 'Creation had always had the feeling that various journalists should be there for all the big events. Security was quite tight around the band, but basically if you behaved – even if you were a punter – you were in. If you didn't get in people's faces, you were part of the party. That night in Dublin was when I thought: shit, this is going to change. There was huge great big trauma. No one could get into the hotel. And that's when it all changed. It was laminates and big blokes on doors.'

'Was that the turning-point?' wonders Hopkins. 'I don't think it was. But it was certainly a funny night.' Tim Abbot, who was in Dublin with his own parents, thinks there had been a change for the worse even before the *News Of The World* affair. Abbot had become disenchanted by the number of show business stars that now surrounded Oasis offstage and backstage, and wondered how many of them knew or cared about music. 'Absolutely,' agrees Hopkins. 'Some of it was good: it kind of fitted the band in with the lineage of the Stones and the Faces, and it fitted with where I thought they'd go. But it went far beyond what anyone would have thought. It took it over.'

Tim and Chris Abbot couldn't compete for the Gallaghers' attention when all around stood film stars, models, media clubbers and other scions of high society. To the Abbots, the Gallaghers were becoming strangers. 'Tim was still important on a vibe level,' says Hopkins. 'He had a great creative brain and he was a really inspiring person to work with. He was very involved in the build-up to ... *Morning Glory?*.' Nevertheless, Tim Abbot sensed he was on borrowed time. Intellect and background had never come between him and the Gallaghers. But all their new friends could and did.

'I noticed this marginalisation of myself more and more,' he says. 'My role as cheeky-chappie and gang leader was narrowing, and there was now a space for Alan [McGee] to become the gang leader. The other element was Patsy, who was working on a completely other tangent. It was like: "Do we need the Abbots?" There was far too much coke – even for us. They'd got all this security round them. All of a sudden it changed from being gregarious, "family" kind of nights into showy, who-are-the-most-important-people-in-the-room-oh-fucking-hell-we-are. It was absolutely sickening. Me and Chris ... commented on their selection of friends and the sellout of it all.'

The re-emergence of McGee in Oasis' circle was interesting. With his wealth and fame, he was in one sense closer to the Gallaghers than Tim Abbot could hope to be. McGee's money did not just talk – it roared. The market shares for the first quarter of 1996 showed Creation to be the sixth most successful record company in Britain for albums, and the fifth for singles. It was presently lying ahead of the major labels Polydor, RCA, London, East West and Mercury.

Oasis had monopolised the album chart number 1 position for almost the entire quarter, selling twice as much as their nearest challenger, Alanis Morissette.

Although Oasis would release only one single in Britain that year ('Don't Look Back In Anger'), one could have been fooled into thinking they had released over a dozen. Creation re-promoted the group's previous eight singles at several points, obtaining Top 75 placings nearly every time. 'Live Forever' alone re-charted in 1996 on five occasions, while the Oasis catalogue as a whole was displayed prominently in stores from January to Christmas. 'We did campaigns: three-for-£10 campaigns on the singles,' says Emma Greengrass, 'one of which had already run when I joined and which had been a great success. Promoting the singles was as much of a job as promoting the albums.'

By dint of having so many singles on the market at once, Oasis broke the all-time record for weeks spent on the UK chart in a year, with 134. Their closest rival was Michael Jackson on 43. The last time an act had spent more than 100 weeks on the chart had been Elvis Presley in 1957.

It was Creation's first experience of the mass market; its first experience, too, of the dawdling consumers who spell the difference between quintuple and octuple platinum. From one end of the year to the other, it was as if Creation and Ignition refused to believe that there was a punter anywhere in Britain who could not be sold an Oasis record. 'What it came down to, ultimately, was mass radio-play for "Wonderwall" and "Don't Look Back In Anger",' says Greengrass. 'They are the lowest common denominator type of music. There's nothing wrong with that – they're good songs – but they appeal to a certain person that very rarely buys a CD. But when they do, it means you sell a couple of million copies. They're more desirable, in a way, than the people who buy the CD on the first day.'

At no stage was ... Morning Glory? advertised on TV. It didn't have to be: with an aggregate of 49 weeks on the chart, 'Wonderwall' and 'Don't Look Back In Anger' were the soundtrack to British life for most of the year. In its twenty-second week of release, when a drop-off in sales would have been realistic, ... Morning Glory? still managed to shift 100,000 copies. 'We worked out at one point what percentage of households owned a ... Morning Glory? album,' says Greengrass. 'It was pretty bloody frightening. Something like 40 per cent.'

In the midst of such marketing blanket-bombing, the only thing that Marcus Russell could find to complain about was that ... Morning Glory? was not stocked by a petrol station he'd driven through on the way to Wales. The oversight was soon corrected.

Creation took on more staff in specialist areas, even employing the third Gallagher brother, Paul, as A&R man for the north of England.

But the more-hands-on-deck approach could not hide the fact that no act besides Oasis was selling many records. With the exception of the two Oasis albums, the Boo Radleys' *Wake Up!* and a compilation of Saint Etienne's singles, no Creation album since 1995 had passed the 100,000 mark. Heavy Stereo, the Diggers, Crawl and Wireless were all signed in the post-Oasis period, only to find the going tough and the music press yawning with unconcern. Indeed, the underperforming Heavy Stereo released their debut album, *Déjà Voodoo*, at the precise moment when virtually no one in the country wanted to hear it.

'The album was dead by the time it came out,' says John Andrews. 'The band had been turned into a joke by the press and the media in general.' McGee's much-promised Oasis Mark II had not lived up to their billing, but it didn't matter in the least to Sony – Oasis Mark I was all it needed. 'We were getting all the loans back that we'd poured in. We were selling records internationally. We were kings of the castle,' says Jeremy Pearce.

Yet the damp squib of Heavy Stereo had created a problem for Creation that was to become more common in the second half of the decade. In an effort to get into the Top 40, the bank vaults had been opened wide. 'We had spent a fortune on marketing Heavy Stereo,' says Andy Saunders. 'We were so far in the hole on them.' And Heavy Stereo were not the only ones. 'It's one of those things where you can't get the genie back in the bottle,' remarks James Kyllo. 'Once you've started spending so much money to market things – as we did with Oasis – we kept doing the same thing on other groups that didn't sell as many as Oasis. Heavy Stereo sold less than 5,000 albums. It had a lot to do with doing things by rote: "Oh, that worked, so this is what you do." '

'It took a long time for the company to adjust to the success of Oasis,' says Tones Sansom, who was promoted to regional publicist in 1996. 'When you're really busy, other things perhaps slip by. The Super Furries were doing very nicely but by no means brilliantly. We sold 60,000 copies of [their debut album] *Fuzzy Logic*. It felt a little like the company was cruising. But that's not due to laziness on anyone's part. We were still furiously busy with Oasis as a press office. Every day there would be something in the papers.'

Tim Abbot believes the problem lay deeper. In a tirade that cannot be judged simply as sour grapes from a disgruntled former star pupil, he says: 'The great thing about Creation when I was there was that we would punt on 80 per cent nonsense, but the other 20 per cent would be *Beaster* by Sugar, or Andy Weatherall's "Soon" remix – the great records that you can never take away from Creation. But there's Old Creation and New Creation. The brand equity of Old Creation was about having no profit ethic; it was lunacy and mismatches and experiences second to none. New Creation was, to me,

80s yuppie materialism. It had no emotional spirit. It wasn't driven by art.'

Erstwhile dependables like Bob Mould and Ride had left or were leaving the scene. Primal Scream, once the most important act on the company's books, were holed up in their studio in Primrose Hill, deconstructing and experimenting yet again. Word had it that they were planning a return to the dance beats of *Screamadelica*, but Paul Mulreany, who was playing drums for them, recalls the mood being one of whatever happens, happens. 'I was actually working with them for about two years before anything started to go to tape,' he says. 'A lot of it was just mucking about and hanging around. It was a youth club mentality. It was somewhere to go, in a good area with good pubs. There wasn't a big masterplan in the slightest.'

Whereas in days gone by everything would have hinged on a Primal Scream album, by 1996 Creation could afford to forget about the band for months on end. Even so, as Mulreany remembers, 'at one point Creation was like: "Where the fuck's our album?" I had a big conversation with Alan at the *(What's The Story) Morning Glory?* launch, and I was saying: "If it wasn't for Primal Scream, you wouldn't have been in a position to sign Oasis." Alan was on a downer with Primal Scream. He really had the hump with them.'

Just as peppery as McGee's relationship with the Scream were Tim Abbot's dialogues with Liam Gallagher. Abbot had met Robbie Williams, a singer in Take That, at the Glastonbury festival the previous summer when Williams danced onstage during Oasis' set. Abbot was now trying to prise Williams out of Take That's contract with BMG and reposition him in the media as a decadent and humorous talent liberated from the shackles of boy-band monotony. 'Managing Robbie was the only thing I've ever done for the cardinal sin of greed,' says Abbot. 'I just thought: great, here is this guy who is going to be the next George Michael. He ended up being George Formby.'*

The ubiquity of Williams had drawn an increasingly cool response from Liam Gallagher, but Abbot scarcely had time to notice the portcullis begin its descent. He only realised the extent of his unpopularity when Oasis played two outdoor shows at the Manchester City football stadium Maine Road in April. 'The paranoia now was incredible,' Abbot says. 'They'd had a threat to be kidnapped. A massive Manchester gang – very heavy-duty – said: "We're going to kidnap one of them." Shit went on behind the scenes. The security was tripled up. I know people who were doing the merchandising who subbed in ex-SAS people. It was an incredibly heavy gig.

---

* The management contract between Abbot and Williams was terminated in 1998 when Williams argued that he had signed it under the effects of cocaine supplied to him by Abbot. The two parties settled out of court.

'It was celebsville backstage,' he goes on. 'The women were now running the whole pitch – the "cliterati", me and our Chris used to call them. Where we had always phoned up and got full access passes, now it was: "Who do you want them for?" We got Joe Soap passes, basically. It was Creation's coming-home gig – Alan was very much in the area – and there were all these different floors of executive entertaining, corporate entertaining. Maine Road was the start of the *über*-guest-lists.'

For about a year, the gadget-loving Abbot had been filming his escapades with Oasis on a Sony video camera. He was not proposing to do anything with the tapes as such; they were for his private collection and would sometimes be shown to friends in his Bethnal Green flat. However, Abbot did intend to write a book about Oasis, which inevitably put him on a collision course with Ignition. The list of journalists, insiders and ex-associates planning Oasis books was long and growing longer. Their former security man, Ian Robertson, was shortly to publish an account of his life in the eye of the hurricane, *Oasis: What's The Story?*, to the fury of Ignition. To ward off similar indiscretions, confidentiality agreements were distributed by Ignition to the Oasis road crew. Much to his indignation, Tim Abbot received one and threw it in the bin. 'Cheeky cunts,' he says. 'I've gone: "What's this? I don't even work for you. I work for myself." I wouldn't stand for that ever in life.'

The official history of Oasis was being written by the journalist Paolo Hewitt, who had travelled with the band and become a trusted friend. Abbot envisaged his own book being primarily photographic and – whatever Ignition might have imagined – relentlessly upbeat. But there was no way he was going to sign a confidentiality agreement. 'It was about civil liberties,' he says. 'For fuck's sake, it's only music. We're not talking about GM food formulas.'

'I think people did try and squeeze Tim out, definitely,' says Hopkins. 'I think the confidentiality clause may have been a convenient hook ... It did seem strange. I think he was made a scapegoat. By that time, there was a lot of politics going on around that band. It's possible that certain people within that new circle tried to edge Tim and Chris out.'

In the months that followed, Tim Abbot's freelance marketing consultancy with Oasis was terminated. He was not invited to the band's August shows at Loch Lomond and Knebworth, but was asked to return his video camera to Sony and give the film footage to Creation. Abbot refused to do either. His demonisation was all over bar the shouting.

'It was a shame that Tim got moved out,' says Hopkins. 'You have to remember that it was Tim that brought Noel back from San Francisco, put that tour back on the road and put that band back together. Tim did the 40 days in the wilderness with Noel. He was there for him and he brought him back.'

'My flight-plan, which I think was equivalent to Marcus' at the time, was that Oasis could go on to be the next U2,' says Abbot. 'But they had no political axe and they're not great intellectuals. The capacity of that band was consumed by materialism and showbiz and *Hello!* and *OK!*, whereas a band like Blur, if they'd been in that position, could have intellectualised it and turned it into something far greater.'

Whatever he was turning into, Noel Gallagher was no longer voting Abbot.

There were three possible outcomes to the end of the Creation–Sony deal in the summer of 1996. Firstly, the companies could remain partners on the same terms as before. Secondly, Sony could buy the 51 per cent of Creation that it did not already own, relying on its money to pacify Alan McGee and Dick Green into staying on as diminished figureheads. And thirdly, McGee and Green could walk away – to PolyGram, or to start another record label under a different name.

But in January, Jeremy Pearce had notified McGee and Green of a fourth option – one which would really have put the cat among the pigeons. Pearce was leaving Sony in April to head up Richard Branson's as-yet-unnamed new company, and wondered if it would be possible to take Creation with him: McGee, Green, Oasis, the works.

'The plan which I came up with involved Branson buying Creation from Sony,' says Pearce. 'Creation would be our UK company and we would license the rights to Sony internationally. And the reason we could do this was because Alan would go to Sony and do his usual shouting and screaming, "fuck you" bit; Oasis would do their bit because they liked us and we would give them some shares; and Branson would say to Sony: "Don't worry, you're not going to lose the band. You haven't got the UK anyway – because that's [licensed to] Creation – and you'll still get the international rights." And it would have been a really sexy, great company.'

Assuming that McGee and Green said yes to this – and the friendship between Pearce and McGee was not quite as solid as Pearce thought – the Oasis factor would be a colossal obstacle. Branson might be able to buy Creation from Sony, but why would Sony let Britain's most famous entrepreneur have Oasis? And that was before Branson even got round the table with Marcus Russell.

But the more he developed his idea, the more Pearce was certain that Oasis would pose a huge headache for Sony if it decided to go ahead with a Creation buy-out. McGee and Green would surely quit on the spot, leaving Sony with an internationally successful group with which it had no personal contact. 'There wasn't a key man clause, so Oasis couldn't have left with Alan,' Pearce points out. 'But on the other hand, it would have been a real mess for Sony. My theory was that Sony might have said: "We haven't got Oasis for the UK anyway. This way, we get Branson's new company internationally as well as Creation." There might have been a deal.'

The inducements for McGee and Green were to be a seven-figure signing fee apiece and shares in the Branson company, the UK operation of which they and Pearce would run as a team. 'I took Alan in to meet Branson, who was mad for it – loved the idea,' says Pearce. 'Alan was . . . he liked it, but he was worried, I think, by it. He's not a particularly imaginative businessman. It's not his thing. But he liked Branson a lot, and Branson said: "All right, we'll have a go." '

True, McGee warmed to Branson and thought the company sounded exciting. But several things disturbed him. For a start, he was anxious to know if Sony was intending to buy out Creation or not. If not, there would be no reason for him and Green to leave. 'We didn't want to go,' he says. 'We were having the time of our lives. ...Morning Glory? was on the way to being the biggest record of the 90s in Britain. We obviously didn't want to walk away from that. It was the Creation dream coming true.'

Another thing that made McGee uneasy was Jeremy Pearce's belief that Oasis would consent to be part of the arrangement. This certainly didn't square with the Oasis or the Marcus Russell that McGee knew. 'Jeremy's idea that he could have got Oasis was an absolute, utter delusion,' he says. 'The bottom line is Marcus is an astute businessman. He's just sold fifteen million (sic) copies of ... Morning Glory? Why would he change the distribution service?'

The third thing that worried McGee was that Creation's lawyer, John Kennedy, was also acting for Pearce. And to complicate matters even further, Kennedy was soon to become chairman of PolyGram UK, which had been making inquiries about headhunting McGee and Green since the autumn. McGee was looking to Kennedy, whom he trusted implicitly, to advise him which offers to take seriously, but Kennedy was honour-bound to say only so much. The result was that McGee got cold feet about Pearce and Branson.

When McGee ruled out any involvement with Branson, Pearce felt let down and humiliated, fearing that he had been made to look foolish in Branson's eyes. 'The carpet was pulled from under me,' he says. 'But Alan's not a sophisticated man. He doesn't think in those terms. He's a fighter. He thought: I'm not going to let Jeremy fuck this up with Sony for me.' Indeed, McGee fretted that the amorous intentions of Branson and of PolyGram had sent out a negative message to Sony. He was right. 'Sony thought we didn't want to carry on,' he says. 'We thought Sony didn't want to carry on. So we were getting into this situation where nothing was happening.'

Had the Sony contract been due for renegotiation earlier, Pearce estimates that McGee and Green would have been lucky to get £2.5

million for their remaining shares. By now, however, *(What's The Story) Morning Glory?* had completely transformed the picture; Creation was due 'an absolute fortune ... something like six or seven million' from Sony, McGee recalls, for sales of the Oasis album to date. In the financial year to 30 June, 1996, Creation would show a pre-tax profit of £7 million on turnover of £32 million – compared to a pre-tax profit of £424,000 for the year to 30 June, 1995, and a pre-tax loss of £1.9 million the year before that. Entirely thanks to the Oasis effect, Creation was now valued at £50 million. 'It suddenly made it very expensive for Sony to buy the company,' says Pearce, 'because Oasis were so big in England. The international sales weren't a big issue, but UK sales were – because that's where they can make your profit.'

By April, McGee was sure that Sony's silence indicated that it was going to purchase Creation and absorb it into the corporation. 'Alan did a terrible thing, really,' says Pearce. 'He went and told [Paul] Russell that I was trying to steal Creation ... He went to Russell and said: "Look, I want you to know that Jeremy's doing this, but it's nothing to do with me – and in fact, you know, I hate the guy, because it's terrible. I love Sony. I love *you*, Paul." Which he's said pretty consistently from that day on. I think he suddenly thought: fucking hell, I'm not going to get any *money* out of all this ...'

McGee's plan of action was actually a great deal more subtle – and a lot more bloody-minded – than that.

The body language of Sony had made McGee paranoid at first, but close friends now saw him turn incandescent with rage. Seeming to have forgotten that a buy-out of Creation was Sony's contractual right, which he himself had sanctioned in 1992, McGee thought only of the death of his label and determined to do whatever it took to prevent it. 'I fought Sony the only way I could,' he later said. 'Very hard, very dirty.'

He also fought Sony the only place he knew where: in the pages of the music press. Andy Saunders recalls: 'Alan came to me and said: "Those fuckers at Sony are insulting me. They want to buy my shares and I don't want to sell them. I need to do something to tell them that I'm not happy." I said to him: "We should go – under very controlled circumstances – and do something in the *NME*. We should take the moral high ground." He agreed.'

Saunders rang an *NME* news reporter, summoning him to a meeting with McGee in the Pembroke Castle, a pub near the Creation offices. To guard against misquotes, Saunders taped the interview while McGee read from a prepared statement. 'It was designed to hurt [Sony],' says Saunders, 'but not to libel.'

In the *NME* story, which ran in the 27 April issue under the headline 'Creation In Sony Share Shambles', the journalist quoted McGee warning of a 'bloodbath' unless Sony allowed him and Green to keep their shares. 'Creation is an A&R company,' McGee said. 'The moment I let some corporate fucking arsehole in New York run the record company, I will resign.' He added: 'Bad blood is developing rapidly ... It seems as if they are refusing to negotiate, and it seems to be saying they don't want me and Dick at Creation. We are Creation. If we go, I believe most of the artists and senior staff at the company will want to leave.' He named Oasis, Primal Scream and the Boo Radleys as some of the artists in question. 'We now need to have a crisis meeting with Sony,' McGee went on, 'to find out if this can be resolved.'

Symmetrically, Sony sources chose that very week to embark on a series of tactical briefings against Creation in *Music Week*. In a report headlined 'Sony Aims To Complete £12m Creation Buy-Out', the trade magazine wrote: 'Sony Music has confirmed it is set to acquire the rest of Creation. Paul Russell has said Sony will become sole owner within weeks.' However, there were two errors in the story. Firstly, *Music Week* suggested that only 49 per cent of the Creation shares remained to be acquired; and secondly, it alleged that McGee and Green were in a hurry to sell their shares before July, as any acquisition that took place after that date might see an increase in their capital gains tax if an autumn general election were to return a Labour government. 'Total bollocks,' says McGee flatly. 'We don't think like that.'

With the score at one-all, McGee was ready to up the stakes by giving stories to the *Financial Times* journalist Alice Rawsthorn, whose analyses of the music world reached every corridor of the industry and were widely seen as unequalled. With Rawsthorn on his side, McGee would not be an easy opponent. 'I knew at the end of the day that Sony could not have another high-publicity disaster,' he says. 'They'd had the court case with George Michael. They'd had Michael Jackson. They'd had the Pulp thing with Jarvis.* The last thing they needed was me going to the *Financial Times* and going to the High Court for a big battle about shares. That was the undercurrent of what I was about: if you want to come into the deep waters with me, I'm a lunatic and I'll fucking fight you.'

The High Court was only a paper threat, since McGee was on thin ice legally. But his position as an ethical refusenik was strengthened by events at Sony LRD, where Jeremy Pearce was leading an exodus

---

* Jarvis Cocker had walked onstage during Michael Jackson's performance at the 1996 Brit Awards, revolted by the latter's messianic stage show. Cocker was extensively congratulated for cocking a snook at the pomposity of Jackson, a Sony artist. The Jackson 'high-publicity disaster' to which McGee refers concerns unproven allegations of sex abuse against children, which were reported in 1993 and investigated by the Los Angeles Police Department.

of staff away to Branson's newly-named company, V2. 'LRD was dec-imated,' says Pearce. 'Nearly everyone came with me to V2, so there was no contact [between Sony and] either Creation or Oasis.' McGee could now play Oasis' loyalty to him as his ace in the hole, confident that a fear of antagonising the Gallaghers and Marcus Russell would force Sony to reconsider its buy-out.

There was just one magnificent flaw in McGee's poker hand. Whereas the likes of Martin Carr would have gone to the ends of the earth for him, Oasis were supremely harder hitters. Far from aban-doning Sony if the renegotiation went awry, Oasis would not have budged one inch. McGee's bid was a gigantic bluff – but he knew that Sony would not think of calling it. 'Sony didn't understand Oasis,' he says. 'They thought that if I went "boo", Oasis would follow. But I understand the way that working-class people think. And I knew that as much as the Gallaghers love me to pieces, and as much as I got on great with Marcus, there was absolutely not a hope in hell of them walking away. No matter what loyalty they have towards me, they wouldn't have walked out on the system that had made them rich guys. I was playing Sony by threatening things that were really just total nonsense.'

McGee recalls Marcus Russell being less than overjoyed by his chi-canery, but Noel Gallagher appeared to relish Sony being duped by a skilled amateur. Jeremy Pearce was lapping it up, too, particularly when he heard that McGee and Green were demanding an enor-mous cheque from Sony to keep the terms of the 1992 deal as they were. 'I remember Alan saying: "This is what I'm going to do – what do you think?" ' Pearce recalls. 'I said: "It's great, they'll be pissing themselves." It was all very funny. And I was still vaguely hanging in there in case there were any crumbs to bring to V2.'

McGee, Green and John Kennedy met Paul Russell on the Tuesday afternoon after McGee had vented his spleen to the *NME*. Tuesday was when the paper was published in London, and McGee was curi-ous to see if Russell had read his copy. 'John Kennedy was sitting with me and he goes: "If he's read it, it'll be lively",' McGee says. 'Russell came in and he looked at me – and I could tell he knew. He went out to get himself a cup of tea and I said to John: "He definitely knows." And John went: "He doesn't know." I went: "John, he *knows*." ' Returning to the room, Russell asked Dick Green: 'Who's your publicist?' Green pointed to McGee and said: 'He is.' McGee felt Kennedy's foot nudge his under the desk.

'Respect to Paul Russell, because if I had said those things in the *NME* about somebody like Rob Dickins, he would have slapped my head and taken his ball off the football pitch,' says McGee. 'But with Paul Russell, he was just like: "Well, you rough little bastard, I sort of respect you – now let's do the deal." He knew that it wasn't personal.'

The upshot of the meeting was that both parties accepted that there had been a misunderstanding of the other's wishes, which the mutual dropping of stories to the press had only exacerbated. There would be no buy-out. As McGee now puts it: 'When me and Paul Russell get in a room, it's fine. It's just all the foreplay that's a bit messy.'

The contract between Creation and Sony was duly renegotiated in accordance with a formula agreed in 1992. The formula had been weighted to Sony's considerable advantage at the time, but it had left a loophole for a major change of circumstances – and that change of circumstances was the phenomenal success of *(What's The Story) Morning Glory?*. 'It was a bit like a dartboard,' says McGee. 'If you throw three 50s, somebody's going to pay you £14.5 million. And we unbelievably threw three 50s.'

Just as McGee and Russell were agreeing that the scenario was less complex than it had appeared, stories emerged in the press that suggested some commentators were still baffled by the complexities. A report in one of the Sunday newspapers in the first week of May claimed that Sony had mistakenly thought it had bought a controlling stake in Creation in 1992 and now realised that it had not – as if such absent-mindedness were likely. The article went on to venture that the third Creation shareholder, John McGee, held the fate of the label in his hands with his two-and-a-half shares.

More erroneous by far was a story composed by *Music Week* for its front page towards the end of that month. As McGee and Green attended the meeting on Friday, 31 May that would decide the terms of the new deal, *Music Week* writer Paul Gorman believed he had enough information to predict the result in advance. 'Paul Gorman rang me up and said: "So Creation are going to sell their shares?",' recalls Andy Saunders. 'I said: "Under absolutely no circumstances are Creation going to sell their shares." And he said to me: "Well, I've been told by a source within Sony that they will." I said: "Well, that source is lying, mate. And don't you dare fucking print that." Of course, it came out on the Monday.'

On 3 June, a week after *(What's The Story) Morning Glory?* had gone nine times platinum in the UK for sales of 2.7 million, *Music Week* revealed that Creation was about to be ushered into complete Sony ownership as a result of Friday's talks. It also reported that McGee and Green would stay with the label for 'a period believed to be five years' and receive more than £12 million for their combined shares. According to *Music Week*, the acquisition would be done and dusted early the next year.

The truth about the 31 May talks was quite different. After what a joint statement from Sony and Creation called 'a short, amicable and constructive meeting', Sony agreed to pay McGee and Green £14.5 million to extend the contract for another five years, and to increase their royalty rate on Sony's sales of Creation-signed acts outside the UK. No buy-out. The industry was shell-shocked.

'Creation has pulled off the deal of the year,' began a *Music Week* story the following Monday, which ran alongside a full retraction and apology. 'Contrary to expectations ... Creation emerged from talks late last Friday night with a package which extends its existing deal until 2001 ...' The *Sunday Times* called it 'a stunning *coup de grâce*', adding: 'When singer George Michael attempted to leave Sony for a new label it took him 75 days in court and cost him £35 million. When McGee decided to break a contractual promise to the same company, all he needed was a hint of defiance and the knowledge that ultimately there are few in the music industry who dare challenge his ear for success.'

Jeremy Pearce was among the congratulators. 'I don't think Sony imagined,' he says, 'that Alan would be so totally unreasonable as to think that he could stop them exercising their right *and* take money. To be fair, most people wouldn't have the balls to do that. I mean, it was outrageous really.'

'All business is poker,' McGee said in July. 'Everybody's bluffing. You have to work out who will execute their threat. At the end of the day, Sony realised I was crazy enough to destroy the label, so they backed down. I mean, who would be daft enough to alienate the man who discovered Oasis?'

A business journalist on the *Sunday Times* later wrote: 'For the first time since setting up Creation, McGee was playing among the cream of the industry.' McGee had played by the rules of the street, however, and that was what had given him his edge. Not for the first time in his life, and not for the last, he delighted in the contrast in social backgrounds between himself and those whom he had overcome. 'Most of the music industry is all public-school,' he says now. 'They've all been buggering each other for years. I'm an oik off a council estate in Glasgow. I don't sound like one of them, I don't look like one of them and I've got outspoken opinions that piss them off.'

As was his way, Dick Green elected not to share the headlines with his Creation partner. Still, he was able to come to the phone when *Music Week* asked for a comment on the £14.5 million payment to him and McGee. After giving it some thought, just as he gave everything some thought, Green admitted that the money was 'a nice amount'. Even from one of the most reticent multimillionaires in the UK entertainment industry, it was some understatement.

Alan Horne seldom leaves his house in Glasgow any more. The forgotten man of Scottish independent music spends his days caring for Paul Quinn, who has had multiple sclerosis for several years. There was a reactivation of Postcard by Horne in the early 90s, but it did not compare to the 80s model in reputation, and only an Orange

Juice retrospective in 1993, *The Heather's On Fire*, created much publicity.

'I think when Alan revived Postcard he thought it would completely eclipse Creation and he would attract all the Creation fans,' says Edwyn Collins. 'He didn't realise that times had moved on: you can't rely solely on press any more. He spent a lot on packaging, but he wouldn't really promote the records and wouldn't advertise. None of the groups toured outside Glasgow. He had lost nearly all the ground that he ever had. Postcard was only a small, culty thing compared to what Creation had become.'

Horne's disdain for Alan McGee had not softened with the years. Rather, it hardened when he heard of an interview McGee had given to the Scottish magazine *M8* in 1994. Talking just weeks before his breakdown, McGee condemned Horne as 'a complete fucking dickhead', adding: 'At the end of the day, the guy's never had a hit and he's never going to have a hit, and he's never really made a classic record, although Orange Juice came close. He'll be an old age pensioner and he'll still be trailing Postcard around with him ...'

Horne waited more than two years to shove those words back down McGee's throat. In June 1996, his opportunity arrived. Edwyn Collins took Horne to the Silver Clef Awards in Edinburgh, where Collins was receiving a gong for his contribution to Scottish music and for sales of his hugely successful comeback hit, 'A Girl Like You'. The Horne that walked into that Edinburgh hotel was a much changed man from the Horne of old. Having given up any pretence of liking rock or indie music, he had steeped himself in black culture. It exemplified the overall disgust he felt for white people as human beings. To Collins' regret, Horne now dismissed the work of Postcard out of hand, claiming it to be worthless save for a moderate historical value. 'I think it was the best we could have done at the time, being Scottish and being white and being da-da-da,' Horne says. 'But I couldn't listen to those records now. It would just depress me. I'd rather listen to En Vogue.'

As to his own fabulously uncompromising behaviour in the Postcard days, Horne was keen to draw a line under it and move on. 'The reputation I had with certain people was based on the fact that I was a horrible, overcompensating, shy person who was speeding out of my head all the time,' he says. 'When we were doing the label, I was the head of a gang of people who were not the best-adjusted people. I really wanted to prove that I was the leader, so I pushed myself and pushed myself, and became a monster. And that's what people met in those days. It took me until my 30s before I got any kind of balance.'

A skinny, drawn man in his early forties, Horne prefers a slower life to the years when he made his deals on speed. But his cattiness and alertness are still to be feared, even if his self-worth has taken some knocks since his heyday. 'It's this thing about always looking for peer group approval but not being able to find a peer group,' he says. 'I'm like that. I can't find my peer group. It's possibly the thing that undermines my whole existence.' Other than Quinn and a few friends, he concedes that he simply doesn't like people very much.

At the Silver Clef Awards ceremony in 1996, Horne was collared by Postcard fans, some of whom had hero-worshipped him in the early 80s. Among them were Wet Wet Wet, who were picking up an award themselves. 'I was standing there having to deal with them saying: "You were a real influence on us, man – put it there, pal. Do you want to come to the football with us?" ' Horne recalls with a shudder. 'I'm not exaggerating, it was like that. Then Edwyn says: "You know who the other person getting a prize is? Alan McGee." '

Collins had not seen McGee in some years and was surprised by his diffidence. McGee was still inclined to feel uncomfortable in crowded places, and had taken several friends and family members with him for support, including his father, Ed Ball, Kle Boutis and Creation's regional plugger Anita Heryet. 'It was the first time I'd seen a completely teetotal, reformed, sober McGee,' says Collins. 'He was very nervous when he made his acceptance speech. Horne was at my table, which was adjacent to McGee's. McGee's dad kind of broke the ice: he put one arm round me and one arm round Alan [McGee], and he said: "The boys done well." '

Collins introduced the two Alans to one another. It was the first time they had met properly and there was only one topic of conversation on Horne's agenda. 'I asked him why he had said those things,' Horne recalls. 'He said, "Oh, that was the drugs, man. I had a really bad time. No, you've been a big influence ..." It wasn't a satisfying result.' Horne insisted on a formal apology. 'He asked for an apology about three times,' McGee remembers, 'and I had to say, "Look, man, I've apologised. I'm sorry, I was a drug addict, all right?" '

Horne was still not satisfied. 'He proceeded to get far too drunk, so drunk that McGee didn't want anything to do with him,' says Collins. 'Horne eventually ended up in tears. It was sad. It was almost like, every dog has his day.'

Like every other Glasgow punk, McGee had been denied a chance of seeing the Sex Pistols in his home city. When they reformed in 1996 for a tour of the world, McGee had grave reservations and decided to avoid their open-air show in London's Finsbury Park. He was still a fan of the original Pistols – he had signed the bassist, Glen Matlock, to a solo deal the previous year – but their '96 tour had been receiving mocking reviews in the press and ticket sales for some European dates had been sluggish. McGee felt he was missing nothing; most people he asked about the Finsbury Park concert told him it had been awful.

But two people were kinder. Kevin Rowland, whom McGee was close to signing at the time, had enjoyed the show and Noel Gallagher said he thought the band had been great but was too drunk to be sure. When the Pistols played a low-key gig at the Empire in Shepherd's Bush in July, McGee went along to see if they could still muster up a thunderstorm, taking Gallagher with him.

At eight o'clock the following morning, Andy Saunders was phoned at home by a ranting McGee, who told him he had just seen one of the greatest concerts of his life, and wanted to review it for the *NME*. When the rest of the music business woke up, Saunders called an amused Steve Sutherland, who suggested McGee send his 'review' to the paper's letters page like any other reader. 'No,' said McGee. 'I want it to be a review ... In fact, fuck it, I'll take out an advert.'

Romanced as 'McGee's most outrageous act of '96' – by Sutherland himself – a £5,000 full-page ad was placed in the *NME*, wherein McGee reviewed the Sex Pistols as only the former editor of *Communication Blur* could. 'The band was amazing-looking and -sounding,' he wrote. 'Paul Cook: shaved head and soul. The Sex Pistols changed my life in 1977 and in 1996. They are the Gods to a man. Rock 'n' roll should always be this great.'

Although the advertisement was lampooned – what exactly was a shaved soul? – it reminded those who had forgotten that McGee was still a mad music fan. The pan-Oasis climate of the previous nine months had seen few spur-of-the-moment outbursts from the President; by giving his review the headline 'A Creation Records Statement', he did the label's reputation as a music-led company more good than harm. 'That advert garnered a massive amount of media attention,' says Saunders. 'It paid for itself in terms of Creation branding. I told him to give it a catalogue number, so he gave it CRE 1976.'

McGee later told Sutherland: 'No other record company in the world would take out an advert for a band on another label.' Perhaps not, but once he'd finished eulogising the Virgin America-signed Sex Pistols in the advert, McGee moved the subject on to one of Creation's newest acts, the unknown Three Colours Red, whom he called one of the best live bands in the country.

McGee heard from a third party that John Lydon had read the advert, saying: 'Never trust Alan McGee. He's a very clever man.' McGee was thrilled that Lydon even knew who he was. However, he was being modest. The people who knew of McGee – and who wanted to get to know him in person – by now included secretaries of state, one or two opposition ministers and the leader of the Labour Party himself.

Opening his mail one day in June, McGee saw that he had received an invitation to a reception for record company bosses hosted by the Government's secretary of state for national heritage,

Virginia Bottomley. He wasn't sure how to respond. 'Alan brandished this letter to me,' recalls Andy Saunders, 'and said: "I've been invited to 10 Downing Street to take part in a music industry forum." I said to him: "You can't do it." And he said: "Oh . . ." – genuinely shocked – ". . . why not?" I said: "Because it's the fucking *Tories*. You can't go and sit down with the Tories." He immediately said: "No, you're right." '

Saunders advised McGee to go public on the matter and issue a press release crucifying Bottomley and her party. McGee was agreeable, and circulated a statement which read in part: 'I refuse to be used merely as photo fodder for the self-publicity of someone who has no understanding of, or compassion for, the people of this country.' Later that same month, he told the *Sunday Times*: 'The Tory barbarians have done nothing for the music industry – in fact, the Criminal Justice Act made it more difficult to hold concerts – and now they are chasing the youth vote. Well, she can just fuck off.'

McGee's hatred of the Conservatives was sincere, if somewhat abstract at times, and was explained variously by him as having to do with their closure of hospitals; the effect of some of their urban policies on parts of Scotland; and the high numbers of muggings that had blighted Oasis' Maine Road concerts in April, which McGee blamed on a mood of hopelessness that pervaded the nearby Moss Side estate after 17 years of Tory rule. Interested in the possibility of helping Labour to power in some way, McGee thought of funding a nationwide campaign of posters, which would show Noel Gallagher and Damon Albarn glowering at each other, with a slogan underneath reading: 'The only people they hate more than each other are the Tories'.

The most celebrated example in British history of a political leader using pop music celebrities to attract young people was the photograph of Labour prime minister Harold Wilson with the Beatles in the 60s. In the main, however, Wilson's Cabinet had been full of middle-aged men with no conception of the Swinging 60s, Beatlemania or even pop. 'With the exception of [home secretary] Roy Jenkins' liberal reforms,' wrote an *Observer* journalist three decades later, 'the Wilson Government contributed little to the shape or content of a decade it never really understood.'

In the 80s, during its long decade in opposition, the Labour Party was linked to youth-catching movements such as CND and the striking miners, and made well-publicised attempts to defend the young unemployed from Conservative attack. But despite the music press and the majority of young pop musicians being pro-Labour, the party lost the confidence and even the interest of young people in the run-up to the 1983 general election. By the mid-80s, the Labour leader Neil Kinnock was making overtures to the youth by associating with Billy Bragg and appearing in a video by the singer Tracey Ullman. As the *NME* wrote in 1985: 'Political debate is largely won or lost in the media, and pop music saturates [the] media.'

Labour's links with pop were cemented by Red Wedge, a group of Labour-supporting musicians headed by Bragg and Paul Weller which toured to raise political awareness in the 18 months leading up to the 1987 general election – an election Labour expected to win. However, the Conservatives were returned by more than 100 seats, stupefying Labour and finishing Red Wedge. Moreover, it could be said that pop culture was Kinnock's Waterloo in 1992 when, addressing an eve-of-election rally in Sheffield, he let excitement get the better of him and started shouting like Mick Jagger at a Stones gig. The Tories won a fourth term; it was later estimated that 43 per cent of people under the age of 25 – about 16 per cent of the electorate – had failed to vote.

One of the principal problems with Red Wedge had been that the musicians who made up the group shared an earnest, even prosaic image. Bragg was a soapbox orator – articulate but pedantic – while Weller's Style Council, Tom Robinson and the Communards were all synonymous with stern attitudes and dour benefit gigs at the Hackney Empire. Red Wedge had not cost Labour the election by any means, but nor had it been of much use in canvassing the apathetic. The Britpop wave of the mid-90s was entirely different. With its often zany songs and videos, Britpop was essentially optimistic and unquestionably superficial. That, as it turned out, was just what New Labour was looking for.

In 1995, sales of records in the UK had reached £1 billion, a rise of 11 per cent on 1994, and exports had increased by 25 per cent to £354 million, due mostly to Britpop bands like Oasis and Blur. While the growth in 1996 was not as impressive, exports continued to rise as Oasis were joined as an international force by the Spice Girls. Labour and the Tories had been courting the music industry since the early 90s: the BPI had welcomed politicians to its annual general meetings, while, as *Music Week* was to remark in 1997, 'so many MPs and ministers now sashay along to the Brit Awards that it has become one of the quietest nights of the year in the Commons'.

Unlike the film industry, the music business was self-financed and rarely sought or took government advice. Its many fetishes and dark secrets – for example, ridiculously high CD pricing, into which Labour MP Gerald Kaufman had led a campaign that ended in a Monopolies and Mergers Commission investigation in 1993 – were no business, it felt strongly, of politicians. What was more serious in the music industry's view was the effectiveness of the 1988 Copyright Act in the light of new developments in the information superhighway. The industry was keen to support a party that would stop it from losing revenue.

But the most frequent complaint from the music business was that

the Conservative Government had failed to acknowledge its economic importance. So out of touch with current music were the
Tories that in 1987 Margaret Thatcher had named her favourite pop
song as 'Telstar' by the Tornados, a record released before many pre-
sent-day stars had been born. Both Labour and Conservative mani-
festos for the 1997 general election would mention the music
business in a favourable light. However, despite the Labour leanings
of musicians, music papers and the younger music executives, the
industry as a whole was pro-free enterprise and pro-Tory. And
whether Alan McGee knew it or not, two Tory voters worked for
Creation.

Tony Blair had played in a rock group as a student, and was the
first Labour leader to number people from the music business
among his personal friends. More accessible to the industry – and
younger in both years and demeanour – than his predecessor John
Smith, Blair had been guest of honour at the annual Q magazine
awards in 1994, where he made a witty speech and was greeted
warmly by some of the musicians and MDs. By 1996, an election victory for Blair was seen as probable if not inevitable, but after the cat-
astrophic complacency of 1992 Labour was at greater pains than ever
to target the youth vote by the use of music. That summer, McGee
and Andy Saunders attended a Labour fund-raiser at the Hilton
Hotel in London, where they spoke to Blair for the first time.

In August, a week after *(What's The Story) Morning Glory?* was certified ten times platinum in the UK, making it one of the seven highest-selling albums in chart history, Oasis played two concerts at
Knebworth, an estate near Stevenage in Hertfordshire, before a total
of 250,000 people. Billed as the largest national live event of the
decade, Knebworth confirmed Oasis as the most popular band
Britain had known since the Beatles.

'You certainly couldn't do anything bigger than Knebworth,' says
Johnny Hopkins. 'There was incredible demand for tickets.' Two million ticket applications were made: Oasis could have performed at
Knebworth every day for a fortnight and still left a quarter of a million people disappointed. McGee was to say of Knebworth: 'It represented our crowning achievement. Everything we'd been doing
since 1983 had been setting the scene for Oasis, beginning with
pressing 700 records for Jasmine Minks, the Legend! and Primal
Scream. And thirteen years later, fifteen million people* were buying into the Creation vision of music – a sexy singer, guts, rock 'n' roll
and a fuck-you attitude.'

---

* McGee is referring here to the fifteen million people who bought *(What's The Story)
Morning Glory?*

Coordinated by Meg Matthews, the backstage hospitality at Knebworth was centralised from a marquee bearing the Creation slogan of 1996, 'Creation Records – World Class', which had first appeared in a brochure for the *Music Week* awards back in March. The marquee was bigger than the venues played by many Creation bands, and was described by the *Independent* as 'the kind that is usually seen at race meetings and polo matches'. The journalist added cuttingly: 'Within, specially invited members of the music business made merry while a clutch of VIPs – Kate Moss, Mick Hucknall – partied behind a length of scarlet rope'. Marquee security was so stringent that McGee was three times denied entry. 'Knebworth was just too big,' says Tones Sansom. 'I think the guest-list was 7,000.'

The five members of Oasis each had a personal trailer in which to prepare for the shows, with a garden outside. In the areas where the public was allowed, punters queued for hamburgers at a fiver a throw. The great British rock concert had traced a full circle back to the Rolling Stones and Led Zeppelin gigs of the 70s, when fans would wait hours for the pleasure of queuing for another hour-long wait. A different *NME* – a different Britain; a different Alan McGee – would have gazed down through the ages upon Knebworth and asked profound questions of the revolution.

'I don't think people should be afraid of being big,' says Hopkins in defence of Oasis and Creation. 'To go out there and put on a good show, which they did, that's cool. I suppose it was Zeppelin-esque, but I think it was something they had to do. It was a one-off: you don't try and follow that up with anything similar. That's what we discussed at the time. It was the right thing to do, and everybody knew that whatever they did next had to be different ... And fucking hell, Creation *was* a world-class record label. Look at the history: *Screamadelica, Isn't Anything, Bandwagonesque, Loveless, Grand Prix*. There's a lot of labels that have been going a lot longer and can't claim to have put out stuff like that.'

Tim Abbot had managed to get Knebworth tickets for himself and a girlfriend, but found the circus to be rather on the hollow side. Abbot left the vast site that night in a Cherokee Jeep with Pulp members Jarvis Cocker and Steve Mackey, all of them shaking their heads in disbelief at the ostentation of the Oasis corporate rock show. To Abbot, there was nothing world-class about Creation any more. 'Nobody could ever recreate what Creation had been before the day of the earthquake in Los Angeles,' he says. 'It had gone. Creation ended then as I see it, because Alan never came back. The drugs stories of Oasis were *nothing* compared to the two, three years prior to that. Primal Scream. Chris Abbot. Norman of the Fanclub on E. That's what Creation was made up of. By the time of Knebworth, it was an old carcass being dragged along by a load of opportunists.'

Emma Greengrass, exhausted, fell ill not long after Knebworth.

Meg Matthews started to appear at Creation less and less, to the detriment of office morale. 'It was another character gone,' says a mournful Hopkins. Life in Primrose Hill became mundane. What Hopkins and Sansom call the 'boring years' had begun.

By the end of the year, McGee was admitting that Oasis would probably never do anything on the scale of Knebworth again, and that similarly high sales for the next album were out of the question. Some of his staff agreed with him. 'The signs were there in the attitude of Noel and Liam,' says John Andrews. 'They were leaving a bad taste in people's mouths. Whereas before they'd been seen as great guys who had come from the street and made it, they just didn't carry it off with any sense of grace. That's why there had to be a downfall. Because it was vulgar.'

'In his time,' says Tim Abbot, 'Noel Gallagher was incredibly on top of his game. He read situations intuitively. He had a humility in his soundbites that was kind of cool. But when you start shopping for England, coming out of Harrods saying: "Well, fuck you, I've got 30 million" – *that's* how they lost it. They were out of tune because everyone around them was in this false, materialistic economy – the crapocracy of low-talent celebrity. You just alienate people. There's a great Walsall Market expression: "Never make a mug of your punter." '

The first suggestions were now being voiced that Oasis – and Creation for that matter –had peaked at Knebworth. However, it could be argued that the peak had come some time before: possibly with 'Wonderwall', possibly at Maine Road. 'I think the peak was probably in between "Roll With It" and "Wonderwall",' says Andrews, 'when everybody was warming to Oasis. People who had slagged them off before were saying: "No, they are actually brilliant", and people could compare them to the Beatles without sniggering. By the time Oasis got to Knebworth, they were so big that they had just become too arrogant. It was like Rome. The Empire has spread, but it's so far removed from what it came from that it's got to crumble at some point.'

A few weeks after Knebworth, McGee was asked by New Labour to organise an event for the party conference in Blackpool at the end of September. He later recalled: 'They said: "Can you put your name on the tickets? Can you sort out the music? Can you do some sort of photo with Tony? And by the way, will you go £10,000 towards sponsoring it?" We thought about it for about an hour and we thought: all right, we're up for it.'

What New Labour wanted was for Noel Gallagher to sing Oasis songs at the event, but the band was about to start recording a new album and Gallagher was too tired to appear. Andy Saunders had the idea of presenting Blair with an Oasis platinum disc to show that they – and Creation – were firmly in his corner. For live entertainment, meanwhile, Labour would have to settle for 18 Wheeler.

The Creation-sponsored Youth Experience Rally in Blackpool's Norbreck Castle Hotel on 28 September was attended by around 200 young people from the town's two marginal constituencies, who were given free drinks and kept amused by Steve Coogan's spoof chat-show host Alan Partridge, arguably the most credible TV personality Blair could have wished for. Blair himself made his way to the stage as 'Don't Look Back In Anger' was piped over the PA. He was handed his Oasis platinum disc by McGee, and said of Creation: 'It's a great company. We should be really proud of it. Alan's just been telling me he started twelve years ago with a £1,000 bank loan and now it's got a £34 million turnover. Now *that's* New Labour.'

It was nothing of the sort. As one broadsheet writer waspishly pointed out, Blair and McGee had two things in common: they were both failed musicians and they had both come to prominence as a result of Thatcherism. 'I am absolutely a product of Thatcherism,' McGee later admitted. 'She would have loved me.' (He soon decided this didn't play too well. By May the following year, he was claiming that Creation had achieved its success 'despite the Conservative Government'.)

The handover of the platinum disc completed, Blair announced 18 Wheeler from the stage. 'It's a fantastic label, they've got some great acts and this is going to be one of the biggest,' he said, before faltering. ' ... Wheeler 18, isn't it?' When a frantically mouthing McGee put him right, Blair introduced the band under its correct name, left the ballroom and was not seen again all night.

The Youth Experience Rally was the first instance of a UK record company throwing its support behind a future prime minister. More importantly for Blair, Oasis were in the ring too. '[Labour] were really worried that they were going to look like Red Wedge in the 80s – the Hackney Empire, social worker kind of thing,' McGee said that month. 'They want Creation, Ministry Of Sound DJs ... Obviously, I know to a certain extent that I'm being used, but I'm willing to go along with it.' He even said publicly that he would not cavil at paying 50 per cent income tax if the money trickled down to people who needed it.

McGee currently lived in a mansion apartment block in Bickenhall Street, off Baker Street, where his neighbours included Gary Glitter. McGee's lifestyle was compartmentalised and geared towards maximum efficiency. At the root of it lay a healthy diet and a daily fitness regime. He drank herbal tea every day, and regularly enjoyed two-hour walks in Regent's Park. McGee can neither drive nor swim; nor, funnily enough, can Noel Gallagher.

For his meetings and interviews, McGee used either the Landmark Hotel, where the tea-room waiters greeted him deferentially and where he was partial to the mirror-panelled gymnasium; or his own office in Berkley Grove, a cul-de-sac in Primrose Hill a minute's walk from Creation. '[The office's] contents reveal his lack of concern for the financial side of his business,' wrote a *New Statesman* journalist in all innocence. 'There is no desk, no filing cabinet, just a pair of sofas facing each other across a coffee table. To one side of the sofas are a hi-fi, speakers and an electric guitar; to the other stands a cabinet on which is mounted a photo of Chelsea striker Gianluca Vialli. On the walls hang three gold and platinum discs ... commemorating land-mark sales of records that McGee particularly cares about: the Jesus and Mary Chain's 1985 album *Psychocandy*, Primal Scream's *Screamadelica* and Oasis' *(What's The Story) Morning Glory?'*

Those journalists who met McGee at the Landmark would invari-ably open their articles in the same fashion: a slow panning shot of the hotel's lobby and its American and oriental tourists and sharp-suited businessmen; the journalist somehow contriving to miss the entrance of a rather nondescript-looking gentleman with a faint fuzz of ginger hair and spectacles; and finally, the journalist's realisation that this man is probably wealthier than anyone else in the building. Asked by a magazine in the summer of 1996 how much he earned a year, McGee replied: 'I don't know any more.'

Most of the articles would be illustrated by a photograph of McGee taken in his office. He would look into the camera impassively – well, perhaps a slight frown – and bring his hands together as if in prayer, the fingers interlocking under his chin. He had moved into the office in the late summer of 1996. 'It was hugely symbolic,' says Andy Saunders. 'He was removing himself from the very fabric of Creation.'

McGee's political ambitions appeared to go no further than per-suading people to vote Labour in May. 'I've done my bit now,' he told the *New Statesman*. 'I've got no plans to do anything else.' McGee and Saunders expected to hear no more from Labour in the months before the general election. 'We were very, very fringe members of the Labour elite,' says Saunders. 'We didn't think they'd need to come back to us.' But come back they would.

23 Control

THE NUMBER OF CREATION staff had increased to 35, and McGee implied that he would like to see it rise still higher. In November 1996 he claimed that Creation was poised to make the transition from an indie label to a major in size and effect – a transition made in the 80s by Island and Virgin. McGee suggested that Creation was 'probably as big as Island now'; elsewhere he mentioned Stax, Motown and Sire as labels whose growth inspired him. However, his real aim was for Creation to become 'as big and as dynamic' as Atlantic had been under Ahmet Ertegun, while avoiding the modern trap of being so efficient as to become faceless.

Being Creation, there was little chance of over-efficiency. 'As Creation expanded, it became more inefficient,' says John Andrews. 'The expansion was the cornerstone of the inefficiency of the label. How not to manage a record label.'

The perception of Creation outside Primrose Hill – and certainly in New Labour's headquarters in Millbank – was that it was a byword in British success and a company inexorably on the march. Replying in March to a journalist's question about independence, once the most urgent criterion of the label, Andy Saunders had put it in perspective by saying: 'Indie is a bit of a swear-word to us. It denotes underachievement. It's as if you're saying the band you're pushing has limited potential.'

Neither Saunders nor anyone else in the press department wavered from the belief that Oasis-sized success was attainable for the other acts on the roster. What annoyed Saunders more than any of his colleagues, however, was when certain acts made diffuse and intentionally uncommercial music that appeared to have underachievement as its guiding principle. Saunders was not always right about this, but it didn't stop him from being angry. And when he heard the album that the Boo Radleys were releasing as their follow-up to the chart-topping *Wake Up!*, Saunders thought it a disgrace.

The Boo Radleys were one of several bands that had undergone a rethink following their Britpop success in 1995. Pulp, unsettled by fame and media intrusion, were planning to return with some of their darkest music ever, while Damon Albarn had said in private that he was prepared to lose half a million Blur fans on their next album, providing it allowed the group to break new musical ground. Martin Carr was coming from a similar angle: restless in his pop pigeon-hole, he wanted no more trumpet fanfares or snappy hooks.

'This was one of the things I would have talked to Noel and Liam about that night in Glasgow [in 1994],' Carr says. 'Bands have a duty to change and challenge themselves and try and do something new. I firmly believed it. And a band like us, with the kind of ambition that we had musically, it would have been silly to try and harness us.' Empowered by the Old Creation attitude to A&R – let the band make the record it wants to make – which New Creation had yet to get around to resetting, the Boo Radleys delivered a harsh and uncompromising album called *C'mon Kids*.

John Andrews, their marketing manager, might have been expected to blanch at some of its more discordant passages, but no: he considered it a shrewd move on the part of Carr and the band to prolong their life as musicians and artists. Carr himself was hopeful that *C'mon Kids* would sell in droves, but knew that it would take several listens to make its point. Saunders was the one who heard only gratuitous turmoil and mischief in its grooves. He almost wished he hadn't been reinstated as the Boo Radleys' publicist.

'When I came to promote it,' he says, 'Mark Sutherland, who was the features editor of the *NME*, said to me: "Andy, there's one story. They were a pop band who had success and now they're not. That's the only story that any decent journalist is going to write about this album." It died on its arse.' With no 'Wake Up Boo!' to drive sales, the way was paved by the raucous, angular single 'What's In The Box?' In what may have been a gesture of sheer goodwill, Radio 1 put it on its heavy rotation A-list.

'People believed in that single,' says Andrews. 'Simon Mayo – and I'm not saying he's a great cultural spokesman – said on Radio 1: "This is the best single since the Sex Pistols' 'Anarchy In The UK'." At that point I thought: we're going to educate the public, and they're going to buy this record and buy Beach Boys records and understand a little bit more.' 'What's In The Box?' spent only two weeks in the Top 75.

That Carr had shot the golden goose didn't matter too much to a label that was being bankrolled by Oasis at the time. But it mattered to the Boo Radleys, who lost 100,000 fans on *C'mon Kids* and returned to being a cult band. When their UK tour was in the process of being set up, they found that Creation was suddenly turning down some of their requests – for instance, using the DJs Propellerheads as an opening act to give the shows a *Screamadelica* feel – blaming financial considerations.

'Although we'd made quite a bit of money personally, the band itself was pretty skint,' says Carr. 'What we decided to do in America was support people. We hadn't supported anyone for years and we thought: the gigs that we're doing aren't getting any bigger; we need to start playing to more people.' On a tour of Europe in October, the Boo Radleys supported Suede, whose third album, *Coming Up*, had debuted in the UK at number 1. But even Suede were feeling the pinch. *Coming Up* was their first album without guitarist and songwriter Bernard Butler, whose bitter departure had been one of the longest-running music press stories of the mid-90s. 'When we played in Germany,' recalls Carr, 'this guy in the audience had a sign, and every time they played a Bernard song he'd hold up this sign saying: "You Are Great". Then when they played one of the new songs, he'd turn it round and it said: "You Are Shit". Brett tried to reach down and grab it – he was getting really pissed off – and the bloke grabbed his mike and starting shouting German into it. Best Suede gig ever.'

But the tour had set a pattern. The Boo Radleys were now no more than they had been in 1992: a support band for hire.

Nineteen-ninety-six ended with ... *Morning Glory?* twelve times platinum. It had become the fifth-highest-selling album in UK history, and possibly even the fourth. (No figures exist to prove conclusively how many copies of *Sgt. Pepper's Lonely Hearts Club Band* were sold in the 60s.) At Christmas, the entire Oasis catalogue was re-promoted successfully, adding more height to an already formidable mountain. 'Some people thought that was pushing it a bit too far,' notes Emma Greengrass. 'But it made money for the company. If that's what people wanted me to do, I did it.'

Oasis excepted, few UK artists had broken through internationally in 1996. The Scots-American band Garbage and the grunge throwback act Bush (British but signed to an American label) were the only non-established groups to release million-selling albums in the US. Of 31 UK albums to have charted in the American Top 100 over the previous twelve months, only four had been made by bands less than three years old. The industry worried that the talent might be drying up – or, like Blur and Pulp, be too English-sounding to achieve international renown. 'It's clear we can no longer assume we are the first or most important repertoire source,' said John Kennedy, chairman of the market-leading PolyGram. 'Arrogance or complacency come at a very high cost ... We can't sit here arrogantly saying to the world: "Because we like it, you should like it."' In December, the trade magazine *MBI (Music Business International)* warned that British indie and alternative music had peaked in America, and that mainstream pop was back with a bang. 'The feelgood factor which permeated the UK over the past couple of years has been based on buoyant domestic sales,' it reminded everyone. 'With sales growth now slowing, UK companies are faced with a stark choice – either trim costs drastically or convert UK sales into international success.'

Unable to do the latter with any consistency, Creation did the former by dropping Heavy Stereo. It was an act of great significance. Creation dropped Heavy Stereo for the same reason that major labels drop bands: because their album sales and singles performances fall far short of the marketing spend. 'Heavy Stereo were pitched too high too soon,' says Johnny Hopkins. 'The whole thing with Oasis is that it was taken really slowly. It might not have appeared that way, but there was a lot of thought put in from May–June '93. We all had the brakes on because we'd seen so many bands – like Suede, in a way – go too quickly. "Supersonic" came out and didn't get *Top Of The Pops*. Doesn't matter; we'll try on the next one.' Creation had indeed kept trying with Heavy Stereo, but their fourth single, 'Mouse In A Hole', had missed the Top 40 like their previous three.

The failure of Heavy Stereo was viewed by the press as more the band's fault than Creation's, and no one was rash enough to predict the label's relegation simply on the basis of one own-goal. McGee certainly had bigger fish to fry, rolling out the statistics for the benefit of the London *Evening Standard*. 'Oasis sold seven million copies of the last album outside America and four [million] there,' he said. 'That still hasn't put us up with Hootie and the Blowfish or Alanis. We've always wanted to be the biggest and the best. Next year we've got to gauge our success against those people.'

By then, McGee had heard six tracks from the next Oasis album and was sufficiently excited to tell the *Standard*: 'They're absolute genius. They've moved on, but I still heard four number 1 singles.' However, while Oasis had given McGee a phenomenal year – and might give him another in 1997 – it remained the case that Creation had not broken an act in the UK since the Boo Radleys' flirtation with the mainstream in 1995. As usual, Oasis were distorting the picture. Creation was a hugely important company whenever it released a record by Oasis; a good deal less important when it released a record by anyone else. 'The whole thing about Oasis was they were the right band on the right record company at the right time in the right place,' says Tones Sansom. 'With … *Morning Glory?*, suddenly the mainstream had swung round to us.' And just as suddenly, it now swung away.

Emma Greengrass was perhaps the first person in Primrose Hill to notice things 'tightening up' at Radio 1 for some of the other Creation acts she had recently started marketing. She knew that a revival of mainstream pop was taking place that might make it harder to get on the A- and B-lists; what she hadn't bargained for was a backlash against Creation as a label. The press department was next to notice it: there was increasing amusement in the media about Creation bands' chart positions. One journalist called it the 'Creation curse', writing: 'Much like the *Hello!* curse, where couples happily profess their everlasting love for one another in a six-page photo special and then split up the very next week ... Creation bands go on *Top Of The Pops* and their singles then go tumbling down the charts the next week.'

'Creation was always a very narrow taste-band,' says Sansom. 'But [the backlash] had as much to do with the branding of Creation as Oasis' record label, I felt. It was no longer a cool underground thing. With every band after the Super Furries, it was like: "That's on Oasis' record label." They became bigger than the Creation name. Oasis brilliantly walked the line between credibility and success for longer than most bands can manage to – let's say three years – but suddenly, with a staff to support and with the hope of repeating Oasis' success, it was all eyes on the chart and on the radio. It was a pointless way for a company like Creation to be thinking.'

The marketing department was not allowed to refer to Oasis by name in campaigns for other acts, so even those Creation bands that might have appealed to Oasis fans were denied the opportunity to slipstream their way into the public consciousness. Noel Gallagher had given his seal of approval to Heavy Stereo and 18 Wheeler at different times, but his words had travelled no further than the pages of the *NME* and *Melody Maker*, whose readers had made up their minds about those bands months before. Unable to use the Oasis brand name as a recommendation to consumers of the other goods in its aisles, Creation experienced the inevitable results of having a disastrously top-heavy roster: the loss of its cachet as a connoisseur's label, the loss of its credibility and the loss of its identity.

The more Creation wagered on the weekly Top 40 rundown, the more it stood to lose. Quick-moving charts were giving a confusing view of which singles were genuinely popular and which were selling to genre-hoggers or individual fanbases (hence the Creation curse), making the commercial status of certain artists terribly hard to judge. Were Shed Seven a successful pop band? Yes, because they'd had four Top 20 hits. No, because only their fans could remember any of them. With constant increases in the amount of singles being released per week – an average of 134 in November 1996, up 20 on the year before – leading retailers like Woolworths had become far more selective about which ones they stocked. Woolworths took only twelve new singles a week, creating a logjam of record companies desperate to steal a march on their rivals by offering retailers extravagant discounts. The alternative – a reduced or non-existent chart position – was not an option. Meanwhile, the entry of supermarkets into the music retail equation, with their focus on a narrow range of pop and MOR product on which they demanded substantial discounts, was good news in the short term for the consumer, who could buy a chart album for £9.99 rather than

£13.99, but bad news in the long term for music and musicians, since A&R departments were encouraged to sign only the most conservative, supermarket-friendly acts. Tesco, Sainsbury, Safeway and Asda, each using music as a loss leader, had such a powerful effect on the charts by 1996 that the term 'Asda artist' was coined to describe titanic product-shifters such as Mariah Carey and the Lighthouse Family, who were bought and sold with salad lettuce and chicken tikka masala. The next Oasis album would confirm them as Asda artists – but the only way Creation's other bands would get into Asda was by shopping there.

Many record companies had called for an end to retail discounts, but in 1996 only one of the majors – Robson and Jerome's label BMG – made a stand. It was too late to go back. Discounting would finally devalue the single in 1997, a year in which almost 200 entered the Top 10 in their first week of release, compared to 20 in 1988. But if the singles chart seemed meaningless as a result, its importance to Creation was still implicit. Or to be more precise, implicit and mortal.

'When I worked for Creation, I worked on 75 singles,' says John Andrews. 'Of those, 38 were Top 40 hits, and out of the remaining 37 only six never made it into the Top 75. That tells you more about the label than anything else. We felt that chart success for singles would drive album sales, and album sales would keep the label going. That was true in '95, and to a degree in '96. But after that, the market changed and I don't think we understood that.'

It was the beginning of a market-wide move away from guitar music to pop, MOR, American R&B and production-line dance, and Radio 1 would react to it and accelerate it by playing less and less guitar music as time went on. Creation – the label with the blockbuster rock 'n' roll band, the world-class reputation and the ear of the future government – was more vulnerable than anyone realised.

One of the first Creation artists who attempted to adapt to the changes in the company – and to the changes in the market – was Andy Bell. He had been blown away by Noel Gallagher's ability to write songs that the whole country sang, expressing himself simply and directly and waiting for time and repetition to render his lyrics more profound. Bell had never been a populist, but he felt it was time to become one.

After the break-up of Ride, Bell was the only member that Creation wanted to keep. While he wrote and recorded demos, McGee placed an advert in the music papers asking for talented young rock 'n' roll musicians to get in touch. The advert yielded Alex Lowe, an ex-boxer from Scotland with a mile-wide attitude and a strong singing voice. A band was put together around Lowe and Bell, which eventually settled on the name Hurricane #1. For Bell, Hurricane #1 were to be the opposite of everything he'd known in Ride.

'It was Alan's and my band,' he says. 'It was: "Let's follow all the rules." I was very malleable. Having never experienced the record company marketing side of things at first hand, I was just like: "Whatever. I trust you. Do whatever you want." I was completely on a rebound.' The obverse to the Creation bands of the late 80s and early 90s, who had chosen their own singles and cracked the whip of indie policy, Hurricane #1 would go along with formatting and pricing tactics, and allow the emphasis to be put on releasing singles that were liked by Radio 1. Although Bell stresses that the band was not tailor-made for commercial success ('it was tailor-made for the buzz of hearing it,' he says), he vowed that there would be no Ride-like obstinacy standing in Hurricane #1's way. For one thing, Creation would not have tolerated it. 'Creation had grown in status and power worldwide,' Bell points out. 'Fighting it would have been like fighting a tidal wave.'

John Andrews was Hurricane #1's marketing manager. 'For a period I thought they had a lot of potential,' he says. 'I thought they were very exciting. Within the framework, I felt we could do reasonably well.' But because of the Creation curse and the market's gradual renunciation of guitar groups, it was likely to take three or even four singles – and the same number of expensive videos – to build up awareness for a Hurricane #1 album that in previous years would have been promoted by one single and a complimentary feature in the *NME*. Chas Banks' prophecy of doom had come true: an indie band had to fight hard for its media space these days.

'What would happen with a band like Hurricane was you'd go to a meeting two months ahead of the release,' recalls Tones Sansom. 'The radio people are saying: "Yep, we'll get it on the B-list," and the press people are saying: "Yeah, it's getting there." Then, a month before the release, it's like: "We-ell, let's re-evaluate it. Let's go for a Top 40." Two weeks before the release, it's like: "OK, so we're not going to get in the 40 with this one. Let's think about the next single." ' The procedure would then be repeated three months later.

If 1997 was to be a boom year for Creation financially, which the summer release of an Oasis album practically guaranteed, there would be all the more scrutiny of debut albums by Hurricane #1 and Three Colours Red, not to mention the long-awaited comeback of Primal Scream, from those in the media who felt the label had coasted through 1996. Journalists who had been close to Creation in former years had noticed a change in its atmosphere, and were not slow in saying so. A commonly written criticism was that Creation had become as arrogant as its most famous band. The more wounding remarks taunted McGee for not having discovered a major act since 1993.

McGee sensed that all was not well with Creation, but he remained stoical about the chances of Hurricane #1 and Three Colours Red.

What gave him pause for thought – in fact, it came to him in an epiphany – was the balance of the company's personnel. At Creation's Christmas 1996 party in Julie's Restaurant in west London, McGee counted 38 members of staff and worked out that he liked only five of them as people. That was not so important for the moment: McGee worked from his own office and did not have to meet the staff on a daily basis. But it would become very important a year or so later, when he started telling the press that half of his employees might as well be working for Railtrack, or making tea bags for Tetley, for all that they cared about his label.

'What made him uneasy,' says John Andrews, 'was that people who joined Creation after a certain time didn't understand the culture, didn't understand the heritage of the label, didn't have the mentality that we were *not* part of the music industry. They didn't have the sensibility and the intellect that Alan liked.' These employees worked in every part of the company, Andrews believes. 'He had a downer on people who didn't take Creation seriously, who just enjoyed their job – for them it was a job in the music business that allowed them to hang out, get pissed, get loaded and have a good time. He didn't like people like that. Maybe he resented the fact that they could do things that he had once done, or maybe he felt that they hadn't ... suffered.'

With an Oasis album approaching, McGee told few people about his real feelings for the staff. But his epiphany came as no surprise to Andy Saunders. 'He had started to say: "I either want Creation to be massive or I want it to be two people",' Saunders recalls. 'He was toying with the idea of whether to go for it completely, or whether to scale it right down ... He used to make me very uncomfortable by singling out people he didn't like: "Fucking accounts people. What do I want accounts people for? They're not *creative* people." ' It was clear that McGee couldn't have it both ways: Creation could not grow into an Island or an Atlantic without employing more of the music industry careerists who disheartened him.

Deciding which of the two routes to take was one of the greatest problems facing McGee as he prepared for Creation and Britain to go Oasis-crazy once again. Atlantic or a small pond? 'I think it was a dilemma that everybody was in,' ventures Johnny Hopkins sympathetically. 'It's a case of finding out how to make it work. We didn't quite get there.'

In February 1997, Andy Saunders organised the historic meeting of the music industry and New Labour. It took place in the House Of Commons, where around 50 high-ranking music executives – Rob Dickins, BMG chief John Preston, Virgin MD Paul Conroy and Alan McGee among them – listened to a speech from shadow heritage secretary Jack Cunningham. He assured those who were concerned about copyright and piracy that he would look at those issues, and promised that a Labour government would give the industry strong representation in the European community. 'We'd said "no press", but we had somebody there from PA [Press Association],' Saunders recalls. 'The guy from PA said to me: "Any Tories here?" I said: "Look around you, mate. They're all Tories." '

That month, Creation gave £15,000 to the Scottish Labour Party, whose conference included a performance from Teenage Fanclub. McGee was courted anew by Tony Blair and his campaign strategist Peter Mandelson as a celebrity, a successful businessman and a friend of Oasis with the music-loving youth of Britain in his pocket. New Labour had a song they wanted him to hear: not a Britpop anthem but a 1994 hit by the dance act D:ream.

'Myself and Alan went to see Peter Mandelson at Millbank,' says Saunders. 'We got taken by Mandelson and Margaret McDonagh, Labour's key seats campaigner, to view a film that was going out as a party political documentary – on a CD-ROM – to young Labour supporters. It was the first time we heard "Things Can Only Get Better", which they were using as their campaign song. I said: "You shouldn't use that, it's crap. You should use 'Wake Up Boo!' because it's 'wake up, it's a beautiful morning'." We were like: "You've got to tap into the *Zeitgeist* . . .!" '*

In March, McGee donated £50,000 of his own money to New Labour's campaign, seeking and receiving an assurance that it would be spent in Scotland. 'Alan has been tremendously supportive in the last few years,' Blair was quoted as saying. 'It is particularly good to have the backing of someone who is doing so much for British music – and the balance of trade.' According to one report, Blair had said privately: 'Everything is from the heart with McGee.'

McGee's donation made him one of a select and high-profile band of Labour entrepreneur-backers, putting him in the company of Lord Attenborough, the designer Paul Smith, the publisher Paul Hamlyn, the supermarket millionaire David Sainsbury and the Body Shop founder Anita Roddick. McGee's support for Labour was seen as being most influential in Scotland, where he was given the front page of the *Daily Record* to explain his hatred for the Tories in detail.

'By this time, we were mates with New Labour,' says Saunders. 'We'd taken Margaret McDonagh to the football and stuff. She came to Chelsea–Wimbledon with her dad. She became a very good friend of Alan's, along with [media entrepreneur] Waheed Alli, who was part of Margaret's coterie at the time. We were like this little gang of people that were supporting New Labour in the media industries. And I was the only one who wasn't earning 20 million quid a year.'

---

* 'Wake Up Boo!' was subsequently used in a televised Labour Party political broadcast, playing on a radio in the background.

On election day, 1 May, McGee was at the Royal Festival Hall for New Labour's victory party, where he rubbed shoulders with fellow backers from the arts and former leader Neil Kinnock. They were celebrating the Conservatives' worst defeat since 1906 and counting up the score of big scalps – Michael Portillo, Norman Lamont, Jeremy Hanley and Malcolm Rifkind among others – who had lost their seats to the new guard. Prior to that night, McGee had envisaged himself retreating from politics and resuming his life and career as before. 'I can't see myself being involved any more,' he told *Melody Maker*. 'Basically, it's just a case of: "Vote Labour and by the way, I fucking hate the Tories." That's me. I just want the Tories out.'

New Labour, however, had other plans for him. As Martin Jacques of the *Observer* was later to write: 'After the election, the Government sought to popularise the notion that we were entering a new era – culturally as much as politically. The chosen symbols were corporate executives and cultural celebrities, including Britpop stars. A government's ability to move from the political to the cultural is a defining moment: it enables its appeal to transcend political divisions and become national, rather than partisan. Blair played this card for all it was worth.'

In July, McGee was one of six captains of industry asked to assist Chris Smith, the Government's secretary of state for culture, media and sport, offering their advice on which groups from the worlds of music, fashion and cinema should receive subsidies. The six-man think-tank was named the Creative Industries Task Force. 'The music industry hated Alan for that,' says Andy Saunders, 'because he was the only music industry representative on the task force. He represented music! The music industry were up in arms – they said it should be somebody from the BPI or one of their existing organisations.'

It did seem ironic that the interests of the music business were in the hands of a man whose goal had once been to destroy it in a bloody revolution. McGee, who described himself that summer as 'a capitalist with a conscience', saw his purpose on the Creative Industries Task Force as being 'to make it easier for musicians and managers – small businesses – to set up labels and bands; to get them training in a largely self-taught industry'. Saunders recalls him being infuriated by the poor quality of managers in Britain.

Chris Smith, a former shadow health minister, had been invited by Blair to head the department of culture, media and sport a mere three days after the election victory. It was quick work even for a Government so anxious to examine the creative industries' economic potential. Smith himself said: 'It is a department concerned with many of the things that affect people's day-to-day lives, like sport, television, films and the lottery. Its interest now is to promote everything from beefeaters to Britpop.' The feeble alliteration would soon give way to a new Government catchphrase: 'Cool Britannia'.

Still, if the commission of a Creative Industries Task Force indicated that the arts were seen by the Government as a vital cog in the British economy, rather than as leisure or self-indulgence, that was fine by McGee. The *Observer* would later write: 'In the twelve months after the general election, McGee was seen by Labour as the touchstone of all things fashionable.' He now had power. He also had the determination to use it.

On 24 July, a week before a drinks party at 10 Downing Street to which McGee and Noel Gallagher had been invited, the Tory-supporting *Daily Mail* published a salacious cut-out-and-keep guide to thirteen of the creative people whom the Blair Government now considered its friends. The paper brusquely thumbnailed a one-time actor in *EastEnders* as 'Gay Ex-Soap Star'. The recently departed chief executive of Channel 4 became 'Pornographer-In-Chief'. The designer Vivienne Westwood was styled as 'Knickerless Exhibitionist'. McGee was at number 1 (which pleased him), listed as 'Drug User' – which delighted him. He framed the article and hung it in his office.

The Downing Street party on 30 July saw McGee, his girlfriend Kate Holmes, Noel Gallagher and Meg Matthews mingle with 100 guests from many walks of life besides the arts. However, it was the media stars – and Gallagher and McGee more than any – who stole the headlines the following morning. A photograph of Gallagher talking to Blair was on the front page of the *Sun*, the *Mirror*, the *Times* and even the prudish *Daily Mail*.

Tim Abbot flew into London from America that day, glancing at the papers with a groan. He thought about how far Gallagher and McGee had come, and how much Oasis and Creation had lost. 'The reinvention of that company was second to none,' Abbot says. 'Me and our Chris refer to it as Pol Pot. It was Year Zero: nothing happened until 1995. The new rebirth. It was politics, football ... Alan never *went* to the fucking football. We didn't *talk* about politics. The Clash was our politics. Creation might have been marketing a new ethic – but at what cost, when they'd lost the old ethic?'

It was unfortunate that McGee had a sense of humour. Recalling the Downing Street party in the *Observer* a week later, he made some typically exaggerated wisecracks that managed only to strike a jarring tone. 'Noel and Meg, Liam and Patsy,' he said, 'are the alternative royal family ... I would be lying if I said it wasn't one of the best ligs I've ever been to. It was a gas to have Cabinet ministers coming up and saying hello instead of the usual rock casualties I have to deal with ...'

'One of the photos taken at the event,' a journalist for the *Independent* later wrote, 'embodies an occasion that looks like something from another era: Gallagher, dressed more like a footballer than a rock star, shaking hands with Blair while McGee looks on, oozing pride. It represented both the high point of British music's cultural impact and its effective castration – for if rock stars were now friends of the Government, how could they continue to be truly exciting?'

In view of the Oasis album that Creation was to release on 21 August, it was an extremely good question.

McGee, Dick Green, Emma Greengrass and Johnny Hopkins heard the contents of *Be Here Now* at Noel Gallagher's house in north London. Everyone else made do with a playback at Quo Vadis, a West End restaurant, where employees of Creation mixed with people from Ignition, Anglo and Creation's twin-distributors Vital and 3MV. *Be Here Now* was 72 minutes in length, submerged in superfluous guitar overdubs and didn't sound like another ... *Morning Glory?* at all. 'Everybody was like: "These songs are seven minutes long. This is *bloated* ..."', recalls James Kyllo. However, they kept their doubts to themselves. Tones Sansom remembers 'a lot of nodding of heads, a lot of slapping of backs'.

Hopkins liked the album, but had no idea whether that was because it was good or because it was Oasis. 'After everything that had happened in the intervening two years, it was just impossible to take a record as a record,' he says. He had been worked to stretching-point since January, fending off press inquiries about Liam Gallagher's cocaine arrest after the Q awards, his marriage to Patsy Kensit in April and – in June – the wedding of Noel Gallagher and Meg Matthews. Afer that little lot, a deafening 72-minute album almost came as light relief.

But the feelings of Hopkins about *Be Here Now* were a flea-bite next to the widely reported feelings of Alan McGee. At first, he'd had misgivings. 'There was so much coke around then that it was completely out of control,' he later said. 'I heard it in the studio and I remember saying: "We'll only sell seven million copies" ... I thought it was too confrontational.' When he heard Liam Gallagher sing along to some of the tracks, McGee set his sights much higher. Publicly, controversially, he predicted that *Be Here Now* would sell 20 million.

McGee's indiscretion is explained by Emma Greengrass as being the principal reason why the marketing campaign for *Be Here Now* took shape the way it did. 'The band got pissed off about that because they thought it was hyping the album, quote unquote,' she says. 'I don't think anybody thought it would sell that many. My thoughts were that we'd be lucky if we sold two million in the UK. How the hell could we equal ... *Morning Glory?* or beat it? It's impossible. It ain't going to happen. It was never going to be the same because ... *Morning Glory?* was a time, a place, a moment, a feeling.'

McGee was accused by Oasis and Ignition of hyping *Be Here Now* in a way that was potentially injurious. But John Andrews says to that: 'It's complete rubbish. He hyped *everything*. He always said that about records. If you'd had any experience of dealing with Alan, you'd know to take anything he said with a pinch of salt.' McGee was not to get a chance to set the record straight. Little of him would be seen in the campaign planning meetings. 'He was getting shut out by that point,' says Johnny Hopkins. 'I think there was a bit of exclusion going on. I don't know whether it was an orchestrated plan exactly ... The management of big bands tend to call the shots.'

The *Sunday Times* was to call the build-up to *Be Here Now* 'the most carefully planned and executed publicity campaign the music business has ever seen'. It was right about the planning, but totally wrong about the execution. The objective of Ignition – for Creation had no say whatsoever in the campaign at any stage – was to suppress publicity in all forms by withholding music and information from anyone who was not part of the preordained marketing plot. Beneath it all was Ignition's peculiar conviction that *Be Here Now* should be approached by the media and by the public as a regular, everyday collection of tunes. The marketing spend on the album was to be nothing extraordinary; although it would be advertised by thousands of street posters, there would be no billboards and no TV advertising around the release.

'It was decided very early on that we don't want to hype this album,' says Greengrass. 'We don't want to overexpose it. We want to keep it low-key. We want to try and keep control of the whole mad thing.' As strange as this desire for undervaluation sounds, it was the perfect complement to Ignition's other great fear: bootlegging. By controlling the dissemination of the music, Ignition would minimise the chances of rogue copies of *Be Here Now* appearing on market stalls and internet websites.

Yet Ignition's obsession with control had a consequence that a ten-year-old could have foreseen. It generated more hype for *Be Here Now* than most members of the media had ever known. And whether it was positive or negative, the hype was never other than grotesquely overpitched. The *Mail On Sunday* wrote of Marcus Russell in July: '[He] has a mind like a steel trap and the organisational skills of Winston Churchill.' In reality, Russell's organisation of the *Be Here Now* campaign was more reminiscent of Neville Chamberlain: his directive to Creation and everyone else – 'No hyping of this album' – was not worth the paper it was written on. And by using the iron fist when words failed, Ignition succeeded only in making enemies in every section of the media.

The first single to be taken from *Be Here Now* was 'D'You Know What I Mean?', released on 7 July. Radio played a key part in the marketing strategy, Greengrass explained to *Music Week*: the campaigners had decided on a late release to radio so as not to give the single too much advance exposure. Ignition wasn't joking about this, and its tactics were to be heavy-handed. When three radio stations – Radio Forth in Edinburgh, Capital in London and City FM in Liverpool – broke the 23 June airplay embargo on the single by three days, Ignition called in the police.

'Does it matter that radio stations broke the embargo? Sitting here now? Couldn't give a fuck. Who cares?' says Greengrass. 'But at the time, we'd been in these bloody bunker meetings for six months or something, and our plot was blown. "Shit, it's a nightmare!" Of course it's not a nightmare. Who cares?'

In the meantime, Johnny Hopkins was servicing the music magazines with advance cassettes of the album. If there was one certainty about *Be Here Now*, it was that reviews would be unimportant – the combined readership of the UK music titles was less than a million, while ... *Morning Glory* had sold four times that. Nevertheless, journalists were asked by Ignition to sign contracts (a rarity in the UK music press) making certain promises about the cassette they were about to receive. And these were not contracts that reflected well on Creation. As John Andrews says: 'In terms of the way that the product was positioned – i.e. the way that it was presented to the press, to radio – it was complete paranoia.'

'To be fair to him, Johnny did introduce this in a very by-the-by kind of way,' recalls Andrew Perry, the reviews editor of *Select*. 'He said: "There's just one thing. I'm going to fax this thing over. Just sign it and fax it back." There was literally a clause in there which appeared to be a joke. It said not to discuss the album with anyone – including your partner at home. It basically said don't talk to your girlfriend about it when you're in bed.'

It was this clause that convinced John Andrews that Ignition's supposed intention to market *Be Here Now* in a low-key, understated fashion was a load of disingenuous garbage. 'How can a campaign be understated when you have to sign a contract if you're going to listen to a cassette?' Andrews says. 'You're making it sound like the most important release since ... You know, it's unbelievably pompous.'

The *Select* reviewer signed the contract – as did reviewers on all the other music publications – and a tape of *Be Here Now* was sent over. 'It seemed, particularly once you heard the album, that this was cocaine grandeur of just the most ludicrous degree,' says Andrew Perry. 'I remember listening to "All Around The World" and laughing – actually quite pleasurably – because it seemed so ridiculous. The [contract] seemed almost like an extension of that. You just thought: Christ, there is so much coke being done here.'

Ignition had given Radio 1 a CD containing four songs from *Be Here Now*, which it was allowed to start playing ten days before the album's release – on one condition. The station was told to inter sperse jingles among the tracks to prevent listeners making mint copies. When Radio 1 refused to comply, Ignition took the CD back.

The embargoes extended to retail. Several stores – including Oasis' new mates Asda – had broken the embargo on 'D'You Know What I Mean?', selling it earlier than they were permitted to. Ignition now demanded that Creation ask retailers to sign contracts – an unprecedented event in the label's history – before they received their copies of *Be Here Now*. Retailers were also ordered not to sell the album any earlier than eight o'clock on the morning of release, ruling out popular midnight opening sessions. A director of the distributor Vital warned that strong action would be taken against retailers who signed the agreement and broke the embargo, including an indefinite early deliveries ban on all future new releases not only from Creation but from Vital and 3MV.

'There wasn't just an embargo on the press,' says John Andrews. 'There wasn't just an embargo on radio. There wasn't just an embargo on retail. There was an embargo on the other people on the fucking label. I remember one day when somebody came round to check our phones because they thought the *Sun* had tapped them. It was Ignition's paranoia about Creation and ... it made people despise Oasis within Creation before the record was released. You had this Oasis camp headed by Emma, which also included Johnny, that was like: "I'm sorry, you're not allowed to come into the office between the following hours. You're not allowed to mention the word Oasis." If you'd heard the tape, you weren't allowed to talk about it amongst yourselves. It was like a fascist state.'

Andy Saunders uses a different word: 'Stalinist'. He says: 'It was a reign of terror. You couldn't step out of line and people were constantly looking over their shoulders. The influence that Ignition had on the company as a whole was very destructive. A lot of people were worried about what [Ignition] were doing ... It was all about control. Ignition terrorised people – passively-aggressively, they call it in America – and it created a horrible climate.'

Cassettes of *... Morning Glory?* had been played freely on the Creation stereo in the summer of 1995 as songs were mixed and completed. *Be Here Now* was something quite different. To hear 'D'You Know What I Mean?', the staff had had to go to the Sony building in Great Marlborough Street; and no advance tapes of the album had been played in the Creation office. 'It made it less organic for the people working at Creation,' says Tones Sansom. 'It wasn't as much fun to work on. After *... Morning Glory?*, Oasis was just a rather tedious admin job ... There were all kinds of things going on. Ignition certainly were playing things very, very close to their chest – with who heard things, and when. We were very limited in what we could do according to their wishes.'

'D'You Know What I Mean?' had debuted in the charts at number

1. *Be Here Now* was expected to follow suit, even though it would be on sale for only three days of the week of chart qualification. It was being released on a Thursday all across the world; this, too, was about control. Because America ships albums to retail earlier than the UK, Ignition wanted to make sure that no import copies came back to Britain on a speedy 747.

At last, on the eve of release, came what the *Sunday Times* called the 'final twist ... BBC television gave 40 minutes to a documentary about the band: uncritical, unfocused, it proved little more than a promotional video subsidised by licence-payers'. ('Of course it was part of the marketing campaign,' says Greengrass. 'Every TV appearance is part of the marketing campaign. Those kind of things get done all the time. [Producer] Mark Cooper gave the band a very favourable viewing. That's how he saw them. And we were accused of showing the band through rose-tinted spectacles. I suppose we were a bit naive.')

One reason why Ignition had forbidden stores to open at midnight to sell *Be Here Now* was because it was horrified by the thought of news cameras turning up to interview queuing fans: queues meant news meant hype. Instead, as the aforementioned ten-year-old could probably have predicted with confidence, the cameras simply rolled up at eight in the morning – to find that hardly anybody was in the shops. 'I went down to the Virgin Megastore and it was empty,' says Greengrass. 'There was a load of cameras and of course they all reported: "Ooh, the shops are empty. The Oasis album might be a flop." '

It was at lunchtime that *Be Here Now* really started to sell – and in the most unexpected places. The City of London's branch of Our Price rang 3MV four times to say that it had sold out. The mother of mass market products, *Be Here Now* was being scarfed up by investment bankers, commodities brokers and couriers from office blocks the length and breadth of the City. Around the country, Asda and other supermarkets did stunning business. The newsagent John Menzies sold amounts far out of proportion to its market share. By the end of the first day, 350,000 copies of *Be Here Now* had been bagged up and handed over the counter, making it Britain's fastest-selling album ever.

After three days, it had sold 696,000. On the Sunday, it shot in at number 1 with higher sales than many chart-topping albums achieve in a year. By the end of the month, it had passed 800,000 in the UK, earning McGee an estimated personal windfall of £2 million in eleven days.

The astonishing figures for *Be Here Now* were not celebrated at Creation, where Oasis no longer had the respect or the support they'd had during the ...*Morning Glory?* period. 'We weren't part of the process,' says Andy Saunders, speaking for many, 'so we didn't really care.' If there was any pleasure to be had by the staff, it was only in knowing that *Be Here Now* had made their jobs safe for another year.

Soon the realisation set in among buyers that the album was not the masterpiece they had assumed it to be. '... *Morning Glory?* was a great big step into the unknown, whereas *Be Here Now* was kind of a step back,' says James Kyllo. 'And in the wide world, after the initial excitement, there was profound disappointment.' Perhaps Oasis missed having Blur to compete with. Perhaps, as Hopkins suggests, they had come back too soon after their omnipresence in 1996. After seven million sales of *Be Here Now* had been racked up around the world, it was reported by *Melody Maker* in 1999 to be the album most sold to second-hand record shops.

The *Be Here Now* UK tour was in two legs – one in September, ending in Birmingham; and one in December, ending at Wembley Arena. 'It was a drudge,' says Tones Sansom, who saw every show. 'Johnny, Vanessa [Cotton] and I would be at the gigs from night to night, and you end up in a worse state than the bloody band. There was an after-show party every night, so next day you've got a hangover and you've got to face all these people wondering why they're not on the guest-list. It was quite ferocious, quite nasty.'

By December, Oasis had been 'eclipsed in global importance, class and kudos', as the critic Nick Kent put it, by Radiohead – whose album *OK Computer* had come out in June, left listeners alternately delirious and scratching their heads, and ultimately been near-unanimously decreed the best album of the year. 'The latter was adventurous-sounding and looked to the future,' wrote Kent, 'whereas Oasis sounded like they were stuck in some time-warp 70s pub ... There had always been a fiercely arrogant side to the Gallaghers; it was part of what made them so attractive. But once that arrogance got mixed up with too much success, cocaine and alcohol, it turned into a kind of sneering contempt.' Tim Abbot is more scathing. 'Oasis were raw art that transferred into shit,' he says. 'They came down as little matchstick men and became a Koons.'

Even those who found Radiohead too highbrow had another arrogant northern band to distract them from the Gallaghers. More soulful and less macho than Oasis had become by 1997, the Verve sold more copies of *Urban Hymns* in Britain than Oasis had of *Be Here Now*, staying on the album chart for a year. The Oasis phenomenon was drawing to a close.

Recalling the *Be Here Now* campaign from two years' distance, Emma Greengrass now admits that serious mistakes were made. 'In retrospect a lot of the things we did were ridiculous,' she says. 'We sit in [Oasis] meetings today and we're like: "It's on the Internet. It's in Camden Market. Whatever." I think we've learned our lesson.'

But the sour experiences of people in the media who had dealt with Oasis and Ignition during the *Be Here Now* campaign had a negative impact on Creation that damaged the careers of certain other bands on the label irreparably. Johnny Hopkins concedes that this happened. It remains for John Andrews to say the words that would have stuck in Hopkins' throat:

'Oasis made Creation, you could argue. But they also killed it.'

24 The New Deal

I N THE THIRD QUARTER of 1997, Creation was second only to Virgin in market share of album sales. In the final quarter, by which time sales of *Be Here Now* had slowed to a drizzle, Creation disappeared from the Top ten. After that, it kept falling. 'It started to become clear that there wasn't going to be an enormous pool of money around forever,' says James Kyllo. Mark Taylor explains: 'Essentially, the money that we made from the Oasis record covered previous debts. It was resolving a problem rather than creating a platform.'

The multimillion-unit success of *Be Here Now* had given a false picture – when did an Oasis album not – of how Creation was faring as a whole in a market-place that associated it with the three-year-old Britpop wave, a disappointing follow-up to ... *Morning Glory?* and a once-powerful amalgam of music and arrogance that had flown too close to the sun. With the end of Oasis' predominance came the fall from relevance of some of Creation's more overt values. Not to mince words, the label had become yesterday's papers.

'There's a book by Nelson George about Motown called *Where Did Our Love Go?*' says Johnny Hopkins. 'It talks about the beginnings of Motown, and about how it diversified and moved to LA. One of the chapters is titled "Just Another Record Company", because one of the people in the book says that's what it became. I don't think Creation – even at its worst point – was like anything else. But people *perceived* it to be just another record company.'

The goalposts of perception had moved so far that Creation's music could not keep up with the changes. Had *C'mon Kids* been released in 1993, it would have been greeted as an envelope-pusher and an artistic triumph. Coming out in 1996 after the success of *Wake Up!*, it was perceived as a bullet to the foot. Primal Scream's 1997 album *Vanishing Point* contained some of the most unbridled and intoxicating music the band had ever made – but it was not the only avant-garde rock album to feel the shut-out from a pop-obsessed media. At least it had debuted at number 2, a merciful feat at a time when almost all bands and record companies were being judged by their chart position.

'You're only as good as the records that you're able to sell,' says Mark Taylor. 'Whilst you can fill some gaps with compilations and best ofs, you still need to be generating success from your new artists. We felt we could achieve that with bands like the Super Furries, for example, but ultimately it was too little and too late.'

Creation might have coped with one backlash. It was hard pushed to cope with four: in 1998 there were simultaneous backlashes against Creation, Oasis, Britpop and guitar groups in general. Albums by Garbage and Catatonia sold fewer than 35,000 copies to get to number 1. Underachieving bands on Polydor and Mercury had their contracts terminated. Any group foolish enough to attempt a new direction – and to suggest that their next album would 'surprise a lot of people' – found punters unwilling to risk their money. The rock bands that were breaking through (Catatonia, Travis, Stereophonics) were mid-range, mid-tempo and unenterprising, tending to pick a musical theme and stick to it.

With the walls closing in on guitar groups, the industry was supported by a young audience in thrall to boy bands and girl bands, and by a Radio 1 that was reverting to its pre-Britpop policy of crude humour and personality-led presentation. Mark Radcliffe, one of the station's more credible presenters, was permitted to air only four non-playlisted records in any one programme. As record labels signed more and more of what the listeners seemed to like – boy bands and girl bands singing sugary ballads and cover versions – the industry all but cast adrift the over-twenties. And as teen magazines and TV shows proliferated, acts such as B*Witched, Billie and Steps emerged from talent schools and dance lessons to find careers already in place for them. Pete Waterman, the producer of Steps, was once again the king of UK pop.

The Creation curse had become the curse of all too many labels. Whereas in the 70s and 80s a chart entry or an appearance on *Top Of The Pops* would have signalled the start of the public's long relationship with a song, by 1998 these were often the last occasions it would ever be seen or heard. By taking a fortnight's holiday, it was possible to miss the entire chart lifetime of some Top 20 hits. Many singles were given to radio and MTV so far upfront that their actual release came as little more than a marketing afterthought.

John Andrews feels that the seriousness of the situation took a long time to dawn on Creation. 'We still had success, albeit on a small level, with certain artists,' he says. 'We still had critical acclaim from some areas of the press. Just when you thought it was all over, there was always something that would offer a glimmer of hope.'

Shortly after Christmas 1997, McGee phoned Andy Saunders from the Caribbean to tell him that he and Kate Holmes had got married. 'And he said: "... and I've found a superstar on the beach",' Saunders recalls. 'I'm like: "Really?" He goes: "Yeah, he's a reggae guy and he's a genius." I'm thinking: oh, *fuck*. Well, let's concentrate on the good things. It's Christmas. The guy's got married. He's happy ... I didn't have a lack of faith. I just wondered if this was another impetuous McGee situation like the ones we'd been in many times before.'

McGee's excitement about the reggae singer Mishka had a sort of logic to it. If Creation could launch acts in other areas besides guitar rock, it might stand a chance of survival in the market-place. McGee was fond of saying that a man who had found the new Beatles could probably find the new Elton John – in other words a pop act with mass market potential. There had simply been a slight change of plan: McGee had instead found the new Bob Marley.

Not that he was intending to debut Mishka just yet. Other signings were going to be given their head in the hope of making a commercial splash. Bernard Butler had been licensed to Creation as a solo artist by Sony, to which he had signed as a member of Suede in 1992, and had started to write his own lyrics and sing his own songs. The Jesus and Mary Chain had returned to Creation after 13 years on Blanco y Negro, bringing with them an album that Geoff Travis had dismissed as unreleasable. Kevin Rowland of Dexys Midnight Runners had been signed by McGee in person, making up a trio of stars from the 80s on the Creation roster – the others were Nick Heyward and the former Dream Academy frontman Nick Laird-Clowes.

McGee was elated to have the Mary Chain back, seeing them as charms that could rekindle some of the early Creation fire and assuage him of the spiritual emptiness he had felt during and after the *Be Here Now* campaign. Butler could, he was sure, sell a lot of records. Laird-Clowes, who recorded under the name Trashmonk, would be a cult trophy at worst; a surprise hit if Creation was lucky. But it was the wild talent of Rowland that excited McGee the most.

Rowland's life had hit rock bottom in the 90s through a combination of cocaine and low self-esteem. He had lost his home to the Inland Revenue and moved into a squat, later joining a religious cult and spending eight months in rehab. In 1996, when McGee made his move for him, Creation was riding high and able to afford an eccentric artist with a glittering back catalogue. 'We had eight million quid in the bank,' McGee later recalled, 'and I thought: money's no object – who do I really want to sign? There's only three. I'd like to sign Neil Young, I'd like to sign Paul Weller and I'd like to sign Kevin Rowland.' Unlike Young and Weller, Rowland was available.

McGee invited him to a meeting, to which Rowland arrived in a full-length fake fur coat. When Andy Saunders was tapped on the shoulder and swivelled round in his chair to face the artist whose work he was to publicise, he thought he was looking at Henry VIII. 'He was really fragile and brittle,' McGee said of Rowland. 'He was clean [of drugs] but you just didn't want to say the wrong thing ...

You really didn't want to hurt his feelings. He was close to the edge.'

More than six months of negotiation followed, during which Rev-Ola reissued the third and final Dexys Midnight Runners album, *Don't Stand Me Down*, from 1985. Saunders wrote a press release to announce that Rowland was now a Creation artist, and faxed it to him for his perusal. 'I took my kids to the zoo,' Saunders says, 'and I got a call on my mobile from Kevin. He started to go through this press release word for word. I said to my wife: "Give me 15 minutes", so she took the kids off to look at the monkeys. And I had the most ridiculous conversation with Kevin. He'd say: "You've put in here that Kevin is currently working on new material." I said: "Yes. Because you are, obviously, if you've signed a record deal." He went: "Yeah, but I don't need the pressure, man. I don't need the fucking pressure. Take that out." "O ... K ..." And he went through it right to the end, where it said: "For further information, please call Andy Saunders at Creation Records." Kevin said: "I'm not comfortable with that, Andy." I'm like: "Why?" He goes: "Because there ain't no further information." '

The press release was reduced from a page of type to the bald statement: 'Kevin Rowland has signed to Creation Records. We have no further information.' McGee would hear no new music from Rowland for two years.

One reason why Creation had not been revolutionised or purged after McGee's epiphany in Julie's Restaurant at Christmas 1996 was because much of his time was being occupied by matters of political, cultural and sartorial importance. He had become a celebrity in 1997, not least in Scotland, where his views on devolution were sought by the press throughout that summer. He had developed a taste for clothes made by Hugo Boss and Paul Smith, and in September was named the year's most stylish entrepreneur by *Elle* magazine.

McGee sat alongside Smith, Waheed Alli, Richard Branson, the film producer Lord Puttnam and the publisher Gail Rebuck on the Government's Creative Industries Task Force. McGee described the meetings of the task force as 'two worlds colliding', explaining: 'All the people like me, Paul Smith and Waheed just tell it as if from the shop floor. So I'll talk about training for rock 'n' roll managers [and] the need to understand publishing. And then the Government people talk about "the remit of the document" and get really vague. They're so bogged down ... They move at tortoise pace, while we are all entrepreneurs. We think about something, then do it.'

Since the election, McGee had unilaterally widened his brief to include advising the Government on drugs and on the National Health Service. 'He was flexing the muscles he felt he'd earned by his loyalty and his money,' says Andy Saunders. 'He felt he was due payback.' Concerned about the NHS, McGee stressed the need for free health care for people who had suffered drug-induced break-downs but had – unlike him – been unable to afford £300-a-day hospital treatment. 'If the National Health Service and the local authorities don't have money to provide a service, then you have to change the system,' he had said before the election. 'You have to bring back some humanitarian values.'

As famous for his former lifestyle as for being Oasis' record boss – he called himself 'one of Britain's most celebrated cocaine addicts' – McGee was a figure of some intrigue to the likes of Jack Straw, the Government's puritanical home secretary. At the Downing Street party in July, Straw had asked McGee why he had allowed himself to become addicted to drugs. McGee replied that he had enjoyed taking them. In public, McGee criticised Keith Hellawell, the Government's 'drugs czar', for lambasting Noel Gallagher, who had said that taking drugs was as commonplace as having a cup of tea.

In a speech at the In The City seminar in Glasgow on 28 September, McGee made a much more controversial criticism of the Government, calling for it to give income support to aspiring musicians. The Government was planning to launch its New Deal for the unemployed, a branch of its Welfare To Work policy, in early 1998. This would oblige all jobless 18–24-year-olds to join Welfare To Work schemes, feeding them into employment, the voluntary sector, environmental groups or full-time further education. The failure to take one of these four options would result in the loss of the weekly Jobseeker's Allowance. Not even the Tories had gone that far.

McGee made it clear he supported the New Deal but felt there should be a get-out clause for anyone who wanted to make a career out of music. 'It is incredibly hard to survive as a musician when you first start out,' he said at In The City. 'I know from personal experience. It takes time to perfect your art. It takes time to make a good enough demo to send out to record companies. It takes time to arrange and play gigs. Bands like Oasis make millions for this country in export sales and tax, but they started off like almost every other band – rehearsing hard and slogging up and down motorways in a transit van to play gigs to half a dozen people ... If we want the benefits that music brings – the money, the cultural diversity, the respect from overseas – we have to allow the musicians to eat.' (The speech, which had been written by Andy Saunders, was delivered by McGee 24 hours later to a meeting of the Fabian Society at the Labour Party conference in Brighton. It went down so badly that McGee has called it the most embarrassing ten minutes of his life.)

McGee raised the issue of income support for musicians at the inaugural meeting of the Creative Industries Task Force on 8 October, which was attended by Chris Smith and Peter Mandelson. Speaking to the *Melody Maker* the following day, McGee explained the main thrust of his argument: that young musicians should not have to lie about their status in order to get benefit. 'It's almost like this assault course for artists,' he said, 'to make it as difficult as possible for them to succeed, instead of trying to help them ... The Government's got to legitimise the idea of creative industries. It's essential.' Another suggestion he raised at the task force meeting was training courses for managers.

As the implications of what McGee was saying sank in, it was widely felt that the training of managers seemed certain to rid the music industry of inspired amateurs like Malcolm McLaren, Andrew Loog Oldham and McGee himself, replacing them with sober yuppies who made only the commercially shrewdest of moves. 'People like me probably wouldn't go on the courses,' McGee now speculates. 'But there are so many people that I know – who will remain nameless – that come to me three years after their band breaks up and say: "Alan, we've got a £40,000 tax bill because the manager spent the money." Not because he stole the money. But because he never saved the money.' All the same, in portraying a Government-approved music industry apparently without danger, random factor or belligerence, McGee was asking for criticism – and he got it from an old friend who had been a musician and a manager himself.

Now 44, Bill Drummond had become a curmudgeonly recluse from the business. But he had not lost his sense of theatre. He was about to release his first record in four years, entitled – contrary to the optimistic spirit of Cool Britannia – 'Fuck The Millennium'. On 10 October, he and McGee clashed on Radio 4's *Today* programme. Drummond attacked the creative industries' cosiness with the Government, arguing that Blair's co-opting of the arts left little margin for mavericks and had major ramifications for a stratum of society that was used to standing outside the establishment.

'Right now it seems that there is no creative opposition,' Drummond said. 'As soon as you start becoming part of the PR of the Government, it's a slippery slide.' He went on to say emphatically: 'It is the job of rock 'n' roll to stay outside of any Government-supported schemes and to not be financially assisted or helped.' McGee brushed the comments aside – 'The basic difference between me and Bill is that I don't actually see myself as a rebel,' he quipped to the gallery – but Drummond's point had been serious and well made.

'I think Bill was right,' says McGee with hindsight. 'But at the time, we were on a political mission to change things and we thought we could. The last person I wanted at quarter to eight in the morning was Bill fucking Drummond. I was *cringing*. The only person worse than Drummond to get at quarter to eight in the morning is McLaren.'*

* In 2000, McGee helped to finance McLaren's short-lived bid to become London's first elected mayor.

The bugbear of financial support for musicians resurfaced in January 1998 when the Government launched the New Deal in twelve pilot areas around Britain. McGee told Q that if Labour did not start making a noticeable difference for the better, it would not be getting his £50,000 next time. Conceding that he and Noel Gallagher had been 'nurtured ... for the party's benefit', he concluded: 'Practically speaking, what can they do for us?'

A similar question would be asked by the NME in March, on the front page of its most provocative issue in a decade.

While McGee kept his various political irons in the fire, Creation soldiered on into the spring of 1998 knowing that cost-cutting was paramount. The wealthy face of a deceptively needy label, McGee was as peripheral to the day-to-day requirements of Creation as he ever had been. 'Since Alan's illness, Creation had functioned without him from the actual getting-on-with-it point of view,' says James Kyllo. 'Where Alan's involvement had mostly been was with the art, with the music, which is outside the office day-to-day. Alan hadn't been in the office every day for many, many years.'

McGee had put down roots, buying property in Wales for £370,000 in 1997 and later a house in St. John's Wood. McGee, Dick Green and Andy Saunders had become partners in a photographic agency, Reaction, which was based in Primrose Hill and managed by Anita Heryet. In 1998, McGee was part of a consortium which bid unsuccessfully for an FM radio licence to broadcast indie music to Scotland. Having rented an executive box at Chelsea's football stadium since 1996, McGee bought a quarter of a million shares in the club for £250,000 the following year. He dreamed of buying Glasgow Rangers outright. 'He was deeply uncomfortable with the amount of money he had made,' says Saunders. 'He told me it was all sitting in the bank and he didn't know what to do with it.' What Creation Records didn't add to McGee's wealth, Creation Songs did. The publishing company he co-owned with Green made around £500,000 a year. In November 1997 they had briefly considered floating the company on AIM, the junior stock market.

As McGee continued to flex the muscles of wealth and power, it was his forays into politics that drew most opprobrium in the first months of 1998. In January, the NME journalist Steven Wells, a devout socialist, accused him of gravy-training. McGee responded with a stiff letter insisting that he was committed to 'protecting the rights of unemployed musicians'. He added: 'If I cannot affect (sic) any change, I'll resign [from the Creative Industries Task Force], simple as that.'

But the suspicion that McGee was a toothless lion lingered at the NME. He had started to talk of his admiration for Richard Branson, whom he had dismissed as 'just an entrepreneur' a year before. He now referred to Mick Hucknall and Wet Wet Wet as 'great guys', where once he would have called for them to be given acid baths.

Other analysts, however, were of the belief that McGee still had bite. In the same month that Wells made his accusation, McGee was invited to sit on a second Government task force. Reporting to Chris Smith, the Music Industry Forum was a 14-strong group whose members included McGee, Hucknall, Rob Dickins, Martin Mills of Beggars Banquet, Sir Tim Rice and the EMI Music publisher Peter Reichardt. Predicting that McGee would be the biggest handful of the lot, *The Times* wrote: '[He] is certainly a controversial character for any politician to embrace ... [The] marriage between Mr McGee *et al* and the Government still looks uneasy, and may well end in tears.'

It had become apparent to many who had voted for it – and to many who had not – that Blair's Government was a particularly high-minded and slick operation. Brought to power on a wave of euphoria, it had an obsession with control that would have shamed Marcus Russell, and its re-branding of Britain as Cool Britannia was seen as a sleight-of-hand ruse to distract attention from its failure to tackle serious issues concerning health and education. *Private Eye* satirised the Government's leadership brilliantly in its regular column 'St Albion Parish News', in which Blair appeared as the power-crazed vicar of a local church; and certain influential figures from the creative industries, such as the Red Or Dead designer Wayne Hemmingway, had voiced scepticism about New Labour's preference for the superficial over the substantial. By February, even McGee was saying that Blair was 'all surface'.

Just as Labour supporter Sir Peter Hall was claiming that the Government's budget-squeezing arts policy was worse than the excesses of Thatcherism, McGee absented himself from a 17 February meeting with employment minister Andrew Smith, as a protest against the New Deal. In a statement, McGee called the scheme 'soul-destroying ... incredibly naive ... ill-judged, unfair and draconian ... penalising the lifeblood of our cultural future'. Smith's spokesman rejected McGee's assertion that the New Deal would hamper musicians, saying: 'No one can expect the tax payer to subsidise musicians in the vague hope that they are discovered.'

Refusing to meet Smith until he agreed to 'look long and hard' at the policy, McGee also missed the first meeting on 28 February of the Music Industry Forum – where the New Deal topped the agenda – as he was in New York on business. But he was only too happy to tell the *NME* about his feelings. 'On this issue they're worse than the last Government,' he said. 'The Government is aware of my opinions on Welfare To Work and they're not happy ... I couldn't give a fuck. At the end of the day, if you're going to ask me to the party don't ask me to shut up.' Phoning *Melody Maker* next, he promised: 'I will keep hammering away about Welfare To Work and the drug issue – for legalisation. I'm up on the fox-hunting issue too . . .'

In early March, following two weeks of repeated criticism by McGee of the New Deal, Chris Smith suggested a one-off meeting between himself, Andrew Smith, McGee, Waheed Alli and John Glover (chairman of the International Managers' Forum) to discuss the New Deal's implications for the music business. Before the meeting could take place, the *NME* – which was about to launch a full-colour redesign – made the headlines in every daily newspaper with a publicity coup worthy of the Government itself.

'[A] resentment was manifesting itself in the interviews we did with bands,' editor Steve Sutherland explained. 'We have always been strong in our support of the Labour Party, going right back to Neil Kinnock and Red Wedge. But something had to be said. We don't want to go back to the dark old days when young people couldn't see the point in voting.'

Resentment about the Government had been expressed by almost all of the *NME*'s regular British cover stars. Damon Albarn – who had turned down an invitation to the Downing Street party, probably because Noel Gallagher had accepted it – had slammed the Government's Education Bill for its plan to abolish student maintenance grants and introduce £1,000-a-year tuition fees that would leave students heavily in debt at the end of their courses. The bill was of huge significance to the *NME*'s readership. Speaking at a press conference in February, Albarn, whose parents are university lecturers and whose band includes three former students, said: 'Before the last election there was a lot of talk about the new mood in this country. Since that time, politicians of all parties have tried to claim popular culture for themselves. They even invented a patronising name for it: Cool Britannia . . . Now the politicians who claim that art for their own ends ought to ask themselves how much of it was possible because of free education. A career in the arts is difficult to get started and the fear of a lifetime of debt is going to be a major deterrent to most people.'

Coming from Albarn – one of the chief architects of Britpop – this was a considerable development and one which went a long way beyond the Blur-Oasis rivalry. The *NME* decided to ask other pop stars what they thought of the Government. It received a shower of anti-Blair invective – from Bobby Gillespie, Jarvis Cocker, Ian Brown, Catatonia's Cerys Matthews, the Charlatans' Tim Burgess and the Lightning Seeds' Ian Broudie among others – which it sold with one of the most political covers in its history. A photograph of an expressionless Tony Blair was headlined with an old quote of Johnny Rotten's: 'Ever Had The Feeling You've Been Cheated?'

Composed by eight of the paper's writers, the lengthy article began with a slight case of revisionism. In February, Danbert

Nobacon of Chumbawamba had thrown an ice bucket full of cold water over John Prescott, the deputy prime minister, at the Brit Awards, claiming to represent the emotions of everyone from single mothers to sacked Liverpool dock workers. The incident had been seen – even within the music industry – as a meaningless stunt by a publicity-seeking member of a notoriously gimmicky band. However, the *NME* now gave it some importance.

'New Labour might be ... advised to treat the soaking as a warning from us all,' it wrote. 'As a warning that the New Labour honeymoon is over. That rock music's decades-old, instinctive and deep-seated pro-Labour sympathies have, in the past nine months, been chipped away to almost nothing.' Nearly all of the musicians interviewed were unhappy about the Government's performance, and about the New Deal in particular. Of 25 bands and artists taking part in the survey, the vast majority had spent between three and five years on the dole, which they saw as having been essential to their growth as musicians and writers. One of them, Andrew 'Tiny' Wood of Ultrasound, who had been unemployed for the entire 18-year duration of Margaret Thatcher's time in Downing Street, suggested that stopping young musicians' benefit would 'probably kill people'.

Support for the musicians' argument came from the Government's own arts minister, Mark Fisher, whose stepson Crispin Hunt was the singer in the Britpop band Longpigs. 'There is undoubtedly a difficulty in that a lot of bands struggle for a long time and have benefited from being able to claim benefit,' Fisher had said in February. 'My own son is the leader of a group – for eight years a struggling Sheffield band – existing on no money at all and often claiming benefit and getting Government schemes such as Lady Thatcher's business enterprise scheme.'

The *NME* also criticised the Government for refusing to open a debate on drugs; and for proposing curfews for under-18s that would give the police power to stop and search any teenager on the street after hours. (The scheme was being piloted in Scotland at the time.) 'Tony Blair has warned us repeatedly that New Labour is in the business of making "hard choices",' the *NME* wrote. '... But Tony Blair has already made his "hard choices" and he has chosen Uncool Britannia – the rich, the powerful, the established, the privileged and the reactionary – every single time. And still Blair continues to bask in the reflected glory of Cool Britannia. The question being – how long are we going to let him get away with it?'

New Labour's policies on the young unemployed had in fact been made clear before the election, while Jack Straw had been explicit about drugs and curfews. Blair himself had announced as far back as March 1997 that Labour would, if elected, appoint an overlord to coordinate the efforts of all Government anti-drugs agencies, ensuring more convictions. Only the issue of tuition fees could have been called a bolt from the blue, since there had been no mention of it in the manifesto. The complaints of the musicians showed as poor an understanding of Blair's politics as he had shown in taking their loyalty as read.

This was the view taken by a *Times* editorial on 12 March, the day after the *NME* was published. 'In their expensively-trashed hotel rooms, nursing a collective hangover after the euphoria of last May, Britain's rock stars have at last woken up to smell the coffee ..' it chided. 'Their anger may be sincere, but their judgment is all to pot.' Accusing the stars of being misinformed (' ... the prime minister cannot be blamed if they could not see he was also a Christian traditionalist with a huge streak of social moralism. He has always been more Cliff Richard than Keith Richards'), *The Times* suspected they were soft-headed 90s rock rebels acting to type, chickening out of serious politics – in a way their anti-Vietnam War forebears of the 60s had not – and whining piteously for their jobs to be made easier. Indeed, McGee had been asked as early as October 1996 why he was backing a party whose social authoritarianism ran contrary to the anti-establishment spirit of his record company. McGee had admitted that his support for Labour was founded on a hatred of the Tories, and that he wasn't about to pore over the small print.

Guilty of myopia or not, the *NME* article was hailed that Sunday as 'the most important political event this week'. *Observer* writer Martin Jacques went on: 'Such was the ferocity of the assault that there is surely no way back ... In what amounts to a manifesto, Britpop has severed its links with New Labour less than a year after the election ... The event ... marks the beginning of the end of Cool Britannia.' There was certainly no denying that. What was Cool Britannia without cool Britons? An ice-cream flavour.

The Government's official comment was that Blair had not read the *NME*, but McGee was pretty sure he had. The grapevine told McGee that Blair was 'furious': he had cruised to victory on a Britpop ticket only to see the Britpop stars deserting. 'Sometimes these guys think they are more in tune than they might be,' said his spokesman. 'What you don't do is elect a new government and suddenly the world is all put to rights.'

A week later, the Government was looking a bit more flexible. Chris Smith conceded that the musicians had a 'valid point' and that it was possible the New Deal might be amended. McGee, thrilled by the thought of changing Government policy, was invited to a meeting with Andrew Smith on 19 March, and in the intervening week was asked to come up with ideas of how young musicians might be exempted. The proposal drawn up by McGee, Andy Saunders, John Glover and Stuart Worthington – an expert in training and employment and a consultant to the International Managers' Forum – was that the Government should give musicians two years' leniency, during which they would continue to draw benefit, in effect mirroring the Conservatives' Enterprise Allowance Scheme which had provided a launchpad for McGee in the 80s.

McGee and Saunders attended the 19 March meeting together with Glover and Worthington. 'We went in fairly hard-arsed about it,' recalls Saunders. 'What they said to us was: "Yes, fine, in principle. But we need to make it fit into the existing New Deal." And we said: "Well, we don't see how it can. What you're asking us to do is put a square peg in a round hole." And they're saying: "There is no flexibility on this. Essentially, there is a New Deal and we cannot move outside its remit." We were a little bit exasperated, going: "Well, what we're proposing simply doesn't fit into that. We're asking for something a lot more radical." It was going around in circles quite a lot.'

Andrew Smith insisted that there must be visible results at the end of the two-year leniency period; he was not prepared to give young people benefit for two years without a guarantee of some qualification or improvement. A follow-up meeting was arranged for April.

McGee and Dick Green had begun to have nervous conversations about low sales and other difficulties faced by Creation. In March, the company had made three of its 40 members of staff redundant, with others expected to follow. None of the artists bar Bernard Butler – whose album *People Move On* was released in the first week of April – was selling many records, and McGee and Green debated the wisdom of a large, marketing-geared company continuing to release A&R-led music to a public that did not want it. One of the most interesting things about some of these discussions was the involvement of Joe Foster.

Foster had been at the Christmas party in 1996, and had since listened often as McGee and Green chewed over various points of dissatisfaction about the label's expansion. 'It was very much one culture confronting another,' Foster says. 'A culture of: "No one's important unless they've got loads of money thrown at them ... Do three singles and that's the end of their career" – which is never what we were all about. It was getting to the stage where people were being dropped from the label simply because they weren't going to be on Radio 1. The entire culture was wrong. The Christmas party the year after that was fucking awful. I was in a room full of ponytails, drones and users, all standing around going: "More champagne!" I'm standing with Ed Ball and we're drinking mineral water. It was like: "Fuck, man. I slept on sofas and put records in plastic bags for this?" '

McGee was now being heard complaining that Creation was an impersonal organisation dribbling to death in a marketing vortex. It was a convenient point for him to be making – and he would make it in many interviews over the next two years – but it could be turned on its head easily enough. Indeed Emma Greengrass, her assistant Bronwin Hayes and John Andrews would have argued that the only thing keeping Creation alive was the sales of the albums they had marketed between them. And they would have had the full support of Mark Taylor.

'I disagree with Alan on this,' says Taylor. 'Alan has always been music-based. That's where Alan comes from. He's very creative and he is by his own admission an A&R person. It was obvious that he was driving the company forward on that basis, and the marketing department was struggling to keep up with him ... In terms of effort and thought and commitment, the marketing department couldn't be faulted. From an employer's point of view, they did everything I could have asked of them.'

It was hardly the fault of Greengrass, Andrews and Hayes that Radio 1 was not playing Creation's singles on the hour every hour. Nor was it their fault that the new intake of Creation bands – Hurricane #1, Three Colours Red and the tuneful but rather anonymous three-piece Arnold – lacked the personality of the Gallaghers and therefore had to build a career slowly and make headway in the media by stealth. And nor was it the fault of Greengrass that the seven million worldwide sales of *Be Here Now* had made McGee worry that part of Creation's soul had ebbed away.

'We helped him to sell a lot of records, which apparently is a nasty thing to do,' says Greengrass witheringly. 'Ultimately, all I've ever done is try my hardest to sell as many records for Alan as possible. And for him to turn round and accuse the marketing people of taking away the soul of Creation ... All we were doing was marketing the records we were given in the best way possible – and constantly being told to spend more money.'

As far as Greengrass was aware, McGee had not given the offending revenue from *Be Here Now* to charity. He certainly had not given any of it to her. She had been on the same performance-related bonus scheme as the rest of the Creation management team: 25 per cent of her salary if profits reached a certain level. 'One year we got it, after *Be Here Now*,' says Andy Saunders. 'But of course we were making a massive loss after that, so it never came into play.'

In tandem with the bilious Joe Foster, who is not averse to making comments like 'my granny's cat could have marketed Oasis', McGee had taken an immutable position on late-90s marketing that brought both men back to their Beaconsfield Road all-night sleeve-folding sessions of 1984. Foster is downright derisive of the work the Creation marketing department was doing: 'When you get an email memo saying: "We've got Bernard Butler on the Z-list at Atlantic 252 – well done, everybody" ... I mean, I've worked at ad agencies like that. It's self-congratulation. "We've sold five baked beans this week. Well done, everyone." Delusional behaviour.'

'On the record, I like Emma Greengrass,' says McGee. 'She's a good person. John Andrews? I don't even like John Andrews – I *love* John Andrews. Bronwin? She doesn't have a bad bone in her body. But marketing as a concept, I think, destroys what's great about record companies, because it brings it all down to nuts and bolts. And record companies are about magic.'

It was in the March 1998 issue of Q magazine that the Creation staff finally learned of McGee's discontent. In an interview conducted in January, he said: 'Something has to change. Creation is now a big machine – because we have one of the biggest groups in the world – and I'm not a big machine type person. It's not my idea of why I get out of bed and go to work. When it started in 1984, it was me. By 1989, I had ten of my pals in. Now there are 40 people working for me, and everybody is great at their job. But there's at least 20 who could be working at Tetley's, or anywhere ... They don't understand what Creation has been through.' Describing some of the staff as 'glamour bunnies', he did not foresee long careers at Creation for many of them. And for the first time, he spoke of the possibility of closing Creation and starting afresh.

The glamour bunnies remark did not go down well in Primrose Hill at all. 'That upset a lot of people who weren't at managerial level,' says John Andrews. 'There were people there who worked on a normal level who could quite easily have been part of the original Creation, in terms of their energy and desire. They had a lot to give. And I think they were alienated by what they perceived as the management.' They could hardly turn for reassurance to Dick Green. The thought of having to deal with other people's problems alarmed him at the best of times. A fractious staff was a social horror from which he instinctively recoiled.

Tones Sansom was confident that McGee's comments did not refer to him, but as one of the lowest-ranking employees he felt they could have been better phrased. 'Everyone was working very hard and doing their best under difficult circumstances,' Sansom says. 'But Alan was obviously frustrated. With Oasis, it *was* frustrating on a day-to-day basis. Alan had the sensation that aspects of the direction of the company had been taken out of his hands, and those remarks were born out of that frustration.'

McGee had come to the conclusion that each new month for Creation represented a stay of execution. The more he talked to Foster – and was reminded of their conversations in Tottenham 14 years earlier – the more McGee felt that the label had gone too far in the wrong direction. 'Really, I should have left after Knebworth,' he says. 'The ideology of Creation was always that punk-rock-psyche-delic thing, and we'd taken it to its natural conclusion. What we didn't know is that little bands like Arnold and Trashmonk were never, ever going to get a fair crack of the whip. It was like having a

Zeppelin hanging over your head called Oasis. Everything was in the shadow of it. It got to 1998 and I realised that everything we were putting out was getting killed by this monolithic beast above our heads.'

Desperate times called for desperate measures. If there is a perfect example of how Creation in 1998 allowed itself to make serious misjudgments that would not have been made in a lower-pressure environment, it is the chain of events that began when Andy Bell of Hurricane #1 picked up a ringing telephone in February. The caller was from his management company, Ricochet, telling him to get everyone in the band round to his house for some good news.

Hurricane #1's next single was to be a Bell-written ballad, 'Only The Strongest Will Survive'. As the four members of the band sat in Bell's house, a package arrived containing a video of a projected TV advert for the *Sun*. Lilting over scenes of a varied population reading the newspaper – young and old; male and female; white and black – were the strains of 'Only The Strongest Will Survive'. 'It was a bit bemusing to see what they'd said was such good news,' admits Bell.

After they had watched the tape a couple of times, Bell started getting more phone calls. The first was from McGee, who urged him to agree to the advert. 'They need to know by tonight,' Bell remembers him saying. 'You basically have to decide within the next hour about this.' Ricochet rang next, telling Bell that Creation would not finance a third Hurricane #1 album – the second had yet to be released – if they turned the advert down. (Mark Taylor denies that Creation made such an ultimatum.) 'We were told: "Decide now, because there are 30 other bands bigger than you who want it",' says Bell.

Two members of the band, *Sun* readers themselves, were in favour of the advert. The exposure for Hurricane #1 would be daily and prime-time, and would guarantee a warm relationship between the tabloid and the band for a long time to come. The problem was that the *Sun* was a right-wing tabloid drenched in controversy, which had taken the Government's side in the miners' strike, had often fabricated stories about pop musicians and other celebrities, and had claimed responsibility for the Conservatives' victory in 1992. For over twenty years it had been synonymous with racism, homophobia, ignorance and hatred. And while pop groups of varying size and reputation had cooperated with the paper when obliged to, no band on Creation – nor on any other Labour-supporting label – had ever promoted the home of the Page 3 girl so blatantly.

Bell took advice. He was assured by Creation and by Ricochet that the *Sun* was now a pro-Labour paper with a broad, inclusive editorial policy. 'It was like: "Andy, you've got to understand, the *Sun* is changing",' he says. ' "They're getting rid of the Page 3 girls. You've got to do it." Ninety per cent of the money from it was going to go to Creation. It was going to go to our account in Creation, but the fee was basically so that they could put some money in the pot and afford to give us a third album. And I was persuaded.'

Matthew Wright, the showbiz columnist on the *Mirror*, was not slow in making capital out of Hurricane #1's participation. 'Given my understanding of the Creation ethos, I found it hugely surprising that Hurricane #1 should be chosen to be part of a *Sun* advert,' he told *Melody Maker*. 'I can only imagine that at some point money talks louder than politics, perhaps, or belief.' But Wright's sarcasm was as nothing compared to the anger and disbelief of former Creation friends and allies, who knew Hurricane #1's credibility would never recover. 'It killed the band,' says Jeff Barrett. 'Over. Done. Finished. Bang. *Finito*. Terrible, terrible, terrible thing.'

Andy Bell contends that the damage to credibility was minimal for a band that had little to begin with. Noel Gallagher had publicly scorned Hurricane #1's releases. Unfavourable comparisons between Hurricane #1 and Oasis had been instantaneous, curdling Bell's opinion of the press so badly that he feels nothing but contempt for journalists today. But either way, the *Sun*-advertising Hurricane #1 were dead meat.

McGee at first attempted to wash his hands of the affair ('It's down to individual artists to decide if they want to appear in adverts or not,' he said in March), but admitted 18 months later that advising Bell to do the advert had been 'the biggest mistake I made in the whole 17 years of Creation ... I got the *Sun* thing completely wrong. The band got £150,000 and the press came down horribly on them. It killed the group'.

It didn't do much for Creation either.

Since 1997, several people at Creation had been given new job titles. Johnny Hopkins was now head of press. Andy Saunders had been made head of communications. Emma Greengrass had been promoted to general manager. 'As companies grow, they start to embrace the concept of office politics, unfortunately,' says Mark Taylor, who oversaw the changes. 'Job titles had become an issue.'

The office was deeply factionalised, during working hours and after. Ironically, the long-running tension between Hopkins and Saunders had eased, and they were now able to work side by side without tempers fraying. The mood of the office, however, was more tepid than placid. 'This is quite indicative of how Creation had become,' says Hopkins, 'and of the kind of people that were around – i.e. people who weren't particularly into music. Whenever a new record came out, whether it was the Boos or the Fanclub or Oasis, you wouldn't hear it in the office. People didn't play music in the office. Quite often I'd put on a record and people would tell me to take it off because they were trying to work. It was like, fucking hell, we're a *record* company ...'

For all the boredom, there was one major flashpoint in early 1998. Coordinating a photo session for the Jesus and Mary Chain in the Reaction offices around the corner, Andy Saunders happened to comment on the late arrival of the stylist, Emily Hughes. The girlfriend of Bobby Gillespie, she did not take kindly to being criticised by Saunders. After an exchange of words, he apologised and made her a cup of tea. 'I went over to the Creation office at the end of the shoot,' he says, 'and was just taking my coat off when I got shoved in the back. I turned round and there's Bobby Gillespie with blazing eyes, going: "If you ever fucking speak to my girlfriend like that again, I'll have you killed." '

The other press officers – Hopkins, Tones Sansom, Vanessa Cotton and Susie Roberts – looked up from their work. Sansom seems to recall a smirk crossing Hopkins' face. ('Then we got under our desks,' he adds.) Saunders stood helplessly as Gillespie raged at him. 'I said: "Listen, Bobby, it wasn't like that at all. If you'll let me explain . . ." At which point he said: "You fucking cunt, I'm going to have you stabbed." '

The heavy-set doorman wandered across, but wasn't sure whom he was supposed to be protecting. 'Wayne was an absolute lunatic who would think nothing of drinking a bottle of Scotch in about 20 minutes,' remembers Sansom. 'His hobby was crashing cars. He was standing there but he didn't know what to do. Artist. Staff. Does not compute.'

Gillespie disappeared upstairs to the mezzanine, fuming. Saunders left the building for two hours to calm down, but returned later to tell Dick Green that it simply wouldn't do for artists to threaten the lives of members of staff. To Saunders' dismay, Green took the side of Gillespie – as did almost everybody else. 'Andy should have thought before he said anything to Emily,' remarks Sansom. 'But that's Andy. I'm sure there's 101 tales of journalists who have been threatened with being thrown under a train.'

McGee, who was in New York at the time, heard about the incident and phoned Saunders for more details. At last Saunders found a supporter. 'He was absolutely furious. He goes: "It's all coming to a head. It's just one more nail in the coffin. Bobby has been really rude to my wife, he's been rude to me, he's been rude to everybody else. I'm sick of him and I'm not going to take his shit any more." ' McGee told Saunders he would phone Gillespie and have it out with him.

For the next 45 minutes, McGee and Gillespie screamed at each other down the phone lines. The most personal of accusations were levelled: that neither had been there during the other's time of crisis; that each had been too selfish and too drugged to offer friendship; that each was a self-seeking hypocrite who had lost control of his life. 'Alan rang me back,' recalls Saunders, 'and said: "I got a lot of things off my chest. You didn't even come up in the conversation." They ended up having a mutual home truths session and the situation with Bobby was reconciled. It was the outcome I secretly didn't want.'

In August 1997, some months before their reconciliation, McGee had said of Gillespie: 'He's a hard person to work out. As we grow older, me and Bobby grow further and further apart as people. We have definitely taken separate paths. With the drugs that infiltrated Primal Scream between 1991 and 1996, I went from not getting on with him to the point where I didn't really like him.' Today, McGee says: 'When you fall out with people that you're as close to as me and Bobby, it's fucking intense. But we'll probably be friends till the day we die.'

But there was one matter on which they would not be reconciled. Creation was a long way from being Primal Scream's favourite record label. It was the reason their publicity and A&R were handled out-of-house by Jeff Barrett, and there was no sign of the Scream softening in their attitude. 'Primal Scream exist outside of Creation,' said Barrett in 1998, 'because they've been there for so long and they demand so much. Nobody at the record company is ever told how much they demand. All anybody's ever told is: "They're difficult – and they're right." '

With their *Vanishing Point* album, Primal Scream had re-established themselves as one of Creation's top two acts, albeit one that bore a weight of history, comradeship, madness and shared experience that not even Oasis could match. But even now that his complicated friendship with McGee was back on the rails, there was rarely a flicker of emotion from Bobby Gillespie any more for the label he privately called Cremation Records.

Creation had operated a website since January 1995. John Andrews had been in charge of its upkeep in the early days, setting up an online chat with Slowdive to promote their third album, *Pygmalion*. However, the site had brought no tangible results from a marketing perspective, and Andrews had soon got bored with it. In the ensuing three years, as the internet began to expand at the rate of one new site per minute, Creation made no effort to be competitive. One visiting reviewer called its site 'a surprisingly boring place to be, considering the supposedly radical nature of the company'. Other than a history of the label by Ed Ball and an occasional studio diary by Martin Carr, there was not a great deal to be said for the digital Creation.

McGee, more technophobic than Luddite, had not been fully recovered from illness when the site had opened, and paid it no attention for the first couple of years. 'I thought computers were for people like James Kyllo and Mark Taylor – super-bright, geeky people,' he says. 'I thought: I'm Alan McGee, I write everything down in a list and I'm not that clever. Then Kate got a little Apple Mac out and put my name in. She said: "Look at all these things people are saying about you on the internet." I was scrolling down the pages, going: "That's not *true* ..." After about an hour, I suddenly looked at it and thought: my God, I can work the internet. It was so easy. Then Kate showed me how to log on and log off. The next day, I ordered a computer and for the next six months I hardly left the house.'

Talking to the *Guardian* in March 1998, McGee praised the internet for its 'direct interaction ... beyond the reach of censorship', but went no further than that. The following month, in an article reporting the first instance of an entire album being posted on a record company website prior to commercial release (Massive Attack's *Mezzanine*), Alice Rawsthorn of the *Financial Times* noted that many companies had, after an initial burst of exuberance, allowed their sites to grow stale or lapse from topicality. A case in point was Creation's site, where McGee was still running his 'Predictions For 1997' in April 1998. He was not the only offender. Joe Foster recalls: 'It got to the point where the most happening website of any of the Creation bands was the Millennium, a band on Rev-Ola that split up 33 years ago.'

It took a few months for McGee to realise that the internet could have a serious impact on the business of selling and distributing music. There were two ways in which music could be delivered over the net: it could be ordered online and sent to the buyer by post, or it could be downloaded on to a personal computer using compressing technology such as Liquid Audio or MP3, whence it could be transferred to CD. McGee got Creation's press department to cut out newspaper reports on each technological innovation as it arrived. 'I just thought: wait a minute. This is another culture. This is a revolution coming about,' he says.

A few indie labels in the States had already decided to dispense with formal distribution channels and sell music on the internet, hoping to cut their costs by up to 70 per cent. 'There's nothing that stands between you and getting your music out there other than your own willpower,' David Turin, the owner of the Los Angeles-based internet label People Tree, told the *Guardian* later that year. 'It's not about getting signed any more, it's not about getting accredited by any kind of deal, it's about how good your stuff is. This paves the way for an incredibly exploded music industry. We're not going to be looking to Capitol or Geffen to tell you what's available. We're going to have search engines digging out who's done what, where, and who's got this cool song on their web page. We're just on the cusp of that now.' Turin's next remark would surely have caught the eye of *Guardian* reader Alan McGee. 'It's akin to the punk movement ...' he said. 'The implications are astounding.'

McGee could not have discovered the internet at a more volatile time in the life of Creation. Amid low sales and high costs, most of the label's acts were unrecouped and some were being asked to consider putting out compilation albums in lieu of new material. There was trepidation on the shop floor, inflamed by the March redundancies and by McGee's Tetley comments. 'In the last couple of years,' says Tones Sansom, one of a handful of cigarette smokers at the company, 'all the fag-breaks were about: "Right, this is costing this much money ... and that's costing that much money ... and we're releasing them and they're not selling any copies whatsoever ..." There was a general feeling of how much longer can this go on?'

In May, during a week when several other labels were downsizing, Creation released three acts – 18 Wheeler, Nick Heyward and Toaster – from their contracts. Martin Carr of the Boo Radleys, who had been asked to write more commercial songs for their next album, *Kingsize*, was startled when McGee critiqued the results as still not commercial enough. 'Who do you think is going to buy it?' he asked Carr. 'The kids,' Carr suggested. McGee was scornful. 'What – you mean the 10,000 fans you've got in this country who can put you in the charts at number 31 for one week? Is that what you want?' When Carr told him he wanted a track entitled 'The Future Is Now' to be the A-side of the first single, McGee snorted: 'A-side? It's not even a C-side.'

A four-page Creation news letter, 'Creation For The Nation', was distributed to the industry that summer. It led with a heartfelt message from McGee. 'Creation is what it always was,' he wrote. 'A label of misfits, drug addicts, dysfunctional human beings and out-and-out losers.' He meant it as the strongest possible recommendation, but it was just another way of saying commercial boat-missers and old-timers. Of the artists advertised inside, only Bernard Butler was not in his thirties. 'Alan, Dick and I were talking in vague terms about different ways of doing things,' says Joe Foster. 'And we were basically saying: "Well, it's all over." '

Even the sanguine *NME* had to admit that the post-Britpop lull was verging on disaster. Summer festivals were being cancelled due to low ticket sales, and the lack of a dominant scene had forced the music papers to give front covers to minor bands with nothing to say to – or for – Britain's youth. The market had returned to the levels of the early 90s, when only hardcore music enthusiasts had bought records regularly. Although Ocean Colour Scene and Cast had sold a lot of albums in 1996, and the Verve in 1997 and 1998, a surfeit of rash signings and sub-Oasis also-rans had confused the public and made it lose heart.

It was ridiculous to expect bands like Gene, the Bluetones and Shed Seven to regenerate the summer of 1995 and carry a putative new Britpop movement on their shoulders. But that is just what their record companies demanded of them; the result was widespread drowning. A massive swing to dance music was compounded by apathy among fans of guitar music, whose tendency to resist buying a band's second and third albums would scupper many a career. Meanwhile, after years of conservatism, bad planning and bizarre decisions, the major labels had now become vulnerable to technology that made them look elderly and slow.

As an ex-punk with personal and professional connections to erstwhile angry young men like Bobby Gillespie and the Reid brothers, McGee was struck by the lethargy of the young generation, which he blamed on drugs and Thatcherism. He might have blamed some of it on Oasis for closing the generation gap and nailing up the door. In a letter that symbolised the death of the Creation dream, even if it did not mention any of its stars by name, a 45-year-old *NME* reader pilloried young people for their complacency ('. . . content to sit in their bedsits, colleges and bedrooms and wait for [record] companies to present them with music') – a tirade which the *NME*'s letters editor was too weary to contradict.

McGee, who had been hit as hard as any label boss by the problem of selling records to uninterested consumers, wrote a piece for the *NME* in June, in which he outlined his vision of the future. Listing some recent disappointing sales figures for albums by top-line groups, and citing the pop-and-more-pop policy of Radio 1 as a brutal kick in the teeth for guitar music, he then unleashed one of the most confrontational arguments ever put forward by a major music business player. 'There is a crisis in the industry and it's so huge that nobody knows it's happening,' he wrote. 'There's a revolution happening and nobody's recognising it. Technology is overriding the development of music and we should be asking ourselves: are there actually going to be any record companies in ten years' time? I don't think so.' Pooh-poohing modern rock as 'a dilution of a dilution of a dilution', he argued that it had lost its sense of rebellion, creating identical record collections between parents and children – and that rebellion now lay not in music but in owning a laptop. 'If you're 15 years old and you buy a laptop, your mum doesn't even know how to turn it on, man! That's rock 'n' roll!'

Much of the rhetoric was typical McGee. He made it sound as if he alone had woken up to the possibilities of the internet while his record company peers were still watching Betamax and using abacuses. ('It was nothing that we hadn't been hearing for two years,' says Martin Carr. 'It was just McGee being a bit behind as usual. Except that when he says something, everybody hears it.') What was shocking, however, was McGee's use of two Creation bands to illustrate his premonition. 'In ten years' time, forget it if you think that Oasis or Primal Scream are going to be on a record label,' he wrote. 'They know their fanbase and they're going to download their records to their fans for £10 a shot.'

Breaking ranks with the industry's magic circle – which had sworn never to admit that music was overpriced – he continued: 'It'll be sexier for bands to download their music on the internet: cut out the middle man, the record company, and deliver straight to the fans for a cheaper price.' If this would be sexier for bands, and sexier for fans, the implication was that it would be sexier for Alan McGee too. Without saying in so many words that Creation's days were numbered, he gave the strong impression that he would not be one of the last to join the lifeboats. 'There's a worldwide recession in the music industry,' he went on. 'They might be all smiley-smiley at the Brits, but it's an industry in absolute crisis ... The people at the top recognise that the internet is going to change the whole way that music is sold to people, and they're getting out now while the going's good.'

McGee's naivety and honesty made for stirring reading. By affixing a ticking bomb to the music business in language that leapt off the page, he had virtually assured his ostracism by every governing body and establishment spokesman. But he had never sounded more convincing than when he spelled out the mathematics to the *Observer* a few days later. He calculated that an indie label selling 5,000 albums over the internet at £10 a time would make £45,000 'in one fell swoop' – with its only costs being £1 to cut each CD. No marketing department. No plugger. No play-list.

The BPI retorted to McGee's article by saying that it had received no official indication of a decline in record sales. Chairman Rob Dickins pointed out that Creation and other indies might be in trouble but worldwide sales of singles remained buoyant. He dismissed McGee's essay as irrelevant and uninformed. Ed Bicknell, the manager of Dire Straits, called the predictions 'nonsensical, simplistic and alarmist'. Several industry figures suggested that McGee had overlooked one crucial fact – that a record is a complete package that comes with artwork, annotation and have-in-your-hand ownership, things which no cheap, downloaded CD could emulate.

'The laptop is a Dansette record player,' said Dickins later that year. 'It's a fanzine. It's access. It's being with a peer group. It's being away from your parents. It's all those great things that make things happen. I think it's going to change record distribution and record retailing, and maybe – way beyond our time – it's going to replace the shop. But Alan went further than he needed to go.'*

McGee was made a pariah by the industry. In his speech at the BPI's annual general meeting on 8 July, Dickins called McGee's prophecy 'an absurd, ignorant point made by [someone] who should know better'. And in an echo of Margaret Thatcher's outburst against the 'moaning minnies' who had found fault with society under the

---

* The research consultancy Market Tracking International estimated that the internet would account for 0.1 per cent (or £53.4 million) of worldwide record sales in 1998, and 7.3 per cent (£2.4 billion) by 2005.

Conservatives, *Music Week* labelled McGee a 'doom merchant' whom it would be better off without. 'Alan described himself at the time as being the David Beckham of the music business,' says Andy Saunders. 'It was just after Beckham had been sent off in the World Cup and the whole country hated him.' Rumours persist that the Government was asked by a senior music industry executive to remove McGee from the Creative Industries Task Force. They have always been denied.

In August, as Creation announced six further redundancies and four additional staff departures, *Music Week* editor Ajax Scott wrote ironically: 'Alan McGee's projection that record companies will go bust in ten years looks likely to come back to haunt him. With Creation laying off a third of its workforce last week, the timescale for his company could be shorter than 2008 ... Some suspect McGee has simply lost interest in the record business.' Scott's editorial was headlined 'Pack Up Or Shut Up'.

A few days after *Music Week* was published, two photocopies of Scott's editorial were posted anonymously to McGee and Saunders. Written on each one were the words 'Hope you saw this, you cunt'.

Employment expert and music industry consultant Stuart Worthington had formulated in detail the plan to give young musicians two years' leniency from the terms of the New Deal relating to loss of benefit. When the McGee camp and Andrew Smith met again, Worthington was the chief negotiator. 'The whole thing started rolling forward,' says Andy Saunders, 'and we started to talk about things like keeping activity logs and having regular meetings. The activity log became the central issue.'

It was agreed that young musicians could continue to draw the Jobseeker's Allowance for another 13 months provided they could show evidence to the department of education and employment of their commitment and talent. As well as being able to opt for self-employment, full-time education or training, they could choose an 'open learning' option, whereby they would keep an activity log itemising rehearsals and songwriting sessions, reporting every two months to employment service advisers.

The amendments to the New Deal were condemned on all sides. As Smith unveiled the soon-to-be-nicknamed 'rock 'n' dole' scheme on 15 June, a Conservative spokesman called it 'a charter for scroungers'. Others made the point that McGee's two major campaigns of 1998 appeared to be mutually exclusive. His beloved internet might conceivably get rid of corporate conservatism and make music exciting again – but the musicians themselves would, thanks to McGee and the employment service advisers, be required to do homework as though they were studying for rock GCSEs. 'The idea that in order to claim their dole money would-be musicians are going to have to submit planned work schedules and daily diaries of their practice sessions is just laughable,' wrote a critic of the scheme in the *Scotsman*. 'One or two highly motivated lyricists might manage it. No drummer ever will.'

As the public face of the four negotiators of the 'rock 'n' dole' scheme, McGee took all the brickbats and received what little kudos there was to go round. Ignoring Stuart Worthington's important role in the negotiations, the few favourable news reports credited McGee's 'ferocious criticism' of the New Deal as the clincher that had forced the Government to grant musicians preferential treatment. The New Deal For Musicians was launched at the Sound City music festival in Liverpool on 27 October by employment minister Tessa Jowell.

'What we did – me and Saunders – was pretty brilliant,' says McGee today. 'It was unbelievable that two little indie punk rock kids managed to change Government legislation and create a model scheme for other creative artists. But we've never had any credit from the media. If anything, we've been slagged off for being involved in it. It's one of the best and most selfless things I've ever done, and I've never had a pat on the back from anybody.'

Four days after the launch of the New Deal For Musicians, McGee was placed eighty-seventh in a list compiled by the *Observer* of the 300 most powerful people in Britain. It was implied that his £50,000 donation to New Labour had been a contributing factor to his membership of the Creative Industries Task Force.

The relationship between the McGee-Saunders axis and the Government seemed to become healthier as a result of the New Deal For Musicians – so healthy, in fact, that Saunders was employed as a consultant to the department of education and employment to help get some positive coverage in the media. The nation's students were not so fortunate. The Teaching and Higher Education Bill, which phased out grants and introduced tuition fees, had been voted through the Commons by a large majority in June, despite last-minute protests from Damon Albarn, Bobby Gillespie and the Chemical Brothers.

McGee gradually stopped attending meetings of the Creative Industries Task Force and the Music Industry Forum, but would donate £20,000 to the Labour Party the following March. By the end of December 1998, stung by repeated criticism of its 'beefeaters to Britpop' image and by the resignation of Peter Mandelson from the Cabinet after revelations of an undeclared £373,000 loan, New Labour was reported to be rethinking its emphasis on style and spin, and to be admitting that Cool Britannia and other elitist, superficial forms of presentation had been a mistake. As Martin Jacques of the *Observer* had written, New Labour's attachment to the cultural symbols of Britpop, Britlit and Britart 'have been used as a substitute for a clear and distinctive strategy or a worked-out set of policies'.

At any rate, if the Government thought Britpop still had a heart-beat, it obviously hadn't seen the sales figures for the Boo Radleys' *Kingsize*, which stood at only 10,000 after a month. Exactly, in fact, what McGee had forecast.

For the first time since 1994, Creation had discussed with Sony the possibility of being advanced some short-term funding. Sony's response was that it would rather not go through all that again. With only one expected big-selling album in the pipeline – a compilation of Oasis B-sides in November – Creation was once again dogged by rumours that it was about to close.

More truthfully, it was trying to experiment and learn. While Rob Dickins was arguing that the internet was a modern-day Dansette, and other industry veterans were viewing it as no more a threat to the status quo than Sonic the Hedgehog, McGee had become con-vinced that the internet was a Dansette; the shop in which the Dansette was sold; the bank from which the money to buy it was withdrawn; the high street in which both shop and bank were situ-ated; and the arbiter of what would happen to that high street in the next millennium.

In July 1998, Creation announced plans to join Island and Sony's MiniDisc division in the small movement of UK labels offering an internet sales facility. To be opened in the autumn, the Creation site would play new music, transmit live recordings and allow customers to order CDs using a credit card. Spokesman Andy Saunders envis-aged that CD prices would be lower than in high-street shops. Fatefully, the facility would be available to people living outside the UK.

Two weeks later, in what was seen as a precedent-setting move, Creation abandoned its plans after Sony claimed it would be in breach of the 1992 and 1996 contracts. 'Sony said we didn't hold licences outside the UK and we said that was their prerogative,' Andy Saunders told the *Scotsman*. 'I am sure we would have addressed it ... We are investing a lot of time and money into an internet site that competes. We will work within the parameters we are given.'

A piqued McGee elected to go ahead with the site, selling to cus-tomers within the UK only. In September, he revealed that Creation would be selling music on the internet by the end of the month. 'We want to get in at the beginning of what we consider to be a revolution in the music business,' Saunders explained. 'We want to make sure we are a presence on the internet and that our name is known at the start.' Neither Saunders nor McGee predicted significant sales for the first couple of years.

Creation's big plans for the website were a McGee-Saunders pro-ject in the main. At Mark Taylor's end of the company, the internet had little part to play in the overall strategy of keeping Creation functioning. Having pruned the headcount from 40 to 25 in six months, Taylor saw only one way forward: to start shifting product fast. 'When we made the redundancies,' he says, 'I tried to encourage the focus to be: "We've done the cost-cutting, it's all dependent on us selling records. It's not about having beautiful marketing campaigns or fantastic records. It's all about sales now." '

But bands were still being let go. Arnold, whose poignant *The Hillside Album* had been one of the most popular releases of the late 90s among the staff, were dropped before they could make another, causing a disapproving Tones Sansom to protest to McGee and Green in turn. He got two very different reactions. Green agreed that it was a crying shame. McGee, however, replied that he had a business to run and told Sansom not to take it so personally.

According to Johnny Hopkins, another much-liked Creation band might have been dropped too, had its members not already decided to break up. After an in-store appearance at the Virgin Megastore and a final concert in Paris, the Boo Radleys called it a day shortly after Christmas 1998.

Dick Green, who had hastened their decision by declining to release any more singles from *Kingsize*, had started to take more and more time off work. He was tired and had a woebegone air. McGee had seldom been in the office all year, spending his time either squinting at websites or being followed around London by a camera crew from the BBC *Omnibus* programme, which was making a documentary about him.

'It was becoming ridiculous,' says Andy Saunders. 'Creation was a rudderless ship. Dick simply wasn't coming into work. You had Mark Taylor being burdened – or I should say overwhelmed – with the uncertainty of the situation, and a staff who were saying to him: "What's going on?" He was in no position to tell them. What we really needed there was strong leadership, and what we didn't *get* was strong leadership.'

The behaviour of McGee was particularly evasive and changeful, making some Creation employees wonder if the label's demise would happen within the year. When the *Omnibus* documentary, 'The Man Who Discovered Oasis', was broadcast in September, the staff watched it more for clues than entertainment.

'The Man Who Discovered Oasis' took a broad view of McGee's life and work, interviewing only two musicians in an hour-long programme and condensing the long and painful story of Creation into half a dozen bullet-points. Much of the programme was centred around football, New Labour and the executive health-freak lifestyle that McGee had lived since 1995. The camera followed him from room to room, from office to stadium, yet was unable to give satisfactory answers to the questions of who he was, what he had done and whether or not anyone else could have done it. 'McGee will probably be happy about this very flattering ... portrait,' speculated a journalist who had known him in the days of the Living Room. 'But when you know what is missing, it is frustrating. The Creation story is a modern fable of a boy in the big city, and the heart of that tale is absent.'

McGee loved the documentary, not just because it flattered him but because it showed him poised excitingly at a crossroads. He had already spoken of his ambition to branch into film production, and had admitted that age might soon count against him as a talent-spotter in the music business. The perceptive Matthew Lynn of the *Sunday Times*, who had profiled McGee the previous year, had written: 'McGee is certainly a successful entrepreneur, a wealth-creator. But he is also a rebel, an iconoclast who is always likely to veer off in different and unexpected directions.'

It was the thought of these unexpected directions that dominated the conversations of Creation employees as they discussed the *Omnibus* programme over the next few days. 'The key thing was when he said: "When I'm 40, I'm not going to be running Creation," or words to that effect,' says John Andrews. McGee was just about to turn 38.

Andy Saunders had been involved in the filming of the documentary, so McGee's comments had not come as a surprise to him. Saunders would remain close to McGee, hearing new decisions as soon as they were made. Almost everybody else at the company was in the difficult situation of having to guess what the man would do next. That had been a tradition at Creation since day one – but it had never been less enjoyable than in 1998 and early 1999. 'There was a sense of fear that just spread,' says one staff member. 'There were so many different moods and feelings, and it changed every day of every week.'

25 Slaying The Dinosaur

B Y THE END OF 1998, many commentators agreed that MP3 would
spell the end of the traditional album; that music was about to
enter a jukebox era in which consumers would pay for each
song, or cluster of songs, as it was offered for downloading. The five
major record companies – Sony, Warners, EMI, BMG and Universal –
struggled to exert control over their music and to come to terms with
a form of distribution that threatened to overturn the long-held practices of signing artists to contracts and releasing and promoting product at the most commercially opportune times of year.

By the beginning of 1999, it was estimated that every major label
was represented on the internet, along with almost half of the small-
to-medium-sized labels. After seeing a presentation of distribution
technology developed by Liquid Audio, Creation planned to upgrade
its website to start digital distribution that year. It would be the first
established UK record label to do so.

The all-new Creation website had opened in December, immediately promising to be much more sophisticated than the old model.
Built by Kleber Designs, which had overseen sites for the Warp and
China labels, it allowed fans to search through catalogues and hear
30-second clips before purchasing online. Transactions were handled
by Datacrash, an online credit card encryption company. The site
included a webcam surveying office life.

However, Creation's plans for the site were to cause great controversy. Aside from intending to upload recordings of Creation bands
taped live the previous night, it planned to post its new singles free
of charge for a month prior to release – another UK record company
first. Other labels expressed concern that the practice would deter
people from buying the singles when they came out. McGee coun-
tered that it would be just like hearing them on the radio. And Sony,
which had the loudest voice of all, told him he couldn't do it.

Sony was not the only music corporation wielding the rolling-pin.
The Beastie Boys had been pressured by their label Capitol to take
songs off their website that had been put there to preview their *Hello
Nasty* album. Downloadable on MP3, the tracks could have been

bootlegged and cost Capitol royalties. In December, Capitol had linked up with other major labels in the Secure Digital Music Initiative (SDMI) which policed the internet on the lookout for copyright infringement. Chuck D of Public Enemy said that month: '[The major labels] are running scared. The retail and record companies have scammed the public for years with the CD [overpricing] scandal. Now with MP3 the chickens are coming home to roost.' Public Enemy's label Universal had just taken five unreleased songs by the group off the net.

There was no way of ensuring that MP3 soundfiles were not copied illegally, and in America, where some 100 million people used the net, millions of illicit soundfiles were being downloaded every week. Alan McGee would have been happy to give away music in this fashion – indeed, he saw it as essential if Creation was to be in the vanguard of new developments in digital distribution. Above all, he preached that digitally sold music would cost fans less and give them more. He hoped to start distributing Creation albums digitally in the spring. And Sony said no to that, too.

'It was a very tricky situation,' says Andy Saunders. 'I was told I was not allowed to go to war with Sony on this. I had to phrase it in such a way that it became a mutual agreement. I said: "Look, this is not something that Sony have prevented us from doing. They have merely asked us to put a hold on it until they clarify their global situation." Which was my way of saying: "They've told us to fuck off." '

Thwarted again, McGee lamented the fact that all Creation's site could offer was mail order record sales and a webcam that looked down on the marketing department beavering away on the mezzanine. 'I think it was one of the things that made Alan think: hang on, what is the point of being in bed with Sony?' says Saunders. Clearly, Creation was not going to be in as strong a renegotiating position in 2001 as it had been in 1996. But far from running to the *NME* to complain, as he had done then, a disaffected McGee was virtually admitting that proceeding with Sony was pointless.

The employees, however, were able to find much to amuse them in the webcam. Messages started to appear on the noticeboard from fans purporting to be in love with Bronwin Hayes. She acquired the name Hoity-Toity Bird. 'There were lots of messages like: "I want to shag Hoity-Toity Bird",' says John Andrews, whom the messages renamed Skinny Boy. 'Alan got very excited by it all. He was going: "Great, great, it's turning into a cyber-soap-opera. We're going to be in the *Daily Mirror*." '

Andrews admits he posted a lot of the messages himself.

Emma Greengrass was not visible on the webcam, as it was positioned over her head. She had taken maternity leave in 1998, and had returned to be told that McGee wanted her to work on a new act:

Mishka, the reggae-singing free spirit whom he had found on a Caribbean beach. It was not a prospect that filled Greengrass' heart with joy.

Mishka was to be an attempt by McGee to ease Creation through the doldrums by debuting an act with appeal to radio rather than to indie fans. Mishka also fitted in with McGee's desire to build a broad-rostered Atlantic or Island – a dream that still flickered in his mind – but it would mean re-branding Creation at a uniquely difficult point in its life.

Journalists were told that McGee had found the gifted Rastafarian singing to himself on the Caribbean island of Nevis, oblivious to his surroundings, a true uncorrupted genius of the elements. This was not incorrect, but there was a bit more to the story. Mishka was the brother of the singer-songwriter Heather Nova – the best friend of McGee's wife Kate Holmes – and came from a wealthy Bermudan family. And there was another thing that critics would be bound to remark on: Mishka was a white man.

'I didn't understand it,' says Greengrass. 'I'd heard some demos which turned out to have been something that [manager] Richard Gordon wasn't supposed to have played to anybody because it was so shit. I went to Dick and said: "I don't get this. I don't understand what to do with it." And Dick said: "I don't get it either." '

By the time Mishka's first single 'Give You All The Love' came out in April, McGee had spent almost six months talking it up. He had received extremely positive reactions from Sony in America, and from Radio 1 at home, and was expecting a UK number 1 and an international super-hit.

'Give You All The Love' charted low, however. In a dismissive review of Mishka's album, Andrew Perry wrote in *Select*: 'In a time when major-label A&R policies have rarely been more mainstream, it's the likes of Creation we look to for the light to see us out of the darkness.' For many people besides Perry, Mishka's record illuminated nothing. The bewilderment outside Creation was matched by the derision inside. 'Everybody in the office, bar one or two people, thought it was a complete joke,' says John Andrews, a rare Mishka champion. 'The Oasis camp slagged Mishka off beyond belief. That really got my back up, because I think they sensed the end of Oasis so they were turning on other things. I was angry that they were slagging off an artist that Alan had signed.'

Worse, some of McGee's revelations in the press – particularly that he had spotted Mishka while sunning himself in the West Indies – suggested he had lost touch with street-level indie record-buyers. That perception was seen to grow stronger, this time to McGee's considerable anger, when Creation put out a record by Technique, a dance-pop duo featuring Kate Holmes.

Holmes had kept her own surname when she married. Yet the

NME referred to her provocatively as Kate McGee, infuriating her and her husband. Even the *Guardian* did the same, accusing McGee in passing of cronyism worthy of Tony Blair. The gossipers might have been surprised by the truth. Technique had been signed to Creation for an infinitely more pressing reason than favouritism: they were supposed to race neck and neck with Mishka into the Top 10. 'Technique were two pretty girls singing hummable music,' says Andy Saunders. 'Alan thought he could have a massive pop hit with it.'

Technique's first single, 'The Sun Is Shining', became a big hit on the club charts but not on Gallup. The scenario was repeated on the follow-up. 'I think Alan then realigned his gunsights,' suggests Saunders. And this is where McGee's attempts to re-brand Creation ran aground. As the marketing department can vouch, the records by Technique and Mishka were not released surreptitiously like those by Bill Drummond and Les Zarjaz back in the day, but were instead marketed and promoted at appreciable expense. Mishka's videos cost £80,000 each. Technique's album was produced not by Joe Foster in Alaska but by heavyweights Owen Morris and Stephen Hague – and that was before some of the country's leading remixers were commissioned to work on the singles.

'There was an unbearable amount of pressure heaped on John Andrews,' says Saunders, 'and he was coming close to cracking at points. The fact that results didn't happen on Technique – and he was spending a shit-load of money on the videos and photo sessions – was making him start to panic. He was looking at his marketing costs spiralling upwards and his returns diminishing.'

The pressure may not have been quite so severe on McGee, but the realisation had hit him that Creation was not a label that could be re-branded at a stroke. 'The perception of Creation was white boys with guitars and you can't change that ...' he later said. 'Before we got really massive and mainstream we could put out more diverse albums, but after we'd sold fifteen million albums with ... *Morning Glory?* you couldn't go on just making interesting records. I started chasing the market and Creation was never about the market.'

But if the attempt at re-branding had been a failure, the worry was that Creation had now lost sight of its doctrine. The beauty of Creation had always been that even when it was unable to manage its business professionally, it could at least deliver on the music – in other words, give the public something it would never have got from another record label. It was clear that Creation could no longer do this. By encroaching on mainstream pop and soft reggae, it had become neither one thing nor the other. Neither an indie label with relevance to teenagers, nor a commercial label churning out hit after hit.

'To some extent,' says James Kyllo, 'you could see it as being an attempt to deal with the realities of the Sony situation. We were not getting any international income because we weren't selling records abroad, and one way of trying to keep the label alive was to make records that were understandable and saleable by a major company in foreign territories.'

Perhaps a different label could have succeeded. Creation could not. Creation never would. 'If Mishka had been on S2 or Virgin, he would be huge,' argues John Andrews. 'Let's look at the artists on those labels. Jamiroquai was a complete joke when he started. Des'ree. Kelis, who is on Virgin now ... But the view in the media was that you can't have a reggae-type artist on an indie label.'

What really brought it home to McGee was a number 1 hit in the summer of 1999 for 'King Of My Castle', a remixed Ibiza dance track by the Wamdue Project. The original version had been released exactly a year earlier on Eruption, a dance offshoot of Creation, but had failed to chart in the Top 100. McGee would later say: 'That was divine intervention. It was like a shining light from heaven beaming down and saying: "Alan – go." '

But there was to be one last hurrah.

Kevin Rowland's 1999 album *My Beauty* consisted of cover versions only. It is fair to say that this was not what McGee had expected, but they were singularly passionate and sincere cover versions and it didn't take him long to get used to the idea. John Andrews, who had been a big fan of Dexys Midnight Runners, was thrilled to hear that one of the songs Rowland had recorded was 'You'll Never Walk Alone'.

'I honestly thought we could have another social phenomenon on a par with Oasis,' Andrews says. 'He'd had two number 1 singles with different types of music. He was an unexploited 80s artist in the same way that Paul Weller had been. He had a huge fanbase that hadn't been regenerated. His records were driven by idealism. And I think the fallout from the Oasis era was an intellectual backlash against "let's go out and do loads of charlie". It was like: "Let's be a bit more considered about life." I felt Kevin Rowland could maybe tune in to that in a popular way.'

Andrews had a specific image in mind. He pictured the TV sets of the nation keyed into BBC or ITV on Millennium Eve, and the population silenced and awed by clips of man's greatest accomplishments of the television age: the moon landing, the first human heart transplant, the birth of the first test-tube baby. And there would be other stories of drama and emotion: Solidarity in Poland, the dismantling of the Berlin Wall, the long walk to freedom of Nelson Mandela. 'My vision was that everyone would be listening to "You'll Never Walk Alone",' says Andrews. 'The video would be all the key moments of the late twentieth century – and Kevin Rowland would be singing a folk song about it.'

When Rowland's album was finished, it was played to only three people at Creation: McGee, Dick Green and Mark Bowen. Andy Saunders was excluded; he had been told by McGee at Easter that Rowland preferred the idea of a female publicist, and McGee had recommended Vanessa Cotton. Rather hurt, Saunders accused McGee of undermining him. 'At this point Alan said: "Andy, there is something that is going to happen with this project that is going to blow your mind. When you know what it is, you'll be so relieved that you're not doing the press." '

Saunders asked McGee what it was. McGee replied that he was not at liberty to say. Saunders blew up at him. 'Alan said: "All right, I'll tell you. Kevin dresses as a woman." Of course I burst out laughing. Alan goes: "It isn't funny." I said: "What do you mean, a woman?" Alan goes: "He's absolutely serious. He dresses as a woman. That's how he wants to be perceived. As a woman." I said: "As a woman?" Alan goes: "As a woman. Well, no, not actually as a woman. As a man dressing as a woman." '

When Saunders returned from holiday, Rowland had been photographed for an article in *Dazed And Confused* magazine wearing fishnet stockings, panties and lipstick. It transpired that while he had been recording his album, he had been changing into these clothes in a tent so that the engineers wouldn't see him. 'We saw the photos and it was mass hilarity,' says Saunders. 'I've got to be honest: it was mass hilarity.' McGee assumed that Rowland must be homosexual. Rowland told him he was not.

John Andrews was shown the cover of the album before he heard any music. It was a carbon copy of the *Dazed And Confused* session. Andrews was shocked – on a personal level; as a former Dexys fan; and as a marketing manager. He knew at once that his Millennium Eve dream would never happen. 'I was shocked and I was exhilarated,' he says, 'because it meant that we were dealing with an *artist*, somebody who was beyond the parameters of promotion and positioning, somebody who had outrageous demands ... There was suddenly no chance of us having a hit. With those photos, he turned into an avant-garde, marginalised figure.'

Rowland's astonishing new image made him one of the biggest stories in the music business that summer. He was much interviewed by a stupefied and uncomfortable press, promoting an album that looked likely to finish his career. 'I wouldn't have him another way,' said McGee in the *NME*. 'It's brought out a telling reaction in people who are unsure of their sexuality, who are homophobic. I'd say two-thirds of Creation are disgusted with the project. But it's rock 'n' roll. It's supposed to be offensive.'

It was not homophobia, however, that made people at Creation squirm. It was the reports of Rowland simulating cunnilingus on women in the video for his single 'Concrete And Clay'. 'People just began to see him as a bit of a sad old git,' says Emma Greengrass, who was among those most revolted. Tones Sansom remembers spending an hour in an editing suite picking out the best shots in the video of Rowland's bottom. 'We watched the video and were just like: "Fucking hell ...",' he says. 'I think it was shown once on BBC Wales and that was it.'

McGee, as mystified as anyone, told the *NME*: 'I took his photos and record to the German managing director and he threw them straight in the bin. These are choice moments. At Reading, he's going to get up in white stockings and white panties and sing to 40,000 people for his comeback. Well, respect. That's double punk rock.' At the Reading festival three days later, Rowland did just that – with two scantily clad women gyrating as he licked their legs. His first billed live performance since 1985, it descended into tragedy as bottles were thrown, splashing orange juice on Rowland's dress as he sang 'You'll Never Walk Alone'. There were cheers from the crowd as each missile landed.

'Concrete And Clay' was played by no national radio stations whatsoever, and by only a couple of regional ones. It sold 500 copies, taking Creation back to the days of the Legend! and other try-outs, why nots and eccentric shots in the dark. Following unprecedented resistance from retailers for an artist of Rowland's stature, a total of 700 copies of the album was sold. Creation made no effort to dispute the figures. (In July, Creation switched its distribution from Vital back to Pinnacle. Mark Taylor insisted it was no criticism of Vital's distribution of Rowland.)

'People were sniggering because it was a bloke in a dress who hasn't got a sense of humour,' says Andrews. 'But you're talking about a very complex personality – hugely sensitive – and a great artist who really belongs in the art world. He doesn't belong in the music industry. The thing that I learned at Creation is that the music industry is not the place where artists belong. If you're a true artist, you might by sheer luck survive in the music industry, but ultimately it's about a few multinational record labels divvying out their market share and lording it up at the Brits.'

With Rowland's sales figures so damningly low, McGee was presumed to have egg on his face. In fact, the saga had afforded him more excitement and satisfaction than any Creation record since ... *Morning Glory?*. It would be the last time the President would be so excited and satisfied by a little artifact called Creation.

Creation had launched its own internet radio show in June, broadcasting a new programme on the first of each month thereafter. Featuring interviews with Creation artists and music from the catalogue, they were hosted by McGee and Joe Foster. The two presenters made for such a good double act that the BBC station GLR

invited them to sit in for one of their holidaying DJs that summer.
McGee enjoyed Foster's company immensely.

Foster had earlier looked into the possibility of signing a few small-
scale indie artists to Rev-Ola, chiefly from the American underground. He had gone to International Pop Overthrow, a festival in
Los Angeles, and found a couple of suitable bands. Back in London,
Foster, McGee, Dick Green and Mark Bowen had discussions about
how this lo-fi, unpretentious music might be able to fit into Creation.
Why not? Everything else they had tried had failed.

'We were going to do it as a bit of an adventure,' says Foster, 'and
who knows, we might have found a big band out there. But the path
seemed blocked every way we turned. It didn't seem to be a runner.
Shortly after that, Alan and Dick started talking seriously of winding
Creation down.'

By October, the only people who knew for certain that Creation
was to close were McGee, Green, Foster and Andy Saunders.
Saunders had been told by McGee at the Labour Party conference in
Bournemouth that if he fancied a job with another company, now
might be a good time to start looking. Saunders was given to understand that McGee and Green would be leaving Creation in April or
May the following year.

'It obviously wasn't working as a 25 person record company,' says
McGee. 'Paul Russell wanted to take it to a six, eight-man team. We
would have had to redefine it, and the bands we would probably have
kept were the Fanclub, Oasis, the Primals, the Super Furries and
Bernard, plus a couple of others. But you know what? As I said to
Paul, we'd had the glory years.'

For McGee, dealing with Sony was a reprise of the running battles
of the 80s between the majors and the second tiers. He found Sony
incredibly restrictive: his aspirations to start a film company and to
get involved in dot.com culture were dependent on Sony waiving its
rights to any Creation music used in these projects, which it was not
prepared to do. 'There's a lot of ground between me and Sony at this
point,' he said in October. 'I would now argue that whoever you go
into bed with, you ultimately – unfortunately – start to look like
them. Because by being with Sony we're becoming a fucking
dinosaur.'

With an April departure looking probable, McGee and Green went
to see Paul Russell. McGee recalls: 'I said to Russell: "I've had it with
Creation. It's a redundant idea creatively. We've achieved everything
we're ever going to achieve. We've sold 35 million albums. We've
made you over £100 million. We've made ourselves about £20 million. Let's quit while we're all ahead."

'He didn't like it. He wanted us to stay. Six or eight people. His
concept – which is right – is that if you can find one superstar you
can find two. You've just got to hang in there long enough. Which is

fine, but I just didn't want to do it with Sony. Anyway, he agreed that we would go in April. Then, through different particular management ... The way Sony works, they all delegate. So it ended up that the accountant went into negotiation with Dick. And the accountant, off his own bat, looked at the bottom line, saw that the overhead at Creation is £1 million a year and decided to bring it forward six months. Me and Dick were looking at each other, going: "This is fucking amazing. We're going to get out six months earlier." '

While the two parties negotiated a settlement, Sony advised McGee to notify Marcus Russell of the decision. McGee wanted to put off telling Russell for as long as possible. News travelled – and there were people in the Oasis camp who had long been suspected of leaking stories to the tabloids. On 21 November, a few weeks after McGee and Green had spoken to Paul Russell, McGee met the Oasis manager and told him it was all over. 'I said: "Marcus, I've had enough. I'm bored. I want out. I should have left in '96 after Knebworth. I want to go and start a new label. I want it to be six people. I want it to be terrorist action. I want to be against the charts. I want to fuck off Radio 1." Marcus said: "I don't blame you. Sometimes I get bored out of my tits too." '

The following day, McGee spoke to Noel Gallagher. 'Noel was great about it,' he says. 'There's a classic Noel comment. I said: "Sony are fucking raging." And he goes: "We won. They didn't." ' That evening, McGee had a conversation with Mark Chung, the senior vice-president of SINE.* Chung was having to face the likelihood that Oasis would set up their own label, licensing it to SINE. 'He would rather let them have their own label deal than go outside SINE,' said McGee. 'Oasis are funding the whole SINE organisation because they sell five, six, seven million every record. They're funding all these other bands. So Marcus' big stick is: "If you don't let [Oasis start a new label], I'm going to go off and sign direct to Epic" – which then would bring the demise of SINE.'

The day after his conversations with Gallagher and Chung, McGee was asked by several unrelated music industry people if it was true that he and Green were about to leave Creation. He had no idea how they had heard. Sensing that a story was about to break, he took a meeting with SINE. 'There were six things on the agenda,' he recalls. 'We said: "You *have* to deal with this. This is going to leak." It was almost too big for them to deal with.' After some four hours, it was agreed that McGee and Green would issue a statement the next day. 'We were praying that it wouldn't leak beforehand,' says McGee.

The majority of the Creation staff – including everyone below management level – had no suspicion of the company's imminent

---

* Sony LRD had been renamed Sony Independent Network Europe (SINE) in 1997.

closure. John Andrews had now been put in the picture; McGee had suggested he look for another job. Andrews replied that he wanted to stay to the very end.

The following day – 25 November – McGee phoned Marcus Russell to tell him something amusing about the Sony negotiation. Russell asked him if he had seen that morning's *Sun*. No, said McGee – why? Russell told him that the *Sun* had a story about Oasis leaving Creation to start their own label. McGee thought: fuck.

Johnny Hopkins had certainly not expected the *Sun* story. Nor had he expected any significant upheaval at Creation before the spring of 2000 at the earliest. He got a call from Marcus Russell later that morning telling him not to worry – whatever happened, he would be taken care of.

McGee rang Andy Saunders and asked him: 'What do we do?' Saunders told him it was time to issue a press release announcing the end of Creation. If McGee deliberated, it would look as though Oasis had jilted him, which would damage the credibility of Creation, McGee, Green and the staff.

James Kyllo walked into the Creation office that morning to be asked by Mark Taylor if he had seen the *Sun*. Taylor had it up on his computer screen. The paper reported that Oasis had left Creation after growing unhappy with the label's handling of *Be Here Now*. Tones Sansom turned up for work to find McGee outside in the street. McGee told him that he and Green were leaving Creation with immediate effect. 'McGee goes to me: "I've blown your mind this time, haven't I, Tones?" ' Sansom recalls.

Andy Saunders drafted a press release and had it approved by McGee and Green. In the meantime, McGee made a speech to the staff. He announced that Creation was to continue with a depleted workforce until June 2000 – without him but perhaps with Green as a consultant – to market and promote new albums by Oasis and Primal Scream, a single by Super Furry Animals and one or two compilation albums.

The press release was issued at eleven o'clock. That afternoon, there was a meeting at Creation attended by Hopkins, Greengrass, Hayes, Cotton, Sansom, Taylor, Green, McGee and production manager Clare Rowell. 'We were told that we would all be kept on at Creation – along with a handful of others – to do the Oasis record and Primal Scream and the Super Furries,' says Hopkins. 'Dick was going to stay on as a consultant. There were going to be compilation albums by the Boos and the Valentines.' The others who would be staying included James Kyllo and Mark Bowen.

As luck would have it, the Creation credit cards – which a few senior staff members had in their possession – were due to expire at the end of the week. There was a mass movement to the local pub to spend as much money on the cards as possible. 'The ladies were in tears,' says Sansom. 'We ended up in the Pembroke, demanding Oasis and Primal Scream to be played non-stop. It was very, very emotional.'

The end of Creation made all the papers the following day. The *Guardian*, which had an interview with McGee, revealed that he was about to launch himself as a multimedia entrepreneur. 'The way that I perceive the future,' he said, 'is having a record company, having a publishing company, having my internet start-up companies, having a film company and having a management company. The future for me is multimedia; the future is not being one-dimensional and having one record company. It's worked for the last 25 years, but it doesn't make sense any more. You have to be in lots of different areas to give yourself leverage. If you're not in all these businesses at the same time, you're going to be left behind'.

McGee had already embarked on his new career by investing in the UK music site Clickmusic along with Bob Geldof, Richard Branson and others. He had also found a young computer wizard from Hackney and was in the process of 'inventing something for the internet. I've got venture capitalists all over it.'

More than anything, McGee felt vindicated. 'The things that I predicted 18 months ago have now happened ... I said there would be a consolidation and there has been. In the last year and a half, probably 20 to 30 per cent of people have lost their jobs, about 20 to 30 per cent of bands have lost their contracts, there's been a huge bloodletting and there will continue to be.' He predicted that 'every band that's got any clue whatsoever' would leave Creation at the earliest opportunity.

'He is a man convinced of his vision,' wrote Simon Waldman of the *Guardian*, 'and with some justification. His real talent seems to be spotting something in its infancy and latching on to it, making himself a small fortune in the meantime ... He realised the net was going to change the music industry while most of his peers [had] still to learn how to turn on a PC. And given that simply attaching his name to an internet start-up will probably add a zero to its value, it is likely that he will soon be joining the ranks of internet millionaires.'

By the end of November, McGee was pretty certain that Creation's final album release would be Primal Scream's *Exterminator* in February. The compilation albums by My Bloody Valentine and the Boo Radleys would not be appearing. Oasis – now with Gem Archer of Heavy Stereo and Andy Bell in their line-up – were shortly to establish their own label, Big Brother, on which they would release their new album *Standing On The Shoulder Of Giants*. It was not a record in which McGee had been greatly involved.

'*Standing On The Shoulder Of Giants* was delivered to me in compilation, in sequence and completely mixed and mastered,' he says.

'The thing is, if I wanted to be a distribution company I would have called myself Rough Trade.' Rumours spread – denied by McGee – that he and Oasis had had a bitter falling-out.

The departure of Oasis from Creation effectively removed the necessity – and unquestionably removed the financial wherewithal – to employ the remaining staff on full contracts until the summer. To their surprise and anger, they arrived for work on 22 December to learn that they were all being made redundant. 'Technically, the last day of Creation was the Wednesday before Christmas,' says Hopkins. 'Everyone came in that day to be told that Creation was over.'

Hopkins, Sansom and Cotton were retained as freelancers to work on Oasis and Primal Scream. Then, in January, a stunned Hopkins was informed over the phone by Ignition that he was no longer Oasis' press officer. An independent PR firm, Hall Or Nothing, had already been hired. Ignition had taken care of Hopkins as promised. Very good care of him.

The previous October, the *Observer* had published its annual list of the 300 most powerful people in Britain. In the true spirit of the Creation curse, McGee dropped 211 places to number 298. There are some things even he cannot blame on a marketing-based culture.

His new label Poptones, named after a track on P.i.L.'s 1979 album *Metal Box*, is a partnership with Joe Foster. Five people from Creation, including James Kyllo, publicist Susie Roberts and McGee's former PA Vanessa Budinger, have made the short walk to new employment in Poptones' offices on the site of the old Reaction photo agency.

'We're going for a completely different audience,' says Foster. 'We don't need to be up against S Club 7. I would think that we'll sell records – all our acts will sell records. We'll come up with more and more acts. Some will sell more than others ... The internet will be very important. Even the most culty thing will be on a cult level worldwide. We have a worldwide audience that will buy things to our taste. And if we've got something that will only appeal to nutters – fine. They'll appeal to every nutter in the world.'

On 19 February, with the Creation office all but deserted, McGee took a measured look around his life and liked what he saw. 'The seven years I was at Sony have been very good for me,' he said. 'I'm sitting in my house in St John's Wood – where the Beatles used to live – and I'm happy. I was in the pop business and I've made a lot of money out of it. I don't know if I'm going to be in the pop business again. I had a really big think at Christmas when Richard Ashcroft's management came up for grabs. Do I phone Richard up and say "I'd really love to manage you," or do I go and do this Poptones thing which is totally anti-establishment, anti-music business, totally left-field and I might never have another hit record in my life? And you know what I've chosen.'

Ironically, right at the death, Primal Scream's *Exterminator* showed how Creation might have had a future by revisiting some of its past. A supergroup personnel – augmented by Kevin Shields on guitar – dazzled audiences with some of the most menacing and highly charged rock 'n' roll shows of the band's career, selling more than 100,000 albums almost entirely without the help of daytime radio. A press-led sensation to compare with *Psychocandy*, *Exterminator* missed out on a number 1 chart position by only a few hundred sales.

Standing On The Shoulder Of Giants was the other side of the coin: an uninspired album by a band that people were already starting to talk of in the past tense. Few at Creation regretted their passing. 'When I was 24, Oasis were the most important thing in my life,' says Tones Sansom. 'But when we were sacked at the start of this year, it was like: "Well, actually, what have I lost?" The first two albums were an absolutely phenomenal time in my life, but I had been suspending disbelief for quite a while.'

In March, Teenage Fanclub began talks with Sony about their future. The end of Creation has not affected them drastically, but it saddens them all the same. 'It's going to leave a massive hole and there ain't no one going to fill it,' says Chas Banks. 'We'll be all right, but there are a lot of people who aren't going to be all right. There isn't going to be a vehicle for all those people like Kevin Rowland. It's the final nail in the coffin for somebody saying: "I think that's a great idea. It sounds like a bit of a laugh. Let's do it." They're sanitising those people out of the business.'

Dick Green, who had contemplated joining McGee and Foster in their new venture, chose instead to start a new label with Mark Bowen. One of the aims of Wichita is to reconnect Green with some of the uncomplicated indie values of the 80s that were lost in the 90s. While McGee looks to the digital frontier, Green is getting back to basics.

As for McGee, the pop art fan who destroyed one label in order to create another, he opened Poptones officially on 15 May 2000. But the ending and the beginning are perhaps not as sharply defined as all that. You just have to look at who's missing. 'Poptones is Creation minus Dick and Sony,' a former colleague of McGee's points out. 'What Alan has done is regain control of Creation.'

Acknowledgements

The author is very grateful to the following people for their contributions to the book, research assistance, excellent advice and/or kindness.

Tim Abbot
Gary Ainge
Mike Alway
Dave Anderson
Emma Anderson
John Andrews
Paul Apperley
Keith Armstrong
Pete Astor

Steven Baker
Dave Balfe
Ed Ball
Chas Banks
Dave Barker
Jeff Barrett
Dave Bates
Jim Beattie
Dave Bedford
Andy Bell
Laurence Bell
Terry Bickers
Karen Bignall
Derek Birkett
Jake Black
Johnny Black
Norman Blake
Julie Bland
Sarah Bloomfield
Brian Bonnar
Michael Bonner
Peter Buck
Adrian Bushby

Martin Callomon
Keith Cameron
Cerne Canning
Bill Carey
Graham Carpenter

Martin Carr
Guy Chadwick
Barbara Charone
Gabby Chelmicka
Penelope Chong
Karen Ciccone
Loz Colbert
Sylvia Coleman
Pat Collier
Edwyn Collins
Martin Costello
Gail Colson
Glen Colson
Julian Cope
Vanessa Cotton
Keith Cullen
Nick Currie

Steven Daly
Mark Dennis
Rob Dickins
Colin Dobbins
Ian Donaldson
Bill Drummond
Malcolm Dunbar
Anjali Dutt

Danny Eccleston
Stephen Edney
Simon Edwards
James Endeacott
Dave Evans
Pete Evans
Hugh Fielder
Piotr Fijalkowski
Pat Fish
Guy Fixsen
Tony Fletcher
Alex Forsyth

Joe Foster
Peter Fowler
Dave Francolini
Andy Fraser

Mark Gardener
Rick Gershon
Suzi Gibbons
Robin Gibson
Ian Gittins
Dave Goulding
Derek Green
Dick Green
Emma Greengrass
Sid Griffin
Mick Griffiths
Chris Groothuizen
Ronnie Gurr

Arthur Haggerty
Stephen Hague
Iona Hames
Dave Harper
Belinda Harris
John Harris
Melissa Harrison
Douglas Hart
Jowe Head
Robyn Hitchcock
Max Hole
Duncan Holland
Johnny Hopkins
Alan Horne
Mick Houghton

Sir Jeremy Isaacs
Nina Jackson
Andy Jarman
Howard Johnson

Danny Kelly
James King
Phil King
Dave Knight
James Kyllo

Clive Langer
Andrew Lauder
Lawrence
Sara Lawrence
Cat Ledger
Robert Lloyd
Gerry Love
Lenny Love
Chris Lycett

Andy Macdonald
Andrew Male
Eugene Manzi
Grace Maxwell
Joe McEwen
Alan McGee
Raymond McGinley
Iain McNay
Dave Meegan
Mike Mena
Jim Merlis
Stuart Middleton
Rob Mitchell
John Moore
Jonathan Morrish
Chris Morrison
Bob Mould
Alan Moulder
Douglas Muirden
Paul Mulreany
Charles Shaar Murray

Richard Newson
Dave Newton
Richard Norris
Lamees Nuseibeh

Paul O'Duffy
Sean O'Hagan

Dave Padfield
Tim Palmer
Rob Partridge
Stephen Pastel
Jeremy Pearce
Andrew Perry
Scott Piering
Jack Pikus
Dave Pittman
Warren Prentice
Bill Prince

David Quantick
Steve Queralt
Paul Quinn
Peter Reichardt
Jim Reid
John Robb
Nick Robbins
Susie Roberts
Alan Robinson
Johnny Rogan
Andy Rossiter
Jonathan Ruffle
Matthew Rumbold
Paul Russell

Adam Sanderson
Tones Sansom
Andy Saunders

Richard Scott
Ken Sharp
Graham Sharpe
Billy Sloan
Nick Small
Mike Smith
Mat Snow
Clive Solomon
Marion Sparks
Caffy St. Luce
Stephen Street
Andy Strickland
Nikki Sudden
David Swift

Mark Taylor
Neil Taylor
Samantha Taylor
Jerry Thackray
Noel Thompson
Geoff Travis
Debbie Turner

Tommy Udo
Tim Vass
Sarah Vaughan
Laurence Verfaillie

Rob Wakeman
Simon Walker
Ben Wardle
Ben Watt
David Westlake
Dave Whitehead
Ivor Wilkins
Andy Wilkinson
Phil Wilson

Sources

MAGAZINES AND NEWSPAPERS
The following magazine articles and newspaper reports proved invaluable, and many of them are quoted in the book. They are listed in the order that they appear.

Chapter 1
- Alan McDermid, "Glasgow Branded 'Slum Capital Of Europe'", *Glasgow Herald*, 30/3/76.
- unattrib., "The Whiff Of Death", *Evening Times*, 10/6/76.
- Robbie Benson and Nigel Wallace, "The 25p Turn-On", *Evening Times*, 16/6/76.
- Tom Fullerton, "Glue-Sniff Disc Shocker", *Evening Times*, 19/8/76.
- Jim Davis, "Storm As Filth Tour Heads North", *Daily Record*, 3/12/76.
- John McCalman, "Sex Pistols Sent Packing", *Glasgow Herald*, 7/12/76.
- unattrib., "Pistols Silenced", *Glasgow Herald*, 7/12/76.
- Bob Edmands, "Singles", *NME*, 29/1/77.
- Gordon Blair, "Glasgow Strangles The New Wave", *Daily Record*, 23/6/77.
- Graham Scott, "Never Again – It's Just Pure Punk", *Evening Times*, 23/6/77.
- Michael Bonner, "The True Adventures Of Primal Scream", *Uncut*, November 1999.
- Ian MacFadden, "Licence Ban Prevents Glasgow Punk Show", *Music Week*, 13/8/77.
- Iain Gray, "The Punk World", *Glasgow Herald*, 22/8/77.
- Simon Williams, "Material World", *NME*, 7/10/89.

Chapter 2
- Jon Hunter, *Bandits One To Five* fanzine, summer 1986.
- Mat Snow, "Bridge On The River Clyde", *NME*, 11/2/84.
- Ian Cranna, "Scotland Holds Its Own: The Rezillos Walk The Line", *NME*, 27/8/77.
- Chas de Whalley, "Mr Know-It-All", *Music Week*, 27/6/92.
- Chris Bohn, "From A Loser To A King", *NME*, 15/5/82.
- Phil Sutcliffe, "Life After Debt?", *Q*, August 1991.
- Johnny Rogan, "Rough Trade Records", *Record Collector*, May 1990.
- Danny Baker, "Singles", *NME*, 1/3/80.
- Dave McCullough, "Singles", *Sounds*, 1/3/80.
- Chris Bohn, "Singles", *Melody Maker*, 15/3/80.
- Vivien Goldman, "Jah Punk – New Wave Digs Reggae, OK?", *Sounds*, 3/9/77.
- unattrib., *V Sign* fanzine, issue 1, 1979.
- unattrib., *New Wave* fanzine, issue 9, 1977.
- Phil McNeill, "Looks Like Independents Day", *NME*, 3/9/77.
- Dave McCullough, "Postcard From Paradise", *Sounds*, 30/8/80.
- Kirsty McNeill, "Scotland's New Role In The Performing Arts", *NME*, 9/5/81.

- Kirsty McNeill, Robert Sharp and Robert Hodgens, *Ten Commandments* fanzine, issue 5, 1980.
- Robert Yates, "The Agony And The Ecstasy", *Q*, August 1998.
- Dave McCullough, "Going Underground", *Sounds*, 21/3/80.
- Charles Shaar Murray, untitled article about independent music, *NME*, 24/12/77.
- Bill Black, "Still Waters Run Deep", *Sounds*, 4/8/84.

Chapter 3
- unattrib., "Nightlife Selections", *Time Out*, 25/9-1/10/81.
- Paul Morley, "Ice Cream: The Body Electric!", *NME*, 25/7/81.
- unattrib., "McGee's Creation", *Strange Things Are Happening*, May/June 1988.
- David Quantick, "Televisionaries", *NME*, 11/2/84.
- Julian Cope, "Tales From The Drug Attic", *NME*, 3/12/83.
- Tony Fletcher, "A Statement", *Jamming!*, issue 13, summer 1982.
- Alan McGee and Jerry Thackray, *Communication Blur* fanzine, issue 1, 1982.
- Snoo Wilson, "Psychedelic Revival", *Time Out*, 25/9-1/10/81.
- Amrik Rai, "If Nightingales Could Fly", *NME*, 12/3/83.
- Tony Fletcher, "Singles", *Jamming!*, issue 15, summer 1983.
- Jowe Head, "I Was A Teenage Television Personality", *Eskimo Chain* fanzine, issue 3, 1997.
- Adrian Thrills, "Young, Gifted And... White?", *NME*, 27/8/83.
- Chris White and Jim Evans, "UK Independents", *Music Week*, 21/1/84.
- Chris White and Jim Evans, "Cherry Red – In The Process Of Indie Evolution", *Music Week*, 21/1/84.
- unattrib., "Record News", *NME*, 27/8/83.

Chapter 4
- Rodney Burbeck, "1983 – What A Year!", *Music Week*, 24/12/83.
- unattrib., "Two Cheers For The Second Quarter", *Music Week*, 17/9/83.
- Jim Evans, John Best and Chris White, "Best Of British", *Music Week*, 4/8/84.
- Edwin Pouncey, "Albums", *Sounds*, 23/6/84.
- Mat Snow, "Paint It Black", *NME*, 5/7/86.
- unattrib., "Living In East Kilbride", *Glasgow Herald*, 2/3/84.
- David Cavanagh, "The Dark Side", *Select*, May 1992.
- David Quantick, review of Jesus and Mary Chain, *NME*, 8/9/84.
- Ian Penman, "Into Battle", *NME*, 8/9/84.
- Bruce Dessau, "Lions In Our Own Garden", *NME*, 3/11/84.
- Stuart Maconie, "Good Vibrations", *NME*, 11/2/89.
- Keith Cameron, "Songs In The McGee Of Life", *NME*, 12/2/94.
- Danny Kelly, "Singles", *NME*, 6/10/84.
- Jane Simon, review of Jesus and Mary Chain, *Sounds*, 3/11/84.
- Neil Taylor, review of Jesus and Mary Chain, *NME*, 3/11/84.
- Neil Taylor, "Vile Evil From East Kilbride", *NME*, 8/12/84.
- Biba Kopf, "Chapter, Verse And Worse", *NME*, 16/2/85.

Chapter 5
- unattrib., "Tour News", *NME*, 27/10/84.
- Sandy Robertson, interview with Jesus and Mary Chain, *Sounds*, 9/2/85.
- Carol Clerk, "Bible Bashers", *Melody Maker*, 16/3/85.
- Martin Dunn, "Chain Gang On Rampage", *Sun*, 29/1/85.
- Billy Mann, review of Jesus and Mary Chain, *NME*, 9/2/85.
- The Legend!, review of the X-Men, *NME*, 8/9/84.
- Quentin McDermott, "Coming Of Age", *NME*, 21-28/12/84.
- Biba Kopf, review of "Concerto For Machinery And Voice", *NME*, 14/1/84.
- Neil Taylor, "SPK Riot At ICA", *NME*, 13/10/84.
- Neil Taylor, "Jesus And Mary! A Riot", *NME*, 23/3/85.
- John Harris, "Eyewitness: The Jesus and Mary Chain Riot", *Q*, December 1995.

- unattrib., *Surfin' Swordfish* fanzine, issue 1, August 1985.
- unattrib., news story, *NME*, 30/3/85.
- Neil Taylor, "Liplash!", *NME*, 21/9/85.
- Mat Snow, "Death Of A Salesman", *NME*, 17/8/85.
- Adrian Thrills, "Singles", *NME*, 26/1/85.
- Danny Kelly, "Warning: This Group Will Self-Destruct In The Next Song", *NME*, 6/7/85.

Chapter 6
- Neil Taylor, "Young, Loud And Snotty", *NME*, 3/8/85.
- Neil Taylor, "Wholesale Harmony", *NME*, 17/8/85.
- The Legend!, review of the Pastels, *NME*, 25/7/85
- Don Watson, "Unchained Melody", *NME*, 14/9/85.
- Jack Barron, "Mary Chain Massacre!", *Sounds*, 21/9/85.
- Danny Kelly, review of Jesus and Mary Chain, *NME*, 21/9/85.
- unattrib., "Chain Reaction", *Sounds*, 21/9/85.
- Dave Thomas, review of "Week Of Wonders", *Melody Maker*, 9/11/85.
- Simon Murphy, *Adventure In Bereznik* fanzine, issue 5, 1986.
- Kevin Pearce, *Hungry Beat* fanzine, issue 3, 1986.
- Danny Kelly, "Memphis – Two Over Par", *NME*, 25/5/85.
- William Reid, "Shrink Rap", *Melody Maker*, 28/9/85.

Chapter 7
- Neil Taylor, "Suck On The Pastels", *NME*, 25/1/86.
- David Quantick, "Singles", *NME*, 26/4/86.
- Jane Simon, "Heavy Weather", *Sounds*, 21-28/12/85.
- Mat Snow, "Up The Hill Backwards", *NME*, 12/10/85.
- Donna Andronowski, letter, *NME*, 1/3/86.
- David Swift, "Screaming Secrets", *NME*, 24/5/86.
- S. Fahy, M. Houlihan, M. O'Keefe and A.J. Nicholson, "A Layperson's Guide to Sarcoidosis", *Irish Medical Journal*, Vol. 90 No. 6, October 1997.
- Amrik Rai, "Germ-Free Adolescents", *NME*, 24/3/84.
- Morrissey's "Best Of 1984" questionnaire, *NME*, 23/2/85.
- Adrian Thrills, "The Music Of Sound", *NME*, 8/3/86.
- unattrib., *Blah-De-Blah* fanzine, July 1986.
- Neil Taylor, "Monkey See Monkey Do", *NME*, 7/6/86.
- Chris Heath, "The Jesus And Mary Chain", *Smash Hits*, Vol. 8. No. 15, 1986.
- unattrib., "Should We Scrap The Royal Family?", *Smash Hits*, Vol. 8 No. 15, 1986.

Chapter 8
- Danny Kelly, "Rumbling The Antiseptic Beauty", *NME*, 8/11/86.
- Pinnacle advertorial, *Music Week*, 27/1/90.
- Phil McNeill, "The King Of Indies", *Music Week*, 23/11/91.
- "Pinnacle In Receivership", *Music* Week, 10/11/84.
- Adrian Thrills, "Major Crisis For Indies", *NME*, 17/11/84.
- Len Brown, "Singing In The Rain", *NME*, 28/3/87.
- Danny Kelly, "Masters Of Ceremony", *NME*, 27/6/87.
- Steve Lowe, "It Couldn't Be You!", *Select*, December 1998.
- David Quantick, "Money, Love And Fun", *NME*, 18/7/87.
- Paul Du Noyer, "Reviews", *Q*, October 1986.
- Danny Kelly, "Elevation Don't Go To My Head", *NME*, 11/4/87.
- Danny Kelly, "Al's Angels", *NME*, 11/4/87.
- Jane Solanas, review of Baby Amphetamine, *NME*, 18/7/87.

Chapter 9
- Gavin Martin, news story, *NME*, 8/3/86.
- unattrib., "Kissed Off!", *NME*, 3/10/87.

- John Peel, review of House Of Love, *Observer*, 22/5/88.
- Stuart Maconie, "Primal Solution", *NME*, 5/8/89.
- Jack Barron, "Acid Upstarts", *NME*, 16/7/88.

Chapter 10
- unattrib., "Come On Pete, Give Us A Record", *Music Week*, 27/1/90.
- "Question Time: Wilson Puts The Bosses On The Spot", *Music Week*, 10/3/90.
- Len Brown, review of House Of Love, *NME*, 21/5/88.
- Ben Thompson, "Alive And Kicking At The Country Club", *NME*, 20/8/88.
- Chris Roberts, "Glide On Time", *Melody Maker*, 28/4/90.
- Jack Barron, "Dream Demons", *NME*, 10/12/88.
- Simon Reynolds, "Suicide Kisses", *Melody Maker*, 15/10/88.
- Dave Laing, "A&R's Permanent Fixture", *Music Week*, 16/7/88
- Mr Spencer, "Is There A Comedian In The House?", *Sounds*, 8/10/88.
- unattrib., article on acid house, *NME*, 16/7/88.

Chapter 11
- Stuart Maconie, "The Artery Of Noise", *NME*, 21/4/90.
- Alan DiPerna, "Dinosaur Jr's J Mascis and My Bloody Valentine's Kevin Shields Speak Softly – Very Softly – But Carry Big Axes", *Guitar World*, April 1993.
- Cliff Jones, "Valentine's Day", *Guitar*, July 1992.
- Mandi James, "Britain's Cupidest Band!", *NME*, 9/2/91.
- Garry Bushell and Rick Sky, "It's Groovy And It's Cool – It's Our Acid House T-Shirt!", *Sun*, 12/10/88.
- Sue Evison and Peter Willis, "Evil Of Ecstasy", *Sun*, 19/10/88.
- Steven Wells, Sean O'Hagan and Paolo Hewitt, "Get Right Off One Chummy", *NME*, 19/11/88.
- Len Brown, "Tomorrow Belongs To Us", *NME*, 7/1/89.
- unattrib., "Public *NME*", *NME*, 30/7/88.

Chapter 12
- Jack Barron, "Bliss This House", *NME*, 10/6/89.
- Pat Gilbert, "Ossifaction", *Mojo*, December 1999.
- Andy Beevers, "Primal Scream Therapy", *Music Week*, 24/2/90.
- Jack Barron, "Bob's Full House", *NME*, 17/2/90.
- Rupert Howe, "An Audience With Lord Sabre", *Select*, October 1993.
- Audrey Witherspoon, "Sex, Lies... And Gaffer Tape", *NME*, 7/10/89.

Chapter 13
- unattrib., "Distributors 'Swamped' By Releases", *Music Week*, 30/6/90.
- unattrib., "Indie Stores Go Bust At Rate Of One A Day", *Music Week*, 22/9/90.
- unattrib., "Pinnacle Man Trades Places", *Music Week*, 28/4/90.
- unattrib., "PolyGram Ends Year At Top Of Pile", *Music Week*, 27/1/90.
- Robin Gibson, "Brothers Of Mercy", *Sounds*, 19/9/87.
- Steven Wells interviews James Havoc, *NME*, 11/3/89.

Chapter 14
- Martin Aston, "My Bloody Valentine", *The Catalogue*, issue 67, 1989.
- Gina Harp, "Lush Life: My Bloody Valentine's Pink Elephants", *Mondo 2000*, 1992.
- Steve Lamacq, "Ride On Time", *NME*, 13/1/90.
- Len Brown, "In The Land Of The Riding Sons", *NME*, 10/3/90.
- Norman Cook, "Singles", *NME*, 17/2/90.
- Simon Reynolds, "The Final Frontier", *Melody Maker*, 1/6/91.
- Dele Fadele, "Dub Demons From Atlantis", *NME*, 12/5/90.
- Simon Williams, "Four Play", *NME*, 7/4/90.
- Steve Lamacq, "Isis Breakers", *NME*, 27/10/90.

- Nick Duerden, "Creation", *Record Mirror*, 2/3/91.
- Steve Lamacq, "Madhattan's Tea Party", *NME*, 4/8/90.

Chapter 15
- Roger Morton, "High Generation", *NME*, 28/7/90.
- Simon Williams, "Into The Thames Valley", *NME*, 15/12/90.
- Roger Morton, "Aaaarghbibblewibble!", *NME*, 20/10/90.
- David Stubbs, "Glorious Swansongs", *Melody Maker*, 31/8/91.
- Paul Mathur, "Knocked Out Loaded", *Melody Maker*, 3/8/91.
- John Harris, "Vanishing Point", *Select*, February 2000.
- Stud Brothers, "All Tomorrow's Parties'", *MM*, 3/8/91.

Chapter 16
- unattrib., "Sleeping Bag Splits From Rough Trade", *Music Week*, 4/8/90.
- unattrib., "Revolver Deserts Rough Trade", *Music Week*, 15/12/90.
- unattrib., "Sabotage Follows Sackings At RT", *NME*, 15/12/90.
- unattrib., "Cooking Vinyl Blames Lay-Offs On Rough Trade", *Music Week*, 3/11/90.
- unattrib., "40 Jobs Axed At Rough Trade', *Music Week*, 23/2/91.
- unattrib., "Rough Trade Seeks Cash Aid", *Music Week*, 16/2/91.
- unattrib., "RT Slims To Survive", *Music Week*, 13/4/91.
- unattrib., "Heath Plumps For Sony", *Music Week*, 27/4/91.
- unattrib., "Rough Trade: Death By Committee", *Music Week*, 1/6/91.
- unattrib., "Kimpton-Howe Jumps Ship", *Music Week*, 4/5/91.
- unattrib., "RT Labels Opt For Pinnacle", *Music Week*, 18/5/91.
- unattrib., "Travis 'Waives' £1m RTD Claim", *Music Week*, 11/7/92.
- unattrib., "Rough Trade Rescue Fails", *Music Week*, 1/6/91.
- Martin Aston, "The Definition Of Sound", *Music Week*, 13/7/91.
- unattrib., "Pinnacle Strikes Deal For European Foothold", *Music Week*, 7/9/91.
- unattrib., "Pinnacle Squares Up To Majors", *Music Week*, 7/9/91.
- unattrib., "Christmas Valentines", *Melody Maker*, 28/9/91.
- Miranda Sawyer, "Out Of Our Heads", Q, December 1991.
- Paula McGinley, "Creation Dives In To US Via SBK Link", *Music Week*, 30/11/91.
- Andrew Collins, "World War Skreeeee!", *NME*, 9/11/91.
- Andrew Perry, "All The President's Men", *Select*, April 1994.
- Danny Kelly, "Twenty Flute Rock!", *NME*, 14/12/91.
- Mark Kemp, "The Beauty And The Beast: My Bloody Valentine Strikes A Nerve", *Options*, 1992.

Chapter 17
- Caroline Sullivan, "The Genesis Of Creation", *Guardian*, 25/2/94.
- Andrew Collins, "Anyone For Tennessee?", *NME*, 4/1/92.
- Paul Gorman, "Big Planet Calls For Small Licensing Deals", *Music Week*, 19/3/94.
- Paul Gorman, "'Authenticity' Is The Essence Of Creation", *Music Week*, 19/3/94.
- Max Bell, "Creative Accounting", *Vox*, April 1994.
- Roger Morton, "Better Venerate Than 'Never'", *NME*, 25/4/92.
- unattrib., "Single Sales Fall To Seventies Low", *Music Week*, 22/8/92.
- unattrib., "Slump Bites Deeper", *Music Week*, 30/5/92.
- unattrib., "20 Out As EMI Buys Chrysalis", *Music Week*, 30/11/91.
- unattrib., "EMI Buys Virgin", *Music Week*, 14/3/92.
- unattrib., "Roles Merged As Slump Hits Heath", *Music Week*, 15/8/92.
- unattrib., "State Of Indie Pundits", *NME*, 25/7/92.
- Simon Reynolds, "The Indie Alternative", *Guardian*, 19/12/91.
- unattrib., "Indie Majors Split On Chart", *NME*, 25/7/92.
- Paula McGinley, "A Law Unto Himself", *Music Week*, 28/3/92.
- Steve Redmond, "War Of Roses Tips Balance Of Power", *Music Week*, 16/5/92.
- Keith Cameron, "O Sucre Man!", *NME*, 25/7/92.
- Steven Daly, "Scurf's Up", *NME*, 6/6/92.

Chapter 18
- unattrib., "Primal Win Lifts Mercury Profile", *Music Week*, 19/9/92.
- unattrib., "Dooley's Diary", *Music Week*, 24/4/93.
- James Oldham, "I Want 'Swastika Eyes' To Be Number 1 All Around The World", *NME*, 13/11/99.
- Joan Tarshis, "God's Right Hand. . .", *Mojo*, September 1995.
- Sean O'Hagan, "The Father Of Creation", *Guardian*, 5/7/97.
- John Hatfield, "The Music Man", *Scotland On Sunday*, 8/10/95.
- Carole Morin, "The Man Who Created Oasis", *Telegraph Magazine*, 30/11/96.
- John Robb, "State Of The Nation", *Melody Maker*, 2/10/93.

Chapter 19
- Matthew Lynn, "Mr Rock 'N' Roll Plays The Tycoon", *Sunday Times*, 16/3/97.
- David Belcher, "Making Quite A Spectacle Of Himself", *Glasgow Herald*, 29/5/93.
- Johnny Cigarettes, "Hip Pop. . . Hooray!", *NME*, 11/12/93.
- Andrew Perry, "Greenock Rave On", *Select*, February 1994.
- Alan McGee, "Cocaine Supernova", *Guardian*, 14/3/98.

Chapter 20
- David Belcher, "Creative, Undecayed", *Glasgow Herald*, 5/3/94.
- Pjem, "Lord Of All Creation", [Edinburgh] *Student*, 17/2/94.
- Adam Higginbotham, "Radio One 'No Longer Crap'?", *Select*, March 1994.
- John Harris and Ted Kessler, "Rehabsolutely Fabulous", *NME*, 4/6/94.
- Steve Sutherland, "Flop Of Detox", *NME*, 11/6/94.
- Phil Sommerich, "Warner Sets 2.3m Target For Tenors", *Music Week*, 23/7/94.
- unattrib., "Creation Rubbishes Acquisition Talk", *Music Week*, 27/8/94.

Chapter 21
- Robert Yates, "Cash For Questions", *Q*, March 1998.
- Sam Taylor, "The Creation Myth", *Esquire*, December 1996.
- Paul Gorman, "Indie Pioneer's Ambitions Go Beyond Hitting Number One", *Music Week*, 26/8/96.
- Andy Richardson, "The Battle Of Britpop", *NME*, 12/8/95.
- Siân Pattenden, "What's The Story?", *Select*, October 1995.
- Alan McGee, "Oasis V. Blur: Round Two! Seconds Out. . .", *NME*, 26/8/95.
- Mark Ellen, "Through The Past Darkly", *Mojo*, January 1995.
- Steve Sutherland, "Definitely McGee", *Vox*, January 1997.

Chapter 22
- Emma Cook, "What's In, What's Out?", *Independent On Sunday*, 4/2/96.
- Ted Kessler, "We Do Give A Puck!", *NME*, 16/5/98.
- Alice Rawsthorn, "An Ear To The Underground", *Financial Times*, 19/2/96.
- unattrib., "McGee Celebrates As Oasis Clinch Hat-Trick", *Music Week*, 16/3/96.
- Selina Webb, "EMI And Virgin Set The Pace For 1996", *Music Week*, 27/4/96.
- Alice Rawsthorn, "Creation Ponders Music Publishing Float", *Financial Times*, 25/11/97.
- unattrib., "Creation In Sony Share Shambles", *NME*, 27/4/96.
- Paul Gorman, "Sony Aims To Complete £12m Creation Buy-Out", *Music Week*, 27/4/96.
- Adam Sherwin, "Sony Bid Hits Wonderwall", *Sunday Business*, 5/5/96.
- Paul Gorman, "Creation Rolls With Sony", *Music Week*, 8/6/96.
- Alice Rawsthorn, "Record Company Extends Sony Deal", *Financial Times*, 5/6/96.
- unattrib., "Creation And Sony Renew Deal", *Music Week*, 15/6/96.
- Allan Brown, "In Record Time", *Sunday Times*, 28/7/96.
- Jeff Clark-Meads, "Sony, Creation Renew Alliance", *Billboard*, 15/6/96.
- unattrib., "Creation Finds The Perfect Partner", *Music Week*, 15/6/96.
- Martin Jacques, "Pop Blows Out Blair", *Observer*, 15/3/98.

- Gavin Martin, "Life And Soul Of The Party", *NME*, 24/8/85.
- Alice Rawsthorn, "Blair Stages Pre-Election Gig For Music's Head Honchos", *Financial Times*, 27/1/97.
- Martin Talbot, "Can They Give Us What We Really Really Want?", *MW*, 3/5/97.
- unattrib., "You've Got To Fight For Your Right To (Political) Party!", *NME*, 12/10/96.
- unattrib., "Noises Off", *Sunday Times*, 23/6/96.
- unattrib., "Going Into Labour", *Melody Maker*, 5/4/97.
- Martin Talbot, "Oasis Go Into Orbit", *Music Week*, 17/8/96.
- John Harris, "It's Over (Definitely Maybe)", *Independent*, 26/11/99.
- Sue Mott, "No Looking Back In Anger", *Scotland On Sunday*, 30/3/97.
- unattrib., "The Creation Of New Labour... And Wheeler 18", *Melody Maker*, 5/10/96.
- Alan McGee, "Talking About My Generation", *Independent*, 2/5/97.
- James Brown, "My Brilliant Career", *Loaded*, September 1996.
- Andrew Mueller, "Music: The New Wonder Drug", *Men's Health*, January-February 1998.
- Michael Hann, "Interview: Alan McGee", *New Statesman*, 1/11/96.

Chapter 23
- Louise Gray, "State Of Independence", *Independent*, 22/3/96.
- unattrib., "United Kingdom", *MBI*, December 1996.
- Max Bell, "What's The Story? More Glory", *Evening Standard*, 10/12/96.
- Annabel Levy, "Creation For The Nation", *10-15*, August 1996.
- Simon Sebag Montefiore, "Mr Blair's Shakermaker", *Sunday Times*, 26/10/97.
- ed. Tom O'Sullivan, "How Are The Mighty Fallen After A Year Of Lording It", *Observer*, 24/10/99.
- Alan McGee, "Top Lig, Tone", *Observer*, 3/8/97.
- John Harlow, "Campaign Supernova", *Sunday Times*, 24/8/97.
- Adrian Deevoy and Paul Du Noyer, "The Top 50 Groovers And Shakers", *Mail On Sunday*, 13/7/97.
- Martin Talbot, "Oasis Call For Police Action", *Music Week*, 5/7/97.
- Paul Williams, story about Oasis, *Music Week*, 2/8/97.
- Nick Kent, "It Was All Over By 1997", *Guardian*, 26/8/99.

Chapter 24
- unattrib., "Music Charts", *Guardian*, 22/5/98.
- Will Woodward, "High Wireless Act", *Guardian*, 4/1/99.
- Ted Kessler, "Rowland's Gift", *NME*, 11/9/99.
- unattrib., "McGee Wants To Be Like Commons People", *NME*, 2/8/97.
- unattrib., "Job Creation Scheme", *Melody Maker*, 18/10/97.
- unattrib., "Drummond Blasts McGee's Party Politics", *NME*, 25/10/97.
- Steven Wells, "Banging On", *NME*, 31/1/98.
- Alan McGee, "What A Swells Party This Isn't!", *NME*, 14/2/98.
- Barry Didcock, "Why Oasis Hit Man Joins The Blair Mafia", *Scotsman*, 26/3/97.
- Chris Ayres, "Politics And Pop Could Clash", *Times*, 16/1/98.
- Robert Yates, "Oi Tony. About That Fifty Grand...", *Observer*, 1/2/98.
- Stephen Castle and Paul Routledge, "What A Party...", *Independent On Sunday*, 15/2/98.
- Robert Ashton, "McGee Pushes Labour On Benefit Breaks Plan", *Music Week*, 28/2/98.
- Alan McGee, "If You're Going To Ask Me To The Party, Don't Ask Me To Shut Up", *NME*, 14/3/98.
- unattrib., news story about the New Deal, *Melody Maker*, 7/3/98.
- Carol Midgley, "Blair's Rock Rebellion", *Times*, 13/3/98.
- Ben Willmott and Mat Smith, "We Should Have Free Education Just Like We Have A Free Health Service", *NME*, 7/3/98.

- Jim Alexander, Mark Beaumont, April Long, Paul Moody, James Oldham, Mat Smith, Steven Wells and Ben Willmott, "Betrayal: The Labour Government's War On You", *NME*, 14/3/98.
- Peter Riddell, "'Cool Britannia' Image Has Helped To Foster False Hope", *Times*, 13/3/98.
- unattrib., "The *NME* Within: Cool Britannia Has Lost Its Verve", *Times*, 12/3/98.
- Will Woodward, "Uncool Britannia", *Mirror*, 12/3/98.
- unattrib., "*NME* Force Labour Rethink", *NME*, 21/3/98.
- unattrib., news story about Hurricane #1, *Melody Maker*, 14/3/98.
- Jake, *Blah Blah Blah*, July 1996.
- David Hemingway, "My Media", *Guardian*, 16/3/98.
- Alice Rawsthorn, "Online Promotion Is A Site For More Ears", *Financial Times*, 9/4/98.
- Jim Alexander, April Long, Steve Sutherland, Mat Smith, Jody Thompson and Ben Willmott, "The Great Rock 'N' Roll Dwindle", *NME*, 13/6/98.
- Ted Gibbons, "Methuselah Says", *NME*, 11/7/98.
- Alan McGee, "This Is The Revolution. There Will Be No Record Companies In Five Or Ten Years", *NME*, 13/6/98.
- Martin Wroe, "You Gotta Scroll With It. . .", *Observer*, 14/6/98.
- Peter Foster, "Pop Industry Rocked By Recession", *Times*, 13/6/98.
- Edward Helmore, "Stop Thief!", *Guardian*, 20/11/98.
- Paul Williams, "Dickins Defends Industry Against 'Doom Merchants'", *Music Week*, 18/7/98.
- Ajax Scott, "Pack Up Or Shut Up", *Music Week*, 22/8/98.
- Lucy Ward, "Labour Offers New Deal To Rising Stars On Dole", *Guardian*, 22/5/98.
- Alice Rawsthorn, "It's Only Rock 'N' Dole But Traditionalists May Not Like It", *Financial Times*, 15/6/98.
- Rachel Sylvester, "Rock 'N' Dole Attacked As Charter For Scroungers", *Daily Telegraph*, 16/6/98.
- Tom Morton, "Dope's Record As The True Mother Of Pop Invention", *Scotsman*, 17/6/98.
- Jon Craig, "Blair's Rock 'N' Dole Stars", *Express On Sunday*, 14/6/98.
- unattrib., "Pop Wannabes Get Help From Blair", *NME*, 6/11/99.
- David Hencke and Nicholas Watt, "Labour's Rethink On Spin", *Guardian*, 28/12/98.
- Alice Rawsthorn, "Creation Label Plans To Set Up Internet Site To Sell Music", *Financial Times*, 6/7/98.
- unattrib., "Threat To High Street As Creations Plans Net Sales", *Music Week*, 18/7/98.
- Alice Rawsthorn, "Creation Curbs Internet Plans", *Financial Times*, 20/7/98.
- David Shand, "Sony Halts Plan To Sell CDs Abroad On Net", *Scotsman*, 21/7/98.
- Jon Rees, "Creation Sells Music On The Net", *Business Life*, 20/9/98.
- Bruce Dessau, "Me And Alan McGee", *Time Out*, 9-16/9/98.

Chapter 25
- Gerard Grech, "Net Unveils New Electronic Retail Culture", *Music Week*, 13/1/99.
- unattrib., "The Record Company Is Dead: Long Live The Internet", *NME*, 9/1/99.
- Alice Rawsthorn, "Creation To Put Singles On Internet", *Financial Times*, 21/12/98.
- unattrib., "Capitol Punishment For Beasties", *NME*, 16/1/99.
- Andrew Perry, review of Mishka, *Select*, June 1999.
- unattrib., "Creation Switches To Pinnacle Distribution", *Music Week*, 5/6/99.
- unattrib., "Oasis Quit Label", *Sun*, 25/11/99.
- Simon Waldman, "What's The Story? Multimedia Glory", *Guardian*, 26/11/99.

BOOKS

- Jon Savage, *England's Dreaming: Sex Pistols And Punk Rock* (London: Faber and Faber, 1991).
- Russell Leadbetter, *You Don't Have To Be In Harlem: The Story Of The Most Celebrated Rock Venue In Britain* (Edinburgh: Mainstream, 1995).
- Brian Hogg, *All That Ever Mattered: The History Of Scottish Rock And Pop* (London: Guinness, 1993).
- Johnny Rogan, *Morrissey & Marr: The Severed Alliance* (London: Omnibus, 1992).
- Johnny Rogan, *The Smiths: The Visual Documentary* (London: Omnibus, 1994).
- Johnny Rogan, *Starmakers & Svengalis* (London: Queen Anne Press, 1988).
- Barry Lazell, *Indie Hits 1980-1989* (London: Cherry Red Books, 1997).
- Charlie Gillett and Simon Frith, *Rock File 4* (London: Panther, 1976).
- *Rock: The Rough Guide* (London: Rough Guides, 1996).
- *Virgin Rock Yearbook* (London: Virgin, 1986).
- Stuart Maconie, *Blur: 3862 Days* (London: Virgin, 1999).
- Bill Drummond, *From The Shores Of Lake Placid and Other Stories* (Liverpool: Penkiln Burn, 1998).
- Julian Cope, *Head-On* (Wiltshire: Magog, 1994).
- Julian Cope, *Repossessed* (London: Thorsons, 1999).
- Colin Larkin, *The Virgin Encyclopaedia Of Eighties Music* (London: Virgin, 1997).
- Matthew Collin and John Godfrey, *Altered State: The Story Of Ecstasy Culture And Acid House* (London: Serpent's Tail, 1997).
- Jane Bussman, *Once In A Lifetime: The Crazy Days Of Acid House And Afterwards* (London: Virgin, 1998).
- Mick Middles, *From Joy Division To New Order: The Factory Story* (London: Virgin, 1996).
- Martin C. Strong, *The Great Rock Discography* (London: Canongate, 1998).
- Tim Abbot, *Oasis. Definitely* (London: Pavilion, 1996).
- Paolo Hewitt, *Getting High: The Adventures Of Oasis* (London: Boxtree, 1997).
- *Guinness British Hit Singles*, ed. Helen Weller (London: Guinness, 1997).

AUDIO

- Alan McGee in conversation with Iain McNay and Mike Alway, *The Ruling Class: The Very Best Of él Records* (Cherry Red Records ACME 27CD, 1998).

TV

- "Jock 'n' Roll", *Spectrum*, BBC Scotland, 1981 (dir. Ken MacGregor, ed. James Hunter, presenter B.A. Robertson).

SLEEVENOTES AND OTHERS

- Nigel Smith and James Neiss, *Young And Stupid* by Josef K (LTMCD 2307, 1990).
- Alan McGee, *Alive In The Living Room* by Various (CRE LP 001, 1984).
- Mark Lewisohn, *The Beatles Anthology 1* (Apple 724383444526, 1995).
- Iain McNay, "The Cherry Red Story", *Cherry Red Records Catalogue*, 1997.

Index